36: *British Novelists, 1890-1929: Modernists,* edited by Thomas F. Staley (1985)

37: *American Writers of the Early Republic,* edited by Emory Elliott (1985)

38: *Afro-American Writers After 1955: Dramatists and Prose Writers,* edited by Thadious M. Davis and Trudier Harris (1985)

39: *British Novelists, 1660-1800,* 2 parts, edited by Martin C. Battestin (1985)

40: *Poets of Great Britain and Ireland Since 1960,* 2 parts, edited by Vincent B. Sherry, Jr. (1985)

41: *Afro-American Poets Since 1955,* edited by Trudier Harris and Thadious M. Davis (1985)

42: *American Writers for Children Before 1900,* edited by Glenn E. Estes (1985)

43: *American Newspaper Journalists, 1690-1872,* edited by Perry J. Ashley (1986)

44: *American Screenwriters,* Second Series, edited by Randall Clark, Robert E. Morsberger, and Stephen O. Lesser (1986)

45: *American Poets, 1880-1945,* First Series, edited by Peter Quartermain (1986)

46: *American Literary Publishing Houses, 1900-1980: Trade and Paperback,* edited by Peter Dzwonkoski (1986)

47: *American Historians, 1866-1912,* edited by Clyde N. Wilson (1986)

48: *American Poets, 1880-1945,* Second Series, edited by Peter Quartermain (1986)

49: *American Literary Publishing Houses, 1638-1899,* 2 parts, edited by Peter Dzwonkoski (1986)

50: *Afro-American Writers Before the Harlem Renaissance,* edited by Trudier Harris (1986)

51: *Afro-American Writers from the Harlem Renaissance to 1940,* edited by Trudier Harris (1987)

52: *American Writers for Children Since 1960: Fiction,* edited by Glenn E. Estes (1986)

53: *Canadian Writers Since 1960,* First Series, edited by W. H. New (1986)

54: *American Poets, 1880-1945,* Third Series, 2 parts, edited by Peter Quartermain (1987)

55: *Victorian Prose Writers Before 1867,* edited by William B. Thesing (1987)

56: *German Fiction Writers, 1914-1945,* edited by James Hardin (1987)

57: *Victorian Prose Writers After 1867,* edited by William B. Thesing (1987)

58: *Jacobean and Caroline Dramatists,* edited by Fredson Bowers (1987)

59: *American Literary Critics and Scholars, 1800-1850,* edited by John W. Rathbun and Monica M. Grecu (1987)

60: *Canadian Writers Since 1960,* Second Series, edited by W. H. New (1987)

61: *American Writers for Children Since 1960: Poets, Illustrators, and Nonfiction Authors,* edited by Glenn E. Estes (1987)

62: *Elizabethan Dramatists,* edited by Fredson Bowers (1987)

63: *Modern American Critics, 1920-1955,* edited by Gregory S. Jay (1988)

64: *American Literary Critics and Scholars, 1850-1880,* edited by John W. Rathbun and Monica M. Grecu (1988)

65: *French Novelists, 1900-1930,* edited by Catharine Savage Brosman (1988)

66: *German Fiction Writers, 1885-1913,* 2 parts, edited by James Hardin (1988)

67: *Modern American Critics Since 1955,* edited by Gregory S. Jay (1988)

68: *Canadian Writers, 1920-1959,* First Series, edited by W. H. New (1988)

69: *Contemporary German Fiction Writers,* First Series, edited by Wolfgang D. Elfe and James Hardin (1988)

70: *British Mystery Writers, 1860-1919,* edited by Bernard Benstock and Thomas F. Staley (1988)

(Continued on back endsheets)

German Writers in the
Age of Goethe:
Sturm und Drang to Classicism

Dictionary of Literary Biography • Volume Ninety-four

German Writers in the Age of Goethe: Sturm und Drang to Classicism

Edited by
James Hardin
University of South Carolina

and

Christoph E. Schweitzer
University of North Carolina, Chapel Hill

8260

A Bruccoli Clark Layman Book
Gale Research Inc.
Detroit, New York, London

Manufactured by Edwards Brothers, Inc.
Ann Arbor, Michigan
Printed in the United States of America

Copyright © 1990
Gale Research Inc.
835 Penobscot Bldg.
Detroit, MI 48226-4094

Library of Congress Catalog Card Number 90-003382
ISBN 0-8103-4574-9

Contents

Plan of the Series..vii

Foreword...ix

Acknowledgments...xiii

Christian Friedrich von Blanckenburg
(1744-1796)..3
G. L. Jones

Heinrich Christian Boie (1744-1806) 11
Phillip S. McKnight

Ulrich Bräker (1735-1798) 16
James Hardin

Gottfried August Bürger (1747-1794)..............22
John F. Reynolds

Karoline Auguste Fernandine Fischer
(1764-1842)...31
Susanne Zantop

Georg Forster (1754-1794) 36
Thomas P. Saine

Johann Wolfgang von Goethe (1749-1832)........46
Jane K. Brown

Wilhelm Heinse (1746-1803) 67
Rita Terras

Ludwig Christoph Heinrich Hölty
(1748-1776)...72
Bettina Kluth Cothran

August Wilhelm Iffland (1759-1814)...............79
Gerda Jordan

Friedrich Heinrich Jacobi (1743-1819)..............88
Wulf Koepke

Johann Heinrich Jung-Stilling (1740-1817) 96
H. M. Waidson

Immanuel Kant (1724-1804)...........................106
John D. Simons

Friedrich Maximilian Klinger (1752-1831) 121
Edward P. Harris

Adolph Franz Friedrich Ludwig,
Freiherr von Knigge (1752-1796)..............131
Thomas P. Saine

August von Kotzebue (1761-1819) 139
Edward T. Larkin

Sophie von La Roche (1730-1807).................154
Jeannine Blackwell

Johann Anton Leisewitz (1752-1806) 162
Henry J. Schmidt

J. M. R. Lenz (1751-1792)..............................167
Edward P. Harris

Georg Christoph Lichtenberg (1742-1799)......177
Max Reinhart

Karl Philipp Moritz (1756-1793).....................190
Thomas P. Saine

Maler Müller (Friedrich Müller)
(1749-1825)...198
H. M. Waidson

Johann Heinrich Pestalozzi (1746-1827)..........205
Dieter Jedan

Johann Paul Friedrich Richter
(Jean Paul) (1763-1825)...........................213
Wulf Koepke

Friedrich Schiller (1759-1805) 234
John D. Simons

August Wilhelm Schlegel (1767-1845) 257
Thomas G. Sauer

Johann Gottfried Seume (1763-1810) 267
Erich P. Hofacker, Jr.

Christian Graf zu Stolberg
(1748-1821)...276
Herbert Rowland

Friedrich Leopold Graf zu Stolberg
(1750-1819)...279
Herbert Rowland

Friederike Helene Unger (1741?-1813)............288
Susanne Zantop

Heinrich Leopold Wagner (1747-1779) 294
Christopher L. Dolmetsch

Zacharias Werner (1768-1823) 302
Colin Walker

Johann Karl Wezel (1747-1819).....................311
Phillip S. McKnight

Heinrich Zschokke (1771-1848) 327
Donald H. Crosby

Books for Further Reading............................339

Contributors...341

Cumulative Index..345

v

Plan of the Series

. . . Almost the most prodigious asset of a country, and perhaps its most precious possession, is its native literary product—when that product is fine and noble and enduring.

Mark Twain*

The advisory board, the editors, and the publisher of the *Dictionary of Literary Biography* are joined in endorsing Mark Twain's declaration. The literature of a nation provides an inexhaustible resource of permanent worth. We intend to make literature and its creators better understood and more accessible to students and the reading public, while satisfying the standards of teachers and scholars.

To meet these requirements, *literary biography* has been construed in terms of the author's achievement. The most important thing about a writer is his writing. Accordingly, the entries in *DLB* are career biographies, tracing the development of the author's canon and the evolution of his reputation.

The purpose of *DLB* is not only to provide reliable information in a convenient format but also to place the figures in the larger perspective of literary history and to offer appraisals of their accomplishments by qualified scholars.

The publication plan for *DLB* resulted from two years of preparation. The project was proposed to Bruccoli Clark by Frederick G. Ruffner, president of the Gale Research Company, in November 1975. After specimen entries were prepared and typeset, an advisory board was formed to refine the entry format and develop the series rationale. In meetings held during 1976, the publisher, series editors, and advisory board approved the scheme for a comprehensive biographical dictionary of persons who contributed to North American literature. Editorial work on the first volume began in January 1977, and it was published in 1978. In order to make *DLB* more than a reference tool and to compile volumes that individually have claim to status as literary history, it was decided to organize volumes by topic, period, or genre. Each of these freestanding volumes provides a biographical-bibliographical guide and overview for a particular area of literature. We are convinced that this organization—as opposed to a single alphabet method—constitutes a valuable innovation in the presentation of reference material. The volume plan necessarily requires many decisions for the placement and treatment of authors who might properly be included in two or three volumes. In some instances a major figure will be included in separate volumes, but with different entries emphasizing the aspect of his career appropriate to each volume. Ernest Hemingway, for example, is represented in *American Writers in Paris, 1920-1939* by an entry focusing on his expatriate apprenticeship; he is also in *American Novelists, 1910-1945* with an entry surveying his entire career. Each volume includes a cumulative index of subject authors and articles. Comprehensive indexes to the entire series are planned.

With volume ten in 1982 it was decided to enlarge the scope of *DLB*. By the end of 1986 twenty-one volumes treating British literature had been published, and volumes for Commonwealth and Modern European literature were in progress. The series has been further augmented by the *DLB Yearbooks* (since 1981) which update published entries and add new entries to keep the *DLB* current with contemporary activity. There have also been *DLB Documentary Series* volumes which provide biographical and critical source materials for figures whose work is judged to have particular interest for students. One of these companion volumes is entirely devoted to Tennessee Williams.

We define literature as the *intellectual commerce of a nation:* not merely as belles lettres but as that ample and complex process by which ideas are generated, shaped, and transmitted. *DLB* entries are not limited to "creative writers" but extend to other figures who in their time and in their way influenced the mind of a people. Thus the series encompasses historians, journalists, publishers, and screenwriters. By this means readers of *DLB* may be aided to perceive litera-

*From an unpublished section of Mark Twain's autobiography, copyright © by the Mark Twain Company.

ture not as cult scripture in the keeping of intellectual high priests but firmly positioned at the center of a nation's life.

DLB includes the major writers appropriate to each volume and those standing in the ranks immediately behind them. Scholarly and critical counsel has been sought in deciding which minor figures to include and how full their entries should be. Wherever possible, useful references are made to figures who do not warrant separate entries.

Each *DLB* volume has a volume editor responsible for planning the volume, selecting the figures for inclusion, and assigning the entries. Volume editors are also responsible for preparing, where appropriate, appendices surveying the major periodicals and literary and intellectual movements for their volumes, as well as lists of further readings. Work on the series as a whole is coordinated at the Bruccoli Clark Layman editorial center in Columbia, South Carolina, where the editorial staff is responsible for accuracy of the published volumes.

One feature that distinguishes *DLB* is the illustration policy–its concern with the iconography of literature. Just as an author is influenced by his surroundings, so is the reader's understanding of the author enhanced by a knowledge of his environment. Therefore *DLB* volumes include not only drawings, paintings, and photographs of authors, often depicting them at various stages in their careers, but also illustrations of their families and places where they lived. Title pages are regularly reproduced in facsimile along with dust jackets for modern authors. The dust jackets are a special feature of *DLB* because they often document better than anything else the way in which an author's work was perceived in its own time. Specimens of the writers' manuscripts are included when feasible.

Samuel Johnson rightly decreed that "The chief glory of every people arises from its authors." The purpose of the *Dictionary of Literary Biography* is to compile literary history in the surest way available to us–by accurate and comprehensive treatment of the lives and work of those who contributed to it.

The *DLB* Advisory Board

Foreword

DLB 94, German Writers in the Age of Goethe: Sturm und Drang to Classicism, treats thirty-four literary figures whose first works appeared after 1765 and before 1790 and who began their creative life either in the Sturm und Drang (Storm and Stress) or in the epoch of German or Weimar Classicism. The preceding volume in this series, *DLB 90, German Writers in the Age of Goethe, 1789-1832,* deals with forty-seven writers whose first works appeared in or after 1790 and before 1832 and who therefore by and large fell into the "Romantic" era. Although the editors are acutely aware that any attempt to place writers into presumed literary "periods" is arbitrary, we have made no effort to dispense with the traditional terms. As in other *DLB* volumes on German and Austrian literature, however, we have used a historical rather than an aesthetic line of demarcation. In the volumes on the Age of Goethe the dividing line is the French Revolution–the break between the ancien régime and the modern age. After much deliberation on the title for these volumes we decided that *The Age of Goethe* is, whatever its inadequacies, the most appropriate description of the unprecedented German cultural efflorescence from the Sturm und Drang through Romanticism–though we concede that, for example, Victor Lange's use of the term *classicism* to refer to the entire period from 1740 to 1815 has much to be said for it.[1]

There has been considerable debate and reevaluation in recent years about the nature and significance of the Sturm und Drang and Classicism. Although the Sturm und Drang movement had no close parallel in other European countries, its tendencies had long been present and came largely from outside Germany: Jean-Jacques Rousseau's views on nature and freedom from France; Edward Young's gloomy and effusive *Night Thoughts* (1742-1745) from England; Robert Burns's poetry from Scotland; the poetry and critical theory of Johann Jacob Bodmer (who was also the translator of John Milton's *Paradise Lost*) and his collaborator Johann Jacob Breitinger from Switzerland; and the vogue of folk literature in Europe in general. Within Germany such seminal writers and thinkers as Johann Georg Hamann, with his exaltation of the irrational and the cult of genius, and his disciple (and key later influence on the young Goethe) Johann Gottfried Herder, who pointed to the high level of art in folk literature, helped prepare the way for the new movement. At first the phrase *Sturm und Drang* was used to describe a frame of mind, but it came to be used in the early nineteenth century as a label for the literary period roughly from 1769 to 1786–for example, in August Wilhelm Schlegel's *Vorlesungen über schöne Litteratur und Kunst* (Lectures on Belles Lettres and Art), given in Berlin between 1801 and 1803 (published in 1884). Other terms that have been used to characterize the epoch include *Genieperiode* or *Geniezeit* (period or time of genius). The phrase *Sturm und Drang*–which we have used throughout this volume in the original German rather than in its English form, *Storm and Stress*–stems from the title of a 1776 play by F. M. Klinger. The play's original title was *Der Wirrwarr* (Confusion); its final title, suggested by Christoph Kaufmann–a Swiss physician and adherent of J. C. Lavater's pietistic and emotional brand of Christianity–expresses well two major aspects of the new movement: its emotionalism and its stress on action, even physical force. Both can be found not just in Klinger's play (which is set in the travail of the American Revolution) but in those of J. M. R. Lenz, Heinrich Leopold Wagner, and Friedrich (Maler) Müller; in Goethe's first major work, *Götz von Berlichingen* (1773), and in his early lyric poetry; and in Friedrich Schiller's youthful plays *Die Räuber* (The Robbers, 1781) and *Kabale und Liebe* (Intrigue and Love, 1784). The outbursts of feeling so conspicuous in the dramas of the period, outbursts that at first glance do not appear well motivated, are now seen as a long-suppressed reaction to the dry rationalism and prissy rococo tastes of the preceding decades. The stormy and usually young male protagonists proclaim the superiority of individual taste and genius to the imitation typified by the many seventeenth- and eighteenth-century poetics–books that purported to teach the reader how to create poetry through the skillful use of rhetorical techniques and the emulation of the works of classical antiquity. These protagonists are in revolt against prevailing aesthetic precepts based on reason and "good taste," and, less openly, against political reaction and religious orthodoxy. The moody young Werther made notorious in Goethe's *Die Leiden des jungen Werthers* (The Sorrows of Young Werther, 1774) is perhaps the Sturm-und-Drang protagonist par excellence: a man to whom, as to Goethe's Faust, feeling is everything; a man who is moved to commit suicide as much by anger at social injustice as by despair over a tragic love affair.

But, again, one must be cautious about oversimplifying a complex situation. Not so long ago authoritative literary histories tended to depict the Sturm und Drang largely as a reaction to the Enlightenment. It is now clear that the German Enlightenment, which can be interpreted as a much-delayed German Renaissance, began in the latter half of the seventeenth century and persisted into the nineteenth, and that similar progressive tendencies–toward greater political and religious freedom, tolerance, and increasing reliance on reason–can be traced through the entire one-hundred-fifty-year period. The Sturm und Drang built on the individualism that had arisen through eighteenth-century rationalism; in turn, it served as a preparatory stage for the subsequent literary period. The idealism and altruism that were to mark some of the most significant works of Classicism were by no means new with those works: the two greatest writers of the Geniezeit, Goethe and Schiller, who went on to write works that provide the very definition of German Classicism, began to write Classical works while still in the hold of the Sturm und Drang. It has long been a favorite exercise in German literature classes to contrast the Storm-and-Stress and Classical aspects of Schiller's play *Don Carlos* (1787) and of Goethe's rather similar drama *Egmont* (1787), which he had begun work on before moving to Weimar in 1775. Both plays were conceived in the spirit of the Sturm und Drang but received their final, polished form in the period of Classicism.

It can be seen, then, that the line of demarcation between Sturm und Drang and Classicism is ill defined and fluid. Still, a clear if perhaps not broadly based aesthetic and philosophical development can be traced in the chief literary works of the late eighteenth century that culminated in a very different conception of literature from that of the Sturm und Drang, particularly as to form.

It has been mentioned that the term *Classicism* can be construed to refer to the entire span of German literature from before mid century to around 1815. More frequently, however, the labels *German* or *Weimar Classicism* (the latter designation the better one, since the chief works of the period are those of Goethe and Schiller, both of whom lived in Weimar) are used to describe the epoch between Sturm und Drang and Romanticism, roughly from 1786 to 1805. Goethe's sojourn in Italy in 1786-1788 provides one important date to mark his turn to Classicism. Perhaps equally significant is the appearance in 1787 of Schiller's *Don Carlos*, a work written in iambic pentameter rather than in the prose of the Sturm-und-Drang plays. Goethe's *Iphigenie auf Tauris* (Iphigenia in Tauris), also in iambic pentameter, was published in the same year. Although Goethe's philosophical and poetic interests–and the two can never be separated–follow a remarkably consistent pattern over a long period of time, his views on art did change markedly from those of his Sturm und Drang phase, when his models were Shakespeare and James MacPherson's fictive Celtic bard "Ossian." Like Schiller, who arrived at similar conclusions in a series of aesthetic and philosophical essays, Goethe came to believe that the literature of classical antiquity can provide both a suitable form and content (that is, material with timeless, prototypical themes, such as Orestes fleeing the Furies) for the purposes of modern writers. Building in the 1790s on ideas of the art historian and supreme European Hellenist Johann Joachim Winckelmann and on the historical theories of Goethe's one-time mentor Johann Gottfried Herder, Goethe and Schiller insisted that the new *classical* literature (Klassik) must not be a mere imitation of antique models in the manner of the *classicism* (Klassizismus) of seventeenth-century French tragedy; rather, it would combine the ageless aspects of art with an ethical, humanitarian component. Thus, Goethe's *Iphigenie auf Tauris* furnishes Euripides' play with a philosophical underpinning that is quite modern. Victor Lange analyzes the play this way:

> Against a background of two modes of divine authority, one "barbarian" and the other Greek, the meaning of an inescapable bondage to "fate" in the minds of its victims and agents is meticulously explored. The experience of a ritualistic compulsion is here entirely internalized, modifying the familiar impulses of the classical model,

and resolved through the gradual recognition of moral and psychological counter-resources.... This formidable argument is in the play made explicit by four characters, each contending in a different key, but all seeking to deal with what seems inexorable, in a growing awareness of their critical, their "humane" capacities. Thoas, the king of Tauris, moves from archaic ritualism to a tentative understanding of alternative attitudes, Orestes from being agonized by the horror of the Furies to a comprehension of the nature of his obsession: he is relieved of the awesome burden of the curse not so much, as has often been thought, by Iphigenie's "humanity" as by his own efforts at articulating his condition. His friend Pylades, a cunning pragmatist, learns to respect moral obligations. While Iphigenie herself at first acquiesces in her fateful assignment as the exiled priestess of Diana, she gradually transcends her absolute submission by discerning the "mythical" nature of the power of the gods.

It is clear that Goethe here deals with an issue of far more than "classicist" implications, an issue that was at the very centre of eighteenth-century theology: the autonomous modern consciousness faces a divinity which, in the sense of ancient belief as well as contemporary Protestant orthodoxy, is an implacable and arbitrary power. How can the "enlightened" mind cope with such a fatalistic prospect?[2]

As can be seen from this example, Weimar Classicism was to link literature with philosophy in a way designed to be helpful to society. The stage was to become again, as in the Greece of Sophocles "eine moralische Anstalt" (a moral institution), to use Schiller's famous phrase. It was Schiller who made the greatest contributions to this kind of drama (and most of his plays were performed in the distinguished Weimar theater directed by Goethe). Schiller's *Wallenstein* trilogy (1798-1799), *Maria Stuart* (1800), *Die Jungfrau von Orleans* (The Maid of Orleans, 1801), and *Die Braut von Messina* (The Bride of Messina, 1803) all combine in an unprecedented way antique form (including even the Greek chorus in the last play) with contemporary theories of morality. The end of Weimar Classicism is usually linked with the untimely death of Schiller in 1805. Goethe continued to write in his grand, eclectic way until his death in 1832, and the vogue of Romanticism had commenced before Schiller's demise; but the form of literature theorized about and written by Goethe and Schiller ceased to be a force to be reckoned with in 1805.

As in the seven previous *DLB* volumes on German and Austrian writers, we have made an effort to include not only authors who appear in virtually every literary history–writers of unquestioned literary significance; those who are notable for their influence on contemporary writers and the public; and lesser talents who are especially typical of a given movement or tendency– but also unjustly neglected writers who may have received little attention either in English, or, in some cases, in German literary histories. The contributors to this volume have attempted to look at the authors with fresh eyes, to reexamine their place in the literary canon, to examine the works themselves rather than the secondary literature about them. They have also devoted special attention to the primary bibliography of each author, as in some cases it was discovered that no reliable bibliography existed. Under the heading BOOKS, the bibliography at the beginning of each entry lists in chronological order all first editions of the author's independently published works. When contemporary English translations of a work exist, the first American and/or British editions are listed together with the original work. Important later translations are also included. Translations into German, important forewords, contributions to collections, and books edited by the author are listed under OTHER. Significant works by the author that made their first appearance in periodicals are listed under PERIODICAL PUBLICATIONS. As a result of our stress on the bibliographical aspect of each author's literary production, even the specialist will find information in some entries that was previously unavailable in English or German reference works.

The editors and contributors have attempted to present the articles in a way that will be understandable and useful. Assuming that many readers will have little or no knowledge of German, we have included translations of all German titles (except for titles of periodicals) mentioned in the text of each entry and of all quotations. Important secondary literature is listed at the end of each entry. The location of the letters and other papers (the Nachlaß, to use the more specific German term) has been provided in all cases where it is known. The editors are grateful to the contributors and to the publisher for their efforts to unearth bibliographical data, to verify heretofore unsubstantiated information on the lives of the writers, and to provide interesting illustrations for the entries.

—*James Hardin*
Christoph E. Schweitzer

1. Lange writes: "German literary historians have in the past been anxious to interpret this 'classical' phase of German letters as a series of efforts to assert a specifically native genius, gradually freeing itself of what was felt to be an alien rationalism of the (French) Enlightenment, and achieving characteristic works of 'natural' poetic force.

"The rebellious voices of the 'Sturm und Drang' playwrights are, in this view, the first indicators of a new belief in exuberant creativity against which the 'rococo' sensibility seemed merely mannered, anti-social or obsolete. Herder appears in this design as the magisterial defender of national or populist ideas while the anti-naturalistic postulates of Goethe's and Schiller's 'classicist' programme were regarded as a mistaken effort to reinstitute norms emphatically discredited by the German advocates of spontaneity and passion.

"This historical scheme is no longer convincing. The continuity of ideas and postulates of the European tradition of Enlightenment is in Germany far more compelling and striking than the centrifugal tendencies which in literary as well as social postulates challenge its abuses.... The German classical age begins with the assertion of a sense of the new in Lessing's incomparable defence of rational pragmatism; it ends with a disavowal of the social instrumentality of reason in the subjective idealism of the romantic doctrine." *The Classical Age of German Literature* (New York: Holmes & Meier, 1982), pp. 2-3.

2. Lange, pp. 102-103.

Acknowledgments

This book was produced by Bruccoli Clark Layman, Inc. Karen L. Rood is senior editor for the *Dictionary of Literary Biography* series. Philip B. Dematteis was the in-house editor.

Production coordinator is James W. Hipp. Systems manager is Charles D. Brower. Photography editor is Susan Brennen Todd. Permissions editor is Jean W. Ross. Layout and graphics supervisor is Penney L. Haughton. Copyediting supervisor is Bill Adams. Typesetting supervisor is Kathleen M. Flanagan. Typography coordinator is Sheri Beckett Neal. Information systems analyst is George F. Dodge. Charles Lee Egleston is editorial associate. The production staff includes Rowena Betts, Anne L. M. Bowman, Teresa Chaney, Patricia Coate, Sarah A. Estes, Mary L. Goodwin, Cynthia Hallman, Susan C. Heath, David Marshall James, Kathy S. Merlette, Laura Garren Moore, John Myrick, Cathy J. Reese, Laurrè Sinckler, Maxine K. Smalls, John C. Stone III, Jennifer Toth, and Betsy L. Weinberg.

Walter W. Ross and Parris Boyd did the library research with the assistance of the following librarians at the Thomas Cooper Library of the University of South Carolina: Gwen Baxter, Daniel Boice, Faye Chadwell, Cathy Eckman, Gary Geer, Cathie Gottlieb, David L. Haggard, Jens Holley, Jackie Kinder, Thomas Marcil, Marcia Martin, Laurie Preston, Jean Rhyne, Carol Tobin, and Virginia Weathers.

The editors are grateful for the biographical work of Valerie M. Bernhardt, Jeffrey Lopes, and William N. Wallace. The University Research Council of the University of North Carolina at Chapel Hill provided a grant which was instrumental in the completion of this book.

Dictionary of Literary Biography • Volume Ninety-four

German Writers in the
Age of Goethe:
Sturm und Drang to Classicism

Dictionary of Literary Biography

Christian Friedrich von Blanckenburg
(26 January 1744 - 4 May 1796)

G. L. Jones
University College of Wales, Aberystwyth

BOOKS: *Versuch über den Roman*, as B. (Leipzig & Liegnitz: Siegert, 1774; edited by Eberhard Lämmert, Stuttgart: Metzler, 1965);

Beyträge zur Geschichte des teutschen Reiches und teutscher Sitten: Ein Roman. Erster Theil (Leipzig & Liegnitz, 1775; reprinted, Frankfurt am Main: Minerva, 1970);

Litterarische Zusätze zu Johann George Sulzers Allgemeiner Theorie der schönen Künste, in Einzelnen nach alphabetischer Ordnung der Kunstwörter auf einander folgenden Artikeln abgehandelt, 3 volumes (Leipzig: Weidmann, 1796-1798; reprinted, Frankfurt am Main: Athenäum, 1972).

OTHER: Samuel Johnson, *Biographische und critische Nachrichten von einigen englischen Dichtern*, translated by Blanckenburg, 2 volumes (Altenburg, 1781-1783);

"Schreiben über Lessings verloren gegangenen Faust," in Johann Wilhelm von Archenholz, *Literatur und Völkerkunde*, volume 5 (Leipzig, 1784), pp. 82-84; republished in Gotthold Ephraim Lessing, *Gesammelte Werke*, edited by Paul Rilla, 10 volumes (Berlin: Aufbau, 1954-1958) II: 560-562;

Johann Georg Sulzer, *Allgemeine Theorie der schönen Künste in Einzeln, nach alphabetischer Ordnung der Kunstwörter auf einander folgenden Artikeln abgehandelt*, edited by Blanckenburg (4 volumes, Leipzig: Weidmann, 1792-1794; reprinted, 5 volumes, Hildesheim: Olms, 1967).

Christian Friedrich von Blanckenburg, 1790; oil painting by Ernst Gottlob (Gleimhaus, Halberstadt)

PERIODICAL PUBLICATIONS: "Besprechung des Werther," *Neue Bibliothek der schönen Wissenschaften und der freyen Künste*, 18 (1775): 46-95;

"Über die historische Gewißheit," *Neues Deutsches Museum,* 2 (June 1790): 638-680.

Christian Friedrich von Blanckenburg's reputation as a man of letters rests primarily on his *Versuch über den Roman* (Essay on the Novel, 1774). Although it is a work of considerable length, Blanckenburg did not regard it as an exhaustive and systematic treatment of the subject but as an attempt to stimulate critical reflection on a popular genre which had attracted little serious attention in Germany during the eighteenth century. This neglect Blanckenburg ascribes to the belief that the novel is written for "die Unterhaltung der Menge" (the entertainment of the masses) and did not warrant the attention of the literary critic. Blanckenburg considers this neglect reprehensible: should it not be our first duty, he asks, to provide "gesunde Nahrung" (healthy nourishment) for the largest part of the human race? In his view the popular novel of the age, the romance, exerted a pernicious influence on both the aesthetic taste and the moral standards of its readers. Its preoccupation with amorous adventures in exotic settings could, he believed, be countered if the novel were led back to truth and nature. In this way the novel could become both a very pleasant and a very instructive pastime not only for the "Müßiges Frauenzimmer" (idle female) but also for the "denkenden Kopf" (thinking head). With characteristic modesty Blanckenburg addresses his "Bemerkungen" (observations) not to the "Meister der Kunst" (masters of the art) but to aspiring novelists.

Blanckenburg was born in Pomerania on 26 January 1744 at the family estate of Moitzelin, two miles south of Colberg. His father was Dionysius Friedrich von Blanckenburg; his mother's name is not known. A degree of uncertainty is attached to the spelling of the name Blanckenburg; this orthographical ambiguity is not unusual as far as proper names in the eighteenth century are concerned. Although the author's name appears nowhere in *Versuch über den Roman,* the form *Blankenburg* (without the *c*) does occur elsewhere in his published works and is widely used by his contemporaries. This form was adopted by critics and scholars in the nineteenth century and remained in vogue until 1965, when *Versuch über den Roman* was reprinted. The editor of this reprint, Eberhard Lämmert, based his choice of the form *Blanckenburg* (with the *c*) on the biographical research of Jürgen

Sang, whose dissertation on the author was completed in 1967. Since the mid 1960s the form *Blanckenburg* has been gaining ground and is now generally accepted as the standard spelling.

After attending the Military Academy in Berlin, Blanckenburg joined the Regiment of Dragoons, under the command of Anton von Krockow, as a cornet in 1759. He served in the Prussian army until 1776 and advanced to the rank of captain. During the Seven Years War he was injured at the battle of Kunersdorf. Like his distant and more renowned uncle, Ewald von Kleist, he combined the profession of soldier with a love of literature. While stationed at Bunzlau, Silesia (now Bolestawiec, Poland), he amassed a library of approximately six thousand volumes, which were destroyed in a fire. He subsequently collected another forty-five hundred books, which were auctioned at his death. Blanckenburg's most significant works were published before he left the army: his treatise on the novel was published in 1774; in the following year appeared the first volume of his unfinished novel, *Beyträge zur Geschichte des teutschen Reiches und teutscher Sitten* (Contributions to the History of the German Empire and German Manners), and his perceptive review of Goethe's novel *Die Leiden des jungen Werthers* (The Sorrows of Young Werther, 1774).

In *Versuch über den Roman* Blanckenburg's approach is not prescriptive but descriptive: he does not set out rules by which novels should be judged but studies the novels themselves. Before he began writing his book, he says in the preface, he read the most important works in this genre, particularly Christoph Martin Wieland's *Geschichte des Agathon* (History of Agathon, 1766-1767) and Henry Fielding's *The History of Tom Jones, a Foundling* (1740). His insights into the craft of fiction are derived from the practice of Wieland and Fielding. Above all, it is in describing Wieland's work that he arrives at his own understanding of the novel. Although he draws extensively on the writings of established critics such as Henry Home, Moses Mendelssohn, Gotthold Ephraim Lessing, Denis Diderot, and Lord Shaftesbury, he repeatedly stresses the primacy of genius over criticism. For example, in his discussion of humorous characters in the English tradition he expresses the belief that such characters would lack probability if depicted in a German novel; having made this point, he immediately reminds himself in a footnote that genius knows of no such limitations and that he has no desire to be a legislator.

Title page of Blanckenburg's essay on the novel, the work on which his reputation primarily rests

Nevertheless, Blanckenburg felt constrained to include much critical ballast in his essay to lend validity to a genre which had previously been dismissed by critics as trivial. Similarly, in an endeavor to legitimize the new genre he takes many of his examples not from novels but from dramas; he defends this procedure on the grounds that the latter are better known than the former. But while he enlists the support of the literary critic and the dramatist, he places at the center of *Versuch über den Roman* Wieland's *Geschichte des Agathon*, which he describes as the only work which possesses all the essential characteristics of the genre. It is Wieland's practice and not the "rules" of any critic which guide Blanckenburg in his thinking on the nature of the novel.

Blanckenburg not only seeks to distance the novel from the romance but also to distinguish between the novel on the one hand and the epic and the drama on the other. Although he acknowledges that the novel is the modern descendant of the ancient epic, he takes pains to elucidate the differences between them. These differences emanate from the different manners of the ages which brought them into existence. The Greek epic deals with "öffentliche Thaten und Begebenheiten" (public acts and occurrences), that is, with the actions of the "Bürger" (political being); the modern novel deals with "das Seyn des Menschen; das Innre des Menschen" (the being and inner condition of the human being), that is, with his actions and emotions. Blanckenburg argues that the novel is less limited in scope than the epic because it depicts the individual as a human being and not simply as the citizen of a particular state. The epic is by definition national and so is limited in its appeal to a particular culture and society. How, Blanckenburg asks, could a Moslem reader derive any pleasure from the Christian epic? The novel knows no such restriction; its concern is not with public deeds and political actions but with the emotions of the private individual. In this sense its appeal is universal. In typical manner Blanckenburg proves his point empirically by referring to Fielding. What interests us in *Tom Jones,* he declares, are not the external actions and occurrences but "Dieser Jones selbst, dieser Mensch mit seinem Seyn und seinen Empfindungen" (this Jones himself, this human being with his existence and his emotions). Blanckenburg's insistence on the universal dimension of the novel as opposed to the national limitation of the epic is difficult to reconcile with his advocacy elsewhere in *Versuch über den Roman* of German subjects for the aspiring novelist. He is critical of writers who locate their novels in foreign countries, particularly of the vogue for English settings and characters; he argues that the aspiring German novelist should concentrate on the world he knows best–Germany. This contradiction appears again in Blanckenburg's discussion of individuality and universality of character. In spite of his emphasis throughout the work on the individual character which is fashioned by a particular set of circumstances, he also argues that the novel will become realistic if the writer concentrates not on individual eccentricity but on the most typical cases. In other words, the probable is more acceptable than the possible. The argument derives from Aristotle, and it is clear that this contradiction between the national and the human or the individual and the universal is a reflection of the conflicting demands of the neoclassicism of the Enlightenment on the one hand and of the new subjectivism of the Sturm und Drang on the other.

So much of *Versuch über den Roman*, especially the first part, is devoted to the analysis of the depiction of sublime emotions in individual plays that the reader might be forgiven for wondering whether Blanckenburg will ever distinguish unequivocally between the novel and the drama. Indeed, Blanckenburg declares as late as part 2, chapter 9 that there is no real difference between the reader of a novel and the reader of a drama. Elsewhere his interest in the emotional impact of a literary work, dramatic or narrative, prompts him to advocate not simply the expunging of narrative elements from drama but also the introduction of dramatic elements (soliloquy and dialogue) into the novel. Not until part 2, chapter 10 does he attempt to set out clearly the main difference between the novelist and the dramatist. The dramatist, he argues, is mainly concerned with presenting an action–he uses characters to bring an action to life; what lends unity to a dramatic work is the action, not the characters. The novelist is primarily concerned with depicting the development of a character–he is only interested in actions insofar as they contribute to the formation of character; it is character which lends unity to the novel, not the actions or occurrences. The dramatist is prevented from depicting the inner development of character by the exigencies of time and place. Since the dramatic action must unfold quickly and within a restricted physical space, the dramatist cannot depict the development of character; characters in drama are of necessity fully formed. What distinguishes the novelist is his ability to depict "die Veränderung des innern Zustandes seiner Personen" (change in the inner condition of his characters). Although this distinction between the novelist and the dramatist does not occur until fairly late in the book, it is implicit in all that Blanckenburg writes about individual novels and particularly about *Geschichte des Agathon*. In the first chapter he says: "Wenn wir den Agathon untersuchen: so findet es sich so-gleich, daß der Punkt, unter welchem alle Begebenheiten desselben vereinigt sind, kein andrer ist, als das ganze jetzige moralische Seyn des Agathon, seine jetzige Denkungsart und Sitten, die durch all' diese Begebenheiten gebildet, gleichsam das Resultat, die Wirkung aller derselben sind, so daß diese Schrift ein vollkommen dichterisches Ganzes, eine Kette von Ursach und Wirkung ausmacht" (If we examine *Agathon*: then it emerges immediately that the focal point of all occurrences is none other than the whole present moral being of Agathon, his present thinking and behavior which are formed by all these occurrences, which are, as it were, the result, the effect of the same, so that this work constitutes a completely poetic whole, a chain of cause and effect). Whereas Wieland is to be praised for showing his readers how circumstances fashion character, for example, in Agathon's love for Danae, Samuel Richardson is to be censured for failing to depict, in *The History of Sir Charles Grandison* (1753-1754), how Grandison's love for Henrietta comes into being and develops: Richardson merely tells his readers that Grandison loves Henrietta because she is a lovable young lady. Thus, Richardson ceases to be a "Dichter" (poet) and degenerates into a "bloßer Erzehler" (mere narrator). The narrator is inferior to the "Romanen-dichter" (novelist) because he fails to reflect in his work that chain of cause and effect which links the formation and development of character to a specific set of circumstances. A genuine novel will only be produced if the author bases his work on this concept of causality. Blanckenburg provides a clear definition of the novel in his comment on Johann Timotheus Hermes's plan to write a work titled "Geschichte des H. Groß" (History of Mr. Groß): "Wir sollen nämlich in diesem Werke eine Reihe von Begebenheiten und Vorfällen sehen, wodurch H. Groß gleichsam geführt wird, um am Ende, durch ihre Einwirkung auf ihn, vor unsern Augen, das zu werden, was er ist. Natürlich wird also diese Reihe von Begebenheiten, eine, durch die Person des H. Groß verbundene Kette von Ursach und Wirkung seyn, deren Resultat der Charakter des H. Groß ist" (In this work we shall see a series of events and occurrences through which Mr. Groß will be led, as it were, in order to become finally, by their influence upon him, before our very eyes the person that he now is. Of course, this series of events will, therefore, be a chain of cause and effect connected by the person of Mr. Groß, and the character of Mr. Groß will be the result of this chain).

For Blanckenburg the Leibnizian principles of continuity and sufficient reason are not a figment of the philosophical imagination but a true account of the workings of Nature itself. His aim of leading the novel "back to truth and nature" can only be fulfilled if the novelist emulates the work of the divine Creator and bases his fictional world on the structure of the created universe. "Dichter," he declares, "heißen so gerne Schöpfer. Ich glaube, daß sie nur dann diesen Namen verdienen, wann sie ihren Werken so viel Aehnlichkeit, als es möglich ist, mit den Werken des *Uneingeschränkten* zu geben wissen. . . . Wir sehen [im all] eine, bis ins Unendliche fortgehende Reihe verbundener Ursachen und Wirkungen. . . . Wenn der so gepriesene Grundsatz der Nachahmung irgend einen Sinn hat: so ists wohl kein andrer, als der: verfahret in der Verbindung, der Anordnung eurer Werke so, wie die Natur in der Hervorbringung der ihrigen verfährt. . . . Das Werk des Dichters muß eine kleine Welt ausmachen, die der großen so ähnlich ist, als sie es seyn kann" (Poets like to be called creators. I believe that they only merit this name when they give their works as much similarity as possible to the works of the Infinite. . . . We see [in the universe] an infinite series of linked causes and effects. . . . If the much praised principle of imitation has any meaning: then it must be: proceed in the linking and ordering of your works in the same way as Nature proceeds in the execution of hers. . . . The work of the poet must be a small world which is as similar to the large world as it possibly can be). Blanckenburg places two demands on the novelist: first, that he should reflect in the finite world of his fictional creation the causal structure of the infinite world of the divine Creator, and second, that he should show in a concrete, sensuous manner how the chain of cause and effect is directed toward a particular purpose. The universe is structured teleologically, although man, with his finite understanding, cannot always perceive this structure; human weakness prevents him from comprehending the great chain of being in its entirety. In the fictional world, however, Blanckenburg demands that the reader be granted this comprehension by the novelist: "Nur müssen wir in dieser Nachahmung der großen Welt mehr sehen können, als wir in der großen Welt selbst, unsrer Schwachheit wegen, zu sehen vermögen" (Only we must be able to see more in this imitation of the great world than we are able to see—on account of our weaknesses—in the great world itself). Thus, the novelist is required to imitate the causal structure of the universe and also to emulate the purpose of the Infinite Creator. In the context of this discussion Blanckenburg poses the question: at what point should the novelist end his portrayal of his main character? The answer is that the reader should be left at the end of the novel not in a state of agitation but in one of calm satisfaction. This state of calm will not be achieved if the novel ends in death or destruction: "Der Gedanke, die Vorstellung von einer Verwandlung in Nichts, ist für die Menschheit, in aller Art, der trostloseste, der schrecklichste aller Gedanken. Wir können ihn nicht aushalten, nicht ertragen.–Die gütige Vorsicht hat ihn uns unbegreiflich gemacht" (The thought, the idea of a transformation into nothing, is for mankind in every way the most disconsolate, the most terrible of all thoughts. We cannot bear it, we cannot endure it.–Kind Providence has rendered it incomprehensible for us). Blanckenburg shares the optimism of the Enlightenment and argues that the individual will at the end of his life be in as perfect a state as is compatible with the specific circumstances in which he finds himself. Blanckenburg's thinking on the structure and purpose of the fictional world forms a close parallel to Lessing's arguments in *Hamburgische Dramaturgie* (Hamburg Dramaturgy, 1769) on the providential structure and purpose of the dramatic world. It is typical of Blanckenburg's critical flexibility, however, that he is prepared to modify his opinion in the light of creative practice; he concedes the possibility that the inner state of the individual may be such that he cannot be "in dieser Welt . . . befestigt" (preserved in this world). The novelist would be justified in allowing such a person to die, for only in this way would he be able to satisfy his readers.

The great chain of being is not only the guarantor of truth and reality in the structure of the fictional world; it is also the source of both the pleasure and the instruction which the reader should receive from the novel. In contemplating the reciprocal relationship between circumstances and character, the reader will derive pleasure from the activation of his intellectual powers. Furthermore, such contemplation will help him to refine his own moral sensibility: it will prevent him from passing precipitate and ill-founded judgments on the actions of his fellowmen, and it will enable him to perfect his own being by avoiding those causes which produce deleterious effects; even if a particular set of circumstances has no direct relevance to his own life, the reader will have learned how to think by contemplating the relationship between cause and effect. Pleasure and instruction are indivisible. The novelist will not achieve his didactic end by overt moralizing; Richardson is criticized for placing moral sermons in

Frontispiece and title page for Blanckenburg's only published novel

the mouths of his characters, and Jean-Jacques Rousseau is censured for introducing a treatise on dueling in *Julie, ou la Nouvelle Héloïse* (1761). Moralizing in the novel must arise naturally from the characters and situations; it must not be imposed on them extraneously. Blanckenburg contrasts the instructive pleasure afforded by a novel such as *Geschichte des Agathon* with the "Vergnügen der Ueberraschung" (the pleasure of surprise) which is to be found in most historical novels. This pleasure of surprise is produced by unexpected twists in the narrative and is described by Blanckenburg as "höchst armselig" (highly impoverished). It will cloy after the first reading, whereas the pleasure which comes from observing the chain of cause and effect cannot even be felt entirely at the first reading and demands repeated readings if it is to be experienced fully. Blanckenburg stresses that the novelist must present his ideas in a concrete, graphic manner. If he fails to do so, his novel will provide neither pleasure nor instruction.

Versuch über den Roman stands midway between the rationalism of the Enlightenment and the subjectivism of Sturm und Drang. In his enthusiasm for Shakespeare, his stress on the emotive power of literature, his concentration on the individual character and its development, and his advocacy of the depiction of national manners and

characteristics, Blanckenburg is shown to be influenced by that same zeltgeist that influenced his contemporary, Johann Gottfried Herder (both men were born in 1744). At the same time he remains indebted to the philosophical thought and language of the Enlightenment. Blanckenburg makes no secret of his admiration for Lessing. Stylistically, *Versuch über den Roman* is much closer to Lessing's *Hamburgische Dramaturgie* than to the essays in Herder's *Von deutscher Art und Kunst* (On German Character and Art, 1773). In many ways Blanckenburg is that "denkende Kopf" (thinking mind) for whom *Geschichte des Agathon* had, according to Lessing, been written. Wieland himself was not slow to recognize Blanckenburg's achievement. In a 19 May 1774 letter to the dramatist Tobias Philipp, Freiherr von Gebler he comments: "Das Seltsamste an der Sache ist, daß dieser Leutnant mehr Kenntnisse, Geschmack und Kritik hat, als irgend einer von unsern Professoren, Kunstrichtern und Recensenten" (The strangest thing about it is that this lieutenant has more knowledge, taste, and critical sense than any one of our professors, critics, or reviewers).

In 1775 Blanckenburg demonstrated his acumen as a reviewer with his discussion of Goethe's *Die Leiden des jungen Werthers* in the *Neue Bibliothek der schönen Wissenschaften und der freyen Künste*

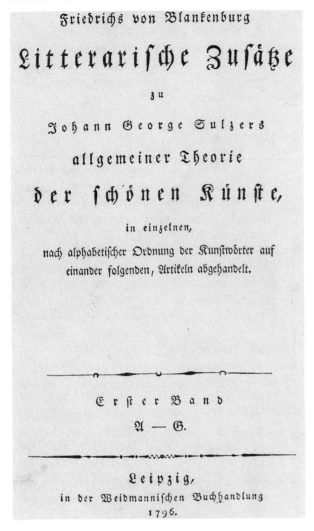

Title page for Blanckenburg's addenda to a work on aesthetics by Johann George Sulzer

(New Library of Belles-lettres and the Liberal Arts). Blanckenburg praises Goethe for showing how Werther's character and eventual death are fashioned by and follow necessarily from the circumstances in which he finds himself. Blanckenburg may not be able to condone Werther's suicide in purely rational terms, but he responds sympathetically and with considerable understanding to Goethe's artistic achievement. Goethe's novel also obliged Blanckenburg to revise his negative opinion on the validity of the epistolary novel. In *Versuch über den Roman* he had criticized such novels on three counts: first, the characters are too involved emotionally in their fates to be able to give a coherent account of cause and effect; second, they can only recount past events, and consequently, the emotional impact on the reader is reduced–all the reader hears is "narration"; third, the characters are obliged to talk about themselves and thus cannot avoid the charge of garrulity and arrogance. These objections are overruled in Blanckenburg's review of *Die Leiden des jungen Werthers*. How else, he asks, could Goethe have allowed Werther to pour out his heart in such a graphic manner than by writing letters to his friend?

Blanckenburg's perspicacity as a reviewer was not matched by his effort to write creatively. His only extant novel, *Beyträge zur Geschichte des teutschen Reiches und teutscher Sitten*, designed as a satirical exposé of the manners of the contemporary German rural gentry, fails because its author is too intent on exploring the motivation of his characters and the causality which lies behind the events. It is as if Blanckenburg consciously set out to exemplify in his novel the theory he had advanced so persuasively in *Versuch über den Roman*. *Beyträge zur Geschichte des teutschen Reiches und teutscher Sitten* is, as Peter Michelsen says, the work of a theoretician, lacking in creative power. That it never proceeded further than the first part probably indicates its author's awareness of his own limitations as a writer of fiction.

In 1776 Blanckenburg resigned his commission; he had been suffering from ulceration of the lungs for some time and had been advised by his doctors to rest and not to participate in the spring exercises of the Prussian cavalry. He settled in Leipzig in 1778 and remained there until his death on 4 May 1796. In Leipzig he could enjoy the company of many like-minded friends, foremost among them Christian Felix Weiße, the editor of the *Neue Bibliothek der schönen Wissenschaften und der freyen Künste*. His publications during the Leipzig years attest to the breadth of his literary interests. In 1781 and 1783 his translation in two parts of Samuel Johnson's *Prefaces, Biographical and Critical, to the Works of the English Poets* (1779-1781) appeared; in 1784 he published "Schreiben über Lessings verloren gegangenen Faust" (Letter on Lessing's Lost *Faust*), which contains an outline of Lessing's fragmentary drama. This letter testifies to Blanckenburg's interest in contemporary German literature and also to his profound admiration for Lessing. In the year of his death the first of three volumes of addenda to an established work on aesthetics was published under the title *Litterarische Zusätze zu Johann George Sulzers Allgemeiner Theorie der schönen Künste* (Literary Addenda to Johann George Sulzer's General Theory of the Fine Arts).

Weiße's obituary of Blanckenburg in the *Neue Bibliothek der schönen Wissenschaften und der freyen Künste* praises not only Blanckenburg's qualities as a Prussian officer and the breadth of his scholarly pursuits but also the congeniality of his character. In spite of his learned interests, Weiße wrote, Blanckenburg was no recluse; the stress he placed in his theoretical writings on social virtues was no doubt a reflection of his own character. He possessed "die seltene Gabe, sich Personen von ganz verschiedenen Fähigkeiten und Kenntnissen . . . mitzutheilen" (the rare gift of being able to communicate with people of quite different abilities and knowledge), which made him "nicht nur zum Freunde aller hiesigen Gelehrten, sondern auch zum willkommenen Gesellschafter in den besten Familienzirkeln jedes Standes" (not only the friend of all local scholars but also a welcome guest in the best family circles of every social class).

In 1776, in response to a request for information about himself to be published in Karl Konrad Streit's *Alphabetisches Verzeichnis aller im Jahr 1774 in Schlesien lebender Schriftsteller* (Alphabetical Index of All Writers Living in Silesia in the Year 1774, 1776) Blanckenburg had written self-effacingly: "Ich pfuschere . . . so ein bisgen ins Handwerk, wie der Bauernadvocat ins Handwerk des Rechtsgelehrten; höchstens bin ich Dilettante. Und von meiner Schriftstellerey Ihnen mehr zu sagen, als was die Welt schon so sehr wider meinen Willen weiß, und was Ihnen allenfalls das Titelblatt meines Versuchs sagen kann, würd ich mir als eine bloße Eitelkeit anrechnen, die wohl dem Gelehrten, nur nicht dem bloßen Liebhaber zu vergeben ist. Ich weiß auch wirklich von der Geschichte meiner Autorschaft, und meinem—wenn Sie wollen, Gelehrtenleben nichts hinzusetzen, das verdiente, dem Setzer und Drucker einige Mühe zu machen. Der Zuschnitt zum Gelehrten ist bey mir nie gemacht worden: was ich bin, bin ich so von ungefehr, durch mich selbst geworden"

(I meddle . . . a little in my craft, as the country lawyer does in the craft of the jurist; at best, I am a dilettante. And to tell you more about my efforts at writing than the world already knows against my will and what can be found on the title page of my *Versuch*, I would regard as mere vanity which may well be forgiven in the scholar but not in the mere amateur. I really know of nothing that might be added to the history of my authorship or, if you wish, of my scholarship, which would merit the efforts of the compositor or the printer. I have never regarded myself as a scholar; what I am, I have become more or less by my own efforts).

References:

Richard Ellis Dye, "Blanckenburgs 'Werther'-Rezeption," in *Goethezeit: Studien zur Erkenntnis und Rezeption Goethes und seiner Zeitgenossen. Festschrift für Stuart Atkins*, edited by Gerhart Hoffmeister (Bern & Munich: Francke, 1981), pp. 65-80;

Jürgen Jacobs, "Die Theorie und ihr Exempel: Zur Deutung von Wielands *Agathon* in Blanckenburg's *Versuch über den Roman*," *Germanisch-Romanische Monatsschrift*, 31 (1981): 32-42;

Dieter Kimpel, *Der Roman der Aufklärung* (Stuttgart: Metzler, 1967), pp. 97-104;

Wolfgang Lockemann, *Die Entstehung des Erzählproblems* (Meisenheim: Hain, 1963), pp. 166-184;

Peter Michelsen, *Laurence Sterne und der deutsche Roman des achtzehnten Jahrhunderts* (Göttingen: Vandenhoeck & Ruprecht, 1962), pp. 141-176;

Jürgen Sang, *Christian Friedrich von Blanckenburg und seine Theorie des Romans: Eine monographische Studie* (Munich: Schön, 1967);

Max Sommerfeld, "Romantheorie und Romantypus der deutschen Aufklärung," *Deutsche Vierteljahrsschrift*, 4 (1926): 459-490;

Wilhelm Vosskamp, "Blankenburg und Blankenburgrezeption: Probleme der Romanpoetik im 18. und frühen 19. Jahrhundert," *Akten des V. Internationalen Germanisten-Kongresses*, 3 (1976): 193-200;

Christian Felix Weiße, "Einige Nachrichten von dem Leben des Hrn. von Blankenburg, während seines Aufenthaltes in Leipzig, und seinem Tode," *Neue Bibliothek der schönen Wissenschaften und der freyen Künste*, 59 (1797): 304-311.

Papers:
A few of Christian Friedrich von Blanckenburg's letters have been preserved in the Nicolai-Nachlaß, Tübingen, and the Eschenburg-Nachlaß, Wolfenbüttel.

Heinrich Christian Boie
(19 July 1744 - 3 March 1806)

Phillip S. McKnight
University of Kentucky

BOOK: *Lieder der Freude: Gesungen zu Meldorf am 28. und 29. Januar 1804* (Friedrichstadt: Bade & Fischer, 1804).

OTHER: *Göttinger Musenalmanach*, edited by Boie (Göttingen: Dieterich, 1770-1775);
Deutsches Museum, edited by Boie and Christian Wilhelm von Dohm (Leipzig: Weygand, 1776-1788);
Richard Chandler, *Reisen in Klein-Asien unternommen auf Kosten der Gesellschaft der Dilettanti und beschrieben von Richard Chandler,* translated by Boie (Leipzig: Weygand, 1776);
Chandler, *Reisen in Griechenland,* translated by Boie (Leipzig: Weygand, 1777);
Christian and Friedrich Leopold Grafen zu Stolberg, *Gedichte,* edited by Boie (Leipzig: Weygand, 1779);
Neues Deutsches Museum, edited by Boie (Leipzig: Göschen, 1789-1791).

Heinrich Christian Boie was, by his own admission, a poet possessed of only moderate skills of versification and inclined to the light and elegant expression of second- and third-rank eighteenth-century poets. Nevertheless, his literary stature has been secured by his activity as editor of two of the most important literary journals of the century, the *Göttinger Musenalmanach* (Göttingen Almanac of the Muses) and the *Deutsches Museum* (German Museum). With his tireless efforts to support and encourage young talent and his remarkable ability to attract all the major writers of his time, regardless of their conflicting viewpoints, Boie worked unselfishly to promote the development of German literature.

Boie was born on 19 July 1744 in Meldorf, Holstein, the son of a preacher, Johann Friedrich Boie, and Engel Katharina Haberkorn Boie. In 1757 his father received a promotion and moved to Flensburg; he was eventually appointed church provost by the king of Denmark, a connection Boie would later use to further his own ca-

Dithmarscher Landesmuseum, Meldorf

reer. His schooling in Flensburg proved to be weak in the classical languages; Boie became proficient in French, English, and Italian, however, and his interest in French and English writing never waned in spite of the changing reception of these two literatures in Germany and his own close association with many of the young anti-French writers.

Boie enrolled in the school of theology at the University of Jena on 23 May 1764 but soon

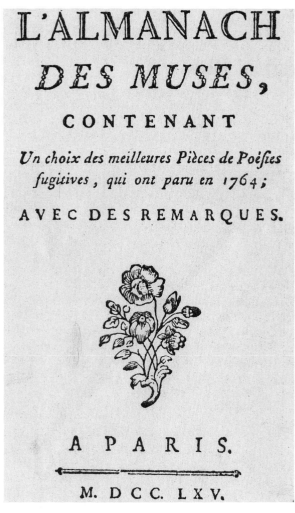

L'ALMANACH DES MUSES,

CONTENANT

Un choix des meilleures Pièces de Poésies fugitives, qui ont paru en 1764;

AVEC DES REMARQUES.

A PARIS.

M. DCC. LXV.

Title page of the first issue of the French literary journal that became the model for Boie's Göttinger Musenalmanach

switched to law, which he thought would provide more financial security. At the end of 1767 he undertook the first of several educational journeys, stopping to make the acquaintance of Christian Adolf Klotz in Halle, Ludwig Gleim in Halberstadt, Johann Joachim Eschenburg in Brunswick, and Gotthold Ephraim Lessing in Hamburg. On 17 April 1769 he transferred to the University of Göttingen; for the next five years he earned a modest living as a private tutor to several young Englishmen, from whom he had occasional difficulty extracting obedience and timely remuneration. In Göttingen his interest in literature soon brought him into contact with the poet, dramatist, and translator Friedrich Wilhelm Gotter. Abraham Gotthelf Kästner, a professor at Göttingen, introduced Boie and Gotter to the French literary journal *Almanach des Muses ou Choix de Poésies fugitives* and urged them to estab-

lish a similar publication in Germany to display the year's best poetry. Boie quickly became the driving force behind the organization of the journal. To gain national support he undertook a prolonged trip with Gottfried August Bürger to Berlin, where he established contact with Friedrich Nicolai, Moses Mendelssohn, and Anna Luise Karsch. There he was invited to the "Mittwochsgesellschaft" (Wednesday Society), which included such prominent figures as Karl Wilhelm Ramler, Johann Heinrich Lambert, Johann Georg Sulzer, and Karl Gotthelf Lessing, the younger brother of Gotthold Ephraim Lessing. Ramler—whose poetry Boie valued almost as highly as that of Friedrich Gottlob Klopstock—and Karsch became important contributors to his journals.

When Christian Heinrich Schmid's *Almanach der deutschen Musen auf das Jahr 1770* (Almanac of German Muses for the Year 1770) in Leipzig made it to press before Boie's *Göttinger Musenalmanach*, Boie accused Schmid of having obtained galley proofs of his almanac and of appropriating his idea. Klotz's polemical response in the *Deutsche Bibliothek der schönen Wissenschaften* (German Library of Belles Lettres) backfired, actually increasing interest in Boie's journal. Boie, who eliminated the generally superficial book reviews carried by the Leipzig and French journals, has deservedly received credit as the creator of a publication format that remained popular for more than a hundred years and a journal that became the central publishing outlet for the members of the "Göttinger Hainbund" (Göttingen Grove League) as well as other prominent and promising writers.

By 1772 the almanac had begun to cover a wide diversity of poetic trends, with contributions by Matthias Claudius, Bürger, Eschenburg, Gleim, Gotter, Ramler, and Karsch, and even epigrams and riddles by Lessing. Even more significantly, Boie had drawn a circle of students and young poets to the almanac, one of whom was Johann Heinrich Voß, who came to Göttingen at the beginning of the summer semester of 1772. Voß, who later married Boie's sister, Ernestine, was instrumental in the formation of the Göttinger Hainbund. Although Boie was not present at the founding of the group during the famous moonlit walk under the oaks on 12 September 1772, he was given honorary membership with the name of Werdomar, after the leader of the bard's chorus in Klopstock's drama *Herrmanns Schlacht* (Herrmann's Battle, 1769). Besides

Title page of the first issue of Boie's journal

the *Teutsche Merkur* for distribution in Göttingen in 1773, during the height of the group's anti-Wieland polemic. The *Musenalmanach* reached the apex of its success in 1774 with Bürger's gruesome ballad "Lenore" and contributions from Goethe and Johann Heinrich Merck. Shortly thereafter Boie turned the editorship over to Voß, partly because he felt that the Hainbund had begun to propagate an affected bardic tone more closely resembling Johann Michael Denis and Karl Friedrich Kretschmann than Klopstock, and partly because Voß, during Boie's absence, had included his poem "Michaelis," with its barb directed at Wieland.

Boie's energetic collection of subscriptions for Klopstock's much-heralded but poorly received *Die deutsche Gelehrtenrepublik* (The German Republic of Scholars, 1774) enhanced his reputation as a mediator between writers and the public. Boie also negotiated publishing contracts for writers; according to Boie's biographer, Karl Weinhold, Johann Gottfried Herder received a substantially smaller honorarium, smaller print, and a more poorly printed copy for the second part (1779) of his *Volkslieder* (Folk Songs) than he had for the first part (1778), the contract for which had been negotiated by Boie.

In 1775 Boie met Christian Wilhelm von Dohm in Göttingen, and they began to formulate plans for a new journal, the *Deutsches Museum*, which, as Boie wrote to Voß on 27 August 1775, would disseminate German spirit and knowledge and create a common bond among Germans. His public call for contributions sent out on 12 September 1775 stated his intention to create a German national journal which would publish articles of current political, social, economic, and scientific interest in addition to poetry, fiction, and philosophical articles. Appearing monthly, the *Deutsches Museum* led off in January 1776 with Bürger's translation of Homer's *Iliad* and soon became one of the most important periodicals in eighteenth-century Germany, publishing contributions by virtually every major writer. Owing to their different interests, Dohm edited the political treatises and statistical data, and Boie edited the literary pieces. Eventually the editors encountered difficulty in agreeing on selections of contributions. After alternating the editorship of the issues for a time in 1777, they signed a contract which left Dohm as a consultant to the journal. By 1781 the *Deutsches Museum* was no longer able to maintain its original circulation of one thousand copies, and in December 1788 the pub-

Boie and Voß, the group included Carl Christian Clausewitz, Karl Friedrich Cramer, Johann Friedrich Hahn, Ludwig Christoph Heinrich Hölty, Johann Anton Leisewitz, Johann Martin Miller, Gottlob Dietrich Miller, Christian and Friedrich Stolberg, and Johann Thomas Ludwig Wehrs. In addition, Ernst Theodor Johann Brückner, Karl August Wilhelm von Closen, Christian Hieronymus Esmarch, Schack (Jacques) Hermann Ewald, Leopold Friedrich Günther Goeckingk, Friedrich Wilhelm Gotter, Christian Adolf Overbeck, Gottlob Friedrich Ernst Schönborn, Johann Gottfried Friedrich Seebach, and Anton Matthias Sprickmann were associated with the group.

Although Boie supported the Göttinger Hainbund's espousal of God, country, virtue, and friendship, he was less inclined to sympathize with the missionary zeal with which his compatriots spread this message. He maintained his contacts with other writers, notably Christoph Martin Wieland, from whom he ordered fifty copies of

Manuscript for a poem by Boie (Gustav Könnecke, Bilderatlas zur Geschichte der deutschen Nationallitteratur
[Graz: Akademische Druck- und Verlagsanstalt, 1981])

lisher, Weygand, ended the journal without telling Boie. In July 1789 Boie began the *Neues Deutsches Museum* (New German Museum), using a smaller format and Göschen as the publisher. With the attention of Europe riveted on the French Revolution, the political content of the journal became the dominant feature. The journal lasted until June 1791.

Unable to support himself entirely from the *Deutsches Museum*, Boie had moved to Hannover in February 1776 to work as staff secretary for Field Marshal Freiherr August von Spörken. There he began a sentimental friendship with Luise Mejer, who turned down his proposal of marriage because of her poor health. The year 1776 was a difficult one for Boie, whose friend Hölty died in his arms in September after a long bout with tuberculosis.

In May 1781 Boie moved to Meldorf to take a job as high bailiff in Süderdithmarschen. For a

while he contemplated marrying Annalie Schlegel to stabilize his shaky financial condition; but Luise Mejer's health took a sudden turn for the better, and they married in June 1785 after a three-year engagement. The marriage ended a year later when Luise died in childbirth, unable to deliver the baby. In 1788 Boie married Luise's friend, Sara von Hugo, with whom he raised seven children. In 1790 he was appointed royal commissioner by the king of Denmark.

Boie gave up a plan to publish his collected poetry in 1788 in recognition that, although it might have been relevant to do so ten years before, the poems no longer had much value. He did publish four poems dedicated to King Christian VII of Denmark in 1804 under the title *Lieder der Freude* (Songs of Joy). He died in Meldorf on 3 March 1806. A substantial portion of his poetry was published in Weinhold's biography (1868).

Letters:

Ich war wohl klug, daß ich dich fand: Heinrich Christian Boies Briefwechsel mit Luise Mejer, 1777-1785, edited by Ilse Schreiber (Munich: Biederstein, 1961);

Heinrich Christian Boie: Briefe aus Berlin 1769-70, edited by Gerhard Hay (Hildesheim: Gerstenberg, 1970);

"11 Briefe von Heinrich Christian Boie und Luise Mejer an Sophie La Roche (1779-1788)," *Wolfenbüttler Studien zur Auflklärung,* 3 (1976): 67-99;

Gerhard Steiner, "Johann Karl Wezel und Heinrich Christian Boie: Bisher ungedruckte Briefe mit Erläuterungen," in *Neues aus der Wezelforschung,* volume 2 (Sondershausen: Arbeitskreis des Kulturbundes der DDR, 1984), pp. 48-58.

Biography:

Karl Weinhold, *Heinrich Christian Boie: Beitrag zur Geschichte der deutschen Literatur im achtzehnten Jahrhundert* (Halle: Verlag des Waisenhauses, 1868).

References:

Jürgen Behrens, "Johann Heinrich Thomsen, Heinrich Christian Boie und Friedrich von Hahn," in *Festschrift für Detlev Schumann zum 70. Geburtstag,* edited by Albert R. Schmitt (Munich: Dalp, 1970), pp. 83-88;

Hans Grantzow, *Geschichte des Göttinger und des Vossischen Musenalmanachs* (Berlin: Ebering, 1909);

Walter Hofstaetter, *Das Deutsche Museum und Das Neue Deutsche Museum* (Leipzig: Voigtländer, 1908);

Alfred Kelletat, ed., *Der Göttinger Hain* (Stuttgart: Reclam, 1979);

Robert Prutz, *Der Göttinger Dichterbund* (Leipzig: Wiegand, 1841; reprinted, Bern: Lang, 1970);

Wolfgang Vulpius, ed., "Heinrich Christian Boie: Stammbuch. Mit Ergänzungen von Ursula Schulz," in *Genio huius loci: Dank an Leiva Petersen,* edited by D. Kuhn and B. Zeller (Vienna & Cologne: Böhlau, 1982), pp. 33-78;

Jürgen Wilke, *Literarische Zeitschriften des 18. Jahrhunderts (1688-1789), Teil II: Repertorium* (Stuttgart: Metzler, 1978).

Papers:

Most of Heinrich Christian Boie's papers are in the Staatsbibliothek Preußischer Kulturbesitz, West Berlin, and include several hundred letters to Bürger, Gerstenberg, Herder, Nicolai, and family members, as well as five files of hand-copied poems.

Ulrich Bräker

(22 December 1735 - circa 11 September 1798)

James Hardin
University of South Carolina

BOOKS: *Lebensgeschichte und natürliche Ebentheuer des armen Mannes im Tockenburg*, edited by Hans Heinrich Füßli (Zurich: Orell, Geßner & Füßli, 1789); translated by Derek Bowman as *The Life Story and Real Adventures of the Poor Man of Toggenburg* (Edinburgh: Edinburgh University Press, 1970);

Tagebuch des armen Mannes im Tockenburg, edited by Füßli (Zurich: Orell, Geßner & Füßli, 1792);

Der arme Mann im Tockenburg: Nach den Originalhandschriften, edited by Eduard Bülow (Leipzig: Wigand, 1852);

Etwas über William Shakespeares Schauspiele, von einem armen ungelehrten Weltbürger, der das Glück genoß, ihn zu lesen, edited by Hermann Todsen (Berlin: Meyer & Jessen, 1911); translated by Bowman as *A Few Words about William Shakespeare's Plays: By a Poor Ignorant Citizen of the World Who Had the Good Fortune to Read Him* (London: Wolff, 1979; New York: Ungar, 1979);

Leben und Schriften Ulrich Bräkers, des armen Mannes im Tockenburg, edited by Samuel Voellmy, 3 volumes (Basel: Birkhäuser, 1945)—comprises volume 1: *Lebensgeschichte und natürliche Ebenteuer des armen Mannes im Tockenburg*; volume 2: *Umwelt und Tagebücher*; volume 3: "Die Freunde"; "Der Wanderer"; "Bräker und Lavater: Gespräch im Reiche der Toten"; "Etwas über William Shakespeares Schauspiele."

Editions and Collections: *Etwas über William Shakespeares Schauspiele, von einem armen ungelehrten Weltbürger, der das Glück genoß, ihn zu lesen*, edited by Walter Muschg (Klosterberg & Basel: Schwabe, 1942);

Etwas über William Shakespeares Schauspiele, von einem armen ungelehrten Weltbürger, der das Glück genoß, denselben zu lesen: Anno 1780, edited by Claus Träger (Leipzig: Insel, 1964);

Bräkers Werke, edited by Hans-Günther Thalheim (Berlin & Weimar: Aufbau, 1964);

Ulrich Bräker; portrait by Heinrich Füßli (Schloßmuseum, Thun; photo by A. Müller, Lichtenstieg)

Lebensgeschichte und natürliche Abenteuer des armen Mannes im Tockenburg, edited by Werner Günther (Stuttgart: Reclam, 1965);

Ulrich Bräker Lesebuch, edited by Heinz Weder (Frankfurt am Main: Fischer, 1973);

Chronik Ulrich Bräker: Auf der Grundlage der Tagebücher, 1770-1798, edited by Christian Holliger and others (Bern: Haupt, 1985);

Raisonierendes Bauerngespräch über das Bücherlesen und den äusserlichen Gottesdienst, 2 volumes, edited by Alois Stadler and Peter Wegelin (St. Gall: Erker, 1985);

Die Gerichtsnacht oder Was ihr wollt, 2 volumes, edited by Stadler and Wegelin (St. Gall: Erker, 1987).

PERIODICAL PUBLICATION: "Das Shakespeare-Büchlein des armen Mannes im Toggenburg vom Jahre 1780," edited by E. Götzinger, *Jahrbuch der deutschen Shakespeare-Gesellschaft,* 12 (1877): 100-168.

Ulrich Bräker is one of the most remarkable figures in the history of German literature: a self-taught man of humble origin who wrote one of the most absorbing autobiographies of the eighteenth century, a provincial laborer and goatherd who was among the first in the German-speaking lands to recognize the greatness of Shakespeare, a voracious reader and tireless writer whose thirty-five-hundred-page diary is a uniquely detailed document of his time. Although he is increasingly the object of scholarship, it is still difficult to assess Bräker's writings in their totality since two-thirds of the diary and a novel–"Jaus der Liebensritter" (Jaus the Knight of Love)–have yet to be published.

Bräker was born in Wattwil in the Toggenburg area of eastern Switzerland on 22 December 1735 to Johannes Bräker, a farm laborer, and Anna Bräker. He grew up almost entirely without formal education and had to work hard for his living from an early age. On the first page of his autobiography he writes: "Mein Vater war sein Tage ein armer Mann; auch meine ganze Freundschaft hatte keinen reichen Mann aufzuweisen" (My father was a poor man all his days; and there wasn't a single rich man in my entire family). But in the winters he attended school and learned to read and write. He read primarily the Bible and devotional literature, dreaming of becoming a preacher. In the meantime his father, struggling desperately to secure a living for his wife and eight children, worked at a variety of jobs, including the preparation of saltpeter, spinning, and raising cattle. Bräker had to care for the cattle and work in the field.

At the age of seventeen Bräker began to receive religious instruction from a preacher from Zurich, Heinrich Näf. Bräker's autobiography gives an unforgettable description of the deep impression Näf made on the boy and conveys the enthusiasm and joy in learning that were to characterize Bräker for the rest of his life. "Er unterrichtete mich gut und gründlich, und war mir in der Seele lieb. Oft erzählt' ich meinem

Bräker and his wife, Salome Ambühl Bräker (portrait by Joseph Reinhard, Bernisches Historisches Museum, Bern)

Vater ganze Stunden lang, was er mit mir geredet hatte; und meynete dann, er sollte davon so gerührt werden wie ich . . . aber ich merkte wohl, daß es ihm nicht recht zu Herzen gieng. . . . Noch auf den heutigen Tag ist meine Liebe zu ihm nicht erloschen. Viel hundertmal denk' ich mit gerührter Seele an dieses redlichen Manns Treu und Eifer; an seinen liebevollen Unterricht, welchen ich von seinen holdseligen Lippen sog, und den mein damals gewiß auch für das Gute weiche und empfängliche Herz so begierig aufnahm" (He taught me well and thoroughly, and I was very fond of him. I often told my father for hours at a time what he had discussed with me; and thought then, that he would be as touched by it as much as I was . . . but I then noticed that it did not really make much of an impression on him. . . . To this very day my love for him [Näf] has not faded. Many hundreds of times I think with devotion of this upright man's faithfulness and zeal; of his loving instruction, that I drew from his sweet lips, and

Butler's *Hudibras* (1663-1664, 1678), Tobias Smollet's *The Expedition of Humphry Clinker* (1771), Heinrich Jung-Stilling's early autobiographical writings (1777-1789), Karl Philipp Moritz's *Anton Reiser* (1785-1790), and Miguel de Cervantes's *Don Quixote* (1605, 1615).

The autobiography would likely have remained in obscurity were it not for a preacher, Martin Imhof, who in 1783 sent excerpts from Bräker's writings to the Zurich publisher Hans Heinrich Füßli. The latter was impressed by the vigor and freshness of the work and published excerpts in an almanac, then brought out a portion of the work as a book.

The diary, even in truncated published form, is a significant document in eighteenth-century cultural history. It combines characteristics of the picaresque novel with probing pietistic self-analysis, elements of the travel novel, and even the worldly urbanity of a work by Wieland. Bowman points out that *Lebensgeschichte und natürliche Ebentheuer des armen Mannes im Tockenburg* conveys both in style and content a sense of the intellectual and moral growth of its author. There are the simple, rustic beginnings–strikingly reminiscent of the first pages of Hans Jakob Christoffel von Grimmelshausen's novel *Der abentheuerliche Simplicissimus Teutsch* (1669; translated as *The Adventurous Simplicissimus*, 1912); the lively depiction of the world and Bräker's fall from innocence, recounted in realistic, earthy language; and the reflective later chapters that treat in more complex style the author's growing awareness of the labyrinthine nature of worldly affairs and that reveal his increasing wisdom.

A second volume, *Tagebuch des armen Mannes im Tockenburg* (Diary of the Poor Man in Toggenburg, 1792), was much less successful than the first, and Füßli, in spite of Bräker's pleas, decided against continuing publication of the diary. But the success of the earlier work brought Bräker into contact with well-known Swiss writers and scholars such as Johann Caspar Lavater and Hans Caspar Hirzel. His fame had reached its peak, and he made several trips, mostly on foot. He was still poor, but an entry dated 1788 in the appendix to *Lebensgeschichte und natürliche Ebentheuer des armen Mannes im Tockenburg* reveals a relatively contented, purposeful view of life: "Lesen und Schreiben ist mir wieder mehr als jemals zum unentbehrlichen Bedürfniß geworden. Und sollt' ich auch die gleichgültigsten Dinge in mein Tagebuch kritzeln, oder in alten Kalendern studiren! Doch, ich habe keinen Mangel an Bü-

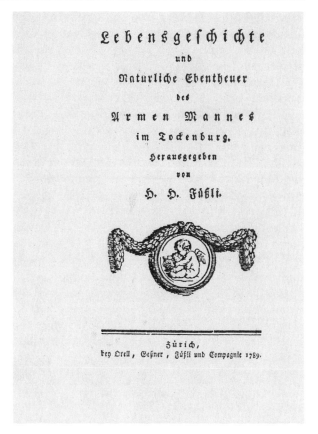

Title page for Bräker's autobiography (Schweizerische Landesbibliothek, Bern)

chern. Wenn mir schon mein geringes Vermögen keinen eignen Vorrath gestattet, giebt's Menschenfreunde in der Nähe und Ferne genug, die meiner Wiß- und Neugierde fröhnen. . ." (Reading and writing have become, more than ever, an absolute need for me. And even if I scribble the most indifferent things in my diary or read in old calendars! But I have no lack of books. Even if my small fortune allows me no stock of my own, there are philanthropists enough near and far who will satisfy my thirst for knowledge and my curiosity . . .).

In his later years Bräker found himself in an odd no-man's-land between the middle class, of which he was not a full-fledged member, and the rural peasantry from which he had emerged. He was neither entirely a writer nor entirely a yarn dealer and could not make a living from either profession. In 1798 he declared bankruptcy and in the same year saw French troops invade the Toggenburg. His diary becomes increasingly preoccupied with thoughts of death. The last entry, for 14 August 1798, has to do with still another financial problem. The exact date of

Bräker's death is unknown; he was buried in Wattwil on 11 September 1798.

Biography:

Holger Böning, *Der arme Mann aus dem Toggenburg: Leben, Werk, Zeitgeschichte* (Königstein: Athenäum, 1985).

References:

Eric A. Blackall, "Ulrich Bräker und Eschenburg," *Shakespeare-Jahrbuch*, 98 (1962): 93-109;

Fritz Ernst, "Um Ulrich Bräker: Zu Samuel Voellmys Biographie von Daniel Girtanner," in his *Essais*, volume 1 (Zurich: Fretz & Wasmuth, 1946), pp. 100-109;

Heinz Graber, Claudia and Christian Holliger-Wiesmann, and Karl Pestalozzi, eds., *Chronik Ulrich Bräker: Auf der Grundlage der Tagebücher Bräkers aus den Jahren 1770-1798* (Bern & Stuttgart: Haupt, 1985);

Walter Hinderer, "Leben und Werk des Naturdichters Ulrich Bräker," in his *Über deutsche Literatur und Rede: Historische Interpretationen* (Munich: Fink, 1981), pp. 39-65;

Hinderer, "Ulrich Bräker," in *Deutsche Dichter des 18. Jahrhunderts: Ihr Leben und Werk*, edited by Benno von Wiese (Berlin: Schmidt, 1977), pp. 371-392;

Erwin Jaeckle, "Der arme Mann im Tockenburg," in his *Bürgen des Menschlichen* (Zurich: Atlantis, 1945), pp. 9-15;

Hans Mayer, "Aufklärer und Plebejer: Ulrich Bräker, Der arme Mann im Tockenburg," in his *Studien zur Literaturgeschichte* (Berlin: Rütten & Loening, 1954), pp. 63-67;

Walter Muschg, "Ulrich Bräker, Etwas über William Shakespeares Schauspiele," in his *Pamphlet und Bekenntnis* (Olten & Freiburg: Walter, 1968), pp. 259-269;

Hans-Günther Thalheim, "Ulrich Bräker: Ein Naturdichter des 18. Jahrhunderts," in his *Zur Literatur der Goethezeit* (Berlin: Rütten & Loening, 1969), pp. 38-84;

Samuel Voellmy, *Daniel Girtanner von St. Gallen, Ulrich Bräker und ihr Freundeskreis: Ein Beitrag zur Geschichte der Aufklärung in der Schweiz in der zweiten Hälfte des 18. Jahrhunderts* (St. Gall: Fehr, 1928);

Voellmy, *Ulrich Bräker: Der arme Mann im Tockenburg. Ein Kultur- und Charakterbild aus dem achtzehnten Jahrhundert, nach den Handschriften dargestellt* (Zurich: Seldwyla, 1923).

Papers:

The Bräker manuscripts are in the Stadtbibliothek Vadiana and in the Staatsarchiv, St. Gall. Twenty-five letters are the Zentralbibliothek, Zurich.

Gottfried August Bürger

(31 December 1747 - 8 June 1794)

John F. Reynolds
Longwood College

BOOKS: *Zum Gedächtnis meines guten Großvaters, Jakob Philipp Bauers, Hofesherrn zu St. Elizabeth in Aschersleben* (Göttingen, 1773);

Das Lob Helenens: An dem Tage ihrer Hochzeit gesungen, anonymous (Sennickerode, 1773);

Neue weltliche hochteutsche Reime, enthaltend die ebentheyerliche doch wahrhaftige Historiam von der wunderschönen Durchlauchtigen Kaiserlichen Prinzessin Europa und einem uralten heydnischen Gözen Jupiter item Zeus genannt, als welcher sich nicht entblödet, unter der Larve eines unvernünftigen Stieres an höchstgedachter Prinzessin ein crimen raptus, zu teutsch: Jungfernraub auszuüben. Also gesetzet und an das Licht gestellet durch M. Jocosum Hilarium, anonymous (Göttingen: Dieterich, 1777);

Gedichte (Göttingen: Dieterich, 1778);

Geweihtes Angebinde, zu Louisens Geburtstage (Göttingen: Dieterich, 1783);

Über Anweisung zur deutschen Sprache und Schreibart auf Universitäten: Einladungsblätter zu seinen Vorlesungen. Erstes Blatt (Göttingen: Dieterich, 1787);

Gesang am heiligen Vorabend des fünfzigjährigen Jubelfestes der Georgia Augusta (Göttingen: Dieterich, 1787);

Ode der fünfzigjährigen Jubelfeier der Georgia Augusta am 17. September 1787 gewidmet von nachbenannten zu Göttingen Studierenden (Göttingen: Dieterich, 1787);

An den Apollo: Zur Vermählung meines Freundes, des Herrn Doctor Althof mit der Demoiselle Kuchel. Am 17ten Mai (N.p., 1789);

Gedichte, 2 volumes (Göttingen: Dieterich, 1789);

Actenstücke über einen poetischen Wettstreit: Geschlichtet auf dem deutschen Parnaß, anonymous (Berlin: Maurer, 1793);

Gottfried August Bürger's sämmtliche Schriften, 4 volumes, edited by Karl Reinhard (Göttingen: Dieterich, 1796-1802; reprinted, Hildesheim & New York: Olms, 1970);

Hauptmomente der kritischen Philosophie: Eine Reihe von Vorlesungen, vor gebildeten Zuhörern gehalten (Münster: Waldeck, 1803);

Painting by Anton Graff (Deutsche Fotothek, Dresden)

Gedichte von Schofelschreck, Menschenschreck und Frau: Als Anhang zu den Gedichten von Gottfried August Bürger, anonymous (Delmenhorst: Jöntzen, 1808);

Lehrbuch der Ästhetik, edited by Reinhard (Berlin: Schüppel, 1825);

Lehrbuch des Deutschen Styles, edited by Reinhard (Berlin: Schüppel, 1826);

Ästhetische Schriften: Ein Supplement zu allen Ausgaben von Bürgers Werken, edited by Reinhard (Berlin: Bechtold & Hartje, 1832);

Bürger's sämmtliche Werke: Einzig rechtmäßige Gesammt-Ausgabe in einem Bande, edited by August Wilhelm Bohtz (Göttingen: Dieterich, 1835);

Werke, 2 volumes, edited by Eduard Grisebach (Berlin: Grote, 1872);

Die Weiber von Weinsberg: Gedichte, Prosa, Briefe, edited by Wolfgang Widdel (Gütersloh: Prisma, 1983).

Edition in English: *A Collection of Select Pieces of Poetry by Schiller and Bürger, Together with Some Characteristic Poems of the Most Eminent German Bards, Translated in the Metre of the Original*, translated by George P. Maurer (New York: Lange, 1848).

OTHER: Xenophon of Ephesus, *Anthia und Abrokomas: Aus dem Griechischen*, translated anonymously by Bürger (Leipzig: Weygand, 1775);

Göttinger Musenalmanach, edited by Bürger (Göttingen: Dieterich, 1779-1794);

William Shakespeare, *Macbeth: Ein Shauspiel in fünf Aufzügen nach Shakespeare*, translated by Bürger (Göttingen: Dieterich, 1783);

Rudolf Erich Raspe, *Wunderbare Reisen zu Wasser und Lande, Feldzüge und lustige Abentheuer des Freyherrn von Münchhausen, wie er dieselben bey der Flasche im Cirkel seiner Freunde selbst zu erzählen pflegt: Aus dem Englischen nach der neuesten Ausgabe übersetzt, hier und da erweitert und mit noch mehr Kupfer geziert*, translated and augmented by Bürger (London [actually Göttingen]: Dieterich, 1786; enlarged, 1789);

Virgil, *Des Publius Virgilius Maro Lehrgedicht vom Landbau*, translated by C. G. Bock, foreword by Bürger (Leipzig: Benth, 1790);

Akademie der schönen Redekünste, edited by Bürger (Berlin: Königliche preußische akademische Kunst- und Buchhandlung, 1790-1791);

Benjamin Franklin, *Benjamin Franklin's Jugendjahre, vom ihm selbst für seinen Sohn beschrieben*, translated by Bürger (Berlin: Rottmann, 1792);

Alexander Pope, *Heloise an Abelard: Nach Pope frey übersetzt*, translated by Bürger (Zurich: Orell, Füssli, 1803).

PERIODICAL PUBLICATIONS: "Stutzertändelei," *Hamburger Unterhaltung* (1770);

"Lenore," *Göttinger Musenalmanach* (1773); republished as *Lenore: Ein Gedicht* (London: Gosnell, 1796); translated by William Robert Spencer as *Leonora* (London: Printed by T. Bensley for J. Edwards and E. and S. Harding, 1796); translated by Sir Walter Scott as "William and Helen," in *The Chase, and William and Helen: Two Ballads, from the German of Gottfried Augustus Bürger* (Edinburgh: Printed by Mundell and Son for Manners and Miller, 1796); translated by Henry D. Wireman as *Lenore: A Ballad* (Philadelphia: Kohler, 1870);

"Aus Daniel Wunderlichs Buch," *Deutsches Museum* (1776);

"Der Raubgraf," *Göttinger Musenalmanach* (1776); translated anonymously as "The Freebooter," in *The Freebooter: From the German of Bürger; Friendship Preferred to Love: A Canzonette. Translated from the French of the Abbé Parrini* (Glasgow: Printed for and sold by Brash & Reid, 1810);

"Des Pfarrers Tochter von Taubenheim," *Göttinger Musenalmanach* (1781); translated anonymously as *The Lass of Fair Wone; or, the Parson's Daughter Betrayed: A Celebrated Ballad, Translated from the German* (Glasgow: Brash & Reid, 1796);

"Der wilde Jäger," *Göttinger Musenalmanach* (1785); translated by Scott as "The Chase," in *The Chase, and William and Helen*; translated anonymously (attributed to Henry James Pye) as *The Wild Huntsman's Chase* (London: Low, 1798); translated by Charles J. Lukens as *The Wild Huntsman* (Philadelphia: Collins, printer, 1870).

One of the most significant poets and literary figures of the eighteenth century, Gottfried August Bürger is most remembered today for his popular folk ballad, "Lenore" (translated as *Leonora*, 1796), published in the *Göttinger Musenalmanach* in 1773. The son of Johann Gottfried Bürger, pastor in Molmerswende, and Gertrud Elisabeth Bürger, née Bauer, Bürger attended the Latin school in Aschersleben for one year. He then matriculated at the Pädagogium in Halle, a school noted for its discipline and strong Protestant theology, on 8 September 1760. Bürger flourished at this school, becoming particularly expert in classical languages, and wrote his first serious poems there. In Halle, Bürger befriended the young Leopold Friedrich von Goeckingk, who later became a Prussian civil ser-

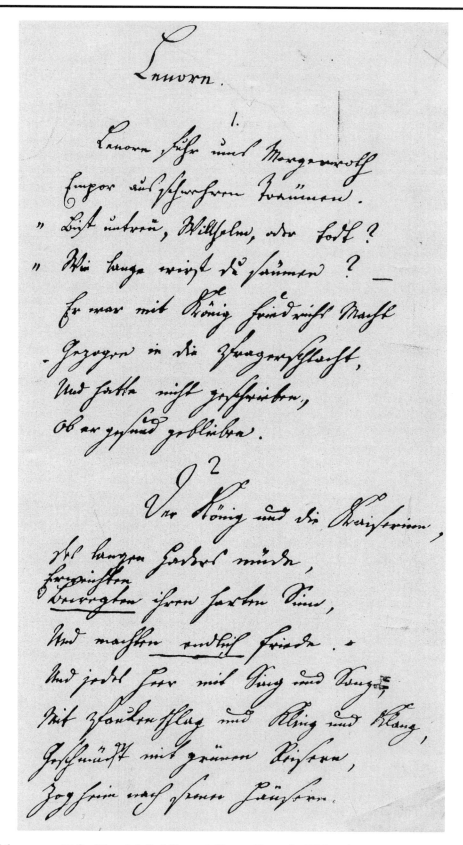

First page of the manuscript for Bürger's ballad "Lenore" (Gustav Könnecke, Bilderatlas zur Geschichte der deutschen Nationallitteratur *[Graz: Akademische Druck- und Verlagsanstalt, 1981])*

vant and a member of the poetic circle known as the "Göttinger Hainbund" (Göttinger Grove League). In 1764, after four years at the Pädagogium, Bürger entered the University of Halle as a theology student. Christian Adolf Klotz, professor of philosophy and rhetoric, had a profound influence on Bürger, encouraging him to translate Homer and various Latin texts into German. Most important, he urged Bürger to study the *Fragmente* (1767) of the philosopher Johann Gottfried Herder. Herder's call for an end to the prolonged French and Greco-Roman hegemony in Germany and for poetry more accessible to ordinary people, based on the here and now, was to be enthusiastically answered by Bürger. Klotz was one of the foremost Latin scholars of his day; but his reputation as a dissolute was widespread, and Bürger, a frequent guest in Klotz's house, became tainted by this reputation.

Bürger's studies at Halle ended in July 1767 when he was found guilty of being a member of an outlawed student society. He returned home for a brief period before entering the University of Göttingen in 1768 as a law student. In Göttingen he took a room at the house of Klotz's mother-in-law. The house was inhabited mainly by wealthy, undisciplined Russians, and Bürger soon neglected his studies and began amassing huge debts. He would have been financially and morally ruined had not three friends come to his aid: Heinrich Christian Boie, a poet and promoter of the *Göttinger Musenalmanach*, whom Bürger had met at Klotz's home in Halle; the literary critic Johann Erich Biester, later editor of the *Berliner Monatsschrift*, who with Bürger founded the "Shakespeare-Klub" in 1770; and the historian Matthias Christian Sprengel, who also became a member of the "Shakespeare-Klub." Almost immediately Bürger's literary productivity increased dramatically; he nearly completed his translation of Xenophon of Ephesus's *Anthia and Abrocomas* (1775); he taught himself Italian and Spanish and wrote a novella in the latter language; and he published the poem "Stutzertändelei" (The Dandy's Dalliance) in the *Hamburger Unterhaltung* in 1770.

At this time the poet and supporter of the arts Johann Wilhelm Ludwig Gleim took notice of Bürger's achievements. Gleim traveled to Göttingen to meet Bürger and spoke of a possible position for him in Magdeburg. Because of his tremendous outstanding debts, however, Burger was compelled to remain in Göttingen. Faced with financial ruin, Bürger was saved by

Engraving by Daniel Chodowiecki to illustrate Bürger's "Lenore" (Gustav Könnecke, Bilderatlas zur Geschichte der deutschen Nationalliteratur [Graz: Akademische Druck- und Verlagsanstalt, 1981])

Boie, who recommended him for the position of rural magistrate in the village of Altengleichen, in the territories of the von Uslar family. The magistrate's office was at Gelliehausen, about a mile from Göttingen.

What appeared at first to be the solution to Bürger's financial difficulties turned out to be a torment for the poet. Members of the von Uslar family were in constant battle with each other and almost at once turned upon the new magistrate, accusing him of incompetence, lack of experience, and neglect. Perhaps even worse than his problems with the von Uslars were Bürger's difficulties with Ernst Ferdinand Listn, the administrator who was responsible for paying Bürger's salary. During the first year of his job Bürger received no money. When Listn declared bankruptcy in 1775, he had defrauded Bürger out of more than twelve thousand talers.

Despite his harrowing living situation, Bürger produced his best work in 1773: the ballad "Lenore," published in the *Göttinger Musenalmanach*. Based on the Scottish ballad "Sweet William's Ghost," it tells of Lenore's grief after her lover, Wilhelm, is killed in battle during the Seven Years War. After renouncing her belief in God's mercy, Lenore goes to bed. Wilhelm returns and carries her off on his horse to a cemetery, where she dies after seeing him transformed into the figure of Death. In this poem Bürger successfully assimilated the literary traditions of Moritat (sensational ballads about murders or executions), romance, and folk ballad and endowed the ballad form with a seriousness of tone and purpose unknown in Germany up to that time. Published only a few months after Goethe's Sturm und Drang play *Götz von Berlichingen mit der eisernen Hand* (Götz von Berlichingen with the Iron Hand, 1773), the ballad incorporates the rebellious spirit of the times. Its controversial questioning of God's goodness and the horrible consequences of man's challenging the divine plan, told in fast-paced, clear lyrics, brought Bürger instantaneous fame and great popularity. The ballad received international acclaim and was translated into English by Sir Walter Scott in 1796. Even though he finished many other poems in the same year, including "Des armen Suschens Traum" (Poor Little Susan's Dream), "Minnesolde" (Love's Wages), "Gegenliebe" (Mutual Love), and in 1776 a second ballad, "Der Raubgraf" (translated as "The Freebooter," 1810), Bürger never regained the force and haunting atmosphere attained in "Lenore."

Almost immediately after completing "Lenore," Bürger began work on another ballad, "Der wilde Jäger" (translated as "The Chase," 1798). The poem took five years to write and was not published until 1785 in the *Göttinger Musenalmanach*. The ballad concerns a nobleman who disregards repeated warnings to control his passion for the hunt and, in his zealous pursuit of his prey, ruins farms, flocks, and finally a hermit's hut. The judgment is pronounced on him that he will be the hunted, not the hunter, for all eternity. Like "Lenore," the poem deals with the human soul; but in "Der wilde Jäger" the theme has been expanded to include a concern for social justice. The same concern is expressed in the poems "Der Bauer: An seinen durchlauchtigen Tyrannen" (The Peasant to his Illustrious Tyrant, written in 1773, published in Bürger's *Gedichte* [Poems, 1778]) and "Des Pfarrers Tochter von Taubenheim" (The Pastor of Taubenheim's Daughter, 1781; translated as "The Lass of Fair Wone, 1796). In comparing the ballads, Bürger referred to "Lenore" as his moon and "Der wilde Jäger" as his sun.

In 1774, at the height of his poetic career, Bürger moved out of Listn's house in Gelliehausen and settled in the nearby village of Niedeck. There he began a friendship with the magistrate Johann Karl Leonhart and his daugh-

Auguste Wilhelmine Eva Leonhart (Molly) in 1774, the year Bürger married her older sister Dorette even though he was in love with Molly. Dorette died in 1784, and Bürger and Molly were married the following year; six months later Molly died. After a painting by H. F. L. Mathieu (Joseph Kürschner, ed., Deutsche National-Litteratur *[Berlin: Spemann, n.d.])*

ters Dorothea Marianne (Dorette) and Auguste Wilhelmine Eva (Molly). At the time Bürger met them, Dorette was sixteen years old and Molly was fourteen. Bürger was attracted to both young women. Although he had stronger feelings for the younger sister, he married Dorette on 22 November 1774. After the birth of a daughter, Antoinette Caecilia Elisabeth, in May 1775, Bürger moved to the village of Wöllmershausen. There he expressed his love for Dorette's sister in the first of his approximately thirty "Molly-Lieder" (Songs to Molly). In Wöllmershausen he also composed two ballads, "Der Ritter und sein Liebchen" (The Knight and His Sweetheart) and "Die Weiber von Weinsberg" (The Wives of Weinsberg).

The emotional torment produced by Bürger's being married to one sister while in love with the other was compounded by lawsuits and continuous accusations of incompetence by his superiors. In spite of these difficulties, Bürger produced voluminous amounts of poetry during this period, including more "Molly-Lieder" and several ballads, including "Lenardo und Blandine." Goethe collected money from the court at Weimar to reduce Bürger's financial worries and encouraged him to complete a translation of the *Iliad*. Bürger's daughter died on 12 December 1777.

By 1778 Bürger was ready to publish a collection of his poetry. *Gedichte* (Poems), which contained sixty-six poems, received high critical acclaim. In the same year Bürger assumed editorship of the *Göttinger Musenalmanach*; he remained editor of this journal until his death and greatly improved the quality of the publication. A second daughter, Marianne, was born in March 1778.

At this point several incidents occurred which affected Bürger's health and well-being. His attempts to find a new position failed, and he alienated his friends in Weimar by venting his rage over his situation in a letter to Goethe. An effort to obtain a position in Prussia was sabotaged by negative reports of his performance of his magisterial duties in Altengleichen. Finally, his unrestrained love affair with his wife's sister, which was going on in his home, had become well known. Bürger was at least able to come to an agreement with Dorette and Molly to resolve his domestic situation. This agreement was actually a recognition and acceptance of the status quo and established a ménage à trois in which Dorette played a subordinate role. In May 1782 Molly gave birth to a son, Emil. Finally, in 1784, after another complaint was lodged against him, Bürger stepped down from his post. Through the assistance of Christian Gottlob Heyne, professor of classics at Göttingen and director of the university library, and the mathematician Abraham Gotthelf Kästner, dean of the school, Bürger received an unsalaried position as teacher of German history and language; his pay came from student fees.

On 29 April 1784 Dorette gave birth to a third daughter, Auguste Wilhelmine, and did not recover; she died on 30 July. The baby died less than two weeks later. Bürger moved to Göttingen, where he began his duties on 29 September. On 27 June 1785 he married his beloved Molly. His future looked bright: his lectures at the university were well received, his financial situation was improving, his international reputation was solid, and he was married to the woman he had always loved. Disaster, however, was not long in coming. After giving birth to a daughter, Auguste Anna Henriette Ernestine, on Christmas

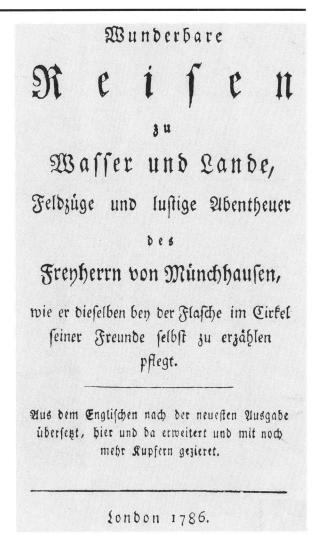

Title page for Bürger's translation and adaptation of Rudolf Erich Raspe's English version of the adventures of Baron Münchhausen

Day 1785, Molly developed a high fever; she died on 9 January 1786.

Bürger's position among his colleagues at the University of Göttingen was awkward. Having no academic credentials, he was regarded with disdain by the faculty—with the exception of Heyne, Kästner, and the physicist Georg Christoph Lichtenberg, a writer of aphorisms whom Bürger had met in Hannover some years earlier. Finally, in September 1787, the title of doctor was conferred on him in recognition of two poems, *Gesang am heiligen Vorabend des fünfzigjährigen Jubelfestes der Georgia Augusta* (Ode on the Evening before the Fiftieth Anniversary of the George August University) and *Ode der fünfzigjährigen Jubelfeier der Georgia Augusta am 17. September 1787* (Ode on the Fiftieth Anniversary of the George August University on September 17,

1787). In 1789 he was promoted to professor extraordinarius, still without salary.

After Molly's death Bürger had begun an adaptation of a remarkable work which had appeared in England in 1786 under the title *Baron Munchausen's [sic] Narrative of his Marvelous Travels and Campaigns in Russia*. These tales had first appeared in German in volumes 8 and 9 of the *Vademecum für lustige Leute* (Vade Mecum for Jolly People) in 1781 and 1783 and had been translated into English by Rudolf Erich Raspe. By 1786 two English editions of the complete tales were in print. Bürger adapted the second of these editions as *Wunderbare Reisen zu Wasser und Lande, Feldzüge und lustige Abentheuer des Freyherrn von Münchhausen, wie er dieselben bey der Flasche im Cirkel seiner Freunde selbst zu erzählen pflegt* (The Marvelous Adventures at Sea and on Land, the Campaigns and Amusing Adventures of Baron von Munchhausen, as He Enjoys Telling Them over a Bottle in the Company of His Friends). The work, based on the real-life–and, at the time, still living–Baron Karl Friedrich Hieronymus von Münchhausen, consists of two parts: the baron's tales of his campaigns and adventures in Russia and his adventures at sea. The tales in the first part, presented in a single continuous narrative, center on often perilous incidents in battle or during the hunt, from which the baron extricates himself through his wit, skill, and great strength. The second part, a series of separate chapters, is more exotic than the first, containing descriptions of journeys to the Far East, to Egypt, even to the moon and to the center of the earth. Bürger's skill in adapting the tales of Münchhausen and making them attractive to the Germans resulted in the book's becoming a genuine "Volksbuch" (popular prose romance). He added so much of himself that for years it was thought that Bürger had been the author of the English version as well as of the German one.

In the spring of 1789 Bürger published a second collection of his poems in two volumes. The critical reception was mixed, although August Wilhelm Schlegel wrote a favorable review of the book. Bürger decided to travel, visiting Jena and then Weimar, where he hoped to rekindle his friendship with Goethe. The elder poet received Bürger coolly, however, remembering the money he had sent Bürger to finish the translation of the *Iliad*–a work which Bürger did not complete. Bürger left Weimar downcast and angry. On his way back to Göttingen he composed a bitter epigram against Goethe.

Engraving after a painting of Bürger by Fiorelli

Back in Göttingen, Bürger received a flattering anonymous poem from a young woman in Stuttgart. He soon discovered that her name was Elise Marie Christiane Elizabeth Hahn and became infatuated with her even before he met her. In early 1790 he sent her his "Beichte" (Confessions), a lengthy autobiographical apologia. Although warned by friends not to proceed with this romance with a girl twenty-two years his junior, Bürger went to Stuttgart, became engaged to Elise, and married her in September 1790. The couple moved to Göttingen, where it soon became clear that the young, attractive Elise preferred a life-style quite opposite that of her husband. By the winter of 1790-1791 Elise's affairs were the scandal of Göttingen. In March 1792 Bürger divorced Elise, who had returned to Stuttgart in February of that year–deserting their son, Agathon, who had been born on 1 August 1791.

While his marriage was disintegrating before his eyes, Bürger was silenced as a poet by Friedrich Schiller's review of his second poetry collection. The review appeared anonymously in the

Allgemeine Literatur-Zeitung in January 1791, but Bürger soon learned the name of the author. Schiller not only criticized Bürger's poetry but also questioned Bürger's right to call himself a true "Volksdichter" (national poet). He found Bürger's poems immature and lacking in refinement and poetic idealization. He criticized the sensuality of the poems and said the poet's involvement in his poetry was too immediate. Bürger published a hasty reply in the *Allgemeine Literatur-Zeitung* on 6 April 1791 which did more harm than good. Schiller's reply accused Bürger of trying to be clever rather than reasonable and of avoiding direct answers to the criticism made in the review.

After 1791 Bürger wrote few works, mostly inconsequential epigrams, translations, and adaptations. He felt that his creative vein was exhausted and spent a great deal of time revising his earlier poems with Schiller's criticism in mind. Rather than attempt new works, Bürger set his hopes on a final luxury edition of his poems. He did not live to see it published. On 8 June 1794 he died of consumption at age forty-six.

Letters:

Briefe von Gottfried August Bürger an Marianne Ehrmann: Ein merkwürdiger Beitrag zur Geschichte der letzten Lebensjahre des Dichters. Mit einer historischen Einleitung, edited by Theophil Friedrich Ehrmann (Weimar: Verlag des Industrie-Comptoirs, 1802);

Gottfried August Bürgers Ehestands-Geschichte: Geschichte der dritten Ehe Gottfried August Bürger's. Eine Sammlung von Acten-Stücken (Leipzig: Schulz, 1812; reprinted, Berlin: Frensdorff, 1905);

Bürger und Müllner: Ein Briefwechsel. Nebst Beilagen (Jüterbog: Colditz, 1833);

Briefe von und an Gottfried August Bürger: Ein Beitrag zur Literaturgeschichte seiner Zeit. Aus dem Nachlasse Bürger's und anderen, meist handschriftlichen Quellen, 4 volumes, edited by Adolf Strodtmann (Berlin: Paetel, 1874; reprinted, Bern: Lang, 1970);

"Ungedruckte Briefe Gottfried August Bürgers," *Euphorion*, 1 (1894): 309-337;

Gottfried August Bürger und Philippine Gatterer: Ein Briefwechsel aus Göttingens empfindsamer Zeit, edited by Erich Ebstein (Leipzig: Dieterich, 1921).

References:

Lief Ludwig Albertsen, "Pervigilium Veneris und 'Nachfeier der Venus': Gottfried August Bürgers Liedstil und sein lateinisches Vorbild," *Arcadia*, 16 (1981): 1-12;

Otto Bieler, "Bürgers Lyrik im Lichte der Schillerschen Kritik," *Germanisch-Romanische Monatsschrift*, 13 (1927): 259-274;

Peter Boerner, " 'Les morts vont vite' or the European Success of Bürger's Ballad 'Lenore,' " *Studies on Voltaire and the 18th Century*, 216 (1983): 448-449;

Oscar Cargill, "A New Source for 'The Raven,' " *American Literature*, 8 (1936-1937): 291-294;

Ruth P. Dawson, "Rudolf Erich Raspe and the Münchhausen Tales," *Lessing Yearbook*, 16 (1984): 205-220;

Wilhelm Dilthey, *Die große Phantasiedichtung* (Göttingen: Vandenhoeck & Ruprecht, 1954), pp. 229-236;

Friedrich Wilhelm Ebeling, *Gottfried August Bürger und Elise Hahn* (Leipzig: Warting, 1868);

Wolfgang Friedrich, "Zu Gottfried August Bürgers Aufsatz 'Die Republik England,' " *Weimarer Beiträge*, 2 (1956): 214-232;

Klaus F. Gille, "Schillers Rezension 'Über Bürgers Gedichte' im Lichte der zeitgenössischen Bürger-Kritik," in *Wissen aus Erfahrung: Wortbegriff und Interpretation heute*, edited by Alexander von Bormann (Tübingen: Niemeyer, 1976), pp. 174-191;

Karl Goedeke, *Gottfried August Bürger in Göttingen und Gelliehausen* (Hannover: Rumpler, 1873);

Eduard Grisebach, "Gottfried August Bürger," in *Die deutsche Litteratur 1770-1870: Beiträge zu ihrer Geschichte mit Benutzung handschriftlicher Quellen*, edited by Grisebach (Vienna: Rosner, 1876), pp. 108-174;

Friedrich Gundolf, "Bürgers 'Lenore' als Volkslied," in *Beiträge zur Literatur und Geistesgeschichte*, edited by Victor Schmitz and Fritz Martini (Heidelberg: Schneider, 1980), pp. 277-298.

Elke Haas, "Die Rhetorik in Bürgers ästhetischen Anschauungen," *Rhetorik*, 3 (1983): 97-109;

Emil Hardina, *Dämonen der Tiefe, ein Gottfried August Bürger Roman* (Reichenberg: Stiepel, 1922);

Walter Hinderer, "Die projizierte Kontroverse: Text und Kontext von Schillers Bürger-Kritik," in *Kontroversen*, edited by Albrecht Schöne, Helmut Koopman, and Franz Josef

Worstbrock (Tübingen: Niemeyer, 1986), pp. 180ff;

Hinderer, "Schiller und Bürger: die ästhetische Kontroverse als Paradigma," *Jahrbuch des Freien Deutschen Hochstifts* (1986): 130-154;

Alfons Höger, " 'Und etwas anders noch . . .': Galanterie und Sinnlichkeit in den Gedichten Gottfried August Bürgers," *Text und Kontext*, 9 (1981): 250-270;

Christian Janentzky, *G. A. Bürgers Ästhetik* (Berlin: Duncker, 1909; reprinted, Hildesheim: Gerstenberg, 1978);

Evelyn B. Jolles, *G. A. Bürger's Ballade 'Lenore' in England* (Regensburg: Carl, 1974);

Paul Jung, "Strukturtypen der Komik: Ein Beitrag zur formalen Analyse der 'lustigen Geschichten,' " *Deutschunterricht*, 25, no. 1 (1973): 44-66;

Lore Kaim-Kloock, *Gottfried August Bürger: Zum Problem der Volkstümlichkeit in der Lyrik* (Berlin: Rütten & Loening, 1963);

Hermann Kinder, ed., *Bürgers Liebe: Dokumente zu Elise Hahns und G. A. Bürgers unglücklichem Versuch, eine Ehe zu führen* (Frankfurt am Main: Insel, 1981);

Gerhard Kluge, "Gottfried August Bürger," in *Deutsche Dichter des 18. Jahrhundert: Ihr Leben und Werk*, edited by Benno von Wiese (Berlin: Schmidt, 1977), pp. 594-618;

Gerhard Köpf, "Friedrich Schiller: 'Über Bürgers Gedichte,' Historizität als Norm einer Theorie des Lesers," *Jahrbuch des Wiener Goethe-Vereins*, 83 (1979): 263-273;

Hartmut Laufhütte, "Vom Gebrauch des Schaurigen als Provokation zur Erkenntnis G.A. Bürgers 'Des Pfarrers Tochter von Taubenhain,' " in *Gedichte und Interpretationen*, volume 2, edited by Karl Richter (Munich: Reclam, 1983), pp. 393-410;

William A. Little, *Gottfried August Bürger* (New York: Twayne, 1974);

Wolfgang Martens, "Zur Metaphorik schriftstellerischer Konkurrenz 1770-1880. (Voss, Bürger, Schiller)," in *Kontroversen*, pp. 160-171;

Georg Mayer, "Bürger's 'Lenore'–eine Visionäre Ballade," *Neue Jahrbücher für Wissenschaft und Jugendbildung*, 3 (1927): 153-158;

Andrew Nicholson, " 'Kubla Khan': The Influence of Bürger's 'Lenore,' " *English Studies*, 64 (1983): 291-295;

Anele Nikogda, "Ein Plebejer 'con amore': Gottfried August Bürgers Ballade 'Leonardo und Blandine,' " *Wissenschaftliche Zeitschrift*, 33 (1984): 2-6;

Karl Nutzhorn, "Aus Bürgers Amtmannstätigkeit," *Hannoversche Geschichtsblätter*, 9 (1903): 385-424;

Hermann Pongs, "Bürgers Lenore," in his *Das Bild in der Dichtung*, volume 3 (Marburg: Elwert, 1969), pp. 71-83;

John K. Primeau, "The Influence of G. A. Bürger on the 'Lyrical Ballads' of William Wordsworth: The Supernatural vs. the Natural," *Germanic Review*, 58 (Summer 1983): 89-96;

Heinrich Christian Friedrich Pröhle, *Gottfried August Bürger: Sein Leben und seine Dichtung* (Leipzig: Mayer, 1856);

Helmut Schelsky, "Selbstgespräch eines alten Mannes: Zu einem Sonett von G. A. Bürger," in *Noch gibt es Dichter: Außenseiter im Literaturbetrieb*, edited by Gerd-Klaus Kaltenbrunner (Munich: Herder, 1979), pp. 129-132;

Friedrich Schiller, "Über Bürgers Gedichte," in *Friedrich Schillers Werke*, fourth edition, volume 4, edited by Hans Mayer (Frankfurt am Main: Insel, 1966), pp. 970-972;

Emil Staiger, *Stilwandel* (Zurich: Atlantis, 1963), pp. 75-119;

Eduard Stäuble, "Gottfried August Bürgers Ballade, 'Lenore,' " *Deutschunterricht*, 10 (1958): 85-114;

Barbara L. Swowska, "Bürgers 'Lenore'–ein wichtiger Impuls zur Herausbildung der polnischen Romantik," *Filologia Germanska*, 4 (1978): 61-72;

Wolfgang Trautwein, *Erlesene Angst-Schauerliteratur im 18. und 19. Jahrhundert: Systematischer Aufriß. Untersuchungen zu Bürger, Maturin, Hoffmann, Poe und Maupassant* (Munich & Vienna: Hanser, 1980);

Erwin Wackermann, "Frühe illegale Münchhausen-Ausgaben: Kleine Schritte zu einer Volksausgabe," *Philobiblon*, 23 (1979): 266-278;

Wolfgang Wurzbach, *Gottfried August Bürger: Sein Leben und seine Werke* (Leipzig: Dietrich, 1900).

Papers:

Most of the known papers of Gottfried August Bürger are in the Universitätsbibliothek Göttingen. A collection of manuscripts and letters is held in the Goethe and Schiller Archive in Weimar, East Germany.

Karoline Auguste Fernandine Fischer

(9 August 1764 - 25 May 1842)

Susanne Zantop
Dartmouth College

BOOKS: *Gustavs Verirrungen: Ein Roman* (Leipzig: Gräff, 1801);

Vierzehn Tage in Paris (Leipzig: Gräff, 1801);

Die Honigmonathe, 2 volumes (Posen & Leipzig: Kühn, 1802); republished as *Die Honigmonate* (Hildesheim, Zurich & New York: Olms, 1987);

Der Günstling (Posen & Leipzig: Kühn, 1809; reprinted, Hildesheim: Olms, 1988);

Margarethe (Heidelberg: Mohr & Zimmer, 1812; reprinted, Hildesheim: Olms, 1989);

Kleine Erzählungen und romantische Skizzen (Posen & Leipzig: Kühn, 1818; reprinted, Hildesheim: Olms, 1989).

PERIODICAL PUBLICATIONS: "Selim und Zoraïde," anonymous, *Journal der Romane*, 10 (1802);

"Krauskopf und Goldlöckchen," anonymous, *Journal der Romane*, 10 (1802);

"Paridamia oder die Krebsscheeren," anonymous, *Journal der Romane*, 10 (1802);

"Bemerkungen, von der Verfasserin von Gustavs Verirrungen," anonymous, 11 installments, *Zeitung für die elegante Welt*, nos. 241, 244, 246, 253 (7-24 December 1816);

"Bemerkungen, von der Verfasserin von Gustavs Verirrungen," anonymous, 7 installments, *Zeitung für die elegante Welt*, nos. 24, 25, 27, 52, 67, 110, 119 (3 February-21 June 1817);

"Rieckchen: Eine Erzählung," 4 installments, *Zeitung für die elegante Welt*, nos. 46-49 (6-9 March 1817);

"William der Neger: Eine Erzählung," 5 installments, *Zeitung für die elegante Welt*, nos. 97-101 (19-24 May 1817); translated as "William the Negro," in *Bitter Healing: German Women Writers from 1700 to 1830*, edited by Jeannine Blackwell and Susanne Zantop (Lincoln: University of Nebraska Press, forthcoming 1990);

"So viel Noten als Text: Von der Verfasserin von Gustavs Verirrungen dem Verfasser der Schuld, mit Bitte um Prüfung und Zurecht-

weisung, vorgelegt," anonymous, *Zeitung für die elegante Welt*, no. 68 (7 April 1818): 540-542;

"Danksagung der Verfasserin von Gustavs Verirrungen, an den Verfasser der Schuld," anonymous, *Zeitung für die elegante Welt*, no. 146 (28 July 1818): 1136-1164;

"Bemerkungen von der Verfasserin von Gustavs Verirrungen," anonymous, *Zeitung für die elegante Welt*, no. 161 (1818): 1306;

"Wien im Anfange des vorigen Jahrhunderts: Eingesandt von der Verfasserin von Gustavs Verirrungen," anonymous, 3 installments, *Zeitung für die elegante Welt*, nos. 62-64 (27-30 March 1819): 489-507;

"Das Kästchen: Eine Erzählung," as Karoline Auguste, 7 installments, *Zeitung für die elegante Welt*, nos. 200-206 (11-19 October 1819);

"Maja und Jazintha: Neugriechische Sage," as Karoline Auguste, 3 installments, *Zeitung für die elegante Welt*, nos. 234-236 (27-30 November 1819);

"Klagen und Geständnisse eines berühmten Staatsmannes: Mitgetheilt von Karoline Auguste," 5 installments, *Zeitung für die elegante Welt*, nos. 56-60 (20-25 March 1820).

Although her works surpass those of other late eighteenth- and early nineteenth-century German women authors in their radical presentation of women's social and moral conflicts and in their expressive power, Karoline Auguste Fernandine Fischer (her first name is also spelled Caroline) remained practically forgotten until very recently. Despite attempts by Christine Touaillon to resuscitate her reputation in the early 1900s, it took nearly two hundred years and a different public—one more interested in women's historic role in society and more sensitized to their peculiar perspective—to understand and fully appreciate the life and works of this innovative, passionate, uncompromising, and in some ways surprisingly modern writer.

Karoline Auguste Venturini was born on 9 August 1764, the second child of Karl Heinrich Ernst Venturini (1734-1801), court violinist at the Duchy of Brunswick, and Charlotte Juliane Wilhelmine Köchy Venturini (1742-1825), the daughter of a local tailor, who had married Venturini in 1761. Although Karoline Venturini was raised in a large lower-middle-class family (six of the eight children seem to have survived into adulthood), she must have received an education well beyond her station, as is attested by the wide range of subject matter and the considerable historical and literary knowledge displayed in her writings. Among her brothers, Carl became a well-known theologian and writer; Johann Georg Julius, a military strategist; and Heinrich August Wilhelm, an engineer.

While nothing is known about Fischer's childhood and youth, her adult life reads like a novel—indeed, like one of her own. It is marked by the tension between women's intellectual or artistic aspirations and emotional longings on the one hand, and the limitations imposed on women by society's expectations on the other. In the early 1790s she married the Lutheran theologian and educator Christoph Johann Rudolph Christiani. In 1793 Christiani became a court preacher in Copenhagen, where he founded and directed a boys' school. The marriage was unhappy owing to the incompatibility of their characters: Christiani's sense of propriety and duty clashed with his wife's desire for emotional adventure and an unconventional life. The couple separated in 1798, after having two children: a daughter, Gustava, who was born in 1792 and died at age three, and a son, Carl Rudolph Ferdinand, who was born in 1797. In 1799, two years before the divorce became official, Karoline Christiani left her husband and son and moved back to Germany. (The son became a lawyer and politician in Lüneburg, befriended the poet Heinrich Heine, and married Heine's cousin Charlotte.)

By 1801 Karoline was living in Dresden with Christian August Fischer, a prolific writer of travelogues, popular scientific tracts, and imitations of French erotic novels which he published under the pen name Christian Althing. Thanks to Fischer's contacts, Karoline Christiani was able to place her first three novels, *Gustavs Verirrungen* (Gustav's Aberrations, 1801), *Vierzehn Tage in Paris* (A Fortnight in Paris, 1801), and *Die Honigmonathe* (The Honeymoons, 1802), with Leipzig publishers. Her books were so well received that she could advertise all subsequent writ-

ings with the label "by the author of Gustav's Aberrations and The Honeymoons." In 1803 she accompanied Fischer to Heidelberg, but she stayed behind with her newborn illegitimate son, Albert, when Christian Fischer left to become a professor in Würzburg. In 1808, however, she followed him to Würzburg and married him, possibly to secure financial support for their child. The marriage lasted only seven months. In early 1809 Karoline Fischer returned to Heidelberg, and in 1814 she was back in Würzburg. Her attempts to make a living by running a girls' school in Heidelberg, opening a lending library in Würzburg, and writing apparently failed. Her novel "Clementina," announced as forthcoming in 1809, and a tract titled "Über die Weiber" (On Women), supposedly written in 1813, probably never appeared. Shunned by society, with few financial resources, suffering from severe depressions, Fischer spent her last years moving back and forth between Würzburg and Frankfurt, where her son Albert took up residence, and in and out of mental institutions. She did not publish anything after 1820 and died impoverished and forgotten in a Frankfurt hospital on 25 May 1842.

Fischer's literary production, which started when she was thirty-seven years old, was as erratic and controversial as her life-style. Sudden bursts of energy were followed by years of silence. Constantly moving, and in constant financial and emotional distress, Fischer obviously did not enjoy the conditions necessary for a sustained creative effort. Yet while there is no continuity in her artistic productivity, the works exhibit considerable thematic unity, an almost obsessive preoccupation with the same interrelated topics: the incompatibility between pursuit of happiness and pursuit of virtue, between desire and duty; the destructive potential of gender roles; and the tragedy of the creative woman who is forced to choose between the lonesome existence of the artist and the confined, stifling life of wife and mother. In one of her late aphorisms Fischer defined women's condition as a "no-win" situation: "Sie sollen das Härteste und Weichste, das Furchtsamste und Herzhafteste, das Oberflächlichste und Tiefste seyn. Hart gegen ihre beiden größesten Feinde, ihr eignes weiches Herz und den geliebten Verführer; weich, um alle mögliche Formen, die ihnen ihr künftiger Herr zu geben gesonnen ist, anzunehmen; furchtsam, weil ihnen nicht leicht etwas besser als die Furchtsamkeit steht, und sich ihr Beschützer dabei in dem ihm

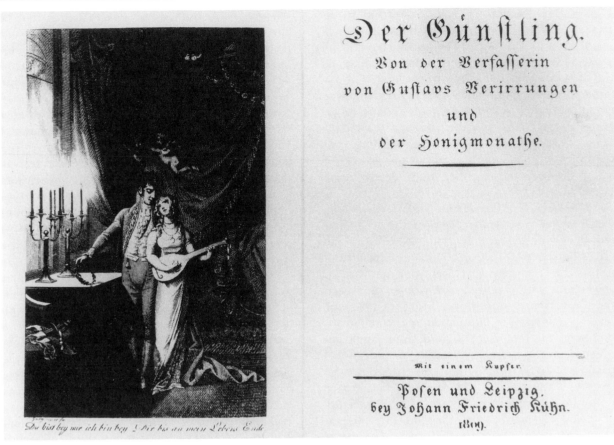

Du bist bey mir ich bin bey Dir bis an mein Lebens Ende

Der Günstling.
Von der Verfasserin
von Gustavs Verirrungen
und
der Honigmonathe.

Mit einem Kupfer.

Posen und Leipzig,
bey Johann Friedrich Kühn.
1809.

Frontispiece and title page for Fischer's novel about the Russian czarina's uncontrollable passion for her councillor

angemessensten Lichte zeigen kann; herzhaft (aber ja recht heimlich) wenn sie dem Tode entgegen gehn; welches bei den verheiratheten Frauen vor jedem Kindbette der Fall ist; oberflächlich und leichtsinnig, wenn sie an ihr Alter und an den Tod ihrer Schönheit denken; der schrecklichste für sie, da sie ihn oft überleben, entfernt von den Wissenschaften und von Allem, was den Geist stärken und erheben kann; gleichwohl mit tiefer Empfindung begabt, damit sie wirklich, gleichviel ob einen Untreuen, lieben und zu jeder Art von Aufopferung geneigt seyn können.–Und das Alles würde von ihnen gefordert?–Fragt die Geschichte, fragt Euch selbst und sagt: Nein! wenn Ihr könnt" (They are supposed to be both extremely unyielding and extremely pliant, extremely timid and extremely courageous, extremely superficial and extremely profound. Unyielding toward their two greatest enemies: their own soft heart and the beloved seducer; pliant, so that they can assume all the shapes their future master deigns to give them; timid, because little is more becoming to them and because it al-

lows their protector to appear all the more protective; courageous [but secretly, please], when they face death, which married women must do at every childbirth; superficial and carefree when they think of old age and the death of their beauty, which is the most horrible death for them, for they often survive it, bereft of knowledge and of anything that could strengthen and uplift their spirit; and yet endowed with the most profound feelings so that they can truly love even an unfaithful man and be ready to make any sacrifice.–And all of this is required of them?–Go and ask history, ask yourselves and say "No!" if you can).

Traditional dualistic images of femininity (saint-whore, angel-devil, Mary-Eve) and the tensions arising from conflicting expectations form the background against which individual desires are acted out. Like plays, Fischer's narratives move with frantic pace toward their final, tragic denouements. Short dramatic episodes dominate the earlier works; rapid exchanges of letters, the later ones. In *Gustavs Verirrungen* and *Vierzehn*

Tage in Paris Fischer occasionally switches to direct scenic dialogue to underscore the sense of dramatic interaction; in her epistolary novels she often reduces the letters to short exclamations full of pathos to create a sense of "orality." The letters appear to be utterances that express extreme emotional states rather than explorations of an inner world. They provide no detailed descriptions of character or setting but reveal the conflicts of their protagonists, who, in the process of acting out socially prescribed roles, destroy each other.

Fischer's first two works, *Gustavs Verirrungen* and *Vierzehn Tage in Paris*, tell of the trials and moral downfalls of male protagonists from the men's perspective. In five "autobiographical" episodes, the irresponsible Gustav narrates his involvements with five different women; the relationships seem to repeat over and over again the same vicious circle of infatuation, seduction, abandonment, and remorse. Caught in the struggle between desire and virtue, yet unable to restrain his passions, Gustav destroys not only the women he loves but also himself. On a similar but lighter note, the protagonist of *Vierzehn Tage,* a recently ennobled German baron, narrates his "aberrations" in postrevolutionary Paris, where his inexperience and vanity lead him into a life of dissipation until he is saved by a virtuous young woman. Fischer's central thesis in this story—"In jedem Manne liegt–nicht blos in so fern er Mensch, sondern vielmehr in so fern er Mann, und je mehr er es ist–ein Fond von Bösartigkeit, der nur durch die Liebe zu einem reinen weiblichen Wesen getilgt werden kann" (In every man–not just because of his human nature, but because he is a man, and the more so the more a man he is–there lies a residue of evil which can only be redeemed through the love of a pure woman)–combines the fairy-tale motif of the beauty and the beast with Romantic notions of the eternal feminine. The ideas of man's basic immorality and insatiable drive for conquest and of women's moral power are further elaborated in Fischer's subsequent novels, although her skepticism about human nature prevents her from believing in the ultimate success of women's redemptive labor of love.

In 1800 Christian August Fischer had published an anonymous treatise, *Über den Umgang der Weiber mit Männern* (On Women's Association with Men), as a second part to Karoline von Wobeser's best-seller *Elisa oder das Weib wie es seyn sollte* (1795; translated as *Eliza; or, The Pattern of Women,* 1802). Both works define "true"–that is, "natural"–femininity in Rousseauean terms, suggesting that women willingly subordinate themselves to men to the point of suffering abuse in abject, albeit "heroic," silence. Although Karoline Fischer repeatedly affirms the idea that men are born to be active and women to suffer, her novels *Die Honigmonathe, Der Günstling* (The Favorite, 1809), and *Margarethe* (1812) also actively polemicize against this image of passive endurance. Fischer does so by confronting women characters who embody the ideal of "Entsagung" (renunciation) or "Gelassenheit" (composure, equanimity) with passionate, articulate heroines who strive for self-realization as artists and human beings. Although none of these "Machtweiber" (demonic women)–as independent, power-conscious women were termed in men's writings–succeeds in reconciling her desire for independence with her desire to be loved, this confrontation of two images of femininity brings out the inner conflicts and the profound feelings of alienation many women experienced under the prevailing double standard. Thus, in *Die Honigmonathe* the passively suffering Julie is juxtaposed to Wilhelmine, the rational, active, independent woman. Although Wilhelmine does not elicit from men the same kind of passionate response as the vulnerable, "feminine" Julie, she manages to steer free of the confining and ultimately destructive marriage Julie is locked into and in the end freely chooses a man with whom she hopes to create an egalitarian relationship.

Fischer's last two novels present a similar confrontation and eventual dissolution of two female stereotypes, yet without a conciliatory ending. In *Der Günstling* the powerful Czarina Iwanowa, modeled after Catherine II of Russia, is unable to control her consuming passion for her councillor, Prince Alexander. When Alexander falls in love with his ward, the "angelic" Maria, Iwanowa has them both poisoned. In *Margarethe,* Fischer's most ambitious and ambiguous novel, the dual image of femininity is acted out by innocent, pious Margarethe and the experienced dancer Rosamunde. Both women are loved by the painter Stephani and the Prince. Both refuse to respond: Margarethe because her philanthropy has no sexual component, Rosamunde because she fears to be destroyed by the men's possessiveness. As Fischer makes clear, the two women embody in the eyes of society the "saint-whore" opposition. They are images that the male protagonists literally produce, possess, and exchange–in the form of portraits Stephani paints and the Prince commissions or buys. Yet while the two female characters are introduced as literary stock types, they transcend stereotyping when they articulate the inner struggle between what they feel to be their calling and what they know to be society's expectations. In an "autobiographical" insert, a Künstlerroman (artist novel) in miniature, Rosamunde explains how she became a performing artist and why she cannot compromise her art for love. Margarethe, on the other hand, is given ample opportunity to disclose through her letters to her mother the psychological roots of her extreme altruism, her need to embrace the whole world instead of one man, and her complete lack of sexual desire. Fischer's novel thus provides insights not only into the conflicts of the female artist but also into the deformation experienced by women who, like Wobeser's Elisa, are socialized into the role of selfless "saint."

Like Mary Wollstonecraft, whose *A Vindication of the Rights of Woman* (1792) she must have known, Fischer explores the threat of "romantic love" to women in the 1800s. When the Prince admonishes Rosamunde to give up her independence and surrender to the passionate courtship of the painter Stephani, claiming that a woman's beauty belongs to the man, she responds defiantly: "Ich glaube . . . sie gehöret ihr selbst; so wie ihr Herz und ihr Leben. Wem sie es auch giebt, es ist ein freies Geschenk; oder es giebt keine Freiheit mehr auf Erden!" (It belongs to her herself, I believe; just as her heart and her life are her own. If she gives it to somebody, it must be a free gift; otherwise, there is no more freedom on earth!). Both Margarethe and Rosamunde thus refuse to be appropriated: Rosamunde because she does not want to compromise her art, Margarethe because she will not limit her love of humanity to one individual. In acting out their respective roles to the extreme–the "public woman" Rosamunde belongs to the whole public, the "redeemer" Margarethe redeems everybody–both women show the contradictions in the role women are expected to play. A reconciliation of artistic ambition and family life, of desire for freedom and desire for love, Fischer argues, is impossible under present (that is, nineteenth-century) conditions.

Fischer's short stories reiterate the same themes and obsessions. Over and over Fischer recreates the conflicts between love and duty, individual desire and social constraints. The doubling into a conformist self and a rebellious other is depicted in racial terms in the short story "William der Neger" (1817; translated as "William the Negro," forthcoming 1990), while "Justine," which appeared in her *Kleine Erzählungen und romantische Skizzen* (Little Stories and Romantic Sketches, 1818), focuses again on the unbridgeable gap between the role of woman artist and that of wife and mother.

Curiously, none of Fischer's artist protagonists are writers. Most, in fact, claim that they were unable to express themselves in the language given to them and were forced to find their own means of expression. Yet when they choose wordless media such as music or dance, it is not to perform someone else's work: they themselves create something genuine and new. Thus, the marginalized Molly creates in her compositions a world of harmonious sounds that nobody but another outsider, the black ex-slave William, can understand; similarly, the haunted Rosamunde discovers dance as a means of escaping reality and entering into her "eigene, heilige Welt" (own sacred world). Art, which Fischer defines as the creation of beauty, is a means of escaping the uninspiring role of wife, housewife, and mother. While the premature deaths of Fischer's women artists, a formula favored by the Romantics, may suggest that women who try to live independently will invariably fail, it is still Fischer's unique achievement to have created models of women who dared to live by their own dictates–and who succeeded, albeit for a short time.

References:
Else Hoppe, "Caroline Auguste Fischer: Eine vergessene Braunschweiger Dichterin," *Niedersachsen,* 65, no. 4/5 (1965): 444-450;

Clementine Kügler, "Caroline Auguste Fischer (1764-1842): Eine Werkbiographie," Ph.D. dissertation, Free University of Berlin, 1989;

Oskar Meyer, "Die Herkunft des 'Mirabeau der Lüneburger Haide,' Carl Rudolph Ferdinand Christiani (1797-1851)," *Lüneburger Blätter,* 6 (1955): 80-97;

Anita Runge, Afterword to Fischer's *Der Günstling* (Hildesheim: Olms, 1988);

Runge, Afterword to Fischer's *Die Honigmonathe* (Hildesheim: Olms, 1987);

Runge, "Die Dramatik weiblicher Selbstverständigung in den Briefromanen Caroline Auguste Fischers," in *Die Frau im Dialog: Studien zur Theorie und Geschichte des Briefs,* edited by

Runge and Lieselotte Steinbrügge (Weinheim: Belz, forthcoming 1990);

C. W. O. A. von Schindel, *Die deutschen Schriftstellerinnen des neunzehnten Jahrhunderts*, volume 1 (Leipzig: Brockhaus, 1823), pp. 127-130;

Christine Touaillon, *Der deutsche Frauenroman des 18. Jahrhunderts* (Vienna & Leipzig: Braumüller, 1919), pp. 578-629.

Georg Forster

(27 November 1754 - 10 January 1794)

Thomas P. Saine
University of California, Irvine

BOOKS: *Characteres generum plantarum, quas in itinere ad insulas maris Australis collegerunt, descripserunt, delinearunt, annis MDCCLXXII-MDCCLXXV*, by Forster and Johann Reinhold Forster (London: White, Cadell & Elmsly, 1776);

A Voyage round the World, in His Britannic Majesty's Sloop Resolution, Commanded by Capt. James Cook, during the Years 1772, 3, 4, and 5, 2 volumes (London: White, Robson, Elmsly, Robinson, 1777); translated by Forster and Rudolf Erich Raspe as *Johann Reinhold Forster's, Doctor Der Rechte und Georg Forsters Reise um die Welt während den Jahren 1772 bis 1775, in dem von Seiner itzt regierenden Großbrittannischen Majestät auf Entdeckungen ausgeschickten und durch den Capitain Cook geführten Schiffe the Resolution unternommen: Beschrieben und herausgegeben von dessen Sohn und Reisegefährten George Forster. . . . Vom Verfasser selbst aus dem Englischen übersetzt, mit dem Wesentlichsten aus des Capitain Cooks Tagebüchern und andern Zusätzen für den deutschen Leser vermehrt und durch Kupfer erläutert*, 2 volumes (Berlin: Haude & Spener, 1778-1780);

Antwort an die Göttingischen Recensenten (Göttingen: Dieterich, 1778);

A Letter to the Right Honourable the Earl of Sandwich, First Lord Commissioner of the Board of Admiralty, &c. (London: Printed for G. Robinson, 1778);

A Reply to Mr. Wales's Remarks (London: White, Robson & Elmsly, 1778);

Georg Forster (Paul Zincke and Albert Leitzmann, eds., Georg Forsters Tagebücher)

Leben Dr. Wilhelm Dodds, ehemaligen Königl. Hofpredigers in London (Berlin: Haude & Spener, 1779);

Vom Brodbaum (Cassel, 1784);

Florulae insularum Australium prodromus (Götting-
en: Dieterich, 1786);

De plantis Magellanicis et Atlanticis commentationes
(Göttingen: Dieterich, 1789);

*Kleine Schriften: Ein Beytrag zur Völker- und Länder-
kunde, Naturgeschichte und Philosophie des Lebens*, 6 volumes, volume 1 edited by Forster,
volumes 2-6 edited by Ludwig Ferdinand
Huber (volume 1, Leipzig: Kummer, 1789;
volumes 2-6, Berlin: Voß, 1794-1797);

*Ansichten vom Niederrhein, von Brabant, Flandern,
Holland, England und Frankreich, im April,
Mai und Junius 1790*, 3 volumes, volume 3
edited by Huber (Berlin: Voß, 1791-1794);

*Ueber das Verhältniß der Mainzer gegen die Franken:
Gesprochen in der Gesellschaft der Volksfreunde
den 15ten November 1792* (Mainz, 1792);

*Erinnerungen aus dem Jahr 1790 in historischen Gemäl-
den und Bildnissen von D. Chodowiecki, D. Berger, Cl. Kohl, J. F. Bolt und J. S. Ringck* (Berlin: Voß, 1792 [dated 1793]);

*Anrede an die Gesellschaft der Freunde der Freiheit
und Gleichheit am Neujahrstage 1793* (Mainz,
1793);

*Discours adressé aux Commissaires de la Convention
Nationale, aux guerriers français et aux corps ad-
ministratifs à Mayence, réunis à la Société des
Amis de la Liberté et de l'Égalité de cette ville,
avant de se mettre en marche pour aller planter
l'arbre de la Liberté, le 13. Janvier, 1793, l'an
deuxième de la République française, par le Citoyen George Forster, président de la société*
(Mainz, 1793);

*Georg Forster's sämmtliche Schriften: Hrsg. von dessen
Tochter und begleitet mit einer Charakteristik Forster's von G. G. Gervinus*, 9 volumes, edited
by Therese Forster (Leipzig: Brockhaus,
1843);

*Briefe und Tagebücher Georg Forsters von seiner Reise
am Niederrhein, in England und Frankreich im
Frühjahr 1790*, edited by Albert Leitzmann
(Halle: Niemeyer, 1893);

Georg Forsters Tagebücher, edited by Leitzmann
and Paul Zincke (Berlin: Behr, 1914; reprinted, Nendeln: Kraus, 1968);

*Georg Forsters Werke: Sämtliche Schriften, Tagebücher,
Briefe*, 18 volumes projected, 16 volumes to
date, edited by the Deutsche Akademie der
Wissenschaften zu Berlin, Institut für deutsche Sprache und Literatur (Berlin: Akademie-Verlag, 1958-   );

Werke in vier Bänden, 4 volumes, edited by Gerhard Steiner (Frankfurt am Main: Insel,
1967-1970).

OTHER: Per Kalm, *Travels into North America; Containing Its Natural History, and a circumstantial
Account of its Plantations and Agriculture in general, with the Civil, Ecclesiastical and Commercial State of the Country, the Manners of the Inhabitants, and several curious and important
Remarks on various Subjects*, 3 volumes, translated by Forster (Warrington: Eyres, 1770-
1771);

Louis-Antoine de Bougainville, *A Voyage round the
World: Performed by Order of His most Christian
Majesty, in the Years 1766, 1767, 1768, and
1769. By Lewis de Bougainville . . . Commodore
of the Expedition, in the Frigate La Boudeuse,
and the Store-ship L'Etoile*, translated by Forster and Johann Reinhold Forster (London:
Nourse & Davies, 1772);

Gebhardt Friedrich August Wendeborn, *Beyträge
zur Kenntniß Großbrittaniens vom Jahr 1779:
Aus der Handschrift eines Ungenannten*, edited
by Forster (Lemgo: Meyer, 1780);

Neue Beiträge zur Völker- und Länderkunde, 13 volumes, edited by Forster and Matthias Christian Sprengel (Leipzig: Kummer, 1780-
1793);

Georges-Louis Leclerc, Comte de Buffon, *Naturgeschichte der vierfüßigen Thiere: Mit Vermehrun-
gen aus dem Französischen übersetzt*, translated
by Forster (Berlin: Pauli, 1780);

*Göttingisches Magazin der Wissenschaften und Littera-
tur*, 4 volumes, edited by Forster and Georg
Christoph Lichtenberg (Göttingen: Dieterich, 1780-1785);

*Johann Reinhold Forsters Bemerkungen über Gegen-
stände der physischen Erdbeschreibung, Naturgeschichte und sittlichen Philosophie auf seiner
Reise um die Welt gesammelt: Übersetzt und mit
Anmerkungen vermehrt von dessen Sohn und Reisegefährten Georg Forster*, translated and annotated by Forster (Berlin: Haude & Spener,
1783);

*Herr Graf Morozzo an Herrn Macquer über die Zerle-
gung der fixen und Salpeterluft: Aus dem Französischen*, translated by Forster (Stendal: Fran-
zen & Grosse, 1784);

Anders Sparrmann, *Reise nach dem Vorgebirge der
guten Hoffnung, den südlichen Polarländern
und um die Welt, hauptsächlich aber in den Ländern der Hottentotten und Kaffern in den Jahren
1772 bis 1776*, translated from the Swedish
by C. H. Groskurd, foreword by Forster (Berlin: Haude & Spener, 1784);

*Des Capitain Jacob Cook's dritte Entdeckungs-Reise, wel-
che derselbe auf Befehl und Kosten der Großbrit-*

tannischen Regierung in das stille Meer und nach dem Nordpol hinauf unternommen und mit den Schiffen Resolution und Discovery während der Jahre 1776 bis 1780 ausgeführt hat: Aus den Tagebüchern des Capitain Cook und der übrigen nach seinem Ableben im Commando auf ihn gefolgten Befehlshabern Clerke, Gore und King, imgleichen des Schiffswundarztes Herrn Anderson herausgegeben. Mit Zusätzen für den deutschen Leser, imgleichen mit einer Einleitung des Uebersetzers vermehrt und durch Kupfer und Charten erläutert, 2 volumes, translated by Forster (Berlin: Haude & Spener, 1787-1788);

Eugène Louis-Melchior Patrin, *Zweifel gegen die Entwicklungstheorie: Ein Brief an Herrn Senebier von L. P. aus der französischen Handschrift übersetzt*, translated by Forster (Göttingen: Dieterich, 1788);

Charles Marguerite Jean Baptiste Mercier Dupaty, *Briefe über Italien vom Jahr 1785: Aus dem Französischen*, 2 volumes, translated by Forster (Mainz: Universitätsbuchhandlung, 1789-1790);

Nachrichten von den Pelew-Inseln in der Westgegend des stillen Oceans: Aus den Tagebüchern und mündlichen Nachrichten des Capitains Heinrich Wilson, und einiger Officiere, welche daselbst mit ihm im August 1783 in der Antelope, einem Postschiff der englischen ostindischen Compagnie, Schiffbruch litten, zusammengetragen von Herrn Georg Keate . . . und aus dem Englischen übersetzt von D. Georg Forster . . . Mit einer Karte und Kupfern (Hamburg: Hoffmann, 1789);

Geschichte des Schiffbruchs und der Gefangennahme des Herrn von Brisson: Aus dem Französischen, translated by Margarete Sophia Forkel, foreword by Forster (Frankfurt am Main: Andreä, 1790);

Des Grafen Moritz August v. Benyowsky, Ungarischem und Pohlnischem Magnaten, und Eines von den Häuptern der Polnischen Conföderation, Schicksale und Reisen von ihm selbst beschrieben, 2 volumes, translated, with a foreword, by Forster (Leipzig: Dyk, 1790 [dated 1791]);

Esther Lynch Piozzi, *Bemerkungen auf einer Reise durch Frankreich, Italien und Deutschland*, 2 volumes, translated by Forkel, foreword and annotations by Forster (Frankfurt am Main & Mainz: Varrentrapp & Wenner, 1790);

William Forsyth, *Über die Krankheiten und Schäden der Obst- und Forstbäume, nebst der Beschreibung eines von ihm erfundenen und bewährten Heilmittels: Aus dem Englischen*, translated by Forster (Mainz & Leipzig: Fischer, 1791);

Geschichte der Reisen, die seit Cook an der Nordwest- und Nordost-Küste von Amerika und in dem nördlichen Amerika selbst von Meares, Dixon, Portlock, Coxe, Long u. a. m. unternommen worden sind, 3 volumes, edited and translated by Forster (Berlin: Voß, 1791);

Kalidasa, *Sakontala oder der entscheidende Ring, ein indisches Schauspiel von Kalidas: Aus den Ursprachen Sanskrit und Prakrit (durch William Jones) ins Englische und aus diesem ins Deutsche übersetzt mit Erläuterungen*, translated and annotated by Forster (Mainz & Leipzig: Fischer, 1791);

William Robertson, *Wilhelm Robertson's Historische Untersuchungen über die Kenntnisse der Alten von Indien, und die Fortschritte des Handels mit diesem Lande vor der Entdeckung des Weges dahin um das Vorgebirge der guten Hoffnung: Nebst einem Anhange, welcher Bemerkungen über die gesellschaftlichen Verhältnisse, die Gesetze und gerichtlichen Verfahrensarten, die Künste, Wissenschaften und gottesdienstlichen Einrichtungen der Indier enthält. Mit zwei Karten. Aus dem Englischen*, translated by Johann Daniel Sander, foreword by Forster (Berlin: Voß, 1791);

Thomas Paine, *Die Rechte des Menschen: Eine Antwort auf Herrn Burke's Angriff gegen die französische Revolution. Nebst der von Ludwig XVI. angenommenen Konstitutions-Acte*, translated by Forkel, foreword by Forster (Berlin: Voß, 1792);

Constantin François de Chasseboeuf, Comte de Volney, *Die Ruinen, aus dem Französischen*, translated by Forkel, foreword by Forster (Berlin: Vieweg, 1792);

Thomas Anburey, *Anburey's Reisen im inneren Amerika: Aus dem Englischen übersetzt*, translated by Forster and Forkel (Berlin: Voß, 1792);

Die neue Mainzer Zeitung oder Der Volksfreund, edited by Forster, 38 issues (1 January-29 March 1793);

"Parisische Umrisse" and "Ueber die Beziehung der Staatskunst auf das Glück der Menschheit," in *Friedens-Präliminarien*, 10 volumes, edited by Ludwig Ferdinand Huber (Berlin: Voß, 1793-1796), I: 317-365; II: 54-58, 152-169; VI: 373-406.

Georg Forster became an important eighteenth-century German author rather by accident after growing up and beginning his writing career in England. He saw more of the world than any other German writer of his time and played a significant role in transmitting non-European cultures to the contemporary audience. A cosmopolitan intellectual who was nowhere truly at home, he became famous for his account of Capt. James Cook's second Pacific voyage, infamous for his role in the attempt to turn part of the German Rhineland into a republic on the French model in 1792-1793. He made his mark on German letters with his travel books, his translations from English and French, and his urbane essays on topics in anthropology, natural history, history, politics, art, and literature. Only three years after his death Friedrich Schlegel was calling him a "classic" German writer.

Until he was nearly twenty-five years old Forster's life and career were inextricably linked to his father's fortunes. Johann Georg Adam Forster was born in Nassenhuben, a Polish village close to Danzig (today Gdansk), the oldest of the seven children of Johann Reinhold Forster, the village pastor, and Justine Elisabeth Nicolai Forster. Reinhold Forster was descended from George Forster, a Scottish adherent of Charles I who had immigrated to this region in the 1640s. Although Reinhold Forster was by profession a theologian, his real passions were languages, geography, and natural science. He knew the rudiments of seventeen languages and seems to have spent all his money on books. In 1765 he eagerly accepted a commission from the Russian government to tour the newly established German settlements on the Volga and draw up plans for their orderly development; he took Georg along as his companion and assistant. Upon returning to St. Petersburg to make his report and receive his due reward—it seems he expected to play an important role in carrying out the plans he was drafting—he quickly antagonized influential persons and was put off by the government bureaucracy. Learning that he had been replaced as pastor in Nassenhuben for overstaying his leave, he took ship for England with Georg to seek his fortune in the land of his ancestors.

After arriving in England in October 1766, Reinhold taught for a while at the Dissenters' Academy in Warrington, where he was a colleague of the scientist Joseph Priestley and the future French revolutionary Jean-Paul Marat. He soon quit and sought to make a living for himself and his family, the rest of whom had come over from Nassenhuben, by translating and giving language instruction. After a short period as an apprentice to a London merchant Georg was pressed into service to help support the family

and published his first independent translation before he was thirteen. In 1770 the family moved to London, where Reinhold established himself in scientific circles. His big opportunity came when he was invited to be the scientific director on Cook's second Pacific expedition after Sir Joseph Banks, who had accompanied Cook on his first voyage, withdrew two weeks before the scheduled departure. Reinhold accepted on the condition that he might take Georg along as his assistant. Thus Georg Forster, at the age of seventeen, set out on a voyage to the South Pacific, New Zealand, Tahiti, and the Antarctic regions which lasted from 13 July 1772 to 30 July 1775.

Reinhold Forster had joined the Cook expedition in the expectation that he would be in a position to reap the literary and scientific rewards of the undertaking by writing about it afterward. Soon after returning to England, however, he quarreled with Cook and the Admiralty and was forbidden to write any account of the voyage. Georg, not feeling bound by the prohibition, stepped in and wrote the two-volume *A Voyage round the World, in His Britannic Majesty's Sloop Resolution, Commanded by Capt. James Cook, during the Years 1772, 3, 4, and 5* (1777), making use of his and his father's diaries and probably with some assistance from Reinhold. Almost simultaneously with the writing of this work Georg and Rudolf Erich Raspe worked on a German version, which was published in two volumes in 1778 and 1780 by Johann Karl Philipp Spener in Berlin. Written in the form of a journal, the work contains some acute anthropological and ethnological observations. Probably most interesting for the contemporary audience was the portrayal of Tahiti. While admiring certain aspects of Tahitian society, Forster was far from considering it a paradise—he noted social inequality and economic exploitation even there. Forster's account of the Cook expedition and Louis-Antoine de Bougainville's *Voyage autour du monde* (1771), the account of his 1766-1769 expedition to the South Pacific—which the Forsters had translated into English in 1772 and which also appeared in that year in a German translation—largely determined the eighteenth century's ideas about Tahiti and contributed significantly to the direction of utopian thinking.

By 1778 the Forster family was in dire financial straits. Georg's trip to Paris in the fall of 1777 in search of buyers for South Pacific artifacts and specimens and a publisher for a French translation of *Voyage round the World* had been only moderately successful—he had met many in-

Forster (right) with his father, Reinhold Forster, serving as science officers on James Cook's second Pacific expedition; aquatint by D. Beuel after a painting by J. F. Rigau

fluential people, including Benjamin Franklin, and joined the Freemasons, but the trip yielded no significant financial results. In 1778 he went to Germany to look for a position for his father and for assistance in paying off the latter's debts so that he could leave England. The first volume of the German version of *Voyage round the World* had just come out, and Forster was an instant celebrity. In Cassel, on the way to Berlin, he accepted a professorship of natural history at the Collegium Carolinum, a flourishing academy which boasted a fine faculty. In Berlin he lobbied the Prussian government for a position for his father, who was eventually offered a professorship at Halle and also received some aid from German Freemasons to help him pay his debts. Reinhold Forster moved to Halle in 1780 and taught there until his death in 1798.

Georg Forster remained in Cassel from 1778 to 1784. In an effort to educate himself more thoroughly for his profession he made frequent visits to Göttingen, where he became acquainted with most of the professors. He was on especially friendly terms with Georg Christoph Lichtenberg, with whom he coedited the *Göttingisches Magazin der Wissenschaften und Litteratur*

(Göttingen Magazine for Sciences and Literature) from 1780 to 1785. In Göttingen he became attracted to Therese Heyne, the teenage daughter of the classical philologist and university librarian, Christian Gottlob Heyne. Heyne edited the *Göttingische Anzeigen von gelehrten Sachen*, the journal of the Göttingen Academy of Sciences, for which Forster wrote many reviews over the years. Early in his Cassel period Forster became active in the local Masonic lodge and, along with his close friend Samuel Thomas Sömmerring, a leading medical scientist and anatomist, became a member of the Rosicrucians. On the whole Forster was unhappy in Cassel, and the involvement with the Rosicrucians—who were politically rather reactionary, prayed for the restoration of religious orthodoxy, and practiced alchemy—was ruinous for his finances and became downright onerous for him and Sömmerring. When he was offered a professorship at the Polish university of Vilna he readily accepted; at about the same time, Sömmerring moved to Mainz. The break with the Rosicrucians caused both men considerable anguish: they feared that they would not be left alone by their erstwhile brothers, even though they had signed promises never to reveal the order's secrets. Forster left Cassel in April 1784 and arrived in Vilna in late October after a journey through Halle, Dresden, Prague, and Vienna, where he spent several weeks and was sorely tempted to stay and seek his fortune. He was acclaimed everywhere he went.

In Vilna Forster soon began to complain of complete isolation from his intellectual and cultural world. He was not impressed by his colleagues at the university, who were mostly former Jesuits, and the Polish government did not make good on its promises to provide the equipment and resources he needed. Yet he had committed himself to an eight-year contract and was deeply in debt. He traveled to Germany in 1785 and married Therese Heyne. On the way back to Vilna they stopped in Halle, where Forster submitted the obligatory dissertation for a doctorate in medicine; he hoped to earn supplementary income by practicing on the Poles (perhaps fortunately, he never did). A daughter, Therese, was born on 10 August 1786. The Forsters were liberated from their exile when the Russian government engaged Georg as chief scientist for a projected four-year Pacific expedition, bought out the rest of his contract at Vilna, and advanced him money to procure equipment and make preparations for the voyage. The Forsters left Vilna at

Letter from Forster to his publisher, Johann Karl Philipp Spener (Horst Fiedler, ed., Georg Forsters Werke, *volume 15)*

A row of professors' houses in Mainz, in one of which Forster lived while he was librarian at the University of Mainz (Stadtarchitekt Jürgen Hoffmann, Mainz)

the end of August 1787 for Göttingen, where the two Thereses were to stay with the Heyne family while Georg was away. Forster planned to join the Russians in England in the fall and sail from there in early 1788.

By this time, however, Russia was at war with Turkey, and Forster remained in Göttingen. After several months of uncertainty he was informed in the spring of 1788 that the expedition was being canceled. The Russians offered him a position in St. Petersburg, which he declined, and allowed him to keep the money they had advanced him. For the first time in his life Forster was free of debt. After negotiating with the Spanish government about an expedition to the Philippines, Forster accepted a position as university librarian in Mainz. He moved there in October 1788 after taking a crash course in university librarianship from his father-in-law.

Mainz was the capital of Electoral Mainz, a leading German ecclesiastical state, and Forster's appointment was one of the Catholic elector's pieces of window dressing to improve his image in Protestant Germany. Forster was as dissatisfied in Mainz as he had been everywhere else. His sec-

ond daughter, Klara, was born in 1789; two other daughters died in infancy. Forster made a journey with Alexander von Humboldt which he related in *Ansichten vom Niederrhein, von Brabant, Flandern, Holland, England und Frankreich, im April, Mai und Junius 1790* (Views of the Lower Rhine, Brabant, Flanders, Holland, England and France, in April, May and June 1790), published 1791-1794. The book, written as a series of letters, represented a significant departure in travel literature: Forster analyzed the culture and the political and social conditions of the areas through which he had traveled, and the work is full of descriptions of works of art he saw. Belgium was in political turmoil at the time of his trip because of Belgian resistance to the reforms undertaken by Emperor Joseph II during the 1780s, and a significant part of Forster's preparation for writing his book consisted of research on recent events in Belgium and the development of political factions there. Forster was sympathetic to Joseph's efforts to modernize conditions in his possessions and regarded the Belgians' resistance as a reactionary movement inspired by their priests, whom Joseph had also attempted to

Ludwig Ferdinand Huber, a writer and diplomat for whom Forster's wife, Therese, left him (Horst Fiedler, ed., Georg Forsters Werke, *volume 15)*

reform. Forster originally expected to have the work published by his old friend Spener, but Spener refused to meet his financial demands (he perhaps also feared that Forster's political views would prove too controversial). As a result the book was published in Berlin by Voß, which published most of his works from that time on; Christian Friedrich Voß, Jr., became one of Forster's most valued friends and correspondents. The first two volumes appeared in 1791 and 1792 (although the second volume has 1791 on the title page). Forster never finished the third volume; it was put out in fragmentary form in 1794, after his death.

Following the retreat of the Prussian and Austrian armies from the ill-starred invasion of France they had launched in August 1792, the French Rhine Army under Adam-Philippe de Custine invaded the Rhineland; it captured Mainz on 21 October, after the elector and leading officials had fled to safety. Within days a "Gesellschaft der Freunde der Freiheit und Gleichheit" (Society of the Friends of Liberty and

Equality) had been established along the lines of the French Jacobin clubs, and the occupiers began drawing up plans for governing the occupied territories pending elections to determine their ultimate status. After some hesitation Forster accepted the post of vice-president in the provisional administration and joined the club, where he delivered several inspirational speeches. He was active in the government and in the club through the winter of 1792-1793 and published a newspaper, *Die neue Mainzer Zeitung oder Der Volksfreund* (The New Mainz Journal, or Friend of the People), from January to March 1793. He was a delegate to and became vice-president of the Rhenish-German National Convention which met in March 1793 to settle the political future of the occupied territories. The territories were declared to constitute a republic independent of the Holy Roman Empire, and Forster and two other delegates were sent to Paris to petition the National Convention to annex the new Rhenish Republic to the French Republic. Forster left Mainz on 25 March, expecting to remain away only a short time; he hoped to return to run for election to the National Convention after the Rhenish Republic was part of France. Although the mission to Paris was successful, the Prussian and Austrian armies encircled Mainz shortly after Forster's departure, and he was forced to remain in France. Meanwhile Therese Forster, who had gone to Strasbourg in December 1792, had moved on to Neuchâtel, Switzerland, to be close to Ludwig Ferdinand Huber, a former Saxonian legation secretary in Mainz with whom she had begun an affair while Forster was on his Rhine trip. She was pressing Forster for a divorce.

Forster was in Paris during the spring of 1793, when the Gironde and Mountain factions in the National Convention were struggling for supremacy. He spent part of the summer and fall in French Flanders conducting negotiations with the English and made a brief, surreptitious trip to meet Therese and Huber at the Swiss border in late November to try to salvage his family situation. In Flanders he began his "Darstellung der Revolution in Mainz" (History of the Revolution in Mainz), but he had access to none of his papers or other relevant documents and materials. The work remained a fragment and was first published in the Gervinus edition of his works in 1843. Back in Paris after his visit with Therese and Huber he completed a substantial essay, "Ueber die Beziehung der Staatskunst auf das Glück der Menschheit" (On the Effect of Statecraft on the Happiness of Mankind), in which he spoke out against monarchical and ecclesiastical despotism. He also wrote most of a collection titled "Parisische Umrisse" (Parisian Sketches), a sympathetic appraisal of the course of the French Revolution between the fall of the Gironde and late 1793; by that time most German observers had become disillusioned with the revolution and were dismayed at the Montagnards' rise to power. The "Parisische Umrisse" and the "Staatskunst" essay were published in Huber's *Friedens-Präliminarien* (Peace Preliminaries, 1793-1796) after Forster's death, along with many lengthy and informative letters Forster had written to Therese during his last months. Forster worked through December 1793 on his various projects while turning over in his mind alternatives for leaving European turmoil behind and beginning a new life elsewhere. During December he came down with a cold, which may have developed into pneumonia; also suffering from the effects of the scurvy which had plagued him off and on since his voyage with Cook, he was confined to bed. He died on 10 January 1794, possibly of a stroke.

Forster published only two major works, *A Voyage round the World* and *Ansichten vom Niederrhein*. The former made him famous; the latter had just appeared when Forster became involved in the Mainz revolution and was never properly taken note of by the contemporary audience. Forster's writing was far and away superior to that of most German authors of his time—probably Lichtenberg and Christoph Martin Wieland were his only equals as stylists—and he was a versatile and engaging essayist who could write well on practically any subject. Much of his best writing consisted of essays which appeared in the *Göttingisches Magazin*, in Johann Wilhelm von Archenholtz's *Neue Literatur- und Völkerkunde* (News About Literature and Peoples) and *Annalen der Brittischen Geschichte* (Annals of British History), in Wieland's *Teutscher Merkur* (German Mercury), and in other periodicals. Throughout his life Forster engaged in translating, primarily travel literature but during his last years also political, historical, and even literary works. Kalidasa's *Sakontala*, which he translated from its English translation (1791), was the first work of Sanskrit literature to be made accessible to German readers. It made a significant impact on Johann Gottfried Herder and the Romantics and was an early stimulus to Sanskrit studies in Germany. Some of his most important essays were written as introduc-

tions to translations—for example, a major piece on history and the Enlightenment, "Cook, der Entdecker" (Cook the Discoverer), which was published with Forster's translation (1787-1788) of materials dealing with Cook's last voyage. Even *Ansichten vom Niederrhein* is essayistic in nature, and it shows the mature Forster's intellectual and stylistic qualities at their best. Forster's reputation as a revolutionary largely obscured the enduring interest of his work, much of which is still eminently readable. His early death was a great loss for German letters.

Letters:

Johann Georg Forster's Briefwechsel: Nebst einigen Nachrichten von seinem Leben, 2 volumes, edited by Therese Huber (Leipzig: Brockhaus, 1829);

Georg Forster's Briefwechsel mit S. Th. Sömmerring, edited by Hermann Hettner (Brunswick: Vieweg, 1877);

Ludwig Geiger, *Therese Huber, 1764 bis 1829: Leben und Briefe einer deutschen Frau* (Stuttgart: Cotta, 1901);

Georg Forsters Briefe an Christian Friedrich Voß, edited by Paul Zincke (Dortmund: Ruhfus, 1915);

Georg Forster nach seinen Originalbriefen, 2 volumes, edited by Zincke (Dortmund: Ruhfus, 1915).

Bibliographies:

Horst Fiedler, *Georg Forster Bibliographie 1767 bis 1970* (Berlin: Akademie, 1971);

Gerhard Steiner, *Georg Forster* (Stuttgart: Metzler, 1977).

Biographies:

Kurt Kerster, *Der Weltumsegler: Johann Georg Adam Forster, 1754-1794* (Bern: Francke, 1957);

Klaus Harpprecht, *Georg Forster oder Die Liebe zur Welt: Eine Biographie* (Reinbek: Rowohlt, 1987).

References:

Eberhard Berg, *Zwischen den Welten: Über die Anthropologie der Aufklärung und ihr Verhältnis zu Entdeckungs-Reise und Welt-Erfahrung mit besonderem Blick auf das Werk Georg Forsters* (Berlin: Reimer, 1982);

Sabine Dorothea Jordan, *Ludwig Ferdinand Huber (1764-1804): His Life and Works* (Stuttgart: Akademischer Verlag Hans-Dieter Heinz, 1978);

Christa Krüger, *Georg Forsters und Friedrich Schlegels Beurteilung der Französischen Revolution als Ausdruck des Problems einer Einheit von Theorie und Praxis* (Göppingen: Kümmerle, 1974);

Helmut Peitsch, *Georg Forsters "Ansichten vom Niederrhein": Zum Problem des Übergangs vom bürgerlichen Humanismus zum revolutionären Demokratismus* (Frankfurt am Main, Bern & Las Vegas: Lang, 1978);

Detlef Rasmussen, *Der Stil Georg Forsters: Mit einem Anhang, Georg Forster und Goethes "Hermann und Dorothea." Ein Versuch über gegenständliche Dichtung* (Bonn: Rohrscheid, 1983);

Rasmussen, ed., *Goethe und Forster: Studien zum gegenständlichen Dichten* (Bonn: Bouvier, 1985);

Rasmussen, ed., *Der Weltumsegler und seind Freunde: Georg Forster als gesellschaftlicher Shriftsteller der Goethezeit* (Tübingen: Narr, 1988);

Wolfgang Rödel, *Forster und Lichtenberg: Ein Beitrag zum Problem deutsche Intelligenz und Französische Revolution* (Berlin: Rütten & Loening, 1960);

Thomas P. Saine, *Georg Forster* (New York: Twayne, 1972);

Saine, "Georg Forster," in *Deutsche Dichter des 18. Jahrhunderts: Ihr Leben und Werk,* edited by Benno von Wiese (Berlin: Schmidt, 1977), pp. 861-880;

Saine, "Georg Forster und die Mainzer Revolution," *Juni*: Magazine für Kultur und Politik, 3 (1989): 80-95;

Gerhard Steiner, *Freimaurer und Rosenkreuzer: Georg Forsters Weg durch Geheimbünde. Neue Forschungsergebnisse auf Grund bisher unbekannter Archivalien* (Berlin: Akademie-Verlag/Weinheim: Acta humaniora der VCH Verlagsgesellschaft mbH, 1985);

Ludwig Uhlig, *Georg Forster: Einheit und Mannigfaltigkeit in seiner geistigen Welt* (Tübingen: Niemeyer, 1965);

Ralph-Rainer Wuthenow, "Georg Forster," in *Deutsche Dicthter*, volume 4: *Sturm und Drang, Klassik*, edited by Gunter E. Grimm and Frank Rainer Max (Stuttgart: Reclam, 1989), pp. 215-230;

Wuthenow, *Vernunft und Republik: Studien zu Georg Forsters Schriften* (Bad Homburg, Berlin & Zurich: Gehlen, 1970);

Paul Zincke, *Georg Forsters Bildnis im Wandel der Zeiten: Ein Beitrag zur Geschichte des öffentlichen Geistes in Deutschland* (Reichenberg: Sudetendeutscher Verlag, 1925).

Papers:

The only substantial collection of Georg Forster's letters, papers, and manuscripts is at the Academy of Sciences in East Berlin.

Johann Wolfgang von Goethe

(28 August 1749 - 22 March 1832)

Jane K. Brown
University of Washington

SELECTED BOOKS: *Neue Lieder in Melodien gesetzt von Bernhard Theodor Breitkopf* (Leipzig: Breitkopf, 1770);

Positiones juris (Strasbourg: Heitzius, 1771);

Von deutscher Baukunst. D.M. Ervini a Steinbach, anonymous (Frankfurt am Main, 1773);

Brief des Pastors zu *** an den neuen Pastor zu ***: Aus dem Französischen, anonymous (Frankfurt am Main, 1773);

Zwo wichtige bisher unerörterte Biblische Fragen zum erstenmal gründlich beantwortet, von einem Landgeistlichen in Schwaben, anonymous (Lindau am Bodensee, 1773);

Götz von Berlichingen mit der eisernen Hand: Ein Schauspiel, anonymous (Darmstadt, 1773); translated by Sir Walter Scott as *Goetz von Berlichingen* (London: Bell, 1799);

Prolog zu den neusten Offenbarungen Gottes verdeutscht durch Dr. Carl Friedrich Bahrdt, anonymous (Giessen, 1774);

Götter Helden und Wieland: Eine Farce, anonymous (Leipzig, 1774);

Clavigo: Ein Trauerspiel (Leipzig: Weygand, 1774); translated by Carl Leftley as *Clavidgo: A Tragedy in 5 Acts* (London: Johnson, 1798);

Neueröffnetes moralisch-politisches Puppenspiel, anonymous (Leipzig & Frankfurt am Main, 1774);

Die Leiden des jungen Werthers, anonymous (Leipzig: Weygand, 1774); translated by Richard Graves as *The Sorrows of Werther*, 2 volumes (London: Dodsley, 1779);

Erwin und Elmire: Ein Schauspiel mit Gesang, anonymous (Frankfurt am Main & Leipzig, 1775);

Nicht ich, sondern Heinrich Leopold Wagner hat den Prometheus gemacht (Frankfurt am Main: Goethe, 1775);

Stella: Ein Schauspiel für Liebende in fünf Akten (Berlin: Mylius, 1776); translated anonymously as *Stella* (London: Hookham & Carpenter, 1798);

Claudine von Villa Bella: Ein Schauspiel mit Gesang (Berlin: Mylius, 1776);

Proserpina: Ein Monodrama, anonymous (N.p., 1778);

Johann Wolfgang von Goethe; oil painting by Heinrich Kolbe, circa 1822-1826 (Goethe-Museum, Düsseldorf)

Aufzug des Winters mit seinem Gefolge (N.p., 1781);

Aufzug der vier Weltalter (N.p., 1782);

Die Fischerinn: Ein Singspiel. Auf dem natürlichen Schauplatz zu Tiefurth vorgestellt (N.p., 1782);

Goethe's Schriften, 8 volumes (Leipzig: Göschen, 1787-1790)–includes in volume 2 (1787), *Die Mitschuldigen: Ein Schauspiel*; in volume 3 (1787), *Die Geschwister: Ein Schauspiel*, translated anonymously as *The Sister* in *Dramatic Pieces from the German* (Edinburgh & London: Printed for William Creech and T. Cadell, 1792); *Iphigenie auf Tauris: Ein Schauspiel*, translated by W. Taylor as *Iphigenia: A Tragedy* (London: Johnson, 1793); in volume 4 (1787), *Der Triumph der Empfindsamkeit: Eine dramatische Grille*; *Die Vögel: Nach dem Aristophanes*; in volume 5 (1788), *Egmont: Ein*

Trauerspiel in fünf Aufzügen, translated anonymously as *Egmont* (London: Saunders & Otley, 1848); in volume 6 (1790), *Torquato Tasso: Ein Schauspiel*, translated by J. Cartwright as *Torquato Tasso* (London: Nutt, 1861); in volume 7 (1790), *Faust: Ein Fragment*; *Jery und Bätely: Ein Singspiel*; *Scherz, List und Rache: Ein Singspiel*;

Das Römische Carneval, anonymous (Berlin: Unger/ Weimar & Gotha: Ettinger, 1789);

Versuch die Metamorphose der Pflanzen zu erklären (Gotha: Ettinger, 1790);

Beyträge zur Optik, 2 volumes (Weimar: Industrie-Comptoir, 1791-1792);

Goethe's Neue Schriften, 7 volumes (Berlin: Unger, 1792-1800)–includes in volume 1 (1792), *Der Groß-Cophta: Ein Lustspiel in fünf Aufzügen*; as volume 2 (1794), *Reineke Fuchs*, translated by Thomas Arnold as *Reynard the Fox* (London: Natali & Bond, 1855; New York: Appleton, 1860);

Der Bürgergeneral: Ein Lustspiel in einem Aufzuge. Zweyte Fortsetzung der beyden Billets, anonymous (Berlin: Unger, 1793);

Wilhelm Meisters Lehrjahre: Ein Roman, 4 volumes (Berlin: Unger, 1795-1796); translated by Thomas Carlyle as *Wilhelm Meister's Apprenticeship* (Edinburgh: Oliver & Boyd / London: Whittaker, 1824; Boston: Wells & Lilly, 1828);

Epigramme: Venedig 1790 (Berlin: Unger, 1796);

Taschenbuch für 1798: Hermann und Dorothea (Berlin: Vieweg, 1798); translated by Thomas Holcroft as *Hermann and Dorothea* (London: Longmans, 1801; Richmond, Va.: Enquirer Press, 1805);

Neueste Gedichte (Berlin: Unger, 1800);

Was wir bringen: Vorspiel, bey Eröffnung des neuen Schauspielhauses zu Lauchstädt (Tübingen: Cotta, 1802);

Taschenbuch für das Jahr 1804: Die natürliche Tochter. Trauerspiel (Tübingen: Cotta, 1804);

Goethe's Werke, 13 volumes (Tübingen: Cotta, 1806-1810)–includes in volume 4 (1806), *Die Laune des Verliebten*; in volume 7 (1808), *Der Zauberflöte zweyter Theil*; in volume 8 (1808), *Faust: Eine Tragödie*, translated by Lord Francis L. Gower as *Faust*, in *Faust; and Schiller's Song of the Bell* (London: Murray, 1823); in volume 10 (1808), "Achilleis";

Sammlung zur Kenntniß der Gebirge von und um Karlsbad (Carlsbad: Franiecki, 1807);

Die Wahlverwandtschaften: Ein Roman, 2 volumes (Tübingen: Cotta, 1809); translated anonymously as "Elective Affinities," in *Novels and Tales* (London: Bohn, 1854);

Maskenzug zum 30sten Januar 1810 (N.p., 1810);

Pandora: Ein Taschenbuch für das Jahr 1810 (Vienna & Trieste: Geistinger, 1810);

Zur Farbenlehre, 2 volumes (Tübingen: Cotta, 1810); translated by Sir Charles L. Eastlake as *Goethe's Theory of Colours* (London: Murray, 1840);

Philipp Hackert: Biographische Skizze, meist nach dessen eigenen Aufsätzen entworfen (Tübingen: Cotta, 1811);

Aus meinem Leben: Dichtung und Wahrheit, 3 volumes (Stuttgart & Tübingen: Cotta, 1811-1813); translated anonymously as *Memoirs of Goethe: Written by Himself*, 2 volumes (London: Colburn, 1824; New York: Collins & Hannay, 1824);

Gedichte (Tübingen: Cotta, 1812);

Des Epimenides Erwachen: Ein Festspiel (Berlin: Duncker & Humblot, 1815);

Gedichte, 2 volumes (Stuttgart & Tübingen: Cotta, 1815);

Goethe's Werke, 20 volumes (Stuttgart & Tübingen: Cotta, 1815-1819)–includes in volume 10 (1817), *Die Aufgeregten*;

Aus meinem Leben, zweyter Abtheilung erster Theil, zweyter Theil: Italienische Reise, 2 volumes (Stuttgart & Tübingen: Cotta, 1816-1817); translated by Alexander James W. Morrison as *Travels in Italy* (London: Bohn, 1846);

Bey Allerhöchster Anwesenheit Ihro Majestät der Kaiserin Mutter Maria Feodorowna in Weimar Maskenzug, anonymous (Stuttgart: Cotta, 1818);

West-östlicher Divan (Stuttgart: Cotta, 1819);

Wilhelm Meisters Wanderjahre oder Die Entsagenden: Ein Roman. Erster Theil (Stuttgart & Tübingen: Cotta, 1821); translated by Carlyle as *Wilhelm Meister's Travels; or, The Renunciants* (Edinburgh & London: Tait, 1827);

Aus meinem Leben, zweyter Abtheilung fünfter Theil: Campagne in Frankreich 1792; Belagerung von Mainz (Stuttgart & Tübingen: Cotta, 1822); translated by Robert Farie as *The Campaign in France in the Year 1792* (London: Chapman & Hall, 1849);

Werke: Vollständige Ausgabe letzter Hand, 60 volumes, volumes 41-60 edited by Johann Peter Eckermann and Friedrich Wilhelm Riemer (Stuttgart & Tübingen: Cotta, 1827-1842)–includes in volume 15 (1828), "Novelle," translated by Carlyle as "Goethe's Novel," *Fraser's Magazine*, 6, no. 34 (1832): 383-393; in volumes 21-23 (1829), revised and enlarged version of *Wilhelm Meisters Wanderjahre oder Die Entsagenden*; as volume 41 (1832), *Faust: Eine Tragödie. Zweyter Theil in fünf Akten*, translated anonymously, with Part I, as *Faust Rendered into English Verse*, 2 volumes (London: Printed by Arthur Taylor, 1838); as volume 48 (1833), *Aus meinem Leben: Dichtung und Wahrheit. Vierter Theil*;

Faust in ursprünglicher Gestalt nach der Göchenhausenschen Abschrift, edited by Erich Schmidt (Weimar: Böhlau, 1887);

Werke: Hg. im Auftrage der Großherzogin Sophie von Sachsen. Weimarer Ausgabe, 143 volumes (Weimar: Böhlau, 1887-1919)–includes in Part I, volume 37, "Buch Annette";

Goethe über seine Dichtungen: Versuch einer Sammlung aller Äußerungen des Dichters über seine poetischen Werke, 9 volumes, edited by Hans Gerhard Gräf (Frankfurt am Main: Literarische Anstalt, 1901-1914; reprinted, Darmstadt: Wissenschaftliche Buchgesellschaft, 1968);

Sämtliche Werke: Jubiläums-Ausgabe, edited by Eduard von der Hellen, 40 volumes (Stuttgart: Cotta, 1902-1912);

Sämtliche Werke: Propyläen-Ausgabe, 48 volumes (Munich & Berlin: Propyläen, 1909-1932);

Wilhelm Meisters theatralische Sendung (Stuttgart: Cotta, 1911);

Gedenkausgabe der Werke, Briefe und Gespräche: 28 August 1949, edited by Ernst Beutler, 24 volumes (Zurich: Artemis, 1948-1964);

Werke: Hamburger Ausgabe, edited by Erich Trunz and others, 14 volumes (Hamburg: Wegner, 1949-1964; revised edition, Munich: Beck, 1982);

Gesamtausgabe der Werke und Schriften, 22 volumes (Stuttgart: Cotta, 1950-1968);

Corpus der Goethezeichnungen, edited by Gerhard Femmel, 6 volumes (Leipzig: Seemann, 1958-1970);

Sämtliche Werke nach Epochen seines Schaffens, edited by Karl Richter, 25 volumes projected, 13 volumes to date (Munich: Hanser, 1985-);

Sämtliche Werke, Briefe, Tagebücher und Gespräche, 40 volumes projected, 8 volumes to date (Frankfurt am Main: Deutscher Klassiker Verlag, 1985-).

Selected Editions in English: *Autobiography and Works*, translated anonymously, 3 volumes (London: Bohn, 1848-1850);

Works, translated anonymously, 14 volumes (London: Bohn, 1848-1890);

Dramatic Works, translated by Anna Swanwick and Sir Walter Scott (London: Bohn, 1850);

Poems of Goethe, translated by Edgar Alfred Bowring (London: Parker, 1853; revised and enlarged edition, London: Bohn, 1874; New York: Lovell, 1884)–revised edition includes "Hermann and Dorothea" and "West-Eastern Divan";

Novels and Tales, translated by R. Dillon Boylan and others (London: Bohn, 1854);

Works: People's Edition, 9 volumes, edited by F. H. Hedge and Leopold Noa (Boston: Cassino, 1882);

Works: Illustrated by the Best German Artists, 5 volumes, edited by Hjalmar Hjorth Boyesen (Philadelphia & New York: Barrie, 1885);

Reineke Fox, West-eastern Divan, and Achilleid: Translated in the Original Metres, translated by Alexander Rogers (London: Bohn, 1890);

Works: Weimar Edition, 14 volumes, edited by Nathan Haskell Dole (Boston: Niccolls, 1902);

Goethe's Literary Essays, edited by Joel E. Spingarn (London: Milford/New York: Harcourt, Brace, 1921);

Faust, translated by Philip Wayne, 2 volumes (Harmondsworth, U.K.: Penguin, 1949, 1959);

The Sorrows of Young Werther and Selected Writings, translated by Catherine Hutter (New York: New American Library, 1962);

Elective Affinities, translated by Elizabeth Mayer and Louise Bogan (Chicago: Regnery, 1963);

Goethe, edited by David Luke (Harmondsworth, U.K.: Penguin, 1964);

Elective Affinities, translated by R. J. Hollingdale (Harmondsworth, U.K.: Penguin, 1971);

The Sorrows of Young Werther and Novella, translated by Mayer, Bogan, and W. H. Auden (New York: Vintage, 1973);

Faust: A Tragedy. Backgrounds and Sources, the Author on the Drama, Contemporary Reactions, Modern Criticism, translated by Walter Arndt, edited by Cyrus Hamlin (New York: Norton, 1976);

Goethe's Collected Works, 12 volumes, edited by Victor Lange, Eric Blackall, and Cyrus Hamlin (New York: Suhrkamp, 1983-1989)–comprises volume 1, *Selected Poems*, edited by Christopher Middleton, translated by Middleton, Michael Hamburger, David Luke, J. F. Nims, V. Watkins (1983); volume 2, *Faust I & II*, edited and translated by Stuart Atkins (1984); volume 3, *Essays on Art and Literature*, edited by John Gearey, translated by E. and E. H. von Nardhoff (1986); volumes 4 & 5, *From My Life: Poetry and Truth; Campaign in France 1792; Siege of Mainz*, edited by Thomas Saine and Jeffrey Sammons, translated by Saine and R. Heitner (1987); volume 6, *Italian Journey*, edited by Saine and Sammons, translated by Heitner (1989); volume 7, *Early Verse Drama and Prose*, edited by Hamlin and F. Ryder, translated by R. M. Browning, Hamburger, Hamlin, and Ryder (1989); volume 8, *Verse Plays and Epic*, edited by Hamlin and Ryder, translated by Hamburger, Luke, and H. Hannum (1987); volume 9, *Wilhelm Meister's Apprenticeship*, edited by Lange, translated by Blackall and Lange (1989); volume 10, *Wilhelm Meister's Journeyman Years*, edited by Jane K. Brown, translated by Krishna Winston, J. van Heurck, and Brown (1989); volume 11, *The Sorrows of Young Werther; Elective Affinities; Novella*, edited by D. Wellberry, translated by Lange and J. Ryan (1988); volume 12, *Scientific Studies*, edited and translated by D. Miller (1988).

OTHER: James Macpherson, 4 volumes, *Works of Ossian*, edited anonymously by Goethe and J. H. Merck (volumes 1-2, N.p.; volumes 3-4, Leipzig: Fleischer, 1773-1777);
Die Propyläen: Eine periodische Schrift, 3 volumes, edited by Goethe (Tübingen: Cotta, 1798-1800);
Voltaire, *Mahomet: Trauerspiel in fünf Aufzügen*, translated by Goethe (Tübingen: Cotta, 1802);
Voltaire, *Tancred: Trauerspiel in fünf Aufzügen*, translated by Goethe (Tübingen: Cotta, 1802);
Benvenuto Cellini, *Leben des Benvenuto Cellini Florentinischen Goldschmieds und Bildhauers von ihm selbst geschrieben: Übersetzt und mit einem Anhange*, translated by Goethe, 2 volumes (Tübingen: Cotta, 1803);
Taschenbuch auf das Jahr 1804, edited by Goethe and Christoph Martin Wieland (Tübingen: Cotta, 1803);
Winckelmann und sein Jahrhundert: In Briefen und Aufsätzen herausgegeben, edited by Goethe (Tübingen: Cotta, 1805);
Denis Diderot, *Rameaus Neffe: Ein Dialog von Diderot. Aus dem Manuskript übersetzt und mit Anmerkungen begleitet*, translated by Goethe (Leipzig: Göschen, 1805);
Ueber Kunst und Alterthum, 6 volumes, edited by Goethe (Stuttgart: Cotta, 1816-1832);

Zur Naturwissenschaft überhaupt, besonders zur Morphologie: Erfahrung, Betrachtung, Folgerung, durch Lebensereignisse verbunden, 2 volumes, edited by Goethe (Stuttgart & Tübingen: Cotta, 1817, 1824);
Hans Sachs, *Der deutsche Gilblas oder Leben, Wanderungen und Schicksale Johann Christoph Sachse's, eines Thüringers: Von ihm selbst verfaßt*, introduction by Goethe (Stuttgart & Tübingen: Cotta, 1822);
N. A. von Salvandy, *Don Alonzo oder Spanien: Eine Geschichte aus der gegenwärtigen Zeit*, foreword by Goethe, 5 volumes (Breslau: Max, 1825-1826);
J. C. Mämpel, *Der junge Feldjäger in französischen und englischen Diensten während des Spanisch-Portugiesischen Kriegs von 1806-1816*, introduction by Goethe, 6 volumes (volumes 1-4, Leipzig: Fleischel; volumes 5-6, Brunswick: Verlags-Comptoir, 1826-1831);
Memoiren Robert Guillemard's verabschiedeten Sergeanten: Begleitet mit historischen, meisten Theils ungedruckten Belegen von 1805 bis 1823. Aus dem Französischen, introduction by Goethe, 2 volumes (Leipzig: Weygand, 1827);
Alessandro Manzoni, *Opere poetiche*, introduction by Goethe (Jena: Frommann, 1827);
Manzoni, *Der fünfte May: Ode auf Napoleons Tod*, translated by Goethe and others (Berlin: Maurer, 1828);
Thomas Carlyle, *Leben Schillers: Aus dem Englischen*, introduction by Goethe (Frankfurt am Main: Wilmans, 1830).

PERIODICAL PUBLICATIONS: "Römische Elegien," *Die Horen* (1795); translated by Leopold Noa as *Roman Elegies Translated in the Original Metres* (Boston: Schoenhof & Moeller, 1876);
"Unterhaltungen deutscher Ausgewanderten," *Die Horen* (1795);
"Xenien," by Goethe and Friedrich Schiller, *Musenalmanach auf das Jahr 1797* (1796);
Madame de Staël, "Versuch über die Dichtungen," translated by Goethe, *Die Horen*, 5 (1796): 20-55;
"Zum Schäkespears Tag," *Allgemeine Monatsschrift für Wissenschaft und Literatur* (April 1854): 247ff.

Johann Wolfgang von Goethe is widely recognized as the greatest writer of the German tradition. The Romantic period in Germany (the late eighteenth and early nineteenth centuries) is

Pastel drawing of Charlotte (Lotte) Buff, with whom Goethe fell in love in Wetzlar in 1772 before discovering that she was engaged to his friend Johann Georg Christian Kestner (Gustav Könnecke, Bilderatlas zur Geschichte der deutschen Nationallitteratur [Graz: Akademische Druck- und Verlagsanstalt, 1981])

In September 1771 Goethe returned to Frankfurt, ostensibly to begin a law career but in fact to begin the most visible literary career in German history. The four years between his return and his departure for Weimar contain the first flowering of his genius and constitute for many critics the high point of his career. During this time Goethe began to practice law both in Frankfurt and in Wetzlar, seat of the supreme court of the Holy Roman Empire; he also wrote book reviews, engaged in constant visiting with literary friends, functioned as the center of the Sturm und Drang movement, and traveled on the Rhine and in Switzerland. The autobiography describes three emotional entanglements in this period. In Wetzlar in 1772 he met Charlotte (Lotte) Buff and fell in love with her before discovering that she was engaged to his friend Johann Georg Christian Kestner. In 1774 he became involved in an uncomfortably close friendship with Maximiliane Euphrosine von La Roche Brentano, daughter of the novelist Sophie von La Roche

and future mother of the poet Clemens Brentano, while she was adjusting with difficulty to her marriage to Peter Anton Brentano, a wealthy Frankfurt merchant. The following year he became engaged to Anna Elisabeth (Lili) Schönemann, the daughter of a wealthy banker; although it inspired a spate of wonderful poems, the engagement was broken off in September 1775. Goethe had begun his career both as a great personality and as a great writer.

The Sturm und Drang movement aimed at establishing new political, cultural, and literary forms for Germany. Following the intellectual lead of Rousseau, Herder, and Hamann, it looked to the ancients, to England, and to the German past for models to replace the French neoclassical tradition. Hence, Goethe studied Shakespeare, Homer, Pindar, and Hans Sachs (a sixteenth-century German writer of farces) and rejected the classicism of his former hero, Wieland. In 1773 Goethe published an essay on the Strasbourg Cathedral, *Von deutscher Baukunst* (On German Architecture), in which he praised the Gothic style; it also appeared the same year in the manifesto of the Sturm und Drang movement, *Von deutscher Art und Kunst* (On German Culture and Art), edited by Herder. Besides Herder Goethe's collaborators included Johann Heinrich Merck, Johann Georg Schlosser (who married Cornelia Goethe in 1773), Friedrich Maximilian Klinger, Jakob Michael Reinhold Lenz, and Heinrich Leopold Wagner. There was a dimension of religious and moral concern in the movement, which resulted in Goethe's two pleas for religious tolerance, *Brief des Pastors zu *** an den neuen Pastor zu **** (Letter from the Pastor of *** to the New Pastor of ***, 1773) and *Zwo Wichtige bisher unerörterte Biblische Fragen* (Two Biblical Questions Not Previously Expounded, 1773). He studied the works of Emmanuel Swedenborg and Benedict de Spinoza and established connections with the theologian Johann Caspar Lavater, the educator Johann Bernhard Basedow, and the philosopher Friedrich Heinrich Jacobi, and with such members of the older generation of poets as Friedrich Gottlieb Klopstock, Heinrich Christian Boie, and Matthias Claudius.

His first contribution in the 1771-1775 period was to unleash the Shakespeare mania for which the Sturm und Drang movement is famous. His speech "Zum Schäkespears Tag" (For Shakespeare's Day, 1854) was presented two months after his return from Strasbourg; a dithyrambic celebration of Shakespeare as a poet of nature, it has remained one of the great milestones of German Shakespeare criticism. Even more influential was the Shakespearean history play *Götz von Berlichingen mit der eisernen Hand* (Götz von Berlichingen with the Iron Hand; translated as *Goetz von Berlichingen,* 1799), first drafted in November 1771 and published in a revised version two years later. The play is based on a sixteenth-century chronicle in which the old baron Götz tries to maintain his independence in the face of the encroaching empire. In the resulting conflict between tradition and law Götz's side degenerates, against his will, into open rebellion. The evil of the court is embodied in the beautiful Adelheid, who seduces Götz's old friend Weislingen into breaking his engagement to Götz's sister Marie. After Weislingen marries Adelheid, she poisons him. Götz dies in prison, welcoming the freedom of a higher world. The play is written in prose (the form of Wieland's translation of Shakespeare), with explosive diction and many short scenes. The emphasis on the prosaic aspects of Shakespearean diction and structure shows that the play is not only a statement in favor of Shakespeare but also a rejection of the orderly elegance of French neoclassical form for German drama.

Goethe's other dramas of the early 1770s are of three types: short satires, mostly from 1773, on literary and cultural themes in prose or in Knittelverse, the doggerel couplets made popular by Hans Sachs; incomplete poetic dramas on great figures such as Caesar, Mahomet, Prometheus, Egmont, and Faust, the extant fragments of which are among Goethe's finest poems of the period; and a group of completed plays of more conventional form–the tragedy *Clavigo* (1774; translated as *Clavidgo,* 1798), the drama *Stella* (1776; translated, 1798), and the operettas *Erwin und Elmire* (1775) and *Claudine von Villa Bella* (1776). *Clavigo* and *Stella* both deal with men like Weislingen who cannot be decisively faithful to a woman. In the first version of *Stella* the shaky hero is finally shared peacefully by the two women he has married; in 1787 Goethe gave the play a more conventional tragic ending. These four plays mark the beginning of a long series of operettas and operatic plays in Goethe's oeuvre.

Goethe's poems of this period set new standards for the genre in Germany. There are ballads, such as "Der König in Thule" (The King of Thule, 1782; later included in *Faust*); love poems, many of which were later set to music by Beethoven and Schubert; and occasional poems, such as

Title page of the novel that made Goethe famous

the masterpiece "Auf dem See" (On the Lake), written in response to a boat trip on the Lake of Zurich in the summer of 1775. There are also, finally, the great Pindaric hymns–among them "Wanderers Sturmlied" (Wanderer's Storm Hymn, included in volume 2 of *Goethe's Werke* [Goethe's Works, 1815-1819], 1815), "Prometheus," and "Ganymed" (both included in volume 8 of *Goethe's Schriften,* 1789).

Goethe's most famous work of the 1771-1775 period is *Die Leiden des jungen Werthers* (translated as *The Sorrows of Werther,* 1779), published in 1774. In this paradigmatic novel of eighteenth-century sensibility, Werther traces in a series of letters the course of his love for Lotte, who is already engaged to a solid young official when Werther meets her. Misled by the warmth of Lotte's friendship but most of all by his own intense imagination—which projects upon Lotte all the ideals garnered from his reading of Homer, Goldsmith, and Ossian—Werther gradually loses touch with the world around him, ceases to narrate coherently (an editor takes over the narration), and finally shoots himself. The novel is based on Goethe's relationship with Charlotte Buff and her fiancé, Kestner; the suicide for love of an acquaintance, Karl Wilhelm Jerusalem, provided the model for Werther's death. As important as the personal experiences for the novel are the literary experiences: the epistolary novel of sensibility from Samuel Richardson through Rousseau reaches its zenith in this novel. Through the passion of Werther the basic patterns of eighteenth-century subjectivity are called into question. The same conflicts and torments that Werther suffers in his relationship with Charlotte he also suffers in his relationships with nature and God. Through Werther's destructive preoccupation with himself Goethe offers a sympathetic yet penetrating commentary on the effusive introspectiveness of eighteenth-century consciousness, with its burgeoning psychology and crumbling metaphysics. By dramatically shortening the form, composing with a tight but elaborate symmetrical structure, incorporating foreign material such as translations from Ossian, inserting subordinate narratives, and especially by allowing Werther no respondents and then interrupting the flow of letters with a third-person narrator, Goethe simultaneously brought the epistolary tradition to its peak and to an end. The novel established Goethe as a European celebrity virtually overnight. To his distress it was widely misunderstood to glorify, rather than criticize, the fashionable melancholy of the age; he revised it extensively for the 1787 edition, the version in which it is now read. For his entire lifetime and beyond, *Die Leiden des jungen Werthers* was the work by which Goethe was known to the non-German world; only *Faust* has come to command the same kind of attention.

In the fall of 1775 Goethe left Frankfurt to visit Weimar at the invitation of the young duke Karl August. He quickly became the duke's close personal friend, the general court wit, and the organizer of court theatricals. In 1776 he was awarded the rights of citizenship and assigned administrative responsibilities in the tiny duchy. Weimar was already a center for the arts, since the duke's mother, Anna Amalia, had brought Wieland to be her son's tutor; Goethe soon per-

Duke Karl August of Sachsen-Weimar, who invited Goethe to Weimar in 1775; drawing by Johann Heinrich Lips (Gustav Könnecke, Bilderatlas zur Geschichte der deutschen Nationallitteratur [Graz: Akademische Druck- und Verlagsanstalt, 1981])

suaded Herder to accept a position there as well. Much of Goethe's time was spent traveling, either for official reasons or in company with the duke. He also made two journeys of literary interest: to the Harz mountains in the winter of 1777 and to Switzerland in the fall of 1779. Shortly after his arrival in Weimar he had entered into an intense friendship with Charlotte von Stein, the wife of a court official; this relationship dominated his emotional life for the next twelve years, transforming him from the ebullient Sturmer und Dranger of the 1770s into the reserved, polished courtier of his last four decades. Humanity, virtue, and self-control were the code words of this relationship, as they were to be for much of Goethe's subsequent writing. By the early 1780s Goethe was in charge of mines, roads, war, and finance; in 1782 the duke procured for him a patent of nobility (allowing him to add "von" to his name). Just as important for his future development as the new location, occupation, and personal relationships was the broadening of Goethe's intellectual interests in Weimar: for the first time he became consistently interested in science. As when he studied alchemy, his interest extended beyond reading to collecting and experimenting; but unlike his alchemical studies and some phrenological work he had undertaken for Lavater, his work in geology, anatomy, and botany led not only to literary results but to discoveries and scientific publications. In 1784 he demonstrated the existence of the human intermaxillary (premaxillary) bone and thereby the continuity of anatomical structures across species (unbeknownst to him the discovery had already been made in Paris in 1780), and in 1787 he conceived an influential theory of metamorphosis in plants.

The productivity of the early 1770s abated in Weimar—not surprisingly, given Goethe's many other responsibilities—but it by no means collapsed. Here he wrote many of his best-loved ballads, songs, reflective nature lyrics, and love poems. While the sublimity, irony, folk-song qualities, pathos, and broad humor of his earlier poetry often persist, there is also a new reflectiveness that moderates the emotion of the earlier poems. Goethe continued to write operetta librettos and occasional satires for court entertainments; to his repertory of "minor" drama he added court masques, which he continued to write until late in his life; he also wrote a free adaptation of Aristophanes' *The Birds* (1787). He worked intermittently on *Egmont* (1787; translated, 1848), which he had begun shortly before leaving Frankfurt; on successive versions, mainly in prose, of *Iphigenie auf Tauris*, published in its final blank verse version in 1787 (translated as *Iphigenia: A Tragedy*, 1793); and on *Torquato Tasso* (1790; translated, 1861). He also wrote *Wilhelm Meisters theatralische Sendung* (Wilhelm Meister's Theatrical Mission, 1911), a lively fragment about the state of the German theater.

The pressure of all these competing interests finally became too great, and Goethe fled to Italy, leaving Carlsbad in secret early in the morning of 3 September 1786. He recorded his impressions at the time in a diary for Frau von Stein; later he drew heavily on this diary for his *Italienische Reise* (1817; translated as *Travels in Italy*, 1846). In his reflections on Italy and his experiences there the interests and developments of the previous twelve years coalesce and become clearly articulated. Goethe had always expected to complete his education with a journey to Italy, as his father had, and twice before he had almost set out

Goethe at age thirty; oil painting by G. Oswald May (Gero von Wilpert, Deutsche Literatur in Bildern *[Stuttgart: Kröner, 1965])*

on that journey. The trip came to signify for him a rebirth, not only into a new life but into what he was always going to become: at several levels it was a journey of self-recovery. But it was in no sense a journey into himself, for his main concern was to look at objects as much as possible for themselves—at the rocks and the plants; the customs, theatricals, and festivals of the people (but never their feelings or political concerns); architecture, sculpture, and, to a lesser extent, painting. His Italy was the Italy of the high Renaissance, which included and subsumed ancient Roman Italy. Apart from brief stays in Venice and Naples and a tour of Sicily, Goethe spent all of his time in Rome, visiting galleries and monuments to study painting and sculpture. For most of his stay he socialized only with the German art colony, especially with Wilhelm Tischbein and Angelika Kauffmann. He revised and completed *Egmont, Iphigenie auf Tauris,* and part of *Torquato Tasso* for the edition of his works that was underway (1787-1790); he also added two scenes to the version of *Faust* that he had composed before he left

Goethe on his Italian journey, 1786-1788; oil painting by J. H. W. Tischbein (Gero von Wilpert, Deutsche Literatur in Bildern *[Stuttgart: Kröner, 1965])*

Frankfurt for Weimar, and selected from his Faust materials scenes that he published in preliminary form as *Faust: Ein Fragment* (1790).

The three plays Goethe revised are usually considered the core of his "classical" works, the first efflorescence of the objective style he developed in Italy. *Egmont* is still concerned with the tragedy of the genius too great for the world around him and with the problem of his consciousness, but from the opposite point of view from that of *Die Leiden des jungen Werthers*. If the latter portrays tragic preoccupation with the self, *Egmont* articulates the tragedy of what Goethe called "das Dämonische" (the demonic), that pure unconsciousness that is in direct contact with the wellsprings of being. Comparing himself to a sleepwalker, Egmont, prince of Garve, refuses to be self-conscious, refuses to be interpretable, or to interpret the behavior of others. Immensely popular with the people of the Netherlands, who are suffering under the rule of Philip

II of Spain, Egmont ignores warnings that neither his rank, his record of service, nor his standing with the people can save him when the regime decides he is too dangerous. Rejecting all intrigue, he walks blindly into a trap set by the wily Duke of Alba; but, like Götz von Berlichingen, he finds freedom just before his death in a vision of his mistress, Klärchen, as Freedom personified. The classicism of this play may best be identified in its symbolic, operatic, yet still intensely psychological language and themes. The play, which is in rhythmic prose, ranges in tone from Shakespearean mob scenes to what Friedrich Schiller called a "salto mortale in eine Opernwelt" (somersault into opera) at the end; actually, in their choral effects and the way that they symbolize the situation of the hero, the mob scenes are already operatic. Goethe was no longer imitating Shakespeare but had absorbed him into a new dramatic form of his own making.

*Christiane Vulpius, who became Goethe's mistress in 1788
and his wife in 1806; pastel drawing by F. Bury, 1800
(Gustav Könnecke,* Bilderatlas zur Geschichte der
deutschen Nationallitteratur *[Graz: Akademische Druck-
und Verlagsanstalt, 1981])*

Iphigenie auf Tauris combines the same intense psychological concerns with a symbolic
form derived less from Shakespeare than from
Euripides. Goethe is generally understood to
have internalized and psychologized Euripides'
drama, in which Orestes comes to barbarian
Tauris in search of a statue of Apollo's sister and
finds his own sister there. By making the Furies invisible and by reinterpreting the oracle so that
Orestes and Iphigenie do not have to steal the
statue of Diana, Goethe has indeed collapsed the
mythological level of the action into the human
level; but at the same time by replacing
Euripides' deus ex machina with humans telling
the truth, interpreting, and granting grace, he
has raised the human level to the mythological:
by their acts Iphigenie, Orestes, and the king of
Tauris have civilized the world. The end of this
play anticipates Faust in its celebration of the creative power of the human mind and will. In Italy
Goethe recast the play into blank verse. The
meter had been established in German drama by
Lessing in *Nathan der Weise* (1779; translated as *Nathan the Wise,* 1781); Goethe showed it capable of
a sublimity and complexity of diction previously
achieved only in the classical meters of Klopstock
and of his own Pindaric hymns.

The power and flexibility of Goethe's new
dramatic language emerges fully in *Torquato
Tasso,* which he finished revising after he returned from Italy in the spring of 1788. The
play shows Renaissance poet Tasso when he has
just completed his great epic, *La Gerusalemme
liberata.* He is unable to come to terms either with
the real political world embodied in the statesman Antonio Montecatino, or to find a satisfac-
tory relationship with his inspiring ideal, the princess Leonore d'Este, sister of his patron, Duke
Alfonso. Caught in complex intrigues, both real
and imagined, Tasso attempts to fight a duel with
Antonio and is placed under arrest by the duke;
later, he impulsively embraces the princess. Seemingly abandoned by the duke and the princess,
he turns to Antonio for support as he sinks into
madness. The blank verse and the Renaissance setting frame a much more objective version of the
problem of *Egmont.* Egmont's freedom and lack
of self-consciousness appear here as the idealism
of the poet, who is above the vagaries and political demands of the real world. Tasso's opposite,
the consummate courtier Antonio, is not seen as
evil, as Alba was in *Egmont,* but rather as the
other half of Tasso's incomplete personality.
(Faust was later to speak of the two souls in his
breast, the one that sought the heavens and the
other that clung to the world.) The two women
in the play, both named Leonore, are likewise com-
plementary personalities; bound together by
their love for Tasso and for one another they
seek to draw Tasso in opposite directions. By placing his hero between embodiments of his own
drives toward the ideal and the real, Goethe transformed his earlier realistic psychology into a symbolic representation of psychological analysis. As
a result, he was able to dispense with the Shakespearean mob scenes he used so effectively in
Egmont; in *Torquato Tasso* the psychological aspects
appear visibly on the stage instead of being mir-
rored in minor characters. Thus it is that despite
their seeming lack of stage action *Iphigenie auf
Tauris* and *Torquato Tasso* are among the most compelling plays in the German language.

Goethe returned from Italy as, he declared, an artist. Karl August relieved him of all official obligations except the directorship of the court theater, which was officially established in 1791, and of libraries and natural-historical and artistic collections in the duchy, including those at the University of Jena. Goethe returned to emotional dislocations and resentments occasioned both by the changes he had undergone and by his decision to go to Italy alone and in secret. Most severe among these was the rupture with Frau von Stein, who could not forgive his having left her side—let alone his open installation of a mistress, Christiane Vulpius, in his house shortly after his return. Only in the mid 1790s was any relationship with Frau von Stein reestablished, and then on a rather distant basis. Christiane bore Goethe several children, only one of whom—Julius August Walther, born in 1789—survived, and remained his companion until her death. Their marriage in 1806 did little to moderate the Weimar court's disapproval of Goethe's scandalous liaison with his uneducated "dicke Hälfte" (fatter half), as she was cruelly called, but their persistence in this situation is a measure both of their devotion to one another and of Goethe's distance from his immediate circle.

Indeed, he lived thereafter in a world of ideas and intellectual activities rather than in a world of events. Even the Italian journey, which he treasured for the rest of his life, was important to him as a remembered experience: he was not at all pleased when the duke dispatched him to Venice in 1790, though he used the time to learn more about Venetian painting. In Weimar he devoted his energy to studies of all sorts. In addition to his earlier interests in geology, botany, and comparative anatomy he became passionately interested in optics, and in 1790 he began publishing increasingly anti-Newtonian essays about the theory of color and scientific method in general. Much of his time was devoted to studying Kant, Plato, and Homer. His other major area of interest was art. This more academic development of his interests was reflected in his new friendships with the educator and statesman Wilhelm von Humboldt and the art historian Hans Meyer; the latter, whom he had met in Italy, lived in his house from 1791 until 1802. The French Revolution was the one political event that necessarily impinged on Goethe's life, not only because it was a topic of constant interest in all circles but also because the duke, who had entered the Prussian army, insisted that Goethe accompany him on campaigns to France in 1792 and to the Rhine in 1793. Goethe reported on these events in "Campagne in Frankreich 1792" (translated as *The Campaign in France in the Year 1792*, 1849) and "Belagerung von Mainz" (Siege of Mainz), published together in 1822. He continued his optical and artistic studies while trudging around after the army; his refusal to be submerged in military activity enabled him to present a clear picture of the daily reality of the campaigns.

Goethe's literary output in the early 1790s was relatively sparse. Two short plays, *Der Groß-Cophta* (The Great Cophta, 1792) and *Der Bürgergeneral* (The Citizen General, 1793), and a dramatic fragment, *Die Aufgeregten* (The Excited Ones, published in 1817), deal with the French Revolution in poetic terms. The verse epic *Reineke Fuchs* (1794; translated as *Reynard the Fox*, 1855), does so more effectively. This translation and adaptation into hexameter of a Low German version of the old story of the fox at the court of the lion is the first result of Goethe's study of Homer. But the most important poetry of these years is the cycle of love poems "Römische Elegien" (1795; translated as *Roman Elegies Translated in the Original Metres*, 1876), written in the first year of his relationship with Christiane. The poems describe the gradual acceptance of a German visitor into the Roman world of history, love, art, and poetry. As the poet takes possession of his Roman beloved, so too does he enter into the cultural heritage represented by Rome to the eighteenth century and everything represented by the south to the Gothic north. Written in the elegiac couplets of Propertius, Catullus, and Ovid, and in their frank manner, the poems transmute their Roman predecessors with the same facility and success as Goethe's classical plays appropriate their predecessors. They created something of a scandal when they were published but are now recognized as the greatest love poems of the generation.

The year 1794 marks the beginning of Goethe's friendship with Schiller. Schiller had come to Jena in 1789 as professor of history on an appointment arranged by Goethe, but the older poet had had two reasons for keeping his distance from the newcomer: not only had Schiller made his reputation as a powerful Sturm und Drang poet a decade after Goethe had renounced the movement, but he had recently given up poetry for immersion in Kant. Only in 1794 did a conversation after a lecture in Jena bring the two together into what rapidly became a mutually supportive and productive relationship. Much of Goethe's energy in the following years was devoted to Schiller's journal *Die Horen,* published from 1795 to 1797, and then to his own successor journal, *Die Propyläen,* published from 1798 to 1800. The program of these journals and of the poets' other work together was nothing less than the establishment of a classical German literature in the sense that the literature of fifth-century Athens had been classical: a literature that both represented and shaped a nation. While neither poet ever really spoke for or influenced the nation in the way to which they aspired, their mutual encouragement and criticism resulted in the greatest masterpieces of both men's careers.

Their excitement and productivity derived, however, not only from their friendship but also from the simultaneous emergence, largely under Goethe's supervision, of the University of Jena as the major center in Germany for the study of philosophy and science. Johann Gottlieb Fichte, Friedrich Wilhelm Joseph Schelling, and Georg Wilhelm Friedrich Hegel spent substantial parts of the 1790s in Jena, Fichte and Schelling in appointments arranged in part by Goethe. Drawn to Jena by their presence and by Goethe's presence in nearby Weimar were, at various times, the major Romantic poets—August Wilhelm and Friedrich Schlegel, Ludwig Tieck, Clemens Brentano, Novalis (Friedrich von Hardenberg), Friedrich Hölderlin, and Heinrich von Kleist. Drawn there also for frequent visits were Wilhelm von Humboldt and his brother, the naturalist Alexander von Humboldt. Goethe himself frequently visited Jena to attend lectures and discussions on philosophy, science, and literature. His scientific and literary studies continued unabated, with extensive reading in Greek literature, and, under the influence of A. W. Schlegel, renewed study of Shakespeare and the discovery of Calderón. He also devoted much time to running the court theater—producing, directing, and training the company both in the great modern repertory created by Mozart, Lessing, Schiller, and himself and also in the classics from the Greeks through Shakespeare and Racine. Even more than in Frankfurt in the 1770s Goethe was at the center of German intellectual life. His poetic achievement in all areas in this period is staggering. Against a rich background of "minor" works—scientific papers; important theoretical essays on art and literature; translations of works by Madame de Staël, Denis Diderot, Benvenuto

Cellini, and Voltaire; a fragmentary sequel to Mozart's *Die Zauberflöte* (The Magic Flute); and a spectacular torso of a drama about the French Revolution, *Die natürliche Tochter* (The Natural Daughter, 1804)—Goethe produced masterpieces which set the standards for most of the nineteenth century in lyric poetry, prose narrative, and drama.

In addition to the flow of occasional and personal poems, Goethe and Schiller wrote a large collection of satiric epigrams titled "Xenien" (Xenias, 1796) and a series of famous ballads. Goethe also continued his study and practice of classical meters with a series of elegies and "Achilleis" (1808; translated as "Achilleid," 1890), a fragment in hexameter on the death of Achilles. But his most important work in this genre is *Hermann und Dorothea* (1798; translated as *Hermann and Dorothea,* 1801) a hexameter idyll in nine cantos. About an innkeeper's son in a small German town who courts a refugee fleeing the French, the poem constitutes Goethe's most important poetic response to the revolution. At the same time its delicately ironic double vision, in which its characters appear both as limited, very German bourgeois and yet also as Homeric figures, makes the poem the paradigmatic achievement of Goethe's classicism.

Goethe's prose narratives of the 1790s are no less remarkable. For Schiller's *Die Horen* he wrote "Unterhaltungen deutscher Ausgewanderten" (1795; translated as "The Recreations of the German Emigrants," 1854), a collection of novellas in a frame narrative about refugees—this time aristocrats instead of bourgeois—from the French Revolution; the cycle focuses on the development of individual virtues such as cooperativeness and self-control as the basis for social order. But it is more important for formal reasons than for its content: it established the novella as a significant genre in German literature, and the fairy tale with which it concludes was the inspiration and model for similar works into the twentieth century. Nevertheless, in the context of the 1790s "Unterhaltungen deutscher Ausgewanderten" ranks as one of Goethe's minor works, for the great narrative of the decade was *Wilhelm Meisters Lehrjahre* (1795-1796; translated as *Wilhelm Meister's Apprenticeship,* 1824), the revision of the novel Goethe had drafted before he went to Italy. He had begun the revision in 1791, but the most significant part was completed in 1795 in the first flush of his friendship with Schiller. As the new title suggests, the novel no longer deals

Pencil sketch by Goethe of the Earth Spirit appearing to Faust in Part 1 of Faust *(Nationale Forschungs- und Gedenk-Stätten der klassischen deutschen Literatur in Weimar)*

just with the theater but explores the modes of being that are open to a thoughtful member of the middle class at the close of the eighteenth century. In this respect the novel is like *Die Leiden des jungen Werthers*, but Wilhelm's problem is not the destructive unity of a world projected by his own solipsism; it is, rather, how to make sense out of a world and circumstances which seem to lack any coherence whatsoever. The paradigmatic example of the European Bildungsroman, *Wilhelm Meisters Lehrjahre* follows its hero through a series of love affairs from late adolescence to early manhood as he flees his wealthy middle-class home to become an actor, outgrows the narrow circumstances of the German theater, and joins a secret society composed mainly of landed aristocrats committed to developing new forms of stability in a changing world. As in *Torquato Tasso*,

the various figures he encounters embody different possible modes of being for Wilhelm himself—ranging from the loose actress Philine to the poetic child Mignon to the pious "schöne Seele" (beautiful soul) to the ideal woman Natalie, to whom he becomes engaged. First the theater, a traditional metaphor for life, then the mysterious secret society of the tower provide the focus for Wilhelm's journey through art and poetry toward active participation in the world. The novel encompasses a vast range of individuals, character types, settings, episodes, and kinds of narrative, as well as inserted songs. The Romantics immediately hailed the novel as an immeasurably great achievement and then, in a series of imitations, struggled with the challenges it posed. The novel sums up and combines, as no single English novel before Charles Dickens's late works did, the achievements of Fielding, Sterne, and Goldsmith; although it was fashionable for English novelists in the nineteenth century to deplore Goethe's novel for its loose morals, it established the tradition of the Bildungsroman on which they all depended.

Faust is Goethe's best-known work of the 1790s. The core of the tragedy of Margarete had been written in prose before Goethe left Frankfurt; a manuscript of this version, known as the *Urfaust* (original *Faust*), was discovered and published in 1887. Parts of this version plus the two scenes composed in Italy had been published in 1790 as *Faust: Ein Fragment*. From 1797 to 1801, with Schiller's encouragement, Goethe rewrote the existing scenes, expanding some of them, and added the prologues, the pact scenes, and the Walpurgis Night segment to complete Part I of the drama, which was published in 1808. He introduces several important changes in the old legend of the scholar who makes a pact with the devil Mephistopheles: his Faust seeks not power through knowledge but access to transcendent knowledge denied to the human mind; the pact is transformed into a bet under the terms of which Faust will be allowed to live as long as Mephistopheles fails to satisfy his striving for transcendence. Most significantly, Goethe makes the second half of Part I into a love tragedy: Faust seduces Margarete, an innocent young girl who embodies for him the transcendent ideal that he seeks; she is condemned to death for killing their infant, but at the last moment, as Faust and Mephistopheles abandon her in prison, a voice from above declares that she is saved. *Faust,* in typical Romantic fashion, conflates Neoplatonism, which opposes a transcendent mind to an immanent world, with Kantianism, which opposes an internal subject to an external object; thus, sometimes Faust has two souls, one of which longs for transcendence, the other for the world (the Neoplatonist version of the Romantic dialectic), and at other times he feels imprisoned within himself and unable to apprehend the world outside his mind (the Kantian version of the Romantic dialectic). Both sets of oppositions are resolved in play or art. Faust's pact with the devil commits him, a striver after transcendent absolutes rather like Werther, to submerge himself restlessly in the reality of the world, like Wilhelm Meister. His opposing souls come into brief moments of harmony with one another but in moments that, by the terms of his pact with Mephistopheles, must not last. The tragedy of Part I, and the tragedy of Margarete, is that the eternities of the spirit must be subject to the destruction of time if they are to be perceived in the world. The intellectual complexity is matched by the stylistic complexity: Goethe transformed the unreflected, rather primitive Shakespeareanism of the early Sturm und Drang version into the highly sophisticated, "classical," thoroughly catholic text of Part I, which appropriates and transmutes vast numbers of texts from the entire Western tradition (excepting only the Greeks, whom Goethe reserved for Part II). Similarly, the Faust theme, which Lessing and after him the Sturm und Drang movement had identified as the quintessential German theme, becomes in Goethe's treatment a bond to link Germany to the European tradition. At the same time the unreflected neoclassical definition of tragedy in the early version is transformed into a renovation of non-Aristotelian forms, ranging from mystery play and Corpus Christi play to eighteenth-century operetta. In *Faust* Goethe established yet again a new genre, a world theater of such complexity that it has had few successors—certainly none of equal stature.

The death of Schiller in 1805 and the defeat of the Prussians at Jena in 1806 mark another major turning point in Goethe's life. The concentration of leading German intellectuals at the University of Jena gradually dispersed, so that Goethe's loose ties to the younger Romantic generation were maintained at an increasing distance. Furthermore, his sympathy with Napoleon, his insistence on the independence of art from politics, and his unorthodox social and religious attitudes alienated him from an ever-increasing portion of his public; by the time of his death he was clearly Germany's greatest, but not its most popular, writer. For most of the nineteenth century, in fact, Heinrich Heine's label for Goethe, "der große Heide" (the great pagan) stuck, with *pagan* generally understood in its most pejorative sense. Nevertheless, for the next thirteen years Goethe continued his activities in art, history, science, and literature at what for anyone else would be considered a prodigious rate. He maintained his interest in classical art, wrote a biography (1811) of Philipp Hackert, an artist he had known in Italy, and took great interest in the emerging talents of Caspar David Friedrich and Philipp Otto Runge. Through his friendship with Sulpiz Boisserée, his early interest in Gothic art was reawakened; from 1816 until his death he edited a journal, *Ueber Kunst und Alterthum* (On Art and Antiquity), devoted to these interests. He collected manuscripts and coins, and began reading more widely in history.

He also became more conscious of his own historic role, perhaps partly as a result of being summoned to meet Napoleon in 1808. Around this time his friend Friedrich von Müller began keeping records of his conversations with Goethe, and Goethe started writing his autobiography. The first installment, *Dichtung und Wahrheit*, appeared in 1811. Apart from the information this work offers about Goethe and his interpretation of himself, it is important for the view of his times that it contains. Goethe's great contribution to the development of autobiography was his recognition that the individual can only be understood in his historical context and that all autobiographical writing is historiography.

Goethe worked steadily in the five years following Schiller's death to complete his vast *Zur Farbenlehre* (1810; translated as *Goethe's Theory of Colours*, 1840), which he sometimes called his single most important work. It consists of three parts: an exposition of Goethe's own theory of color, a polemic against the Newtonian theory that white light is a mixture of colors, and a collection of materials on the history of color theory from antiquity to Goethe's own time. While Goethe's theory has never been accepted by physicists, his insights on the perception of color have been influential, as has his recognition that scientific ideas are conditioned by their historical contexts.

As in art, Goethe's tastes in literature remained open to Romantic influence; to his continuing interest in Shakespeare and Calderón he added the medieval German epic the *Nibelungenlied*. He also followed the work of the new generation of poets, inside and outside of Germany, with great interest. In the theater he produced a series of plays by Calderón, stimulating thereby a lasting revival of his works; in addition, he produced plays by younger Romantic dramatists, such as Heinrich von Kleist and Zacharias Werner. He continued writing court masques, but only one major dramatic work, the operatic fragment *Pandora* (1810). He wrote poems steadily, experimenting with new forms in his first group of sonnets and trying out Persian attitudes and forms in the *West-östlicher Divan* (1819; translated as "West-Eastern Divan," 1874), a book of poems composed in response to the German translation of Hafiz. Like the "Römische Elegien," these poems, many of them masterpieces, are arranged into a sketchy plot that articulates the

Goethe at age seventy-seven; pastel drawing by Ludwig Sebbers (Gero von Wilpert, Deutsche Literatur in Bildern *[Stuttgart: Kröner, 1965])*

poet's encounter with Hafiz and the culture he represents. The collection embodies better than any of his work except *Faust* the aging poet's passionate concern for "Weltliteratur" (world literature), by which term Goethe summarized his belief in a literary tradition that transcended national boundaries. The *West-östlicher Divan* also contains "Noten und Abhandlungen" (Notes and Treatises), brief essays on the history of Persian life and letters. As in his autobiographical and scientific writings, historical context had become indispensable to Goethe.

Before Schiller's death Goethe had begun planning a sequel to *Wilhelm Meisters Lehrjahre* that was, however, to be a cycle of novellas rather than a novel. Several of these novellas were written in the succeeding decade, but one of them so absorbed Goethe's interest that it developed into a novel in its own right: *Die Wahlverwandtschaften* (1809; translated as "Elective Affinities," 1854). The title refers metaphorically to the capacity of certain elements to displace others during chemical reactions. A young girl,

Ottilie, and an unnamed captain arrive at the estate of Eduard and Charlotte, and a double displacement ensues: Eduard and Ottilie are attracted to each other, as are Charlotte and the captain. When Charlotte gives birth to her and Eduard's child, it bears, paradoxically, the features of Ottilie and the captain, with whom the spouses have committed adultery only in spirit. The situation is resolved only when Ottilie forbids Eduard to divorce Charlotte and then starves herself to death. The novel retraces the concerns of *Die Leiden des jungen Werthers*, but in a more abstract and symbolic fashion, as a third-person narrative with only inserted, impersonal diary passages and a full-scale inserted novella. Eduard is a middle-aged Werther who has survived the loss of his beloved Charlotte to marry her on the rebound from her first marriage. Confronting his selfishness and subjectivity is an inscrutable moral law embodied in a powerful natural environment and in the equally inscrutable Ottilie. The novel subtly leaves open to question the extent to which this law is not inherent in nature, but projected by the characters themselves. With its paradoxical double adultery, its frank treatment of divorce, its suicide, and its apparent apotheosis, the novel scandalized most of its readers; despite its undeniable and significant influence in the nineteenth century, especially in England and America, it only became a respectable object of study in the twentieth. It is now considered one of Goethe's major works.

Goethe's wife died in 1816; the following year their son August married Ottilie von Pogwisch, who then ran the household she and August shared with Goethe. Also in 1817 Goethe resigned as director of the court theater after some forty years of supervising Weimar's theatrical life. In the wake of the Wartburg celebration of 1817, an expression of German liberal and national sentiment, Goethe became even more alienated from the political aspirations of his younger countrymen. He spent his last years almost as a living monument to himself, sitting for portraits and busts and receiving the visits of young intellectuals from near and far. This impression is heightened by his extensive autobiographical activities in his last decade. He completed *Dichtung und Wahrheit* and *Italienische Reise* and wrote "Campagne in Frankreich 1792" and "Belagerung von Mainz," as well as shorter reports of his activities year by year. He also organized his papers; published what he could; supervised the early stages of a complete edition of his works, the *Werke:*

Vollständige Ausgabe letzter Hand (Works: Complete Edition with Final Touches, 1827-1842); and arranged for the publication of other papers after his death. Finally, he spent much time in conversations that he knew were being recorded for posterity; the most famous of these are the ones with Johann Peter Eckermann, beginning in 1823.

But these last years were not devoted only to fixing the image of the great personality. Goethe read widely and voluminously: classical authors, Shakespeare, Calderón, his beloved English novelists, and contemporary writers such as Lord Byron, Alessandro Manzoni, Sir Walter Scott, and Victor Hugo. Between 1817 and 1824 he published essays on morphology and general scientific topics in two series, continued his work in optics, read extensively in medicine, and began reading and writing about meteorology. He continued to write literary essays, reviews, and major poems. The most important among the latter are "Urworte Orphisch" (Orphic Utterances), "Trilogie der Leidenschaft" (Trilogy of Passion), "Chinesisch-Deutsche Jahres und Tageszeiten" (Sino-German Seasons and Times of Day), and the poems written in Dornburg after the death of Carl August in 1828. A masterly novella, called simply "Novelle" (Novella, 1828; translated as "Goethe's Novel," 1832), was written in 1826-1827. But Goethe also completed two major large-scale works, *Wilhelm Meisters Wanderjahre oder Die Entsagenden* (1821; translated as *Wilhelm Meister's Travels; or, The Renunciants*, 1827) and *Faust*, Part II (1832; translated, 1838).

Like Goethe's other novels, *Wilhelm Meisters Wanderjahre* represents a significant advance in the nature and structure of the European novel, though it took a long time for its true importance to be recognized. Goethe had begun planning sequels to both *Wilhelm Meisters Lehrjahre* and *Unterhaltungen deutscher Ausgewanderten* before Schiller's death. The result was *Wilhelm Meisters Wanderjahre*, which appeared in a first version in 1821 and in a substantially revised and expanded version in 1829. The frame is a loose narrative of Wilhelm's journeymanship, his travels to increase his mastery of life in company with his son Felix. On his way he is offered innumerable novellas, reports, and collections of aphorisms to read, all of which are included and many of whose characters, along with old friends from *Wilhelm Meisters Lehrjahre*, wander in and out of the frame narrative. The end of Wilhelm's journey, his reunion with his beloved Natalie, is delayed to some indefinite time beyond the end of the

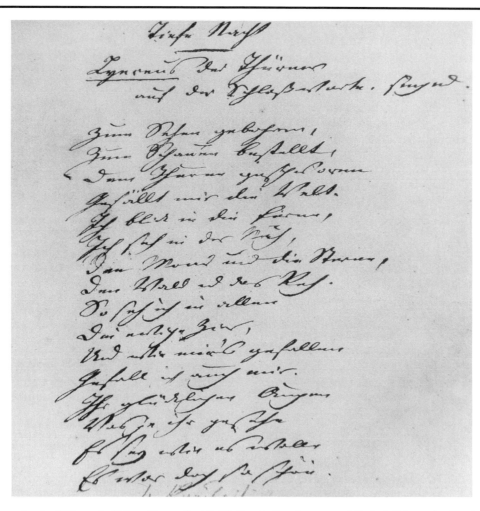

Manuscript page for the "Türmerlied" from Faust, *Part 2 (Nationale Forschungs- und Gedenk-Stätten der klassischen deutschen Literatur, Weimar)*

novel. With this loose structure Goethe questions the possibility of individual development in the fragmented society that Europe had become during his lifetime and thus calls into question the ideals of his earlier novel and of his cultural program of the 1790s. It no longer seems possible for individual development and education to lead to social cohesion and order. Sympathetic parodies of eighteenth-century writers in the novel mourn the loss of subjectivity imposed by the new historical conditions: the problem is exactly the reverse of that in *Die Leiden des jungen Werthers*. Its complex ironies of tone and structure made the novel inaccessible to early audiences. Only in the twentieth century, as the accuracy of Goethe's reading of the nineteenth century became clear, was it taken seriously; and only since World War II have its literary merits begun to be appreciated.

The second part of *Faust*, completed in 1831 and published posthumously at Goethe's desire, has had a similar–though, perhaps because of its undeniable stylistic virtuosity, not quite so extreme–pattern of reception. Begun in the later stages of composition of Part I but completed only between 1825 and 1831, it is an elaborate unfolding and historicizing of the first part. It shows Faust first at the imperial court, then at the "Klassische Walpurgisnacht" (classical witches' sabbath), where he ransacks Greek mythology to find Helena, who bears him a son. Later he returns to the wars of the emperor, then spends his old age supervising land-reclamation projects. Satisfied that he is working for the benefit of humanity, despite the murder of an elderly couple (killed in a fire started by Mephistopheles' henchmen). At the end of his life Faust renounces magic and dies, still striving to improve his lands. Divine Grace, however, saves his soul, which is shown ascending in pursuit of an ever-receding ideal embodied once more in Margarete, "das Ewig-Weibliche" (the eternal feminine). Most of the play, from the middle of Act I to the beginning of Act IV, grounds both itself and all of modern European literature in the classical tradition, going back to what was understood at the time as the oldest levels of classical mythology. This undertaking is possible only on the basis of Goethe's extensive learning, his ability to absorb and recreate literary styles, and his understanding of the nature of allegory, a mode of writing that had been virtually lost in the eighteenth century. But not only does the play sum up Goethe's and Europe's relation to the classical tradition; it also reflects, like *Wilhelm Meisters Wanderjahre*, on the state of European culture and politics in Goethe's last years, and on the human condition in general. Despite the richness of the text, it never loses sight of the central issues of Part I. Over and over it makes the points that pure truth cannot be permanently manifested in time–the tragedy of the historicist; that truth can be known only temporally and imperfectly in the world–the tragedy of the Platonist; and that truth can only be known through the mental projections of the seeker himself–the tragedy of the Kantian. Nowhere are the central concerns of European Romanticism more cogently summed up in all their ramifications than in Goethe's last masterpiece. On 22 March 1832, less than two months after making his final revisions of *Faust*, Goethe died, probably of a heart attack.

Like all Romantics, Goethe was a profoundly dialectical thinker. For a variety of reasons, including the power of his personality, his preference for concrete detail over broad abstraction, the complexity of his views, and the uncongeniality of some of his attitudes in the prevailing political and social climate, his dialectic was disassembled and his works fragmented into the separate statements of a sage. Thus, opposing readings of Goethe have developed–as serene Olympian or tortured nihilist, as the embodiment of nineteenth-century culture or as utterly out of touch with the world around him, as concerned or indifferent–and there has been a long tradition of ambivalence toward him in Germany. The nineteenth century had strong reservations about the unconventionality of his moral stance and about his rejection of a strong nationalist position, while later generations have had more difficulty with his lack of direct political engagement. But both the vehemence of these reactions and

the continuing vitality of his work testify to a power of thought that he was aware of from the earliest years of his career. An acquaintance speaks of his drive in the early 1770s "die Gedanken selbst, wie sie wären, zu denken und zu sagen" (to think and say the thought itself as it really is). This effort to articulate "the thought itself as it really is" is the challenge his writing still presents.

Letters:
Werke: Hq. im Auftrage der Großherzogin Sophie von Sachsen. Weimarer Ausgabe, Part 4, 50 volumes (Weimar: Böhlau, 1887-1912).

Interviews:
Johann Peter Eckermann and Frédéric Jacob Soret, *Gespräche mit Goethe in den letzten Jahren seines Lebens: 1823-1832*, 3 volumes (Leipzig: Brockhaus, 1837-1848); translated by John Oxenford as *Conversations of Goethe with Eckermann and Soret*, 2 volumes (London: Smith, Elder, 1850);

Flodoard Freiherr von Biedermann, Max Morris, Hans Gerhard Gräf, and Leonhard L. Mackall, eds., *Goethes Gespräche: Gesamtausgabe*, 5 volumes (Leipzig: Biedermann, 1909-1911);

Ernst and Renate Grumach, eds., *Goethe: Begegnungen und Gespräche*, 5 volumes (Berlin: De Gruyter, 1965-1985);

Conversations and Encounters, edited and translated by David Luke and Robert Pick (Chicago: Regnery, 1966; London: Wolff, 1966).

Bibliographies:
Karl Goedeke, *Grundriß zur Geschichte der deutschen Dichtung*, third edition, volume 4, part 3 (Dresden: Ehlermann, 1912); volume 4, part 5 (Berlin: Akademie, 1957);

Hans Pyritz, Heinz Nicolai, and Gerhard Burkhardt, *Goethe-Bibliographie*, 2 volumes (Heidelberg: Winter, 1965-1968); continued in *Goethe: Neue Folge des Jahrbuchs der Goethe Gesellschaft* (1955-   );

Waltraud Hagen, *Die Drucke von Goethes Werken* (Berlin: Akademie, 1971).

Biographies:
George Henry Lewes, *The Life and Works · of Goethe*, 2 volumes (London: Nutt, 1855);

Albert Bielschowsky, *Goethe: Sein Leben und seine Werke*, 2 volumes (Munich: Beck, 1896-1904); translated by W. Alpha Cooper as *The Life of Goethe*, 3 volumes (New York &

London: Putnam's, 1905-1908; reprinted, 1970);

Richard Friedenthal, *Goethe: Sein Leben und seine Zeit* (Munich: Piper, 1963); published simultaneously in English as *Goethe: His Life and Times* (Cleveland: World, 1963);

Robert Steiger, ed., *Goethes Leben von Tag zu Tag*, 5 volumes to date (Zurich: Artemis, 1982-   ).

References:

Frederick Amrine, Francis Zucker, and Harvey Wheeler, eds., *Goethe and the Sciences: A Reappraisal*, Boston Studies in the Philosophy of Science, no. 97 (Boston: Reidel, 1987);

Stuart P. Atkins, *Goethe's Faust: A Literary Analysis* (Cambridge: Harvard University Press, 1958);

Atkins, *The Testament of Werther in Poetry and Drama* (Cambridge: Harvard University Press, 1949);

Benjamin Bennett, *Goethe's Theory of Poetry: Faust and the Regeneration of Language* (Ithaca, N.Y.: Cornell University Press, 1986);

Eric A. Blackall, *Goethe and the Novel* (Ithaca, N.Y.: Cornell University Press, 1976);

Jane K. Brown, *Goethe's Cyclical Narratives: The Unterhaltungen deutscher Ausgewanderten and Wilhelm Meisters Wanderjahre*, University of North Carolina Studies in the Germanic Languages and Literatures, no. 82 (Chapel Hill: University of North Carolina Press, 1975);

Brown, *Goethe's Faust: The German Tragedy* (Ithaca, N.Y.: Cornell University Press, 1986);

Walter H. Bruford, *Culture and Society in Classical Weimar, 1775-1806* (Cambridge: Cambridge University Press, 1962);

Pietro Citati, *Goethe*, translated by Raymond Rosenthal (New York: Dial, 1974);

Allan P. Cottrell, *Goethe's Faust*, University of North Carolina Studies in the Germanic Languages and Literatures, no. 86 (Chapel Hill: University of North Carolina Press, 1976);

Wilhelm Emrich, *Die Symbolik von "Faust II": Sinn und Vorformen* (Frankfurt am Main & Bonn: Athenäum, 1957);

Barker Fairley, *A Study of Goethe* (Oxford: Clarendon Press, 1947);

John Gearey, *Goethe's Faust: The Making of Part I* (New Haven: Yale University Press, 1981);

Ilse Graham, *Goethe: A Portrait of the Artist* (Berlin & New York: De Gruyter, 1977);

Ronald D. Gray, *Goethe the Alchemist: A Study of Alchemical Symbolism in Goethe's Literary and Scientific Works* (Cambridge: Cambridge University Press, 1952);

Harry G. Haile, *Invitation to Goethe's Faust* (University: University of Alabama Press, 1978);

Harold Jantz, *The Form of Faust: The Work of Art and Its Intrinsic Structures* (Baltimore: Johns Hopkins University Press, 1978);

Elise von Keudell, *Goethe als Benutzer der Weimarer Bibliothek* (Weimar: Böhlau, 1931);

Victor Lange, *The Classical Age of German Literature, 1740-1815* (New York: Holmes & Meier, 1982);

Lange, ed., *Goethe: Twentieth Century Views* (Englewood Cliffs, N.J.: Prentice-Hall, 1968);

Meredith Lee, *Studies in Goethe's Lyric Cycles*, University of North Carolina Studies in the Germanic Languages and Literatures, no. 93 (Chapel Hill: University of North Carolina Press, 1978);

Wolfgang Leppmann, *The German Image of Goethe* (Oxford: Clarendon Press, 1961);

Karl Robert Mandelkow, *Goethe im Urteil seiner Kritiker*, 4 volumes (Munich: Beck, 1975-1984);

Eudo C. Mason, *Goethe's Faust: Its Genesis and Purport* (Berkeley: University of California Press, 1967);

Hans Mayer, ed., *Spiegelungen Goethes in unserer Zeit* (Wiesbaden: Limes, 1949); revised and enlarged as *Goethe im XX. Jahrhundert* (Hamburg: Wegner, 1967);

Clark S. Muenzer, *Figures of Identity: Goethe's Novels and the Enigmatic Self* (University Park: Pennsylvania State University Press, 1984);

Ernst M. Oppenheimer, *Goethe's Poetry for Occasions* (Toronto: University of Toronto Press, 1974);

T. J. Reed, *The Classical Centre: Goethe and Weimar 1775-1832* (London: Croom Helm / New York: Barnes & Noble, 1980);

Paul Requadt, *Goethes "Faust I": Leitmotivik und Architektur* (Munich: Fink, 1972);

Hans Ruppert, *Goethes Bibliothek* (Weimar: Arion, 1958);

Emil Staiger, *Goethe*, 3 volumes (Zurich: Atlantis, 1952-1959);

Fritz Strich, *Goethe und die Weltliteratur* (Bern: Francke, 1946); translated by C. A. M. Sym as *Goethe and World Literature* (London: Routledge & Kegan Paul, 1949; reprinted, 1972);

Karl Viëtor, *Goethe: Dichtung, Wissenschaft, Weltbild* (1949); translated by Moses Hadas as *Goethe, the Poet* (Cambridge: Harvard University Press, 1949; reprinted, 1970), and by Bayard Quincy Morgan as *Goethe, the Thinker* (Cambridge: Harvard University Press, 1950);

Elizabeth M. Wilkinson and Leonard A. Willoughby, *Goethe: Poet and Thinker* (New York: Barnes & Noble, 1962);

Alfred Zastrau, ed., *Goethe-Handbuch* (Stuttgart: Metzler, 1955-).

Papers:

The bulk of Goethe's papers are in the Goethe-und-Schiller-Archiv, Weimar, German Democratic Republic. The Goethe Museum, Düsseldorf, Federal Republic of Germany, houses a major collection of manuscripts, portraits, and first editions. A smaller collection of Goethe manuscripts is at the Freies Deutsches Hochstift Frankfurter Goethemuseum (the museum is the house in which Goethe grew up), Frankfurt am Main, Federal Republic of Germany. The Speck Collection in the Beinecke Rare Books Library, Yale University, contains first editions and a substantial collection of Goetheana.

Wilhelm Heinse
(15 February 1746 - 22 June 1803)

Rita Terras
Connecticut College

BOOKS: *Sinngedichte* (Halberstadt: Groß, 1771);

Die Kirschen: Eine Romanze, anonymous (Berlin, 1773);

Laidion oder Die Eleusinischen Geheimnisse: Erster Theil, anonymous (Lemgo: Meyer, 1774);

Ardinghello und die glückseeligen Inseln: Eine Italiänische Geschichte aus dem sechszehnten Jahrhundert, anonymous (2 volumes, Lemgo: Meyer, 1787; revised, 1794; edited by Max L. Baeumer, 1 volume, Stuttgart: Reclam, 1975);

Fiormona oder Briefe aus Italien, anonymous (Berlin: Nauck, 1794);

Hildegard von Hohenthal, anonymous, 3 volumes (Berlin: Voß, 1795-1796);

Anastasia und das Schachspiel: Briefe aus Italien, vom Verfaßer des Ardinghello, anonymous, 2 volumes (Frankfurt am Main: Varrentrapp & Wenner, 1803);

Musikalische Dialogen. Oder: Philosophische Unterredungen berühmter Gelehrten, Dichter und Tonkünstler über den Kunstgeschmack in der Musik. Ein Nachlaß, edited by Ignaz Theodor Arnold (Leipzig: Gräff, 1805; reprinted, Hildesheim & New York: Olms, 1977);

Wilhelm Heinse's sämmtliche Schriften, 10 volumes, edited by Heinrich Laube (Leipzig: Volckmar, 1837-1838);

Sämmtliche Werke, edited by Carl Schüddekopf (13 volumes, Leipzig: Insel, 1902-1925; reprinted, 12 volumes, Munich: Omnia-Minireprint, 1977);

Briefe aus der Düsseldorfer Gemäldegalerie, 1776-1777: Mit einer Skizze der deutschen Geniezeit, des Lebens und der Werke Heinses und einer Entwicklungsübersicht der ästhetischen Grundbegriffe im 18. Jahrhundert, edited by Arnold Winkler (Leipzig: Schmid, 1912);

Aphorismen, 3 volumes, edited by Albert Leitzmann, (Leipzig: Insel, 1925);

Aus Briefen, Werken, Tagebüchern, edited by Richard Benz (Stuttgart: Reclam, 1958).

OTHER: Petronius, *Begebenheiten des Enkolp: Aus dem Satyricon des Petron,* 2 volumes, translated anonymously by Heinse (Schwabach, 1773); republished as *Geheime Geschichte des römischen Hofs unter der Regierung des Kaisers Nero: Aus dem Lateinischen des Petron übersetzt mit einigen Anmerkungen,* 2 volumes (Rome, 1783);

Abbé J. F. P. A. de Sade, *Nachrichten zu dem Leben des Franz Petrarca aus seinen Werken und den gleichzeitigen Schriftstellern: Erster Band,* translated anonymously by Heinse (Lemgo: Meyer, 1774);

Erzählungen für junge Damen und Dichter gesammelt und mit Anmerkungen begleitet: Komische Erzählungen, edited anonymously by Heinse (2 vol-

Wilhelm Heinse; 1780 oil painting by Johann Friedrich Eich (Gleimhaus, Halberstadt)

umes, Lemgo: Meyer, 1775; reprinted, 1 volume, Stuttgart: Metzler, 1967);

Theorie des Paradoxen, edited anonymously by Heinse (Leipzig: Dyk, 1778);

Torquato Tasso, *Das befreyte Jerusalem: Mit allerhöchstem kaiserlichen und höchstem kuhrfürstlichpfälzischen Privilegium,* 4 volumes, translated anonymously by Heinse (Mannheim: Verlag der Herausgeber der ausländischen schönen Geister, 1781);

Ludovico Ariosto, *Roland der Wüthende: Ein Heldengedicht von Ludwig Ariost dem Göttlichen. Aus dem Italiänischen aufs neue übersetzt,* 4 volumes, translated by Heinse (Hannover: Helwing, 1782-1783).

Intrigued all his life by the idea of the *bellum omnium contra omnes* (war of all against all)—he read Thomas Hobbes's *Leviathan* (1651)—Wilhelm Heinse has often been called a typical writer of the Sturm und Drang movement. While his reputation as an individualist and sensualist, as well as the fact that most of his major works were written and published during the Sturm und Drang period, may justify such an opinion, Heinse defies classification and remains an enigma to critics and literary historians. Struggling against bigotry and limitations of his freedom, Heinse led a relatively quiet life dominated by fiscal difficulties and social inadequacy. He was neither noteworthy as a scholar nor successful in his profession. As a writer, however, he enjoyed the respect and, in some instances, the admiration of his contemporaries, as well as the reputation of a controversial figure, an interesting author with a tendency toward libertinism.

Johann Jakob Wilhelm Heintze (he later changed the spelling of his last name) was born on 15 February 1746 in Langewiesen to Johann Jakob Heintze, city clerk and organist in the small Thuringian town, and Barbara Katharina Jahn Heintze. In 1768 Heinse was sent to Jena University to study law; but being more interested in literature and philosophy, in 1769 he followed his most distinguished professor, Justus Riedel, to the progressive Erfurt University. Christoph Martin Wieland soon arrived there as a new faculty member. Wieland became Heinse's teacher and occasional mentor and, with his friend Riedel, helped launch the young man's career as a writer. Heinse remained at the university until 1771.

It is not possible to determine whether Heinse accepted a publisher's suggestion that he translate part of Petronius's *Satyricon* merely out of a dire need for money, as he maintained later, or because this piece of lubricious literature challenged him as a translator and, at the same time, appealed to his youthful inclination to shock. In any case, the effect of Heinse's brilliant translation, published as *Begebenheiten des Enkolp* (Enkolp's Affairs) in 1773, was electrifying. Wieland was outraged; Johann W. L. Gleim, another of Heinse's early mentors, was somewhat disturbed; most others were enchanted. Heinse's remains the most popular German translation of the *Satyricon.*

By this time Heinse's readers were ready to welcome an original work by the young author. His letters to Gleim indicate that he had in preparation two major projects begun in Erfurt and continued while traveling with an unsavory character named Liebenstein who became involved in a fraudulent lottery scheme in 1771-1772. (This involvement forced the author to adopt the name Rost for a while.) Heinse completed both works during the happiest episode in his life, the years 1772 to 1774 that he spent in Halberstadt as a

Erzählungen
für
junge Damen und Dichter
gesammelt

und mit Anmerkungen begleitet.

Erster Band.
Komische Erzählungen.

Vadano a volo i canti. Anima pura
Sempre è sicura.
Chiabrera.

LEMGO,
in der Meyerschen Buchhandlung, 1775.

Title page for the first volume of a collection of stories edited by Heinse

tutor in the household of Councillor von Massow and his young wife, whom Heinse called the Muse. Both works reflect the spirit of this time. *Musikalische Dialogen* (Musical Dialogues, 1805), which was completed by 1773, consists of five dialogues in which such prominent Enlightenment figures as Jean-Jacques Rousseau and Nicola Jommelli appear. Rousseau, the author of the *Dictionnaire de Musique* (1767), a work marked by its carefully formulated definitions of accent, song, and voice, is confronted by Jommelli, the musical genius who has no explanation for his talent. Representing Heinse's position, Jommelli convinces Rousseau that the main goal of music is the imitation and arousal of passion.

Heinse described the epistolary novel *Laidion oder Die Eleusinischen Geheimnisse* (Laidion; or, The Eleusinian Mysteries, 1774), completed

in 1771 and revised in 1773, as the realization of a dream of the rapturous union between Johann Joachim Winckelmann's Bacchus and Wieland's goddess of love. Laidion, a courtesan, writing after her death as a member of Aspasia's Eleusinian circle on Mount Venus, is an ingenious narrator and an effective defender of a hedonistic worldview. She satirizes Plato's utopian republic with its machinelike human beings who "so gerecht, so ordentlich leben, so mässig essen und trinken, und so ordentlich ohne Leidenschaft und Wollust lieben, als wenn sie nichts davon empfänden" (ever so righteous, live ever so respectably, eat and drink ever so moderately, and love ever so properly without passion or lust, as if they never knew of the existence of the senses). The novel is obviously indebted to Wieland's *Geschichte des Agathon* (History of Agathon, 1766-1767) and other rococo works. But in *Laidion* Heinse also attempts to combine elements of the epistolary novel, developed by Samuel Richardson and Rousseau, with those of the Bildungsroman. This combination foreshadows the individual style of writing evident in Heinse's most successful work, *Ardinghello und die glückseeligen Inseln* (Ardinghello and the Islands of the Blest, 1787).

From 1774 to 1780 Heinse lived in and near Düsseldorf, where he worked with Johann Georg Jacobi on the latter's periodical *Iris*. At the Düsseldorf Gallery, then the most famous German collection of paintings, Heinse found a new love: the visual arts. In 1776-1777 some letters from Heinse on paintings in the Düsseldorf Gallery appeared in Wieland's *Teutscher Merkur*, a highly regarded publication. Concerned with Rubens, Raphael, Michelangelo, Titian, and others, the letters tell much about Heinse's aesthetic theory, the central idea of which is that art is essentially imitation of nature. Nature, in eighteenth-century terminology, refers to the universe in its entirety, exclusive of the supernatural. Heinse's rediscovery of Rubens is consistent with his naturalistic-relativistic concept of art. On the one hand, his relativism made possible a positive evaluation of Rubens, who, in general, did not appeal to eighteenth-century artistic sensibilities; on the other hand, his mimetic approach limited his perception and left him without any appreciation of spiritual and symbolic values in art.

In 1780 Heinse departed on a three-year journey, mostly on foot, to Switzerland and Italy. Supporting himself by challenging strangers to games of billiards, he visited the waterfalls at

Schaffhausen, walked to Geneva, and continued across the St. Gotthard pass to Genoa. In May 1781 he arrived in Venice, then went on to Florence, Rome, and Naples. All the while he was taking copious notes on Italian history and art that were published in 1909 as *Tagebücher von der italienischen Reise* (Diaries of the Italian Journey) in Carl Schüddekopf's edition of Heinse's works. The Italian notebooks as well as the diaries of his later years reveal that in Italy Heinse also heard a great deal of music and developed a taste for opera. His passion for both the graphic and the performing arts stayed with him and is strongly reflected in the novels of his mature years.

Heinse's most successful novel, *Ardinghello und die glückseeligen Inseln,* written between 1783 and 1785, fully preserves its fictional character while discussing architecture, sculpture, and painting as the author encountered them on his journey through Italy; it is usually considered the first German Künstlerroman (novel about artists). Heinse's contemporaries, impressed by the novel's subtitle, *Eine Italiänische Geschichte aus dem sechszehnten Jahrhundert* (A Sixteenth-Century Italian Story), emphasized its Renaissance character. Both labels are correct. The protagonist, Ardinghello, is a painter (and a poet and a singer) born into two noble Florentine families, the Frescobaldis and the Abizzis. Both families are deeply involved in scandalous political affairs, with the Medicis among others. The action of the novel begins in Venice in 1574 and ends on the island of Paros in 1578. Ardinghello is a political refugee whose amorous and heroic adventures force him into a constant change of scenery until the ardent republican, with the help of friends, can found his own utopia. The novel is a collage of historical, philosophical, and artistic elements intended to present the image of a genius, a great Renaissance man whose efforts on behalf of humanity end with the realization of his dream: a utopian state on the Islands of the Blest. Ardinghello's endeavors as a painter are part of the mosaic of a hedonist's life, in which art is a vehicle to erotic adventures. The contemplation of nature, discussions of eighteenth-century issues, and occasional stints as a warrior take up the rest of the protagonist's time. In Ardinghello's utopian state on the islands of Naxos and Paros the inhabitants live in harmony, united in their reverence for nature, voluntary acceptance of law and order, and sense of equality (women have ten percent of the vote!). The freedom of the individual to lead a life of pleasure is the most important

Engraving of Heinse by Friedrich Christian Gottlieb Geyser, after a painting by Eich

principle of the community. Fiordimona, Ardinghello's ladylove, rejects marriage in favor of a full experience of life, including single motherhood. Ardinghello advocates constant war to keep humanity from sinking into idleness. During Heinse's lifetime *Ardinghello und die glückseeligen Inseln* went into a second authorized and several unauthorized editions. It was translated into French in 1800 and 1944 and into Russian in 1935. As yet there is no translation into English.

Heinse's Italian journey did not improve his financial or social position. Returning home, he once again had to depend on the generosity of friends, in particular Friedrich Heinrich Jacobi in Düsseldorf. Finally, in 1786, the historian Johannes von Müller was able to secure for Heinse a permanent position, first as reader and then, in 1788, as librarian in the household of the Archbishop of Mainz.

In 1792, when Mainz was occupied by the French revolutionary army, Heinse left the city to stay with friends. He did not return until 1794, and then only to move the archepiscopal library to Aschaffenburg. He never shared the enthusiasm for the ideals of the French Revolution displayed by many of his contemporaries and decided to withdraw from the unrest of the 1790s into the world of the last novel to be published during his lifetime: *Hildegard von Hohenthal* (1795-1796). The locale of this apolitical tale is a small German principality; the time is between 1770 and 1780. There are few social conflicts; the characters exude confidence and enjoy the pleasures of life. The performing arts, especially opera, come under scrutiny. The protagonist, Hildegard, is able to make a career as a soprano by pretending to be a castrated male. Heinse's overwhelming concern with musical theory, his inability or unwillingness to integrate analysis and action in his text, and his rather traditional concept of music (he saw Mozart as a mere imitator of Christoph Gluck and said that he paid too much attention to effect and too little to substance) were immediately noticed by critics. The novel enjoyed no more than moderate success.

Heinse's final novel was published posthumously in 1803. *Anastasia und das Schachspiel* (Anastasia and the Chess Game) consists almost exclusively of play-by-play descriptions of famous chess games. With no character development and little action, the work's classification as a novel is hardly justified.

Following Heinse's death in Aschaffenburg on 22 June 1803, his friend and physician Samuel Thomas Sömmering became executor of his will and administrator of his literary estate. In 1805 Sömmering had Heinse's skull removed from his grave and sent to the Seckenberg Museum in Frankfurt am Main, where, for 140 years, it was displayed with the inscription "Wilhelm Heinse, Poeta summus." The skull disappeared during an air raid in 1945.

Letters:

Briefe zwischen Gleim, Wilhelm Heinse und Johann von Müller: Aus Gleims litterarischem Nachlasse, 2 volumes, edited by Wilhelm Körte (Zurich: Geßner, 1806-1808):

Briefwechsel zwischen Gleim und Heinse, edited by

Carl Schüddekopf, 2 volumes (Weimar: Felber, 1894-1895).

Biographies:

Johann Schober, *Johann Jakob Wilhelm Heinse: Sein Leben und seine Werke. Ein Cultur- und Litteraturbild* (Leipzig: Friedrich, 1892);

A. Jolivet, *Wilhelm Heinse: Sa vie et son oeuvre jusqu'en 1787* (Paris: Rieder, 1922).

References:

Max L. Baeumer, *Das Dionysische in den Werken Wilhelm Heinses: Studie zum dionysischen Phänomen in der deutschen Literatur* (Bonn: Bouvier, 1964);

Baeumer, *Heinse-Studien* (Stuttgart: Metzler, 1966);

Walter Brecht, *Heinse und der ästhetische Immoralismus: Zur Geschichte der italienischen Renaissance in Deutschland* (Berlin: Weidmann, 1911);

Manfred Dick, *Der junge Heinse in seiner Zeit: Zum Verhältnis von Aufklärung und Religion im 18. Jahrhundert* (Munich: Fink, 1980);

Henry C. Hatfield, *Aesthetic Paganism in German Literature from Winckelmann to the Death of Goethe* (Cambridge: Harvard University Press, 1964), pp. 73-82;

Harold von Hofe, "Heinse, America, and Utopianism," *PMLA,* 72 (June 1957): 390-402;

Otto Keller, *Wilhelm Heinses Entwicklung zur Humanität* (Bern: Francke, 1972);

Heinrich Mohr, *Wilhelm Heinse: Das erotisch-religiöse Weltbild und seine naturphilosophischen Grundlagen* (Munich: Fink, 1971);

Eugene E. Reed, "The Transitional Significance of Heinse's *Ardinghello,*" *Modern Language Quarterly,* 16 (September 1955): 268-273;

Rita Terras, *Wilhelm Heinses Ästhetik* (Munich: Fink, 1972);

Rolf Wiecker, *Wilhelm Heinses Beschreibung römischer Kunstschätze: Palazzo Borghese—Villa Borghese* (Copenhagen: Text & Kontext, 1977).

Papers:

Wilhelm Heinse's papers are in the archives of the Stadt- und Universitätsbibliothek, Frankfurt am Main.

Ludwig Christoph Heinrich Hölty

(21 December 1748 - 1 September 1776)

Bettina Kluth Cothran
Georgia State University

BOOKS: *Auf den Tod Seiner Excellenz des Herrn Premierministers Gerlach Adolph Freiherrn von Münchhausen* (Göttingen, 1770);

Sämtlich hinterlassene Gedichte, nebst einiger Nachricht aus des Dichters Leben, 2 volumes, edited by Adam Friedrich Geisler (Halle: Hendel, 1782-1783);

Gedichte: Besorgt durch seine Freunde Friedrich Leopold, Grafen zu Stolberg und Johann Heinrich Voß (Hamburg: Bohn, 1783);

Gedichte von Ludewig Heinrich Christoph Hölty: Neu besorgt und vermehrt, edited by Johann Heinrich Voß (Hamburg: Bohn, 1804);

Gedichte: Erste vollständige Ausgabe mit erweiterten biographischen Nachrichten literarisch-kritisch eingeleitet, edited by Friedrich Voigts (Hannover: Meyer, 1857);

Gedichte von Ludewig Heinrich Christoph Hölty: Nebst Briefen des Dichters, edited by Karl Halm (Leipzig: Brockhaus, 1869);

Ludwig Christoph Heinrich Hölty's sämtliche Werke: Kritisch und chronologisch herausgegeben, 2 volumes, edited by Wilhelm Michael (Weimar: Gesellschaft der Bibliophilen, 1914-1918; reprinted, Hildesheim: Olms, 1969);

Werke und Briefe, edited by Uwe Berger (Berlin & Weimar: Aufbau, 1966).

OTHER: Richard Hurd, *Moralische und politische Dialoge: Aus dem Englischen,* 2 volumes, translated by Hölty (Leipzig: Weygand, 1775);

Der Kenner, eine Wochenschrift, von Town dem Sittenrichter: Aus dem Englischen, translated by Hölty (Leipzig: Weygand, 1775);

Der Abentheurer: Ein Auszug aus dem Englischen, 2 volumes, translated anonymously by Hölty (Berlin: Himburg, 1776);

Anthony Ashley Cooper, Lord Shaftesbury, *Philosophische Werke: Aus dem Englischen,* 3 volumes, translated anonymously by Hölty (Leipzig: Weygand, 1776-1779).

Joyful praise of the beauties of spring mixed with a melancholy presentiment of an early death is the predominant mood of the poetry of Ludwig Christoph Heinrich Hölty. In spite of a short life and a relatively slim output, he is represented in most collections of German poetry. Indeed, some of his poems set to music by Johann Friedrich Reichardt and Wolfgang Amadeus Mozart have become familiar as folk songs; most notable among them is the first stanza of "Der alte Landmann an seinen Sohn" (The Old Farmer to His Son), beginning with the words "Üb' immer Treu und Redlichkeit" (Be steadfast in faithfulness and honesty).

Born into times of political and social changes, Hölty was instrumental in paving the way for a poetry that reflected a new spirit. Along with nationalistic enthusiasm, characterized by heralding the tradition of bards and minnesingers, Hölty's poetry evidences a preference for an uncomplicated rural life. Hölty's poems are credited with expressing a new personal, intimate tone and possessing an innate quality of sound and rhythm which proved to be an inspiration not only to his contemporaries, including Johann Wolfgang Goethe, but to generations of lyric poets to come, among them Friedrich Hölderlin, Eduard Mörike, and Annette von Droste-Hülshoff.

Hölty was born on 21 December 1748, the first child of the Protestant pastor Philipp Ernst and Elisabeth Juliane Goessel Hölty. Of Hölty's five brothers and sisters only two sisters survived the first childhood years, and in 1757 their mother died of tuberculosis. In February 1758 Hölty's father married Maria Dorothea Niemann, who raised the children from her husband's first marriage along with their own four sons and four daughters. Hölty enjoyed a happy childhood in the village of Mariensee, near Hannover, where his father had been called in 1742 as the pastor of the village and of a former convent which, since the Reformation, housed unmarried daughters of mostly Protestant noble families. The old church of the convent; the new buildings in the baroque style; the adjacent pastor's house, a roomy two-story building surrounded by a sizable garden; and the lovely valley of the Leine River provided the boy with the first impressions of the peaceful pastoral setting that is reflected in many of his poems.

According to his stepmother, Hölty was an obedient and good-natured child who was well liked by all around him. He was also said to have been of an angelic beauty until the age of nine, when he contracted smallpox. The disease not only left indelible marks on the child's face but also severely impaired his vision; for two years he was practically blind. After regaining his eyesight Hölty was able to return to his favorite pastime, reading. He seemed to want to make up the time he had lost during his illness. It was not uncommon for him to stay up until two or three o'clock in the morning reading, against his parents' wishes. When they sought to assure that he had no candles to read by, he fashioned crude lanterns out of hollowed beets. He also tied a stone around his arm so that he would wake up early in the morning when turning over in bed, all in an effort to maximize studying time. In spite of his avid reading habits, he enjoyed the outdoors; he could often be found walking in the woods, where he sometimes read aloud to himself. He also developed early on a fancy for churchyards and would roam among the graves, occasionally costumed as a ghost.

He first showed signs of interest in poetry as a child, versifying the alphabet and writing poems on the church walls (paper was a scarce commodity). His earliest poem, dating approximately from his eleventh year, is a four-line inscription on the death of his favorite dog. The profession of a poet was, however, not what his father had in mind for Hölty: as the eldest son, he was destined to follow in his father's footsteps and become a pastor. According to the customs of the time, he was taught by his father at home until he turned sixteen, when he was sent to the public school in nearby Celle. There Hölty stayed with his mother's brother, an attorney. The reputation of the "Lateinschule in der Kalandgasse" (Prep School in Kaland Street) reached beyond the borders of the small city. J. H. Steffens, the director of the school, had a keen interest in classical and contemporary literature; thus, Gotthold Ephraim Lessing's dramas were read and performed, sometimes in a Latin version translated by the students, and Henry Fielding's *Tom Jones* (1749) was dramatized and performed. Inasmuch as the elector of Hannover was, as George II, also the king of England, the English language was one of the subjects taught. In spite of his exposure to city life, Hölty never adopted the refined manners of a young man of society; in fact, his disregard for outward appearance went so far that on occasion he was mistaken for a servant or worse.

Before enrolling at the University of Göttingen as a student of theology Hölty, whose health was always fragile, rested up for six months with his family in Mariensee. There, in May 1768, he met the one girl he would ever love, though only from afar. Anna Juliane Hagemann was the younger sister of the wife of one of his neighbors. The picture of the beautiful young woman as he first saw her would forever be with him: "Es war ein schöner Maiabend, die Nachtigallen begannen zu schlagen und die Abenddämmerung anzubrechen. Sie ging durch einen Gang blühender Apfelbäume und war in die Farbe der Unschuld gekleidet. Rote Bänder spielten an ihrem schönen Busen . . ." (It was an enchanting evening in the month of May: nightingales were beginning to sing and the dusk was falling. She was walking among blooming apple trees; she was dressed in the color of innocence. Red ribbons adorned her beautiful bosom).

Hölty was in no position to think of marrying at the time, and he never confided his feelings to his beloved. At Easter 1769 he went to Göttingen. An obedient son, Hölty attended all the lectures prescribed for the study of theology, although he never wholeheartedly pursued the profession chosen for him. He expanded his knowledge of foreign languages by adding Spanish and Italian, and translated from the Italian of Torquato Tasso and Ludovico Ariost. At the end of the three years of study allotted to him and funded by his father, he wished to stay in Göttingen and study subjects of his own choosing. By this time he was convinced, as he later confessed to his father, that he would never be a successful pastor; if for no other reason, his frequent coughing would never have allowed him to preach. He obtained a small stipend, which, together with income from tutoring, provided him with a meager subsistence. In 1774 he contracted with the Leipzig publisher Weygand for translations from the English; he translated portions of the *Connoisseur* as *Der Kenner* (1775), Richard Hurd's *Dialogues* (1775), and the first part of Shaftesbury's *Works* (1776-1779).

His attraction to Göttingen was to be found not only in the seemingly unlimited access to knowledge but also in the close association with his friends. The proverbial cult of friendship in this so-called age of sentimentality played an overwhelming role in Hölty's life. In 1771 he had met Gottfried August Bürger and Johann Martin Miller; later he had added to his circle of friends Johann Heinrich Voß, Heinrich Christian Boie, Johann Friedrich Hahn, Johann Anton Leisewitz, Karl Friedrich Cramer, and the brothers Christian and Friedrich Leopold von Stolberg. The circle of friends was formalized and received its true mission as the "Göttinger Hain" (Göttingen Grove), also known as the "Göttinger Hainbund" (Göttingen Grove League), on 12 September 1772. This important event for German literature occurred on a pleasant evening when Hölty, Voß, Hahn, Miller and his cousin Gottlob Dietrich Miller, and Johann Thomas Ludwig Wehrs were taking a walk and having a heated discussion. Suddenly they happened upon a particularly beautiful oak tree and, moved by patriotic enthusiasm, decided to form a dignified association dedicated to the fatherland. The group's name was taken from Friedrich Gottlob Klopstock's ode "Der Hügel und der Hain" (Hill and Grove, 1767). From then on the group met every Saturday to discuss topics from the arts and sciences, to read to each other, and to evaluate critically their literary productions. Those that met with general approval were formally entered into the Bundesbuch (official book of the association). Later, members who were not active contributors were also admitted, among them Cramer, Leisewitz, Christian Hieronymus Esmarch, Carl Christian Clausewitz, Karl August Wilhelm von Closen, Christian Adolf Overbeck, and Anton Matthias Sprickmann. Even Klopstock asked to be included after he read a volume of poems sent to him by the Stolbergs. Bürger, although never a formal member, was in frequent contact with the "Bund." The journal *Der Göttinger Musenalmanach* became the primary outlet for their publications.

Central to the Hainbund was an adoration of Klopstock, the most influential German poet of his time. A forerunner of the Sturm und Drang movement, he, along with others such as Lessing, vigorously proclaimed sentiments that had just begun to surface: a rejection of the restrictions of the French neoclassicists, a return to nature, and a turn toward passion and lyricism and away from convention and didacticism. The mood had swung against the perceived frivolity of Christoph Martin Wieland; it is alleged that members of the Hainbund even burned books of this author, whom they branded a perverter of youth and public morals. Klopstock's poetry, on the other hand, was rooted in the religious fervor of Pietism and in nationalism. His religious epic *Der Messias* (The Messiah, 1748) was regarded as the epitome of exalted theme and style. To express the religious visions and the lofty themes of friendship and nature adequately, different forms of poetic expression had to be found. One of these forms was the classical ode, which Klopstock was largely responsible for introducing to German poetry. Whereas up to his time an ode was more or less synonymous with Lied (song), afterward the genre could be characterized as a spoken verse that expressed the inner turmoil of the speaker. Thus it was to be distinguished from the song, which suggested a setting to music. Klopstock used all three classical forms of the ode: the alcaic, asclepiadic, and sapphic. In keeping with the classical models the tone imitated that of Horace, and the invocation of Greek gods and goddesses further enhanced the elevated style. One of Klopstock's major innovations was the creation of a free rhythm charac-

Manuscript of a poem by Hölty (Gustav Könnecke, Bilderatlas zur Geschichte der deutschen Nationallitteratur *[Graz: Akademische Druck- und Verlagsanstalt, 1981])*

terized by a lack of rhyme and by verses of uneven length. The Anacreontic poets, especially those of the Hain, later reintroduced rhyme into their poems, reserving Klopstock's model of the free rhythm for odes written in the classical manner only. Of the twenty-five poems Hölty wrote in 1772, eighteen were unrhymed; in 1773, however, only four of twenty-six poems were not rhymed. In his later poems Hölty shows a decided preference for rhyme.

In his youth Hölty wrote odes in the manner of Horace glorifying joy, imagination, and inner peace; but in his later years the elegiac ode seemed better suited to express his melancholy sentiments. In "Das Traumbild" (The Dream Vision), for example, he pays tribute once more to his distant beloved after the model of Petrarch:

Im jungen Nachtigallenhain,
Und auf der öden Wildniß,
Wo Tannenbäume Dämmrung streun,
Umflattert mich das Bildniß.

Es tanzt aus jedem Busch hervor,
Wo Maienlämmlein grasen,
Und wallt, verhüllt im leichten Flor,
Auf jedem grünen Rasen.

Wann mich, mit meinem Gram vertraut
Zur Stunde der Gespenster,
Der liebe helleo Mond beschaut,
Bebt's durch mein Kammerfenster,
Und malt sich an die weiße Wand,
Und schwebt vor meinen Blicken,
Und winkt mir mit der kleinen Hand,
Und lächelt mir Entzücken.

Mein guter Engel, sage mir,
Wo Luna sie beflimmert,
Und wo, von ihr berührt, von ihr!
Die Blume röther schimmert.
Erschaff' ihr Bild aus Morgenlicht,
Ihr Kleid aus Ätherbläue,
Und zeig in jedem Nachtgesicht
Mir meine Vielgetreue.

75

Wo pflückt sie, wann der Lenz beginnt,
Die ersten Maienglocken?
Wo spielst du, lauer Abendwind,
Mit ihren blonden Locken?
O eilt, o flattert weg von ihr,
Geliebte Maienwinde,
Und sagt es mir, und sagt es mir,
Wo ich das Mädchen finde!

(In the young groves of the nightingales,
And in the dreary wasteland,
Where fir trees spread twilight,
Her image surrounds me.
It dances forth from every bush,
Where the lambs of May graze,
And flows, veiled in blooms,
Over each flowering meadow.

When, well acquainted with my sorrow,
At the hour of ghosts,
The beloved bright moon beholds me,
Her image trembles through my bedroom window,
And paints itself upon the white wall,
And is suspended before my eyes,
And waves at me with its little hand,
And smiles enchantment at me.

My good angel, tell me,
Where Luna shines on her,
And where, touched by her, by her!
The flower glows a deeper red.
Fashion her likeness from morning light,
Her dress from the blue ether,
And show me in every dream
My true beloved.

Where does she pluck, when spring begins,
The first lilies of the valley?
Where do you play, warm evening wind,
With her blonde locks?
Oh hurry, oh rush away from her,
Dear winds of May,
And tell me, and tell me,
Where I can find the girl!)

Here all of the main ingredients of Hölty's poems of unrequited love are united: the lovely month of May, the moon, trees, soft winds, nightingales, and his own loneliness. He was one of the first German poets to combine the themes of lingering melancholy and tender love with a sentimental feeling toward nature.

The first poem by Hölty to carry the subtitle "eine Ballade"–actually the first German poem to do so–is "Töffel und Käthe" (1772). This poem is reminiscent of the Greek myth of Philemon and Baucis. It represents the humorous version of the ballad genre, much in the style of Johann Wilhelm Ludwig Gleim and his imitators. In Hölty's ballad "Adelstan und Röschen" (1771) a country maiden, seduced and abandoned by a knight, dies of a broken heart; her remorseful lover kills himself beside her grave. The title character of "Die Nonne" (The Nun, 1773) is also seduced by an unfaithful knight; but whereas Röschen's despair over her lost love is the focus of the first ballad, the emphasis in the second is the nun's hate and revenge. By describing the knight's bragging about his success with the nun, Hölty provides a psychologically accurate explanation of the unusually cruel deeds of the woman: the betrayed nun is not satisfied with the murder of her former lover but exhumes him, tears out his heart, and tramples it. She repeats this gruesome ordeal nightly at midnight. Hölty's nun is thus a variation on the theme of the "rasende Weib" (furious woman) represented by the title character in Johann Elias Schlegel's *Dido* (1744), Marwood in Lessing's *Miß Sara Sampson* (1755), Isabella in Friedrich Maximilian Klinger's *Simsone Grisaldo* (1776), and Adelheid in Goethe's *Götz von Berlichingen mit der eisernen Hand* (Götz von Berlichingen with he Iron Hand, 1773). The insatiable thirst for revenge and the outburst of boundless emotion are themes later taken up by the Sturm und Drang.

The ballad, however, was not Hölty's preferred genre of poetry. In an April 1774 letter to Voß he writes: "Ich soll mehr Balladen machen? Vielleicht mache ich einige, es werden aber sehr wenige sein. Mir kommt ein Balladensänger wie ein Harlekin, oder wie ein Mensch mit einem Raritätenkasten vor. Den größten Hang habe ich zur ländlichen Poesie, und zu süßen melancholischen Schwärmereien in Gedichten" (I am supposed to write more ballads? Maybe I'll write some, but certainly not many. To me, a singer of ballads is like a harlequin or a man with a box full of rarities. I feel most inclined toward poems extolling rural situations and sweet, melancholic sentiments). "Ländliche Poesie" (pastoral poetry) is indeed best suited to Hölty's temperament. In his Lieder (songs) his personal tone, his praise of spring and of Laura as the ever-distant beloved, and a pervasive melancholy find their most touching expression. Of Hölty's 140 poems, 12 mention May in their titles. As one example, "Maylied" (May Song, 1773) expresses a simple and untainted joy of life. For Hölty, this joy is to be found in the country rather than in the city and is marked by a childlike trust in God, whose grace is reflected in glorious nature:

Engraving by Daniel Chodowiecki (1777), based on Hölty's death mask

Der Anger steht so grün, so grün,
Die blauen Veilchenglocken blühn,
Und Schlüßelblumen drunter,
Der Wiesengrund
Ist schon so bunt,
Und färbt sich täglich bunter.

Drum komme, wem der May gefällt,
Und freue sich der schönen Welt,
Und Gottes Vatergüte,
Die diese Pracht
Hervorgebracht,
Den Baum und seine Blüte.

(The meadow is so green, so green,
The blue violets are blooming,
The meadowland
Is already so sprinkled with colors,
And grows more colorful every day.

Come there, those who enjoy the month of May,
And rejoice in the beautiful world,
And in God's grace,
Which brings forth
This splendor,
The tree and its blossom.)

Rhythm and sound carry the sentiment succinctly expressed here. Frequently Hölty seems to transpose his inner vision into nature around him; in

the poem "An den Mond" (To the Moon, 1775) melancholic sentiments and the vision of his own death rise in the poet's soul upon visiting the arbor where he used to meet his beloved. Nature adorned in the splendor of spring reminds the poet painfully of his own youth, unfulfilled by love. Time and again in his poems Hölty invokes "Laura," the graceful phantom of his love. She will never be his in a happily fulfilled life on this earth, but she remains a poetic inspiration as expressed in the song "Sehnsucht nach Liebe" (Longing for Love):

... flattert mir das Phantom
Todter Freuden schon wieder
Vor den Augen der Phantasie?

Rosicht schwebt es herauf.–Laura, die Grazie,
Laura hüpft daher, die mir den ersten Rausch
Überirdischer Wonne
Durch die bebende Seele goß. . . .

(. . . flutters the phantom
Of dead joys once more
Before the eyes of inspiration?

In a rosy light it floats toward me.–Laura, the
  grace,
Laura skips along, who poured the first frenzy
Of heavenly joy
Through my trembling soul. . . .)

Ardently longing for someone to share his emotions, Hölty remained alone. After 1774, which was probably the high point in the Hainbund's existence and included a visit from Klopstock, the circle of friends thinned; with the exception of Voß and Boie, most moved to other universities. To see a little more of the world himself, Hölty in 1774 accompanied Johann Martin Miller to Leipzig, where the latter was planning to study. While in Leipzig, Hölty met with the publisher Weygand and contracted to translate Plato's *Republic* and the rest of Shaftesbury's works.

The last two years of Hölty's life were marked by friendship with a young girl, Charlotte von Einem, whom Hölty and Voß met in October 1774 in her hometown, Hannoversch Münden. A lively correspondence ensued, and Hölty's fourteen letters tell of a relationship that was certainly an inspiration to the poet though it never reached beyond feelings of brotherly affection. In February 1775 Hölty's father died, and his own health deteriorated. He felt responsible for the care of his younger siblings and stipulated that the greater part of his inheritance of 600 talers be used for their education. In April, Hölty went to Mariensee to recuperate. Although he was admired by the citizens of Mariensee, he lamented the provincial atmosphere and lack of friends there and made plans to relocate to Hamburg or to Wandsbek, where his idol Matthias Claudius lived a pastoral life. Though he had been told by two doctors that he had a severe case of tuberculosis, Hölty seems to have ignored the serious nature of his illness. In the summer he felt that he had almost entirely recovered and went to Hamburg for two weeks, where he spent "Göttertage" (heavenly days) with Voß and Klopstock. He subsequently experienced a relapse and returned to Mariensee; later he went to Hannover, where he entrusted his medical care to the famous Dr. Johann Georg Zimmermann. Zimmermann's diets and medicines were ineffective, however, and Hölty died on 1 September 1776. He was buried in an unmarked grave in the Nicolai cemetery in Hannover. In 1901 a bronze statue of a youth was erected there in his memory, with Nikolaus Lenau's poem engraved in its base:

Am Grabe Höltys
Hölty, dein Freund, der Frühling, ist gekommen!
Klagend irrt er im Hain, dich zu finden.
Doch umsonst! Sein klagender Ruf verhallt
In einsamen Schatten.

(At Hölty's Grave
Hölty, your friend, the spring, has arrived!
Lamenting, he searches for you in the grove.
In vain! His lamenting call fades away
In lonely shadows.)

Hölty stood on the threshold of a time that was to give new emphasis to the emotions. After starting out as a poet reflecting predominantly anacreontic, rococo sentiments, Hölty turned to "Empfindsamkeit" (sentimentality), embracing the theory advanced by Shaftesbury that feeling was dominant over reason. The inclusion of nature is probably Hölty's most important contribution to the development of German poetry. The interplay between moods in nature and the human mind, so often the central idea in Hölty's Lieder, point the way to Goethe's "Elebnislyrik" (poetry of experience) and further to Friedrich Hölderlin and Eduard Mörike. In 1836, sixty years after Hölty's death, Mörike dedicated the poem "An eine Lieblingsbuche meines Gartens in deren Stamm ich Höltys Namen schnitt" (To the Favorite Beech Tree in My Garden, in Whose Trunk I Cut Hölty's Name) to his favorite poet, who sang the praises of nature.

References:
Ernst Albert, *Das Naturgefühl Höltys* (Dortmund: Ruhfus, 1910);
Dietmar Goltschnigg, "Die Entwicklung der deutschen Kunstballade von Gleim bis Hölty," *Jahrbuch des Wiener Goethe Vereins*, 77 (1973): 43-64;
Paul Merker, "Höltys Elegie auf ein Landmädchen," *Zeitschrift für Deutschkunde*, 40 (1926): 260-274;
Ernst Müller, *Ludwig Christoph Heinrich Hölty: Leben und Werk* (Hannover: Schlüter, 1986);
Thymiane Oberlin-Kaiser, "Ludwig Christoph Heinrich Hölty," Ph.D. dissertation, University of Zurich, 1964;
Hans-Jürgen Schrader, "Mit Feuer, Schwert und schlechtem Gewissen: Zum Kreuzzug der Hainbündler gegen Wieland," *Euphorion*, 78 (1984): 325-367;
Theodor Simon, "Stil und Sprache der Poesie Höltys," Ph.D. dissertation, University of Münster, 1923;
Ludwig Völker, *Muse Melancholie–Therapeutikum Poesie: Studien zum Melancholie-Problem in der deutschen Lyrik von Hölty bis Benn* (Munich: Fink, 1978).

Papers:
Most of Ludwig Christoph Heinrich Hölty's papers are at the Staatsbibliothek in Munich.

August Wilhelm Iffland

(19 April 1759 - 22 September 1814)

Gerda Jordan
University of South Carolina

BOOKS: *Albert von Thurneisen: Ein bürgerliches Trauerspiel in vier Aufzügen* (Mannheim: Schwan, 1781);

Verbrechen aus Ehrsucht: Ein ernsthaftes Familienge-mählde in fünf Aufzügen (Mannheim: Schwan, 1784); translated by Maria Geisweiler as *Crime from Ambition: A Play in Five Acts* (London: Printed by G. Sidney, 1800);

Die Jäger: Ein ländliches Sittengemälde in fünf Aufzügen (Berlin: Decker, 1785); translated by Bell Plumptre as *The Foresters: A Picture of Rural Manners. A Play in Five Acts* (London: Vernor & Hood, 1799); German version reprinted, edited by Jürg Mathes (Stuttgart: Reclam, 1976);

Liebe um Liebe: Ein ländliches Schauspiel in einem Aufzuge (Mannheim: Neue Hof- und akademische Buchhandlung, 1785);

Fragmente über Menschendarstellung auf den deutschen Bühnen (Gotha: Ettinger, 1785);

Die Mündel: Ein Schauspiel in fünf Aufzügen (Berlin: Decker, 1785); translated by Hannibal Evans Lloyd as *The Nephews: A Play, in Five Acts* (London: Printed by W. and C. Spilsbury, 1799);

Bewußtseyn!: Ein Schauspiel in fünf Aufzügen (Berlin: Rottmann, 1787);

Der Magnetismus: Nachspiel in einem Aufzug (Mannheim: Schwan & Götz, 1787);

Reue versöhnt: Ein Schauspiel in fünf Aufzügen (Berlin: Rottmann, 1789);

Liussan, Fürst von Garisene: Prolog in einem Aufzuge, mit Chören (Mannheim: Neue Hof- und akademische Buchhandlung, 1790);

Figaro in Deutschland: Ein Lustspiel in fünf Aufzügen (Berlin: Rottmann, 1790);

Friedrich von Oesterreich: Ein Schauspiel aus der vaterländischen Geschichte in fünf Aufzügen (Gotha: Ettinger, 1791);

Die Kokarden: Ein Trauerspiel in fünf Aufzügen (Leipzig: Göschen, 1792);

Frauenstand: Ein Lustspiel in fünf Aufzügen (Leipzig: Göschen, 1792);

Engraving by Johann Friedrich Bolt, 1798

Herbsttag: Lustspiel in fünf Aufzügen (Leipzig: Göschen, 1792);

Elise von Valberg: Ein Schauspiel in fünf Aufzügen (Leipzig: Göschen, 1792);

Der Fremdling: Lustspiel in vier Aufzügen (Leipzig: Göschen, 1792);

Der Eichenkranz: Ein Dialog zur Eröffnung der Frankfurter National-Schaubühne bei der Krönungsfeier Kaisers Franz des Zweyten, Frankfurt am

Main, den 14. Juli 1792 (Frankfurt am Main: Brönner, 1792);

Blick in die Schweiz: Eine Reisebeschreibung (Leipzig: Göschen, 1793);

Die Hagestolzen: Ein Lustspiel in fünf Aufzügen (Leipzig: Göschen, 1793); translated anonymously as *The Bachelors: A Comedy in Five Acts* (London: Printed by J. W. Myers, 1799);

Die Verbrüderung: Ein Schauspiel in einem Aufzuge (Mannheim: Schwan, 1793);

Allzu scharf macht schartig: Ein Schauspiel in fünf Aufzügen (Leipzig: Göschen, 1794);

Scheinverdienst: Ein Schauspiel in fünf Aufzügen (Leipzig: Göschen, 1795);

Dienstpflicht: Ein Schauspiel in fünf Aufzügen (Leipzig: Göschen, 1795);

Die Reise nach der Stadt: Ein Lustspiel in fünf Aufzügen (Leipzig: Göschen, 1795);

Alte Zeit und neue Zeit: Ein Schauspiel in fünf Aufzügen (Leipzig: Göschen, 1795);

Die Aussteuer: Ein Schauspiel in fünf Aufzügen (Leipzig: Göschen, 1795);

Der Vormund: Ein Schauspiel in fünf Aufzügen (Leipzig: Göschen, 1795);

Die Advokaten: Ein Schauspiel in fünf Aufzügen (Leipzig: Göschen, 1796); translated by Conrad Lüdger as *The Lawyers: A Drama, in Five Acts* (London: Printed by J. W. Myers, 1799);

Das Vermächtniß: Ein Schauspiel in fünf Aufzügen (Leipzig: Göschen, 1796);

Antwort des Direktor Iffland auf das Schreiben an ihn über das Schauspiel Der Jude und dessen Vorstellung auf dem hiesigen Theater (Berlin: Unger, 1798);

Der Spieler: Ein Schauspiel in fünf Aufzügen (Leipzig: Göschen, 1798);

Der Veteran: Schauspiel in einem Aufzuge (Berlin: Unger, 1798);

A. W. Ifflands dramatische Werke, 17 volumes (Leipzig: Göschen, 1798-1802)—includes as volume 1, *Meine theatralische Laufbahn* (1798);

Die Geflüchteten: Ein Schauspiel in einem Aufzuge (Leipzig: Göschen, 1799);

Das Gewissen: Ein bürgerliches Trauerspiel in fünf Aufzügen (Leipzig: Göschen, 1799); translated by Benjamin Thompson as *Conscience: A Tragedy in Five Acts* (London: Vernor & Hood, 1800);

Achmet und Zenide: Ein Schauspiel in fünf Aufzügen (Leipzig: Göschen, 1799);

Erinnerung: Ein Schauspiel in fünf Aufzügen (Leipzig: Göschen, 1799);

Hausfrieden: Ein Lustspiel in fünf Aufzügen (Leipzig: Göschen, 1799);

Der Komet: Eine Posse in einem Aufzuge (Leipzig: Göschen, 1799);

Leichter Sinn: Ein Lustspiel in fünf Aufzügen (Leipzig: Göschen, 1799);

Der Fremde: Ein Lustspiel in fünf Aufzügen (Leipzig: Göschen, 1800);

Der Mann von Wort: Ein Schauspiel in fünf Aufzügen (Leipzig: Göschen, 1800);

Selbstbeherrschung: Ein Schauspiel in fünf Aufzügen (Leipzig: Göschen, 1800);

Vaterfreude: Ein Vorspiel in einem Aufzuge (Leipzig: Göschen, 1800);

Die Höhen: Ein Schauspiel in fünf Aufzügen (Leipzig: Göschen, 1801);

Die Künstler: Ein Schauspiel in fünf Aufzügen (Leipzig: Göschen, 1801);

Das Erbtheil des Vaters: Ein Schauspiel in vier Aufzügen (Leipzig: Göschen, 1802);

Das Vaterhaus: Ein Schauspiel in fünf Aufzügen (Leipzig: Göschen, 1802);

Die Familie Lonau: Ein Lustspiel in fünf Aufzügen (Leipzig: Göschen, 1802);

Die Hausfreunde: Schauspiel in fünf Aufzügen (Berlin: Oehmigke, 1805);

Wohin? Ein Schauspiel in fünf Aufzügen (Leipzig: Göschen, 1806);

Die Marionetten: Lustspiel in einem Aufzuge (Berlin: Oehmigke, 1807);

Der Oheim: Lustspiel in fünf Aufzügen (Berlin: Oehmigke, 1808);

Die Brautwahl: Lustspiel in einem Aufzuge (Berlin, 1808);

Die Einung: Ein Schauspiel in einem Aufzuge (Berlin: Braun, 1811);

Liebe und Wille: Ein ländliches Gespräch in einer Handlung (Berlin: Nicolai, 1814);

Theater, 24 volumes (Vienna: Pichler, 1814-1819);

Theorie der Schauspielkunst für ausübende Künstler und Kunstfreunde, 2 volumes, edited by C. G. Flittner (Berlin: Neue Societäts-Verlags-Buchhandlung, 1815);

Theater von August Wilhelm Iffland: 1. vollständige Ausgabe, 24 volumes (Vienna: Klang, 1843).

OTHER: *Almanach fürs Theater*, 5 volumes, edited by Iffland (volumes 1-2, Berlin: Oehmigke, 1806-1807; volume 3, Berlin: Braun, 1808; volume 4, Berlin: Salfeld, 1810; volume 5, Berlin: Duncker & Humblot, 1811);

Beiträge für die deutsche Schaubühne: In Uebersetzungen und Bearbeitungen ausländischer Schauspieldichter, 4 volumes, translated, adapted, and edited by Iffland (Berlin: Braun, 1807-1812).

Enormously popular as an actor and playwright in his own time, August Wilhelm Iffland is remembered today for his contribution to the development of the German theater. His full-length plays, one-acts, and dialogues proved to be ephemeral, but they trained German audiences to expect good acting and quality productions. Iffland's melodramas, along with those of August von Kotzebue, Johann Jakob Engel, Friedrich Ludwig Schröder, and Otto Heinrich Reichsfreiherr von Gemmingen-Hornberg, flooded the German stage for years; they outnumbered by far performances of plays by Shakespeare, Gotthold Ephraim Lessing, Johann Wolfgang Goethe, and Friedrich Schiller because the audiences demanded light fare. Iffland was among the first to appreciate the merits of Sturm und Drang plays, and his theater welcomed Schiller and Goethe; still, the happy-ending bourgeois play dominated the German stage until serious drama was compared with it and recognized as superior to such trivia. Among the services Iffland rendered the German drama with his large output of inferior plays was to provide this contrast.

Iffland was born on 19 April 1759 to the well-to-do registrar of the Royal War Office of Hannover, Christian Rudolf Iffland, and Elisabeth Friederike Karoline Iffland, née Schröder; he was the youngest of four children. He received his early education from private tutors, attended the city Lyceum for several years, and then was put in tutelage to a pastor Richter in the village of Springe to be prepared for the ministry. Iffland agreed with his father's plans for his future, but for the wrong reasons: he enjoyed the histrionics of preaching. From the time of his first visit to the theater at age four he had been fascinated by the stage and had attended as many of the occasional performances in Hannover as he could. In 1775 he returned to the Hannover Lyceum; there he took advantage of every opportunity to read or act before audiences, earning applause especially for his imitations of important local people. He acted in school plays, including Goethe's *Clavigo* (1774). When Konrad Ernst Ackermann's troupe, then at the height of its fame, came to Hannover, the eighteen-year-old Iffland concluded that he must follow an acting career in spite of the objections of his family. He left home secretly on 22 February 1777; on 15 March he was onstage in the court theater of Gotha, under the direction of Konrad Ekhof, playing the Jew Israel in Johann Jakob Engel's *Der Diamant* (The Diamond, 1772). Ekhof was known as a philosophical actor who encouraged a natural delivery, warm expression, and personal dignity—earning him the epithet "the German Garrick"—while at the same time paying attention to the most minute detail of speech and gesture. Ekhof recognized Iffland's talent and became his teacher. Iffland began in roles of servants and Jews, soon proceeding to young lovers, dandies, and comical old men. Apparently he did not fascinate by his looks: he was thickset, in later years even obese; his thighs seemed too slender, his feet too small and delicate for his bulk. His face was round, his nose slender; his voice did not project well but was well modulated. The soul of his acting lay in his talent for mimicry; his expression, projected mainly with his eyes, was always true and psychologically motivated. In spite of his rapidly growing fame his family continued to treat him as an outcast until Iffland forced a reconciliation by visiting his parents in 1779. His father's admonition on this occasion, that he should always keep a pure and pious soul, was unnecessary; it was in Iffland's nature to lead an orderly life, and his ambition was to raise the class of actors to a position of respectability.

Ekhof died on 16 June 1778, and the Gotha court theater was dissolved at Easter 1779. In September Iffland was called to Mannheim, where the elector Karl Theodor had founded a theater the year before and had named Wolfgang Heribert Baron von Dalberg its director. Dalberg's goal was to create a model theater, and Iffland, the student of the great Ekhof, was a welcome addition, especially since he contributed the aura of his good upbringing. Iffland's first appearance at the opening of the new theater brought him a three-minute round of applause, even from rivals, for his role. In December 1779 Goethe and Karl August of Weimar, stopping in Mannheim on their way from Switzerland, attended performances of *Clavigo* and of Friedrich Wilhelm Gotter's *Der Ehescheue* (He Who Fears Marriage, 1778); Goethe praised the young actor and advised him never to play mediocre roles but "immer das Äußerste, das Niedrigstkomische und das Höchsttragische" (always the extreme, the lowest comedy or the highest tragedy).

When he was still in Gotha, Iffland had tried his hand at short essays on the theater, consisting mostly of rules and principles of acting, which he had contributed to journals. Essays

Four engravings by Daniel Chodowiecki to illustrate scenes from Iffland's play Die Jäger *in the* Berliner genealogische Kalender, *1787*

were also encouraged by Dalberg's custom of posing questions; the best answer received a prize. Iffland's first essays were published in 1785 as *Fragmente über Menschendarstellung auf den deutschen Bühnen* (Fragments on the Portrayal of Character on the German Stage). In them he began the sermonizing which he continued in his dramatic writings.

In 1781 he started his successful career as a playwright with *Albert von Thurneisen,* which was performed at Mannheim the same year. Iffland's five-act tragedy, although about war, reveals his inclination to turn away from the show of strength and power favored by the public and toward the portrayal of human destinies, sorrows, and suffering. The hero is a fine officer who, in a moment of confusion, neglects his duty; he is encouraged in his erroneous ways by an envious rival, and his commanding officer sentences him to death. Two other plays, *Wilhelm von Schenck* and *Wie man's treibt so geht's* (You Reap What You Sow), were performed the same year but were not printed.

Iffland continued to gather laurels as an actor. As Franz Moor in the 13 January 1782 premiere of Schiller's *Die Räuber* (The Robbers) he received praise from the author, and Schiller and Iffland became friends. Schiller suggested the title for Iffland's next play, *Verbrechen aus Ehrsucht* (1784; translated as *Crime from Ambition,* 1800), which was so successful at its premiere in March 1784 that it threatened to overshadow Schiller's *Kabale und Liebe* (Intrigue and Love)–for which Iffland had suggested the title–the following month. *Verbrechen aus Ehrsucht* was praised for its high moral content, and Dalberg said that with such plays the stage could become a "wahre Schule der Sitten" (true school for morals). Eduard Ruhberg, a young man with good basic qualities but ambitious and passionate, loves a rich noblewoman and has hopes for her hand in marriage. His mother is flattered by the prospect, but his father, a strict and proud man, advises against the match. The association with the noble family leads Eduard to incur debts, which he pays by stealing funds entrusted to his father. A relative saves the family from ruin; Eduard has to leave home. Critics and Emperor Joseph II found fault with Eduard's light punishment, and Iffland continued the plot in *Bewußtseyn!* (Awareness!, 1787), in which Eduard is haunted by the memory of his crime. His punishment is that he finds no joy in life and has to give up the girl who truly loves him. In 1789 Iffland completed the trilogy with *Reue versöhnt* (Repentance

Reconciles). After exaggerated self-accusations, new complications, and misunderstandings Eduard, who met so much misfortune in the company of nobility, finds new meaning in life and inner peace in the bosom of a good, hardworking bourgeois family.

Iffland wrote such moralistic plays by inclination, especially after he heard Schiller's address, "Die Schaubühne als eine moralische Anstalt betrachtet" (The Stage Regarded as a Moral Institution), in Mannheim in June 1784. Schiller's verdict, "Die Gerichtsbarkeit der Bühne fängt an, wo das Gebiet der weltlichen Gesetze sich endigt" (The legislative powers of the stage begin where the realm of secular laws leaves off), became Iffland's guiding light, and he became in his plays the advocate and avenger of the duped and the oppressed. Schiller's opinion that the stage could show steps to be taken toward a proper moral education generated several of Iffland's plays in which innately good but frivolous young men, spoiled by their mothers and intimidated by overbearing fathers, stray from the virtuous path but are purged by fate and return to righteous ways, or daydreaming, useless, overly sentimental girls are turned to worthwhile lives by learning to do household chores. Schiller hoped that the stage could effect religious tolerance; the pastor in Iffland's *Die Jäger* (1785; translated as *The Foresters,* 1799) speaks conciliatory words to smooth over the contrast between Protestants and Catholics, and the Jewish trader in *Dienstpflicht* (Duty to Service, 1795) is a devout and righteous man. *Kabale und Liebe,* which replaced Lessing's *Emilia Galotti* (1772) as a model for Iffland and for others, furnished Iffland with several motifs that recur again and again in his plays in more or less altered forms: the royal official who rose to his station by not altogether legal means with the help of an underling who now exploits him; a romantically involved, virtuous son who renounces the privileges of nobility in favor of happiness with a simple girl; the outwardly coarse but innately good-hearted bourgeois father. Although Iffland tends to reuse the same themes, he infuses new life into them by showing the poetry of country life, the joys of nature and a harmonious home life, rejuvenation through manual labor, and a restored trust in God. As an actor he knew what was effective onstage, and he had an uncanny ability to give the audience just as much sentimentality as it demanded.

Die Jäger contains what came to be Iffland's stock characters: the mother, a garrulous busy-

Iffland in 1785, the year of publication of Die Jäger; *engraving by A. Karcher of a drawing by M. Kloß (Gustav Könnecke,* Bilderatlas zur Geschichte der deutschen Nationalliteratur *[Graz: Akademische Druck- und Verlagsanstalt, 1981])*

body but basically a good person who is overly concerned with the welfare of her son; her husband, a solid man with good sense; and the evil official serving a good prince. The forester's son Anton and niece Friederike are in love and plan to marry, thereby upsetting the mother's plan for their marriages to the offspring of the official. She objects on the grounds that the lovers are of different religions, and Anton storms out of the house in pursuit of a hunter who had oppressed an old man. The village pastor, Iffland's mouthpiece for religious tolerance, reconciles the mother to the marriage of Anton and Friederike, but in the midst of the family's joyous anticipation of the wedding comes the news that Anton has murdered the hunter. The evil official, delighted to be able to denounce the good forester, is about to send off the report of the murder when the true attacker confesses and the hunter's wounds turn out not to be fatal. Iffland continued the story of Anton and Friederike in *Das*

Vaterhaus (Ancestral Home, 1802). The couple is living in the city; temptation almost leads Anton to be unfaithful to Friederike, but a visit home effects a cure.

The return of a husband about to stray is also the topic of *Frauenstand* (Women's Lot, 1792). A court councillor finds that his domestic bliss is not enough to satisfy him; he longs for more prestige and better connections to the nobility. In pursuit of these ambitions he spends too much money. Furthermore, misled by false friends, he begins to doubt his wife's fidelity. But in the end he realizes that she is the best thing that ever happened to him. In *Herbsttag* (Autumn Day, 1792) the daughter of a bourgeois gentleman-farmer is courted insincerely by a young nobleman; a friend of the girl's family, a philistine but emotional old bachelor, talks sense to the boy before he can do any real damage.

Iffland also wrote one of the many emulations of *Emilia Galotti*. The plot of *Elise von Valberg* (1792) concerns a seduction at court, but unlike Lessing's tragedy it has a happy ending: the prince overcomes his infatuation and returns to his wife. Iffland uses this opportunity to advocate solid bourgeois morals for the marriages of princes so that they can serve as models for their subjects.

Goethe called *Die Hagestolzen* (1793; translated as *The Bachelors*, 1799) Iffland's best play, "das einzige, in dem er aus der Prosa ins Ideelle geht" (the only one in which he leaves the prosaic and reaches the ideal), and Schiller caught glimpses of true poetry in it. Iffland dedicated this "Versuch, Hausglück zu befördern" (attempt to promote domestic happiness) to Friedrich Wilhelm II. The court councillor Reinhold has, unbeknownst to him, been prevented from marrying by his avaricious spinster sister. When he realizes what he has missed and determines to find a wife, the sister offers to speak to the only lady who is available. But she misrepresents her brother so badly that he is put to shame and escapes to his small farm, which is run by a hardworking tenant family. These loving and happy people open up a new world to him, and Reinhold asks the wife's sister to marry him. In this play, rather than sermonizing, Iffland lets the characters act out his message. Iffland's other full-length plays written in Mannheim include *Allzu scharf macht schartig* (Too Much Sharpness Makes One Jagged, 1794), a warning against the consequences of a slanderous tongue; *Scheinverdienst* (Fake Merit, 1795), depicting the down-

Iffland as Franz Moor in Friedrich Schiller's play Die Räuber *in 1806; engraving by Meno Haas of a drawing by F. Patel (Gustav Könnecke,* Bilderatlas zur Geschichte der deutschen Nationalliteratur *[Graz: Akademische Druck- und Verlagsanstalt, 1981])*

fall of a family because the offspring, raised by their mother to be geniuses, strive for goals beyond their station; and *Dienstpflicht*, about a war council having to deal with deceitful army suppliers. Iffland also wrote one-act plays and dialogues for special occasions. The occasion for *Liebe um Liebe* (Love for Love's Sake, 1785) was the marriage of the Count Palatinate Maximilian, later king of Bavaria, to the Princess Auguste of Darmstadt; *Liussan, Fürst von Garisene* (Liussan, Prince of Garisene, 1790) was written to celebrate the elector Karl Theodor's alliance with Prince Ludwig of Saarbrücken; the patriotic *Friedrich von Oesterreich* (Frederick of Austria, 1791), Iffland's only historical play, commemorates the coronation of Emperor Leopold II; the dialogue *Der Eichenkranz* (The Oak Wreath, 1792) was written for the coronation of Franz II and was per-

formed at the opening of Frankfurt's National Stage; *Die Verbrüderung* (The Alliance, 1793) is an allegory of the alliance of Pfalzbayern and Rheinpfalz written for the jubilee of Elector Karl Theodor.

On 21 January 1792 Iffland was elected to the "First Committee" of the Mannheim theater and became its producer. In February 1794 the elector issued orders to close the theater because of financial problems caused by the war with France, but he withdrew the orders in response to the pleas of Iffland, Dalberg, and the Mannheim innkeepers. The French bombardment, frequent temporary closings of the theater, and an uncertain future tempted Iffland to accept one of the offers he received from theaters all over Germany, including Berlin and the Burgtheater in Vienna. Only Dalberg's generosity in supplementing his income from private funds moved him to stay. On 19 May 1796 Iffland married Luise Margarethe Greuhm, a lady's maid to the Duchess Marie Wilhelmine Augusta of Zweibrücken. The marriage, which was arranged by the electress and seems to have been a contented one, was childless.

Between performances in Mannheim Iffland had engagements in Weimar, Hamburg, Vienna, and elsewhere. While he was performing in Berlin, the Royal National Theater offered him the position of director; he accepted and assumed his new duties on 14 November 1796. Under his direction the Berlin stage entered its golden age. Iffland devoted enormous energy and diligence to the position but made time to continue writing. In *Die Advokaten* (1796; translated as *The Lawyers,* 1799) a carpenter's son who has worked his way up in the world becomes dishonest and is brought to his senses by a girl; *Wohin?* (Where To?, 1806) is a political play mirroring the pressures of foreign occupation and the inability of an indecisive government to deal with them. He continued to write plays for special occasions, such as *Der Veteran* (1798), with which he paid homage to Friedrich Wilhelm III of Prussia; *Die Geflüchteten* (The Refugees, 1799), written as a vehicle for the destitute widow of his actor friend David Beil; and *Liebe und Wille* (Love and Will, 1814), in honor of the return of the royal family to Berlin.

Realizing that the public's taste was changing, he gradually removed his own works from the repertoire to make room for the new serious tragedy. He devoted great care and enthusiasm to the preparation of Schiller's plays, from *Wallen-*

Iffland in 1813; color miniature on ivory by Karl Joseph Raabe (Goethe-Museum, Düsseldorf; Anton-und-Katharina-Kippenberg-Stiftung)

stein (1800) to *Wilhelm Tell* (1804), as well as to Goethe's *Iphigenie auf Tauris* (1787), *Egmont* (1788), and *Torquato Tasso* (1790); he was the first to bring to the stage the plays of Zacharias Werner and the translations of Shakespeare by August Wilhelm Schlegel, Dorothea Tieck, and Wolf Heinrich von Baudissin. During the French occupation from 1806 to 1808 he worked late at night translating into German the fashionable little comedies imported from France. He turned down offers from Vienna and Mannheim, where he could have escaped the problems caused by the occupation, remaining loyal to the people of Berlin and to the king, who made sacrifices to keep the theater open. For his patriotic management of the theater he was rewarded on 17 January 1810 with the medal of the Red Eagle Third Class; this was the first time an actor had been thus honored and the first time anyone had been so honored for his activities alone, regardless of social position. On 18 June 1811 he was made general director of all royal stages in Berlin, including the orchestra, ballet, and opera.

In spite of failing health he took part in military exercises in 1813 because he wanted to be involved in the uprising against Napoleon. He had suffered for some time from a lung ailment, and on 22 September 1814 he succumbed to it.

Iffland's plays may be forgotten but not the service he rendered the German stage as a theorist of acting and producing, as a teacher of aspiring actors, and as a promoter of a truly German stage. His essays appear in *Fragmente über Menschendarstellung, Almanach fürs Theater* (Almanac for the Theater, 1806-1811), *Beiträge für die deutsche Schaubühne* (Contributions to the German Stage, 1807-1812), and *Theorie der Schauspielkunst für ausübende Künstler und Kunstfreunde* (Theory of Acting for Practicing Actors and Friends of the Arts, 1815). These essays began as mere observations–for example, that a good comedian could also be a good tragic actor because a natural actor should please any audience–but were transformed by Dalberg's questions, which Iffland answered at length, into statements of his basic concepts concerning acting and actors, producing, and German theater. He says, for example, that the nature of the actor should enter into his art but at the same time should be limited by his art, because only the right amount of his own temper will achieve the right effect. To portray a noble character onstage, Iffland says, the actor must strive to be one himself. Dalberg's question about the performance of French tragedies on the German stage elicits Iffland's claim that French plays are artificial, unnatural, and untrue, and that the German spirit is alien to the French. Among the rules Iffland set up for actors his fundamental one is: "Der Dichter muß ganz gehört werden, sonst ist sein Werk entstellt" (The poet must be heard completely, otherwise his work is distorted). He attacks sloppy conversational tone, but even more so artificial pathos. The most important aspect of acting is to convince the spectator of the character and to make him forget the actor.

Iffland was instrumental in promoting historically correct costuming as opposed to the elegant evening dress used previously. Social contrasts, the age of a character, and the time of day should be distinguishable by costume. The hero should be dressed in light-colored garb, the villain in dark. He criticized actors who stood too close together–namely, near the prompter; he objected to ostentatious entrances and exits; he prescribed pauses in delivery and moderation in weeping, and he acknowledged gradations in passion but said that since passion is in each case accompanied by its own circumstances, it cannot be described or artificially copied. And so it is with all theory: "Sie selbst–die Welt–das ist die einzige mögliche Theorie" (The world itself–that is the only possible theory).

Letters:
Briefe von A. W. Iffland und F. L. Schröder an den Schauspieler Werdy, edited by Otto Devrient (Frankfurt am Main: Rommel, 1881);
A. W. Ifflands Briefe an seine Schwester Louise und andere Verwandte 1772-1814, edited by Ludwig Geiger (Berlin: Gesellschaft für Theatergeschichte, 1904);
A. W. Ifflands Briefe, meist an seine Schwester, nebst andern Aktenstücken und einem ungedruckten Drama: Mit Anmerkungen, edited by Geiger (Berlin: Gesellschaft für Theatergeschichte, 1905);
Ifflands Briefwechsel mit Schiller, Goethe, Kleist, Tieck und anderen Dramatikern, edited by Curt Müller (Leipzig: Reclam, 1910).

Biographies:
Carl Duncker, *Iffland in seinen Schriften als Künstler, Lehrer und Direktor der Berliner Bühne* (Berlin: Duncker & Humblot, 1854);
Adolf Hauffen, *August Wilhelm Iffland: Einleitung* (Stuttgart: Union Deutsche Verlags-gesellschaft, 1891).

References:
Wilhelm Altmann, *Ifflands Rechtfertigung seiner Theaterverwaltung, 1813* (Berlin, 1904);
Walter Horace Bruford, *Theatre, Drama and Audience in Goethe's Germany* (Westport, Conn.: Greenwood Press, 1950; London: Routledge & Kegan Paul, 1950);
Siegfried David, "Ifflands Schauspielkunst bis zum Abschluß der Mannheimer Zeit," Ph.D. dissertation, Heidelberg University, 1931;

Rudolf Genée, *Ifflands Berliner Theaterleitung* (Berlin: Buchdruckerei der National-Zeitung, 1896);
C. A. von Gruber, *Über Ifflands Mimik* (Vienna, 1801);
Heinrich Härle, *Ifflands Schauspielkunst* (Berlin: Elsner, 1925);
Heinz Kindermann, *Theatergeschichte der Goethezeit* (Vienna: Bauer, 1948);
Erwin Kliewer, *A. W. Iffland: Ein Wegbereiter in der deutschen Schauspielkunst* (Berlin: Ebering, 1937);
Wilhelm Koffka, *Iffland und Dalberg: Geschichte der klassischen Theaterzeit Mannheims* (Leipzig: Weber, 1865);
Karl Friedrich Kunz, *Aus dem Leben zweier Schauspieler, A. W. Iffland und Ludwig Devrients* (Leipzig: Brockhaus, 1838);
Sybille Maurer-Schmook, *Deutsches Theater im 18. Jahrhundert* (Tübingen: Niemeyer, 1982), pp. 110, 133, 164, 184-185, 195-197;
Hans Oberländer, *Die geistige Entwicklung der deutschen Schauspielkunst im XVIII. Jahrhundert* (Hamburg & Leipzig: Voß, 1898);
Arthur Stiehler, *Das Ifflandsche Rührstück* (Hamburg & Leipzig: Voß, 1898);
Gisbert Freiherr von Vincke, *Gesammelte Aufsätze zur Bühnengeschichte* (Hamburg & Leipzig: Voß, 1893);
Rudolf Weil, *Das Berliner Theaterpublikum unter Ifflands Direktion, 1796-1814* (Berlin: Elsner, 1932).

Papers:
August Wilhelm Iffland's papers are in the Goethe- und Schiller-Archiv in Weimar, East Germany. The Deutsche Literaturarchiv/Schiller Nationalmuseum in Marbach, West Germany, has a collection of manuscripts, and the Niedersächsische Landesbibliothek in Hannover, West Germany, has an album of Iffland's containing manuscripts and drawings.

Friedrich Heinrich Jacobi

(25 January 1743 - 10 March 1819)

Wulf Koepke
Texas A&M University

BOOKS: *Woldemar: Eine Seltenheit aus der Naturge-schichte. 1. Band,* anonymous (Flensburg & Leipzig: Kerten, 1779); revised as *Woldemar* (2 volumes, Königsberg: Nicolovius, 1794; revised again, 1796; 1779 version reprinted, 1 volume, Stuttgart: Metzler, 1969);

Vermischte Schriften: Erster Theil (Breslau: Löwe, 1781)–comprises "Der Kunstgarten: Ein philosophisches Gespräch," "Eduard Allwills Papiere";

Etwas das Lessing gesagt hat: Ein Commentar zu den Reisen der Päpste nebst Betrachtungen von einem Dritten, anonymous (Berlin: Decker, 1782);

Ueber die Lehre des Spinoza in Briefen an den Herrn Moses Mendelssohn (Breslau: Löwe, 1785; enlarged, 1789);

Friedrich Heinrich Jacobi wider Mendelssohns Beschuldigungen betreffend die Briefe über die Lehre des Spinoza (Leipzig: Göschen, 1786);

David Hume über den Glauben oder Idealismus und Realismus: Ein Gespräch (Breslau: Löwe, 1787; reprinted, New York & London: Garland, 1983);

Eduard Allwills Briefsammlung, herausgegeben von Friedrich Heinrich Jacobi, mit einer Zugabe von eigenen Briefen. 1. Band (Königsberg: Nicolovius, 1792);

Jacobi an Fichte (Hamburg: Perthes, 1799);

Was gebieten Ehre, Sittlichkeit und Recht in Absicht vertraulicher Briefe von Verstorbenen und noch Lebenden?: Eine Gelegenheitsschrift (Leipzig: Göschen, 1806);

Ueber gelehrte Gesellschaften, ihren Geist und Zweck: Eine Abhandlung, vorgelesen bey der feyerlichen Erneuung der Königlichen Akademie der Wissenschaften zu München von dem Präsidenten der Akademie (Munich: Fleischmann, 1807);

Von den Göttlichen Dingen und ihrer Offenbarung (Leipzig: Fleischer, 1811); reprinted in *Streit um die göttlichen Dinge: Die Auseinandersetzung zwischen Jacobi und Schelling,* edited by Wilhelm Weischedel (Darmstadt: Wissenschaftliche Buchgesellschaft, 1967), pp. 91-356;

Friedrich Heinrich Jacobi (Stadtgeschichtliches Museum, Düsseldorf)

Friedrich Heinrich Jacobi's Werke, edited by Friedrich Köppen and Friedrich von Roth (8 volumes, Leipzig: Fleischer, 1812-1825; reprinted, 7 volumes, Darmstadt: Wissenschaftliche Buchgesellschaft, 1976);

Die Hauptschriften zum Pantheismusstreit zwischen Jacobi und Mendelssohn, edited by Heinrich Scholz (Berlin: Reuther & Reichard, 1916);

Friedrich Heinrich Jacobis "Allwill," edited by J. U. Terpstra (Groningen & Jakarta: Walters, 1957).

OTHER: François Hemsterhuis, *Alexis oder Von dem goldenen Weltalter,* translated by Jacobi (Riga: Hartknoch, 1787);

Johann Georg Jacobi, ed., *Überflüssiges Taschenbuch für das Jahr 1800,* foreword by Friedrich Heinrich Jacobi (Hamburg: Perthes, 1799);

"Ueber eine Weissagung Lichtenbergs," in *Taschenbuch für das Jahr 1802,* edited by Johann Georg Jacobi (Hamburg: Perthes, 1801);

"Drey Briefe," in *Schellings Lehre oder Das Ganze der Philosophie des absoluten Nichts: Nebst drey Briefen verwandten Inhalts von Friedr. Heinr. Jacobi,* by Friedrich Köppen (Hamburg: Perthes, 1803), pp. 207-278;

"Fliegende Blätter," in *Minerva: Taschenbuch für das Jahr 1817* (Leipzig: Fleischer, 1816), pp. 259-300.

PERIODICAL PUBLICATIONS: "Betrachtung über die von Herrn Herder in seiner Abhandlung vom Ursprung der Sprache vorgelegte genetische Erklärung der thierischen Kunstfertigkeiten und Kunsttriebe," *Der Teutsche Merkur,* 1 (1773): 99-121;

"Briefe an eine junge Dame," *Der Teutsche Merkur,* 2 (1773): 59-75, 113-119, 235-247;

"Eduard Allwills Papiere," *Iris,* 4, no. 3 (1775): 193-236; revised, *Der Teutsche Merkur,* 14 (1776): 14-75; 15 (1776): 57-71; 16 (1776): 229-262; edited by Heinz Nicolai (Stuttgart: Metzler, 1962);

"Freundschaft und Liebe: Eine wahre Geschichte, von dem Herausgeber von Eduard Allwills Papieren," *Der Teutsche Merkur,* 18 (1777): 97-117; 19 (1777): 32-49, 229-259; 20 (1777): 246-267;

"Ein Stück Philosophie des Lebens und der Menschheit," *Deutsches Museum* (1779): 307-348, 393-427;

"Ueber Recht und Gewalt oder philosophische Erwägung eines Aufsatzes von dem Herrn Hofrath Wieland, über das göttliche Recht der Obrigkeit, im Teutschen Merkur," *Deutsches Museum* (1781): 522-554;

"Ueber und bei Gelegenheit des kürzlich erschienenen Werkes: Des lettres de Cachet et prisons d'état," *Deutsches Museum,* no. 4 (1783): 361-394; no. 5 (1783): 435-476;

"Die beste von den Haderkünsten: Eine Erzählung," *Deutsches Museum* (1787): 49-51;

"Einige Betrachtungen über den frommen Betrug und über eine Vernunft, welche nicht die Vernunft ist, von Friedrich Heinrich Jacobi in einem Briefe an den Herrn geheimen Hofrath Schlosser," *Deutsches Museum* (1788): 153-184;

"Swifts Meditation über einen Besenstiel, und wie sie entstanden ist," *Neues Deutsches Museum* (1789): 405-417;

"Zufällige Ergießungen eines einsamen Denkers in Briefen an vertraute Freunde," *Die Horen,* 3, no. 8 (1795): 1-34;

"Ueber das Unternehmen des Kriticismus, die Vernunft zu Verstande zu bringen, und der Philosophie überhaupt eine neue Absicht zu geben," in *Beyträge zur leichtern Uebersicht des Zustandes der Philosophie beym Anfange des 19. Jahrhunderts,* volume 2, edited by C. L. Reinhold (Hamburg, 1802), pp. 1-110.

Friedrich Heinrich Jacobi is mentioned today mostly as the friend or correspondent of more famous writers, such as Johann Georg Hamann, Gotthold Ephraim Lessing, Moses Mendelssohn, Johann Gottfried Herder, and Johann Wolfgang Goethe. In his own right, he is better remembered in the history of philosophy than in the history of literature. His writings are Gelegenheitsschriften (occasional writings), in a personal, largely autobiographical vein. His significance lies in the fact that he brought up important and controversial issues in philosophy and human relations. In this latter area, he published his views in the form of narratives which might be termed novels. His two most notable works, "Eduard Allwills Papiere" (Edward Allwill's Papers, 1775-1776) and *Woldemar* (1779), are remarkable not so much as literary achievements but as descriptions of characters and conflicts that stimulated other writers. Jacobi's literary and philosophical works grew out of his vast correspondence, and the epistolary form remained his fundamental mode of expression.

Jacobi was born on 25 January 1743 in Düsseldorf to the wealthy merchant Johann Konrad Jacobi and Marie Fahlmer Jacobi. His mother died in 1746, and his father remarried two years later. His older brother, Johann Georg, is known for his anacreontic and sentimental poetry and as an editor of literary periodicals.

Friedrich Heinrich, called "Fritz," was a rather passive child, a dreamer with little motivation for either learning or physical exercise, handicapped by frequent illnesses. He absorbed himself in religious ideas and after confirmation joined a pietistic group from the Reformed Church called "Die Feinen" (The Fine Ones). In

First page of a letter, in French, dated 25 November 1768, from Jacobi in Düsseldorf to Marc Michel Rey in Amsterdam
(Koninklijk Huisarchief, The Hague)

Title page of the issue of Der Teutsche Merkur *containing the first installment of the second version of Jacobi's novel "Eduard Allwills Papiere"*

spring 1759 he was sent to Frankfurt for an apprenticeship in business. He could not get along with his master and obtained permission from his father to be sent to Geneva in fall 1759; he stayed there until 1762. These were beneficial and decisive years. He began to adjust to business activities and to like physical exercise. More important, he began to work to improve his mind. He found a mentor in the famous mathematician George Louis Lesage; he absorbed the works of Charles de Bonnet, notably his essay on palingenesis; and he was one of the enthusiastic readers of Jean-Jacques Rousseau's *Émile* when it appeared in 1761. Jacobi's main focus was the "Profession of Faith of a Savoyan Vicar," Rousseau's pronouncement on "natural religion." He began to develop the bases for his later philosophy of faith: although the existence of God cannot be proven, it must be accepted on faith to assure the existence of the self and the world.

After Jacobi's return to Düsseldorf his father insisted on his entering the family business; in 1764 his father handed the direction of the business over to him. In the same year Jacobi married Helene Elisabeth (Betty) von Clermont, a wealthy heiress from Vaels, near Aachen. It was a happy marriage with many children, four of whom survived into adulthood. Jacobi owned a country house in Pempelfort, outside of Düsseldorf, and loved to have visitors there. In 1770 he initiated a correspondence with Christoph Martin Wieland; Jacobi praised Wieland's accomplishments, and Wieland urged Jacobi to try to write. Jacobi seems to have had the idea of starting a German journal in the manner of the *Mercure de France,* which became Wieland's *Der Teutsche Merkur.* During an attempted coeditorship the two men began to disagree over editorial policy. Jacobi withdrew, and the friendship with Wieland ended.

In 1772 Jacobi was named a member of the Hofkammer (administrative council) of the duchy of Jülich-Berg. He left the family business to a brother-in-law and earned his living from customs duties extracted from boats on the Rhine and other state tariffs. On a personal level, the great event was a visit by Johann Wolfgang Goethe on 22 July 1774. The two young men began an enthusiastic friendship and stayed in contact for the rest of their lives.

Goethe, like Wieland, urged Jacobi to express his creative powers, and Jacobi began an epistolary novel which reflected the deep impression Goethe had made on him. The first installment of "Eduard Allwills Papiere" appeared in 1775 in *Iris,* a journal for ladies, edited by Jacobi's brother; a larger part of the still-unfinished work was published in 1776 in Wieland's *Der Teutsche Merkur.* The success of these samples encouraged Jacobi to include "Eduard Allwills Papiere" in 1781 in the volume *Vermischte Schriften* (Miscellaneous Writings). It was revised and augmented once more in 1792 and given the title *Eduard Allwills Briefsammlung* (Eduard Allwill's Correspondence). This piecemeal method of publication indicates that although the audience responded with interest, Jacobi lost the drive to complete the book. The additions of 1792 are philosophical discussions that do not advance the plot.

The letters in "Eduard Allwills Papiere" are lively, they sound authentic, and they deal with complex human relations in a milieu familiar to Jacobi's readers. Jacobi begins with the descrip-

Copy, executed circa 1842 by Laurentius Schäfer, of a portrait of Jacobi by Johann Friedrich Eich. Jacobi requested the portrait as a gift for his friend Johann Wilhelm Ludwig Gleim; date of the original is unknown (Kunstlerverein Malkasten, Düsseldorf).

tion of the happy family life of Heinrich Clerdon, an honest official, in a series of idyllic, sometimes sentimental scenes. The two characters whose letters make up the work do not quite fit into this picture: Heinrich's widowed sister-in-law, Sylli Clerdon, who is separated from her late husband's family because of a lengthy court case and feels depressed and alienated from society; and Eduard Allwill, the fascinating family friend who follows his own heart, rather than moral principles, as the guide for his actions. He is driven by an inner demon and not always responsible for what he does. He means well, and his spontaneous, almost childlike behavior makes him irresistible to women. But he does not love any of them deeply and after a while leaves them behind. This intriguing and dangerous individual comes close to a portrait of Goethe as Jacobi saw him. The last letters reflect a growing ambivalence on Jacobi's part: Allwill demonstrates Goethe's immense impact on his friends, and also their reactions of bewilderment and self-defense.

Allwill is, above all, the portrait of a genius. "Eduard Allwills Papiere" remained a character sketch, but as such, it appealed to Jacobi's contemporaries. Jean Paul, for example, found in Allwill the inspiration for his novel *Titan* (1800-1803).

Jacobi was not only preoccupied by the idea of the genius; he also shared the intense interest of his age in love and friendship. Friendship had come to include erotic relationships between men and women. Jacobi thrived on sentimental friendship in an intimate circle. His marriage was happy, but he liked to have other women in the household as well. A marriage *à trois* was his ideal, as it was for others in the era. Goethe gave expression to such desires in his play *Stella*, especially in its first (1776) version, which ended with a happy relationship of a man and two women. (Goethe later changed the ending into a tragedy.) Jacobi found allusions to his own life in this play and felt compelled to write his own story. This work was first called "Freundschaft und Liebe" (Friendship and Love), and a fragment of it was published under that title in *Der Teutsche Merkur* in 1777. Again, Jacobi added on to the original nucleus, publishing *Woldemar: Eine Seltenheit aus der Naturgeschichte* (Woldemar: A Rarity from Natural History) in 1779. He reworked the novel in 1794 and revised it once more in 1796. Again, most of the later additions do not advance the plot but are discursive in nature. *Woldemar* introduces the reader to Jacobi's milieu of high officials and businessmen. Woldemar, an able official, is rather misanthropic and, like his author, suffers from frequent depression. In spite of the support of his brother and friends, he despairs of ever finding an adequate human relationship. At last he establishes a platonic friendship with Henriette, who persuades him to marry her friend Allwina. The conflict occurs when Woldemar begins to doubt Henriette's true feelings toward him. In his morbid suspicion he overreacts, and Henriette has to guide him out of this mood. In the end the narrator says, "Ihm schauderte vor dem Abgrunde–an dem er noch stand: *vor den Tiefen seines Herzens!*" (He shuddered before the abyss–where he was still standing: *the depths of his own heart!*).

In the prefaces to both *Eduard Allwills Briefsammlung* and *Woldemar*, Jacobi stated the principle and purpose of his fictional writing in the same words: "Menschheit wie sie ist, erklärlich oder unerklärlich, auf das gewissenhafteste vor Augen zu stellen" (To portray humanity as it is, explicable or inexplicable, as conscientiously as possible). He intended, he said, to create works which

Jacobi in 1781; engraving by Carl Ernst Christoph Hess of a drawing by François Hemsterhuis

were "mit Dichtung gleichsam nur umgeben" (so to speak only surrounded by poetry), meaning that he wanted to present psychologically authentic characters and situations, and that literary form and style were to have only an auxiliary function. This statement may sound like a justification of his own strengths and weaknesses, but there was much literature during the age which could make similar claims—for example, the works of Karl Philipp Moritz or of Jacobi's protégé Wilhelm Heinse.

Besides Heinse, who lived in Jacobi's house for several years, Jacobi's circle of friends and correspondents included the princess Gallitzin in Münster; her protégé François Hemsterhuis; Johann Caspar Lavater; Hamann; and Herder. In 1779 the elector Karl Theodor of Bavaria offered Jacobi the title of Geheimer Rat (privy councillor) and invited him to come to Munich as a Ministerialreferent (assistant minister). It soon became clear, however, that Jacobi's ideas on economic policy differed from those of the Munich officials to such a degree that his employment in Munich would be pointless, and he remained in Düsseldorf. An early adherent of Adam Smith's

ideas, Jacobi opposed state regulation of the economy and protectionism.

On 5 July 1780 Jacobi visited Lessing in Wolfenbüttel. Lessing was sick and depressed following personal tragedies and theological and political disputes. After reading the manuscript of Goethe's "Prometheus," which Jacobi had brought with him, Lessing–according to Jacobi's account–exclaimed that the poem expressed Benedict de Spinoza's philosophy, and that he was in agreement with it. This comment touched off a lively debate between Jacobi and Lessing on Spinoza and the existence of a personal God. After Lessing's death in early 1781 Jacobi wrote down his recollections and sent them to Herder, Goethe, and Mendelssohn, who planned to write a book about Lessing. Mendelssohn found the idea that Lessing might have been a Spinozist repugnant and tried to disprove it in private and in public. Jacobi finally felt compelled to publish *Ueber die Lehre des Spinoza in Briefen an den Herrn Moses Mendelssohn* (On the Doctrine of Spinoza in Letters to Mr. Moses Mendelssohn, 1785). While maintaining that Lessing had been a Spinozist, Jacobi consistently criticized Spinoza's system as atheistic and fatalistic. Jacobi's lively presentation of Lessing's arguments, however, drew much attention to the controversy; attracted the interest of the early Romantics and the Tübingen circle of G. W. F. Hegel, Friedrich Hölderlin, and F. W. J. Schelling; and touched off responses such as Herder's *Gott* (God, 1787).

After the death of Jacobi's wife in 1784, two of his sisters took over the household. Jacobi became more deeply embroiled in the philosophical disputes of the age. His *David Hume über den Glauben* (David Hume on Faith, 1787) defined his own position as anti-Kantian and anti-idealistic. He maintained his philosophy of faith: the limits of human understanding compel us to accept the existence of a reality outside the mind and of God on faith. Thus he turns Hume's skepticism around: for Hume, knowledge is *mere* belief–that is, it is subjective and therefore uncertain. Jacobi says that we have to accept reality on *faith*–that is, belief in a *religious* sense, which is not mixed with uncertainty. Kantian idealism for him was "Nihilismus" (nihilism)–a word to which he gave currency–and he became especially vehement in his attitude toward Kant's followers beginning with Johann Gottlieb Fichte. In *Jacobi an Fichte* (Jacobi to Fichte, 1799) he denounced Fichte's philosophy not only as erroneous but as dangerous.

Plaster bust of Jacobi by G. M. Klauer, 1784 (Goethe-Nationalmuseum, Weimar)

Jacobi was deeply troubled by the outbreak of the French Revolution. When the threat of French occupation of the Rhineland became imminent in 1794, he moved to Eutin in northern Germany. His "Zufällige Ergießungen eines einsamen Denkers" (Accidental Effusions of a Lonely Thinker, 1795), published in Schiller and Goethe's journal *Die Horen*, is an indictment of the revolutionaries, especially of the execution of Louis XVI. Jacobi eventually became an economic victim of the revolution. Having lost two-thirds of his capital, he welcomed the call in 1804 to Munich to become the president of the reorganized Akademie der Wissenschaften (Academy of Sciences) of Bavaria. In 1807 he made a widely noticed and controversial speech to the academy on the purpose and function of learned societies in which he emphasized the importance of pure research which has no immediate practical applications, stressed the moral integrity of scholarship, and said that government should support but not dictate to the sciences. In 1811, as a summary of his philosophical credo, he published *Von den Göttlichen Dingen und ihrer Offenbarung* (Of Divine Matters and Their Revelation), which caused a vio-

lent response by Schelling and a controversy that cost Jacobi his friendship with Goethe, who sided with Schelling, and ended in Jacobi's early retirement in 1812. He devoted his remaining years to a final revised edition of his works, which was completed after his death. He died on 10 March 1819 in Munich.

After a long period of neglect, Jacobi's position in the history of philosophy was reassessed in the late 1960s and the 1970s. Besides his historical merit in generating the Spinoza debate, his anti-Kantian views deserve to be taken as seriously as they were by Hegel and Schelling. While the contemporary audience may have overestimated Jacobi's narrative and essayistic work, he is not a negligible figure in literature. His revisions of "Eduard Allwills Papiere" and *Woldemar* weakened their literary substance, so it makes sense to go back to the first versions of the 1770s. His *Eduard Allwill* is a pivotal figure in the preoccupation with the genius. *Woldemar*, in spite of obvious weaknesses in structure and style which caused Goethe (to whom it was dedicated) to make fun of it in his Weimar circle, has much psychological validity. It offers a good example of the period's preoccupation with the self, with friendship, and with new relationships between the sexes. Bourgeois conventionality after 1815 has obscured the fact that much experimentation with love and friendship was going on before. From a literary point of view, "Eduard Allwills Papiere," the echo of the friendship with Goethe, is Jacobi's best work.

Letters:

Friedrich Heinrich Jacobi's auserlesener Briefwechsel, 2 volumes, edited by Friedrich Roth (Leipzig: Fleischer, 1825-1827);

Briefwechsel zwischen Goethe und F. H. Jacobi, edited by Max Jacobi (Leipzig: Weidmann, 1846);

Aus F. H. Jacobi's Nachlaß: Ungedruckte Briefe von und an Jacobi und Andere. Nebst ungedruckten Gedichten von Goethe und Lenz, 2 volumes, edited by Rudolf Zoeppritz (Leipzig: Engelmann, 1869);

Briefwechsel: Gesamtausgabe, 3 volumes to date, edited by Michael Brüggen and Siegfried Sudhof (Stuttgart: Frommann-Holzboog, 1981-).

References:

Günther Baum, *Vernunft und Erkenntnis: Die Philosophie F. H. Jacobis* (Bonn: Bouvier, 1969);

Otto Friedrich Bollnow, *Die Lebensphilosophie Friedrich Heinrich Jacobis* (Stuttgart: Kohlhammer, 1933);

Theodor Bossert, "Friedrich Heinrich Jacobi und die Frühromantik," Ph.D. dissertation, University of Gießen, 1926;

Alexander W. Crawford, *The Philosophy of Friedrich Heinrich Jacobi* (New York: Macmillan, 1905);

W. Gebhard, ed., "Friedrich Heinrich Jacobi: Acta die von Ihro Churfürstlichen Durchlaucht zu Pfaltz etc. etc. Höchstdero Hof-Cammerrathen Jacobi gnädigst aufgetragnenen Commission, das Commerzium der beyden Herzogthümer gülich und Berg zu untersuchen, betreffend," *Zeitschrift des Bergischen Geschichtsvereins*, 18 (1882): 1-148;

Klaus Hammacher, *Kritik und Leben II: Die Philosophie Friedrich Heinrich Jacobis* (Munich: Fink, 1969);

Hammacher, ed., *Friedrich Heinrich Jacobi: Philosoph und Literat der Goethezeit* (Frankfurt am Main: Klostermann, 1971);

Herta Hartmannshenn, *Jean Pauls "Titan" und die Romane Friedrich Heinrich Jacobis* (Marburg: Bauer, 1934);

Otto Heraeus, *Fritz Jacobi und der Sturm und Drang* (Heidelberg: Winter, 1928);

Harold von Hofe, "Jacobi, Wieland, and the New World," *Monatshefte*, 49 (1957): 187-192;

Karl Homann, *F. H. Jacobis Philosophie der Freiheit* (Munich & Freiburg: Alber, 1973);

Renate Knoll, *Johann Georg Hamann und Friedrich Heinrich Jacobi* (Heidelberg: Winter, 1963);

Heinz Nicolai, *Goethe und Jacobi: Studien zur Geschichte ihrer Freundschaft* (Stuttgart: Metzler, 1965);

Roy Pascal, "The Novels of F. H. Jacobi and Goethe's Early Classicism," *Publications of the English Goethe Society*, new series 16 (1947): 54-89;

Fritz Schulte, "Die wirtschaftlichen Ideen Friedrich Heinrich Jacobis: Ein Beitrag zur Vorgeschichte des Liberalismus," *Düsseldorfer Jahrbuch*, 48 (1956): 280-292;

Hans Schwartz, *Friedrich Heinrich Jacobis "Allwill"* (Halle: Niemeyer, 1911);

Theodor Cornelis van Stockum, *Spinoza–Jacobi–Lessing: Ein Beitrag zur Geschichte der deutschen Literatur und Philosophie im 18. Jahrhundert* (Groningen: Noordhoff, 1916);

Siegfried Sudhof, "Die Edition der Werke F. H. Jacobis: Gedanken zur Neuausgabe des 'Allwill,'" *Germanisch-Romanische Monatsschrift*, new series 12 (1962): 243-253;

Norman Wilde, *Friedrich Heinrich Jacobi: A Study in the Origin of German Realism* (New York: Columbia College, 1894).

Johann Heinrich Jung-Stilling

(12 September 1740 - 2 April 1817)

H. M. Waidson

University of Wales, Swansea

*BOOKS: *Specimen de historia martis Nassovico-Siegenesis quod . . . pro licentia gradum doctoris . . . deffendet Johannes Henricus Jung* (Strasbourg: Heitzius, 1772);

Die Schleuder eines Hirtenknaben gegen den hohnsprechenden Philister den Verfasser des Sebaldus Nothanker (Frankfurt am Main: Eichenberg, 1775);

Sendschreiben an den Herrn Stadtchirurg: Hellmann zu Magdeburg, dessen Urtheil, die Lobsteinischen Staarmesser betreffend (Frankfurt am Main, 1775);

Die große Panacee wider die Krankheit des Religionszweifels (Frankfurt am Main: Eichenberg, 1776);

Die Theodicee des Hirtenknaben als Berichtigung und Vertheidigung der Schleuder desselben (Frankfurt am Main: Eichenberg, 1776);

Henrich Stillings Jugend: Eine wahrhafte Geschichte (Berlin & Leipzig: Decker, 1777);

Oeffentlicher Anschlag bei dem Antritte des Lehrstuhls der praktischen Kameralwissenschaften (Lautern: Auf Kosten der Kameral Hohen Schule, 1778);

Henrich Stillings Jünglings-Jahre: Eine wahrhafte Geschichte (Berlin & Leipzig: Decker, 1778);

Henrich Stillings Wanderschaft: Eine wahrhafte Geschichte (Berlin & Leipzig: Decker, 1778);

Die Geschichte des Herrn von Morgenthau: Von dem Verfasser der Geschichte des Henrich Stillings, anonymous, 2 volumes (Berlin & Leipzig: Decker, 1779);

Rede auf den Namenstag der Durchläuchtigsten Kurfürstin Maria Elisabeth Augusta: Vorgelesen bei der öffentlichen Versammlung der Kurpfälzischen Physisch-Oekonomischen Gesellschaft zu Lautern (Mannheim & Lautern: Verlag der Kameral Hohen Schule, 1779);

Versuch einer Grundlehre sämmtlicher Kameralwissenschaften zum Gebrauche der Vorlesungen (Lautern: Verlag der Gesellschaft, 1779);

Daß die Kameralwissenschaft auf einer . . . Hohen Schule vorgetragen werden müsse (Lautern:

Johann Heinrich Jung-Stilling

Auf Kosten der Kameral Hohen Schule, 1780);

Die Geschichte Florentins von Fahlendorn, as Heinrich Stilling, 3 volumes (Mannheim: Neue Hof- und akademische Buchhandlung, 1781-1782; Reading, Pa.: Printed by J. Schneider, 1797);

Versuch eines Lehrbuches der Forstwirtschaft, 2 volumes (Mannheim & Lautern: Verlag der Gesellschaft, 1781-1782);

Leben der Theodore von der Linden, as Heinrich Stilling, 2 volumes (Mannheim: Neue Hof- und akademische Buchhandlung, 1783);

*Bibliography revised by *DLB staff*

96

Versuch eines Lehrbuchs der Landwirthschaft der ganzen bekannten Welt in so fern ihre Produkten in den europäischen Handel kommen (Leipzig: Weygand, 1783);

Theobald oder Die Schwärmer: Eine wahre Geschichte, as Heinrich Stilling, 2 volumes (Leipzig: Weygand, 1784; Lebanon, Pa.: Printed by Jacob Stöver, 1811); translated by Samuel Schaeffer as *Theobald; or, The Fanatic: A True History* (Philadelphia: Hooker / New York: Saxton & Miles, 1846);

Gemeinnütziges Lehrbuch der Handlungswissenschaft für alle Klassen von Kaufleuten und Handlungsstudirenden (Leipzig, 1785);

Lehrbuch der Vieharzneykunde, 2 volumes (Heidelberg: Pfähler, 1785-1787);

Versuch eines Lehrbuchs der Fabrikwissenschaft zum Gebrauch Akademischer Vorlesungen (Nuremberg: Grattenauer, 1785);

Anleitung zur Cameral-Rechnungs-Wissenschaft nach einer neuen Methode des doppelten Buchhaltens, zum Gebrauch der Akademischen Vorlesungen (Leipzig: Weidmann & Reich, 1786);

Antrittsrede über den Ursprung, Fortgang und die Lehrmethode der Staatswirthschaft (Marburg: Neue Akademische Buchhandlung, 1787);

Blicke in die Geheimnisse der Natur-Weisheit (Berlin & Leipzig: Decker, 1787);

Jubelrede über den Geist der Staatswirthschaft, gehalten den 7ten November 1786 (Mannheim: Neue Hof- und akademische Buchhandlung, 1787);

Eickels Verklärung: Eine Scene aus der Geister Welt (Elberfeld: Giesen, 1788);

Abhandlungen oeconomischen und statistischen Inhalts (Copenhagen & Leipzig: Kröger, 1788);

Lehrbuch der Staats-Polizey-Wissenschaft (Leipzig: Weidmann, 1788);

Henrich Stillings häusliches Leben: Eine wahrhafte Geschichte (Berlin & Leipzig: Rottmann, 1789);

Lehrbuch der Finanz-Wissenschaft (Leipzig: Weidmann, 1789);

Lehrbuch der Cameral-Wissenschaft oder Cameral-Praxis (Marburg: Neue Akademische Buchhandlung, 1790);

Abhandlungen des Staatswirthschaftlichen Instituts zu Marburg, by Jung-Stilling and others (Offenbach: Weiß & Brede, 1791);

Methode den grauen Star auszuziehen und zu heilen (Marburg: Neue Akademische Buchhandlung, 1791);

Die Grundlehre der Staatswirthschaft: Ein Elementarbuch für Regentensöhne und alle, die sich dem Dienst des Staats und der Gelehrsamkeit widmen

wollen (Marburg: Neue Akademische Buchhandlung, 1792; reprinted, Königstein: Scriptor, 1978);

De originibus montium et venarum metallicarum (Marburg: Bayrhoffer, 1793);

Über den Revolutions-Geist unserer Zeit zur Belehrung der bürgerlichen Stände (Marburg: Neue Akademische Buchhandlung, 1793);

Der Tod Ludwigs des Sechszehnten, Königs von Frankreich (Marburg, 1793);

Das Heimweh, as Heinrich Stilling, 4 volumes (Marburg: Neue Akademische Buchhandlung, 1794-1796);

Scenen aus dem Geisterreiche, 2 volumes (Frankfurt am Main: Varrentrapp & Wenner, 1795; enlarged, 1800-1801); translated by Gottlieb Schober as *Scenes in the World of Spirits* (New Market, N.C.: Henkel, 1815);

Der Schlüssel zum Heimweh (Marburg: Neue Akademische Buchhandlung, 1796);

Staatswirthschaftliche Ideen: Erstes Heft (Marburg: Neue Akademische Buchhandlung, 1798);

Die Pilgerreise zu Wasser und zu Lande oder Denkwürdigkeiten der göttlichen Gnadenführung und Fürsehung in dem Leben eines Christen, der solche, auch besonders in seinen Reisen durch alle vier Haupttheile der Erde reichlich an sich erfahren hat: Von ihm selbst beschrieben in Briefen an einen seiner Christlichen Mitbrüder in den Jahren 1797 und 1798 (Nuremberg: Raw, 1799);

Die Siegsgeschichte der christlichen Religion in einer gemeinnützigen Erklärung der Offenbarung Johannis (Nuremberg: Raw, 1799);

Lavaters Verklärung (Frankfurt am Main: Hermann, 1801);

Sendschreiben an die Bürger Helvetiens (Winterthur: Steiner, 1802);

Der christliche Menschenfreund in Erzählunge für Bürger und Bauern, 4 volumes (Nuremberg: Raw, 1803; Hagerstown, Md.: Printed by Johann Gruber, 1807);

Heinrich Stillings Lehr-Jahre: Eine wahrhafte Geschichte (Berlin & Leipzig: Rottmann, 1804);

Taschenbuch für Freunde des Christenthums, 12 volumes (Nuremberg: Raw, 1804-1815);

Erster Nachtrag zur Siegsgeschichte der christlichen Religion in einer gemeinnützigen Erklärung der Offenbarung Johannis (Nuremberg: Raw, 1805);

Heinrich Stillings Leben, 5 volumes (Basel & Leipzig: Rottmann, 1806)—comprises *Heinrich Stillings Jugend, Heinrich Stillings Jünglings-Jahre, Heinrich Stillings Wanderschaft, Heinrich Stil-*

lings häusliches Leben, Heinrich Stillings Lehr-Jahre;

Kleine gesammelte Schriften, 2 volumes (Frankfurt am Main, 1806-1808);

Vertheidigung gegen die schweren Beschuldigungen einiger Journalisten (Nuremberg: Raw, 1807);

Theorie der Geister-Kunde, in einer Natur-Vernunft- und Bibelmäßigen Beantwortung der Frage: Was von Ahnungen, Gesichten und Geistererscheinungen geglaubt und nicht geglaubt werden müsse (Nuremberg: Raw, 1808; Reading, Pa.: Printed and sold by Heinrich B. Sage, 1816); translated by Samuel Jackson as *Theory of Pneumatology, in Reply to the Question, What Ought to Be Believed or Disbelieved Concerning Presentiments, Visions, and Apparitions, According to Nature, Reason, and Scripture* (London: Longman, Rees, Orme, Brown, Green & Longman, 1834; edited by George Bush, New York: Redfield, 1851); German version reprinted (Wiesbaden: Fourier, 1979);

Des Christlichen Menschenfreunds Biblische Erzählungen, 14 volumes (Nuremberg: Raw, 1808-1816);

Apologie der Theorie der Geisterkunde veranlaßt durch ein über dieselbe abgefaßtes Gutachten des Hochwürdigen geistlichen Ministeriums zu Basel: Als erster Nachtrag zur Theorie der Geisterkunde (Nuremberg: Raw, 1809; Reading, Pa.: Printed and sold by Heinrich B. Sage, 1816);

Antwort durch Wahrheit in Liebe auf die an mich gerichteten Briefe des Herrn Professor Sulzers in Konstanz über Katholicismus und Protestantismus (Nuremberg: Raw, 1811);

Erzählungen, 3 volumes (Frankfurt am Main: Hermann, 1814-1815);

Klara: Ein Gedicht (Frankfurt am Main, 1814);

Lehrsätze der Naturgeschichte für Frauenzimmer (Karlsruhe: Braun, 1816);

Schatzkästlein (Nuremberg: Raw, 1816);

Heinrich Stillings Alter: Eine wahre Geschichte. Oder Heinrich Stillings Lebensgeschichte, sechster Band. Herausgegeben nebst einer Erzählung von Stillings Lebensende von dessen Enkel Wilhelm Schwarz . . . Hierzu ein Nachwort von Dr. F. H. C. Schwarz (Heidelberg: Mohr & Winter, 1817); republished as *Heinrich Stillings Alter, von ihm selbst geschrieben: Nebst einer Beschreibung seiner letzten Tage. . . . Herausgegeben von seinem Enkel, Wilhelm Schwarz* (Allentown, Pa.: Printed by H. Ebner, 1821);

Leben und Tod eines christlichen Ehepaares (Stuttgart, 1817);

Chrysäon oder Das goldene Zeitalter: In vier Gesängen nebst einigen Liedern und Gedichten (Nuremberg: Raw, 1818);

Geschichte unseres Herrn Jesu Christi und der Gründung der christlichen Kirche durch die Apostel, nebst der Zerstörung Jerusalems, 4 volumes (Nuremberg: Raw, 1820);

Gedichte, edited by Wilhelm E. Schwarz (Frankfurt am Main: Hermann, 1821);

Sendschreiben geprüfter Christen an weiland den geheimen Hofrath Jung-Stilling: Aus dessen schriftlichem Nachlasse gesammelt und geordnet für seine Freunde. Ein Anhang zu Heinrich Stillings Lebensgeschichte (Karlsruhe: Müller, 1833);

Johann Heinrich Jung's, genannt Stilling, sämmtliche Schriften: Zum erstenmale vollständig gesammelt und herausgegeben von Verwandten, Freunden und Verehrern des Verewigten, 14 volumes (volumes 1 & 2, Stuttgart: Henne; volumes 3-14, Stuttgart: Scheible, 1835-1838);

Johann Heinrich Jung's, genannt Stilling, sämmtliche Werke: Neue vollständige Ausgabe, 12 volumes (Stuttgart: Scheible, 1841-1842);

Lebensgeschichte: Vollständiger Text nach den Erstdrucken, edited by Wolfgang Pfeiffer-Belli (Munich: Die Fundgrube, 1968);

Lebensgeschichte: Vollständige Ausgabe, edited by Gustav Adolf Benrath (Darmstadt: Wissenschaftliche Buchgesellschaft, 1976).

Editions in English: *The Life of John Henry Stilling,* translated by Ernest Lewis Hazelius (Gettysburg, Pa.: Printed at the Press of the Theological Seminary, H. C. Neinstedt, 1831);

Henrich Stilling: His Childhood, Youthful Years and Wanderings, His Domestic Life, and Years of Tuition, translated by Samuel Jackson (London: Hamilton, Adams, 1835);

Sequel to Henrich Stilling, Containing Stilling's Old Age, A Fragment; His Last Hours; A Supplement, by His Son-in-law; and Letters to Stilling, from Lavater, Oberlin, Moser, the Baroness von Krudener, Prince Charles of Hesse Cassel, translated by Jackson (London: Hamilton, Adams, 1836);

Interesting Tales, translated by Jackson (London: Hamilton, Adams, 1837)—comprises "Conrad the Good" ("Konrad der Gute"), "The Emigrant" ("Der Emigrant"), "The Noble Youths" ("Die edlen Jünglinge"), "Blind Leonard and His Guide" ("Leonhard und Bernhardine"), "The Watchman and His Daughter" ("Der Nachtwächter und seine Tochter"), "The Way to the Throne" ("Der

Weg zum Thron"), "Gotthard and His Sons" ("Gotthard und seine Söhne"), "A Holy Family" ("Auch eine heilige Familie"), "The Poor Weaver" ("Der arme Leinweber"), "An Extraordinary Effect of the Imagination" ("Eine außerordentliche Wirkung der Einbildungskraft");

The Autobiography of Heinrich Stilling, translated by Jackson (New York: Harper, 1844);

Mary de Goldenbeck; or, The Portrait of a Noble Lady, translated by Samuel Schaeffer (Philadelphia: Hooker, 1848);

Jung Stilling: His Biography, translated by Robert Oswald Moon (London: Foulis, 1938).

OTHER: *Der Volkslehrer,* edited by Jung-Stilling, 4 volumes (Leipzig: Weygand, 1781-1784);

Virgils Georgica in deutsche Hexameter übersetzt, translated by Jung-Stilling (Mannheim: Neue Hof- und akademische Buchhandlung, 1787);

Der graue Mann: Eine Volksschrift, edited by Jung-Stilling, 30 issues (Nuremberg: Raw, 1795-1800);

H. C. Moser, ed., *Die praktisch-geometrische Aufnahme der Waldungen mit der Bousole und Meßkette,* foreword by Jung-Stilling (Leipzig: Gräff, 1797);

Friedrich de la Motte Fouqué, ed., *Die Jahreszeiten: Eine Vierteljahresschrift für romantische Dichtungen. Frühlings-Heft,* music by Jung-Stilling (Berlin: Hitzig, 1811);

Neues christliches Schatzkästlein auf alle Tage des Jahres in einer Auswahl biblischer Kernsprüche mit Liederversen, foreword by Jung-Stilling (Stuttgart: Steinkopf, 1816).

Johann Heinrich Jung used the name Henrich Stilling when, in his twenties, he wrote the first parts of his autobiography; he derived the name "Stilling" from the phrase "Stillen im Lande" (quiet in the land) of Psalm 35:20. He is best known today for his life story, in which he aimed to demonstrate providential guidance as the major motivating force in his life. Jung-Stilling, as he is generally called, was much influenced by a Protestant Pietism that gave priority to inner conviction rather than to the Bible. He was also familiar with the ideas of the Enlightenment and welcomed Immanuel Kant's attempt at reconciling reason with faith. As a university teacher Jung-Stilling published writings on socioeconomic subjects. His social and religious concerns, together with his emphasis on the family

and education, find ample expression in his autobiography and in the four novels he published from 1779 to 1785. His large-scale account of the development of a young man who becomes the leader of a new Christian community, *Das Heimweh* (Homesickness, 1794-1796), was widely read and of considerable influence. Although his narrative works, including short stories as well as novels, often show the central figure undergoing a series of trials and ordeals, they generally demonstrate the triumph of good over evil.

Jung-Stilling was born on 12 September 1740 in Grund, near Hilchenbach, Westphalia, to Johann Helman Jung, a farmer, tailor, surveyor, and schoolteacher, and Johanna Dorothea Katharina Fischer Jung. After teaching himself Latin and mathematics, at age fifteen he became a schoolteacher in the nearby town of Zellberg. Soon thereafter he left to become an assistant to a steel manufacturer in Plettenberg, then, in succession, a farmer in Stade, an apprentice and journeyman tailor, an apprentice to a merchant, a teacher again, and a private tutor to the children of a merchant in Rade. Acquaintance with a Catholic priest named Molitor who was also an ophthalmologist inspired him to study medicine at the University of Strasbourg from 1769 to 1772; there he met Johann Wolfgang Goethe and Johann Gottfried Herder. In addition to his medical studies, he took courses in forestry, economics, and public finance. In 1771 he married Christine Heyder, the daughter of a manufacturer in Ronsdorf; the couple had a son and a daughter. In 1772 he established a practice as an ophthalmologist in Elberfeld, quickly becoming celebrated for his cataract operations.

Henrich Stillings Jugend (Henrich Stilling's Childhood, 1777)–in the first four volumes of the autobiography Jung-Stilling calls his alter ego Henrich; in the later volumes, and in later editions of the earlier ones, the form *Heinrich* is used– is dominated by the protagonist's grandfather, Eberhard, a Westphalian farmer, and records his tolerance and affection in his reaction to his son Wilhelm's wish to marry Dortchen, a frail and sensitive girl. Her death from a fever leaves Henrich to be cared for by his grandmother. He spends much time with his grandfather, who fascinates him as a teller of tales about their ancestors; Eberhard's death marks the end of this part of the autobiography, which is enlivened by frequent passages of dialogue, two ballads, and an inserted story. Goethe, recognizing the quality of his erstwhile fellow student's manuscript, ar-

The house in Grund, Westphalia, where Jung-Stilling was born

ranged for its publication in 1777; it was an immediate success.

In 1778 Jung-Stilling became a professor of economics and public finance at the school of economics at Kaiserslautern. The same year two further installments of his autobiography appeared: *Henrich Stillings Jünglings-Jahre* (Henrich Stilling's Youth) and *Henrich Stillings Wanderschaft* (Henrich Stilling's Travels). At age fifteen, Henrich is looking forward to making his living as a teacher and a tailor. During the next few years he is in and out of teaching posts and is expected by his father to work at tailoring or farming when unemployed. Henrich is happier when reading or studying, and there are tensions between father and son. at Twenty-one Henrich leaves to try his luck as a journeyman tailor. Some weeks later he has a sudden, overwhelming religious experience: " ... von dem Augenblick an fühlte er eine unüberwindliche Neigung, ganz für die Ehre Gottes und das Wohl seiner Mitmenschen zu leben und zu sterben ... " (from that moment on he felt an irresistible inclination to live and to

die wholly for the glory of God and the well-being of his fellowmen . . .). For a time he works as a tailor's apprentice with Meister Isaak, who shares his religious views. Subsequently he becomes a private tutor in the household of Spanier, a businessman who in 1768 suggests to Henrich that he become a medical doctor. When Molitor, an old pastor, passes on to him the papers of his ophthalmic research, Henrich believes that he has received a sign from heaven. He becomes a medical student at Strasbourg, beset by financial problems but befriended and in part supported by Goethe, with whom he shares a critical view of the rationalism of the Enlightenment.

Die Geschichte des Herrn von Morgenthau (The Story of Lord von Morgenthau, 1779), Jung-Stilling's first novel, opens with the arrival of Morgenthau to live in an undeveloped and largely uninhabited valley in the Duchy of Hochbergen. Through his wisdom a thriving community comes into being. On one occasion he intervenes in person to apprehend three robbers, and the defiance and subsequent repentance of one of

First meeting of Jung-Stilling and Johann Wolfgang Goethe at the University of Strasbourg; drawing by Daniel Chodowiecki that was later engraved for use as the frontispiece in Jung-Stilling's Henrich Stillings Wanderschaft *(Goethe-Museum, Düsseldorf; Anton-und-Katharina Kippenberg-Stiftung)*

them, Falzbein, forms a story in itself. By marrying Johannette, Morgenthau becomes intimately connected with her family, whose senior member is pastor of the Reformed Church at Korndorf, the nearest sizeable locality; the marriage of Johannette's brother allows wider links of friendship to develop. The situation appears to be stable and well under Morgenthau's control; but after the death of Duke Philipp, the hostile aristocrat Löschbrand acquires influence, and members of Morgenthau's circle are subjected to severe harassment. Finally, Morgenthau is revealed

as the legitimate heir to the duchy, and all is well. There are many episodes and minor figures in the novel, and some exposition of religious and philosophical issues. Many tears are shed; the sensitive are vulnerable because of their virtue and probity. The establishment of the new community marks a withdrawal from wider society, especially from court life with its reprehensible standards of behavior. The characters tend to be idealized and are vehicles for the author's advocacy of maximum effort for the ethical transformation of society.

Jung-Stilling's wife died in 1781; the following year he married Selma von St. George, by whom he had a son and two daughters. His second novel, *Die Geschichte Florentins von Fahlendorn* (The Story of Florentin von Fahlendorn, 1781-1782), is more tidily constructed than the first novel and develops considerable elements of tension. It opens with the description of the sad fortitude of a ten-year-old boy in the Vosges mountains who has been left alone in the world after the death of his mother. His encounter with Rosine, a girl the same age as he, leads to his being provided with a good home. Florentin's intelligence and noble elevated spirit are brought to the attention of a generous nobleman, Baron von Beulenburg, who offers care and further education to Florentin and Rosine. In her twentieth year Rosine is stricken by melancholy, which Florentin interprets in the light of a premonition he has had that they are soon to be separated but will later be happily reunited. Shortly afterwards Florentin is impressed into the Dutch army and shipped to Surinam, where he is to serve for three years. Rosine too is tested: she is held against her will by Baron von Columbin, whose advances she steadfastly resists and from whom she eventually escapes. Florentin's experiences in Surinam form an exotic counterpart to the action taking place in Europe: Pilgersheim, a settlement established by a German colonist, is a model community where the principles of an ideal, liberal society are put into practice. Eventually Florentin and Rosine marry. Florentin's identity has been revealed by this time, and he has become entitled to a considerable inheritance; Rosine proves to be a capable household manager and a gifted supervisor of a school and orphanage. Toward the end the narrator sums up the work: "Es enthält ein Muster, wie die allerhöchste Vorsicht die Menschen zu ihrer wichtigen Bestimmung zu leiten pflegt" (It contains a pattern indicating how the highest Providence is accustomed to guide human beings to their significant destinies). This novel, like others of Jung-Stilling's, lays great stress on ethical teaching. Florentin and Rosine are to be viewed as models, the narrator says, for most young persons need guiding away from selfish to ethical behavior.

In *Leben der Theodore von der Linden* (Life of Theodore von der Linden, 1783) Dietrich von der Linden is a wealthy merchant who lives in seclusion. Though good-hearted, he is an impediment to the development of his children, Hans Jakob and Theodore. Dietrich is at first unhappy about Theodore's wooing by Ehrenfried, a young man from court circles, and about Hans Jakob's friendship with Clementine, Ehrenfried's sister; but a genuine friendship grows between Theodore and the Princess of Rheinau and her husband, Wilhelm, a considerate and just governor. An ideal and serene situation seems guaranteed; but there are hostile forces in Rheinau court life, as emerges dramatically with an attempt to poison the princess. Prince Wilhelm's brother, Albert, organizes a conspiracy which leads to Wilhelm's abdicating in favor of Albert. The villainy is finally exposed and punished, and the people of Rheinau are glad to have their former ruler back in charge: " . . . es [das Böse] ist das Läuterungsmittel, wodurch Gott so viele herrliche Menschen bildet und von allen Schlacken reinigt" (. . . it [evil] is the means of purification with which God fashions so many fine people and purifies them from all dross). The narrative implies acceptance of given social circumstances; bad princes have to be endured by their subjects.

In 1784 Jung-Stilling became professor of agriculture at the University of Heidelberg; another novel appeared the same year. *Theobald oder Die Schwärmer* (translated as *Theobald; or, The Fanatic*, 1846) centers on the religious sects that flourished in German Protestant lands in the eighteenth century. Jung-Stilling aims at a balanced assessment of these movements; he sees his own position as lying in the middle, between the extremes of misguided enthusiasm and disbelief. But his narrative certainly presents aspects of religious enthusiasm as damaging to the happiness of well-meaning people. Dietrich Theobald, a farmer's son, falls in love with a young woman of higher social status, Amalie von Wirthen, whom he meets during a church service led by a popular preacher; in their religious fervor it is some time before they realize that their fondness for each

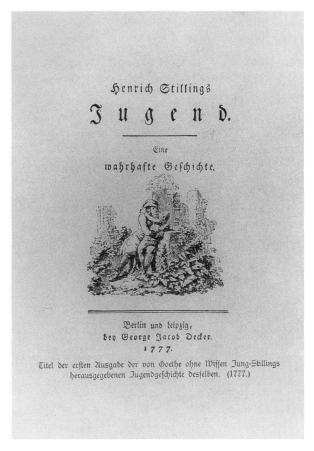

Title page for the first installment of Jung-Stilling's autobiography; Goethe arranged for its publication without knowing the identity of its author

other has a sexual basis. They marry and live quietly on Dietrich's farm. Their son Samuel then becomes the focal point of the action. The harshness of his early education–probably reflecting the secluded and severe conditions of the author's childhood under his father's tutelage–does not have a permanent effect on him; he goes on to study medicine, but his first years in practice are stressful, as were those of Jung-Stilling. Transferring to a different town, Samuel is wrongfully imprisoned because of the malice of members of the sect that is in power there. In a third locality he is again the victim of intrigues; but in due course his sterling qualities find recognition, and he eventually becomes a minister of the monarch.

Jung-Stilling moved in 1787 to Marburg University, where he taught finance and public administration. He brought his life story up to date in the next installment of his autobiography, *Henrich Stillings häusliches Leben* (Henrich Stilling's Domestic Life, 1789).

Jung-Stilling in later years; engraving by L. Schlemmer after a painting by Schröder

Performing his first operation for cataract on a poor woman, Henrich acquires a sense of mission and begins to use his skill widely, making no charge for his services. He is also reluctant to press his regular patients–most of whom are poorer members of the community–for payment of their bills, and in general he is a bad manager of money. In 1778 he takes a post at an academy that is being set up at Rittersburg (Kaiserslautern); his teaching responsibilities include agriculture, technology, commerce, and veterinary science. He is at first confronted by hostility, but he overcomes this problem. His wife, Christine, dies. His second wife, Selma, who has been introduced to him by the novelist Sophie von La Roche, takes over the financial management of his household. Henrich has become a busy academic, an opthalmic surgeon, and a widely known author. In 1787 he moves to a chair of financial and statistical science at Marburg University.

Selma Jung-Stilling died in 1790; shortly thereafter Jung-Stilling married Elisabeth Coing, by whom he had a son and three daughters. His next major work of fiction, the four-volume *Das Heimweh* (1794-1796), is the most ambitiously conceived of his novels. Eugenius leaves his home in rural Germany to go on a long pilgrimage. The

first two volumes of the novel are told in excerpts from Eugenius's diary and show him mainly under the influence of other people; in the two later volumes, after his marriage to Urania, Eugenius is in a position of influence over others, and an omniscient narrator is used. As he leaves home, Eugenius knows that his father is entrusting him to the care of a secret society which has control of underground rooms and passages whose existence is unknown to most people. The journey to the East begins with Eugenius and his servant Hans Ehrlich helping people in distress, though they also encounter worldly temptation. The two travelers are abducted in Hungary and regain their freedom in Constantinople. In Egypt Eugenius is abducted by Arabs and comes to admire their way of life. Nine months later he undergoes a series of fantastic ordeals as he explores the labyrinths in and under one of the Pyramids. Eugenius is now declared to be fully initiated. In secret subterranean quarters in Jerusalem he marries the ideal, noble Urania. His mood is "eine unaufhörliche Empfindung seiner Kleinheit und der Größe seiner Bestimmung" (a continuing feeling of his own smallness and of the greatness of his destiny). The novel now traces his caravan journey to Samarkand, where many European and non-European families come together under his administration to settle on virgin soil and establish the model state of Solyma. There is fear that ideas associated with the French Revolution and rationalism may undermine Eugenius's benevolent autocracy, but a threatened uprising is foiled. The news from Europe is of war-stricken gloom and a decline in traditional religious beliefs, but the essentials of European civilization are developing afresh in Solyma.

Jung-Stilling wrote a detailed commentary on *Das Heimweh*, titled *Der Schlüssel zum Heimweh* (The Key to *Das Heimweh*, 1796), which begins with his conviction that he himself had been the object of divine providential intervention just as Eugenius was guided by the secret society. Eugenius is the Christian church, while the Egyptian pyramids represent the greatest systems of philosophy; the many other characters and subsidiary stories in the novel are also provided with allegorical significance.

In 1803 Jung-Stilling returned to the University of Heidelberg as a professor of political science. The last completed installment of his autobiography, *Heinrich Stillings Lehr-Jahre* (Heinrich Stilling's Apprenticeship, 1804), begins with the protagonist choosing Elise Coing, a friend of

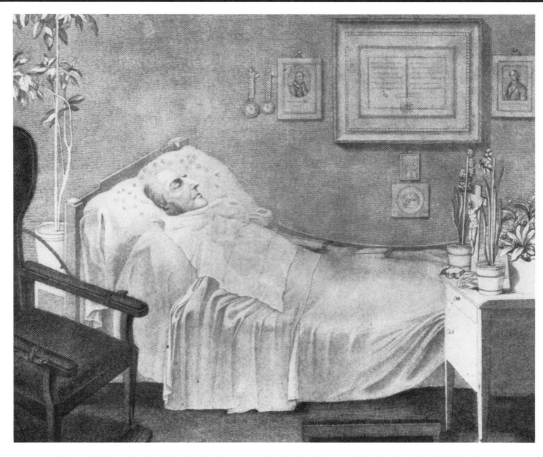

Jung-Stilling shortly after his death; engraving by A. Krüger of a drawing by G. Schmidt

Selma's, to be his third wife. Heinrich records the success of *Das Heimweh* and the unrest emanating from the French Revolution. Henrich's son Jakob with difficulty deflects his fellow students from assaulting Heinrich and his family. Heinrich becomes increasingly involved in religion and no longer finds his academic lecturing rewarding. His father dies in 1802 after a long period of disability. Shortly afterward Heinrich is offered a post at Heidelberg which, although financially less attractive than his position at Marburg, offers him greater freedom. Looking back on his life after sixty-three years, Heinrich affirms his conviction that he has been inspired throughout by divine guidance.

Jung-Stilling retired to Karlsruhe on a pension from the Margrave of Baden in 1806. In his later years he was active as a writer of short fiction. There are tales set in eighteenth-century Germany, describing problems facing the rural poor and their dependence on the good will of neighbors and local land owners; sometimes the devel-

opment of a protagonist takes him from a repressive early environment under a domineering father to substantial achievements and happiness in later life. The theme of the flight of refugees from the French Revolution to Germany, Austria, or North America is a recurring one. Some stories have an oriental background and include fairy-tale fantasy or allegory. Sometimes the author shows the encounters of fictitious characters with major figures of the New Testament. Jung-Stilling also wrote hymns based on Biblical stories and topics, as well as ballads with medieval settings in the manner of the Sturm und Drang movement.

Jung-Stilling was a vigorous opponent of the French Revolution; during the Napoleonic Wars he took a renewed interest in eschatological interpretations of the times. He was the confidant of the princes of Hessen-Cassel and Baden, and in later years he had some influence on the Russian Czar Alexander I. He also gave much of his time and energy to counseling ordinary people, seeing himself as an interpreter of religious and general issues for a wide public. He died in Karlsruhe on 2 April 1817. What was intended as the opening of another volume of autobiography exists as a fragment of a few pages describing the move to Heidelberg in 1803; it was published in 1817 as the beginning of *Heinrich Stillings Alter* (Heinrich Stilling's Old Age). Jung-Stilling's grandson, Wilhelm Schwarz, then takes up the narrative, concluding with his grandparents' illnesses in 1816 that led to their deaths within two weeks of each other in early 1817.

Max Geiger sums up Jung-Stilling's personality: "Arbeiten, Tätigsein, Wirken–und zwar immer für Gott, seine Sache und sein Reich–, darin sieht Johann Heinrich Jung seine lebensaufgabe beschlossen" (Work, activity, influence–and what is more, always for God, His cause and His kingdom influence–and what is–in this Johann Heinrich Jung sees his life's mission).

Letters:

Briefe Jung-Stillings an seine Freunde, edited by Alexander Vömel (Berlin: Weigandt & Grieben, 1905);
Briefe an Verwandte, Freunde und Fremde aus den Jahren 1787-1816, edited by Hans W. Panthel (Hildesheim: Gerstenberg, 1978).

References:

Max Geiger, *Aufklärung und Erweckung: Beiträge zur Erforschung Johann Henrich Jung-Stillings und der Erweckungstheologie* (Zurich: EVZ, 1963);
Hans R. G. Günther, *Jung-Stilling: Ein Beitrag zur Psychologie des Pietismus* (Munich: Federmann, 1848);
Erich Schick, *Jung-Stillings Heimweh und Heimat* (Basel: Majer, 1943);
Anne Marie Stenner-Pagenstecher, *Das Wunderbare bei Jung-Stilling: Ein Beitrag zur Vorgeschichte der Romantik* (Hildesheim, Zurich & New York: Olms, 1985);
Albrecht Willert, *Religiöse Existenzund literarische Produktion: Jung-Stillings Autobiographie und seine früheren Romane* (Frankfurt am Main & Bern: Lang, 1982).

Papers:

Johann Heinreich Jung-Stilling's papers are in the Stadtarchiv Siegen, the Landesbibliothek Dortmund, and the Basel University Library.

Immanuel Kant
(22 April 1724 - 12 February 1804)

John D. Simons
Florida State University

BOOKS: *Gedanken von der wahren Schätzung der lebendigen Kräfte und Beurtheilung der Beweise, deren sich Leibnitz und andere Mechaniker in dieser Streitsache bedient haben, nebst einigen vorhergehenden Betrachtungen, welche die Kraft der Körper überhaupt betreffen* (Königsberg: Dorn, 1747);

Allgemeine Naturgeschichte und Theorie des Himmels, oder Versuch von der Verfassung und dem mechanischen Ursprunge des ganzen Weltgebäudes, nach Newton'schen Grundsätzen abgehandelt, anonymous (Königsberg & Leipzig: Petersen, 1755); translated by William Hastie as *Universal Natural History and Theory of the Heavens* (Ann Arbor: University of Michigan Press, 1969);

Principiorum primorum cognitionis metaphysicae nova delucidatio (Königsberg: Hartung, 1755); translated by John A. Reuscher as "A New Exposition of the First Principles of Metaphysical Knowledge," in *Kant's Latin Writings*, edited by Lewis White Beck (New York: Lang, 1986), pp. 49-110;

Metaphysicae cum geometria junctae usus in philosophia naturali, cujus specimen I. continet monodologiam physicam (Königsberg: Hartung, 1756);

Geschichte und Naturbeschreibung der merkwürdigsten Vorfälle des Erdbebens, welches an dem Ende des 1755sten Jahres einen großen Theil der Erde erschüttert hat (Königsberg: Hartung, 1756);

Neue Anmerkungen zur Erläuterung der Theorie der Winde, wodurch er zugleich zu seinen Vorlesungen einladet (Königsberg: Driest, 1756);

Entwurf und Ankündigung eines Collegii der physischen Geographie nebst dem Anhange einer kurzen Betrachtung über die Frage: ob die Westwinde in unsern Gegenden darum feucht sind, weil sie über ein großes Meer streichen (Königsberg: Driest, 1757);

Neuer Lehrbegriff der Bewegung und Ruhe und der damit verknüpften Folgerungen in den ersten Gründen der Naturwissenschaft, wodurch zugleich seine Vorlesungen in diesem halben Jahre angekündigt werden (Königsberg: Driest, 1758);

Portrait by Döbler, 1791 (from George Whitney and David Bowers, eds., The Heritage of Kant, *1939)*

Versuch einiger Betrachtungen über den Optimismus, wodurch er zugleich seine Vorlesungen auf das bevorstehende halbe Jahr ankündigt (Königsberg: Driest, 1760);

Gedanken bei dem frühzeitigen Ableben des Herrn Johann Friedrich von Funck, in einem Sendschreiben an seine Mutter (Königsberg: Driest, 1760);

Die falsche Spitzfindigkeit der vier syllogistischen Figuren erwiesen (Königsberg: Kanter, 1762); translated by Thomas K. Abbott as "On the Mistaken Subtlety of the Four Syllogistic Figures," in his *Kant's Introduction to Logic* (London: Longmans, 1885), pp. 79-95;

Der einzig mögliche Beweisgrund zu einer Demonstration des Daseins Gottes (Königsberg: Kanter, 1763, actually 1762); translated by G. B. Kerferd and D. W. Wolford as *The Only Possible Ground for a Demonstration of the Existence of God* (New York: Barnes & Noble, 1968);

Versuch, den Begriff der negativen Größen in die Weltweisheit einzuführen (Königsberg: Kanter, 1763);

Beobachtungen über das Gefühl des Schönen und Erhabenen (Königsberg: Kanter, 1764); translated by John T. Goldthwait as *Observations on the Feeling of the Beautiful and Sublime* (Berkeley: University of California Press, 1960);

Nachricht von der Einrichtung seiner Vorlesungen im Winterhalbjahr (Königsberg: Kanter, 1765);

Träume eines Geistersehers, erläutert durch Träume der Metaphysik (Königsberg: Kanter, 1766); translated by Emanuel P. Goerwitz as *Dreams of a Spirit-Seer* (London: Sonnenschein, 1900; New York: Macmillan, 1900);

De mundi sensibilis atque intelligibilis forma et principiis (Königsberg: Hartung, 1770); translated by John Handyside, revised by Lewis White Beck, as "On the Form and Principles of the Sensible and the Intelligible World," in *Kant's Latin Writings*, edited by Beck (New York: Lang, 1986), pp. 145-194;

Von den verschiedenen Racen der Menschen, zur Ankündigung der Vorlesungen der physischen Geographie im Sommerhalbjahr (Königsberg: Hartung, 1775);

Kritik der reinen Vernunft (Riga: Hartknoch, 1781; revised, 1787); translated by J. M. D. Meiklejohn as *Critique of Pure Reason* (London: Bohn, 1855); translated by Norman Kemp Smith as *Immanuel Kant's Critique of Pure Reason* (London: Macmillan, 1929);

Prolegomena zu einer jeden künftigen Metaphysik, die als Wissenschaft wird auftreten können (Riga: Hartknoch, 1783); translated by John Richardson as *Prolegomena to Every Future Metaphysic* (London: Simpkin & Marshall, 1819); translated and edited by Beck as *Prolegomena to Any Future Metaphysic* (New York: Liberal Arts Press, 1950); translated and edited by P. G. Lucas as *Prolegomena to Any Future Metaphysics That Will Be Able To Present Itself*

as a Science (Manchester, U.K.: Manchester University Press, 1953);

Grundlegung zur Metaphysik der Sitten (Riga: Hartknoch, 1785; revised, 1786); translated by H. J. Paton as *The Moral Law* (London: Hutchinson, 1948); Paton translation republished as *Groundwork of the Metaphysic of Morals* (New York: Harper, 1948);

Metaphysische Anfangsgründe der Naturwissenschaft (Riga: Hartknoch, 1786); translated by James Ellington as *Metaphysical Foundations of Natural Science* (Indianapolis & New York: Bobbs-Merrill, 1970);

Kritik der praktischen Vernunft (Riga: Hartknoch, 1788); translated by Beck as *Critique of Practical Reason* (New York: Liberal Arts Press, 1956);

Ueber eine Entdeckung, nach der alle neue Kritik der reinen Vernunft durch eine ältere entbehrlich gemacht werden soll (Königsberg: Nicolovius, 1790);

Kritik der Urteilskraft (Berlin & Liebau: Lagarde & Friederich, 1790); translated by John Henry Bernard as *Critique of Judgement* (London & New York: Macmillan, 1892; revised, 1914); translated by James C. Meredith as *Kant's Critique of Aesthetic Judgement* (Oxford: Clarendon Press, 1911) and *Kant's Critique of Teleological Judgement* (Oxford: Clarendon Press, 1928); Meredith translations republished as *Critique of Judgement* (Oxford: Clarendon Press, 1957);

Die Religion innerhalb der Grenzen der bloßen Vernunft (Königsberg: Nicolovius, 1793); translated by Theodore M. Greene and Hoyt H. Hudson as *Religion within the Limits of Reason Alone* (Chicago: Open Court, 1934; revised by John R. Silber, La Salle, Ill.: Open Court / New York: Harper, 1960);

Zum ewigen Frieden: Ein philosophischer Entwurf (Königsberg: Nicolovius, 1795; enlarged, 1796); translated by Beck as *Perpetual Peace* (New York: Liberal Arts Press, 1957);

Die Metaphysik der Sitten, 2 volumes (Königsberg: Nicolovius, 1797); volume 1 partially translated by J. Ladd as *The Metaphysical Elements of Justice* (Indianapolis & New York: Liberal Arts Press, 1965); volume 2 translated by M. J. Gregor as *The Doctrine of Virtue* (New York: Harper, 1964), and by J. Ellington as *The Metaphysical Principles of Virtue* (Indianapolis & New York: Liberal Arts Press, 1964);

Der Streit der Fakultäten in drey Abschnitten (Königsberg: Nicolovius, 1798); partially translated

The original buildings of the University of Königsberg, in which Kant taught. The university was moved to other quarters in 1844.

by H. B. Nisbet as "The Contest of the Faculties," in *Kant's Political Writings*, edited by Hans Reiss (Cambridge: Cambridge University Press, 1970), pp. 177-190;

Ueber die Buchmacherei: Zwei Briefe an Hrn. Fr. Nicolai (Königsberg: Nicolovius, 1798);

Anthropologie in pragmatischer Hinsicht (Königsberg: Nicolovius, 1798); translated by Gregor as *Anthropology from a Pragmatic Point of View* (The Hague: Nijhoff, 1974);

Logik: Ein Handbuch zu Vorlesungen, edited by G. B. Jäsche (Königsberg: Nicolovius, 1800); translated by R. S. Hartman and W. Schwartz as *Kant's Logic* (Indianapolis & New York: Liberal Arts Press, 1974);

Kant's Werke, 10 volumes, edited by G. Hartenstein (Leipzig: Modes & Baumann, 1838-1839);

Sämmtliche Werke, 12 volumes, edited by Karl Rosenkranz and Friedrich Wilhelm Schubert (Leipzig: Voß, 1839-1840);

Sämmtliche Werke, 8 volumes, edited by Hartenstein (Leipzig: Voß, 1867-1868);

Kants gesammelte Schriften, 23 volumes, edited by the Prussian Academy of Sciences and the Berlin Academy of Sciences (Berlin: Reimer, 1900-1955);

Immanuel Kants Werke, 11 volumes, edited by Ernst Cassirer (Berlin: Cassirer, 1912);

Eine Vorlesung über Ethik, edited by P. Menzer (Berlin: Pan, 1924); translated by Louis Infield as *Lectures on Ethics* (London: Methuen, 1930; New York & London: Harper, 1963);

Sämtliche Werke, 10 volumes, edited by Karl Vorländer (Leipzig: Meiner, 1926).

Editions in English: *Essays and Treatises on Moral, Political, and Various Philosophical Subjects*, 2 volumes, translated by John Richardson (London: Richardson, 1798)—volume 1 includes "What is Enlightening," "The Groundwork of the Metaphysic of Morals," "The False Subtlety of the Four Syllogistic Figures Evinced," "On the Popular Judgment: That May be Right in Theory, But Does Not Hold in the Praxis," "Eternal Peace," "The Conjectural Beginning of the History of Man," "What Means: To Orient One's Self in Thinking," and "An Idea of an Universal Hisory in a Cosmopolitical View"; volume 2 includes "Observations on the Feeling of the Beautiful and the Sublime," "Something on the Influence of the Moon on the Temperature of the Air," "On the Volcanos in the Moon," "On the Failure of All the Philosophi-

Kant in 1768; portrait by I. B. Becker (from George Whitney and David Bowers, eds. The Heritage of Kant, *1939)*

cal Essays in the Theodicae," "The Religion Within the Sphere of Naked Reason," and "The End of All Things";

The Metaphysical Works, translated by Richardson (2 volumes, London: Simpkin & Marshall, 1819; enlarged, 3 volumes, 1836);

Theory of Ethics; or, Practical Politics, translated by Thomas K. Abbott (London: Longmans, 1873; revised and enlarged, 1883);

Principles of Politics, Including His Essay on Perpetual Peace, translated by William Hastie (London: Hamilton, 1891; New York: Scribners, 1891);

Critique of Practical Reason and Other Writings in Moral Philosophy, translated by Lewis White Beck (Chicago: University of Chicago Press, 1949);

Kant on History, translated by Beck (Indianapolis: Bobbs-Merrill, 1963);

Kant's Political Writings, edited by Hans Reiss (Cambridge: Cambridge University Press, 1970);

Perpetual Peace, and Other Essays on Politics, History, and Morals, translated by Ted Humphrey (Indianapolis: Hackett, 1983)–includes "Speculative Beginning of Human History" and "The End of All Things";

Kant's Latin Writings, edited by Beck (New York: Lang, 1986).

PERIODICAL PUBLICATIONS: "Idee zu einer allgemeinen Geschichte in weltbürgerlicher Absicht," *Berliner Monatsschrift,* 11 (November 1784): 386-410; translated by H. B. Nisbet as "Idea For a Universal History With a Cosmopolitan Purpose," in *Kant's Political Writings,* edited by Hans Reiss (Cambridge: Cambridge University Press, 1970), pp. 41-54;

"Beantwortung der Frage: Was ist Aufklärung?," *Berliner Monatsschrift,* 11 (December 1784): 481-494; translated by Lewis White Beck as "What Is Enlightenment?," in *Immanuel Kant: Philosophical Writings,* edited by Ernst Behler (New York: Continuum, 1986), pp. 263-269;

"Über die Vulkane im Monde," *Berliner Monatsschrift,* 12 (March 1785): 199-213;

"Über die Bestimmung des Begriffes einer Menschenrasse," *Berliner Monatsschrift,* 12 (November 1785): 390-417;

"Mutmaßlicher Anfang der Menschengeschichte," *Berliner Monatsschrift,* 13 (January 1786): 1-27;

"Was heißt: Sich im Denken orientieren?," *Berliner Monatsschrift,* 13 (October 1786): 304-330;

"Über das Mißlingen aller philosophischen Versuche in der Theodicee," *Berliner Monatsschrift,* 18 (September 1791): 194-225;

"Über den Gemeinspruch: Das mag in der Theorie richtig sein, taugt aber nicht für die Praxis," *Berliner Monatsschrift,* 22 (September 1793): 201-284; translated by E. B. Ashton as *On the Old Saying: That May Be True in Theory But It Won't Work in Practice* (Philadelphia: University of Pennsylvania Press, 1974);

"Etwas vom Einfluß des Mondes auf die Witterung," *Berliner Monatsschrift,* 23 (May 1794): 392-407;

"Das Ende aller Dinge," *Berliner Monatsschrift,* 23 (June 1794): 495-522.

Widely considered the foremost philosopher since classical antiquity, Immanuel Kant effected a revolution in philosophy. His influence on the development of science, theology, and philosophy is virtually incalculable. He offered solutions to problems that have always had the utmost relevance for the thinker: What are morality and duty? What are truth, beauty, and justice? What can and cannot be known? He clarified the difference between knowledge and faith and established the limits of each; in so doing, he liberated science from religion and religion from science. Then he freed individual conscience from outside authority by placing morality in the disposition of the individual heart. In addressing these and other problems, he terminated the one-sided intellectualism of the eighteenth century. Virtually all thinkers since then who have seriously tackled the fundamental principles in science, theology, and philosophy have done so by starting with ideas first developed by Kant.

Kant was born on 22 April 1724 in Königsberg (today Kaliningrad, U.S.S.R.) as the fourth of nine children, of whom five—two younger sisters, an older sister, and a brother—survived infancy. His father, Johann Georg, had learned the craft of harness making from his father and grandfather. His mother, the former Anna Regina Reuter, the daughter of a saddler, was born in Nuremberg. The future philosopher grew up in a blue-collar district on the edge of town among workers, craftsmen, and shopkeepers whose values revolved about hard work and religious piety.

Fortunately for the young Kant the family pastor, Franz Albert Schultz, was struck by his precocity and convinced the family to send him to school at the Collegium Fredericianum, of which Schultz was the principal. There Kant spent eight years—six days a week from seven in the morning until four in the afternoon—studying Latin, Greek, Hebrew, French, mathematics, and theology. After graduating second in his class, the sixteen-year-old Kant enrolled at the University of Königsberg, where his interest in philosophy and science was kindled by the talented professor Martin Knutzen. Kant spent seven years at the university but did not graduate, owing to financial hardship: his mother had died in 1737 and his father died in 1746. To support himself he had to drop out of school and serve as tutor to the children of well-to-do families in the vicinity of Königsberg. During these years he devoted his considerable free time to independent study and to writing a dissertation. In 1755 he returned to the university, successfully defended the disserta-

tion, and was given the post of Privatdozent (adjunct assistant professor), a lowly position with little prestige and no salary except for student fees. In these early years he taught about twenty-eight hours a week on a wide range of subjects, including philosophy, pedagogy, mathematics, physics, anthropology, mineralogy, and his favorite, physical geography. After classes he enjoyed reading the newspapers over coffee. In the evening he played cards and billiards, often arriving home after midnight mildly intoxicated. Circumstances forced him to live frugally in a one-room apartment furnished only with a bed, table, and chair; except for a silhouette of Jean-Jacques Rousseau, the walls were bare. To supplement his meager income he worked as assistant librarian in the royal castle.

Throughout the 1760s and 1770s he published books and essays on science, philosophy, morality, aesthetics, astronomy, logic, and metaphysics. He was popular with his students not only because his lectures were lively but also because of the many humorous remarks he interjected. Finally, in 1770 he was promoted to the chair of logic and metaphysics with a salary he could live on. As his reputation grew he received offers from other universities; some even promised to quadruple his salary. But in each case his refusal was categorical, imperative as it was for him to remain in the city of his birth: any change in his physical environment, including the arrangement of the furniture, made him uneasy. The following anecdote is typical. In the 1780s he developed the habit of gazing out the window at a distant church steeple as he worked or meditated. After a few years, trees growing in a neighbor's garden obscured the steeple. Kant began to fidget and become restless; he found that he was unable to work. The problem was resolved when the neighbor, who admired the famous man, readily agreed to trim the offending trees. Kant refused to travel. He never saw a mountain or the sea, although the Baltic was only an hour away.

The most important influences on the genesis of Kant's thought were religious, political, and scientific. He was raised in the Pietist tradition, a Protestant movement that emphasized simple piety, the acceptance of one's position in life, and indifference toward ritual and dogma. Politically, Kant was a man of the Enlightenment who spoke up for human rights, professed the equality of man, and advocated representative government. He was most profoundly influenced in these matters by the Swiss-French thinker and political theo-

Title page for Kant's epoch-making first critique, the work
in which he performed a "Copernican Revolution" in
philosophy by showing that the mind helps to create
the reality it experiences

retician Rousseau, who had raised profound questions on the social nature of morality and the problem of individual feeling. In science he studied the works of Sir Isaac Newton, which served as the basis for his lectures in physics and natural philosophy. In 1755 he published his famous vortex theory, which explains the origin of the universe from a rotating nebula. Today this theory is known as the Kant-Laplace hypothesis because in 1796 the French astronomer Pierre-Simon de Laplace published a similar, more-developed model.

Kant's greatest contributions, however, are not in pure science; he was interested in the logic of science, the limits of scientific knowledge, and the relationship of science to morality and religion. Kant opposed all purely abstract speculation. Any philosophy, he said, is suspect if it cannot show how the human mind can have the sort of knowledge that it actually does have. For this reason he was convinced that the major philosophical systems of the seventeenth and eighteenth centuries–rationalism and empiricism–were fundamentally flawed. The rationalists René Descartes, Baruch Spinoza, and Gottfried Wilhelm von Leibniz claimed that certain knowledge can be had only through pure reason–a priori–not through experience. The empiricists John Locke, George Berkeley, and David Hume insisted that all knowledge derives from and is bound by experience. When Kant began to develop his philosophical system, philosophy was polarized around this issue. He was convinced that neither view adequately explains scientific knowledge, which has both a priori and experiential components. In their place he offered his own "kritische Philosophie," which is contained in three monumental "Kritiken" (critiques). For eleven years he collected material and worked out his ideas in every detail; then he wrote out the first of these works, Kritik der reinen Vernunft (1781; translated as Critique of Pure Reason, 1855), in a few months. Such haste explains in large part the difficult and forbidding nature of the book's literary style, as Kant himself later admitted. In 1783 he published the shorter, more carefully composed Prologemena zu einer jeden künftigen Metaphysik (translated as Prologemena to Every Future Metaphysic, 1819), in which he explains the chief ideas of the Kritik der reinen Vernunft in clear terms. The book also serves as a good introduction to his philosophy in general.

In the Kritik der reinen Vernunft Kant argues at length why both rationalism and empiricism are partly right and partly wrong. The rationalists were correct in insisting that reason plays a fundamental role in knowledge, because reason gives form to experience. But they were wrong to exclude sensation, for without it the understanding is devoid of content. The empiricists were right in claiming that knowledge is limited to what can be experienced; but they were wrong to exclude reason, because it is the rational faculty that synthesizes and gives meaning to the material presented to it by the senses. Kant's great contribution to philosophy was to reconcile these views to virtually everyone's satisfaction. Knowledge, he says, is the product of sense and reason: without experience, or sensation, no object can be presented to the mind; without reason, nothing can be thought about. Sensation and understanding operate jointly to combine information and synthesize data into meaningful patterns.

Drawing of Kant by Püttrich (Willibald Klinke, Kant for Everyman, *translated by Michael Bullock [London: Routledge & Kegan Paul, 1951])*

In Kant's scheme the world consists strictly of appearances. That which causes these phenomena, "das Ding an sich" (the thing-in-itself or noumenon), lies beyond the bounds of perception and so is unknowable and incomprehensible. Nor can we arrive at certain knowledge of "das Ding an sich" through reason alone, because the attempt to go beyond the limits of experience leads to insoluable "antinomies," or contradictions, such as the demonstration that time and space are both finite and infinite. The only thing that can be known with certainty is the phenomenal world, the world as we perceive and understand it. Kant's revolutionary insight is that the world conforms to our minds, to our knowing process, not our minds to the world. We cannot know the world unless it is subjected to our patterns of knowing. If any aspect of the world does not restrict itself to our human sensory and intellectual apparatus, it has no existence for us. Metaphysics, therefore, is impossible. Among other things, this anthropocentric explanation makes human be-

ings, rather than divine revelation, the source of the meaning of the world.

When the volume appeared in 1781 it caused an upheaval in the world of philosophy. It was attacked from all sides. The most embittered reaction came from the powerful Wolffian school of philosophy, founded at Halle by the rationalist Christian Wolff, whose entire system of thought Kant had just demolished; enraged, the Wolffians launched two journals whose sole purpose was to refute Kant. The empiricists also flooded the philosophical journals with rebuttals; meanwhile, the popular philosopher Moses Mendelssohn was vainly trying to rescue the traditional philosophical proofs for the existence of God from Kant's criticism of such attempts to go beyond the limits of experience. A Kant fever swept through the German universities. At Jena in 1786 two students fought a duel over the philosopher. In some university towns the authorities became uneasy; in Marburg the local count pronounced Kantian philosophy subversive and forbade its teaching. Nevertheless, in a few years Kant's victory was complete, owing in no small part to the efforts of Johann Schultze and K. L. Reinhold, who recast the ideas of the *Kritik der reinen Vernunft* in simple, straightforward language and spread them throughout the European intellectual community.

Years of living frugally, increases in his salary, and honoraria for his publications enabled Kant in 1783 to buy a house on Prinzessinstraße and to hire a cook. (A few years previous he had employed as his footman Martin Lampe, a retired Prussian soldier remembered for his dullness). At this time Kant reorganized his daily routine, which changed little for the rest of his life. He subjected himself to the severest regimen to maintain his health, for he was a small, frail man with a delicate constitution. He arose punctually at five o'clock and drank a few cups of tea while he thought about the day's lectures. At seven he went downstairs to the room reserved as his classroom and taught until nine. Then he wrote until lunch, which always began precisely at one o'clock. He looked forward to this meal with keen anticipation, not only because it was the only one he permitted himself but because it was a social event. Since he thought conversation aided digestion, and he was gregarious by nature, there were always from three to nine guests—never fewer than the graces, never more than the muses, he explained. As he did not like to talk shop in his free time, he selected the guests

Kant's house in Königsberg (Willibald Klinke, Kant for Everyman, *translated by Michael Bullock [London: Routledge &*
Kegan Paul, 1951])

from a variety of occupations–politicians, doctors, lawyers, officers, merchants, students, colleagues, or anyone who happened to be passing through town and wanted to see him. The food was plentiful, the wine flowed freely, the atmosphere was casual, the conversation was stimulating. Women were not invited. This exclusion, coupled with his lifelong bachelorhood, led to speculation that he disliked women. This notion is incorrect. He often said about himself that when he needed a wife he was too poor to feed one, and when he was at last able to feed one he did not need one anymore.

After lunch came the famous walk, which he took every day regardless of the weather. It lasted precisely one hour, and the route rarely varied. He always walked alone, convinced that breathing through the mouth, which conversation necessitates, was unhealthy. This ritual was not without problems during the summer, for perspiration disgusted him; at the slightest indication he would seek out a shady spot and stand per-

fectly still until he was dry again. He spent the evening reading or writing. At precisely ten o'clock he went to bed. Unlike the rest of the house, the bedroom was never heated, even during frigid weather. The window was never opened, and he refused to keep a candle in the room; if he had to get up during the night he felt his way along a rope running from the bed to the door. When he was ready to fall asleep he always pronounced the name "Cicero" a few times.

Toward the end of the *Kritik der reinen Vernunft* Kant says that his entire philosophical system revolves around three questions. Their profundity is exceeded only by their simplicity: What can I know? What ought I to do? What may I hope for? The first question was explored in the first critique. The second and third are subjects of *Kritik der praktischen Vernunft* (1788; translated as *Critique of Practical Reason*, 1956), and the third is taken up again in *Kritik der Urteilskraft* (1790; translated as *Critique of Judgement*, 1892). In answering the question of what *ought* to be, he says

Kant hosting one of his famous lunches in 1786; painting by E. Dörstling (from George Whitney and David Bowers, eds.,
The Heritage of Kant, *1939)*

that instead of our actions conforming to the facts—the situations in which we find ourselves or the inclinations we happen to have–they should conform to our principles. These principles are derived from reason. A true moral act, he says, depends on the motive of the action, not on the outcome. The only motive that is good in itself, without qualification, is the good will: that is, the desire to act according to duty. Duty is discovered by reason and is the same for everyone at all places and at all times. He formulates the moral law in his famous categorical imperative: "Handle, so daß die Maxime deines Willens jederzeit zugleich als Prinzip einer allgemeinen Gesetzgebung gelten könnte" (Act in such a way that the principle of your will could at any time also become the principle of a universal law). In other words, if an action could not be made universal without contradicting itself, that action is immoral.

Kant illustrates this principle with the example of the false promise. To get himself out of a financial difficulty, a person proposes to borrow some money. He knows that he will never be able to pay the money back, but he also knows that he will not receive the loan unless he promises to repay the lender. Should he, then, falsely promise to pay the money back? A moment's reflection shows that if such an action were made universal–if *everyone* made false promises–the institution of promising would go out of existence, because no one would accept a promise anymore. Thus the false promise would, if made universal, negate or contradict itself; and self-contradiction is the epitome of irrationality. Immorality, then, is equivalent to irrationality. From this first formulation of the categorical imperative Kant derives a second: we should treat all human beings–including ourselves–as ends in themselves, never merely as means. From the categorical imperative follows the moral condemnation of slavery and war, and the demand for equality and representative government. Kant also says that the moral will must be *autonomous*–that is, no behavior can be moral unless it is the result of free choice. If a person is induced or compelled to act in accor-

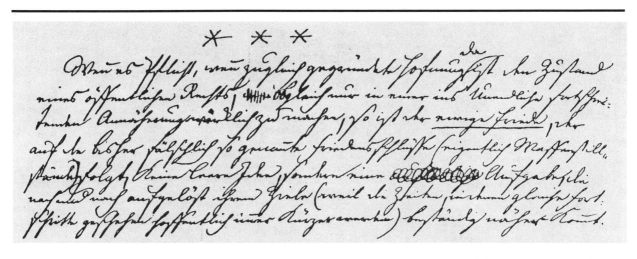

Passage from the manuscript for Kant's 1795 essay Zum ewigen Frieden *(Gustav Könnecke,* Bilderatlas zur Geschichte der deutschen Nationallitteratur *[Graz: Akademische Druck- und Verlagsanstalt, 1981])*

dance with duty—such as through the promise of reward or punishment—he is not acting through a sense of self-legislation. When we act for purposes outside ourselves, we are not free. Only when the will operates in harmony with universal principles that it has created for itself is it self-ruling. Morality makes no sense unless we are free; thus, even though as phenomena we are part of nature and therefore subject to universal physical causation, we are entitled to believe that as Dinge an sich we are free.

Kant argues that we do not need religion to act morally; the categorical imperative is enough. Whatever is done merely to please God is false virtue. Yet we need the idea of God to make the concept of moral perfection thinkable. Also, our moral sense demands that virtue and happiness be conjoined, but we see that this conjunction rarely occurs in this life; thus our moral sense demands that there be a life to come and a God to effect the conjunction of virtue and happiness in that life. Finally, the moral person strives to bring his desires into perfect harmony with his duty; but this is a process that can only be accomplished in an infinite amount of time. Thus, again, morality makes no sense unless there is immortality. Hence, morality leads to religion in that it is the moral law which justifies belief in God and immortality. In the *Kritik der reinen Vernunft* Kant had demonstrated that we can have no certain knowledge of the immortality of the soul or proof of the existence of God, because these matters lie beyond experience. But the *Kritik der praktischen Vernunft* asserts that we have the right, even the duty, to have faith in a su-

preme being and a life to come if we intend to take morality seriously.

The last of the major works on which Kant's fame rests is *Kritik der Urteilskraft*. In the first part he discusses aesthetic judgment, in the second mechanistic and teleological judgment. When we call something—a painting or a sunset, for example—beautiful, it is because the object creates a pleasurable sensation, which derives from the harmonious interplay of the sensate and rational faculties. This condition can arise only if the object is devoid of purpose, transcending any notion of usefulness or gain on the part of the beholder. A sunset cannot be bought, sold, eaten, or traded in on a new model. Beauty is pure "Wohlgefallen ohne Interesse" (disinterested pleasure). Whereas beauty is based on harmony between the rational and the sensate, the sublime is based on their conflict. This conflict occurs when ethical principles collide with and defeat such deterministic forces as fear, inclination, or even self-preservation, as, for example, when we contemplate a violent storm or a raging sea. The victory over these forces evokes in the spectator the pleasurable awareness of the superiority of his reason and the dominion it has over the senses.

In the second part of the critique Kant distinguishes between two kinds of judgment, the mechanistic and the teleological. Man is both Ding an sich and phenomenon and so lives both in the world of freedom and in the world of determinism. Since man has the capacity to conceive of goals and direct his actions toward them, he is telic; but man is also part of nature and so is determined, subject to mechanistic forces beyond his

Front and side views of a bust of Kant, executed in 1801 by Friedrich Hagemann (Willibald Klinke, Kant for Everyman, *translated by Michael Bullock [London: Routledge & Kegan Paul, 1951])*

control. These diametrically opposed facts can be reconciled through "zweckmäßige Urteile" (purposive judgments). Science seeks to systematize its findings so as to reflect a unity and purpose in nature, as if it were designed by a creator; it is impossible to know if there really is a purpose in nature, but it is necessary to ascribe one to it if we are to make sense of it. Yet Kant rejects the notion that purpose is one of the categories by which we understand the world: teleological explanations are prescientific, typical of the Middle Ages (it rains so that the plants will grow). The notion of purposiveness in nature finds its most satisfying explanation in God, though this does not prove His existence. Kant regards man's need to see purpose in nature and to have faith in God as a moral one: if man can regard the world as a stage for his actions, then he is able to view both himself and the world as having been created for some higher purpose and therefore as meaningful. Only in this way can man feel at home in nature.

In the 1790s Kant felt secure enough to attack some ideas long cherished by the state and church. "Über den Gemeinspruch: Das mag in der Theorie richtig sein, taugt aber nicht für die Praxis" (1793; translated as "On the Popular Judgment: That May Be Right in Theory, But Does not Hold in the Praxis," 1798) is concerned with morality, right, and the condemnation of despotism. The state, he says, has no right to decide for its subjects what happiness is and how to pursue it; each person must decide these issues for himself. Even more provocative is "Das Ende aller Dinge" (1794; translated as "The End of All Things," 1798), a masterpiece of philosophical irony that pokes fun at such dogmas as the Last Judgment: to believe in this doctrine is to believe that all creation has been without purpose. Kant parodies the Garden of Eden myth, comparing Earth to a latrine where the offal from other worlds is sent. Such essays infuriated and frightened the authorities. Across the Rhine the French Revolution was raging. The French king

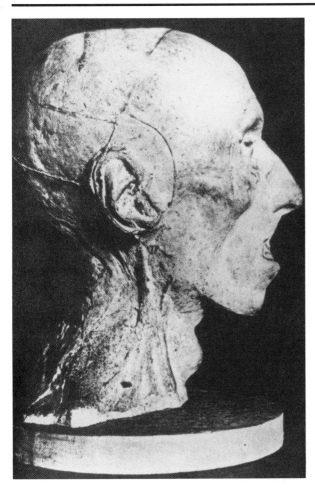

Kant's death mask (Uwe Schultz, Immanuel Kant *[Reinbek: Rowohlt, 1965])*

had been guillotined, the Church was being destroyed, institutions heretofore thought timeless were being swept away. The Prussian authorities had every reason to fear that Kant and other popular German thinkers who had made no secret of their admiration for the French Revolution might ignite a similar situation in their own country. The problem for the government was how to silence the world-famous man without appearing ridiculous. After much hesitation it was decided that Kant would receive a secret letter from King Friedrich Wilhelm II threatening him with unpleasant consequences if he did not desist from ridiculing the Church. The philosopher felt it was his duty to obey the sovereign and promised not to publish any more about religion. But when the king died in 1797, Kant felt free to resume his criticism, since the promise had been made to Friedrich Wilhelm alone.

In 1796, at the age of seventy-two, Kant gave his last lectures. He continued to write and publish until 1800, when the disabilities of old

age made work impossible. His hearing and sight began to fail. Judging from contemporary descriptions of his health, the philosopher was also suffering from Alzheimer's disease. He displayed the classic symptoms of the malady: short-term memory loss and the inability to recognize relatives and close friends. His health and mind deteriorated steadily until his death on 12 February 1804.

Contrary to Kant's wishes for a simple funeral, the entire city took part. He lay in state for sixteen days. Twenty-four students served as pallbearers; they were followed by thousands of citizens, including the entire officer corps of the garrison. At the cathedral the procession was received by the university senate. After the eulogy Kant was buried in the north wall of the cathedral.

The most prominent German philosophers of the late eighteenth and nineteenth centuries–Johann Gottlieb Fichte, Friedrich von Schelling, Georg W. F. Hegel, and Arthur Schopenhauer–all based their systems on Kant's philosophy but modified it considerably. In literature, Kant's most apparent influence is found in Friedrich von Schiller, Johann Wolfgang von Goethe, Wilhelm von Humboldt, and Heinrich von Kleist. Thanks to the efforts of Samuel Taylor Coleridge, Kant was widely recognized and studied in England and later in North America. In the middle of the nineteenth century interest in him decreased, only to rise even higher toward the end of the century when Neo-Kantian movements arose in Marburg and Heidelberg. Unlike the idealists Fichte, Schelling, and Hegel, the Neo-Kantians strove to work only within the philosophical limits set by Kant and to use his system primarily as a means for elucidating Newtonian physics. In 1896 an international Kant society was established; its journal, *Kant-Studien*, is devoted to the study of his thought and influence.

During the first half of the twentieth century interest once again declined, owing to developments in logic instigated by Alfred North Whitehead and Bertrand Russell. The philosophy of science veered toward positivism, while the ethics of William James, G. E. Moore, and John Dewey were at odds with the moral theory of the German philosopher. After World War II interest in Kant increased once again. He is now studied with an intensity accorded few other philosophers.

Letters:
Kant: Philosophical Correspondence 1759-99, edited

117

Kant's tomb at the Königsberg Cathedral (Willibald Klinke, Kant for Everyman, *translated by Michael Bullock [London: Routledge & Kegan Paul, 1951])*

by Arnulf Zweig (Chicago: University of Chicago Press, 1967);

Briefe, edited by Jürgen Zehbe (Göttingen: Vanderhoeck & Ruprecht, 1970).

Bibliographies:

Erich Adickes, *German Kantian Bibliography of Writings by and on Kant* (Würzburg: Liebing, 1896);

Ralph C. S. Walker, *A Selective Bibliography on Kant,* second edition (Oxford: Sub-Faculty of Philosophy, 1978);

Gernot U. Gabel, *Immanuel Kant: Eine Bibliographie der Dissertationen aus den deutschsprachigen Ländern 1900-1975* (Hamburg: Edition Gemini, 1980).

Biographies:

Ludwig Borowski, *Darstellung des Lebens und Cha-*

rakters Immanuel Kants (Königsberg: Nicolovius, 1804);

R. B. Jachmann, *Immanuel Kant, geschildert in Briefen an einen Freund* (Königsberg: Nicolovius, 1804);

E. A. C. Wasianski, *Immanuel Kant in seinen letzten Lebensjahren* (Königsberg: Nicolovius, 1804);

Thomas de Quincey, "The Last Days of Immanuel Kant," in *The Collected Writings of Thomas de Quincey,* 12 volumes, edited by David Masson (Edinburgh: Black, 1890), IV: 323-379;

Ernst Cassirer, *Kants Leben und Lehre* (Berlin: Cassirer, 1918);

Uwe Schultz, *Immanuel Kant in Selbstzeugnissen und Bilddokumenten* (Hamburg: Rowohlt, 1965);

Karl Jaspers, *Kant: Leben, Werk, Wirkung* (Munich: Piper, 1975);

Ralph C. S. Walker, *Kant* (London: Routledge & Kegan Paul, 1978).

Kant's gravestone

References:

Erich Adickes, *Kant und das Ding an sich* (Hildesheim: Olms, 1977);

Michael Albrecht, *Kants Antinomie der praktischen Vernunft* (Hildesheim: Olms, 1978);

Henry W. Allison, *Kant's Transcendental Idealism* (New Haven: Yale University Press, 1983);

Hannah Arendt, *Lectures on Kant's Political Philosophy* (Brighton, U.K.: Harvester Press, 1982);

Karl Aschenbrenner, *A Companion to Kant's Critique of Pure Reason: Transcendental, Aesthetic and Analytic* (Lanham, Md. & London: University Press of America, 1983);

Bruce Aune, *Kant's Theory of Morals* (Princeton: Princeton University Press, 1980);

Thomas Auxter, *Kant's Moral Teleology* (Macon, Ga.: Mercer University Press, 1982);

Peter Bachmaier, *Wittgenstein und Kant: Versuch zum Begriff des Transzendentalen* (Frankfurt am Main: Lang, 1978);

Lewis White Beck, *A Commentary on Kant's "Critique of Practical Reason"* (Chicago: University of Chicago Press, 1960);

Beck, ed., *Kant Studies Today* (La Salle, Ill.: Open Court, 1969);

Gordon G. Brittan, *Kant's Theory of Science* (Princeton: Princeton University Press, 1978);

C. D. Broad, *Kant: An Introduction* (Cambridge: Cambridge University Press, 1978);

Peter Burg, *Kant und die französische Revolution* (Berlin: Duncker & Humblot, 1974);

Edward Caird, *The Critical Philosophy of Immanuel Kant*, 2 volumes (Amsterdam: Rodopi, 1969);

Ernst Cassirer, *Das Erkenntnisproblem in der Philosophie und Wissenschaft der neueren Zeit*, 2 volumes (Berlin: Cassirer, 1911);

Cassirer, *Kants Leben und Lehre* (Berlin: Cassirer, 1918);

H. W. Cassirer, *A Commentary on Kant's Critique of Judgement* (London: Methuen, 1938);

Cassirer, *Kant's First Critique: An Appraisal of the Permanent Significance of Kant's Critique of Pure Reason* (London: Harvester Press, 1978);

Francis Xavier Jerome Coleman, *The Harmony of Reason: A Study in Kant's Aesthetics* (Pittsburgh: University of Pittsburgh Press / London: Feffer & Simons, 1974);

Samuel Taylor Coleridge, *Biographica Literaria* (Bristol: Fenner, 1817);

J. Gray Cox, *The Will at the Crossroads: A Reconstruction of Kant's Moral Philosophy* (Lanham, Md. & London: University Press of America, 1984);

D. W. Crawford, *Kant's Aesthetic Theory* (Madison: University of Wisconsin Press, 1974);

Friedrich Delekat, *Immanuel Kant: Historisch-kritische Interpretation der Hauptschriften* (Heidelberg: Quelle & Meyer, 1966);

Gilles Deleuze, *Kant's Critical Philosophy: The Doctrine of the Faculties* (London: Athlone, 1984);

Alwin Diemer, *Gesamtregister der Kant-Studien* (Meisenheim: Hain, 1969);

J. N. Findlay, *Kant and the Transcendental Object: A Hermeneutic Study* (Oxford: Clarendon Press, 1981);

Gerhard Funke, *Von der Aktualität Kants* (Bonn: Bouvier, 1979);

William A. Galston, *Kant and the Problem of History* (Chicago & London: University of Chicago Press, 1975);

Arsenij Gulyga, *Immanuel Kant: His Life and Thought* (Boston: Birkhäuser, 1987);

Paul Guyer, *Kant and the Claims of Taste* (Cambridge & London: Harvard University Press, 1979);

Martin Heidegger, *Die Frage nach dem Ding: Zu Kants Lehre von den transzendentalen Grundsätzen* (Tübingen: Niemeyer, 1962);

Heidegger, *Kant und des Problem der Metaphysik* (Bonn: Cohen, 1929);

Otfried Höffe, *Immanuel Kant* (Munich: Beck, 1983);

Brigitte Högemann, *Die Idee der Freiheit und das Subjekt: Eine Untersuchung von Kants Grundlegung zur Metaphysik der Sitten* (Königstein: Forum Academicum, 1980);

Karl Jaspers, *Drei Gründer des Philosophierens: Plato, Augustin, Kant* (Stuttgart: Piper, 1957);

Friedrich Kaulbach, *Das Prinzip Handlung in der Philosophie Kants* (Berlin: De Gruyter, 1978);

John Kemp, *The Philosophy of Kant* (Oxford: Oxford University Press, 1968);

Israel Knox, *The Aesthetic Theories of Kant, Hegel and Schopenhauer* (Brighton, U.K.: Harvester Press, 1978);

Johann-Heinrich Königshausen, *Kants Theorie des Denkens* (Amsterdam: Rodopi, 1977);

Stephen Körner, *Kant* (Harmondsworth, U.K.: Penguin, 1955);

Frieder Lötzsch, *Vernunft und Religion im Denken Kants: Lutherisches Erbe bei Immanuel Kant* (Cologne: Böhlau, 1976);

J. D. McFarland, *Kant's Concept of Teleology* (Edinburgh: University of Edinburgh Press, 1970);

Gordon Nagel, *The Structure of Experience: Kant's System of Principles* (Chicago & London: University of Chicago Press, 1983);

H. J. Paton, *The Categorical Imperative* (London: Hutchinson, 1958);

Friedrich Paulsen, *Immanuel Kant: His Life and Doctrine* (London: Nimmo, 1902);

Frank Peddle, *Thought and Being: Hegel's Criticism of Kant's System of Cosmological Ideas* (Washington, D.C.: University Press of America, 1980);

T. N. Pelegrinis, *Kant's Conceptions of the Categorical Imperative and the Will* (London: Zeno, 1980);

Robert B. Pippin, *Kant's Theory of Form: An Essay on the Critique of Pure Reason* (New Haven & London: Yale University Press, 1982);

Gerold Prauss, *Kant über Freiheit als Autonomie* (Frankfurt am Main: Klostermann, 1983);

Prauss, *Kant und das Problem der Dinge an sich* (Bonn, 1974);

Olivier Reboul, *Nietzsche: Critique de Kant* (Paris: Presses universitaires de France, 1974);

K. L. Reinhard, *Briefe über die Kantische Philosophie*, 2 volumes (Leipzig: Göschen, 1790-1792);

John Sallis, *The Gathering of Reason* (Athens: Ohio University Press, 1980);

Ernst Sandvoss, *Immanuel Kant: Leben, Werk, Wirkung* (Stuttgart: Kohlhammer, 1983);

Johann Schulze, *Erläuterungen über des Herrn Prof. Kant. Kritik der reinen Vernunft* (Königsberg: Hartung, 1789);

Schulze, *Prüfung der Kantischen Critik der reinen Vernunft* (Königsberg: Hartung, 1789);

Roger Scruton, *Kant* (Oxford: Oxford University Press, 1982);

Susan Meld Shell, *The Rights of Reason: A Study of Kant's Philosophy and Politics* (Toronto: University of Toronto Press, 1980);

P. F. Strawson, *The Bounds of Sense: An Essay on Kant's "Critique of Pure Reason"* (London: Methuen, 1973);

A. H. Smith, *Kantian Studies* (Oxford: Clarendon Press, 1947);

Norman Kemp Smith, *A Commentary to Kant's Critique of Pure Reason*, second edition (London: Macmillan, 1923);

Karl Vorländer, *Kant, Fichte, Hegel und der Sozialismus* (Berlin: Cassirer, 1920);

Vorländer, *Kant, Schiller, Goethe* (Leipzig: Dürr, 1907);

William Henry Walsh, *Kant's Criticism of Metaphysics* (Edinburgh: Edinburgh University Press, 1975);

W. H. Werkmeister, ed., *Reflections on Kant's Philosophy* (Gainesville: University Presses of Florida, 1975);

Leo Henri Wilde, *Hypothetische und kategorische Imperative: Eine Interpretation zu Kants "Grundlegung zur Metaphysik der Sitten"* (Bonn: Bouvier, 1975);

T. E. Wilkerson, *Kant's Critique of Pure Reason: A Commentary for Students* (Oxford: Clarendon Press, 1976);

Howard L. Williams, *Kant's Political Philosophy* (Oxford: Blackwell, 1983);

T. C. Williams, *The Concept of the Categorical Imperative* (Oxford: Oxford University Press, 1968);

Allan W. Wood, *Kant's Rational Theology* (Ithaca & London: Cornell University Press, 1978).

Papers:

After Kant's death his papers were deposited in the Königsberg university and city libraries, and an exhibit with memorabilia was set up in the library of the royal castle. Virtually all of the papers were destroyed during the thousand-bomber air raid of 29-30 August 1944. The re- maining fraction is deposited at the Bayerische Staatsbibliothek in Munich.

Friedrich Maximilian Klinger
(17 February 1752 - 25 February 1831)

Edward P. Harris
University of Cincinnati

BOOKS: *Otto: Ein Trauerspiel*, anonymous (Leip- zig: Weygand, 1775; edited by B. Seuffert, Nendeln, Liechtenstein: Kraus, 1968);

Das leidende Weib: Ein Trauerspiel, anonymous (Leip- zig: Weygand, 1775);

Die neue Arria: Ein Schauspiel, anonymous (Berlin: Mylius, 1776); translated anonymously as *The Modern Arria: A Tragedy in Five Acts* (Lon- don: Boosey & Escher, 1795);

Simsone Grisaldo: Ein Schauspiel in fünf Aufzügen, anonymous (Berlin: Mylius, 1776);

Sturm und Drang: Ein Schauspiel (Berlin: Decker, 1776; edited by Jörg-Ulrich Fechner, Stutt- gart: Reclam, 1970); translated by Betty Senk Waterhouse as *Storm and Stress*, in *Five Plays of the Sturm und Drang*, edited by Water- house (University Park: Pennsylvania State University Press, 1978), pp. 145-189;

Der verbannte Götter-Sohn: Erste Unterhaltung, anon- ymous (Gotha: Ettinger, 1777);

Orpheus: Eine tragisch-komische Geschichte, anony- mous, 5 volumes (Geneva: Legrand [actual- ly Basel: Thurneysen], 1778-1780); revised as *Bambinos sentimentalisch-politische, comisch- tragische Geschichte: Korrekte, umgearbeitete und vollendete Ausgabe. Erster Theil* (St. Peters- burg: Tornow / Leipzig: Kriele, 1791);

Prinz Seiden-Wurm der Reformator oder Die Kron- Kompetenten: Ein moralisches Drama aus dem fünften Theil des Orpheus, anonymous (Ge- neva: Legrand [actually Basel: Thurneysen], 1780);

Prinz Formosos Fiedelbogen und der Prinzessin Sana- clara Geige, oder Geschichte des großen Königs: Vom Verfasser des Orpheus, anonymous, 2 vol-

Friedrich Maximilian Klinger; engraving by Mayr based on a painting by Guttenbrun

umes (Geneva: Legrand [actually Basel: Thurneysen], 1780);

Der Derwisch: Eine Komödie in fünf Aüfzugen, anony- mous (Basel: Serini, 1780);

Stilpo und seine Kinder: Ein Trauerspiel in fünf Akten (Basel: Thurneysen, 1780);

Plimplamplasko der hohe Geist (heut Genie): Eine Handschrift aus den Zeiten Knipperdollings und Doctor Martin Luthers. Zum Druck befördert von einem Dilettanten der Wahrheit; und mit Kupfern geziert von einem Dilettanten der Kunst, anonymous, by Klinger, Jakob Sarasin, and Johann Kaspar Lavater (Basel: Thurneysen, 1780; edited by Peter Pfaff, Heidelberg, 1966);

Die falschen Spieler: Ein Lustspiel in fünf Aufzügen (Vienna: Kurzbeck, 1782);

Elfride: Eine Tragödie (Basel: Thurneysen, 1783);

Die Geschichte vom goldenen Hahn: Ein Beytrag zur Kirchen-Historie, anonymous (Gotha: Ettinger, 1785); revised as *Sahir, Eva's Erstgeborener im Paradiese: Ein Beytrag zur Geschichte der europäischen Kultur und Humanität*, anonymous (Tiflis [actually Riga: Hartknoch], 1798);

Theater, 4 volumes (Riga: Hartknoch, 1786-1787)—comprises volume 1 (1786): *Konradin, Die Zwillinge, Die falschen Spieler*; volume 2 (1786): *Der Schwur, Die neue Arria, Sturm und Drang*; volume 3 (1787): *Medea in Korinth, Medea auf dem Kaukasos, Der Derwisch, Stilpo*, "Anhang: Scenen aus *Pyrrhus*," *Der verbannte Götter-Sohn*; volume 4 (1787): *Der Günstling, Simsone Grisaldo, Elfride*;

Neues Theater, 2 volumes (St. Petersburg: Tornow / Leipzig: Jacobäer, 1790)—comprises volume 1: *Aristodemos, Roderico*, "Fragment [from *Pyrrhus Leben und Tod*]"; volume 2: *Damokles, Die zwo Freundinnen*;

Oriantes: Ein Trauerspiel in fünf Akten, anonymous (Frankfurt am Main & Leipzig: Jacobäer, 1790);

Medea in Korinth und Medea auf dem Kaukasos: Zwey Trauerspiele (St. Petersburg & Leipzig: Kriele [actually Leipzig: Jacobäer], 1791);

Fausts Leben, Thaten und Höllenfahrt in fünf Büchern (St. Petersburg: Kriele [actually Leipzig: Jacobäer], 1791; revised and enlarged, 1794); translated by George Borrow as *Faustus: His Life, Death, and Descent into Hell* (London: Simpkin & Marshall, 1825);

Geschichte Giafers des Barmeciden: Ein Seitenstück zu Fausts Leben, Thaten und Höllenfahrt, 2 volumes (St. Petersburg [actually Leipzig: Jacobäer], 1792-1794; revised and enlarged edition, N.p., 1810);

Geschichte Raphaels de Aquillas in fünf Büchern: Ein Seitenstück zu Fausts Leben, Thaten und Höllen-

fahrt (St. Petersburg [actually Leipzig: Jacobäer], 1793; revised and enlarged edition, Leipzig, 1799);

Auswahl aus Friedrich Maximilian Klingers dramatischen Werken, 2 volumes (Leipzig: Jacobäer, 1794);

Reisen vor der Sündfluth, anonymous (Bagdad [actually Riga: Hartknoch], 1795); 2 volumes, translated anonymously as *Travels before the Flood: An Interesting Oriental Record* (London: Johnson, 1796);

Der Faust der Morgenlaender oder Wanderungen Ben Hafis, Erzaehlers der Reisen vor der Sündfluth, anonymous (Bagdad, 1797 [actually Riga: Hartknoch, 1796]);

Der Schwur gegen die Ehe: Ein Lustspiel in fünf Akten (Riga: Hartknoch, 1797);

Geschichte eines Teutschen der neuesten Zeit, anonymous (Leipzig: Hartknoch, 1798);

Der Weltmann und der Dichter (Leipzig: Hartknoch, 1798);

Betrachtungen und Gedanken über verschiedene Gegenstände der Welt und der Litteratur: Nebst Bruchstücken aus einer Handschrift, 3 volumes (volumes 1-2, Cologne: Hammer; volume 3, St. Petersburg: Hammer [actually Leipzig: Hartknoch], 1803-1805);

F. M. Klingers Werke, 12 volumes (Königsberg: Nicolovius, 1809-1816);

Fried. Max. Klingers sämmtliche philosophische Romane, 12 volumes (Vienna, 1810);

Sämmtliche Werke (12 volumes, Stuttgart & Tübingen: Cotta, 1842; reprinted, 4 volumes, Hildesheim & New York: Olms, 1976);

Ausgewählte Werke, 8 volumes (Stuttgart: Cotta, 1878-1880);

Friedrich Maximilian Klingers Dramatische Jugendwerke, 3 volumes, edited by Hans Berendt and Kurt Wolff (Leipzig: Rowohlt, 1912-1913);

Werke in zwei Bänden, 2 volumes, edited by Hans Jürgen Geerdts (Weimar: Aufbau, 1958);

Werke: Historisch-kritische Gesamtausgabe, 24 volumes projected, 5 volumes to date, edited by Sander L. Gilman and others (Tübingen: Niemeyer, 1978-).

OTHER: *Die Zwillinge: Ein Trauerspiel in fünf Aufzügen*, in *Hamburgisches Theater*, volume 1, edited by Friedrich Ludwig Schröder (Hamburg: Bode, 1776), pp. 1-88.

PERIODICAL PUBLICATIONS: "Scenen aus Pyrrhus' Leben und Tod, einem Schauspiel" (scenes 1 and 2), *Deutsches Museum*, 1, no. 3 (1776): 236-253;

"Scenen aus Pyrrhus Leben und Tod, einem Schauspiel" (scenes 3-9), *Theater-Journal für Deutschland*, 1 (1777): 17-40; 2 (1777): 101-105; 9 (1779): 38-39.

In 1776 Friedrich Maximilian Klinger donned the blue coat, yellow waistcoat, and white hat with yellow trim prescribed by Johann Wolfgang Goethe as the costume of his sorrowful Werther and rode out to Langen to meet J. M. R. Lenz's coach as it approached Frankfurt. This flamboyant gesture, which underscored the first meeting of the two leading figures of the Sturm und Drang era, was typical of the irrepressible young Klinger. Not only as the author of the play which provided a name for the period but in his ebullience and overweaning enthusiasm as well, Klinger personified the "Genie" (genius) movement and, as its most gregarious representative, provided the major link between the Sturm und Drang writers and those of the Göttinger Hainbund. In ever-widening circles he met and befriended the members of Germany's youthful rebellion against the formal dicta of the Enlightenment: Lenz, Heinrich Leopold Wagner, the Counts Stolberg, Christian Heinrich Boie, Wilhelm Heinse, Johann Georg Jacobi, Johann Heinrich Merck, Johann Martin Miller, and Friedrich (Maler) Müller all succumbed to his sympathetic personality. Klinger is generally known only in the context of his youth, but the bulk of his published work appeared long after Sturm und Drang had ceased to be a force in German literature. Following his move to Russia in 1780 in the imperial entourage, Klinger continued to produce literary works at an impressive rate and at a remove from the mainstream that permitted him to practice a unique style, unaffected by the mystical influences of Romanticism. The plays of his Russian period and the "Dekade" (decade) of satiric novels are only now receiving the critical attention they deserve. Klinger's route to classicism parallels that of Goethe but was subjected to entirely different influences and encountered a wholly dissimilar reception.

One of the few authors of the eighteenth century of proletarian antecedents, Klinger was born in 1752 in Frankfurt am Main to Johannes Klinger, a town constable, and Cornelia Fuchs Klinger, a sergeant's daughter. His father died when Klinger was eight years old; his mother raised her son and two daughters by becoming

Pastel drawing of Klinger by Johann Wolfgang Goethe, 1775 (Goethemuseum, Frankfurt am Main)

a laundress for the well-to-do of Frankfurt—including, perhaps, the Goethes of Hirschgrabenallee. Klinger's academic potential was recognized, and he was awarded a tuition waiver and given odd jobs which enabled him to study at the gymnasium; he also served as a tutor there. His relationship with Goethe during their Frankfurt years is poorly documented, but there was enough contact for Klinger to begin work on his first drama under the influence of Goethe's then-unpublished *Götz von Berlichingen mit der eisernen Hand* (Götz von Berlichingen with the Iron Hand, 1773). And it was with Goethe's financial assistance that Klinger was able to enroll at the University of Gießen in 1774 to study law; his primary interests were, however, the classics and modern literature. He succeeded—again with Goethe's aid—in placing two youthful dramas, *Otto* and *Das leidende Weib* (The Suffering Wife), with the Leipzig publisher Weygand, which had already established itself as the house of the Sturm und Drang by publishing the works of Goethe and Lenz. Weygand announced Klinger's two dramas at the Easter book fair of 1775 as plays in the "Goethean/Lenzian Manner." Thus Klinger made his literary debut as the first transmitter of the new movement. But while the influence of

Engraving by J. Albrecht (1777) to illustrate Act 4, Scene 3 of Die Zwillinge: *having killed his brother, Guelfo searches in the mirror for the mark of Cain on his forehead (Gero von Wilpert,* Deutsche Literatur in Bildern *[Stuttgart: Kröner, 1965])*

muthigen Jüngling denken, der mit verhängtem Zügel dahin schießt, oder als einen Mann, der aus Vorsatz romantisiren wollte, sey ihnen dahingestellt" (Whether they [the readers] choose to view the author [of these two plays] as a youth who gives his imagination free rein or as a man who consciously romanticizes is left up to them).

In 1776 his *Die Zwillinge* (The Twin Brothers) was awarded first place in a nationally advertised competition for original plays sponsored by Sophie Charlotte Ackermann and her son Friedrich Ludwig Schröder of the Ackermann theater troupe in Hamburg. In contrast to his two earlier dramas, this play respects the classical unities and reflects a thoroughgoing understanding of the practical demands of the stage in the size of its cast and the number of set changes. But the highly emotional language of this story of sibling conflict is a veritable paradigm of the Sturm und Drang, and the protagonist is the prototypical "Kraftkerl" (swashbuckler) of the epoch. Guelfo, bewildered by the inheritance of his "elder" brother and urged on by his melancholy friend Grimaldi, becomes a howling force of nature, slays his twin, and is in turn slain by his father. Astonishingly simple in its archetypal plot, the play conveys an emotional force seldom equaled in literature.

The success of *Die Zwillinge*, coupled with the publication in the same year of his plays *Der neue Arria* (translated as *The Modern Arria*, 1795) and *Simsone Grisaldo* as well as the first of several "Scenen aus Pyrrhus Leben und Tod" (Scenes from Pyrrhus's Life and Death) encouraged him to abandon his studies in Gießen and seek a practical career; but he was not sure what that career might be. He first went to Weimar, where he hoped to prosper at Goethe's side. By all accounts an impressively handsome, well-spoken young man, Klinger dreamed of becoming either a military officer or an actor. After disruption of his relationship with Goethe, who had no intention of encouraging his literary compeers to remain at the Weimar court, in October 1776 Klinger joined the traveling theater company of Abel Seyler as a dramaturge with the production rights to his play *Sturm und Drang* (Storm and Stress, 1776). Klinger's original title for this work set in revolutionary America was "Wirrwarr" (Confusion); the one it bears and which it shares with the literary epoch was suggested by Christian Kaufman, the Swiss "Kraftapostel" (Apostle of Power), whom Klinger had met that year. The awkward contours of its plot (a poorly motivated

Goethe and Lenz is clearly present in both plays, these fiery works also demonstrate a devotion to Shakespeare, Rousseau, and Petrarch as well as familiarity with such major German writers of the time as Friedrich Gottlieb Klopstock, Gotthold Ephraim Lessing, Christian Fürchtegott Gellert, Friedrich Nicolai, and Christoph Martin Wieland. It is apparent that Klinger was an avid reader who had studied the contemporary mainstream of German literature and had consciously turned away from it to a socially critical drama in the "open" form. As Lenz's production ebbed and Goethe sought new impetus, Klinger became the primary exponent of the Sturm und Drang. That he deliberately practiced an outrageous approach to his writing is manifest in his only surviving utterance on dramatic theory, a letter to the editor of the *Frankfurter gelehrte Anzeigen* (1775), and is strongly suggested by Weygand's caveat to the public: "Ob sie sich nun den Verfasser als einen

Title page for Klinger's play that gave its name to a literary
movement (Herzog-August-Bibliothek, Wolfenbüttel)

feud between Scottish families), its rhapsodic language, and its contorted characters make it an appropriate touchstone for the departure of a generation of writers from the rational mainstream of
the eighteenth century. While still in Weimar,
Klinger had read aloud from the manuscript of
Sturm und Drang, and Goethe had jumped up
and exclaimed: "Was für verfluchtes Zeug ist's,
was du da wieder einmal geschrieben hast! Das
halte der Teufel aus!" (What kind of rubbish
have you written now! No one can put up with
that!). There is every indication that Klinger was
quite pleased by this reaction. The other plays of
this period are equally outlandish: the heroic
knight Simsone Grisaldo gallops through medieval Spain refreshing himself with lion's blood,
and the earnest young lovers of Die neue Arria

are lost in the turmoil of opaque courtly intrigue
in a vaguely Italian Renaissance setting.

Although he had ample time and motivation to write for the stage while he was with
Seyler, Klinger's literary output during this period was minimal: the fragmentary pamphlet Der
verbannte Götter-Sohn (The Banished Child of the
Gods, 1777), the play Stilpo und seine Kinder
(Stilpo and His Children, 1780), and the
antityrant play, "Der Tyrann von Syrakus," later
reworked as Damokles (1790), are among his least
impressive works.

Becoming dissatisfied with the life of a theater poet with an ambulant troupe, in February
1778 Klinger traveled to Switzerland seeking the
company of his childhood friend, the composer
Christoph Kayser. On the way to Zurich he
stopped off in Emmendingen to see Goethe's
brother-in-law, Johann Georg Schlosser, and
Schlosser took him to Colmar to meet the blind
poet Gottlieb Conrad Pfeffel; Pfeffel corresponded with Benjamin Franklin, and Klinger
hoped to use Pfeffel's influence to get a commission in the American revolutionary army. In
Emmendingen he met Lenz again and was
deeply shaken by the latter's mental illness.
Klinger's attempt to become an officer in the
American army failed, but with Schlosser's assistance he obtained a commission as a lieutenant in
the free corps of Chevalier de Wolter and served
on the side of the emperor in the War of the Bavarian Succession from summer 1778 to spring
1779. Enamored of the soldier's life—"Ich bin
ganz Soldat, denke und empfinde nichts andres"
(I am a soldier with my entire being, think and
feel nothing else)—he vowed to turn his back on literary efforts and claimed to have burned his
works in progress in the fall of 1778. But the
first two volumes of the novel Orpheus (1778-
1780) were in all likelihood written about the
same time as the purported auto-da-fé. In this
fable, based on the myth of Orpheus among the
bacchantes, the eunuch Bambino is slaughtered
because he has awakened desires which he cannot satisfy.

In May 1779 Klinger was mustered out of
the service. He sought a new commission in vain,
traveling first to Ulm seeking the assistance of
Gen. Joseph Heinrich von Ried and going so far
as to plead with his childhood friend Ernst Schleiermacher, an official in Hesse, to help him join
in the American war. Whether he would serve on
the side of the rebels or the English was a matter
of indifference to him. At twenty-seven, frus-

Frontispiece and title page for the satirical pamphlet in which Klinger, Jakob Sarasin, and Johann Kaspar Lavater lampooned the Sturm und Drang

trated in his efforts to secure a military career, he turned back to the theater for a livelihood—this time with a sense of self-irony far removed from his youthful enthusiasm. To the year 1779 belongs *Prinz Seiden-Wurm* (Prince Silkworm, first published as an intermezzo in the fifth part of *Orpheus*, 1780), a comedy with intriguing elements of puppet theater and an odd mixture of political satire and fairy tale. *Der Derwisch* (The Dervish), an excellent example of rococo comedy dating from the second half of the same year, drew its title figure from a character in Lessing's *Nathan der Weise* (Nathan the Wise), which had just appeared. This thoroughly good-humored play is set in a fantastic orient among the Illuminati and much is made of their mysterious ways and vows of silence. In part, the setting was inspired by a visit to the Masonic Lodge "La modestie" in Zurich. The dervish, who possesses the gift of reviving the dead; his friend, the beggar; the sultan; and the sultan's ludicrous attendants owe much to the oriental vogue of the day. During the same year Klinger also completed the remainder of *Orpheus* and its pornographic appendix, *Prinz Formosos Fiedelbogen und der Prinzessin Sanaclara Geige* (Prince Formoso's Fiddlestick and the Princess Sanaclara's Violin, 1780), to which he attached translations of a selection of letters by Crébillon.

He spent part of the summer of 1780 in Pratteln, Switzerland, where he collaborated with Johann Kaspar Lavater and Jakob Sarasin on the satiric pamphlet *Plimplamplasko, der hohe Geist (heut Genie)* (Plimplamplasko, the Lofty Spirit [Called Genius in Our Era], 1780), which marked his final and definitive rejection of the exuberant excesses and subjectivity of the Sturm und Drang. Purporting to be a manuscript from Martin Luther's time, this playful epic is a lampoon on the same Christoph Kaufmann who contributed the title *Sturm und Drang* to Klinger's play and who was probably responsible for Goethe's break with Klinger. Simultaneously, however, it is a satire of Klinger's own style. The comic hero conquers the good genius Puro Senso, chains him like Prometheus to a cliff, and proclaims man's independence from the gods: "Ein hoher Genie bakt sich selber" (The lofty spirit is homemade), he exclaims in a perverse echo of the cult of the genius of only a few years earlier. It was a fitting end for his last year in Germany.

Through the intercession of Duke Friedrich Eugen of Württemberg Klinger joined the entourage of the Grand Duke Paul of Russia as a reader. He arrived in St. Petersburg at the end of September 1780 and was given a naval commission, finally attaining the military status for which he yearned and which was so elusive for the non-nobleman in that era. As a traveling companion to the grand duke and his wife he toured Europe from September 1781 until December 1782. While in Vienna during November and December 1781 Klinger was a daily guest of Friedrich Ludwig Schröder. Klinger presented the famous actor and director with the manuscript of the comedy *Die falschen Spieler* (The Cardsharps, 1782), which Schröder staged at the Hoftheater. Paul's court continued its tour to Venice, Rome, Naples, Florence, and Paris. In Paris Klinger apparently completed the manuscript for the drama *Elfride*, which was based on an account of the legendary daughter of the Earl of Devonshire in David Hume's *History of England* (1754-1762). Schröder was unable to arrange a production of the play, which was published in 1783. On returning to Russia, Klinger was assigned to an infantry regiment. His military career followed a steady path of promotion to the rank of lieutenant general in 1811.

In 1788 Klinger married Elisabeth Alexajef, who was the daughter of Col. Alexander Alexajef and was rumored to be the natural daughter of the empress Catherine II and her lover, Grigori Orlov. Elisabeth bore him three children: only one, Alexander, lived beyond infancy, to fall at Borodino in 1812. Klinger flourished at the court during the reign of the German-born Catherine, but the reactionary internal policies of her successor, Paul I, forced him to proceed carefully. The fear of censorship occasioned the odd games with the places of publication as given in his books beginning in 1796. In 1799 he was made praeses of the Academy of Knights. He was assigned to the corps of cadets as a teacher and was made its director in 1801. Dedicated to the didactic principles of the Enlightenment, he made many suggestions for reforms in the educational system; these suggestions led to his appointment to the governing council of the ministry of education in 1802 and subsequently to the boards of several schools. In 1803 he was named by Czar Alexander I as curator (political overseer/advisor) of the University of Dorpat (present-day Tartu) in Estonia. He held that office until his retirement in 1817.

In Russia the practice of literature became a leisure activity for Klinger, who was a diligent officer and civil servant. But he viewed his writing as an essential element of his life, as "Beweise meines moralischen Daseyns" (proof of my moral existence), and often described it in terms of his professional career: "meine Autorschaft [ist] ein Krieg" (My authorship [is] a war). His literary efforts often took the form of revisions of earlier works for the collections published in 1786-1787, 1790, 1794, and 1809-1816. Klinger's personal library included an enormous range of subject matter in a variety of languages, and his works of the Russian period reflect a cosmopolitan perspective.

In the 1780s Klinger completed three historical plays, two comedies, and five dramas based on themes drawn from classical antiquity. Several of these works are probably recastings of earlier drafts dating perhaps from his days as a theater poet. The histories, *Konradin* (1786), *Der Günstling* (The Favorite, 1787), and *Roderico* (1790), reveal a tendency toward a more abstract and idealistic technique of composition: historical fact fades into the background, and the plots tend to focus on a dialectical colloquy of aspects of statecraft. The comedies, *Der Schwur* (The Vow, 1786), revised as *Der Schwur gegen die Ehe* (The Vow against Marriage, 1797), and *Die zwo Freudinnen* (The Two [Female] Friends, 1790), have little in common with Klinger's earlier attempts in the genre. The first is an effort at a satirical depiction of court life in which the German petty nobility ape French manners, and the second is based on an anecdote from Petersburg society. Both are wordy and miss the mark of comic effect. The five "antikisierende Dramen" (dramas that draw on classical form and themes from antiquity) *Aristodemos* (1790), *Oriantes* (1790), *Medea in Korinth* (Medea in Corinth, 1787), *Medea auf dem Kaukasos* (Medea in the Caucasus, 1787), and *Damokles* (1790) all draw upon an intensive study of classical antiquity. Klinger viewed ancient history as a collection of exemplary incidents which could provide a timeless setting for explorations of social and ethical principles. These plays, composed in the classic five-act structure, are vehicles for Klinger's ideas on history, politics, and morality; the dialogue often resembles the exchanges

*Drawing of Klinger by Johann Heinrich Lips
(Nationalbibliothek, Vienna)*

found in the dialogues of Plato. Klinger considered the Medea dramas to be among his best work. His interest may have been kindled by the 1785 visit to St. Petersburg of Friedrich Leopold von Stolberg, who showed Klinger his adaptations of Aeschylus and discussed the Medea myths with him. Klinger proudly announced in the preface to *Medea in Korinth*: "Ich benutze weder die griechische, noch die lateinische, noch die französische Medea. Diese hier, und wie sie sey, ist mein Werk" (I do not use the Greek, nor the Roman, nor the French Medea. This Medea and her character as depicted is my own work). The second play, of which Klinger wrote "gewiß das beste, . . . was ich je geschrieben habe" (surely the best thing I have ever written), is not a genuine continuation of the first. *Medea auf dem Kaukasos* is a far more philosophical work with little dramatic action, and it comes close to being a didactic parable.

Most of his literary production of the 1780s was published in two collections, *Theater* (1786-1787) and *Neues Theater* (New Theater,

1790). Thereafter, he only returned to the drama to make revisions for two later compendia, *Auswahl aus Friedrich Maximilian Klingers dramatischen Werken* (Selection from Friedrich Maximilian Klinger's Dramatic Works, 1794) and *F. M. Klingers Werke* (F. M. Klinger's Works, 1809-1816). The novel *Die Geschichte vom goldenen Hahn* (The Story of the Golden Cock, 1785) may well have been completed on bivouac in August 1783. This slight work, which shows the same rococo elements found in *Der Derwisch*, is a parodistic fairy tale set in a land of innocent "noble savages." This paradise is destroyed by the incursion of Europeans, whose proselytizing zeal and cult of progress spoil the purity of utopia. One pair of lovers escapes the enlightened world; they return after the inevitable cataclysm and restore the reign of ingenuous nature.

On 7 January 1790 Klinger announced his intention to revise *Orpheus*, "es mit mehr Salz würzen, mehr Philosophie hinein mischen, zwekmäßiger machen, und es vom Satyros durchbeizen lassen" (to add more salt, mix in more philosophy, make it more purposeful, and let Satyros cauterize it). The new version was to be much more topical in its satire. It appeared in 1791 under the title *Bambinos sentimentalisch-politische, comisch-tragische Geschichte* (Bambino's Sentimental-Political, Comic-Tragic Story).

In 1791 Klinger informed his friend Schleiermacher that he had sent a manuscript to his publisher: "Darinnen wirst du nebst einem tiefen Zwek, alles finden, was ich über Wissenschaft, Menschen, Glük, Moral, Religion, Gott und Welt denke . . . . Ich muß nun einige Werke schreiben, um dem deutschen Volke zu zeigen, was ich kann, wenn ich es unternehmen will, zu zeigen" (In it you will find—aside from a deep purpose—all my thoughts on science, humanity, fortune, morality, religion, God and the world. . . . I must now write a few works to show the German people what I can do when I want to demonstrate it). This work, *Fausts Leben, Thaten und Höllenfahrt* (Faust's Life, Deeds, and Descent into Hell, 1791; translated as *Faustus: His Life, Death, and Descent into Hell*, 1825), is the first of an ambitious projected cycle of ten novels. In part Klinger was motivated by the desire to establish his ultimate reputation as a writer; indifferent reception of the collections and individual books published since his move to Russia hurt him deeply, and he hoped for fairer treatment from posterity. Looking back in 1798, he maintained that he had conceived the ten novels from the beginning as a repository for his experience, insight, and wisdom. He sent the manuscript of the first part of *Geschichte Giafers des Barmeciden: Ein Seitenstück zu Fausts Leben, Thaten und Höllenfahrt* (Story of Giafer the Barmecide: A Pendant to Faust's Life, Deeds and Descent into Hell, 1792-1794) to his publisher in January 1792; the second part was completed in 1793. In the meantime, *Geschichte Raphaels de Aquillas in fünf Büchern: Ein Seitenstück zu Fausts Leben, Thaten und Höllenfahrt* (Story of Raphael de Aquilla in Five Books: A Pendant to Faust's Life, Death and Descent into Hell) appeared in 1793. *Reisen vor der Sündfluth* (1795; translated as *Travels before the Flood*, 1796) and *Der Faust der Morgenlaender oder Wanderungen Ben Hafis, Erzaehlers der Reisen vor der Sündfluth* (Faust of the Orient; or, The Travels of Ben Hafi, Narrator of Travels before the Great Flood, 1796) were written in 1794 and 1795. There was then a pause while Klinger revised *Der Schwur*, but he returned to the cycle in 1797. That summer he completed *Geschichte eines Teutschen der neuesten Zeit* (Story of a German of the Current Era, 1798) and in the fall he finished the revision of *Die Geschichte vom goldenen Hahn* as *Sahir, Eva's Erstgeborener im Paradiese: Ein Beytrag zur Geschichte der europäischen Kultur und Humanität* (Sahir, Eva's Firstborn in Paradise: A Contribution to the History of European Culture and Humanity, 1798). In the following spring *Der Weltmann und der Dichter* (The Cosmopolitan and the Poet, 1798) was completed. At that time he wrote: "Da haben Sie nun acht Werke von den zehen—das neunte wird sich bald hervordrängen; aber das Zehente?" (There you have eight of the ten; the ninth will soon emerge; but the tenth?). The implication is a fear of the censor. Part of the tenth work, "Das zu frühe Erwachen des Genius der Menschheit" (The Premature Awakening of the Spirit of Mankind), appeared in 1803 in the first volume of Klinger's *Betrachtungen und Gedanken über verschiedene Gegenstände der Welt und der Litteratur* (Reflections and Aphorisms on Various Subjects of the World and of Literature, 1803-1805), but the whole was never published. The ninth may never have been written, and Klinger offered the three volumes of aphorisms as a substitute for it. (The contention that an anonymously published novel, *Der Kettenträger* [The Chain Bearer, 1796], was the missing work is false.) The unfinished novel cycle represents an attempt by a well-traveled and well-read man of reason to survey the European Enlightenment. It is a pessimistic undertaking, and it ends with resigna-

tion: despite historical change the betterment of mankind is questionable at best, and an ultimate solution defies human capability. The novels stand in the satiric tradition between Wieland and Jean Paul and echo the anticlericalism of Voltaire. *Betrachtungen und Gedanken über verschiedene Gegenstände der Welt und der Literatur* and the twelve-volume *Werke* round out his literary production. In addition, there is a large body of correspondence: with Goethe—with whom the old friendship was restored in 1811—and with the many visitors to St. Petersburg and Dorpat, among them Caroline von Egloffstein; Fanny Tarnow; Johann Gottfried Seume; Ernst Moritz Arndt; and Wilhelm von Wolzogen, who brought greetings from Friedrich Schiller. Klinger died on 25 February 1831 and was buried in Dorpat.

As German literary criticism has turned away from the traditional periodization and the standard progression of development, a renewed interest in Klinger's later works is underway. Studies by Harro Segeberg, David Hill, and Fritz Osterwalder as well as the publication of a historical-critical edition have provided impetus to the study of Klinger and the late Enlightenment. Certainly Klinger's long and productive life, his openness to ideas, and his personal magnetism place him among the most influential literary figures of the late eighteenth century.

Letters:

Briefbuch zu F. M. Klinger: Sein Leben und Werk edited by Max Rieger (Darmstadt: Bergsträsser, 1896).

Biographies:

Max Rieger, *Klinger in der Sturm- und Drangperiode* (Darmstadt: Bergsträsser, 1880);

Rieger, *F. M. Klinger: Sein Leben und Werk* (Darmstadt: Bergsträsser, 1896);

Olga Smoljan, *F. M. Klinger: Leben und Werk*, translated by E. M. Arndt (Weimar, Arion 1962);

Christoph Hering, *F. M. Klinger: Der Weltmann als Dichter* (Berlin: De Gruyter, 1966).

References:

Hans Heinrich Borcherdt, "Klingers Romanzyklus," in his *Der Roman der Goethezeit* (Urach: Port, 1949), pp. 76-103;

Hans Jürgen Geerdts, "F. M. Klingers Faust-Roman in seiner historisch-ästhetischen Problematik," *Weimarer Beiträge*, 6 (1960): 58-75;

Sander L. Gilman and Edward P. Harris, "Klinger's Wieland," *Modern Language Notes*, 99 (April 1984): 589-606;

Karl S. Guthke, "Lektion eines Preisausschreibens: Klingers *Zwillinge*," in his *Literarisches Leben im achtzehnten Jahrhundert in Deutschland und in der Schweiz* (Bern: Francke, 1975), pp. 282-289;

Edward P. Harris, "Der Tyrann von Syrakus: An Unknown Early Version of F. M. Klinger's *Damocles*," *Archiv für das Studium der deutschen Sprachen und Literaturen*, 210, no. 2 (1973): 241-296;

Harris, "Vier Stücke in einem: Die Entstehungsgeschichte von F. M. Klingers *Die Zwillinge*," *Zeitschrift für deutsche Philologie*, 101, no. 4 (1982): 481-495;

R. Herrmann, "Das Bild der Gesellschaft in den Werken des älteren Klingers, besonders in seinen Aphorismen," Ph.D. dissertation, University of Berlin, 1958;

David Hill, *Klinger's Novels: The Structure of the Cycle* (Stuttgart: Heinz, 1982);

Hartmut M. Kaiser, "Studien zu F. M. Klingers Romanen: Eine Analyse der Motive und Charaktere in der Triade *Faust, Raphael, Giafar*," Ph.D. dissertation, Brown University, 1968;

Kurt May, "Die Struktur des Dramas in Sturm und Drang, an Klinger's 'Zwillinge,'" in his *Form und Bedeutung* (Stuttgart: Klett, 1957), pp. 42-49;

May, "Klingers Sturm und Drang," *Deutsche Vierteljahrsschrift*, 11 (1933): 398-407;

Fritz Osterwalder, *Die Überwindung des Sturm und Drang: Zum Werk F. M. Klingers. Die Entwicklung der republikanischen Dichtung in der Zeit der Französischen Revolution* (Berlin: Schmidt, 1979);

Gunter Otto, *Begriffs- und Namenregister zu Friedrich Maximilian von Klingers "Betrachtungen und Gedanken über verschiedene Gegenstände der Welt und der Literatur"* (Hildesheim: Olms, 1981);

Erich Schmidt, *Lenz und Klinger: Zwei Dichter der Goethezeit* (Berlin, 1878);

Harro Segeberg, *F. M. Klingers Romandichtung: Untersuchungen zum Roman der Spätaufklärung* (Heidelberg: Winter, 1974);

David F. Stout, "The Portrayal of the Author Figure in Three Novels by F. M. Klinger," Ph.D. dissertation, Cornell University, 1979;

H. M. Waidson, "F. M. Klinger," in *German Men of Letters*, volume 6 (London: Garland, 1972), pp. 241-261;

Friedrich A. Wyneken, *Rousseaus Einfluß auf Klinger* (Berkeley: University of California Press, 1912).

Papers:

At her husband's request, Klinger's widow destroyed his papers. His personal library is held by the University of Tartu. Major collections of letters are in the Freies Deutsches Hochstift, Frankfurt am Main, and in the Staats- und Universitätsbibliothek Hamburg.

Adolph Franz Friedrich Ludwig, Freiherr von Knigge

(16 October 1752 - 6 May 1796)

Thomas P. Saine
University of California, Irvine

BOOKS: *Theaterstücke, von A. Frhrn. v. K.*, 2 volumes (Hanau & Offenbach: Schulz, 1779-1780);

Allgemeines System für das Volk: Zur Grundlage aller Erkenntnisse für Menschen aus allen Nationen, Ständen und Religionen in einem Auszuge herausgegeben, anonymous (Nicosia, 1873 [actually Hanau: Schulz, 1780?]);

Der Roman meines Lebens, in Briefen herausgegeben, 4 volumes (Riga [actually Frankfurt am Main: Andreä], 1781-1783);

Ueber Jesuiten, Freymaurer und deutsche Rosencreutzer: Herausgegeben von Joseph Aloisius Maier, der Gesellschaft Jesu ehemaligen Mitgliede (Leipzig, 1781);

Geschichte Peter Clausens, von dem Verfasser des Romans meines Lebens, 3 volumes (Frankfurt am Main: Andreä, 1783-1785); translated anonymously as *The German Gil Blas; or, The Adventures of Peter Claus* (London: Printed for C. and G. Kearsley, 1793); German version reprinted (Frankfurt am Main: Minerva, 1971);

Sechs Predigten gegen Despotismus, Dummheit, Aberglauben, Ungerechtigkeit, Untreue und Müßiggang, herausgegeben von A. Freyherrn von K***** (Frankfurt am Main: Andreä, 1783);

Gesammelte poetische und prosaische kleinere Schriften von A. Frhrn. v. K., 2 volumes (Frankfurt am Main: Andreä, 1784-1785);

Sechs Predigten über Demuth, Sanftmuth, Seelen-Frieden, Gebeth, Wohlthätigkeit und Toleranz, herausgegeben von Adolph Freyherrn von K**** (Heidelberg: Pfähler, 1785);

Journal aus Urfstädt von dem Verfasser des Romans meines Lebens, 2 volumes (Frankfurt am Main: Andreä, 1785-1786);

Journal aus Urfstädt als Fortsetzung des Romans meines Lebens und der Geschichte Peter Clausens von eben demselben Verfasser (Frankfurt am Main: Andreä, 1786);

Beytrag zur neuesten Geschichte des Freymaurerordens in neun Gesprächen, mit Erlaubniß meiner Obern herausgegeben (Berlin, 1786);

Adolph Freiherr von Knigge; pastel portrait by an unknown artist (Focke-Museum, Bremen)

Die Verirrungen des Philosophen oder Geschichte Ludwigs von Seelberg, herausgegeben von A. Freiherrn von K****, 2 volumes (Frankfurt am Main: Andreä, 1787);

Dramaturgische Blätter, 3 volumes (Hannover: Schmidt, 1788-1789);

Ueber den Umgang mit Menschen (2 volumes, Hannover: Schmidt, 1788; revised, 1788; revised and enlarged, 3 volumes, Hannover: Ritscher, 1790-1796); translated by Peter Will as *Practical Philosophy of Social Life; or, The Art of Conversing with Men,* 2 volumes (London: Printed for T. Cadell, Jun., and W. Da-

131

vies, 1799; Lansingburgh, N.Y.: Penniman & Bliss, 1805); German first edition reprinted, 1 volume (Darmstadt: Wissenschaftliche Buchgesellschaft, 1976);

Ueber Friedrich Wilhelm den Liebreichen und meine Unterredung mit Ihm: Von J. C. Meywerk, Churf. Hannoverschen Hosenmacher (Frankfurt am Main & Leipzig: Andreä, 1788);

Philo's endliche Erklärung und Antwort, auf verschiedene Anforderungen und Fragen, die an ihn ergangen, seine Verbindung mit dem Orden der Illuminaten betreffend (Hannover: Schmidt, 1788);

*Sechs Predigten über Trost im Leiden, Bezähmung der Leidenschaften, Gute Werke, Verläumdung, Bibelstudium und Schmeicheley, herausgegeben von Adolph Freyherrn von K*****, Dritte Sammlung* (Frankfurt am Main: Andreä, 1788);

Geschichte des armen Herrn von Mildenburg, in Briefen herausgegeben, 3 volumes (volume 1, Hannover: Schmidt, 1789; volumes 2-3, Hannover: Ritscher, 1790);

Benjamin Noldmann's Geschichte der Aufklärung in Abyssinien, oder Nachricht von seinem und seines Herrn Vetters Aufenthalte an dem Hofe des großen Negus, oder Priesters Johannes, 2 volumes (Göttingen: Dieterich, 1791);

Das Zauberschloß oder Geschichte des Grafen Tunger (Hannover: Ritscher, 1791);

Ueber den Bücher-Nachdruck: An den Herrn Johann Gottwerth Müller, Doctor der Weltweisheit in Itzehoe (Hamburg: Hoffmann, 1792);

Die Reise nach Braunschweig: Ein comischer Roman (Hannover: Ritscher, 1792; reprinted, Frankfurt am Main: Minerva, 1971);

Des seligen Herrn Etatsraths Samuel Conrad von Schaafskopf hinterlassene Papiere: Von seinen Erben herausgegeben, anonymous (Breslau, 1792; reprinted, Frankfurt am Main: Insel, 1965);

Josephs von Wurmbrand, kaiserlich abyssinischen Ex-Ministers, jezzigen Notarii caesarii publici in der Reichsstadt Bopfingen, politisches Glaubensbekenntniß, mit Hinsicht auf die französische Revolution und deren Folgen, anonymous (Frankfurt am Main & Leipzig: Helwing, 1792; reprinted, Frankfurt am Main: Insel, 1968);

Briefe, auf einer Reise aus Lothringen nach Niedersachsen geschrieben (Hannover: Ritscher, 1793);

Ueber Schriftsteller und Schriftstellerey (Hannover: Ritscher, 1793);

Geschichte des Amtsraths Gutmann, von ihm selbst geschrieben (Hannover: Ritscher, 1794); translated anonymously as *The History of the Amts-*

rath Gutman, Written by Himself (London: Printed for Vernor & Hood, 1799);

Auszug eines Briefes die Illuminaten betreffend, ohne Einwilligung des Schreibers, aber gewiß in der redlichsten Absicht zum Druck befördert, von seinem Freunde, anonymous (Leipzig: Schäfer, 1794; enlarged, 1795);

Reise nach Fritzlar im Sommer 1794: Auszug aus dem Tagebuch. Durchaus bloß für Freunde von Joach. Melchior Spießglas, hochfürstlicher Cammerjäger und Titular-Ratzenfänger in Peina (N.p., 1794);

Etwas über die Reise nach Fritzlar (N.p., 1795);

Kurze Darstellung der Schicksale, die den Kaufmann, Herrn Arnold Delius in Bremen, als Folgen seiner nordamerikanischen Handlungs-Unternehmungen betroffen haben (N.p., 1795);

Rückblicke auf den, wenn Gott will, für Teutschland nun bald geendigten Krieg: Nebst einigen Erläuterungen, die Propaganda, Jacobiner und Illuminaten betreffend (Copenhagen, 1795);

Manifest einer nicht geheimen, sondern sehr öffentlichen Verbindung ächter Freunde der Wahrheit, Rechtschaffenheit und bürgerlichen Ordnung, an ihre Zeitgenossen, anonymous (Vienna, 1795);

Ueber Eigennutz und Undank. Ein Gegenstück zu dem Buche: Ueber den Umgang mit Menschen (Leipzig: Jacobäer, 1796);

Schriften, 12 volumes (Hannover: Hahn, 1804-1806);

Aus einer alten Kiste: Originalbriefe, Handschriften und Dokumente aus dem Nachlasse eines bekannten Mannes, edited by Hermann Klencke (Leipzig: Kollmann, 1853; reprinted, Kronberg im Taunus: Scriptor, 1979);

Der Traum des Herrn Brick: Essays, Satiren, Utopien, edited by Hedwig Voegt (Berlin: Rütten & Loening, 1968);

Sämtliche Werke, edited by Paul Raabe, Ernst-Otto Fehn, Manfred Grätz, Gisela von Hanstein, and Claus Ritterhoff, 24 volumes projected, 20 volumes to date (Nendeln, Liechtenstein: KTO Press, 1978-   ).

OTHER: *Sammlung ausländischer Schauspiele, für die deutsche Bühne umgearbeitet*, 2 volumes, adapted by Knigge (Heidelberg: Pfähler, 1784-1785);

Das Gemälde vom Hofe: Lustspiel. Aus dem Französischen, translated anonymously by Knigge (Munich: Lindauer, 1786);

Jean-Jacques Rousseau, *Bekenntnisse*, 4 volumes, translated by Knigge (Berlin: Unger, 1786-1790);

Über den gegenwärtigen Zustand des gesellschaftlichen Lebens in den vereinigten Niederlanden. Als ein Anhang zu dem Werke: Über den Umgang mit Menschen, aus dem Holländischen übersetzt, translated by Knigge (Hannover: Ritscher, 1790);

G. F. Niemeyer, *Der Greis an den Jüngling,* foreword by Knigge (Bremen, 1793);

Niemeyer, *Vermächtniß an Helene von ihrem Vater,* foreword by Knigge (Bremen, 1794);

Thomas Sheridan, *Jonathan Swifts Leben,* translated by Philippine Freyin von Knigge, edited by Knigge (Hannover: Ritscher, 1795).

One of the most highly visible late-eighteenth-century German intellectuals, Adolph Franz Friedrich Ludwig, Freiherr von Knigge supported himself for years by his pen before landing a secure, if fairly modest, position in Hannoverian government service. His literary products included dramas; theater adaptations and reviews; novels; moral sermons; works on Freemasonry, the Illuminati, and other secret societies; satires; biting political and social commentary; and an immensely popular book on how to get along with people that was reprinted and bowdlerized until well into the nineteenth century. A talented musical amateur, he composed piano sonatas, concertos for bassoon, symphonies, and Masses, and translated opera libretti. An inspiration to the younger generation of journalists and critics at the end of the century, Knigge was committed to the advancement of the human race in the modern age. Though himself not an exponent of radical ideas, he was so outspoken on social and political issues that at the end of his life—because of the furor over the Illuminati and the fears of conservatives about the effects of the French Revolution on Germany—he was the most attacked and most compulsively reviled figure of the German Enlightenment: a worthy and creditable successor to the notorious Dr. Karl Friedrich Bahrdt, with whom he was associated in the minds of reactionary publicists.

Knigge was born in Bredenbeck, near Hannover, on 16 October 1752 to Philipp Carl Freiherr von Knigge and Louise Wilhelmine, née Freifrau von Knigge. His father, a Hannoverian official who had taken a doctorate in law, owned substantial properties, including estates at Bredenbeck and Pattensen. He had also run up huge debts. Knigge's mother died in 1763, his father in 1766. After the father's death the creditors took possession of the estates as security for the debts, allocating the young Knigge a somewhat niggardly annual allowance of five hundred Reichsthaler. He was to expend considerable energy and ingenuity during his life in vain attempts to regain his patrimony and live the life to which his aristocratic class was accustomed.

Following his father's death Knigge was boarded in Hannover, where he had three years of instruction by tutors beyond what he had received at home. In 1769 he went to the Hannoverian university at Göttingen to study first law, then public finance. While still engaged in his studies he was appointed equerry and assessor in the military and finance department of Hesse-Cassel but was granted leave to continue his academic preparation until 1772, when he moved to Cassel. He remained there until 1775, working mainly on economic matters and as director of the state tobacco manufacture. In 1773 he married Henriette von Baumbach, whose mother owned an estate at Nentershausen, near Bebra. The same year he joined the Freemasons, becoming a member of the lodge "Zum gekrönten Löwen" (At the Crowned Lion), which adhered to the system of the Strict Observance. His daughter Philippine—whose education was to occupy him intensely—was born on 25 February 1775 in Cassel. By the beginning of 1775 Knigge was casting about for employment elsewhere, including Berlin; Friedrich II explained in his response to Knigge's job application that he had to reserve government jobs for his own subjects wherever possible. Knigge left Cassel that year, reputedly because of the intrigue-filled atmosphere at court; he stayed for a time at his mother-in-law's estate in Nentershausen, where he first tried his hand at writing. He also traveled extensively in the Rhineland, Alsace, and Lorraine. In Weimar in early 1776 he was appointed to the honorific post of court chamberlain without remuneration.

From 1777 to 1780 Knigge lived at the court of Hanau without an official position. There he became ever more involved in Masonic affairs, participating in the convention at Brunswick and Wolfenbüttel in 1778. He occupied himself largely with trying to establish an amateur theater and made his debut as an author, putting out two volumes of plays and the short *Allgemeines System für das Volk* (General System for the People, 1780), a "future document" purportedly published in 1873 that describes the moral system and religious beliefs of a small band of concerned men and women who had fled the decadence of northern Europe for the seclusion of Cyprus. Debts and the enmity of influential persons at the small court eventually led Knigge to steal away quietly from Hanau.

There followed ten years of "private" life: in Frankfurt am Main from 1780 to 1783, in Heidelberg from 1783 to 1786, and in Hannover from 1787 to 1790. During these years Knigge supported himself almost exclusively by his writing, publishing a steady stream of novels, moral works, and periodicals such as the *Journal aus Urfstädt* (1785-1786). In Hannover he busied himself in 1788 and 1789 as a theater critic and put out his *Dramaturgische Blätter* (Dramaturgical News). During the Hannover years he also devoted much of his energy to the unsuccessful effort to regain possession of his estates, submitting petitions and complaints about the creditors to the government and even seeking to enlist the support of George III in London.

The years 1780 to 1784 were the period of Knigge's most intensive involvement with Freemasonry and of his efforts to help establish and propagate the Order of the Illuminati as a force of Enlightenment. The Illuminati had been founded in Bavaria in 1776 by Adam Weishaupt, a professor of civil and canon law at the University of Ingolstadt; but owing to Weishaupt's lack of experience and contacts the Order had not been able to establish links with the Masons or spread significantly beyond Bavaria. When Knigge joined in 1780, under the name "Philo," he believed that he had found the true path to happiness and Enlightenment; but he soon discovered that the Illuminati were in total disarray, without inspired leadership, plans, or goals. He undertook to organize them, formulating plans; drafting statutes, rituals, and hierarchies; and recruiting members far and wide among his Masonic acquaintances. As a proselytizer for the new Illuminati system he participated in the important Masonic convention at Wilhelmsbad in 1782. He was easily the most effective and influential member of the Order, but vehement disagreements with Weishaupt ("Spartacus") and the other Bavarian leaders (the "Areopagites") led Knigge to leave the Illuminati in 1784. Deprived of his energetic recruiting and organizing activity, the Illuminati were already in decline when their membership lists and many of their secret documents were discovered and they were banned in Bavaria later that year.

Knigge's involvement with secret societies led to several important works during the 1780s, including the pamphlet *Ueber Jesuiten, Freymaurer und deutsche Rosencreutzer* (On Jesuits, Freema-

Mezzotint of Knigge by Wachsmann, from a drawing by Lahde (Gero von Wilpert, Deutsche Literatur in Bildern [Stuttgart: Kröner, 1965])

sons, and German Rosicrucians, 1781)–after the papal dissolution of the Society of Jesus in 1773 most German Enlighteners saw Jesuits lurking everywhere and suspected they had a hand in every reactionary plot to suppress the Enlightenment–and a set of dialogues which appeared under the title *Beytrag zur neuesten Geschichte des Freymaurerordens in neun Gesprächen* (Contribution on the Recent History of Freemasonry in Nine Dialogues) in 1786. The prominent role played by "Philo" in the secret correspondence and documents published after the banning of the Illuminati made Knigge a target for conservatives. He tried to set the record straight on the innocent nature of the Illuminati, their goals, and the part he had played in the organization in *Philo's endliche Erklärung und Antwort, auf verschiedene Anforderungen und Fragen, die an ihn ergangen, seine Verbindung mit dem Orden der Illuminaten betreffend* (Philo's Final Declaration and Answer to Diverse Demands and Questions Which Have Been put to Him Concerning His Connection with the Order of the Illuminati) of

1788. Although he swore off secret societies after his experiences with the Illuminati, Knigge was involved once again in a controversial undertaking when he became associated around 1790 with Bahrdt's project to form a German Union. By this time the words *Knigge* and *radical* were practically synonymous in the public mind, and Knigge had been set up as a prime scapegoat for conservatives in the campaign to combat the spread of French revolutionary ideas to Germany.

Although he never regained his estates, Knigge finally achieved a measure of financial security when he was appointed the chief Hannoverian official in Bremen and moved there in late 1790. While Bremen was a Free City, Hannover owned pieces of territory there and administered the cathedral (the only Lutheran church in the city) and cathedral school, which became part of Knigge's responsibilities. He fulfilled his duties in Bremen punctiliously, although he already suffered from the illness which was to cause his death at the age of forty-three. He was bedridden for long periods from 1792 on and could travel only in a special carriage equipped with a bed.

Still, during these last years, so full of official duties, pain, and controversy, Knigge never stopped writing. Some of the works of Knigge's Bremen period are among his finest and most influential: the satirical-political novel *Benjamin Noldmann's Geschichte der Aufklärung in Abyssinien, oder Nachricht von seinem und seines Herrn Vetters Aufenthalte an dem Hofe des großen Negus, oder Priesters Johannes* (Benjamin Noldmann's History of the Enlightenment in Abyssinia; or, Report of His and His Cousin's Sojourn at the Court of the Great Negus, or Prester John, 1791); the comic novel *Die Reise nach Braunschweig* (The Journey to Brunswick, 1792); a political satire, *Des seligen Herrn Etatsraths Samuel Conrad von Schaafskopf hinterlassene Papiere* (Posthumous Papers of the Late Finance Counselor Samuel Conrad von Schaafskopf, 1792); a sympathetic analysis of the causes of the French Revolution, *Josephs von Wurmbrand, kaiserlich abyssinischen Ex-Ministers, jezzigen Notarii caesarii publici in der Reichsstadt Bopfingen, politisches Glaubensbekenntniß, mit Hinsicht auf die französische Revolution und deren Folgen* (The Political Credo of Joseph von Wurmbrand, Former Imperial Minister to Abyssinia, Now Notary Public in the Imperial City of Bopfingen, with Regard to the French Revolution and Its Consequences, 1792); and an essay on the court politics, French émigré machina-

tions, and dire miscalculations that had led the German states into their war against revolutionary France in 1792, *Rückblicke auf den, wenn Gott will, für Teutschland nun bald geendigten Krieg* (Retrospective on the War That, God Willing, Will Soon Be Ended for Germany, 1795). The last work was prompted by the prospect of a successful outcome of the Basel peace negotiations between Prussia and France.

Knigge spoke his mind fearlessly on current affairs at a time when many other German writers were inhibited by censorship or political considerations. He was reprimanded by the Hannover government for publishing the Wurmbrand book without the censor's approval and was commanded thenceforth to publish nothing that had not passed the censorship, but he remained undaunted. Several of his more critical late works were published outside of Hannoverian territory. After Johann Georg Zimmermann–who had made his reputation as a popular and progressive writer in the 1750s but turned increasingly conservative with age–defamed him in ferocious attacks published in the *Wiener Zeitschrift* in 1792, Knigge filed suit and eventually obtained a judgment requiring Zimmermann to apologize and retract his statements. Actually, Knigge had earlier been involved, at least tangentially, in an anti-Zimmermann campaign and had satirized Zimmermann's self-important account of conversations he had with Friedrich II during the king's last illness in his spoof *Ueber Friedrich Wilhelm den Liebreichen und meine Unterredung mit Ihm: Von J. C. Meywerk, Churf. Hannöverschen Hosenmacher* (On Frederick William the Loving and My Conversations with Him, by J. C. Meywerk, Electoral Hannoverian Trousers-Maker, 1788). The Knigge-Zimmermann affair gave rise to a flood of controversy in the press and established Knigge as a leading champion of free speech in Germany. He continued to be attacked on virtually every page of such conservative journals as the *Eudämonia* and in pamphlets by the likes of the editor of the *Eudämonia*, F. L. A. von Grolmann. In March 1795 English authorities and the Hannoverian military removed Knigge from Bremen temporarily because they feared that he would fan public protest against the planned Hannoverian occupation of the city. Knigge was summoned to government headquarters at Stade, where he was kept occupied with busywork until he saw through the ruse and demanded to be allowed to return to Bremen; the rumor circulated, however, that he had been arrested. At his death on 6 May 1796

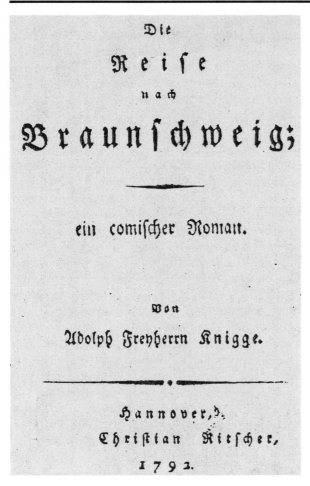

Die

Reise

nach

Braunschweig;

ein comischer Roman.

Von

Adolph Freyherrn Knigge.

Hannover,
Christian Ritscher,
1792.

*Title page for Knigge's comic novel about a group of people
who travel to Brunswick to see a balloon ascent*

Knigge, who was interred in the Bremen cathedral, was mourned by German intellectuals and still feared by the conservatives, who hardly dared hope that he was really dead.

Much of Knigge's literary output deals with issues of the day and cannot be understood by the modern reader without considerable historical background. Though few of his purely literary works have great merit on their own terms, they are consistently interesting to the intellectual and social historian. Until the middle of the twentieth century Knigge was known almost solely for *Ueber den Umgang mit Menschen* (1788; translated as *Practical Philosophy of Social Life; or, The Art of Conversing with Men*, 1799), and this was practically the only work to which scholars had addressed themselves. *Ueber den Umgang mit Menschen* is generally regarded as an etiquette book and has often been the butt of jokes; actually it is a realistic, pragmatic, and often cynical primer on how to survive and make the best possi-

ble impression in this less-than-perfect world. The volume offers a vivid commentary both on Knigge's novels and on the social conditions of his day, and it clearly documents his disillusionment with his society and social class. It also contains much sound advice: for example, on the wisdom of entrusting oneself solely to the care of one competent physician and paying his fees without delay, rather than seeking alternate opinions at every turn. Knigge's last work published during his lifetime, *Ueber Eigennutz und Undank* (On Egotism and Ingratitude, 1796), which he labeled a pendant to *Ueber den Umgang mit Menschen*, is an even more disillusioned social treatise, reflecting Knigge's own rough treatment at the hands of his fellowmen.

Knigge's writing draws heavily on his experiences. Most of the novels deal with members of the lower nobility who aspire to or have had a career at court, are constantly in debt, have been wronged by creditors or lost control of their estates, and are finally done in by court intrigues. A happy ending in a Knigge novel consists of escaping to idyllic retirement and enjoying the life of the country squire to which Knigge himself presumably aspired. Only one novel, *Die Reise nach Braunschweig*, falls outside this pattern: a group of people travels from the countryside to Brunswick to see the Frenchman Blanchard's balloon ascent in 1788; but after all the anticipation and all the rigors of the journey all of the protagonists, for one reason or other, miss out on the momentous event. The most interesting of Knigge's serious novels is the picaresque *Geschichte Peter Clausens* (History of Peter Claus, 1783-1785; translated as *The German Gil Blas; or, The Adventures of Peter Claus*, 1793), the life story of a cobbler's son who rises in society through an incredible series of careers, adventures, and misadventures to marriage, immense wealth, ennoblement, and influence at court, only to fall from favor like other Knigge heroes and retire to the country.

Knigge is most attractive in his late political writing, where he is engaged in the quintessential Enlightenment task of concerning himself with the welfare of his fellow human beings. The most enjoyable of these works is *Benjamin Noldmann's Geschichte der Aufklärung in Abyssinien*, which combines an account of the picaresque career of Joseph Wurmbrand, who ends up as the chief political adviser at the feudal court of Abyssinia, with reflections on the developmental history of the human race, revolutions, and corruption in public life. The corruption of the

Abyssinian government leads to revolution, the institution of a new constitution on the American and French models, and a project of modernizing reform. The book is a compendium of all of Knigge's most advanced and liberal social ideas, and he intended at one point to submit it to the French National Assembly for its consideration in reforming French society.

Knigge used Joseph Wurmbrand again in 1792 as the fictive author of a thoroughgoing defense of the French Revolution (the book that got him into trouble for bypassing the censor): French society and the absolute monarchy under Louis XVI had been so corrupt that the French people had been entirely within their rights to abolish the ancien régime and seek to begin anew. Even after the Jacobin Reign of Terror, Knigge continued to defend the revolution of the French people; in *Rückblicke auf den, wenn Gott will, für Teutschland nun bald geendigten Krieg* he lays the blame for the excesses of the revolutionaries at the door of the decadent aristocracy. Far from preaching revolution to the Germans, however, he consistently appealed to German rulers to learn from the French experience and work to enlighten and improve the condition of their people while there was still time. Like most other German liberals of his day he was a constitutional monarchist at heart, and he praised his own Hannoverian government wholeheartedly (at least in print). If he was inconvenienced by a certain amount of chicanery on the part of that government, he blamed it on advisers and officials who had taken it upon themselves not to carry out the clear policies and intentions of the king. The fearless and outspoken Freiherr von Knigge was a man of his times, speaking to his own time; his admirable qualities are, however, still appealing today.

Bibliography:

Ernst-Otto Fehn and others, eds., *Ob Baron Knigge auch wirklich todt ist? Eine Ausstellung zum 225. Geburtstag des Adolph Freiherrn Knigge* (Wolfenbüttel: Herzog August Bibliothek, 1977).

Biographies:

Philippine Knigge, *Kurze Biographie des Freiherrn Adolph Knigge* (Hannover: Hahn, 1830);

Karl Goedeke, *Adolph Freiherr Knigge* (Hannover: Hahn, 1844).

Title page for Knigge's picaresque novel about the rise and fall of a cobbler's son

References:

Richard van Dülmen, *Der Geheimbund der Illuminaten: Darstellung. Analyse. Dokumentation* (Stuttgart-Bad Cannstatt: Frommann, 1975);

Einige Originalschriften des Illuminatenordens, welche bey Zwack durch vorgenommene Hausvisitation zu Landshut den 11. und 12. Oct. 1786 vorgefunden worden. Auf höchsten Befehl Seiner Churfürstlichen Durchlaucht zum Druck befördert (Munich: 1787);

Leopold Engel, *Geschichte des Illuminaten-Ordens: Ein Beitrag zur Geschichte Bayerns* (Berlin: H. Bermüller, 1906);

Reinhold T. Grabe (Hans Georg Brenner), *Das Geheimnis des Adolph Freiherrn von Knigge: Die Wege eines Menschenkenners* (Hamburg & Leipzig: H. Goverts, 1936);

Friedrich Ludwig Adolph von Grolmann, *Freyherrn von Knigge Welt- und Menschenkenntniß: Ein Pendant zu dem Buche Umgang mit Menschen* (Frankfurt am Main & Leipzig: 1796);

Grolmann, *Die neuesten Arbeiten des Spartacus und Philo in dem Illuminaten-Orden jetzt zum erstenmal gedruckt, und zur Beherzigung bey gegenwärtigen Zeitläuften herausgegeben* (Frankfurt am Main, 1794);

Carl Haase, "Obrigkeit und öffentliche Meinung in Kurhannover 1789-1803," *Niedersächsisches Jahrbuch für Landesgeschichte*, 39 (1967): 192-294;

Ludwig Hammermayer, ed., *Der Wilhelmsbader Freimaurer-Konvent von 1782* (Heidelberg: Lambert Schneider, 1980);

Jörg-Dieter Kogel, *Knigges ungewöhnliche Empfehlungen zu Aufklärung und Revolution* (Berlin: Oberbaumverlag, 1979);

Peter Christian Ludz, ed., *Geheime Gesellschaften* (Heidelberg: Lambert Schneider, 1979);

T. C. Melbert, "Kotzebue and Knigge: Their Role in the Middle Class Identity Crisis," Ph.D. dissertation, Columbia University, 1970;

Nachtrag von weiterer Originalschriften, welche die Illuminatensekte überhaupt, sonderbar aber den Stifter derselben Adam Weishaupt, gewesenen Professor zu Ingolstadt betreffen, und bey der auf dem Baron Bassusischen Schloß zu Sandersdorf, einem bekannten Illuminaten-Neste, vorgenommenen Visitation entdeckt, sofort auf Churfürstlich höchsten Befehl gedruckt, und zum geheimen Archiv genommen worden sind, um solche jedermann auf Verlangen zur Einsicht vorlegen zu lassen, 2 volumes (Munich: Lentner, 1787);

Dietrich Naumann, *Politik und Moral: Studien zur Utopie der deutschen Aufklärung* (Heidelberg: Winter, 1977);

Joseph Popp, "Weltanschauung und Hauptwerke des Freiherrn Adolph von Knigge," Ph.D. dissertation, University of Munich, 1931;

Thomas P. Saine, *Black Bread–White Bread: German Intellectuals and the French Revolution* (Columbia, S.C.: Camden House, 1988);

Saine, Reviews of the Raabe edition of Knigge's *Sämtliche Werke*, *Lessing Yearbook*, 12 (1980): 219-225; 16 (1984): 263-272;

Karl Spengler, "Die publizistische Tätigkeit des Freiherrn Adolph von Knigge während der Französischen Revolution," Ph.D. dissertation, University of Bonn, 1931;

Gerhard Steiner, "Neues vom alten Knigge: Freiherr von Knigge in der Verbannung. Authentisches Material über einen Vorgang zur Zeit der Französischen Revolution," *Marginalien*, 58 (1975): 40-56;

Hedwig Voegt, *Die deutsche jakobinische Literatur und Publizistik 1789-1800* (Berlin: Rütten & Loening, 1955);

Jürgen Walter, "Adolph Freiherrn Knigges Roman 'Benjamin Noldmanns Geschichte der Aufklärung in Abyssinien': Kritischer Rationalismus als Satire und Utopie im Zeitalter der deutschen Klassik," *Germanisch-Romanische Monatsschrift*, new series 21 (1971): 133-180;

E. Yuill, "A Genteel Jacobin, Adolph Freiherr von Knigge," in *Erfahrung und Überlieferung: Festschrift für C. P. Magill*, edited by Hinrich Siefken and Alan Robinson (Cardiff: University of Wales Press, 1974), pp. 42-56;

Barbara Zaehle, *Knigges Umgang mit Menschen und seine Vorläufer: Ein Beitrag zur Geschichte der Gesellschaftsethik* (Heidelberg: Winter, 1933);

Franz Xaver von Zwack, ed., *Anhang zu den Originalschriften des Illuminatenordens, welche auf höchsten Churfürstlichen Befehl zum Druck befördert worden sind* (Frankfurt am Main & Leipzig: 1787).

Papers:

The papers available to Hermann Klencke when he published *Aus einer alten Kiste* in 1853 have since disappeared.

August von Kotzebue

(3 May 1761 - 23 March 1819)

Edward T. Larkin
University of New Hampshire

BOOKS: *Er und Sie: Vier romantische Gedichte* (Eisenach: Wittekindt, 1781);

Erzählungen (Leipzig: Dyck, 1781);

Bibliothek der Journale, 2 volumes (St. Petersburg: Breitkopf, 1783);

Lesbare Sachen beym Verdauungsgeschäfte und am Putztische, anonymous (St. Petersburg & Leipzig: Dyck, 1783);

Der Eremit auf Formentera: Ein Schauspiel mit Gesang in zwey Aufzügen (Reval & Leipzig: Kummer, 1784);

Die Leiden der Ortenbergischen Familie, 2 volumes (St. Petersburg & Leipzig: Kummer, 1785-1786); translated by Peter Will as *The Sufferings of the Family of Ortenberg: A Novel*, 2 volumes (Dublin: Printed for J. Moore, 1799; New York: Printed for Hugh M. Griffith, 1800);

Zaide oder Die Entthronung Muhamed des Vierten: Historische Novelle (Leipzig: Kummer, 1786); translated by Charles Smith as *Zaida; or, The Dethronement of Muhamed IV: A Novel, Founded on Historic Facts* (New York: Burnton & Darling, 1803);

Fliegend Blatt, als Beylage zu der Schrift: Sophisterei in Estland (N.p., 1787);

Kleine gesammelte Schriften, 4 volumes (Reval & Leipzig: Kummer, 1787-1791);

Die väterliche Erwartung: Schauspiel mit Gesang in einem Aufzug (Reval & Leipzig: Kummer, 1788);

Die Geschichte meines Vaters oder Wie es zuging, daß ich gebohren wurde: Ein Roman in zwölf Kapiteln (Reval & Leipzig: Kummer, 1788); translated anonymously as *The History of My Father; or, How It Happened That I Was Born: A Romance* (London: Treppass, 1798);

Ildegerte, Königin von Norwegen: Historische Novelle (Reval & Leipzig: Kummer, 1788); translated by Benjamin Thompson as *Ildegerte, Queen of Norway*, 2 volumes (London: Lane, 1798; Philadelphia: Printed for Robert Campbell, 1800);

August von Kotzebue; engraving by J. B. Bittheuser from a painting by Friedrich Tischbein

Adelheid von Wulfingen: Ein Denkmal der Barbarey des dreyzehnten Jahrhunderts. Trauerspiel in fünf Aufzügen (Reval & Leipzig: Kummer, 1789); translated by Thompson as *Adelaide of Wulfingen: A Tragedy in Four Acts. (Exemplifying the Barbarity Which Prevailed during the Thirteenth Century)* (London: Vernor & Hood, 1798; New York: Printed for Charles Smith & S. Stephens, 1800);

Menschenhaß und Reue: Ein Schauspiel in fünf Aufzügen (Berlin: Himburg, 1789); translated by George Papendick as *The Stranger; or, Misanthropy and Repentance: A Drama* (London:

Wingrave, 1798; Boston: Printed by John Russell, 1799); German version revised (Leipzig: Kummer, 1819);

Die Corsen: Ein Schauspiel in vier Akten (Leipzig: Kummer, 1790); translated anonymously as *The Corsicans: A Drama in Four Acts* (London: Bell, 1799; New York: Longworth, 1814);

Die Indianer in England: Lustspiel in drey Aufzügen. Zum erstenmale aufgeführt auf dem Liebhabertheater zu Reval, im Februar 1789 (Leipzig: Kummer, 1790); translated by Alexander Thomson as *The East Indian: A Comedy* (London: Longman & Rees, 1799; New York: Printed for Charles Smith & S. Stephens, 1800);

Die gefährliche Wette: Ein kleiner Roman, in zwölf Kapiteln (Leipzig: Kummer, 1790);

Doktor Bahrdt mit der eisernen Stirn oder Die Deutsche Union gegen Zimmermann: Ein Schauspiel in vier Aufzügen von Freyherrn von Knigge (Leipzig: Barth, 1790);

Die Sonnen-Jungfrau: Ein Schauspiel in fünf Akten (Leipzig: Kummer, 1791); translated by Anne Plumptre as *The Virgin of the Sun: A Play, in Five Acts* (London: Printed for R. Phillips, sold by H. D. Symonds, 1799; New York: Printed for Charles Smith & S. Stephens, 1800);

Das Kind der Liebe oder Der Straßenräuber aus kindlicher Liebe: Ein Schauspiel in fünf Akten (Leipzig: Kummer, 1791); translated by Plumptre as *The Natural Son: A Play in Five Acts* (London: Phillips, 1798); translated by Thompson as *Lovers' Vows; or, The Natural Son* (London: Vernor & Hood, 1800; Baltimore: Printed for Thomas, Andrews & Butler, 1802);

Bruder Moritz, der Sonderling, oder Die Colonie für die Pelew-Inseln: Lustspiel in drey Aufzügen (Leipzig: Kummer, 1791);

Meine Flucht nach Paris im Winter 1790: Für bekannte und unbekannte Freunde geschrieben (Leipzig: Kummer, 1791);

Ausbruch der Verzweiflung (Leipzig: Cleve, 1791);

Philosophisches Gemälde der Regierung Ludwig des Vierzehnte oder Ludwig der Vierzehnte vor den Richterstuhl der Nachwelt gezogen: Nach dem Französischen des Joseph de la Lalee (Strasbourg: König, 1791);

Der weibliche Jacobiner-Clubb: Ein politisches Lustspiel in einem Aufzuge (Frankfurt am Main & Leipzig: Kummer, 1791); translated by J. C. Siber as *The Female Jacobin-Club: A Political*

Comedy in One Act (Liverpool: Printed by Coddington & Co., sold by W. Jones, 1801);

Der Papagoy: Ein Schauspiel in drey Akten (Leipzig & Frankfurt am Main: Kummer, 1792);

Die edle Lüge: Schauspiel in einem Aufzuge (Leipzig: Kummer, 1792); translated by Maria Geisweiler as *The Noble Lie: A Drama, in One Act* (London: Printed for C. Geisweiler, 1799);

Vom Adel: Bruchstück eines größeren historisch-philosophischen Werkes über Ehre und Schande, Ruhm und Nachruhm, aller Völker, aller Jahrhunderte (Leipzig: Kummer, 1792);

Die jüngsten Kinder meiner Laune, 6 volumes (Leipzig: Kummer, 1793-1797);

An das Publicum von August von Kotzebue (N.p., 1793);

Sultan Wampum oder Die Wünsche: Ein orientalisches Scherzspiel mit Gesang in drey Aufzügen (Frankfurt am Main & Leipzig: Kummer, 1794);

Unpartheiische Untersuchungen über die Folgen der französischen Revolution auf das übrige Europa, anonymous, attributed to Kotzebue (Thorn: Verlagsgesellschaft, 1794);

Graf Benjowsky oder Die Verschwörung auf Kamtschatka: Ein Schauspiel in fünf Aufzügen (Leipzig: Kummer, 1795); translated by Wilhelm Render as *Count Benyowsky; or, The Conspiracy of Kamtschatka: A Tragi-comedy, in Five Acts* (Cambridge: Printed for the author & sold by J. Deighton & J. Nicholson, 1798; New York: Judah, 1799);

Der Mann von vierzig Jahren: Ein Lustspiel in einem Aufzuge. Nach dem Französischen des Frayan (Leipzig: Kummer, 1795); translated by William Poel as *The Man of Forty: A Comedietta, in One Act* (London & New York: French, n.d.);

Armuth und Edelsinn: Ein Lustspiel in drey Aufzügen (Leipzig: Kummer, 1795); translated by Geisweiler as *Poverty and Nobleness of Mind: A Play. In Three Acts* (London: Geisweiler, 1799); translated by Prince Hoare as *Indigence; or, Nobleness of Mind. A Comedy in Five Acts* (New York: Printed for Charles Smith & S. Stephens, 1800);

Die Negersclaven: Ein historisch-dramatisches Gemälde in drey Acten (Leipzig: Kummer, 1796); translated anonymously as *The Negro Slaves: A Dramatic-Historical Piece, in Three Acts* (London: Printed for T. Cadell, Jr., & W. Davies, 1796);

Die Spanier in Peru oder Rolla's Tod: Ein romantisches Trauerspiel in fünf Akten (Leipzig: Kummer, 1796); translated by Matthew Gregory

Lewis as *Rolla; or, The Peruvian Hero: A Tragedy in Five Acts* (London: Printed for J. Bell, and sold by Messrs. Robinsons, Symonds, Longman & Rees, and Hurst, 1799); translated by William Dunlap as *Pizarro in Peru; or, the Death of Rolla* (New York: Printed by G. F. Hopkins for W. Dunlap, 1800);

Die Verläumder: Ein Schauspiel in fünf Akten (Leipzig: Kummer, 1796); translated by Plumptre as *The Force of Calumny: A Play in Five Acts* (London: Printed for R. Phillips, sold by H. D. Symonds & T. Hurst, 1799; New York: Printed for C. Smith & S. Stephens by John Furman, 1800);

Die Wittwe und das Reitpferd: Eine dramatische Kleinigkeit (Leipzig: Kummer, 1796); translated by Plumptre as *The Widow, and the Riding Horse: A Dramatic Trifle in One Act* (London: Printed for R. Phillips, sold by H. D. Symonds, and T. Hurst, 1799; New York: Printed for Charles Smith & S. Stephens, 1800);

Schauspiele, 5 volumes (Leipzig: Kummer, 1797);

Fragmente über Recensenten-Unfug: Eine Beylage zu der Jenaer Literaturzeitung (Leipzig: Kummer, 1797);

Das Dorf im Gebirge: Schauspiel mit Gesang in zwey Akten (Vienna: Schaumburg, 1798);

Der Graf von Burgund: Ein Schauspiel in fünf Akten (Vienna: Doll, 1798); translated by Plumptre as *The Count of Burgundy: A Play, in Four Acts* (London: Printed for R. Phillips, sold by H. D. Symonds, 1798); translated by Smith as *The Count of Burgundy: A Play of Kotzebue* (New York: Printed for Charles Smith & Stephen Stephens, 1800);

Falsche Schaam: Ein Schauspiel in vier Akten (Leipzig: Kummer, 1798); translated anonymously as *False Shame: A Comedy, in Four Acts* (London: Vernor & Hood, 1799; Newark, N.J.: Printed by John Wallis for Charles Smith, New York, 1801);

Der Opfertod: Schauspiel in drey Akten (Leipzig: Kummer, 1798); translated by Henry Neuman as *Self-immolation; or, The Sacrifice of Love: A Play—in Three Acts* (London: Printed for R. Phillips, sold by H. D. Symonds, 1799; Boston: Printed for W. P. and L. Blake, 1799);

La Peyrouse: Ein Schauspiel in zwey Akten (Leipzig: Kummer, 1798); translated by Plumptre as *La-Peyrouse: A Drama, in Two Acts* (London: Printed for R. Phillips, sold by H. D. Symonds, 1799); translated by Smith as *La Peyrouse: A Comedy, in Two Acts* (New York: Printed for Charles Smith & S. Stephens, 1800);

Der Wildfang: Lustspiel in drey Akten (Vienna: Kurzbeck, 1798); translated by R***** H***** as *The Madcap: A Comedy for the Digestion. In Three Acts* (Edinburgh: Printed for C. G. & J. Robinson, London, 1800); translated by Dunlap as *The Wild-Goose Chace: A Play, in Four Acts* (New York: Printed by G. F. Hopkins for W. Dunlap, 1800);

Die Bruderzwist: Ein Schauspiel in fünf Aufzügen . . . Zum Druck befördert von einem Theater-freund oder Die Versöhnung: Schauspiel in fünf Akten (Vienna: Wallishausser, 1798); translated by Conrad Ludger as *The Reconciliation; or, Birthday: A Comedy, in Five Acts* (London: Ridgway, 1799); translated anonymously as *Fraternal Discord: A Comedy, in Five Acts* (New York: Printed for Charles Smith, 1801);

Die Unglücklichen: Ein Lustspiel in einem Akte (Vienna: Wallishausser, 1798);

Die Verwandschaften: Ein Schauspiel in fünf Akten (Vienna: Wallishausser, 1798); translated by Lt. Col. Henry Capadose as *Kindred: A Comedy in Five Acts* (London: Bull, 1837);

Neue Schauspiele, 23 volumes (Leipzig: Kummer, 1798-1819);

Der hyperboreeische Esel oder Die heutige Bildung: Ein drastisches Drama und philosophisches Lustspiel für Jünglinge, in einem Akt (Leipzig: Kummer, 1799);

Die silberne Hochzeit: Ein Schauspiel in fünf Akten (Leipzig: Kummer, 1799); translated by Thompson as *The Happy Family: A Drama in Five Acts* (London: Vernor & Hood, 1799; New York: Printed for C. Smith & S. Stephens, 1800);

Üble Laune: Ein Lustspiel in vier Akten (Leipzig: Kummer, 1799); translated by Ludger as *The Peevish Man: A Drama in Four Acts* (London: Hookham, 1799; Philadelphia: Printed by John Bioren for Henry & Patrick Rice, and James Rice, 1800);

Der alte Leibkutscher Peter des Dritten: Eine wahre Anekdote (Leipzig, 1799);

Über meinen Aufenthalt in Wien und meine erbetene Dienst-Entlassung, nebst A, B, C und D: Eine Vernichtung des im Aprilstück des Berliner Archivs der Zeit gegen mich eingerückten Pasquills (Leipzig: Kummer, 1799);

Der Gefangene: Ein Lustspiel in einem Akt (Leipzig: Kummer, 1800);

Johanna von Montfaucon: Ein romantisches Gemälde aus dem vierzehnten Jahrhundert, in fünf Akten (Leipzig: Kummer, 1800); translated anonymously as *Johanna of Montfaucon* (London: Geisweiler, 1800);

Der Sammtrock: Lustspiel in einem Akt mit Gesang (Vienna: Wallishausser, 1800);

Das Schreibepult oder Die Gefahren der Jugend: Schauspiel in vier Akten (Leipzig: Kummer, 1800); translated anonymously as *The Writing-Desk; or, Youth in Danger: A Play in Four Acts* (London: Printed for G. G. & J. Robinson by G. Woodfall, 1799; New York: Printed for Charles Smith, 1801);

Bayard: Ein Schauspiel in fünf Akten (Leipzig: Kummer, 1801);

Der Besuch oder Die Sucht zu glänzen: Lustspiel in vier Akten (Leipzig, 1801);

Das Epigramm: Ein Lustspiel in vier Akten (Vienna: Wallishausser, 1801);

Die kluge Frau im Walde oder Der stumme Ritter: Ein Zauberspiel in fünf Aufzügen (Vienna: Wallishausser, 1801);

Gustav Wasa: Ein Schauspiel in fünf Akten (Leipzig: Kummer, 1801);

Das merkwürdigste Jahr meines Lebens, 2 volumes (Berlin: Sander, 1801); translated by Benjamin Beresford as *The Most Remarkable Year in the Life of August von Kotzbue: Containing an Account of His Exile into Siberia, and of the Other Extraordinary Events Which Happened to Him in Russia* (London: Phillips, 1802; New York: Hopkins, 1802); German version revised (Berlin: Sander, 1803); edited by Hans Schumann as *Das merkwürdigste Jahr meines Lebens als Verbannter in Sibirien* (Zurich: Manesse, 1989);

Das neue Jahrhundert: Eine Posse in einem Akt (Leipzig: Kummer, 1801);

Die beyden Klingsberg: Ein Lustspiel in vier Akten (Leipzig: Kummer, 1801); translated anonymously as *Father and Son; or, Family Frailties: A Comedy in Five Acts*, in *The New British Theatre*, edited by John Galt, volume 3 (London: Printed for the Proprietors, 1814), pp. 349-408;

Lohn der Wahrheit: Ein Schauspiel in fünf Akten (Leipzig: Kummer, 1801);

Octavia: Ein Trauerspiel in fünf Akten (Leipzig: Kummer, 1801);

Des Teufels Lustschloß: Eine natürliche Zauber-Oper in drey Akten (Leipzig: Kummer, 1801);

Vituvia: Trauerspiel (Leipzig, 1801);

Die Zurückkunft des Vaters: Ein Vorspiel (Leipzig: Kummer, 1801);

Kurze und gelassene Antwort des Herrn von Kotzebue auf eine lange und heftige Schmähschrift des Herrn von Masson (Berlin: Sander, 1802);

August von Kotzebues erste und letzte Beilage zu dem Buche: Das merkwürdigste Jahr meines Lebens, als erste und letzte Antwort für einen nichtswürdigen Pasquillanten, der eigentlich keine Antwort verdient (Berlin, 1802);

Das Fest der Laune: Gegeben zu Weimar, nach der ersten Vorstellung der Jungfrau von Orleans. Mit Prolog, Epilog und Dialog, auch einigen anderen Nebenfeyerlichkeiten, anonymous, attributed to Kotzebue (N.p., 1802);

Der Spiegelritter: Eine Oper in drey Aufzügen (Vienna: Goldmann, 1802);

Almanach der Chroniken für das Jahr 1804 (Leipzig: Kummer, 1803);

Almanach Dramatischer Spiele zur geselligen Unterhaltung auf dem Lande, 18 volumes (Berlin: De la Garde, 1803-1807; Leipzig: Kummer, 1808; Riga: Hartmann, 1809-1812; Leipzig: Hartmann, 1813-1816; Leipzig: Kummer, 1817-1820);

Cleopatra: Eine Tragödie (Vienna: Wallishausser, 1803);

Unser Fritz: Ein Schauspiel in einem Akt (Vienna: Wallishausser, 1803);

Expektorationen: Ein Kunstwerk und zugleich ein Vorspiel zum Alarcos, anonymous (N.p., 1803);

Hugo Grotius: Schauspiel in vier Akten (Leipzig: Kummer, 1803);

Der Hahnenschlag: Schauspiel in einem Akt (Vienna: Wallishausser, 1803);

Die Hussiten vor Naumburg im Jahr 1432: Ein vaterländisches Schauspiel mit Chören in fünf Akten (Leipzig: Kummer, 1803); translated by Frederic Shoberl as *The Patriot Father: An Historical Play in Five Acts* (London: Kirby, 1830);

Die deutschen Kleinstädter: Ein Lustspiel in vier Akten (Leipzig: Kummer, 1803); translated by Oscar Mandel as *The Good Citizens of Piffelheim*, in his *August von Kotzebue: The Man, the Comedy* (University Park & London: Pennsylvania State University Press, 1989);

Die französischen Kleinstädter: Lustspiel in vier Akten nach Picard (Leipzig, 1803);

Die Kreuzfahrer: Ein Schauspiel in fünf Akten (Leipzig: Kummer, 1803); translated anonymously as *Alfred and Emma: A Play in Five Acts, Founded in the Red Cross Knights of Kotzebue* (London: Printed for the author by J. Whitling, 1806);

Don Ranudo de Colibrados: Lustspiel in vier Akten nach Holberg (Leipzig: Kummer, 1803);

Der Schauspieler wider Willen: Ein Lustspiel in einem Akt nach dem Französischen (Leipzig: Kummer, 1803);

Der Wirrwarr oder Der Muthwillige: Eine Posse in vier Akten (Leipzig: Kummer, 1803); translated by E. F. F. as *The Confusion; or, The Wag: A Play in Five Acts* (Cambridge: Hall / London: Whittaker, 1842);

Die schlaue Wittwe oder Die Temperamente: Eine Posse in einem Akt (Vienna: Wallishausser, 1803);

Ariadne auf Naxos: Ein tragikomisches Triodrama (Vienna, 1804);

Erinnerungen aus Paris im Jahre 1804 (Berlin: Frölich, 1804); translated anonymously as *Travels from Berlin through Switzerland to Paris, in the Year 1804*, 3 volumes (London: Printed for R. Phillips, 1804);

Der todte Neffe: Lustspiel in einem Akt (Leipzig: Kummer, 1804);

Pagenstreiche: Posse in fünf Aufzügen (Leipzig: Kummer, 1804);

Rübezahl: Ein Schauspiel in einem Akt (Vienna: Wallishausser, 1804);

Die Tochter Pharaonis: Ein Lustspiel in einem Aufzuge (Vienna: Wallishausser, 1804); translated by Beatrice B. Beebe as *Pharaoh's Daughter* in *Typical Plays for Secondary Schools*, edited by J. P. Webber and H. H. Webster (Boston, 1929);

Die Uhr und die Mandeltorte (Vienna: Wallishausser, 1804);

Der Vater von ungefähr: Ein Lustspiel in einem Akt (Vienna: Wallishausser, 1804);

Erinnerungen von einer Reise aus Liefland nach Rom und Neapel, 3 volumes (Berlin: Frölich, 1805); translated anonymously as *Travels through Italy, in the Years 1804 and 1805*, 4 volumes (London: Phillips, 1806; revised, 1807);

Die hübsche, kleine Putzmacherinn: Ein Lustspiel in einem Aufzuge (Vienna: Wallishausser, 1805);

Mädchenfreundschaft oder Der türkische Gesandte: Ein Lustspiel in einem Akt (Vienna: Wallishausser, 1805);

Heinrich Reuss von Plauen oder Die Belagerung von Marienburg: Ein Trauerspiel in fünf Akten (Leipzig: Kummer, 1805);

Kleine Romane, Erzählungen, Anekdoten und Miscellen, 6 volumes (Leipzig: Kummer, 1805-1809); translated anonymously as *Historical, Literary, and Political Anecdotes, and Miscella-*

nies, 3 volumes (London: Printed for H. Colburn by S. Rousseau, 1807);

Die Stricknadeln: Ein Schauspiel in vier Akten (Frankfurt am Main & Leipzig: Kummer, 1805);

Bonaparte, der du bist im Himmel, geheiligt werde dein Nahme!, anonymous (Rome: Päpstlicher Buchdruckerey [probably Königsberg], 1806);

Carolus Magnus: Lustspiel in drey Aufzügen (Fortsetzung der deutschen Kleinstädter) (Leipzig: Kummer, 1806); revised as *Der Gallatag in Krähwinkel: Ein Lustspiel in drey Akten* (Vienna: Wallishausser, 1809);

Das verlorene Kind: Ein Schauspiel in einem Akt (Vienna: Wallishausser, 1806);

Blinde Liebe: Lustspiel in drey Akten (Leipzig: Kummer, 1806);

Die gefährliche Nachbarschaft: Ein Lustspiel in einem Aufzug (Vienna: Wallishausser, 1806); translated and adapted by William Thomas Moncrieff as *The Party Wall; or, In and Out! A Comic Interlude, in One Act* (New York: Clayton / Philadelphia: Neal, 1842);

Die Organe des Gehirns: Ein Lustspiel in drey Akten (Leipzig: Kummer, 1806); translated by Capadose as *The Organs of the Brain: A Comedy in Three Acts* (London: Bull, 1838);

Das Schmuckkästchen oder Der Weg zum Herzen: Schauspiel in vier Aufzügen (Vienna: Wallishausser, 1806);

Der Deserteur: Eine Posse in einem Akt (Vienna, 1808);

Die Erbschaft: Schauspiel in einem Akt (Vienna, 1808);

Das Gespenst: Romantisches Schauspiel in vier Akten (Leipzig: Kummer, 1808);

Der Leineweber: Ein Schauspiel in einem Akt (Vienna: Wallishausser, 1808);

Das Posthaus in Treuenbrietzen: Ein Lustspiel in einem Akt (Vienna, 1808);

Preußens ältere Geschichte, 4 volumes (Riga: Hartmann, 1808);

Das Standrecht: Schauspiel in einem Akt (Vienna: Wallishausser, 1808);

Der Stumme: Lustspiel in einem Akt (Vienna: Wallishausser, 1808); translated by Beebe as *The Man Who Couldn't Talk: A Comedy in One Act*, *Poet Lore*, 40, no. 2 (1929): 223-236;

Ubaldo: Ein Trauerspiel in fünf Akten (Leipzig: Kummer, 1808);

Die Unvermählte: Ein Drama in vier Aufzügen (Vienna: Wallishausser, 1808);

Leontine: Ein Roman, 2 volumes (Riga & Leipzig: Hartmann, 1808); translated anonymously as *Leontina: A Novel*, 3 volumes (London: Colburn, 1809);

Der blinde Gärtner oder Die blühende Aloe: Liederspiel (Leipzig: Kummer, 1809);

Das Intermezzo oder Der Landjunker zum erstenmale in der Residenz: Ein Lustspiel in fünf Akten (Leipzig: Kummer, 1809);

Philibert oder Die Verhältnisse: Ein Roman (Königsberg: Nicolovius, 1809);

Die Seeschlacht und die Meerkatze: Posse in einem Akt (N.p., 1809);

Der verbannte Amor oder Die argwöhnischen Eheleute: Lustspiel in vier Akten (Leipzig: Kummer, 1810);

Kotzebue's Theater, 54 volumes (Vienna: Doll, 1810-1820);

Herr Gottlieb Merks, der Egoist und Criticus: Eine Burleske in zwey Aufzügen (N.p., 1810); translated by W. H. H. Chambers as *Egotist and Pseudo-critic, Herr Gottlieb Merks* in *The Drama: Its History, Literature, and Influences on Civilization*, edited by Alfred Bates, volume 11 (London: Athenian Society, 1903), pp. 303-336;

Das arabische Pulver: Posse in zwei Akten nach Holberg (Leipzig: Kummer, 1810);

Kleine gesammelte Schriften, 4 volumes (Leipzig: Kummer, 1810);

Sorgen ohne Noth und Noth ohne Sorgen: Lustspiel in fünf Akten (Leipzig: Kummer, 1810);

Die kleine Zigeunerin: Ein Schauspiel in vier Akten (Leipzig: Kummer, 1810);

Clios Blumenkörbchen, 3 volumes (Darmstadt: Leske, 1811-1812);

Pachter Feldkümmel von Tippelskirchen: Ein Fastnachtsspiel in fünf Akten (Leipzig: Kummer, 1811);

Blind geladen: Lustspiel in einem Akt (Leipzig, 1811); translated and adapted anonymously as *How to Die for Love: A Farce, in Two Acts* (London: Chapple, 1812; Philadelphia: Carey, 1812);

Die Belagerung von Saragossa oder Pachter Feldkümmels Hochzeitstag: Lustspiel in vier Akten (Leipzig: Kummer, 1811);

Das zugemachte Fenster: Eine komische Operette (Vienna: Wallishausser, 1811);

Die neue Frauenschule: Lustspiel frei nach dem Französischen (Leipzig & Augsburg: Stage, 1811);

Max Helfenstein: Lustspiel in zwei Akten (Leipzig: Kummer, 1811);

Der Flußgott Niemen und Noch Jemand: Ein Freudenspiel in Knittelversen, Gesang und Tanz (Reval, 1812);

Geschichte Kaiser Ludwigs IV. (Riga: Hartmann, 1812);

Geschichten für meine Söhne (Tübingen: Cotta, 1812);

Die Ruinen von Athen: Ein Nachspiel mit Chören und Gesängen. Zur Eröffnung des neuen Theaters in Pesth. Musik Ludwig von Beethoven (Pesth, 1812); translated by Paul England as *The Ruins of Athens: Cantata by Beethoven* (London: Novello, 1898);

Ungerns erster Wohlthäter: Ein Vorspiel mit Chören. Zur Eröffnung des neuen Theaters in Pesth verfaßt. Musik Ludwig van Beethoven (Pesth, 1812);

Die barmherzigen Brüder: Nach einer wahren, in der National-Zeitung vom Jahre 1802 aufbehaltenen Anekdote (Vienna: Wallishausser, 1812);

Der Brief aus Cadix: Ein Drama in drei Akten (Leipzig: Kummer, 1813);

Politische Ansichten, Gedanken und Meinungen (Berlin, 1813);

Bela's Flucht: Ein Schauspiel in zwei Akten (Leipzig: Kummer, 1813);

Die deutsche Hausfrau: Ein Schauspiel in drei Akten (Leipzig: Kummer, 1813);

Große Hofversammlung in Paris.—Der Abschied aus Cassel: Ein rührendes Singspiel von Friedrich Germanns. Steckbrief der Cassler Bürgerschaft hinter Hieronymus Napoleon nebst Signalement (N.p., 1813);

Possen bey Gelegenheit des Rückzuges der Franzosen: Seitenstück zum Flußgott Niemen und Noch Jemand (N.p., 1813);

An die Deutschen und an die deutschen Blätter (Leipzig: Rein, 1814);

Politische Flugblätter, 2 volumes (Königsberg: Nicolovius, 1814-1816);

Geschichte des deutschen Reiches, von dessen Ursprunge bis zu dessen Untergange, 4 volumes (Leipzig: Kummer, 1814-1832);

Napoleon's Reise-Abentheuer: Eine heroische Tragi-Comödie (Leipzig, 1814);

Noch Jemand's Reise-Abentheuer: Eine heroische Tragi-Comödie. Seitenstück zum Flußgott Niemen und Noch Jemand (Königsberg: Nicolovius, 1814);

Der Schutzgeist: Eine dramatische Legende in sechs Akten nebst einem Vorspiel (Leipzig: Kummer, 1814);

Epilog . . . am Tage . . . von la belle Alliance (Königsberg, 1815);

Opern-Almanach für das Jahr 1815 (Leipzig: Kummer, 1815);

Der Rehbock oder Die schuldlosen Schuldbewußten: Ein Lustspiel in drei Akten (Leipzig: Kummer,

1815); translated and adapted by C. A. Somerset as *The Roebuck; or, Guilty and Not Guilty: A Comedy in Three Acts* (London: Duncombe, n.d.);

Der Schawl: Lustspiel in einem Akt (Vienna: Wallishausser, 1815);

Chroniken: Eine Auswahl historischer und romantischer Darstellungen aus der Vorzeit (Leipzig, 1816);

Romanesken (Vienna: Haas, 1816);

Rudolph von Habsburg und König Ottokar von Böhmen: Ein historisches Schauspiel in sechs Akten (Leipzig: Kummer, 1816);

Des Hasses und der Liebe Rache: Schauspiel aus dem spanischen Kriege in fünf Akten (Leipzig: Kummer, 1816);

Opern-Almanach für das Jahr 1817 (Leipzig: Kummer, 1817);

Gottes-Gericht: Eine Neujahrausgabe für erwachsene Jünglinge und Mädchen (Frankfurt am Main: Körner, 1817);

Pudenda oder Archiv der Thorheiten unserer Zeit (Leipzig: Barth, 1817); excerpts republished as *Magnetisiertes Scheidewasser* (Weimar: Hoffmann, 1819);

Der Rothmantel: Ein Volksmärgen [sic] nach Musäus, für die Bühne bearbeitet in vier Akten (Leipzig: Kummer, 1817);

Der Vielwisser: Ein Lustspiel in fünf Akten (Leipzig: Kummer, 1817);

Gedichte, 2 volumes (Vienna: Wallishausser, 1818);

Der deutsche Mann und die vornehmen Leute: Sittengemälde in vier Akten (Leipzig: Kummer, 1818);

Das Taschenbuch: Ein Drama in drei Akten (Leipzig: Kummer, 1818);

Gisela: Schauspiel in vier Akten (Leipzig: Kummer, 1818);

Switrigail: Ein Beytrag zu den Geschichten von Litthauen, Rußland, Polen und Preußen (Leipzig: Kummer, 1820);

Aus August von Kotzebues hinterlassenen Papieren, edited by L. J. von Knorring (Leipzig: Kummer, 1821);

Sämmtliche dramatische Werke, 44 volumes (Leipzig: Kummer, 1827-1829);

Theater: Mit biographischen Nachrichten. Rechtmäßige Original-Auflage, 40 volumes (Vienna: Klang / Leipzig: Kummer, 1840-1841);

August's von Kotzebue ausgewählte prosaische Schriften. Enthaltend: Die Romane, Erzählungen, Anekdoten und Miszellen, 45 volumes (Vienna: Klang, 1842-1843).

Editions in English: *Collected Dramas*, 6 volumes (London: Printed for R. Phillips, 1798-1799);

The Beauties of Kotzebue: Containing the Most Interesting Scenes, Sentiments, Speeches, &c. in All His Admired Dramas. Freely Translated; Connected and Digested under Appropriate Heads, Alphabetically Arranged; with Biographical Anecdotes of the Author; A Summary of His Dramatic Fables, and Cursory Remarks, edited by Walley Chamberlain Oulton (London: Crosby & Letterman, 1800);

The Dramatic Works of Baron Kotzebue, 3 volumes, translated by Charles Smith and others (New York: Printed for Charles Smith & Stephen Stephens, 1800);

A Selection of the Best Plays of Augustus von Kotzebue, translated by Anne Plumptre and Henry Neuman (London: Phillips, 1800);

Sketch of the Life and Literary Career of Augustus von Kotzebue: With the Journal of His Tour to Paris, at the Close of the Year 1790. Written by Himself, translated by Plumptre (London: Printed by C. Whittingham for H. D. Symonds, 1800; New York: Ward, 1801);

The Dramatic Works of Baron von Kotzebue, 3 volumes, translated by Benjamin Thompson (London: Vernor, 1802);

The Pastor's Daughter, with Other Romances, 4 volumes, translated anonymously (London: Printed for Henry Colburn, 1806);

Novellettes, 3 volumes, translated anonymously (London: Phillips, 1807);

The Beauties of Kotzebue: Consisting of Selections from His Works, edited by Alfred Howard (London: Printed by T. Davison for T. Tegg, n.d.).

OTHER: "Ich, eine Geschichte in Fragmenten, zu Nutz und Frommen der mannbaren Jugend, an's Licht bracht von mir selbst," in *Ganymed für die Nachwelt*, edited by J. G. E. Wittekind (Eisenach: Wittekindt, 1781), pp. 1-100;

Für Geist und Herz: Monatsschrift für die nordischen Gegenden, 4 volumes, edited by Kotzebue (volumes 1-3, Reval: Glehn; volume 4, Leipzig: Breitkopf, 1786-1787);

Johann Karl August Musäus, *Nachgelassene Schriften des verstorbenen Professor Musäus: Herausgegeben von seinem Zögling*, edited by Kotzebue (Leipzig: Kummer, 1791);

G. W. von Derzchavin, *Felizens Bild: Aus dem Russischen*, translated by Kotzebue (Reval & Leipzig: Dyck, 1792);

Derzchavin, *Gedichte des Herrn Staatsraths von Derschawin: Aus dem Russischen*, translated by Kotzebue (Leipzig: Kummer, 1793);

Heinrich Zschokke, *Das rächende Gewissen: Ein Trauerspiel in vier Aufzügen*, revised by Kotzebue (Vienna: Wallishausser, 1799);

Jean Nicolas Bouilly, *Der Taubstumme oder Der Abbé de l'Épee: Historisches Drama in fünf Akten. Aus dem Französischen*, translated by Kotzebue (Leipzig: Kummer, 1800); translated by Benjamin Thompson as *Deaf and Dumb; or, The Orphan: An Historical Drama. In Five Acts* (London: Vernor & Hood, 1801); translation republished as *Abbé de l'Épee; or, The Orphan: An Historical Drama, in Four Acts* (New York: Printed for Charles Smith, 1801);

Louise oder Die unseligen Folgen des Leichtsinns: Eine Geschichte einfach und wahr, 2 volumes, foreword by Kotzebue (Leipzig: Kummer, 1800);

Der Freymüthige oder Berlinische Zeitung für gebildete und unbefangene Leser, edited by Kotzebue (Berlin: Sander, 1803);

Der Freymüthige oder Ernst und Scherz: Ein Unterhaltungsblatt, 4 volumes, edited by Kotzebue and G. Merkel (Berlin: Sander, 1804-1807);

Alexandre Duval, *Eduard in Schottland oder Die Nacht eines Flüchtlings: Historisches Drama in drey Akten*, translated and revised by Kotzebue (Vienna: Wallishausser, 1804); translated and revised by Charles Kemble as *The Wanderer; or, The Rights of Hospitality: A Drama, in Three Acts* (New York: Longworth, 1808);

Jean Baptiste Louvet de Couvrai, *Die Abentheuer des jungen Faublas: Aus dem Französischen*, 2 volumes, translated by P. C. Weyland, foreword by Kotzebue (volume 1, Leipzig & Gotha: Hennings, 1805; volume 2, Hamburg: Herold, 1810);

Bouilly, *Fanchon, das Leyermädchen: Vaudeville in drei Akten. Aus dem Französischen*, translated by Kotzebue (Leipzig: Kummer, 1805);

Molière, *Die Schule der Frauen: Lustspiel in fünf Akten*, translated by Kotzebue (Leipzig: Kummer, 1805);

E. Hennig, ed., *Statuten des deutschen Ordens: Nach dem Originalexemplar. Mit erläuternden Anmerkungen*, foreword by Kotzebue (Königsberg: Nicolovius, 1806);

Taschenbuch auf das Jahr 1807, edited by Kotzebue (Tübingen & Stuttgart: Cotta, 1806);

Die Biene: Eine Quartalschrift, 8 volumes, edited by Kotzebue (Königsberg: Nicolovius, 1808-1810);

Geist aller Journale, 6 issues, edited by Kotzebue (Riga: Hartmann, 1809);

Die Grille, 3 volumes, edited by Kotzebue (Königsberg: Nicolovius, 1811-1812);

Bouilly, *Geschichten für meine Töchter*, 2 volumes, translated by Kotzebue (Leipzig: Hartmann, 1811);

Das russisch-deutsche Volksblatt, 39 issues, 10 supplements, edited by Kotzebue (Berlin: Expedition des R. D. V., 1813);

Bericht an S. M. den König von Schweden: Aus dem Französischen, translated by Kotzebue (Königsberg: Michelsen, 1814);

Richard Cumberland, *Der Westindier: Lustspiel in fünf Akten. Aufs neue für die deutsche Bühne bearbeitet*, revised by Kotzebue (Leipzig: Kummer, 1815);

Kurze Übersicht der Manufakturen und Fabriken in Rußland: Aus dem Russischen, translated by Kotzebue (Königsberg: Nicolovius, 1815);

Generalin Bertrand, *Briefe . . . von der Insel St. Helena, geschrieben an eine Freundin in Frankreich: Aus dem Französischen*, translated by Kotzebue (Königsberg: Universitätsbuchhandlung, 1816);

Moriz von Kotzebue, *Der russische Kriegsgefangene unter den Franzosen: Herausgegeben von dessen Vater*, edited by Kotzebue (Leipzig: Kummer, 1816); translated anonymously as *The Russian Prisoner of War among the French: Edited with the Addition of a Preface and Postscript, by the Author's Father*, A. von Kotzebue (London: Printed for Gale & Fenner by S. Hamilton, 1816);

Louis Benoît Picard, *Der Captain Belronde: Lustspiel in drei Acten nach Picard für die deutsche Bühne bearbeitet*, revised by Kotzebue (Leipzig: Kummer, 1817);

Petr Ivanovich Ricord, *Erzählung des Kapitän Rikord von seiner Fahrt nach den japanischen Küsten in den Jahren 1812 und 1813*, edited by Kotzebue (St. Petersburg & Leipzig: Kummer, 1817);

Alexandru Sturdza, *Betrachtungen über die Lehre und den Geist der Orthodoxen Kirche*, translated by Kotzebue (Leipzig: Kummer, 1817);

Literarisches Wochenblatt, edited by Kotzebue, 3 volumes (Weimar: Hoffmann, 1818-1819).

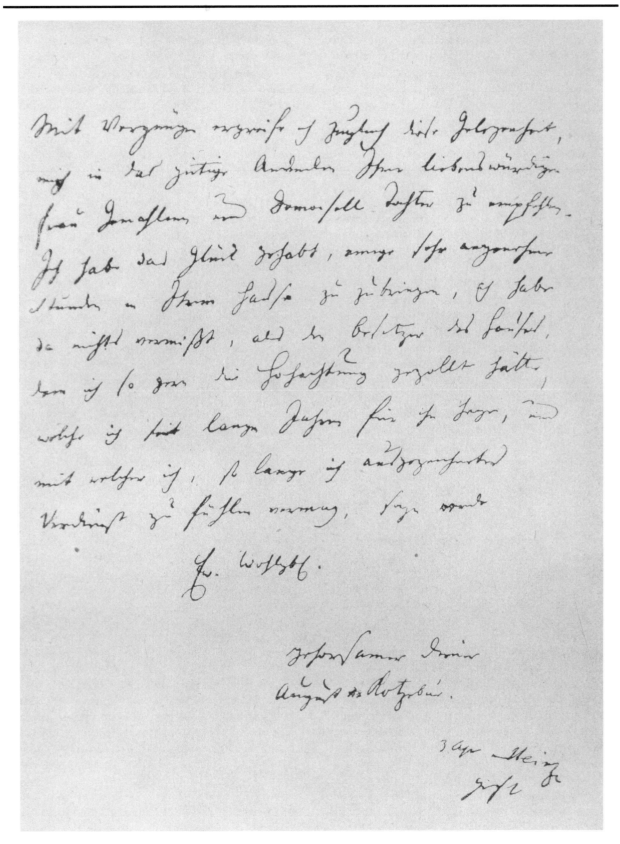

Last page of a letter by Kotzebue (Joseph Kürschner, ed., Deutsche National-Litteratur, *volume 139:* Kotzebue und Collin,
edited by Adolf Hauffen [Stuttgart: Union Verlagsgesellschaft, n.d.])

One of the most prolific writers of the Age of Goethe, August von Kotzebue was the author of short stories, novels, travelogues, historical studies, autobiographical works, essays, and poetry; he also edited newspapers and journals and translated French plays into German. It is, however, for his great facility and voluminous productivity as a dramatist that he is best known. Kotzebue, who once boasted that he could write a comedy in three days, estimated the total number of his dramatic works to be 211; recent scholarship places the figure at 230. While his comedies and melodramas won him acclaim, his few efforts in historical drama and in tragedy were justifiably ignored by the literary establishment. Kotzebue conceded in the foreword to his *Der Graf von Burgund* (1798; translated as *The Count of Burgundy*, 1798) that he was not a writer of masterworks but argued that his ability to create popular, stageworthy productions should earn him a position of honor among the German dramatists.

Kotzebue's plays enjoyed phenomenal success (with all social classes), both national and international. They accounted for approximately one quarter of the repertoire of the German stages from 1795 to 1825 and were equally popular abroad, being translated into English, Russian, Danish, Swedish, French, Spanish, Rumanian, Italian, Dutch, Greek, Bulgarian, and Serbo-Croatian. In England his success aroused the envy and ire of playwrights and critics, and in the New York theaters in 1799 fifty-two of the ninety-four performances were translations or adaptations of Kotzebue's works.

Kotzebue was born in Weimar on 3 May 1761. He was raised by his mother, Christina Krüger Kotzebue, because his father, Levin Karl Christian Kotzebue, the legation secretary to Princess Anna Amalia of Weimar, died when Kotzebue was two years old. Kotzebue received his primary education at the Weimar Gymnasium, where he impressed his teacher, Johann Karl August Musäus, with some of his writings. While not particularly interested in school, the young Kotzebue was a voracious reader. His enthusiastic reading of *Don Quixote* (1605, 1615), *Robinson Crusoe* (1719-1720), and Johann Gottfried Schnabel's *Die Insel Felsenburg* (Felsenburg Island, 1731-1743) later manifested itself in the exotic settings and positive portrayals of natural and unaffected characters in his plays. Because of the father's position, the Kotzebue family maintained close ties to the Weimar court and consequently to Johann Wolfgang Goethe, who arrived in Wei-

mar in 1775. The young Kotzebue's interest in drama was stimulated by his participation as a letter carrier in a production of Goethe's *Die Geschwister* (The Siblings; written in 1776, published in 1787). As a youth he was also deeply moved by a performance of Friedrich Gottlob Klopstock's *Der Tod Adams* (The Death of Adam, 1757) at the Weimar palace, and he is said to have committed to memory Gotthold Ephraim Lessing's *Emilia Galotti* (1772).

At sixteen Kotzebue was sent to the University of Jena, where he studied languages and participated in informal dramatic productions. His efforts to have his writings published in Christoph Martin Wieland's *Der teutsche Merkur* were unsuccessful. After his sister married a gentleman from Duisburg, Kotzebue's mother decided that her son should continue his education at the university in that city. But there he was again distracted from his studies, founding an amateur theater group at a nearby cloister and trying his hand at a novel. In 1779 he returned to Jena and at his mother's encouragement studied law. Kotzebue, however, rarely attended the lectures. Instead, his activities included writing an imitation of *Emilia Galotti* titled "Charlotte Frank" and a ballad, which was judged immoral by the censor at the university, satirizing the women of the Jena-Weimar area. At nineteen he completed his studies and passed an examination which entitled him to practice law.

His attempt to settle in Weimar in 1781 proved unsuccessful, in part because of his earlier offensive characterization of the local women. Through the intercession of Count Goertz, an acquaintance of Kotzebue's father, Kotzebue found employment as the secretary to the governor-general, Friedrich Wilhelm von Bauer, in St. Petersburg. On a trip to Riga the general came across a copy of Kotzebue's *Erzählungen* (Tales, 1781). He was sufficiently impressed with the stories that he entrusted Kotzebue with the management of the German stage in St. Petersburg. In 1783 Kotzebue was appointed counselor and assessor of the chief court in the Duchy of Estonia in Reval (present-day Tallinn) by the empress Catherine II. Finding the cultural conditions in Reval somewhat regressive, Kotzebue again founded a theater. To ensure the approval of the theater by the nobility and religious authorities, he distributed the profits to the poor. In 1785 Kotzebue married Friederike von Essen, a woman of the high Estonian nobility. In the same year he was named chief justice and president of the government-magistrate of the province of Estonia, which entitled him to the privileges of nobility. He was not yet twenty-four years old.

In the winter of 1787-1788, while suffering from a prolonged fever, Kotzebue wrote *Menschenhaß und Reue* (1789; translated as *The Stranger; or, Misanthropy and Repentance*, 1798) and *Die Indianer in England* (1790; translated as *The East Indian*, 1799) for the theater in Reval. *Menschenhaß und Reue* prompted a host of sequels and parodies by other playwrights and established Kotzebue's reputation as a dramatist. The melodrama depicts the reconciliation of Baron Meinau with his wife, whose infidelity had caused the baron to withdraw from the world and disdain humanity.

Menschenhaß und Reue is representative of Kotzebue's conception of melodrama. The play is entertaining, stageable, and sentimental. Kotzebue's chief aim in drama is to involve the spectators emotionally in the play so that they will be entertained and will continue to support the theater. The audience is moved by the inclusion of instances of repentance, magnanimity, and forgiveness. The characters are placed in a seemingly hopeless situation, but the apparent catastrophe is transfigured into personal happiness. Kotzebue's desire to entertain his audience often led him to ignore social reality: the final forgiveness and reconciliation in *Menschenhaß und Reue* contradicted the eighteenth-century attitude toward adultery and laid the seeds of future claims of immorality in his work. While Kotzebue did not hold to the classical view of the stage as a moral institution through which moral precepts are reinforced, he did possess a predilection for sententious statement. Still, morality and education were always subordinate to theatricality and sentimentality. Nor did he consider social criticism essential to drama; only mild and inconsistent criticism of absolutism and class prejudice are found in his dramatic works.

In 1790, as his wife lay dying after the birth of their fourth child in Weimar, Kotzebue underwent a water treatment for his fevers in Bad Pyrmont under the direction of Dr. Johann Georg von Zimmermann, a noted physician and writer from Hannover. Unable to cope with the sufferings of his wife, Kotzebue secretly fled to Paris. In *Meine Flucht nach Paris im Winter 1790* (1791; translated as "My Flight to Paris" in *Sketch of the Life and Literary Career of Augustus von Kotzebue*, 1800) he describes the disruptive impact of the French Revolution on Parisian society and

communicates his sincere sense of loss over the death of his wife. Just before he left Paris in January 1791 there appeared the satiric and virtually pornographic play *Doktor Bahrdt mit der eisernen Stirn oder Die Deutsche Union gegen Zimmermann: Ein Schauspiel in vier Aufzügen von Freyherrn von Knigge* (Doctor Bahrdt with the Iron Forehead; or, The German Union against Zimmermann: A Play in Four Acts by Freiherr von Knigge, 1790). The claim that Kotzebue attributed this work to Adolph Freiherrn von Knigge because of the latter's negative review of *Die Indianer in England* remains disputed. It seems likely that Knigge's name was chosen because he was one of Zimmermann's harshest critics. After Friedrich II had died in 1786, Zimmermann, the king's physician, published three works which, while laudatory of the king, criticized the leading advocates of the Enlightenment, attributing the lack of morality in society, and even the outbreak of the French Revolution, to the propagation of the humanistic principles espoused during the Enlightenment. In response, Knigge, Theodor Gottlieb von Hippel, and Carl Friedrich Bahrdt, the Protestant theologian whose scandal-ridden life was renowned, satirized Zimmermann's medical practices and literary efforts.

Doktor Bahrdt, Kotzebue's unsolicited defense of Zimmermann, depicts a gathering of Zimmermann's enemies at Bahrdt's brothel. Each of the figures–Johann Heinrich Campe, Heinrich Christian Boie, Georg Christoph Lichtenberg, Friedrich Nicolai, Abraham Gotthelf Kästner, and Christian Friedrich von Blanckenberg–is characterized by an ironic or vulgar epithet. Each divulges an incident which suggests his perversity or lack of self-restraint. The characters then swear before a lingam to establish a "German Union against Zimmermann." But the revelers are punished by the spirit of Martin Luther as well as a host of other heavenly figures.

By virtue of its bawdiness and the uncertainty surrounding its authorship, *Doktor Bahrdt* quickly became a best-seller. The satire, typical of Kotzebue's polemic, provoked vociferous protests of indecency and immorality, and a police investigation was initiated to determine the identity of the author. To divert suspicion from himself, Kotzebue had a man named Schlegel in Reval write an article confessing to be the author. When it became clear that Kotzebue did write the play, he fled to St. Petersburg. There he was granted asylum by Catherine II, in whose good graces Zimmermann had stood.

The publication of *Doktor Bahrdt* had long-lasting effects on Kotzebue's career. It solidified his position as an outsider in the literary establishment by alienating him from those whose religious and cultural views were actually similar to his own. Kotzebue was not an ardent advocate of religious orthodoxy and espoused tolerance in religious matters. His position on social issues, particularly on the question of class relations, was at best ambiguous in its support of the privileges of nobility. A further consequence of the publication of *Doktor Bahrdt* was that future reviewers of his other works–including Clemens Brentano, Johann Gottfried Herder, and Friedrich Schleiermacher–repeatedly referred back to the immorality of the play. To counter the negative impact of the text, Kotzebue issued an apology, titled *An das Publicum* (To the Public, 1793), which he distributed at his own expense. In an earlier publication, *Vom Adel* (On the Aristocracy, 1792), Kotzebue had expressed his support of the institution of nobility.

In the summer of 1791 Kotzebue returned to his estate, Friedenthal, in Estonia. In 1794 he married Christina von Krusensten, a noble heiress. After having secured a lifetime pension, Kotzebue resigned his position in Estonia in 1795. He became director of the Imperial Theater in Vienna in 1797 but quit after nine months (also with a pension), apparently because the actors were reluctant to perform a new play every three weeks.

In 1799 Kotzebue purchased a house in Weimar, hoping to settle there; but his wife's desire to see her family in Russia and his own conflicts with Goethe and the early Romantic poets compelled him to leave Weimar after only one year. Goethe had great admiration for Kotzebue's ingenious use of theatrical effects and for his ability to write successful plays; in fact, as director of the Weimar theater he produced eighty-seven of Kotzebue's plays. But Goethe was put off by Kotzebue's arrogance and polemical nature, and he considered Kotzebue's plays lacking in intellectual vitality and aesthetic necessity.

Kotzebue's most blatant criticism of the Romantics can be found in his one-act comedy *Der hyperboreeische Esel oder Die heutige Bildung: Ein drastisches Drama und philosophisches Lustspiel für Jünglinge* (The Hyperborean Donkey; or, Today's Education: A Drastic Drama and Philosophical Comedy for Adolescents, 1799), a denunciation of Romantic aesthetics and philosophy. Karl von Bey returns home after his university studies and is unable to engage in any reasonable conversation with the members of his family. His utterances consist of isolated, incoherent statements from Friedrich Schlegel's novel *Lucinde* (1799) and the Romantic periodical *Das Athenäum*. He is finally institutionalized. Kotzebue's satirical characterization of Romanticism prompted August Wilhelm Schlegel to respond in 1800 with *Ehrenpforte und Triumphbogen für den Theaterpräsidenten von Kotzebue bei seiner gehofften Rückkehr ins Vaterland* (A Triumphal Arch for Kotzebue, President of the Theater, upon His Return to the Fatherland). In this play Schlegel accuses Kotzebue of triviality and lack of imagination.

In April 1800, despite warnings from his friends, Kotzebue departed Berlin with his wife and three children to return to Russia. Suspected of Jacobin sympathies despite his public affirmation of noble privilege, Kotzebue was arrested at the border by the police of the xenophobic Czar Paul I and sent to Siberia without trial. For four months he was held, first in Tobolsk, where his plays were being performed, and then in Kurgan, where, he claims in *Das merkwürdigste Jahr meines Lebens* (1801; translated as *The Most Remarkable Year in the Life of August von Kotzbue*, 1802), he was something of a celebrity. In July Kotzebue was pardoned, richly compensated, and made director of the court theater in St. Petersburg when Paul learned of his comedy *Der alte Leibkutscher Peter des Dritten* (The Old Coachman of Peter the Third, 1799), which celebrates a generous action of the czar's father. Kotzebue was able to leave Russia with his family when Paul's successor, Alexander I, ascended the throne. Returning to Weimar, Kotzebue again failed to gain acceptance with the literary establishment, and in late 1802 he moved to Berlin (where he enjoyed wide acceptance) to become coeditor of the successful periodical *Der Freymuthige*.

In 1803 Kotzebue's most successful play, the comedy *Die deutschen Kleinstädter* (The German Townsfolk, 1803; translated as *The Good Citizens of Piffelheim*, 1989) was performed in Berlin. Its popularity is illustrated by the fact that Johann Nestroy's play *Freiheit in Krähwinkel* (Freedom in Krähwinkel, 1849) and Heinrich Heine's poem "Erinnerung aus Krähwinkels Schreckenstagen" (Memoir of Krähwinkel's Terrible Days, 1854) could presuppose the audience's familiarity with the fictional town in which the play is set. In the manner of a revue this farcical four-act play satirizes bourgeois ceremoniousness, ridiculous pedantry, and philistine behavior. The obsession of

The assassination of Kotzebue by the theology student Karl Ludwig Sand on 23 March 1819 (Städtisches Reiß-Museum, Mannheim)

the townspeople with titles impedes the marriage of the natural and unpresumptuous Sabine Starr to Olmers, a young man from the capital. Olmers comes to Krähwinkel to ask for her hand in marriage, but Sabine has already been promised to Herr Sperling, a quixotic, poetical type, in whom Kotzebue once again criticizes Romantic aesthetics. In a typical case of mistaken identity Olmers is believed to be the king in disguise. But when it becomes evident that he has no title at all, his already slim chances of marrying Sabine are reduced to nil. In the end his fortune is reversed when he is able to save the townspeople from embarrassment by using his influence at the court.

Die deutschen Kleinstädter is representative of Kotzebue's comedies. The middle-class characters are portrayed critically yet sympathetically. The dialogue is witty and fresh, and sentimentality is kept to a minimum. Double meanings, repetition of comical effects, and mistaken identities form the basis of the humor. Catastrophes are only apparent, and the happy ending is never really in doubt. The orderly functioning of the world is

maintained, and the intactness of the family is ensured.

After the death of his second wife in August 1803 Kotzebue traveled again to Paris; his *Erinnerungen aus Paris im Jahre 1804* (Memoirs from Paris in the Year 1804, 1804; translated as *Travels from Berlin through Switzerland to Paris, in the Year 1804*, 1804) details his interest in the French theater and continues his critique of the French Revolution. In Paris he met Napoleon, for whom he had little sympathy and whom he later satirized in *Bonaparte, der du bist im Himmel, geheiligt werde dein Nahme!* (Bonaparte, Who Art in Heaven, Hallowed Be Thy Name!, 1806). In 1804, shortly after returning to Estonia, Kotzebue married Wilhelmina von Krusenstern, a cousin of his second wife. He then traveled to Italy, reporting on the journey in *Erinnerungen von einer Reise aus Liefland nach Rom und Neapel* (Memoirs from a Trip from Livonia to Rome and Naples, 1805; translated as *Travels through Italy, in the Years 1804 and 1805*, 1806). Kotzebue was not enamored of Italy; on the contrary, he takes pains to extol the leadership qualities of Czar Alexander of Russia. When Kotzebue returned north, he was admitted to the Prussian Academy of Sciences and settled in Königsberg, where (with the king's encouragement) he engaged in research for his *Preußens ältere Geschichte* (Prussia's Early History, 1808), a work which found little favor with the public and which was largely ignored by the scholarly community.

In 1816 Kotzebue was rewarded for his opposition to Napoleon in the periodicals *Die Biene* (1808-1810), *Die Grille* (1811-1812), and *Das russisch-deutsche Volksblatt* (1813) with the title Councilor of State of Russia. At his own request he was sent to Germany to be a correspondent for the czar. He settled in Weimar, from where he submitted monthly reports on politics, finance, and warfare in Germany and France. Kotzebue was suspected of spying for the czar in the fall of 1817 when part of one of his reports was published by the liberal establishment. While the details surrounding the incident are unclear, it seems that Kotzebue gave his report to a student to be copied; but the student allowed someone else to read it and copy passages from it. It was then passed on to the liberal Jena professor Heinrich Luden, who wanted to publish it in his journal *Nemesis*. Kotzebue had the page confiscated before Luden could publish it; but it did appear in Lorenz Oken's *Isis* and Ludwig Wieland's *Volksfreund*, and Kotzebue incurred the anger of the liberals, especially of the students. When the first volume of Kotzebue's *Geschichte des deutschen Reichs, von dessen Ursprunge bis zu dessen Untergange* (History of the German Empire from Its Origins to Its Downfall, 1814-1832) was burned at the Wartburg Festival in 1817, Kotzebue made his displeasure with the book burning known, referring to the universities as "Brutstätten der Revolution" (breeding grounds for revolution). These comments, along with the conservative positions he took in his weekly, *Literarisches Wochenblatt*, incited the students. Fearing for the safety of his family, Kotzebue fled with his wife and children to Mannheim at the end of 1818. But in the late afternoon of 23 March 1819 he was stabbed to death in his home by the theology student Karl Ludwig Sand, who had been a volunteer in the Wars of Liberation, a participant in the Wartburg Festival, and cofounder of the Burschenschaft at Erlangen. By temperament he was an improbable assassin but was likely moved to the act by the political excitement generated by the student movement and by the rhetoric of the liberal professors at Jena. Sand was arrested following a failed suicide attempt outside the Kotzebue residence and beheaded in May 1820. He became a hero for the proponents of a constitutional government, and many outspoken liberals wrote on his behalf. History has generally treated Sand favorably. Kotzebue, on the other hand, after having been mourned publicly on many German stages, has been blamed (probably unfairly) for the imposition of the repressive Karlsbad Decrees (1819), which prohibited the "Burschenschaften" (student fraternities), curtailed the autonomy of the universities, and intensified the censorship laws.

Letters:

Der Briefwechsel zwischen August von Kotzebue und Carl August Böttiger (Bern & New York: Lang, 1987).

Biographies:

Benjamin Thompson, *Biographical Account of Baron von Kotzebue* (London: Wright, 1801);

Friedrich Cramer, *August von Kotzebues Leben* (Leipzig: Brockhaus, 1820); translated anonymously as *The Life of August von Kotzebue* (London: Boosey, 1820);

H. Döring, *August von Kotzebues Leben* (Weimar: Hoffmann, 1830);

Charles Rabany, *Kotzebue: Sa vie et son temps, ses oeuvres dramatiques* (Paris: Berger-Levrault, 1893).

References:

Leif Ludwig Albertsen, "Internationaler Zeitfaktor Kotzebue: Trivialisierung oder sinnvolle Entliterarisierung und Entmoralisierung des strebenden Bürgers im Frühliberalismus?," *Sprachkunst*, 9 (1978): 220-240;

Alfred Behrmann, "Kotzebue on the American Stage," *Arcadia*, 4 (1969): 274-284;

Peter Brückner, "–bewahre uns Gott in Deutschland vor irgendeiner Revolution!": Die Ermordung des Staatsrats von Kotzebue durch den Studenten Sand* (Berlin: Wagenbach, 1978);

Gerhard Giesemann, *Kotzebue in Rußland: Materialien zu einer Wirkungsgeschichte* (Frankfurt am Main: Athenäum, 1971);

Giesemann, *Zur Entwicklung des slovenischen Nationaltheaters: Versuch einer Darstellung typologischer Erscheinungen am Beispiel der Rezeption Kotzebues* (Munich, 1975);

A. W. Holzmann, *Family Relationships in the Dramas of August von Kotzebue* (Princeton & London: Princeton University Press, 1935);

Robert Kahn, "Kotzebues Weltanschaung," *Modern Language Forum*, 38 (1953): 41-55;

Karl-Heinz Klingenberg, *Iffland und Kotzebue als Dramatiker* (Weimar: Arion, 1962);

Oscar Mandel, *August von Kotzebue: The Comedy, the Man* (University Park & London: Pennsylvania State University Press, 1989);

Doris Maurer, *August von Kotzebue: Ursachen seines Erfolges, konstante Elemente der unterhaltenden Dramatik* (Bonn: Bouvier, 1979);

James McGoldrick, "Russia in the Writings of August von Kotzebue: A Study of Kotzebue's Satire and Irony," Ph.D. dissertation, State University of New York, Buffalo, 1976;

Thomas C. Melbert, "Kotzebue and Knigge: Their Role in the Middle Class Identity Crisis," Ph.D. dissertation, Columbia University, 1971;

Douglas Milburn, "The Popular Reaction to German Drama in England at the End of the Eighteenth Century," *Rice University Studies*, 55 (1969): 149-162;

Fritjof Stock, *Kotzebue im literarischen Leben der Goetzeit: Polemik–Kritik–Publikum* (Düsseldorf: Bertelsmann, 1971);

Johannes Strohschänk, "Die Kotzebuerezeption am Dunlaps Park Theatre in New York um 1800," Ph.D. dissertation, University of California, Davis, 1986;

Harley U. Taylor, Jr., "The Dramas of August von Kotzebue on the New York and Philadelphia Stages from 1798 to 1805," *West Virginia University Philological Papers*, 23 (1977): 47-58;

Jenny Broekman de Vries, "August von Kotzebue: His Popularity on the Early American Stage," *Schatzkammer*, 2 (1976): 33-42;

Jack Zipes, "Dunlap, Kotzebue and the Shaping of American Theater: A Re-evaluation from a Marxist Perspective," *Early American Literature*, 8 (1974): 272-284.

Papers:

Letters and manuscripts of August von Kotzebue are at the Freies Deutsches Hochstift, Frankfurt am Main.

Sophie von La Roche

(6 December 1730 - 18 February 1807)

Jeannine Blackwell
University of Kentucky

BOOKS: *Geschichte des Fräuleins von Sternheim: Von einer Freundin Derselben aus Original-Papieren und anderen zuverläßigen Quellen gezogen,* 2 volumes, anonymous, edited by Christoph Martin Wieland (Leipzig: Weidmann & Reich, 1771); translated by Edward Harwood as *Memoirs of Miss Sophy Sternheim,* 2 volumes (London: Printed for T. Becket, 1776); German version reprinted, 1 volume, edited by Marlies Korfsmeyer (Munich: Winkler, 1976);

Der Eigensinn der Liebe und Freundschaft: Eine englische Erzählung nebst einer kleinen deutschen Liebesgeschichte, anonymous (Zurich: Füßli, 1772);

Bibliothek für den guten Geschmack, anonymous (Amsterdam & Bern, 1772);

Rosaliens Briefe an ihre Freundin Marianne von St**: Von der Verfasserin des Fräuleins von Sternheim, 3 volumes, anonymous, edited by Johann Joachim Bode (Altenburg: Richter, 1779-1781);

Empfindungen der Verfasserin der Geschichte des Fräuleins von Sternheim, als Joseph II. in Schwetzingen war (Vienna, 1782); republished as *Joseph der Zweyte nahe bei Speyer im Jahre 1781,* anonymous (Speyer: Enderesi, 1783);

Moralische Erzählungen im Geschmacke Marmontels, 2 volumes, anonymous (Mannheim: Goedeke, 1782-1784);

Die glückliche Reise: Eine moralische Erzählung, anonymous (Basel: Serini, 1783);

Moralische Erzählungen der Verfasserin der Pomona (Speyer, 1784);

Die zwey Schwestern: Eine moralische Erzählung, anonymous (Frankfurt am Main & Leipzig, 1784); translated by Jeannine Blackwell as "Two Sisters," in *Bitter Healing: German Women Authors from 1700 to 1840. An Anthology in English,* edited by Blackwell and Suzanne Zantop (Omaha: University of Nebraska Press, forthcoming);

Waldone: Eine moralische Erzählung, anonymous (Speyer: Enderesi, 1785);

Sophie von La Roche; painting by Johann Heinrich Wilhelm Tischbein (Sophie von La Roche, Geschichte des Fräuleins von Sternheim, *edited by Fritz Brüggemann [Leipzig: Reclam, 1938])*

Briefe an Lina: Als Mädchen, als Mutter, 3 volumes, anonymous (Mannheim, 1785-1787); enlarged edition, 2 volumes, as La Roche (Leipzig, 1789-1794);

Neuere moralische Erzählungen, anonymous (Altenburg: Richter, 1786);

Tagebuch einer Reise durch die Schweiz, von der Verfasserin von Rosaliens Briefen, anonymous (Altenburg: Richter, 1787);

*Moralische Erzählungen: Nachlese zur ersten und zwei-
ten Sammlung,* anonymous (Mannheim & Offenbach, 1787);

*Journal einer Reise durch Frankreich, von der Verfasse-
rin von Rosaliens Briefen,* anonymous (Altenburg: Richter, 1787);

*Freunde und Freundinnen von zwei sehr verschiedenen
Jahrhunderten und die Bade-Bekanntschaften*
(Offenbach: Brede, 1788);

*Tagebuch einer Reise durch Holland und England,
von der Verfasserin von Rosaliens Briefen,* anonymous (Offenbach:Weiß & Brede, 1788); excerpts translated by Claire Williams as *Sophie in London, 1786: Being the Diary of Sophie
von La Roche* (London: Cape, 1933);

Geschichte von Miß Lony und der schöne Bund
(Gotha: Ettinger, 1789);

Briefe über Mannheim (Zurich: Füßli, 1791);

Rosalie und Cleberg auf dem Lande (Offenbach:
Weiß & Brede, 1791);

*Erinnerungen aus meiner dritten Schweizerreise:
Meinem verwundeten Herzen zur Linderung,
vielleicht auch mancher trauernden Seele zum
Trost geschrieben* (Offenbach: Weiß & Brede,
1793);

Schönes Bild der Resignation, 2 volumes (Leipzig:
Gräff, 1795-1796; revised, 1801);

*Sendschreiben über die Wieland- und Geßner-, Schlos-
ser- und Nicolovius'schen Verbindungen* (Karlsruhe, 1795);

Erscheinungen am See Oneida, 3 volumes (Leipzig:
Gräff, 1798);

*Reise von Offenbach nach Weimar und Schönebeck
‹Jahr 1799* (Leipzig: Gräff, 1800); also published as *Schattenreise abgeschiedener Stunden
in Offenbach, Weimar und Schönebeck im Jahr
1799;*

Mein Schreibetisch: An Herrn G. R. P. in D., 2 volumes (Leipzig: Gräff, 1799);

Fanny und Julia oder Die Freundinnen, 2 volumes
(Leipzig: Gräff, 1801-1802);

Liebe-Hütten, 2 volumes (Leipzig: Gräff, 1803-
1804);

Melusiens Sommerabende, edited by Wieland
(Halle: Societäts-Buch- und Kunsthandlung,
1806);

Erinnerungen aus meinem Leben (Leipzig, 1807).

OTHER: *Pomona für Teutschlands Töchter,* 24 issues, edited by La Roche (Speyer: Hennings
/ Altenburg, 1782-1784);

Frederike Baldinger, *Lebensbeschreibung von Friederike Baldinger, von ihr selbst verfaßt,* edited by
La Roche (Offenbach: Weiß & Brede, 1791);

Herbsttage, edited by La Roche (Leipzig: Gräff,
1805).

Sophie von La Roche, the first recognized
and acclaimed woman novelist in Germany, was
both a pioneer in the establishment of an independent women's literary public and a conservative
monarchist opposed to full independence for
women. The contradictions in her literary and personal lives reflect those of her era. Born into a
wealthy doctor's family and thus by birth a member of the bourgeoisie, she married into court
life. A devout Pietist from Swabia whose father forbade her marriage to a Catholic, she sent her
daughters to a convent school and married her
children off across religious lines. The sentimental novelist par excellence, she rejected the love
match as a basis for marriage and tried to arrange financially advantageous situations for her
children. A member of the nobility, she became a
widow with no pension who used her writings to
support herself and her children. She spoke and
wrote French, the language of the educated
court lady, as her first language, but learned German orthography slowly and painfully, without
benefit of formal schooling, and had a penchant
for graphic Swabian turns of phrase. These contradictions had much to do with her precarious social and financial standing in the wake of upheav-
als in court life and in the literary scene.

Marie Sophie Gutermann was born in
Kaufbeuren, Swabia, on 6 December 1730; the
first of thirteen children in a wealthy and respected family, she grew up in Augsburg. Her father, Georg Friedrich Gutermann, was a dean of
the medical faculty at the university; her mother,
Regina Barbara Gutermann, née Unold, died
when Sophie was seventeen, probably from complications of childbirth. Sophie, her father's "little
librarian" and a wunderkind, had read the whole
Bible by age five. Her father, who had studied theology at Halle, the Pietist center of Germany, did
not allow her to study with the famous pedagogue and philosopher Jacob Brucker, who had
volunteered to teach her; instead, she learned
the accomplishments of the educated bourgeois
girl: French, dancing, painting, music, sewing,
and cooking. Her father arranged a marriage to
an Italian physician, Gian Lodovico Bianconi,
from whom Sophie learned mathematics and Italian; but the negotiation of a marriage contract
failed over the question of whether the couple's
children would be raised in the Protestant or Catholic faith. The seventeen-year-old Sophie was or-

dered to rip Bianconi's picture to pieces before her father; she refused Bianconi's offer of an elopement.

After a brief engagement in 1750 to her younger cousin Christoph Martin Wieland that was opposed by all their relatives, Sophie Gutermann entered on 27 December 1753 into an arranged marriage with Georg Michael Frank von La Roche, the private secretary and favorite son of the duke of Stadion in Mainz. She bore eight children, five of whom–Maximiliane, Fritz, Luise, Carl, and Franz Wilhelm–survived infancy. In the course of leading salon and dinner discussions she continued her irregular self-education. In 1762 the La Roches followed the duke from Mainz into semiretirement at Warthausen. That Sophie's friendship with Wieland remained intact is witnessed in their lifelong correspondence of more than 5,500 letters; Warthausen and Wieland's home in Biberach were one mile apart. Wieland encouraged her to write German and helped teach her orthography, and their children played together. After the duke's death in 1768, Georg Michael La Roche was appointed minister, and later chancellor, to the prince-elector Clemens Wenzelaus of Trier, with his residence at Ehrenbreitstein.

Sophie La Roche's first publication, *Geschichte des Fräuleins von Sternheim* (1771; translated as *Memoirs of Miss Sophy Sternheim*, 1776), was an immediate best-seller. It is the first German epistolary novel, the first German novel by a writer known to be a woman, and what some critics call the first novel of sentimentality in German. La Roche was acclaimed as a maternal muse by the fiery young Sturm und Drang authors Johann Gottfried Herder, Johann Wolfgang Goethe, J. M. R. Lenz, and the Jacobis. *Geschichte des Fräuleins von Sternheim* was noted particularly for the adeptness with which the main character, whom the author calls "eine schöne Seele" (a beautiful soul), fused the Pietist model of introspection with the bourgeois ideal of the physically attractive sentimental heroine. Sophy Sternheim, like her creator, is poised between the middle-class world of virtue and the vicissitudes of court life. This robust character survives seduction and betrayal by the charmingly evil Lord Derby, pulls herself out of poverty and degradation by becoming a teacher, and restores herself to universal acclaim and vindication as the wife of a handsome young gentleman. Moving precariously between classes, Sternheim embodied for her generation the notion of virtue in distress. But for the mem-

bers of the Sturm und Drang movement, who saw personality and genius as the key to revolt, she was also an integrated soul, one with which Goethe's Werther could have had an affinity.

The popularity of this anonymous novel, the authorship of which soon became widely known, assured La Roche a continuing readership. The growing split in the German reading public and between "high" and "low" literature after 1770 determined, however, that the members of the Sturm und Drang such as Goethe and Lenz would not be the loyal devotees of La Roche's books or of her journal *Pomona für Teutschlands Töchter* (Pomona for Germany's Daughters, 1782-1784). The enlightened, pedagogical bent of La Roche's program for German women of the middle classes was not the goal of the genius cult of the young Goethe or of the Romantics of the 1790s. Where La Roche depicted romantic love as a mode of emotional and social mobility, a test of character, and an education in society for female figures, the genius cult of Goethe and the Romantics saw it as a sensual inspiration of the male poet in his creation of the work of art. The term *Bildung* (education) for La Roche covered a broad sweep of practical accomplishments for the improvement of the middle classes and women; for the genius cult *Bildung* became the aesthetic education of cultural elite best exemplified in the highly autobiographical Bildungsroman. This cultural and social difference of opinion is seen in Goethe's comment on La Roche in a 1799 letter to Friedrich Schiller: "Sie gehört zu den nivellierenden Naturen, sie hebt das Gemeine auf und zieht das Vorzügliche herunter und richtet das Ganze als dann mit ihrer Sauce zu beliebigem Genusse an" (She is one of the sort who levels everything out; she raises the common things and pulls down the superior, and then dishes it all up with her own special sauce).

La Roche's place in literary history has been bound to this division of the reading public, and her work after *Geschichte des Fräuleins von Sternheim* has been ignored. Her close association with Wieland caused her star to rise and fall with his. La Roche was the model for the pastoral figure in Wieland's twelve odes to Doris, written in 1751-1752; a protagonist in Lenz's *Pandaemonium germanicum* (1819); and the bluestocking woman writer portrayed in Schiller's poem "Die berühmte Frau" (The Famous Woman, 1789). Above all, her position within the Goethean Age was determined by her proximity to Goethe and

La Roche (left) with her husband, Georg Michael Frank von La Roche, and their daughter Maximiliane, circa 1770;
painting by Anton Wilhelm Tischbein (Goethemuseum, Frankfurt am Main)

the Romantics: as the mother of Maximiliane, to whom Goethe was briefly attracted when he visited the family in Ehrenbreitstein; as the grandmother, through Maximiliane's 1774 marriage to Pietro Brentano, of Bettina Brentano von Arnim, whose book *Goethes Briefwechsel mit einem Kinde* (1835; translated as *Goethe's Correspondence with a Child,* 1837-1839) shocked the literati of her time; and as the grandmother of Clemens Brentano. She was to remain "the grandmother of the Brentanos" until the 1960s, when sociological analyses of the late-eighteenth-century reading public treated her work in discussions of Trivial-literatur. Only as the concept of triviality itself has been put into question has La Roche's work undergone serious reinvestigation by sociologists of literature and by feminist critics.

Georg Michael La Roche's flourishing career as a diplomat ended in 1780, in the aftermath of the publication of his antimonastic *Briefe über das Mönchwesen* (Letters on Monasticism,

1771). His fall meant a withdrawal to calm small-town life in Speyer and, after 1786, in Offenbach, where Georg La Roche died in 1788. It also meant serious financial setbacks for the family and led to Sophie La Roche's publishing endeavors and her attempts to arrange marriages and professions for her unpropertied children.

Rosaliens Briefe an ihre Freundin Marianne von St** (Rosalie's Letters to Her Friend Marianne von St**, 1779-1781) began La Roche's twenty-five-year career as a self-supporting woman author. Here, as well as in her *Briefe an Lina* (Letters to Lina, 1785-1787) and most of her moral tales of the 1780s, La Roche creates a contrast between the abuses of authority within the bourgeois family in the city, on the one hand, and the idyllic countryside where class and religious differences and the subordination of women are neutralized, on the other. The bourgeois pastoral ideal, in which the home is the core of existence, replicates the rural utopian schemes of many Enlighteners and places La Roche among the most progressive women authors of her day. Yet at the same time her idylls embody a benevolent, enlightened paternalism and the physiognomies of her protagonists, the distribution of virtues among her characters, and the eventual marriage of her heroines to "naturally" noble men reinforce existing class structures. Behavioral reform rather than revolution, flight to the country rather than social conflict are La Roche's aims. The carefully observed architectural, horticultural, and decorative details in La Roche's works underscore her belief in the possibility of realizing this vision.

In her travel writings La Roche, one of the few middle-class women to travel without male companions, opened a field that would become a major literary outlet for authors such as Therese Huber, Fanny Lewald, and Luise Mühlbach. Although her travels within Germany and to England, Switzerland, Holland, and France did not extend as far geographically as the classic male journey, she brought to her predominantly female readership the domestic detail so frequently missing in the standard travelogues. She overcame the geographical limits of her actual travels in her fiction: in *Geschichte des Fräuleins von Sternheim* La Roche realistically creates the impoverished milieu of exploited Scottish tin miners; in an idyll set in America, *Erscheinungen am See Oneida* (Event at Lake Oneida, 1798), her European heroine gives birth assisted by Indian women. She passed on her interest in socially critical travel fiction to her granddaughter Bettina Brentano, whom she helped to raise: Bettina and Gisela von Arnim's novel *Das Leben der Hochgräfin Gritta von Rattenzuhausbeiuns* (The Life of the Countess Gritta von Ratsatourhouse, 1844) incorporates travel and social criticism into the fairy-tale format.

In her later years La Roche promoted younger women authors, publishing Caroline von Günderrode in her anthology *Herbsttage* (Autumn Days, 1805) and Caroline von Wolzogen, Philippine Gatterer Engelhard, Sophie Albrecht, Luise von Göchhausen, and Wilhelmine von Gersdorf in her journal *Pomona*. As influential as La Roche was in the developing years of German women's literature, however, the significance of her own writing faded except with her loyal and aging reading public. The French Revolution separated her politically from the intellectuals with whom she might have had the closest affinity: her correspondence with Georg and Therese Heyne Forster, as well as her sympathetic interest

in Romantics such as Caroline Böhmer Schlegel, ended in 1789. Her previous association with French-influenced German court life made her sympathetic to the royalist cause, even though her family had been disadvantaged within that system; La Roche, like Goethe and many others born before 1750, was not able to accept the end of that epoch. A self-supporting author who was not part of the artistic and critical elite, she continued to write works portraying sentimental yet enlightened notions of virtue, charity, and self-interest; her public remained female and middle-class. Her advocacy of arranged marriages and her rejection of love matches distanced her from the younger generation looking for romance, not virtue and education, in women's fiction.

The deaths of her son Franz in 1791 and her daughter Maximiliane in 1793 after her thirteenth childbed, and the failure of her daughter Luise's marriage to an abusive, alcoholic courtier deeply affected La Roche; her neglect on the literary scene contributed to her sense of loss. In 1795 she lost her small pension from the Trier court when Trier fell into French hands. Yet her belief in the educability of humankind remained firm in her last major work, *Mein Schreibetisch* (My Writing Desk, 1799). She ends this intellectual retrospective with an expression of sentimental virtue: "Ich fühle inn mit 68 Jahren noch ganz, den hohen Werth der Kenntnisse, und ob ich schon mit meiner Eugenia in *Schönes Bild der Resignation* sagen kann: 'Alles, was Menschen mir gaben, haben Menschen mir wieder genommen'; aber der, wie man mich lehrte, einzige Zug Aehnlichkeit mit unserm Urheber, Güte, und die uns von allen anderen erschaffenen Wesen auszeichnenden Gaben, Denken und Wissen, sind mir geblieben. Das Schicksal zerstörte meinen Wohlstand, die Jahre meine Gestalt:—aber meine Seele kennt den wahren Werth aller Dinge dieser Erde, freut sich der vielen vortrefflichen Menschen, welche ich kennenlernte, und zollt ihnen Hochachtung, Liebe und Dankbarkeit. Oft drücke ich die Briefe wohlwollender Freunde mit Entzücken an mein Herz, kenne keinen Neid, keinen Haß, noch Unruhe, denke nur an das Gute, und habe keinen größeren Wunsch, als im Stande zu sein, Leidenden zu helfen, und noch viele Bücher zu lesen" (I still feel with my 68 years the great value of knowledge, and even though I can say with Eugenia in [Beautiful Image of] Resignation: "Everything that people have given me, people have taken away again"; I still possess that

Title page for La Roche's novel set at Lake Oneida, New York

one trait that makes us resemble our Creator, goodness, and the traits that distinguish us from all the rest of creation, thinking and knowing. Fate has destroyed my prosperity, and the years my body, but my soul knows the true worth of all things of this earth, enjoys the many excellent people I have known, and pays tribute to them in admiration, love, and gratitude. I often press letters from supportive friends to my heart, knowing no envy, no hate, no unease; I think only about the good, and have no greater wish than to be in a position to help the suffering, and to keep on reading books).

    Her death at Offenbach on 18 February 1807 was little noticed.

Letters:

"Briefe aus der Weimarschen Literaturepoche l.

Auszüge aus den Briefen von Sophie von La Roche an Wieland," edited by K. W. Bötti-ger, *Morgenblatt für gebildete Leser*, 51 (1857): 950-952;

"Aus alten Briefen: Die Familie La Roche und ihr Freundeskreis in den Jahren 1760-1780," edited by Robert Hassenkamp, *Nord und Süd*, 73 (1895): 323-340;

"Aus dem Nachlaß der Sophie von La Roche," edited by Hassenkamp, *Euphorion*, 5 (1898): 475-502;

"Briefe der Sophie von LaRoche an den Prinzen Friedrich von Gotha-Altenburg," edited by P. von Ebart, *Westermanns Monatshefte*, 89 (March 1901): 771-781;

"Lettres inédites de Sophie de La Roche," edited by J. Dresch, *Revue Germanique*, 11 (1920): 135-147, 220-247; 12 (1921): 16-45; 15 (1924): 434-446; 16 (1925): 26-36, 156-166,

Sophie von La Roche

305-314, 439-452; 18 (1927): 13-19, 114-120;

Lettres de Sophie de La Roche à C. M. Wieland: Précédées d'une étude sur Sophie La Roche, edited by Victor Michel (Nancy: Berger-Levrault, 1938);

"Ein empfindsamer Briefwechsel," edited by Hans Werner Seiffert, *Beiträge zur deutschen und nordischen Literatur* (1958): 153-174;

Wielands Briefwechsel, edited by the Akademie der Wissenschaften der DDR, 5 volumes to date (Berlin: Akademie-Verlag, 1963-　);

Sophie von La Roche: Ihre Briefe an die Gräfin Elise zu Solms-Laubach 1787-1807, edited by Kurt Kampf (Offenbach: Stadtarchiv, 1965);

"Unbekannte Briefe C. M. Wielands und Sophie von La Roches aus den Jahren 1789 bis 1793," edited by Hansjörg Schelle, *Modern Language Notes,* 86 (1971): 649-695;

Ich bin mehr Herz als Kopf: Sophie von La Roche, Ein Lebensbild in Briefen, edited by Michael Maurer (Munich: Beck, 1983).

Biographies:

Kuno Ridderhoff, "Einleitung," in La Roche's *Ge-*

schichte des Fräuleins von Sternheim (Berlin: Behr, 1907), pp. v-xxxix;

Bernd Heidenreich, *Sophie von La Roche: Eine Werkbiographie* (Frankfurt am Main, Bern & New York: Lang, 1986).

References:

Barbara Becker-Cantarino, " 'Muse' und 'Kunstrichter,' Sophie von La Roche und Wieland," *Modern Language Notes,* 99 (April 1984): 571-588;

Becker-Cantarino, "Nachwort," in La Roche's *Geschichte des Fräuleins von Sternheim* (Stuttgart: Reclam, 1983), pp. 318-418;

Becker-Cantarino, "Sophie La Roche, der Beginn der "Frauenliteratur' und der weiblichen Tradition," in her *Der lange Weg zur Mündigkeit: Frauen und Literatur 1500-1800* (Stuttgart: Metzler, 1987), pp. 278-301;

Silvia Bovenschen, *Die imaginierte Weiblichkeit: Exemplarische Untersuchungen zu kulturgeschichtlichen und literarischen Präsentationsformen des Weiblichen* (Frankfurt am Main: Suhrkamp, 1979), pp. 190-200;

Charlotte Craig, "Sophie von La Roche's Enlightened Anglophilia," *Germanic Notes,* 8 (1977): 34-40;

Burghard Dedner, *"Die Geschichte des Fräuleins von Sternheim* und *Rosaliens Briefe:* Die Umdeutung der Tradition im Bereich 'realistischen' Erzählens," in his *Topos, Ideal und Realitätspostulat: Studien zur Darstellung des Landlebens im Roman des 18. Jahrhunderts* (Tübingen: Niemeyer, 1969), pp. 54-87;

Guenter Giesenfeld, "Die Leiden des papiernen Mädchens: Sophie von La Roche, Wieland und die Anfänge des Trivialromans," in *Erfahrung und Ideologie: Studien zur massenhaft verbreiteten Literatur,* edited by Jürgen Schutte (Berlin: Argument, 1983), pp. 7-16;

Peter-Uwe Hohendahl, "Empfindsamkeit und gesellschaftliches Bewußtsein: Zur Soziologie des empfindsamen Romans am Beispiel von *La Vie de Marianne, Clarissa, Fräulein von Sternheim* und *Werther," Jahrbuch der Deutschen Schillergesellschaft,* 16 (1972): 176-207;

Victor Lange, "Visitors to Lake Oneida: An Account of the Background of Sophie von La Roche's Novel *Erscheinungen am See Oneida,"* in *Deutschlands literarisches Amerikabild: Neuere Forschungen zur Amerikarezeption der deutschen Literatur,* edited by Alexander Ritter (Hildesheim: Olms, 1977), pp. 92-122;

Andreas Mielke, "Sophie von La Roche: A Pioneering Novelist," *Modern Language Studies,* 18 (1988): 112-119;

Werner Milch, *Sophie von La Roche: Die Großmutter der Brentanos* (Frankfurt am Main: Societätsverlag, 1935);

Peter Petschauer, "Sophie von La Roche, Novelist Between Reason and Emotion," *Germanic Review,* 57 (Winter 1982): 70-77;

Helene Kastinger Riley, "Tugend im Umbruch: Sophie von LaRoche's *Geschichte des Fräuleins von Sternheim* einmal anders," in her *Die weibliche Muse: Sechs Essays über künstlerisch schaffende Frauen der Goethezeit* (Columbia, S.C.: Camden House, 1986), pp. 27-52;

Lydia Schieth, "Christoph Martin Wieland und die *Geschichte des Fräuleins von Sternheim,*" in her *Die Entwicklung des deutschen Frauenromans im ausgehenden 18. Jahrhunderts.* (Frankfurt am Main, Bern & New York: Lang, 1987), pp. 28-49;

Siegfried Sudhoff, "Sophie von La Roche," in *Deutsche Dichter des 18. Jahrhunderts,* edited by Benno von Wiese (Berlin: Schmidt, 1977), pp. 300-319;

Christine Touaillon, *Der deutsche Frauenroman des 18. Jahrhunderts* (Vienna: Braumüller, 1919);

Ingrid Wiede-Behrendt, *Lehrerin des Schönen, Wahren, Guten: Literatur und Frauenbildung im ausgehenden 18. Jahrhundert am Beispiel von Sophie von LaRoche* (Frankfurt am Main: Lang, 1987).

Papers:

The papers of the La Roche family, including some of Sophie von La Roche's letters, manuscripts, and corrected proofs, are at the Freies Deutsches Hochstift, Frankfurt am Main. Smaller collections are at the Deutsches Literaturarchiv Schiller Nationalmuseum, Marbach; the Stadtarchiv, Offenbach; the Wieland-Museum, Biberach; the Universitätsbibliothek, Freiburg; the Pfälzische Landesbibliothek, Speyer; the Zentralbibliothek, Zurich; the Hessisches Staatsarchiv, Darmstadt (Kammer-sekretariatsakten); the Stadtbibliothek Schaffhausen; and the Bayerische Staatsbibliothek, Munich.

Johann Anton Leisewitz

(9 May 1752 - 10 September 1806)

Henry J. Schmidt
Ohio State University

BOOKS: *Julius von Tarent: Ein Trauerspiel*, anonymous (Leipzig: Weygand, 1776); translated by Peter Will as *Julius of Tarentum: A Tragedy*, in *The German Museum or Monthly Repository of the Literature of Germany*, volume 2 (London: Geisweiler, 1800); German version edited by Werner Keller (Stuttgart: Reclam, 1965); translated by Betty Senk Waterhouse as *Julius of Tarento*, in *Five Plays of the* Sturm und Drang (Lanham, Md.: University Press of America, 1986), pp. 191-229;

Über die bei Einrichtung öffentlicher Armenanstalten zu befolgenden Grundsätze überhaupt und die Einrichtung der Armenanstalt in Braunschweig insbesondere (Brunswick, 1802);

Das Armenwesen der Stadt Braunschweig betreffende Nachrichten: Stück I, by Leisewitz, J. P. Spehr, and J. H. Stähler (Brunswick, 1803);

Darstellung der Grundsätze und Einrichtungen der braunschweigischen Armenanstalt in Beziehung auf die von den Herren Quartierpflegern zu übernehmenden Geschäfte, anonymous (Brunswick: Vieweg, 1804);

Schriften von Johann Anton Leisewitz: Zum ersten Mahle gesammelt, edited by A. Klingemann (Vienna: Kaulfuß & Armbruster, 1816);

Sämmtliche Schriften: Zum erstenmale vollständig gesammelt und mit einer Lebensbeschreibung des Autors eingeleitet, edited by Franz Ludwig Anton Schweiger (Brunswick: Leibrock, 1838; reprinted, Hildesheim: Olms, 1970);

Julius von Tarent und die dramatischen Fragmente, edited by Richard Maria Werner (Stuttgart: Göschen, 1889; reprinted, Nendeln, Liechtenstein: Kraus, 1968);

Johann Anton Leisewitzens Tagebücher, 2 volumes, edited by Heinrich Mack and Johannes Lochner (Weimar: Gesellschaft der Bibliophilen, 1916; reprinted, Hildesheim & New York: Olms, 1976);

Julius von Tarent und die dramatischen Fragmente. Im Anhang: Rede eines Gelehrten an eine Gesellschaft Gelehrter; Nachricht von Lessing's Tod

Oil painting by Schröder (Gustave Könnecke, Bilderatlas zur Geschichte der deutschen Nationallitteratur [Graz: Akademische Druck- und Verlagsanstalt, 1981])

(Darmstadt: Wissenschaftliche Buchgesellschaft, 1969).

OTHER: *Geschichte der Entdeckung und Eroberung der Kanarischen Inseln: Aus einer in der Insel*

162

*Palma gefundenen spanischen Handschrift über-
setzt. Nebst einer Beschreibung der Kanarischen
Inseln von G. Glas. Aus dem Englischen,* translated by Leisewitz (Leipzig: Weygand, 1777).

Johann Anton Leisewitz's place in literary history is secured by a single drama, *Julius von
Tarent* (1776; translated as *Julius of Tarentum,*
1800), which was published when he was twenty-
four. Since the play did not win first prize in a competition to which it was submitted, Leisewitz considered it a failure. Ironically, *Julius von Tarent*
was far more popular on the German stage than
Friedrich Maximilian Klinger's prizewinning play,
Die Zwillinge (The Twins). Both plays centered on
fratricide; in its emotional intensity Klinger's play
was paradigmatic for the Sturm und Drang literary movement, whereas the tone of Leisewitz's
work was more temperate and hence more acceptable to the mainstream theater. The unique balance between Enlightenment "reasonableness"
and Sturm-und-Drang rebellion in *Julius von
Tarent* constitutes its historic importance: it is a
transitional work that pits the Weltanschauungen
of two epochs against each other, maintaining
that each position is destined to collapse not because of its antagonist but because of its own short-
comings. There was little indication in Leisewitz's
writings before *Julius von Tarent* that he was capable of creating a work of such quality; his modest, middle-class aspirations and hypochondriacal
nature prevented him from repeating his one literary success.

He was born in 1752 in Hannover to Jo-
hann Eobald Leisewitz, a wine merchant from
Celle, and Catharina Louisa von der Vecken
Leisewitz. In 1770 he began studying law in
Göttingen. There, on 2 July 1774, he became a
member of the "Göttinger Hain" (Göttingen
Grove), a group of Sentimental poets, including
Ludwig Christoph Heinrich Hölty, Johann
Heinrich Voß, Heinrich Christian Boie, and the
Stolberg brothers, whose literary model was
Friedrich Gottlieb Klopstock. In keeping with
their "bardic" nationalism, Leisewitz began working on a history of the Thirty Years War, a project he never completed. His only contribution to
the Hain's journal, the *Göttinger Musenalmanach*
(1775), consisted of two dramatic scenes comprising a total of three pages: *Die Pfandung* [sic] (The
Seizure of Goods) is a dialogue between a peasant and his wife about the impending confisca-
tion of their bed to pay for their prince's intemper-
ate living; in *Der Besuch um Mitternacht* (The

*Title page for Leisewitz's only significant work, a tragedy
about sibling rivalry*

Midnight Visit) the ghost of Hermann the
Cheruscan appears before a debauched prince to
prophesy a coming age of freedom. Both scenes
express the antifeudal sentiments of the bourgeois intelligentsia of the late eighteenth century.
This Rousseauistic spirit found its way into *Julius
von Tarent,* which Leisewitz submitted in 1775
to the Hamburg impresarios Sophie Charlotte
Ackermann and her son Friedrich Ludwig
Schröder, who had advertised for original tragedies and comedies.

After failing to gain the recognition he expected, he returned to Hannover to work as a lawyer, and in subsequent decades he rose through
the bureaucratic ranks in Brunswick, from district secretary (1778), tutor of the heir apparent

(1786), court counselor (1790), and privy counselor of justice (1801) to president of the Public Health Council (1805). He met regularly with Gotthold Ephraim Lessing, and on his travels he made the acquaintance of Johann Gottfried Herder, Christoph Martin Wieland, and Johann Wolfgang von Goethe. From 1779 to 1781, and sporadically thereafter, he kept a diary in which he meticulously chronicled his daily activities, meals, and physical ailments. He married Sophie Seyler, the adopted daughter of his uncle, in 1781; the marriage was a happy one that lasted until his death but produced no children. The last years of his life were dedicated to the amelioration of poverty in Brunswick. Between 1802 and 1804 he published lengthy analyses of the region's social conditions and proposals for institutional reform. When he died in 1806, thousands of the poor accompanied his burial procession.

Based on an episode from the history of the Medicis in Florence, *Julius von Tarent* counterposes two brothers, Julius and Guido, whose monomaniacal personalities make them appear almost like abstract forces in collision. Both wish to possess Blanca, who has been imprisoned in a nunnery by their father, Prince Constantine of Tarent, because she is not of noble birth. Julius, the eldest, is a Sentimental visionary, luxuriating in his emotions, chafing at his mundane princely duties, and consumed by his love for Blanca. Guido is the quintessential soldier, striving obsessively for honor and glory, demanding Blanca as a prize for his valor. Despite Constantine's machinations, the brothers refuse to yield to each other until filial loyalty is pitted against erotic love. Constantine says, "[sollten] meine Runzeln nichts gegen ihre reizende [sic] Züge, meine Tränen nichts gegen ihr Lächeln–mein Grab nichts gegen ihr Bette (vermögen)?" (Are my wrinkles nothing compared to her beautiful features, are my tears nothing compared to her smile–is my grave nothing compared to her bed?). Guido offers to renounce his claims to Blanca if Julius will do the same, but the latter simply says: "Ich kann nicht" (I cannot). The brothers resume their rivalry. Julius attempts to storm the nunnery, and Guido kills him. In retribution, Constantine executes Guido, turns his kingdom over to the "harte neapolitanische Regierung" (severe Neapolitan government), and enters a monastery.

In its epigrammatic dialogue and balanced dramatic structure *Julius von Tarent* is indebted to the Enlightenment, particularly to Gotthold Ephraim Lessing, whom Leisewitz admired

Depiction by an unknown artist of act 5, scene 4 of the Berlin premiere of Julius von Tarent: *Blanca goes mad on viewing the body of her beloved, Julius, who has been killed by his brother, Guido (Gero von Wilpert,* Deutsche Literatur in Bildern *[Stuttgart: Kröner, 1965])*

greatly. Its conventional aspects–which include the assignment of a levelheaded confidante to nearly every major character–contrast with the subversive nature of Julius's philosophy. He believes in the absolute primacy of individual desire, even when it conflicts with the welfare of the state. He indulges himself in flights of imagination, spurning what he believes to be the slow and cumbersome mechanism of rational thought. Confronting his critics with "die Vernunft der Liebe" (the rationality of love), he dares to extend his ideal of individual fulfillment into the political sphere: "Und mußte denn das ganze menschliche Geschlecht, um glücklich zu sein, durchaus in Staaten eingesperrt werden, wo jeder ein Knecht des andern und keiner frei ist . . . ? Narren können nur streiten, ob die Gesellschaft die Menschheit vergifte–beide Teile geben es zu, der Staat tötet die Freiheit!" (Did the entire human race, just for the sake of happiness, have to be imprisoned in national states in which each person is a slave of another and no one is free . . . ? Only fools can argue whether society poisons mankind–both sides admit: the State kills freedom!). Among the admirers of Julius's pathos of freedom was Friedrich Schiller, who claimed in a 14 April 1783 letter to Wilhelm Friedrich Reinwald that his Dom Karlos "hat . . . von Shakespeare's Hamlet die Seele–Blut und Nerven von Leisewitz, Julius, und den *Puls* von mir" (derived his soul from Shakespeare's Hamlet–his blood and nerves from Leisewitz's Julius–and his *pulse* from me). Yet, as in *Dom Karlos* (1787), idealism in *Julius von Tarent* is fated to end tragically. Unable to control his passion, Julius transgresses against his family, the state, and the Church. The drama's ideological framework–the Christian morality of the ruling class–requires retribution, and Guido is thus merely the instrument of Julius's inevitable downfall.

The tragedy of *Julius von Tarent* is not just that of Julius but also of his father. As in Klinger's *Die Zwillinge* and Schiller's *Die Räuber* (The Robbers, 1781), fraternal animosity between Julius and Guido masks the underlying father-son conflict. Constantine's rational governance may indeed have made his subjects happy "ohne Geräusch, ohne Revolution" (without noise, without revolution), yet Leisewitz demonstrates throughout that this is a manipulative rationality that restricts individuals to their allotted social roles. When personal desire comes into conflict with the ruler's perception of the general welfare, the former must be suppressed. Since, however, such "benevolent despotism" lacks the liberating qualities of imagination and passion, it too is destined to fail. All of Constantine's efforts to deflect Julius from his obsession–removing the object of his affections, offering him a substitute (Countess Cecilia), evoking filial sentiment and biblical and historical precedents–are in vain, because in his righteousness he cannot comprehend Julius's nature. Therefore he must restore moral balance by killing his remaining son, throwing his kingdom to the wolves, and becoming a penitent.

Perhaps the most modern feature of the drama is the usually overlooked characterization of Countess Cecilia. Cast in the mold of Christoph Martin Wieland's Musarion in the poem of that title (1768) and Lessing's Minna von Barnhelm and Countess Orsina in *Emilia Galotti* (1772), this outspoken, intelligent woman encourages Blanca's love of Julius as an act of pure friendship. Refusing to marry Julius or anyone else, she implies that true autonomy might be attained by casting off all predetermined sex

Leisewitz; engraving by Uhlemann of a drawing by Kauxdorf (Gero von Wilpert, Deutsche Literatur in Bildern [Stuttgart: Kröner, 1965])

roles: "O, ich hasse mein Geschlecht, ob ich gleich kein Mann sein möchte" (Oh, I hate my sex, even though I wouldn't want to be a man). From a twentieth-century vantage point, Leisewitz appears to be sensing emancipatory possibilities lying beyond the purview of both the Enlightenment and the Sturm und Drang–and therefore beyond his ability to delineate them more clearly.

Letters:

Johann Anton Leisewitzens Briefe an seine Braut nach den Handschriften, edited by Heinrich Mack (Weimar: Gesellschaft der Bibliophilen, 1906).

Biographies:

Gregor Kutschera von Aichbergen, *Johann Anton Leisewitz: Ein Beitrag zur Geschichte der deutschen Literatur im XVIII. Jahrhundert*, edited by Karl Tomaschek (Vienna, 1876);

Paul W. Noble, "The Life and Works of Johann Anton Leisewitz," Ph.D. dissertation, University of Wisconsin, 1976.

References:

Ulrich Karthaus, "Johann Anton Leisewitz: *Julius von Tarent*," in *Interpretationen: Dramen des Sturm und Drang* (Stuttgart: Reclam, 1987), pp. 99-127;

Margaret Kirby, *"Julius von Tarent* and the Theme of Fraternal Strife in the 'Sturm und Drang,'" *Forum for Modern Language Studies,* 19 (October 1983): 348-363;

Ines Kolb, *Herrscheramt und Affektkontrolle: Johann Anton Leisewitz' "Julius von Tarent" im Kontext von Staats- und Moralphilosophie der Aufklärung* (Frankfurt am Main: Lang, 1983);

Fritz Martini, "Die feindlichen Brüder: Zum Problem des gesellschafts kritischen Dramas von J. A. Leisewitz, F. M. Klinger und F. Schiller," *Jahrbuch der Deutschen Schillergesellschaft,* 16 (1972): 208-265;

Gert Mattenklott, *Melancholie in der Dramatik des Sturm und Drang* (Stuttgart: Athenäum, 1985), pp. 86-121;

A. Menhennet, "Drama between Two Stools: Leisewitz's *Julius von Tarent* and von Gemmingen's *Der deutsche Hausvater,"* Oxford German Studies, 6 (1971-1972): 33-49;

Norbert Oellers, "Johann Anton Leisewitz," in *Deutsche Dichter des 18. Jahrhunderts,* edited by Benno von Wiese (Berlin: Schmidt, 1977), pp. 843-860;

Henry J. Schmidt, "The Language of Rationality: Leisewitz's *Julius von Tarent,"* in *Theatrum Mundi: Essays on German Drama and German Literature,* edited by Edward R. Haymes (Munich: Fink, 1980), pp. 31-39;

Josef Sidler, "Johann Anton Leisewitz, *Julius von Tarent,"* Ph.D. dissertation, University of Zurich, 1966;

Peter Spycher, *Die Entstehungs- und Textgeschichte von J. A. Leisewitz' "Julius von Tarent"* (Bern: Graf-Lehmann, 1951).

Papers:

Johann Anton Leisewitz's papers are in the Brunswick City Archives.

J. M. R. Lenz

(23 January 1751 - 4 June 1792)

Edward P. Harris
University of Cincinnati

BOOKS: *Die Landplagen: Ein Gedicht in sechs Büchern: Nebst einem Anhang einiger Fragmente,* anonymous (Königsberg: Zeisen & Hartung, 1769);

Lustspiele nach dem Plautus fürs deutsche Theater, anonymous (Frankfurt am Main & Leipzig [actually Darmstadt: Wittich], 1774);

Der Hofmeister oder Vortheile der Privaterziehung: Eine Komödie, anonymous (Leipzig: Weygand, 1774; reprinted, Stuttgart: Reclam, 1963); translated by William E. Yuill as *The Tutor* in *The Tutor; The Soldiers* (Chicago: University of Chicago Press, 1972), pp. 1-80;

Der neue Menoza oder Geschichte des cumbanischen Prinzen Tandi: Eine Komödie, anonymous (Leipzig: Weygand, 1774);

Anmerkungen übers Theater nebst angehängten übersetzten Stück Shakespeares, anonymous (Leipzig: Weygand, 1774);

Meynungen eines Layen den Geistlichen zugeeignet: Stimmen des Layen auf dem letzten theologischen Reichstag im Jahr 1773, anonymous (Leipzig: Weygand, 1775);

Eloge de Feu Monsieur **nd Écrivain très célèbre en Poésie et en Prose: Dedié au beau Sexe de l'Allemagne, anonymous (Hanau, 1775);

Menalk und Mopsus: Eine Ekloge nach der fünften Ekloge Virgils, anonymous (Frankfurt am Main & Leipzig: Weygand, 1775);

Petrarch: Ein Gedicht aus seinen Liedern gezogen, anonymous (Winterthur: Steiner, 1776);

Vertheidigung des Herrn W. gegen die Wolken von dem Verfasser der Wolken, anonymous (Lemgo: Helwing, 1776; edited by Erich Schmidt, Nendeln, Liechtenstein: Kraus, 1968);

Die Freunde machen den Philosophen: Eine Komödie, anonymous (Lemgo: Meyer, 1776);

Die Soldaten: Eine Komödie, anonymous (Leipzig: Weidmann & Reich, 1776; reprinted, Stuttgart: Reclam, 1966); translated by Yuill as *The Soldiers* in *The Tutor; The Soldiers,* pp. 81-134;

Pencil drawing by Johann Heinrich Pfenniger (Österreichischen Nationalbibliothek, Vienna)

Flüchtige Aufsäzze von Lenz: Herausgegeben von Kayser (Zurich: Füeßly / Winterthur: Steiner, 1776);

Der Engländer: Eine dramatische Phantasey, anonymous (Leipzig: Weidmann & Reich, 1777);

Jupiter und Schinznach: Drama per Musica. Nebst einigen bey letzter Versammlung ob der Tafel recitirten Impromptüs (N.p., 1777);

Philosophische Vorlesungen für empfindsame Seelen (Frankfurt am Main & Leipzig: Weygand, 1780);

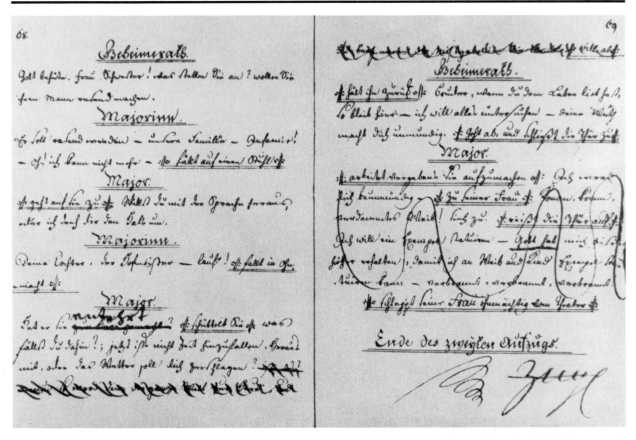

Two pages from the manuscript for Lenz's comedy Der Hofmeister *(Elisabeth Genton,* Jakob Michael Reinhold Lenz et la scène allemande)

Gedichte verschiedenen Inhalts (Altenburg: Richter, 1781);

Pandaemonium germanicum: Eine Skizze von J. M. R. Lenz, Aus dem handschriftlichen Nachlasse des verstorbenen Dichters herausgegeben, edited by G. F. Dumpf (Nuremberg: Campe, 1819);

Gesammelte Schriften, 3 volumes, edited by Ludwig Tieck (Berlin: Reimer, 1828);

Der verwundete Bräutigam, edited by K. L. Blum (Berlin: Duncker & Humblot, 1845);

Dramatischer Nachlaß von J. M. R. Lenz, edited by Karl Weinhold (Frankfurt am Main: Rütten & Loening, 1884);

Gedichte von J. M. R. Lenz: Mit Benutzung des Nachlasses Wendelin von Maltzahns, edited by Weinhold (Berlin: Hertz, 1891);

Ausgewählte Gedichte, edited by Erich Osterheld (Leipzig: Eckardt, 1909);

Gesammelte Schriften, 4 volumes, edited by Ernst Lewy (Berlin: Cassirer, 1909);

Gesammelte Schriften, 5 volumes, edited by Franz Blei (Munich: Müller, 1909-1913);

Über die Soldatenehen, edited by Karl Freye (Hamburg: Privately printed, 1913);

Briefe über die Moralität der Leiden des jungen Werthers: Eine verloren geglaubte Schrift der Sturm- und Drangperiode, edited by Ludwig Schmitz-Kallenberg (Münster: Coppenrath, 1918);

Werke und Schriften, 2 volumes, edited by Britta Titel and Hellmut Haug (Stuttgart: Goverts, 1966);

Werke und Schriften, 2 volumes, edited by Richard Daunicht (Reinbek: Rowohlt, 1970);

Anmerkungen übers Theater: Shakespeare-Arbeiten und Shakespeare-Übersetzungen, edited by Hans-Günther Schwarz (Stuttgart: Reclam, 1976).

OTHER: S. Pletschejew, *Uebersicht des russischen Reichs nach seiner gegenwärtigen Neu eingerichteten Verfassung,* translated by Lenz (Moscow: Rüder, 1787).

PERIODICAL PUBLICATIONS: "Der Versöhnungstod Jesu Christi, besungen von einem Jüngling in Dorpat," *Gelehrte Beyträge zu den Rigischen Anzeigen,* 7 (1766): 49-60;

"Myrsa Polagi oder die Irrgärten," *Liefländisches Magazin der Lektüre*, 1 (1782): 229-281;
"Der Waldbruder: Ein Pendant zu Werthers Leiden," *Die Horen* (1797).

During his brief but intense creative life J. M. R. Lenz wrote some of the most intriguing literary works of the eighteenth century. Before succumbing to madness in 1777 he produced a body of work–including lyric poetry, four dramas, several important essays, excellent adaptations of Plautus, and a novella, as well as a rich legacy of fragments and unpublished pieces–that has helped to define the literary era of the Sturm und Drang. No writer of the period has been "rediscovered" as regularly as Lenz, who attracted the attention and emulation of the Romantics, the "Jung Deutschen" (Young Germans), the naturalists, the expressionists, Frank Wedekind, Bertolt Brecht, and, most recently, Heinar Kipphardt. The scenic techniques he developed in his plays, which with one exception were not performed during his lifetime, have served as models for succeeding generations of playwrights. Notorious in his own time, his reputation faded so rapidly that he was forgotten long before his lonely death. Trying to describe him in part 3 of his autobiography, *Dichtung und Wahrheit* (Poetry and Truth, 1814), Goethe had to resort to the English word *whimsical* to sum up his eccentric personality. According to Goethe, Lenz had "einen entschiedenen Hang zur Intrige, und zwar zur Intrige an sich, ohne daß er eigentliche Zwecke, verständige, selbstische, erreichbare Zwecke dabei gehabt hätte.... Auf diese Weise war er zeitlebens ein Schelm in der Einbildung, seine Liebe wie sein Haß waren imaginär, mit seinen Vorstellungen und Gefühlen verfuhr er willkürlich, damit er immerfort etwas zu tun haben möchte" (a definite propensity for intrigue, intrigue for its own sake, however, for he never had real, discernible, personal, attainable goals.... In this way he was an inveterate knave in his own imagination–his love and his hate were imaginary and he disbursed his fancies and his emotions arbitrarily so that he could always be busy at something). In the first phase of the Sturm und Drang, Lenz and the author of *Die Leiden des jungen Werthers* (The Sorrows of Young Werther, 1774) and *Götz von Berlichingen mit der eisernen Hand* (Götz von Berlichingen with the Iron Hand, 1773) were inextricably linked as purveyors of the "Goethean-Lenzian Manner," which became the generic term for the literary manifestation of a yearning for the national past, passionate worship of nature, and unreflective outpourings of feeling, all with an exuberant echo of Shakespeare, Edward Young, and the folk poetry of Ossian. Lenz chose the drama as his primary medium, for it alone seemed to offer an adequate outlet for his inherent sense of rectitude in conflict. Like Goethe, Lenz often incorporated his own emotional crises in his works as a form of catharsis. Lenz's plays and speculative essays on the theater usher in the "open" form of drama, with scenic mosaics, a realistic idiom, and relevant social themes, which has been handed down through Georg Büchner, Christian Dietrich Grabbe, and Wedekind to Brecht and the present generation. Lenz, as Goethe was the first to note, could imbue the most common of situations with poetry. A moralist, Lenz stood firmly in the didactic tradition of the Enlightenment and directed his energies toward criticism of social inequities and toward a new and drastic formulation of nonillusional theatricality.

Jakob Michael Reinhold Lenz was born 23 January (or 12 January according to the Julian calendar) 1751 in Seßwegen in the Baltic province of Livonia. The son of David Lenz, a pastor, and Dorothea Neoknapp Lenz, Lenz was reared in an atmosphere of Pietism of the variety espoused in Halle, where his father was educated. The family moved to Dorpat (today Tartu), Estonia, in 1759. At about fourteen years of age Lenz began to write poetry reflecting the pious atmosphere of his home and a predilection for the work of Friedrich Gottlob Klopstock. Two of his works from this period are the poem "Der Versöhnungstod Jesu Christi" (The Expiatory Death of Jesus Christ, 1766) and *Die Landplagen* (The Plagues, 1769). He also tried his hand at the drama with *Der verwundete Bräutigam* (The Wounded Bridegroom, 1845). With a stipend from the town of Dorpat, Lenz entered the University of Königsberg in 1768 as a student of theology. Among the lectures he attended were those on logic and metaphysics by Immanuel Kant. There is no evidence that Lenz knew the writer Johann Georg Hamann, who was living in Königsberg at the time, but he did enter into correspondence with Hamann later. In 1771 Lenz left the university one semester short of completing his studies to accompany as tutor two young German nobles, Friedrich Georg and Ernst Nicolaus von Kleist, to Strasbourg, where his charges took up commissions in the French army. In Stras-

Title page for Lenz's essay on German drama, which includes his translation of Shakespeare's Love's Labour's Lost

bourg Lenz was accepted into the literary and philosophical circle around Friedrich Rudolf Salzmann and became acquainted with Goethe. Visiting nearby Sesenheim, Lenz fell in love with Goethe's former beloved, Friederike Brion. He addressed several poems to her which were long believed to be by Goethe. This was the first of a series of hapless relationships with women.

Between 1772 and 1774 he adapted five comedies of Plautus–they are still stageworthy renderings–and wrote *Der Hofmeister* (1774; translated as *The Tutor*, 1972), *Der neue Menoza* (The New Menoza, 1774), and the essays *Anmerkungen übers Theater* (Observations on the Theater, 1774) and *Meynungen eines Layen den Geistlichen zugeeignet* (Opinions of a Layman Dedicated to the Clergy, 1775). They were published, at Goethe's urging, by the Leipzig book dealer Friedrich Weygand. Weygand, the publisher of

choice of the younger generation, had already brought out *Die Leiden des jungen Werthers* and was to publish the first plays of Friedrich Maximilian Klinger.

Der Hofmeister, which was performed in Berlin in November 1778, is a case in point. It begins with the obsequious title figure, Läuffer, who hopes to become tutor to the children of Major von Berg, bowing and scraping before the play's only rational spokesperson, Privy Councillor von Berg, the major's brother. The technique is taken directly from Roman comedy, which Lenz knew well, and serves as an exposition of the ironic subtitle of the play: *Vortheile der Privaterziehung* (Advantages of a Private Education). The privy councillor is, of course, the *raisonneur* familiar from French drama, and his commentary is deliberately didactic. The institution of private tutors for the children of the well-to-do is deleterious for all concerned: the tutor himself, who is nothing more than a servant; the children, who are deprived of a genuine education; and society, for the money thus diverted could better serve the commonweal by helping to educate all. At the root of the problem lies the conflict between the privileged nobility and the middle class: Läuffer is by no means a positive character, but he is nonetheless an exemplar of the willingly exploited and suppressed.

Subsequent events illustrate the play's moral drastically, grotesquely, and, in the final analysis, comically. These events do not proceed in a straight line, however, for Lenz constructs a parallel set of subplots to underscore his point and introduces an overabundance of odd and colorful characters. The tutor is introduced into the Berg household at a crucial point: Gustchen and her cousin Fritz are in love but are kept apart by the privy councillor because Gustchen is far too young. When Fritz departs for the university, the melancholy young girl turns for comfort to her bumbling tutor. She becomes pregnant, and she and Läuffer flee the certain wrath of the major. Läuffer, wounded by the major's pistol and believing that Gustchen is dead, castrates himself in a fit of remorse; he then falls in love with a naive village girl, who agrees to marry him despite his condition. Meanwhile, Fritz has become embroiled in the affairs of a fellow student, Pätus, whose happy future has been endangered by the machinations of a villainous young nobleman and his tutor (the nobleman is also a product of that pernicious system). A timely win in the lottery enables Fritz to extricate himself and his friend from

Title page for Lenz's play about relations between military officers and townspeople

their woes and to return home as the feckless prodigal. The curtain falls on a reconciled Berg family and, as a corollary, a reunited Pätus family as well. Läuffer's fate is not fully explained, but the assumption is allowed that he and his bride will find the happiness implied in her response to his confession that he cannot sleep with her: "So kann Er doch wachen bey mir, wenn wir nur den Tag über beysammen sind und uns so anlachen und uns einstweilen die Hände küssen–Denn bey Gott! ich hab' ihn gern" (Then he can lie awake with me, if only we're together during the day and smile at each other and kiss each other's hands once in a while–for heaven knows, I'm fond of him).

The Pätus and Berg reconciliations stretch out over three generations. Pätus's long-lost grandmother is discovered, and Fritz takes Gustchen's illegitimate child as his own and ends the play with a vow: "Wenigstens, mein süsser Junge!

werd' ich Dich nie durch Hofmeister erziehen lassen" (At least, sweet boy, I'll never have you educated by private tutors). Friedrich Hebbel, the acknowledged master of the "closed" form of dramaturgy, likened *Der Hofmeister* to a game of cards, noting that the characters come together as accidentally as do king, queen, and jack in a deal, "und ihr Schicksal ist dann am Ende auch ein Kartenschicksal, eine rohe willkürliche Kombination des Zufalls" (and in the end their fate is a card-game fate, a crude, arbitrary combination of coincidence). This is, of course, quite true, but it is also Lenz's dramaturgical strategy; the device of the winning lottery ticket is chosen deliberately. If one takes the play on its own terms, noting Lenz's allusions to the fate of Abelard and Héloïse and to Romeo's rival, Count Paris, the play is wholly consistent in its inner logic and makes the point it sets out to make. The plot action and the odd collection of characters complement one another in a complex web of remarkable precision, and the ruinous effects of an outmoded system are not forgotten in the artifice of the happy ending.

Tandi, the young prince of Cumba, is the central figure of *Der neue Menoza*. This "noble savage" is based on the hero of a novel by the Danish writer Eric Pontoppidan in which a young Asian prince visits Europe on an educational tour. The novel was translated into German in 1742 and achieved four printings by 1759. Lenz's variation of this popular Enlightenment approach to cultural criticism brings Prinz Tandi to Europe in search of unaffected goodness and that harmony between heart and mind that he has been told exists in European man. What he finds is indolence and feeble babble. But he also finds a bride in Wilhelmine von Biederling, the daughter of his hosts in Naumburg. The swiftly moving plot first crushes the young couple's happiness with the disclosure that they are brother and sister, then salvages it with the revelation that Wilhelmine was exchanged as an infant. Thus the way is cleared for the happy ending. In his usual manner, Lenz constructs a subplot and adds a few colorful characters as vehicles for his criticism of contemporary society. The play ends with an apparently irrelevant dialogue about the popular theater and the puppet play. But since the comedy draws both character and plot elements from the commedia dell'arte, the conclusion may be taken as Lenz's commentary on the theater and popular taste.

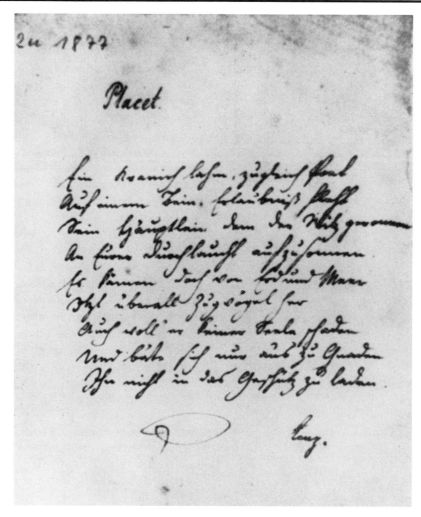

Petition from Lenz informing Duke Karl August that he will arrive in Weimar on 4 April 1776. Lenz sought refuge in Weimar because he feared repercussions from the publication of Die Soldaten *(Goethe-Schiller-Archiv, Weimar).*

Most analyses of *Anmerkungen übers Theater* begin by chiding the author for not having made his theoretical disquisition more systematic. Lenz must also be castigated for not following his reflections on the theater in writing his own plays. But the book is not intended as a methodology or a blueprint for composing a drama; rather, it is a series of notes for a lecture Lenz gave in 1772 for the Société de Philosophie et de Belles-Lettres in Strasbourg. Included in the book as an illustration is Lenz's translation of Shakespeare's *Love's Labour's Lost,* under the title *Amor vincit omnia.* Lenz rejects the dicta of Aristotle, especially as practiced by the French Classical dramatists; these rules are, in Lenz's view, no longer applicable. For the Germans, he argues, they were perhaps never applicable, for the German needs color, individuality, and variety such as

Shakespeare–Germanic in spirit–provides. The traditional unities of time, place, and action have no function in a theater which should attempt to display the fullness of nature. Man is, in the Christian era, master of his fate. Man is also a being of infinite complexity, and the drama that depicts him must show him in a multiplicity of situations, actions, and events. But Lenz also emphasizes that the playwright cannot simply connect odd points of incident according to his own lights; rather: "Er nimmt Standpunkt–und dann muß er so verbinden" (He takes a standpoint–and then he has to make the combinations). Beauty as an ideal has no place in this aesthetic, which places primary importance on displaying the distinctive rather than the typical. The prevailing distinction between comedy and tragedy was still based on class: the upper class alone was suited to the tragic fall, and only the foibles of the middle and lower classes could provoke laughter. Lenz discards that archaic notion and suggests a new paradigm: "Meiner Meinung nach wäre immer der Hauptgedanke einer Komödie eine Sache, einer Tragödie eine Person" (In my view, a comedy is concerned with events, tragedy with characters). To achieve the desired mixture the German dramatist is compelled to write comically and tragically at the same time, because the audience for which he creates is a muddle of culture and coarseness.

Lenz found it difficult to decide whether to call *Die Soldaten* (1776; translated as *The Soldiers*, 1972). a comedy or a tragedy, although he ultimately settled on the former designation. It is perhaps a question of point of view. An officer, Desportes, seduces Marie Wesener, the daughter of a shopkeeper in Armentières. Despite the efforts of Countess La Roche, who takes pity on the girl, Marie is handed around from officer to officer until she is reduced to ruin. A rejected suitor from her own class, Stolzius, joins the army and poisons the villain, taking his own life as well. Marie's father, whose business has been wrecked by this affair, finds her walking the streets as a prostitute. In a final scene, the countess and the regimental commandant discuss the sad fall of the Wesener family. Everything will be done, of course, to help the Weseners reestablish themselves. The countess sees the affair of Marie and Desportes as a consequence of the rule that soldiers must be unmarried. The colonel reluctantly agrees and suggests that it would be a fine idea if the king would set up "eine Pflanzschule von Soldatenweibern" (an establishment of soldiers' women) so that other wives and daughters of civilians would be spared.

The plot of *Die Soldaten* is far simpler than that of *Der Hofmeister,* and most of the characters have a direct relationship to the central events. There are thirty-five scenes, all but one of them requiring a set change. The drama uses pantomime, stage directions, and subtleties of language. The dramatis personae fall into two groups: the officer-gentry and the bourgeois townspeople. The attributes of each group are revealed by the words and actions of its members. The officers are characterized by their unwedded state and by the degree of their preoccupation with the art of seduction, which ranges from Rammler's obsession to Pirzel's apparent unconcern. The group is delineated in a more serious vein in conversations with Chaplain Eisenhardt,

Pencil sketch of Lenz, circa 1777, by an unknown artist (Elisabeth Genton, Jakob Michael Reinhold Lenz et la scène allemande)

who, like the privy councillor in *Der Hofmeister,* represents the voice of reason. Similarly, the dialogue between Stolzius and his mother and between Marie and her sister and father reveals the interdependency and insecurity of the individuals within their own class. But the greatest effect is achieved in those scenes that bring the officers into contact with the townspeople: the aged Jew Aaron, Madame Bischof, and Stolzius are victimized, degraded, and humiliated in all their confrontations with the officers. Signally, in the first meeting between Marie and Desportes the latter appears "im Bürgerkleide" (in civilian dress), the proverbial wolf in sheep's clothing. After her fall, Marie suffers expulsion from her family and her class as well. There is, in her case, an attempt at redemption, but the play leaves the audience with the uneasy feeling that the problem cannot be resolved.

A love affair with Cleophe Fibich, who was engaged to one of the Kleists, influenced the plot of *Die Soldaten*. In 1774 Lenz broke with the Kleists and financed his further studies in Strasbourg from tutorial fees and royalties. In 1775 he fell in love with Goethe's newly married sister, Cornelia Schlosser. In the spring and early summer of that year he met Goethe again; the two men formed a closer friendship, which is reflected in the satirical sketch *Pandaemonium germanicum* (1819), written in 1775, and the novel fragment "Der Waldbruder" (The Hermit, 1797), written in 1776, in that each contains a character modeled on Goethe. In *Pandaemonium germanicum,* a fragmentary three-act sketch which is framed as a dream, Lenz and Goethe climb the heights of Mount Parnassus and meet and argue with philistines and journalists; they then enter the holy region of the Temple of Poetic Fame, where they encounter great writers of the past, such as William Shakespeare, Molière, and La Fontaine. Most of the dialogue is, however, between Lenz and the older generation of German writers. Klopstock, Gotthold Ephraim Lessing, and Johann Gottfried von Herder are praised, while Friedrich Nicolai, Friedrich Heinrich Jacobi, and Christoph Martin Wieland are criticized for their rococo-style writings. Lenz is convinced that Goethe will join the company but is far less certain that he will ever be worthy of Parnassus. During this period Lenz was the leading figure in the literary attacks on Wieland, who was considered by the younger generation to be decadent, gallicized, and a danger to the public morality. In search of "Germanness" Lenz helped to found the Deutsche Gesellschaft (German Society) of Strasbourg. Then, as now, the city was within French borders but had a substantial German intellectual community. Lenz contributed essays on the Alsatian German dialect and other linguistic topics to the group's journal, *Der Bürgerfreund.* Still another hopelessly ineffectual love affair, this one with Henriette Waldner von Freundstein, whom he knew only through letters, seems to have influenced the plots of *Die Freunde machen den Philosophen* (Friends Make the Philosopher, 1776) and *Der Engländer* (The Englishman, 1777).

Lenz's last full-length play, *Die Freunde machen den Philosophen,* is set in Cadiz and Marseilles. A young German, Reinhold Strephon, is in love with Seraphine, the daughter of a Spanish grandee; she returns his affection. But their love can never be fulfilled in marriage because of the difference in their social classes. Seraphine devises an amoral but practical solution: she will marry an impoverished French nobleman who is willing to accept Strephon in a ménage à trois. But Strephon cannot share her. Seraphine therefore marries an old flame in Spain, Don Prado. On their wedding night Strephon enters their bedchamber with a pistol, bent on killing himself in their presence. Don Prado is so touched by the young couple's love that he takes the pistol away from Strephon and magnanimously relinquishes his claim to his bride. The focus of the play is on Strephon, who is a writer and in many respects a self-portrait of Lenz. Fully one-third of the text is composed of monologues by Strephon, and the play's other characters are all foils to his actions— or, rather, his words. The theme of *Die Freunde machen den Philosophen* is ostensibly the evil of class distinctions, but its actual content is a study in introspection.

In April 1776, fearing repercussions from the publication of *Die Soldaten* (he prevailed upon Klinger to claim authorship), he sought refuge with Goethe in Weimar. There he was well received by Duke Karl August, forgiven for his attacks and befriended by Wieland, and employed as a tutor in English by Charlotte von Stein. At the beginning of December he was compelled to leave Weimar after some social outrage, described by Goethe in his diary only as "Lenzens Eseley" (Lenz's asinine behavior).

After leaving Weimar, Lenz visited Goethe's sister and her husband, Johann Georg Schlosser, in Emmendingen, and Gottlieb Konrad Pfeffel in Colmar; he then went on to Zurich, where he stayed briefly with Johann Kaspar Lavater and Christoph Kaufmann. There he suffered his first attack of mental illness in November 1777. (His condition has been diagnosed as catatonia, but such analyses so long after the fact can scarcely be trusted.) The news of the death of his "guardian angel," Cornelia Goethe Schlosser, on 7 June 1777 may have triggered the first episode. Kaufmann made arrangements to send Lenz to Pastor Johann Friedrich Oberlin in Waldersbach im Steintal, where he was cared for from 20 January until 10 February 1778. On 22 January Lenz wrote the ominous lines to Lavater: "Ein Bogen, der immer gleich gespannt bleibt, verliert zuletzt seine Schnellkraft" (A bow under constant tension ultimately loses its spring). Pastor Oberlin carefully recorded Lenz's behavior in his journal; this diary later formed the basis for Büchner's novella "Lenz," written in 1835-1836 and published in 1839.

Lenz's mental disturbances became increasingly acute, with intense feelings of guilt and attempts at suicide. He returned to Schlosser's care and was taken to Riga by his brother in 1779. Vain attempts were made to find a position for him in his home province, where he lived in poverty, with intermittent periods of lucidity, until he was offered—out of charity—an appointment as an instructor at a boarding school near Moscow in 1781. Renewed physical and mental illness devastated him until he died during the night between 3 and 4 June 1792. His body was found in the street in Moscow. In a necrology published in the *Intelligenzblatt der Allgemeinenen Literaturzeitung* (18 August 1892), a Pastor Jerczembski described the lonely end of Lenz's life: "von wenigen betrauert und von keinem vermißt. . . . Von allen verkannt, gegen Mangel und Dürftigkeit kämpfend, entfernt von allem, was ihm teuer war, verlor er doch nimmer das Gefühl seines Wertes. . . . Er lebte von Almosen, aber er nahm nicht von jedem Wohltaten an. . . ." (mourned by few, missed by none. . . . Misjudged by all, battling deprivation and want, far from all he cherished, he never lost the sense of his own worth. . . . He lived from handouts but would not take them from just anyone).

The odd mixture of genius and childishness in Lenz's personality and the pathetic circumstances of his mental deterioration led many of his contemporaries to dismiss his work as equally demented; later generations of critics have approached his writing selectively, lauding strokes of genius and consigning the overall effect to the aberrations of a deranged mind. To be sure, Lenz delighted in achieving shock effects by distortion and by unique combinations of the real and the unreal, but his own image of the "Zerrspiegel" (fun-house mirror) should be taken at face value. His literary efforts between 1774 and 1776 were certainly out of synchronization with his time but are not for that reason to be spurned.

Goethe described Lenz as "nur ein vorübergehendes Meteor" (only a fleeting meteor) which appeared briefly on the horizon of German literature and vanished as quickly as it came. But his two masterpieces, *Der Hofmeister* and *Die Soldaten*, have been revisited consistently by a succession of writers who have drawn on his experiments with dramatic form. Moreover, the pathos of Lenz's life—his madness, loneliness, unre-quited love, the often violent conflict of reality and the poetic imagination, and the incompatibility of his work with his time—has offered an array of symbols to intrigue later generations of writers from Büchner to the present.

Letters:
Lenz in Briefen, edited by F. Waldmann (Zurich: Stern, 1899);
Briefe von und an J. M. R. Lenz, 2 volumes, edited by Karl Freye and Wolfgang Stammler (Leipzig: Wolff, 1918; reprinted, Bern: Lang, 1969).

Bibliography:
David P. Benseler, "J. M. R. Lenz: An Indexed Bibliography with an Introduction on the History of the Manuscripts and Editions," Ph.D. dissertation, University of Oregon, 1971.

Biographies:
M. N. Rosanov, *J. M. R. Lenz, der Dichter der Sturm- und Drangperiode: Sein Leben und seine Werke* (Leipzig: Schulze, 1909; reprinted, Leipzig: Zentralantiquariat der Deutschen Demokratischen Republik, 1972);
Heinz Kindermann, *J. M. R. Lenz und die deutsche Romantik* (Vienna: Braumüller, 1925);
Ottomar Rudolf, *J. M. R. Lenz: Moralist und Aufklärer* (Bad Homburg: Gehlen, 1970).

References:
Roger Bauer, "Die Komödientheorie von J. M. R. Lenz, die älteren Plautus-Kommentare und das Problem der 'dritten' Gattung," in *Aspekte der Goethezeit,* edited by Stanley A. Corngold, Michael Curschmann, and Theodore Ziolkowski (Göttingen: Vandenhoeck & Ruprecht, 1977), pp. 11-37;
Allan Blunden, "Lenz, Language, and *Love's Labour's Lost,*" *Colloquia Germanica,* 8 (1974): 252-274;
Richard Daunicht, "J. M. R. Lenz und Wieland," Ph.D. dissertation, University of Berlin, 1941;
Norman Diffey, *J. M. R. Lenz and Jean-Jacques Rousseau* (Bonn: Bouvier, 1981);
Bruce Duncan, "A 'Cool Medium' as Social Corrective: J. M. R. Lenz's Concept of Comedy," *Colloquia Germanica* (1975): 232-245;
Elisabeth Genton, *J. M. R. Lenz et la scène allemande* (Paris: Didier, 1966);

René Girard, *Lenz: 1751-1792. Genèse d'une dramaturgie du tragi-comique* (Paris: Klincksieck, 1968);

Horst Albert Glaser, "Heteroklisie–der Fall Lenz," in *Gestaltungsgeschichte und Gesellschaftsgeschichte*, edited by H. Kreuzer (Stuttgart: Klett, 1969), pp. 132-151;

Karl S. Guthke, "Myrsa Polagi oder die Irrgärten: Ein J. M. R. Lenz zugeschriebenes Lustspiel," *Jahrbuch des Freien Deutschen Hochstifts* (1964): 59-101;

John Guthrie, *Lenz and Büchner: Studies in Dramatic Form* (Frankfurt am Main: Lang, 1984);

Edward P. Harris, "J. M. R. Lenz in German Literature: From Büchner to Bobrowski," *Colloquia Germanica*, 3 (1973): 214-233;

Walter Hinck, "Materialien zum Verständnis des Textes," in Lenz's *Der neue Menoza* (Berlin: De Gruyter, 1965), pp. 73-95;

Curt Hohoff, *Jacob Michael Reinhold Lenz: In Selbstzeugnissen und Bilddokumenten* (Reinbek: Rowohlt, 1977);

Eva Maria Inbar, *Shakespeare in Deutschland: Der Fall Lenz* (Tübingen: Niemeyer, 1982);

Leo Kreutzer, "Literatur als Einmischung: J. M. R. Lenz," in *Sturm und Drang*, edited by Walter Hinck (Kronberg: Athenäum, 1978), pp. 213-229;

Helga Stipa Madland, *Non-Aristotelian Drama in Eighteenth Century Germany and Its Modernity: J. M. R. Lenz* (Bern: Lang, 1982);

Fritz Martini, "Die Einheit der Konzeption in J. M. R. Lenz 'Anmerkungen übers Theater,' " *Jahrbuch der Deutschen Schillergesellschaft*, 14 (1970): 159-182;

Timm Reiner Menke, *Lenz-Erzählungen in der deutschen Literatur* (Hildesheim: Olms, 1984);

John Osborne, *J. M. R. Lenz: The Renunciation of Heroism* (Göttingen: Vandenhoeck & Ruprecht, 1975);

Inge Stephan and Hans-Gerd Winter, *"Ein vorübergehendes Meteor?" J. M. R. Lenz und seine Rezeption in Deutschland* (Stuttgart: Metzler, 1984);

Britta Titel, " 'Nachahmung der Natur' als Prinzip dramatischer Gestaltung bei J. M. R. Lenz," Ph.D. dissertation, University of Frankfurt, 1961;

Erich Unglaub, *"Das mit Fingern deutende Publicum": Das Bild des Dichters Jakob Michael Reinhold Lenz in der literarischen Öffentlichkeit 1770-1814* (Frankfurt am Main: Lang, 1983);

Franz Werner, *Soziale Unfreiheit und "bürgerliche Intelligenz" im 18. Jahrhundert: Der organisierende Gesichtspunkt in J. M. R. Lenzens Drama "Der Hofmeister, oder, Vorteile der Privaterziehung"* (Frankfurt am Main: Fischer, 1981);

Hans-Gerd Winter, *J. M. R. Lenz* (Stuttgart: Metzler, 1987).

Papers:

J. M. R. Lenz's extant manuscript material is widely scattered; the largest holdings are found in the Staatsbibliothek Berlin.

Georg Christoph Lichtenberg

(1 July 1742 - 24 February 1799)

Max Reinhart
University of Georgia

BOOKS: *Betrachtungen über einige Methoden, eine gewisse Schwierigkeit in der Berechnung der Wahrscheinlichkeit beym Spiel zu heben: Nebst einer Anzeige seiner Vorlesungen* (Göttingen: Dieterich, 1770);

Timorus, das ist Vertheidigung zweyer Israeliten, die durch die Kräftigkeit der Lavaterischen Beweisgründe und der Göttingischen Mettwürste bewogen den wahren Glauben angenommen haben, von Conrad Photorin, der Theologie und Belles Lettres Candidaten (Berlin & Königsberg: Hartknoch, 1773);

Patriotischer Beytrag zur Methyologie der Deutschen: Nebst einer Vorrede über das methyologische Studium überhaupt, anonymous (Göttingen: Dieterich, 1773);

Epistel an Tobias Göbhard in Bamberg über eine auf Johann Christian Dieterich in Göttingen bekannt gemachte Schmähschrift, anonymous (Göttingen: Dieterich, 1776);

Anschlag-Zettel im Namen von Philadelphia, anonymous (Göttingen, 1777);

Über Physiognomik wider die Physiognomen: Zur Beförderung der Menschenliebe und Menschenkenntniß, anonymous (Göttingen: Dieterich, 1778);

De nova methodo naturam ac motum fluidi electrici investigandi, 2 volumes (Göttingen: Dieterich, 1778-1779); translated into German by Herbert Pupke as *Über eine neue Methode, die Natur und die Bewegung der elektrischen Materie zu erforschen* (Leipzig: Akademische Verlagsgesellschaft Geest & Portig, 1956);

Fragmente von Schwänzen: Ein Beytrag zu den Physiognomischen Fragmenten, anonymous (Göttingen: Dieterich, 1783);

Über einige wichtige Pflichten gegen die Augen (Vienna: Hörling, 1792);

Ausführliche Erklärung der Hogarthischen Kupferstiche, mit verkleinerten aber vollständigen Copien derselben von Riepenhausen, 5 volumes (Göttingen: Dieterich, 1794-1799); selections translated by Innes and Gustav Herdan as *The World of Hogarth: Lichtenberg's Commentaries*

Georg Christoph Lichtenberg

on Hogarth's Engravings (Boston: Houghton Mifflin, 1966); republished as *Lichtenberg's Commentaries on Hogarth's Engravings* (London: Cresset, 1966); translated by Arthur S. Wensinger and W. B. Coley as *Hogarth on High Life: The Marriage à la mode Series from Georg Christoph Lichtenberg's Commentaries* (Middletown, Conn.: Wesleyan University Press, 1970);

Dornenstücke, as Paul Ehrenpreis, attributed to Lichtenberg (Mannheim, 1797);

Nicolaus Copernicus (Leipzig: Jacobäer, 1800);

Verteidigung des Hygrometers und der de Luc'schen Theorie vom Regen, edited by Ludwig Christian Lichtenberg and Friedrich Kries (Göttingen: Dieterich, 1800);

Georg Christoph Lichtenberg's vermischte Schriften, nach dessen Tode aus den hinterlassenen Papieren gesammelt und herausgegeben, edited by Ludwig Christian Lichtenberg and Kries (9 volumes, Göttingen: Dieterich, 1800-1806; enlarged, 8 volumes, 1844-1847; reprinted, 9 volumes, Bern: Lang, 1972);

Karikatur-Almanach auf 1801: Aus Lichtenbergs Nachlaß (Hamburg, 1801);

Spiele des Witzes und der Laune (Pest: Hartleben, 1816);

Ideen, Maximen und Einfälle: Nebst dessen Charakteristik, 2 volumes, edited by Gustav Jördens (Leipzig: Klein, 1827);

W. Hogarth's Zeichnungen nach den Originalen in Stahl gestochen: Mit der vollständigen Erklärung derselben von G. C. Lichtenberg, 2 volumes, edited by Franz Kottenkamp (Stuttgart: Literatur-Comptoir, 1840; enlarged, Stuttgart: Rieger, 1857-1858; enlarged again, 1873); translated by Innes and Gustav Herdan as *The World of Hogarth: Lichtenberg's Commentaries on Hogarth's Engravings* (Boston: Houghton Mifflin, 1966);

Gedanken und Maximen: Lichtstrahlen aus seinen Werken, edited by Eduard Grisebach (Leipzig: Brockhaus, 1871);

Aus Lichtenbergs Nachlaß: Aufsätze, Gedichte, Tagebuchblätter, Briefe, zur hundertsten Wiederkehr seines Todestages, edited by Albert Leitzmann (Weimar: Böhlau, 1899);

Georg Christoph Lichtenbergs Aphorismen: Nach den Handschriften, 5 volumes, edited by Leitzmann (Berlin: Behr, 1902-1908; reprinted, Nendeln, Liechtenstein: Kraus, 1968);

Georg Christoph Lichtenberg: Gedanken, Satiren, Fragmente, 2 volumes, edited by Wilhelm Herzog (Jena: Diederichs, 1907);

Aphorismen Briefe, Schriften, edited by Paul Requadt (Stuttgart: Kröner, 1940; revised, 1953);

Der Fortgang der Tugend und des Lasters: Daniel Chodowieckis Monatskupfer zum Göttinger Taschenkalender mit Erklärungen Georg Christoph Lichtenbergs 1778-1783, edited by Ingrid Sommer (Berlin: Der Morgen, 1947);

Georg Christoph Lichtenberg: Gesammelte Werke, 3 volumes, edited by Wilhelm Grenzmann (Frankfurt am Main: Holle, 1949-1953);

Georg Christoph Lichtenberg: Aphorismen, edited by Friedrich Sengle (Stuttgart: Reclam, 1953);

Georg Christoph Lichtenberg: Aphorismen, Essays, Briefe, edited by Kurt Batt (Leipzig: Dieterich, 1963);

Georg Christoph Lichtenberg: Werke in einem Band, edited by Peter Plett (Hamburg: Hoffmann & Campe, 1967);

Schriften und Briefe, 7 volumes to date, edited by Wolfgang Promies (Munich: Hanser, 1967-);

Schriften zum Physiognomik-Streit: Über Physiognomik wider die Physiognomen; Zur Beförderung der Menschenliebe und Menschenkenntnis; Fragment von Schwänzen, edited by Karl Rihe (Steinbach: Anabas, 1970);

Vermächtnisse, edited by Promies (Reinbek: Rowohlt, 1972);

Werke in einem Band, edited by Hans Friederici (Berlin: Aufbau, 1973);

Kalenderaufsätze zu Hogarth, edited by Otto Weber (Darmstadt: Lichtenberg-Buchhandlung, 1974);

Lichtenberg in England: Dokumente einer Begegnung, 2 volumes, edited by Hans Ludwig Gumbert (Wiesbaden: Harrassowitz, 1977);

London-Tagebuch: September 1774 - April 1775, edited by Gumbert (Hildesheim: Gerstenberg, 1979);

Georg Christoph Lichtenberg: Werke in einem Band, edited by Promies and Barbara Promies (Dortmund: Harenberg, 1982);

Schriften und Briefe, 4 volumes, edited by Franz H. Mautner (Frankfurt am Main: Insel, 1983);

Sudelbücher, edited by Mautner (Frankfurt am Main: Insel, 1984).

Editions in English: *The Reflections of Lichtenberg*, translated by Norman Alliston (London: Sonnenschein, 1908);

"Further Excerpts from Lichtenberg's *Notebooks*," "Amintor's Morning Devotion," translated by Joseph Peter Stern in his *Lichtenberg: A Doctrine of Scattered Occasions* (Bloomington: Indiana University Press, 1959), pp. 277-327;

The Lichtenberg Reader: Selected Writings of Georg Christoph Lichtenberg, translated and edited by Franz H. Mautner and Henry Hatfield (Boston: Beacon Press, 1959); republished in abbreviated form as *Lichtenberg: Aphorisms & Letters* (London: Cape, 1969).

OTHER: Tobias Mayer, *Tobiae Mayeri opera inedita*, volume 1: *Commentationes Societati Regiae scientiarum oblatas, quae integrae supersunt*, *cum tabula selenographica complectens*, edited by Lichtenberg (Göttingen: Dieterich, 1775);

Göttinger Taschen Calender, 22 volumes, edited by Lichtenberg (Göttingen: Dieterich, 1778-1799);

Johann Georg Zimmermann, *Versuch in anmuthigen und lehrreichen Erzählungen, launigten Einfällen und philosophischen Remarquen über allerley Gegenstände*, edited by Lichtenberg (Göttingen: Dieterich, 1779);

Göttingisches Magazin der Wissenschaften und Litteratur, 4 volumes, edited by Lichtenberg and Georg Forster (Göttingen: Dieterich, 1780-1785); reprinted, 4 volumes (Osnabrück: Zeller, 1977);

Johann Christian Polycarp Erxleben, *Anfangsgründe der Naturlehre*, third edition, edited by Lichtenberg (Göttingen: Dieterich, 1784; fourth edition, 1787; fifth edition, 1791; sixth edition, 1794); selections from the preface translated as "On the Decomposition of Water," *Journal of the Royal Institution of Great Britain*, 1 (1802): 101-103;

Friedrich Wilhelm Heinrich von Treba and F. H. Spörer, *Beobachtung der Magnetnadel am Harze*, afterword by Lichtenberg (Leipzig: Göschen, 1789);

Samuel Thomas Sömmering, ed., *Adams, Büsch und Lichtenberg über einige wichtige Pflichten über die Augen*, contributions by Lichtenberg (Frankfurt am Main: Varrentrapp & Wenner, 1794).

PERIODICAL PUBLICATIONS: "Versuch einer natürlichen Geschichte der schlechten Dichter, hauptsächlich der Deutschen," *Gelehrte Beyträge zu den Braunschweigischen Anzeigen* (May 1766);

"Von dem Nutzen, den die Mathematik einem Bel Esprit bringen kan," *Hannoverisches Magazin* (August 1766): 981-992;

"Observationes, astronomicae per annum 1772 et 1773 ad situm Hannoverae, Osnabrugi et Stadae determinandum institutae," *Novi Commentari Societatis Regiae Scientiarum Gottingensis: Commentationes physicae et mathematicae classis*, 7 (1776): 210-232;

"Briefe aus England," *Deutsches Museum*, no. 1 (1776): 562-574, no. 2 (1776): 982-992; no. 1 (1778): 11-25, 434-444; selections translated by Margaret L. Mare and William H. Quarrell as *Lichtenberg's Visits to England as Described in His Letters and Diaries* (Oxford:

Clarendon Press, 1938; New York: Blom, 1969);

"Über das Weltgebäude," *Göttinger Taschen Calender* (1779): 1-31;

"Einige Lebensumstände von Capt. James Cook, größtentheils aus schriftl. Nachrichten einiger seiner Bekannten gezogen," *Göttingisches Magazin der Wissenschaften und Litteratur*, 1 (1780): 243-296;

"Simple, jedoch authentische Relation von den curieusen shwimmenden Batterien, wie solche anno 1782 am 13. und 14. Septembris, unvermuthet zu schwimmen aufgehört nebst dem, was sich auf dem Felsen Calpe, gemeiniglich der Felsen von Gibraltar genannt . . . zugetragen," as Emanuel Candidus, *Göttingisches Magazin der Wissenschaften und Litteratur*, 3 (1782): 615-635;

"Vorschlag zu einem Orbis pictus für deutsche dramatische Schriftsteller, Romanen-Dichter und Schauspieler: Nebst einigen Beyträgen dazu," *Göttingisches Magazin der Wissenschaften und Litteratur*, 1 (June 1780): 467-498; 4 (1783): 162-175;

"Gnädigstes Sendschreiben der Erde an den Mond," *Göttingisches Magazin der Wissenschaften und Litteratur*, 1 (1780): 331-346;

"Nachricht von dem ersten Blitz-Ableiter in Göttingen, nebst einigen Betrachtungen dabey," *Göttingische Anzeigen von gemeinnützigen Sachen* (1780): 104-108;

"Über die Pronunciation der Schöpse des alten Griechenlands verglichen mit der Pronunciation ihrer neuern Brüder an der Elbe oder Über Beh, Beh und Bäh, Bäh: Eine litterarische Untersuchung von dem Concipienten des Sendschreibens an den Mond," *Göttingisches Magazin der Wissenschaften und Litteratur*, 2 (1781): 454-479;

"Über einige englische Dichter und ihre Werke, aus Johnson's *Prefaces Biographical and Critical to the Works of the English Poets*," *Göttingisches Magazin der Wissenschaften und Litteratur*, 3 (1782): 62-100;

"Prof. Lichtenbergs Antwort auf das Sendschreiben eines Ungenannten über die Schwärmerey unserer Zeiten," *Göttingisches Magazin der Wissenschaften und Litteratur*, 3 (1782): 589-614;

"Über Hrn. Vossens Vertheidigung gegen mich im März / Lenzmonat des deutschen Museums, 1782," *Göttingisches Magazin der Wissenschaften und Litteratur*, 3 (1782): 100-171;

"Über die neuerlich in Frankreich angestellten Versuche, große hohle Körper in der Luft aufsteigen zu machen, und damit Lasten auf eine große Höhe zu heben," *Göttingisches Magazin der Wissenschaften und Litteratur*, 3 (1782): 783-793;

"Vermischte Gedanken über die aërostatischen Maschinen," *Göttingisches Magazin der Wissenschaften und Litteratur*, 3 (1782): 930-953;

"Kurze Geschichte einiger der merkwürdigsten Luftarten," *Göttinger Taschen Calender* (1783): 48-77;

"Fortsetzung der Betrachtung über das Weltgebäude: Von Cometen," *Göttinger Taschen Calender* (1787): 81-134;

"Leichtgläubigkeit, Aberglauben und Fanatismus: Eine gemischte Gesellschaft," *Göttinger Taschen Calender* (1787): 212-232;

"Amintors Morgen-Andacht," *Göttinger Taschen Calender* (1791): 81-89;

"Einige Neuigkeiten vom Himmel," *Göttinger Taschen Calender* (1792): 81-116;

"Bedlam für Meinungen und Erfindungen," *Göttinger Taschen Calender* (1792): 128-136;

"Warum hat Deutschland noch kein großes öffentliches Seebad?" *Göttinger Taschen Calender* (1793): 92-109;

"Einige Betrachtungen über vorstehenden Aufsatz nebst einem Traum," *Göttinger Taschen Calender* (1794): 134-145;

"Ein Wort über das Alter der Guillotine," *Göttinger Taschen Calender* (1795): 157-165;

"Von den Kriegs- und Fast-Schulen der Schinesen, nebst einigen andern Neuigkeiten von daher," *Göttinger Taschen Calender* (1796): 121-146;

"Rede der Ziffer 8 am jüngsten Tage des 1799ten Jahres im großen Rath der Ziffern gehalten: Die Nulle, wie gewöhnlich, im Präsidenten-Stuhle," *Göttinger Taschen Calender* (1799): 83-111;

"Daß du auf dem Blocksberge wärst: Ein Traum wie viele Träume," *Göttinger Taschen Calender* (1799): 150-180.

In Friedrich Schlichtegroll's *Nekrolog auf das Jahr 1799* (Necrology for the Year 1799, 1805) Georg Christoph Lichtenberg, born on 1 July 1742 as the seventeenth child of the Ober-Ramstadt pastor Johann Conrad and Henriette Catharina Eckhard Lichtenberg, is eulogized as a famous teacher of physics, one of the nation's wittiest writers and scholars, and "einer der glücklichsten Kämpfer gegen jede Torheit" (one

of the most successful warriors in the battle against foolishness). Johann Wolfgang von Goethe admired his uncanny knack for characterization; Arthur Schopenhauer praised his philosophical originality; Tolstoy ranked him with the best German minds; in the twentieth century Karl Kraus, Kurt Tucholsky, André Breton, Sigmund Freud, and Ludwig Wittgenstein acknowledged their indebtedness to him. Lichtenberg, who gave the aphorism its modern form in German literature, was a keen witted writer with inexhaustible insight into the human condition. He was also an astronomer; a mathematician; Germany's first experimental physicist; and an inventor who erected the first lightning rod in Göttingen, imitated and improved on Benjamin Franklin's electrical experiments with the kite, and stood at the forefront of aerostatic research and hot-air-balloon travel. The noted scientists Jean Deluc, Alessandro Volta, and Friedrich Herschel sought his advice, while all educated Germany read his journal essays regularly with great interest. Today only specialists know Lichtenberg as other than a marginal figure, and he is commonly misclassified in literary histories.

The modern image of Lichtenberg at C. M. Wenck's progressive Pädagogium in Darmstadt between 1752 and 1761 is of a prizewinning young scholar, well liked but inclined to depression—a condition exacerbated by a deformed spine and encouraged by his reading of Edward Young's *Night Thoughts* (1742-1746). Like most of his fellow students, Lichtenberg was greatly influenced by the poetry of Empfindsamkeit (Sentimentality), especially *Der Messias* (Messiah, 1751-1773) of Friedrich Klopstock, which he took for a time as his poetic model. As a young man he was also strongly attracted to physiognomy, the practice of deducing character from facial features; this ancient pseudoscience found eager revivalists in the mania of feeling which swept Europe around mid century. Lichtenberg tempered his own observations with empirical criteria, however, and viewed the oracular pronouncements of enthusiastic practitioners with skepticism.

In 1763 the twenty-one-year-old Lichtenberg traveled to Göttingen to enroll as a student of mathematics, astronomy, and natural science at the most progressive university in Germany, the Georgia Augusta; the university was the birthplace of German rationalism and positivism, historical realism, and modern scientific methodology. Lichtenberg's adviser was A. G. Kästner, one of the leading mathematicians and physicists of the period. Upon completion of his studies in 1767 he was offered a professorship in mathematics and English in Geißsen, but he asked for and received a two-year postponement. In the meantime, he worked as an unpaid assistant at his alma mater, where he earned his keep as an instructor and counselor to wealthy students from England. In May 1770, he accepted a poorly remunerated professorship in philosophy in Göttingen, where he was satisfied to teach for the remainder of his life.

Following the death of his mother in 1764 and a period of illness and serious depression—cyclical recurrences in his life—Lichtenberg undertook to keep a Sudelbuch (scribbling book), in which he entered brief (as few as ten, as many as four or five hundred words) and candid thoughts at random. During his first trip to England in 1770 he became acquainted with the retail practice of keeping so-called waste books: "Die Kaufleute haben ihr Waste book . . . darin tragen sie von Tag zu Tag alles ein was sie verkaufen und kaufen, alles durcheinander ohne Ordnung, aus diesem wird es in das Journal getragen, wo alles mehr systematisch steht, und endlich kommt es in den Leidger at double entrance. . . . Dieses verdient von den Gelehrten nachgeahmt zu werden" (The merchants have their waste book . . . in which they enter daily everything that they buy and sell, everything scattered without order; from this book the entries are then carried over into a journal in which everything is more systematic, and then finally into a double-entry ledger. . . . This ought to be imitated by scholars). From that time on he frequently referred to his notebooks as "waste books." Relieved of the duty of immediate systematization, he was free to register and meditate on his observations in a provisional fashion.

Goethe's observation—in his study of comic language in Byron's *Don Juan*—that Lichtenberg could play with words as though they were cards did not mean that he used them capriciously. Lichtenberg's wit, typical of enlightened humor, was characterized, as Freud noted in his 1905 work on joking and the unconscious, by its "Gedankeninhalt" (intellectual content) and was by no means unrelated to systematic thought. The waste-book concept clearly implies system, however postponed the final entries—the conclusions—may be. Lichtenberg often spoke of his "Gedankensystem" (system of thought), and only twice did he use the term *Aphorismus* with reference to his work; the term gained currency only

Caricature of Lichtenberg that has been variously attributed to Georg Heinrich Wilhelm Blumenbach and to Lichtenberg himself (from a photo at the Universitätsbibliothek Göttingen; original lost)

with the publication of Albert Leitzmann's anthology (1902-1908). Taken as a whole, what Joseph Peter Stern calls Lichtenberg's "scattered occasions" form a "doctrine of opinions" whose central principle is relativism based on great knowledge and methodological skepticism.

The Sudelbücher constitute the basis upon which Lichtenberg's reputation rests, for better or for worse, and therein lies the problem of his reception. In spite of the reputation he gained as an essayist, he was an intensely solitary man who published little of the work for which he came to be known. In a well-meaning effort to present to the world a sense of Lichtenberg's immense knowledge and wit, the publisher Johann Christian Dieterich released a collection of his works (1800-1806) that included his fragmentary pieces—the very material, that is, which the author had intended to keep private. What emerged was a picture of a brilliantly insightful but rather quirky and unsystematic mind. Subsequent editors continued to emphasize the fragmentary and private side of Lichtenberg's work, and this unbalanced view persisted until recently.

Lichtenberg's earliest writings are critical of contemporary German culture. His 1765 essay "Von den Charakteren in der Geschichte" (On the Characters of History, collected in *Georg Christoph Lichtenberg: Gedanken, Satiren, Fragmente*, 1907) manifests the epistemological doubt so characteristic of the later writer, a doubt which derived from his ethical reservations about human nature. Albrecht Schöne sees Lichtenberg as a precursor of Robert Musil, the twentieth-century author of *Der Mann ohne Eigenschaften* (1930-1943; translated as *The Man without Qualities*, 1953-1960). In his first published work, "Versuch einer natürlichen Geschichte der schlechten Dichter, hauptsächlich der Deutschen" (Toward a Natural History of Bad Poets, Especially the Germans, 1766), Lichtenberg says that the collective wasted energy of Germany's bad poets has become a national scandal: "täglich wenigstens 30 000 reimende Seelen in Deutschland die gesunden Glieder ihres Körpers dem Staat entziehen, und Vernunft, Papier und Geschmack auf die unerlaubteste Weise mißhandeln" (on a day-to-day basis at least 30,000 rhyming souls in Germany withhold the healthy limbs of their bodies from the nation and abuse reason, paper, and good taste most intolerably). The 1769 essay "Dienbare Betrachtungen für junge Gelehrte in Deutschland, hauptsächlich auf Universitäten" (Useful Observations for Young German Scholars, Especially at the Universities, collected in *Georg Christoph Lichtenberg's vermischte Schriften, nach dessen Tode aus den hinterlassenen Papieren gesammelt und herausgegeben*, volume 3, 1844) is critical of the superficial affectations to which Germany's young writers had become prone. These essays may be seen as early exercises toward the large satirical work, begun around 1774 but never completed, titled "Zum Parakletor oder Trostgründe für die Unglücklichen, die keine Originalgenies sind" (On the Paraclete: Consolation for the Unfortunate Poets Who Are Not Geniuses).

A two-month trip to England in 1770 convinced Lichtenberg that British culture surpassed all others, an opinion he never abandoned. On his return to Göttingen he was appointed to the university faculty in philosophy. A royal commission in 1772 to carry out astronomical and geodetic observations in the electorate territories took Lichtenberg to Hannover, Osnabrück, Hamburg, and the Helgoland. On the way to Osnabrück he crossed paths with Johann Gottfried Herder, one of the key theoreticians of

the Sturm und Drang; in Osnabrück he began a friendship with the writer Justus Möser, whose plain way of life affected Lichtenberg profoundly and led him to prefer the company of ordinary people. In Hamburg he was sought out by his former hero, Klopstock. In September 1773 he was commissioned to edit the scientific papers of the physicist-astronomer Tobias Mayer, and in April 1774 he was elected to membership in the Akademie der Wissenschaften (Academy of Sciences) in Göttingen.

The stimulus of travel and new friendships between 1770 and 1775 resulted in some of the most vividly descriptive letters that a German writer had yet produced. In a 28 June 1773 letter to his landlady in Göttingen he offers a masterful characterization of the exiled Danish queen Mathilda, whom he had observed at a dinner party in Celle: "Ihre Gesichtsfarbe ist gesund, meliert, aber doch mehr weiß als rot. Ihre Augen zwar nicht lebhaft, aber durchdringend und verraten Nachdruck, Feuer und Geist. Der Heroismus, den sie bei ihrer Arretierung bewies (denn sie kriegte den Offizier, der ihr den Arrest ankündigte, beim Schopf zu fassen), ist in ihrem Gesicht, wiewohl mit sehr viel weiblicher Sanftmut verwaschen, ausgedrückt" (Her face has a wholesome blend of colors, rather more of white than red. Her eyes, not exactly animated, but penetrating, suggest firmness, passion, and spirit. The heroism she demonstrated at her arrest [she grasped the arresting officer by the hair of his head] is expressed in her face, although softened considerably with feminine tenderness).

One might say that England took Lichtenberg by storm when he returned there in 1774-1775, for it fundamentally shaped many of his attitudes. There, he explains in his inspired "Briefe aus England" (Letters from England, 1776), he discovered the manifold functions of man. When he was not in the royal train of King George III he found himself lionized by the London aristocracy. He was welcomed into the scientific community of Joseph Priestley and James Watt; made the acquaintance of the crew of James Cook's second world voyage; witnessed the emergence of the industrial revolution in the Bolton steamship factory; visited the Bedlam asylum, where he made observations toward a psychology of abnormal behavior; sat in on Parliamentary debates on the colonial question and concluded, in his polemic *Anschlag-Zettel im Namen von Philadelphia* (Placard in the Name of Philadelphia, 1777), that the American revolutionaries were nothing but misguided idealists; and visited the Margate spa and decided that Germany should also have a public bath, a notion he was still pursuing in 1793 in "Warum hat Deutschland noch kein großes öffentliches Seebad?" (Why Does Germany Still Have No Public Bath?). He took copious notes on David Garrick's acting style and as a result became, with Gotthold Ephraim Lessing, one of Germany's earliest promoters of Shakespeare; his nonelitist conception of genius as "anschauende Kenntnis des Menschen in allen Ständen" (intuitive understanding of people of all classes) also derived from this experience. His opinion, shared with Jean-Jacques Rousseau, that education should be molded to the individual seemed to find confirmation in England, and he believed that he had discovered there a living example of ideas in practice, a nation that produced not bookish minds but great and active men.

Lichtenberg had by this time lost all tolerance for the physiognomic school, whose subjectivistic principles were being exploited by the Christian proselytizing movement under the Swiss clergyman Johann Kaspar Lavater. Lavater hoped to convert those individuals whose facial features indicated to him a nobility of soul. His attempt in the late 1760s to convert the Jewish philosopher Moses Mendelssohn was viewed with alarm by Lichtenberg and occasioned his first public controversy, albeit under the lightly disguised pseudonym "Conrad Photorin." *Timorus, das ist Vertheidigung zweyer Israeliten, die durch die Kräftigkeit der Lavaterischen Beweisgründe und der Göttingischen Mettwürste bewogen den wahren Glauben angenommen haben* (Timorus, Being the Defense of Two Israelites, Who, Induced by the Power of Lavater's Arguments and Göttingen Pork Sausages, Have Accepted the True Faith, 1773) borrows the parodistic strategy used so successfully by the sixteenth-century supporters of the humanist Johannes Reuchlin: by offering only poor arguments against Reuchlin, the *Epistolae obscurorum virorum* (Letters of Obscure Men, 1515-1517) had, in effect, defended him. In *Timorus* the theology student Photorin, a disciple of Lavater, champions the cause of the proselytizing movement in bombastic pronouncements: "Was? keine Proselyten mehr machen? Keine Seelen mehr retten? Wißt ihr, was die Folgen sein würden? der Teufel würde Proselyten zu Tausenden machen. Atheisterei, Toleranz, geistliche Anarchie, allgemeiner Umgang mit Juden, Heiden und Heidamacken, würde daraus

entspringen" (What? make no more converts? save no more souls? Do you realize what would happen? The devil would make converts by the thousands. Atheism, tolerance, spiritual anarchy, common socializing with Jews, infidels, and highway robbers would be the consequence). The effectiveness of this enlightened document brought Lichtenberg quickly to the attention not only of the literary world but to that of theologians and philosophers as well.

In 1777–the same year in which he brought the twelve-year-old flower vendor Maria Stechard off the street and into his home, where she remained his loving mistress until her death in 1782–Lichtenberg established his reputation as a scientist. His investigations into the relationship between positive and negative electrical currents resulted in the discovery of what came to be known as the "Lichtenberg figures," which claimed the attention of the scientific world. Because of the eighteenth century's limited understanding of the nature of electricity, however, the full implications of his discovery were not recognized until much later; for example, Chester F. Carlson has demonstrated the function of the Lichtenberg figures in the development of xerography. When the eminent Göttingen physicist Johann Erxleben died in 1777, Lichtenberg was called upon to edit his friend's great work, *Anfangsgründe der Naturlehre* (Elementary Principles of Natural Science), beginning with the third edition in 1784 and running through the sixth edition in 1794. To Erxleben's text–which Goethe used as his primary reference work on physics– Lichtenberg regularly contributed results of his own research. As a consequence of his editorial responsibilities and those of the chair in experimental physics created for him by the University of Göttingen in 1775, Lichtenberg was never able to complete the manuscript for his own textbook on physics.

Erxleben had founded and edited the *Göttinger Taschen Calender* (Göttingen Pocket Calendar), which combined didacticism with entertainment to appeal to the intelligent lay reader. With Erxleben's death the publisher Dieterich, in whose apartment Lichtenberg lived, convinced his thirty-five-year-old tenant to assume the editorship. The first volume under Lichtenberg's direction attacked Lavater's *Physiognomische Fragmente zur Beförderung der Menschenkenntnis und Menschenliebe* (Physiognomic Fragments on the Furtherance of Human Knowledge and Human Love, 1775-1778). In the lead essay, as he explained in

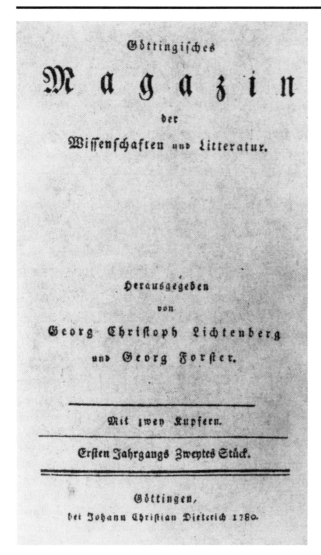

*Title page of the second issue of the magazine Lichtenberg
coedited from 1780 to 1785*

a later review of his own article, he intended to
persuade a popular audience that physiognomic
analysis in the wrong hands lends itself readily to
serious abuse. He argues that human character is
too complex to be fathomed by a facile reading
of external features. The issue sold out; and the
journal soon achieved an enviable circulation of
eight thousand–virtually the whole of educated
Germany–thus securing Lichtenberg's reputation
as a formidable journalist.

The June 1780 number of the *Göttingisches
Magazin der Wissenschaften und Litteratur*, of which
Lichtenberg, together with the writer Georg Forster, had recently become editor, returned to the
theme of his earliest publications. "Vorschlag zu
einem Orbis pictus für deutsche dramatische
Schriftsteller, Romanen-Dichter und Schau-

spieler" (Model of an *orbis pictus* for German Dramatists, Novelists and Actors, 1780) represents the
culmination of his assault on the youthful poets
of the Sturm und Drang and the Sentimentalism
of the Göttinger Hainbund. Measured against
the standard of John Milton and Christoph Martin Wieland, he claims, the fashionable poets be-
tray a ludicrous degree of intellectual laxity.
Lichtenberg accordingly strikes a didactic pose:
by making use of the engravings of Daniel
Chodowiecki, he says he will guide the young
poets toward the creation of an *orbis pictus*, an authentic representation of the world based on accurate and detailed observation. Lichtenberg's formal ideals of nonartificiality and brevity, and his
nonelitist conception of genius–his choice of
Chadowiecki's engravings of servants who in
their speech and dress are "die Spiegel ihrer
Herrschaften" (the mirror images of their masters) mocks the pretenses of the young writers–
prevented him from coming to terms with the
ebullient passion and extravagant style of the
young dramatists and novelists of the Sturm und
Drang.

Over the next two years Lichtenberg be-
came further involved in the struggle against Sentimentalism. Not even Goethe's sensationally popular novel *Die Leiden des jungen Werthers* (The
Sorrows of Young Werther, 1774) escaped his criticism (although he had only high regard for
Goethe's Sturm und Drang drama *Götz von
Berlichingen* [1773]). While he recognized in *Die
Leiden des jungen Werthers* a new and powerful poetic voice, he mistrusted its radical subjectivity.
Lichtenberg's most notable controversy was with
Johann Voß and was sparked by Voß's overfastidi-
ous transliteration of the Greek *eta* as the German *ä* rather than *e* in his translation of Homer's
Odyssey (1781). In his essay "Über die Pronunciation der Schöpse des alten Grienchelands
verglichen mit der Pronunciation ihrer neuern
Brüder an der Elbe oder Über Beh, Beh und
Bäh, Bäh" (On the Pronunciation of the Sheep
of Ancient Greece Compared with that of Their
Modern Offspring on the Elbe; or, On Beh, Beh
and Bäh, Bäh, 1781) Lichtenberg attacked what
he regarded as Voß's deeper pedantic and nationalistic tendencies. Against Voß's alleged nationalism he holds up the standard of cos-
mopolitanism, with its ideals of reason and
tolerance; against narrow subjectivity he insists
upon the balancing of feeling and intellect.

Lichtenberg's health, never robust, began to
fail after 1783. His hopes of traveling to Italy fell

Lichtenberg in 1791 (portrait by A. H. Schwenterley)

through in 1785, and his sketches in that year of an autobiographical novel, "Der doppelte Prinz" (The Double Prince), were discarded. (Wolfgang Promies attributes the abandonment of the latter plans to the awe in which Lichtenberg had come to hold Jean Paul.) On 5 October 1789 he fell ill but by evening was strong enough to marry Margarethe Elisabeth Kellner, a keg-maker's daughter who had been his mistress since 1783 and was already the mother of three of their eventual six children. About this time the private aspect of Lichtenberg's writing becomes more and more dominant, typifying the late-Enlightenment trend toward resignation and divergence from mainstream developments that is also exemplified in the work of peripheral authors such as Johann Karl Wezel and Christian Garve.

Lichtenberg's response to the French Revolution was more or less representative of the political moralism of the German intelligentsia. At first he interpreted the evolution of political events in France as the vindication of reason over tyranny, a predictable response for one who had

begun his philosophical studies with Leibniz. Unlike his friend Forster, however, who was in close personal contact with the revolutionaries and understood the function of violence in the making of a new bourgeois-republican order, Lichtenberg's opinions on popular sovereignty were shaken by the Reign of Terror. In letters to friends he speaks less approvingly of the revolutionaries (they are, for example, often referred to as "der Pöbel" [the mob]) than in his notebooks, which reflect his most private thoughts: "Die französische Revolution wird manches Gute zurücklassen, das ohne sie nicht in die Welt gekommen wäre" (The French Revolution will leave much good behind which otherwise could never have come about). In the end he recommends constitutional monarchy on the English model for the French as he had for the Americans. His caution in practical politics did not, however, keep him from continuing publicly to lampoon the foolishness of feudal tyranny in general. In "Von den Kriegs- und Fast-Schulen der Schinesen" (On the Chinese Schools of War and Starving, 1796) he satirically advises absolutist rulers to establish such schools to force their subjects into submission: "Ich versichere Euch, wir haben auf diesen Akademien Leute gezogen, die, wenn sie von dem Feinde geplündert, gepeitscht und geschunden wurden, anstatt zu heulen und zu wehklagen, sich bloß dabei an die Universitäts-Jahre erinnerten" (I assure you, in these academies we have trained people so that, when they are pillaged, whipped, and fleeced, rather than howl and complain, they do nothing but think back on their old days at the university).

Lichtenberg's writings from the final decade of his life are skeptical as always but give evidence of his having achieved a deeper confidence in the ultimate order of the universe. His philosophical speculations had always been dominated by the question of how much the human being, confined by language, is capable of knowing. After 1780 two names begin to appear regularly in these considerations: Immanuel Kant, from whom Lichtenberg learned that experience cannot be registered outside of the categories of human thought; and Benedict de Spinoza, in whose philosophical monism he discovered the most cogent explanation of how the world nevertheless presents a unified image to our senses. Convinced of the truth of Spinozistic substantialism, he confessed his belief that Kantian philosophy must admit "daß unseren Vorstellungen etwas in der Welt korrespondiert" (that objects in the world correspond to our images of them).

Nowhere in eighteenth-century literature is this unity more confidently expressed than in Lichtenberg's short essay celebrating his recovery from his near-fatal illness, "Amintors Morgen-Andacht" (1791; translated as "Amintor's Morning Devotion," 1959). His prophecy in a letter of 3 July 1786 (in the wake of the Spinoza debate started a year earlier between Friedrich Heinrich Jacobi and Mendelssohn) that natural science would eventually confirm the speculative content of Spinozism was fulfilled, he believed, in a clairvoyant moment of "unbeschreibliche[s] Wohlbehagen" (indescribable well-being). The beatific state sprang from the delightful knowledge, reminiscent of Spinoza's "amor intellectualis Dei," that natural order follows from the order of one's own mind: "meine Ruhe ist das Werk meiner eigenen Vernunft" (my contentment is the work of my own reason). Characteristically for Lichtenberg, however, the pleasure he has found in his personal existence is accompanied by the duty to redouble his efforts to understand that which he may never in fact be able to comprehend: "Freude über *eigenes Dasein,*" he writes, must be "verbunden mit *nicht ängstlicher,* sondern *froher Neugierde . . . , zu erfahren . . . was nun dieses alles sei und werden wolle*" (the pleasure of one's *own existence* must be coupled *not with timid* but *joyful curiosity* to discover *what all of this is and could be*).

In 1793, the year Goethe began to solicit his advice on a doctrine of colors, Lichtenberg was made a member of the Royal Academy of Sciences in London. In the twentieth century Lichtenberg is recognized primarily as a pioneer of modern scientific methodology. His curious personal failure to produce concrete results, while making them possible for others, may be attributed to his philosophical skepticism and his creatively digressive habit of following associative leads arising from his experiments. He also influenced the general education of Germany by popularizing science in his role as editor of the *Göttinger Taschen Calender.*

Lichtenberg's commentaries on engravings by Chodowiecki and William Hogarth were popular features of the *Taschen Calender.* Here he was able to exploit his intuitive powers to achieve an often profound psychological reading of faces and situations. From 1794 until his death in 1799 he devoted himself increasingly to this study, publishing annual collections titled *Ausführliche Erklärung der Hogarthischen Kupferstiche* (Detailed Analysis of the Hogarth Copper Engravings); according to Goethe, the 1795 collection was one of the year's three most popular literary works. Goethe's ambivalent estimation of the Hogarth collections—he rejected Hogarth's Goyaesque perspectives as un-German misanthropy while praising the ethical right-mindedness of Lichtenberg's commentaries—provides a key to understanding the balance in which Lichtenberg held his public and private personae. Although Lichtenberg was fully conscious of the grotesque element in life, as his scribbling books show frequently and unmistakably, in his commentaries this element is transformed into wit. He loathed the young Sentimentalist poets precisely because of their inability or unwillingness to maintain reasonable control over their chaotic, intellectually undisciplined private selves. Lichtenberg was fascinated throughout his life by the abnormal side of consciousness; he could not, however, tolerate its display—at least not in writers.

On New Year's Day 1799, Lichtenberg prophesied his death: "Es geht ans Leben dieses Jahr" (This will be the last year of my life). Just after mid February he suffered a serious chest inflammation, and in five days, on February 24, he died. According to one report, his casket was accompanied to the Bartholomäus-Friedhof (Bartholemew Cemetery) in Göttingen by more than five hundred of the university's approximately seven hundred students (Samuel Taylor Coleridge may well have been among them), a poignant tribute to the regard in which he was held as both a teacher and friend.

The overall importance of Georg Christoph Lichtenberg to the world of learning is currently being reevaluated. Friedrich Schleiermacher's pronouncement in 1801 that Lichtenberg was incapable of "allgemein[e] und groß[e] Ideen" (great universal ideas) has been corrected, and the acknowledged scope of his contributions has been expanded. Nevertheless, a proper understanding of Lichtenberg's place in literary history as one of the supreme writers of the late Enlightenment continues to be distorted by certain bizarre notions. In Richard Newald's *Geschichte der deutschen Literatur* (History of German Literature, 1957) he is classified under "Sturm und Drang," while in Herbert A. Frenzel and Elisabeth Frenzel's *Daten deutscher Dichtung* (Facts about German Writing, 1971) he falls under "Empfindsamkeit" —in spite of the antipathy with which he regarded both of those movements.

Lichtenberg's sensitivity to the complex nature of personality is perhaps matched in the eighteenth century only by Karl Philipp Moritz, while his conjectures on dreams and his acute understanding of the libido, repression, and compensation anticipate Freud. His comprehension of the human-all-too-human side of the species links him with Heinrich Heine and Friedrich Nietzsche. The reflections generated by his epistemological skepticism have been likened to those of Ludwig Wittgenstein and sometimes bear an uncanny resemblance to postmodernist language theory. Because there is a definitive split between mental intentionality and linguistic representation, he observes, "Es wird also von uns immer wahre Philosophie mit der Sprache der falschen gelehrt" (We must always teach true philosophy with the language of false philosophy). Further, his insights into the unfathomable nature of human thought make him a forerunner of modern ideology critique. The redemptive quality of his satirical wit keeps him, however, from sinking into cynicism. If his affinities with the twentieth-century critique of enlightenment were to be traced, he would more accurately be identified with the affirmative criticism of Peter Sloterdijk than with the negative dialectics of Theodor Adorno or the endless language games of Jean-Francois Lyotard.

Letters:

Georg Christoph Lichtenberg's Briefe an Dieterich: 1770-1798, edited by Eduard Grisebach (Leipzig: Dieterich, 1898);

Lichtenberg, Georg Christoph: Briefe, 3 volumes, edited by Albert Leitzmann and Carl Schüddekopf (Leipzig: Dieterich, 1901-1904; reprinted, Hildesheim: Olms, 1966);

Aus G. C. Lichtenbergs Correspondenz, edited by Erich Ebstein (Stuttgart: Enke, 1905);

Lichtenbergs Mädchen: Mit zwölf ungedruckten Briefen Lichtenbergs, edited by Ebstein (Munich: Süddeutsche Monatshefte, 1907);

Lichtenberg, Georg Christoph: Briefe an Johann Friedrich Blumenbach, edited by Leitzmann (Leipzig: Dieterich, 1921);

Georg Christoph Lichtenberg: Briefe an die Freunde, edited by Wilhelm Spohr (Berlin: Hoffmann, 1938);

Georg Christoph Lichtenberg: Briefwechsel, 3 volumes to date, edited by Ulrich Joost and Albrecht Schöne (Munich: Beck, 1983).

Bibliographies:

"The Miscellaneous Works of George Christophe Lichtenberg, Published after His Death," *Edinburgh Review*, 3 (1803/1804): 343-354;

Friedrich Lauchert, *Georg Christoph Lichtenberg's schriftstellerische Tätigkeit in chronologischer Übersicht dargestellt: Mit Nachträgen zu Lichtenberg's "Vermischten Schriften" und textkritischen Berichtigungen* (Göttingen: Dieterich, 1893);

Martin Domke, "Lichtenberg in fremden Sprachen," *Zeitschrift für Bücherfreunde*, 37 (1933): 217-219;

Wilhelm Frels, *Deutsche Dichterhandschriften von 1400 bis 1900* (Leipzig: Hiersemann, 1934), pp. 185-186;

Wolfgang Preisendanz, "Georg Christoph Lichtenberg:" Ein Literaturbericht, *Germanisch-Romanische Monatsschrift*, 37 (1956): 338-357;

Karl S. Guthke, "Georg Christoph Lichtenberg's Contributions to the *Göttingische Gelehrte Anzeigen*," *Libri*, 12 (1962/1963): 331-340;

Rudolf Jung, *Lichtenberg-Bibliographie* (Heidelberg: Stiehm, 1972);

Photorin: Mitteilungen der Lichtenberg-Gesellschaft (1979-).

Biographies:

Victor Bouillier, *Georg Christoph Lichtenberg (1742-1799): Essai sur sa vie et ses oeuvres littéraires, suivi d'un choix de ses aphorismes* (Paris: Champion, 1914);

Paul Hahn, *Lichtenberg und die exakten Wissenschaften: Materialien zu seiner Biographie* (Göttingen: Vandenhoeck & Ruprecht, 1927);

Wilhelm Grenzmann, *Georg Christoph Lichtenberg* (Salzburg: Pustet, 1938);

Otto Deneke, *Lichtenbergs Leben I (1742-1775)* (Munich: Heimeran, 1944);

Carl Brinitzer, *Lichtenberg: Die Geschichte eines gescheiten Mannes* (Tübingen: Wunderlich, 1956; republished, Munich: Heyne, 1979); translated by Bernard Smith as *A Reasonable Rebel: Georg Christoph Lichtenberg* (London: Allen & Unwin, 1960);

Wolfgang Promies, *Georg Christoph Lichtenberg: Mit Selbstzeugnissen und Bilddokumenten* (Reinbek: Rowohlt, 1964; revised, 1987);

Franz H. Mautner, "Georg Christoph Lichtenberg," in *Deutsche Dichter des 18. Jahrhunderts*, edited by Benno von Wiese (Berlin: Schmidt, 1977), pp. 482-506;

Dorothea Goetz, *Georg Christoph Lichtenberg* (Leipzig: Teubner, 1984).

References:

Monika Ammermann, *Gemeines Leben: gewandelter Naturbegriff und literarische Spätaufklärung: Lichtenberg, Wezel, Garve* (Bonn: Bouvier, 1978);

Aufklärung über Lichtenberg: Mit Beitragen von Helmut Heißenbüttel, Armin Hermann, Wolfgang Promies, Joseph Peter Stern, Rudolf Vierhaus (Göttingen: Vandenhoeck & Ruprecht, 1974);

Ernst Bertram, "Georg Christoph Lichtenberg," in his *Georg Christoph Lichtenberg, Adalbert Stifter: Zwei Vorträge* (Bonn: Cohen, 1919), pp. 11-45;

Kurt Besser, *Die Problematik der aphoristischen Form bei Lichtenberg, Fr. Schlegel, Novalis und Nietzsche: Ein Beitrag zur Psychologie des geistigen Schaffens* (Berlin: Juncker & Dünnhaupt, 1935);

Gottlieb Betz, "Lichtenberg as a Critic of the English Stage," *Journal of English and Germanic Philology*, 23 (1924): 270-288;

Ernst Bloch, "Lichtenbergsches herauf, herab," in *Literarische Aufsätze*, volume 9 of his *Gesamtausgabe* (Frankfurt am Main: Suhrkamp, 1965), pp. 201-208;

Carl Brinitzer, *Georg Christoph Lichtenbergs Genialität und Witz* (Munich: Heyne, 1979);

Chester F. Carlson, "History of Electrostatic Recording," in *Xerography and Related Processes*, edited by John H. Dessauer (London: Focal Press, 1965), pp. 15-19;

Josef Dostal-Winkler, *Lichtenberg und Kant: Problemgeschichtliche Studie* (Munich: Rösl, 1924);

Erich Ebstein, "Lichtenberg und Goethe über die Theorie der Farben," *Archiv für die Geschichte der Naturwissenschaft und der Technik*, 3 (1912): 71-78;

Gertrud Fischer, *Lichtenbergische Denkfiguren: Aspekte des Experimentellen* (Heidelberg: Winter, 1982);

Herbert A. Frenzel and Elisabeth Frenzel, *Daten deutscher Dichtung: Chonologischer Abriß der deutschen Literaturgeschichte von den Anföngen bis zur Gegenwart* (Cologne & Berlin: Kiepenheuer & Witsch, 1971);

Sigmund Freud, "Der Witz und seine Beziehung zum Unbewussten," in his *Psychologische Schriften*, volume 4, third edition (Frankfurt am Main: Fischer, 1970), pp. 79-89;

Heinz Gockel, *Individualisiertes Sprechen: Lichtenbergs Bemerkungen im Zusammenhang von Er-*

kenntnistheorie und Sprachkritik (Berlin: De Gruyter, 1973);

Johann Wolfgang von Goethe, "Byrons Don Juan," in his *Werke: Hg. im Auftrage der Großherzogin Sophie von Sachsen*, series 1, volume 41 (Weimar: Böhlau, 1902), p. 248;

Hans L. von Gumbert, *Biblioteca Lichtenbergiana: Katalog der Bibliothek Georg Christoph Lichtenbergs* (Wiesbaden: Harrassowitz, 1982);

Paul Hahn, "Lichtenberg und die Experimentalphysik: Zur 200-jährigen Wiederkehr seines Geburtstages, " *Zeitschrift für den physikalischen und chemischen Unterricht*, 56 (1943): 8-15;

Helmut Heißenbüttel, *Als ich meine Gedanken- und Phantasiekur gebrauchte: Zur Struktur der "Sudelbücher" von Georg Christoph Lichtenberg* (Mainz: Akademie der Wissenschaften und der Literatur, 1985);

Arthur von Hippel and F. W. Merrill, "The Atomphysical Interpretation of Lichtenberg's Figures and Their Application to the Study of Gas Discharge Phenomena," *Journal for Applied Physics*, 10 (1939): 873-887;

Richard Kleineibst, *G. C. Lichtenberg in seiner Stellung zur deutschen Literatur* (Strasbourg: Trübner, 1915);

Rainer Koehne, "Gedanken und Exzerpte zur Bestimmung der philosophiegeschichtlichen Stellung Lichtenbergs," in *Zeugnisse: Theodor W. Adorno zum 60. Geburtstag*, edited by Max Horkheimer (Frankfurt am Main: Suhrkamp, 1963), pp. 133-151;

Franz H. Mautner, "Der Aphorismus als literarische Gattung," *Zeitschrift für Ästhetik und allgemeine Kunstwissenschaft*, 27 (1933): 132-175;

Mautner, "Lichtenberg as an Interpreter of Hogarth," *Modern Language Quarterly*, 13 (1952): 64-80;

Mautner, *Lichtenberg: Geschichte seines Geistes* (Berlin: De Gruyter, 1968);

Mautner, "Lichtenbergs ungedruckte Tagebücher: Bericht und Anfänge einer Deutung," *Euphorion*, 51 (1957): 23-41;

Mautner and F. H. Müller, "Remarks on Georg Christoph Lichtenberg, Humanist-Scientist," *Isis*, 43 (1952): 223-231;

Werner Milch, "Georg Christoph Lichtenberg: On the Occasion of the Two Hundredth Anniversary of His Birth," *Modern Language Review*, 37 (1942): 335-355;

Gerhard Neumann, *Ideenparadiese: Untersuchungen zur Aphoristik von Lichtenberg, Novalis, Frie-*

drich Schlegel und Goethe (Munich: Fink, 1976);

Neumann, ed., *Der Aphorismus: Zur Geschichte, zu den Formen und Möglichkeiten einer literarischen Gattung* (Darmstadt: Wissenschaftliche Buchgesellschaft, 1976);

Richard Newald, *Von Klopstock bis zu Goethes Tod 1750-1832*, in part 1, volume 6 of *Geschichte der deutschen Literatur: Von den Anfängen bis zur Gegenwart*, edited by Helmut de Boor and Richard Newald (Munich: Beck, 1957), pp. 229-232;

Herbert Pupke, "Georg Christoph Lichtenberg als Naturforscher: Zur 200. Wiederkehr seines Geburtstages," *Die Naturwissenschaften*, 30 (1942): 745-750;

Paul Requadt, *Lichtenberg: Zum Problem der deutschen Aphoristik* (Hameln: Seifert, 1948; enlarged edition, Stuttgart: Kohlhammer, 1964);

Peter Rippmann, *Werk und Fragment: Georg Christoph Lichtenberg als Schriftsteller* (Bern: Francke, 1953);

Wolfgang Rödel, *Forster und Lichtenberg: Ein Beitrag zum Problem deutscher Intelligenz und Französischer Revolution* (Berlin: Rütten & Loening, 1960);

Friedrich Schaefer, *Georg Christoph Lichtenberg als Psychologe und Menschenkenner: Eine kritische Untersuchung und ein Versuch zur Grundlegung einer "Empirischen Charakterpsychologie"* (Leipzig: Dieterich, 1899);

Albert Schneider, *G. C. Lichtenberg Penseur* (Paris: Université de la Sarre, 1954);

Schneider, *Georg Christoph Lichtenberg Precurseur du Romantisme: L'Homme et l'Oeuvre* (Nancy: Université de la Sarre, 1954);

Herbert Schöffler, *Lichtenberg: Studien zu seinem Wesen und Geist*, edited by Götz von Selle (Got-

tingen: Vandenhoeck & Ruprecht, 1956);

Albrecht Schöne, *Aufklärung aus dem Geist der Experimentalphysik: Lichtenbergsche Konjunktive* (Munich: Beck, 1982);

Schöne, "Zum Gebrauch des Konjunktivs bei Robert Musil," *Euphorion*, 55 (1961): 196-220;

Joseph Peter Stern, *Lichtenberg: A Doctrine of Scattered Occasions. Reconstructed from His Aphorisms and Reflections* (Bloomington: Indiana University Press, 1959);

Marija Tronskaja, "Georg Christoph Lichtenberg," *Die deutsche Prosasatire der Aufklärung* (Berlin: Rütten & Loening, 1969), pp. 256-325;

Gert Ueding, "Beredsamkeit aus der Erfahrung: Georg Christoph Lichtenbergs *Sudelbücher*," *Photorin* (1985): 1-18;

Rudolf Wildbolz, "Über Lichtenbergs Kurzformen," in *Geschichte, Deutung, Kritik: Literaturwissenschaftliche Beiträge dargebracht zum 65. Geburtstag Werner Kohlschmidts*, edited by Maria Bindschedler and Paul Zinsli (Bern: Francke, 1969), pp. 109-133;

Ralph-Rainer Wuthenow, "Lichtenbergs Skepsis," in *Reise und Utopie: Zur Literatur der Spätaufklärung*, edited by Hans Joachim Piechotta and others (Frankfurt am Main: Suhrkamp, 1976), pp. 151-169;

Jörg Zimmermann, ed., *Lichtenberg: Streifzüge der Phantasie* (Hamburg: Dölling & Galitz, 1988).

Papers:

The Niedersächsische Staats- und Universitätsbibliothek Göttingen has letters from and to Lichtenberg, his diaries, the *Sudelbücher*, notes on various themes, submissions to him for the *Göttingisches Magazin der Wissenschaften und Litteratur*, and drafts of lectures.

Karl Philipp Moritz

(15 September 1756 - 26 June 1793)

Thomas P. Saine
University of California, Irvine

BOOKS: *Tabelle von der Englischen Aussprache; Tabelle von der Englischen Etymologie* (Berlin: 1779);

Unterhaltungen mit meinen Schülern (Berlin: Spener, 1780);

Beiträge zur Philosophie des Lebens, aus dem Tagebuche eines Freimäurers, anonymous (Berlin: Wever, 1780; revised, 1781);

Die Dankbarkeit gegen Gott erhöhet unsre Freuden auf Erden: Eine Predigt, in der St. Katharinen-Kirche zu Braunschweig am 27sten August 1780 gehalten (Berlin: Sander, 1780);

Vom Unterschiede des Akkusativ's und Dativ's oder des mich und mir, sie und ihnen usw. für solche, die keine gelehrte Sprachkenntniß besitzen: In Briefen (Berlin: Wever, 1780);

Anhang zu den Briefen vom Unterschiede des Akkusativ's und Dativ's worin der Unterschied zwischen für und vor erklärt, und die Ursach gezeigt wird, warum durch und für immer den Akkusativ, und von, mit, aus, nach und zu, beständig den Dativ nach sich haben (Berlin: Wever, 1781);

Anweisung zur Englischen Accentuation nebst vermischten Aufsätzen die Englische Sprache betreffend: Als ein Anhang zu dessen Tabellen von der englischen Aussprache und Etymologie (Berlin, 1781);

Über den märkischen Dialekt: In Briefen (Berlin: Wever, 1781);

Anweisung die gewöhnlichsten Fehler, im Reden, zu verbessern, nebst einigen Gesprächen: Als das zweite Stück zu der Abhandlung über den märkischen Dialekt (Berlin: Wever, 1781);

Sechs deutsche Gedichte, dem Könige von Preußen gewidmet (Berlin: Wever, 1781);

Blunt oder der Gast: Ein Schauspiel in einem Aufzuge (Berlin: Wever, 1781);

Kleine Schriften die deutsche Sprache betreffend (Berlin: Wever, 1781);

Deutsche Sprachlehre für die Damen: In Briefen (Berlin: Wever, 1782);

Aussichten zu einer Experimentalseelenlehre, an Herrn Direktor Gedike (Berlin: Mylius, 1782);

Painting by Friedrich Rehberg (Edgar Schröder, Berlin)

Reisen eines Deutschen in England im Jahr 1782: In Briefen an Herrn Direktor Gedike. Mit einem Kupferstich der Castleton-Höhle (Berlin: Maurer, 1783); translated anonymously as *Travels, Chiefly on Foot, through Several Parts of England, in 1782: Described in Letters to a Friend, by Charles P. Moritz, a Literary Gentleman of Berlin. Translated from the German by a Lady* (London: Printed for G. G. and J. Robinson, 1795); translated anonymously as *Travels in England in 1782* (New York: Cassell, 1886); German version reprinted (Nendeln, Liechtenstein: Kraus, 1968);

190

Anleitung zum Briefschreiben (Berlin: Sander, 1783);

Englische Sprachlehre für die Deutschen: Nebst drei Tabellen, die englische Aussprache, Etymologie und Wortfügung betreffend (Berlin: Wever, 1784);

Von der deutschen Rechtschreibung: Nebst vier Tabellen, die deutsche Rechtschreibung, Interpunktion, Deklination, und insbesondere den Unterschied des Akkusativs und Dativs betreffend. Zum Gebrauch der Schulen und für solche die keine gelehrte Sprachkenntniß besitzen (Berlin: Wever, 1784);

Ideal einer vollkommnen Zeitung (Berlin: Voß, 1784);

Anton Reiser: Ein psychologischer Roman, 4 volumes (Berlin: Maurer, 1785-1790); translated by Percy Ewing Matheson as *Anton Reiser: A Psychological Novel* (London & New York: Oxford University Press, 1926; reprinted, Westport, Conn.: Hyperion Press, 1978);

Andreas Hartknopf: Eine Allegorie, anonymous (Berlin: Unger, 1786);

Versuch einer kleinen praktischen Kinderlogik welche auch zum Theil für Lehrer und Denker geschrieben ist (Berlin: Mylius, 1786; reprinted, Frankfurt am Main: Insel, 1980);

Versuch einer deutschen Prosodie (Berlin: Wever, 1786; reprinted, with a preface by Thomas P. Saine, Darmstadt: Wissenschaftliche Buchgesellschaft, 1973);

Fragmente aus dem Tagebuche eines Geistersehers: Von dem Verfasser Anton Reisers, anonymous (Berlin: Himburg, 1787);

Über die bildende Nachahmung des Schönen (Brunswick: Schulbuchhandlung, 1788); excerpts translated by Robert Heitner as "On the Creative Imitation of Beauty," in *Italian Journey* by Johann Wolfgang von Goethe, edited by Thomas P. Saine and Jeffrey L. Sammons (New York: Suhrkamp, 1989), pp. 431-436;

Ueber eine Schrift des Herrn Schulrath Campe, und über die Rechte des Schriftstellers und Buchhändlers (Berlin: Maurer, 1789);

Neues A.B.C. Buch welches zugleich eine Anleitung zum Denken für Kinder enthält (Berlin: Schöne, 1790);

Andreas Hartknopfs Predigerjahre, anonymous (Berlin: Unger, 1790);

Italiänische Sprachlehre für die Deutschen: Nebst einer Tabelle, die italiänische Aussprache und Etymologie betreffend (Berlin: Wever, 1791);

Götterlehre oder Mythologische Dichtungen der Alten (Berlin: Unger, 1791); translated by "C. F. W. J." as *Mythological Fictions of the Greeks and Romans* (New York: Carvill, 1830);

Anthousa oder Roms Alterthümer: Ein Buch für die Menschheit. Die heiligen Gebräuche der Römer (Berlin: Maurer, 1791);

Lesebuch für Kinder: Als ein Pendant zu dessen ABC Buch, welches zugleich eine natürliche Anleitung zum Denken für Kinder enthält (Berlin: Schöne, 1792);

Vom richtigen deutschen Ausdruck oder Anleitung die gewöhnlichsten Fehler im Reden zu vermeiden für solche die keine gelehrte Sprachkenntniß besitzen (Berlin: Verlag der kgl. preuß. akademischen Kunst- und Buchhandlung, 1792);

Reisen eines Deutschen in Italien in den Jahren 1786 bis 1788: In Briefen, 3 volumes (Berlin: Maurer, 1792-1793);

Grammatisches Wörterbuch der deutschen Sprache, volume 1 (Berlin: Felisch 1793; reprinted, Hildesheim & New York: Olms, 1970);

Vorlesungen über den Styl oder Praktische Anweisung zu einer guten Schreibart in Beispielen aus den vorzüglichsten Schriftstellern, 2 volumes, by Moritz and Daniel Jenisch (Berlin: Vieweg, 1793-1794);

Die große Loge oder Der Freimaurer mit Wage und Senkblei: Von dem Verfasser der Beiträge zur Philosophie des Lebens, anonymous (Berlin: Felisch, 1793); enlarged as *Launen und Phantasien*, edited by Karl Friedrich Klischnig (Berlin: Felisch, 1796);

Vorbegriffe zu einer Theorie der Ornamente (Berlin: Matzdorff, 1793);

Allgemeiner deutscher Briefsteller, welcher eine kleine deutsche Sprachlehre, die Hauptregeln des Styls und eine vollständige Beispielsammlung aller Gattungen von Briefen enthält (Berlin: Maurer, 1793);

Die neue Cecilia: Letzte Blätter (Berlin: Unger, 1794); reprinted, Stuttgart: Metzler, 1962);

Schriften zur Ästhetik und Poetik: Kritische Ausgabe, edited by Hans Joachim Schrimpf (Tübingen: Niemeyer, 1962);

Werke in zwei Bänden, 2 volumes, edited by Jürgen Jahn (Berlin: Aufbau, 1973);

Werke, 3 volumes, edited by Horst Günther (Frankfurt am Main: Insel, 1981).

OTHER: *Gnothi Sauton oder Magazin zur Erfahrungsseelenkunde als ein Lesebuch für Gelehrte und Ungelehrte*, 10 volumes, edited by Moritz, C.F. Pockels, and Salomon Maimon (Berlin: Mylius, 1783-1793; reprinted, edited by Anke Bennholdt-Thomsen and Alfredo

Frontispiece, engraved by C. S. Henne, and title page for the book in which Moritz instructed Berlin women how to speak their own dialect

Guzzoni, Lindau im Breisgau: Antiqua, 1978-1979);

John Trusler, *Regeln einer feinen Lebensart und Welt-kenntniß zum Unterricht für die Jugend und zur Beherzigung für Erwachsene von D. John Trus-ler,* translated by Moritz (Berlin: Mylius, 1784);

Denkwürdigkeiten, aufgezeichnet zur Beförderung des Edlen und Schönen, 4 volumes, edited by Moritz and Pockels (Berlin: 1786-1788);

Monatsschrift der Akademie der Künste und mechani-schen Wissenschaftes zu Berlin, 3 volumes, edit-ed by Moritz and J.A. Riem (Berlin: Verlag der kgl. preuß. akademischen Kunst- und Buchhandlung, 1789-1790);

Italien und Deutschland: In Rücksicht auf Sitten, Gebräuche, Litteratur und Kunst, 2 volumes, edited by Moritz and A. Hirt (Berlin: Verlag der kgl. preuß. akademischen Kunst- und Buchhandlung, 1789-1793);

Annalen der Akademie der Künste und mechanischen Wissenschaften zu Berlin, edited by Moritz

(Berlin: Unger, 1791);

Adam Walker, *Bemerkungen auf einer Reise durch Flandern, Deutschland, Italien und Frankreich,* translated by Moritz (Berlin: Voß, 1791);

Mythologischer Almanach für Damen, edited by Mo-ritz (Berlin: Unger 1792);

Salomon Maimon's Lebensgeschichte: Von ihm selbst ge-schrieben und hrsg. von K. P. Moritz, 2 vol-umes, edited by Moritz (Berlin: Vieweg, 1792-1793);

Thomas Holcroft, *Anna St. Ives,* 5 volumes, trans-lated by Moritz (Berlin: Unger, 1792-1794);

Johann Gottfried Bremer, *Die symbolische Weisheit der Ägypter aus den verborgensten Denkmälern des Alterthums: Ein Teil der Ägyptischen Maure-rei, der zu Rom nicht verbrannt worden,* edited by Moritz (Berlin: Matzdorff, 1793).

Hardly any eighteenth-century German writer was as confusingly prolific as Karl Philipp

Andreas Hartknopf.

Eine Allegorie.

Non fumum ex fulgore
Sed ex fumo dare lucem.

Berlin, 1786.
bei Johann Friedrich Unger.

Title page for the first of Moritz's two novels about the preacher Andreas Hartknopf

Moritz, the author of novels; poems—he was one of the few Germans to be praised by Frederick II for his poetry; a playlet; psychological and moral works; books on the German, English, and Italian languages; travel volumes; works on aesthetics and mythology; and the editor of several journals as well. All of this work was produced in a span of less than fifteen years in the chaotic life of one of the more peculiar inhabitants of the world of German letters. Moritz would have been a fit subject for a novel by Jean Paul or E.T.A. Hoffmann and did play the major role in his own most important novel, *Anton Reiser* (1785-1790; translated, 1926).

Moritz was born in Hameln on 15 September 1756 (not in 1757, as is so often stated in the Moritz literature: Hans Joachim Schrimpf published the church records in his 1980 biography of Moritz in an attempt to set the record straight once and for all) to Johann Gottlieb Moritz and his second wife, Dorothee Henriette König Moritz. After the death of his first wife in 1753 Johann Gottlieb, a Hannoverian army musician, had found solace in the Quietist religious teachings of Madame Jeanne Marie de la Mothe-Guyon and her German disciple, Johannes Friedrich von Fleischbein. The father's Quietism caused difficulties in the household, since Dorothee Henriette Moritz remained a church-oriented Lutheran, and the Quietism and the household difficulties were the chief formative influences during Moritz's early childhood. The family moved to Hannover in 1763 after the father's return from active service in the Seven Years War. Johann Gottlieb Moritz refused to send his son to school, although he allowed him to learn to read and write while stuffing him full of Fleischbein's version of Guyon's mystic teachings. At the age of twelve Moritz began to learn Latin. Throughout his childhood he was sickly: he had tuberculosis, and between the ages of eight and twelve he suffered greatly from a scrofulous foot.

In the fall of 1768 Moritz was apprenticed to Johann Simon Lobenstein, a hatmaker in Brunswick. Lobenstein was a Fleischbeinian Quietist of the worst sort, who, at least according to the account in *Anton Reiser*, used religious conviction and exhortation as a means to the more effective economic exploitation of his apprentices and journeymen. Moritz was so unhappy in Brunswick that he tried to commit suicide, whereupon his father—who seems to have taken Moritz's failure to thrive under Lobenstein's harsh domination as a sure indication of his spiritual perdition—was forced to take him back to Hannover. In the spring of 1771 Moritz was admitted to the Hannover gymnasium, against his father's wishes, after being recommended to the school by a military chaplain. Soon after Moritz entered the gymnasium his parents moved away; he was left behind to study in extreme poverty, dependent on charity and choir singing to survive. He painted a depressing picture of his school years in *Anton Reiser*. It was in this period, however, that he became aware of the "Wonne des Denkens" (joy of thinking) and became acquainted with Enlightenment literature and thought. The appearance of *Die Leiden des jungen Werthers* (The Sorrows of Young Werther) in 1774 made an indelible impression on him, and he became Goethe's devoted admirer; he even dreamed of trekking to Weimar to offer himself as Goethe's servant. It was during his years at the gymnasium, where he was the classmate of August Wilhelm Iffland, the future author, actor, and theater director, that he became obsessed with the theater.

In 1776 Moritz matriculated at the University of Erfurt as a student of theology, but he soon left to seek his fortune as an actor with a theater troupe which was already on the verge of disbanding. (This is approximately as much of his biography as is related in *Anton Reiser*.) After some wandering in search of a profession he matriculated at the University of Wittenberg in 1777. Around this time he became acquainted with Johann Bernhard Basedow, the founder of the Philanthropinum, an experimental school in Dessau, where he stayed for a while. He was greatly impressed by Basedow and decided to become a teacher; but he also had severe disagreements with him, and he later satirized Basedow's disciples in his Andreas Hartknopf novels.

In 1778 Moritz got his first job, a temporary appointment at the military orphanage in Potsdam. In November he moved to the gymnasium "Zum grauen Kloster" (At the Gray Cloister) in Berlin; he became deputy rector in 1779, after completing the requirements for the "Magister" degree at Wittenberg, and professor in 1784. During this period he joined the Freemasons—by 1791 he was a leading figure in the Berlin "St.-Johannis-Loge zur Beständigkeit" (St. John Lodge for Steadfastness)—and became an accepted member of Berlin Enlightenment circles, the friend of Moses Mendelssohn and an early member of the famous salon of Henriette Herz (whose husband, Marcus Herz, was Moritz's physician). He became associated with the respected Berlin pedagogues Anton Friedrich Büsching, Friedrich Gedike, and Johann Erich Biester and contributed articles to Gedike and Biester's *Berlinische Monatsschrift*, which began publication in 1783. Moritz's friendship with Mendelssohn in the last years of the latter's life had a great effect both on Moritz's intellectual development and on the style and content of his writing. The influence of Mendelssohn's late metaphysical views, expressed in *Morgenstunden* (Morning Hours, 1785), can be seen in Moritz's *Unterhaltungen mit meinen Schülern* (Conversations with My Students, 1780), a series of dialogues meant to introduce young people to thinking about God and nature; in *Versuch einer kleinen praktischen Kinderlogik* (Attempt at a Short Practical Logic for Children, 1786) and in Moritz's es-

Moritz (standing, with hand in vest) in Rome during his 1786-1788 Italian trip. Standing next to him is the artist Johann Heinrich Wilhelm Tischbein, who painted this picture; seated in front of them is Lord Hamilton. The identity of the dwarf in the background is unknown. (Nationale Forschungs- und Gedenkstätten, Weimar)

says on moral and philosophical subjects in the journal he edited, *Denkwürdigkeiten, aufgezeichnet zur Beförderung des Edlen und Schönen* (Memorabilia Published for the Purpose of Furthering the Noble and the Beautiful, 1786-1788). Mendelssohn also had an impact on Moritz's psychological thought, manifested most clearly in the programmatic announcements of his project to found a magazine for experimental psychology and in the articles he wrote for the magazine after it began appearing in 1783 under the title *Gnothi Sauton oder Magazin zur Erfahrungsseelenkunde*. Most of Moritz's early writing, including his publications on the German language, had a strong pedagogical bent: in *Deutsche Sprachlehre für die Damen* (Elements of German for the Ladies, 1782) Moritz, the Hannoverian, seeks to teach the Berliners how to speak their own dialect properly. After a trip to England he wrote *Reisen eines Deutschen in England im Jahr 1782* (Travels of a German in England in the Year 1782, 1783; translated as *Travels, Chiefly on*

Foot, through Several Parts of England, in 1782, 1795), becoming famous as the sentimental German who traveled on foot.

In 1785 Moritz published the first installment of *Anton Reiser: Ein psychologischer Roman* (Anton Reiser: A Psychological Novel), excerpts of which had already appeared in the *Magazin zur Erfahrungsseelenkunde* under the rubric "Erinnerungen aus den frühesten Jahren der Kindheit" (Earliest Childhood Recollections). The next two installments appeared in 1786; the fourth and last–the novel remained unfinished– came out in 1790. *Anton Reiser* is the story of a desperately deprived and isolated boy's journey through childhood and adolescence. The narrator relates, with an objective and unsparing omniscience that lays bare Reiser's every delusion and self-delusion, the boy's joys and sorrows, his crushing defeats and errors, his twisted relationship with God, his thirst for learning and books, and his consuming passion to represent himself on the stage as a better and more fortunate person than he is in real life. In its unmitigated bleakness it is possibly the most depressing novel in German literature. It obviously draws heavily upon Moritz's own childhood, and most of what is known or surmised about Moritz's first twenty years is gleaned from the novel; yet it would be a mistake to treat *Anton Reiser* as pure autobiography. After all, the book is subtitled "A Psychological Novel." The two Andreas Hartknopf novels, *Andreas Hartknopf: Eine Allegorie* (1786) and *Andreas Hartknopfs Predigerjahre* (Andreas Hartknopf's Preacher Years, 1790) are also autobiographical in their own way: they present an ideal figure, Andreas Hartknopf, who preaches the great lesson of "Resignation" and accepts his fate as a martyr to religious orthodoxy and intolerant Basedowian educators. While *Anton Reiser* is unique in the penetrating realism of its psychological observation, the Hartknopf novels, which fascinated Jean Paul, represent the earliest attempt in modern German literature to narrate on a symbolic-allegorical plane. In the final installment of *Anton Reiser*, written after Moritz had fully developed his theory of artistic genius, the hero is forced to realize and accept his lack of genius for poetry or the theater; Andreas Hartknopf is a spiritual and moral genius of a kind that Anton Reiser is not.

In 1786 Moritz took leave abruptly from the gymnasium "Zum grauen Kloster" to embark on a trip to Italy, which he financed in part with an advance from the Brunswick publisher Joa-

Moritz in 1791; painting by Schumann
(Gleimhaus, Halberstadt)

chim Heinrich Campe for a book describing the journey and his stay in Italy. The only immediate product of the Italian sojourn was the treatise *Über die bildende Nachahmung des Schönen* (1788; excerpts translated as "On the Creative Imitation of Beauty," 1989); the earliest document in the German tradition of idealist aesthetics, it postulates the work of art as a thing-in-itself, independent of any use value or any effect it may exert on the observer. Campe was quite unhappy about the brevity and obscure language of the treatise and later argued publicly with Moritz about what publishers and authors had a right to expect from each other (whereupon Moritz ostentatiously returned Campe's advances). The two years in Italy introduced Moritz to the classical world and left their mark on his aesthetic thinking after he returned to Berlin in 1789. He eventually published an extended work about his Italian journey for another publisher: *Reisen eines Deutschen in Italien in den Jahren 1786 bis 1788* (Travels of a German in Italy in the Years 1786 to 1788, 1792-1793) is interesting and significant above all for its descriptions of classical and Renaissance art; but it has never received the critical or scholarly attention it deserves, overshadowed as it has been by Goethe's much more famous *Italienische Reise* (Italian Journey, 1816-1817). A great personal gain for Moritz in Italy was his friendship with Goethe, who was in Rome at the same time. Goethe claimed to see in Moritz a younger brother who had suffered greatly at the hands of fate whereas he, Goethe, had been blessed. Goethe used Moritz as a sounding board for his theory of plant metamorphosis, and at the end of *Italienische Reise* he reprinted a substantial excerpt from *Über die bildende Nachahmung des Schönen* as an example of his and Moritz's aesthetic thinking during those years. Goethe also said that he would not have been able to transform his prose *Iphigenie auf Tauris* (Iphigenia on Tauris) into a polished "classical" play in blank verse (1787) without Moritz's *Versuch einer deutschen Prosodie* (Attempt at a German Prosody, 1786), which had come out just before Moritz left for Italy. On the way back to Berlin, Moritz was Goethe's guest in Weimar from 4 December 1788 to 31 January 1789, and he impressed leading members of Weimar society with his personableness and the fervor of his devotion to art. He made a triumphal return to Berlin in the company of Weimar's Duke Karl August, who seems to have exerted some influence in securing Moritz's appointment that year as professor of the theory of fine arts at the Berlin Academy of Arts. Moritz eventually also acquired the title of "Hofrat" (Aulic Councillor) and became a member of the Berlin Academy of Sciences.

The desperately poor and socially deprived son of the Hannoverian regimental musician had finally achieved respectability and a degree of economic security. Now that he was established in society he decided that he needed a wife and a household, and after a certain amount of searching he settled on Friederike Matzdorff, the teenaged sister of his publisher. He married her in 1792, saw her run off with an old flame, divorced her, and then remarried her shortly before his death. The earliest fan of Jean Paul, he arranged for his brother-in-law to publish Jean Paul's first novel *Die unsichtbare Loge* (The Invisible Lodge, 1793). He died on 26 June 1793 of the tuberculosis from which he had suffered throughout his life.

Until the 1970s Moritz scholarship was concerned almost exclusively with his aesthetics, as presented in *Über die bildende Nachahmung des Schönen*, and with his novel *Anton Reiser*, which

was usually treated as a piece of psychologizing autobiography. (The *Magazin zur Erfahrungsseelenkunde*, which is considered the earliest journal devoted to empirical psychology, had drawn attention from historians of psychology, but it was not generally well known.) *Über die bildende Nachahmung* and *Anton Reiser* were the only works by Moritz that were widely available, having been reprinted several times since the late nineteenth century, and no one had sought to collect and analyze his myriad other writings in any systematic fashion. Horst Günther's three-volume edition of Moritz's major works (1981) and the 1978-1979 reprint of the *Magazin zur Erfahrungsseelenkunde* now offer more of Moritz than has ever before been readily available, and some of his other works may now receive more attention. The *Magazin*, especially, deserves study because it is a treasure trove of material about the eighteenth-century psyche. The journal solicited contributions from readers, and Moritz wrote articles for it on language from the psychological point of view, on his observations of a young deaf-mute he had taken into his home, and on the psychology of religious experience (including the story of his father's infatuation with Quietism and how he had been cured of it in the last years before his death in 1788).

Moritz was not a first-class talent, and most of his works are flawed. He was always under pressure from his publishers–often from more than one at the same time–to deliver manuscript on a daily basis. He borrowed copiously from his own works–which makes Moritz philology a sometimes frustrating and hazardous undertaking–and from the works of others. One is never quite sure whether he is presenting the warmed-over thoughts of other people in his own special dress, or whether he is being almost brilliantly original. There is in fact something original about practically every one of his works. He cannot be said to have had a great influence on the direction of German letters, although some of his works were reprinted well into the nineteenth century–*Allgemeiner deutscher Briefsteller* (General Guide to German Letter Writing, 1793) and *Götterlehre oder Mythologische Dichtungen der Alten* (Mythology of the Ancients, 1791; translated as *Mythological Fictions of the Greeks and Romans*, 1830) head the list–and he was known to Romantics as late as Heinrich Heine. In its way, *Götterlehre* is perhaps his most accomplished, most impressive, and most satisfying work. While the canonizable output of Karl Philipp Moritz is slender, his work in its entirety is a mirror of late eighteenth-century German intellectual concerns and is worthy of becoming better known to cultural and intellectual historians as well as to literary scholars.

Biographies:

Karl Friedrich Klischnig, *Erinnerungen aus den zehn letzten Lebensjahren meines Freundes Anton Reiser: Als ein Beitrag zur Lebensgeschichte des Herrn Hofrath Moritz* (Berlin: Vieweg, 1794);

Hugo Eybisch, *Anton Reiser: Untersuchungen zur Lebensgeschichte von Karl Philipp Moritz und zur Kritik seiner Autobiographie. I: Moritz' Lebensgang von 1756-1778 (nach den Quellen)* (Leipzig: Voigtländer, 1909);

Hans Joachim Schrimpf, *Karl Philipp Moritz* (Stuttgart: Metzler, 1980).

References:

Raimund Bezold, *Popularphilosophie und Erfahrungsseelenkunde im Werk von Karl Philipp Moritz* (Würzburg: Königshausen & Neumann, 1984);

Adam John Bisanz, *Die Ursprünge der Seelenkrankheit bei Karl Philipp Moritz* (Heidelberg: Winter, 1970);

Mark Boulby, *Karl Philipp Moritz: At the Fringe of Genius* (Toronto, Buffalo & London: University of Toronto Press, 1979);

Joachim Heinrich Campe, *Moritz: Ein abgenöthigter trauriger Beitrag zur Erfahrungsseelenkunde* (Brunswick: Schulbuchandlung, 1789);

Eckehard Catholy, *Karl Philipp Moritz und die Ursprünge der deutschen Theaterleidenschaft* (Tübingen: Niemeyer, 1962);

Josef Fürnkäs, *Der Ursprung des psychologischen Romans: Karl Philipp Moritz' "Anton Reiser"* (Stuttgart: Metzler, 1977);

Ruth Ghisler, *Gesellschaft und Gottesstaat: Studien zum "Anton Reiser"* (Winterthur, 1955);

Joseph Grolimund, *Das Menschenbild in den autobiographischen Schriften Karl Philipp Moritz': Eine Untersuchung zum Selbstverständnis des Menschen in der Goethezeit* (Zurich: Juris, 1967);

Horst Günther, ed., *Insel Almanach auf das Jahr 1981: Karl Philipp Moritz: Wer ist das?* (Frankfurt am Main: Insel, 1980);

Ulrich Hubert, *Karl Philipp Moritz und die Anfänge der Romantik* (Frankfurt am Main: Athenäum, 1971);

Claudia Kestenholz, *Die Sicht der Dinge: Metaphorische Visualität und Subjektivitätsideal im Werk*

von Karl Philipp Moritz (Munich: Fink, 1987);

Egon Menz, *Die Schrift Karl Philipp Moritzens "Über die bildende Nachahmung des Schönen"* (Göppingen: Kümmerle, 1968);

Robert Minder, *Die religiöse Entwicklung von Karl Philipp Moritz auf Grund seiner autobiographischen Schriften* (Berlin: Junker & Dünnhaupt, 1936); republished as *Glaube, Skepsis und Rationalismus* (Frankfurt am Main: Suhrkamp, 1974);

Robert Mühlher, *Deutsche Dichter der Klassik und Romantik* (Vienna: Braumüller, 1976), pp. 79-259;

Klaus-Detlev Müller, *Autobiographie und Roman: Studien zur literarischen Autobiographie der Goethezeit* (Tübingen: Niemeyer, 1976), pp. 145-169;

Lothar Müller, *Die kranke Seele und das Licht der Erkenntnis: Karl Philipp Moritz' Anton Reiser* (Frankfurt am Main: Athenäum, 1987);

Müller, "Karl Philipp Moritz," in *Deutsche Dichter, 4: Sturm und Drang, Klassik* (Stuttgart: Reclam, 1989), pp. 231-251;

Günter Niggl, *Geschichte der deutschen Autobiographie im 18. Jahrhundert theaterische Grundlegung und literarische Entfaltung* (Stuttgart: Metzler, 1977), pp. 65-72;

Bruno Preisendorfer, *Psychologische Ordnung, groteske Passion: Opfer und Selbstbehauptung in den Romanien von Karl Philipp Moritz* (St. Ingbert: Rohrig, 1987);

Peter Rau, *Identitätserinnerungen und ästhetische Rekonstruktion: Studien zum Werk von Karl Philipp Moritz* (Frankfurt am Main: Fischer, 1983);

Thomas P. Saine, *Die ästhetische Theodizee: Karl Philipp Moritz und die Philosophie des. 18 Jahrhunderts* (Munich: Fink, 1971);

Hans-Jürgen Schings, *Melancholie und Aufklärung: Melancholiker und ihre Kritiker in Erfahrungsseelenkunde und Literatur des 18. Jahrhunderts* (Stuttgart: Metzler, 1977), pp. 226-255;

Hans Joachim Schrimpf, "Karl Philipp Moritz," in *Deutsche Dichter des 18. Jahrhunderts: Ihr Leben und Werk*, edited by Benno von Wiese (Berlin: Erich Schmidt, 1977), pp. 881-910;

Dorothee Sölle, *Realisation: Studien zum Verhältnis von Theologie und Dichtung nach der Aufklärung* (Darmstadt & Neuwied: Luchterhand, 1973), pp. 107-167;

Bengt Algot Sorensen, *Symbol und Symbolismus in den ästhetischen Theorien des. 18 Jahrhunderts und der deutschen Romantik* (Copenhagen: Munksgaard, 1963), pp. 71-85.

Papers:
Johann Paul Friedrich Richter (Jean Paul) and Moritz's brother, Johann Christian Conrad Mo-

ritz, collected material for a planned biography of Karl Philipp Moritz. After Richter's death Moritz's literary remains disappeared. There seems to be no collection of Moritz papers or even a substantial collection of Moritz's published works anywhere in the world.

Maler Müller
(Friedrich Müller)
(13 January 1749 - 23 April 1825)

H. M. Waidson
University of Wales, Swansea

BOOKS: *Der Satyr Mopsus: Eine Idylle in drey Gesängen. Von einem jungen Mahler,* anonymous (Frankfurt am Main & Leipzig [actually Mannheim: Schwan], 1775);

Bacchidon und Milon, eine Idylle: Nebst einem Gesang auf die Geburt des Bacchus. Von einem jungen Mahler, anonymous (Frankfurt am Main & Leipzig [actually Mannheim: Schwan], 1775);

Die Schaaf-Schur: Eine Pfälzische Idylle (Mannheim: Schwan, 1775);

Balladen (Mannheim: Schwan, 1776);

Situation aus Fausts Leben (Mannheim: Schwan, 1776);

Niobe: Ein lyrisches Drama (Mannheim: Schwan, 1778);

Fausts Leben, dramatisirt: Erster Theil (Mannheim: Schwan, 1778);

Adams erstes Erwachen und erste seelige Nächte (Mannheim: Schwan, 1778; revised, 1779);

Schreiben von Friedrich Müller Königlich Bayrischen Hofmahler über eine Reise aus Liefland nach Neapel und Rom von August von Kotzebue (Deutschland [Mannheim], 1807);

Mahler Müllers Werke, 3 volumes, edited by Georg Anton Batt, J. P. Le Pique, and Ludwig Tieck (Heidelberg: Mohr & Zimmer, 1811)–comprises in volume 1, "Adams erstes Erwachen und erste seelige Nächte," "Der erschlagene Abel," "Der Faun," "Der Satyr

Mopsus," "Bacchidon und Milon," "Ulrich von Coßheim: Deutsche Idylle," "Die Schaaf-Schur," "Das Nuß-Kernen: Eine Pfälzische Idylle," "Kreuznach"; in volume 2, *Fausts Leben, dramatisirt, Situation aus Fausts Leben, Die Pfalzgräfin Genovefa, Niobe,* "Gedichte"; as volume 3, *Golo und Genovefa;* reprinted, 3 volumes, edited by Gerhard vom Hofe (Heidelberg: Schneider, 1982);

Der hohe Ausspruch oder Chares und Fatime: Eine altpersische Novelle (Karlsruhe: Braun, 1825);

Adonis, die klagende Venus, Venus Urania: Eine Trilogie (Leipzig: Fleischer, 1825);

Dichtungen, edited by Hermann Hettner (2 volumes, Leipzig: Brockhaus, 1868; reprinted, 1 volume, Bern: Lang, 1968);

Der Faun Molon: Eine Idylle. Nach der Handschrift herausgegeben, edited by Otto Heuer (Leipzig: Rowohlt, 1912);

Idyllen: Vollständige Ausgabe in drei Bänden unter Benutzung des handschriftlichen Nachlasses, 3 volumes, edited by Otto Heuer (Leipzig: Wolff, 1914).

Editions and Collections: *Fausts Leben: Situation aus Fausts Leben,* edited by Bernhard Seuffert (Heilbronn: Henninger, 1881);

Maler Müller und Schubart, edited by A. Sauer, volume 81 of *Deutsche National-Litteratur,* edited by Joseph Kürschner (Berlin & Stuttgart: Spemann, 1883);

Goethemuseum, Frankfurt am Main

Werke: Volksausgabe, mit neuer Würdigung des Dich-
ters und Malers, edited by Max Oeser (Mannheim: Schiller, 1916-1918);

Idyllen, Nach den Erstdrucken revidierter Text, edited
by Peter-Erich Neuser (Stuttgart: Reclam,
1977);

Fausts Leben, edited by Johannes Mahr (Stuttgart:
Reclam, 1979).

OTHER: "Der Faun: Eine Idylle," *Die Schreibtafel:*
Zweyte Lieferung (Mannheim: Schwan, 1775),
pp. 8-16;

"Der erschlagene Abel," in *Die Schreibtafel: Dritte*
Lieferung (Mannheim: Schwan, 1775).

Maler Müller was one of the group of
young men in the 1770s whose critical reaction to
the society and literature of the time is usually
seen as forming the Sturm und Drang movement. He wished to give primacy to spontaneous
feeling with an emphasis on nature and the language and manners of the people. Johann

Friedrich Müller was born in Bad Kreuznach on
13 January 1749 to Johann Friedrich Müller, a
baker and innkeeper, and Katharina Margaretha
Roos Müller. Müller's mother died when he was
young. His education at the gymnasium, which
began in 1759, ended when his father died in
1763. The boy's artistic gifts were noticed by a patron of his father's inn, a businessman named
Schmerz, who paid for him to go to Zweibrücken
in 1765 to study art. There he became the court
painter for the duke of Pfalz-Zweibrücken.
Müller fell in love with Charlotte Kärner, but her
father, an ecclesiastical official, did not regard
the young man as an acceptable suitor and did
all he could to prevent the couple from meeting.
In 1774 Müller left Zweibrücken for Mannheim,
where he obtained access to court circles and
soon became an active participant in the city's literary and artistic life. He was a friend of the publisher Friedrich Schwan, who, beginning in 1775,
published Müller's idylls, poetry, and dramatic
pieces. At first the author was given only as "ein
junger Mahler" (a young painter); later Müller
adopted the pseudonym Mahler (modern spelling: *Maler*) Müller, the name by which he is generally known. He was well regarded by Gotthold
Ephraim Lessing, with whom he discussed plans
for theatrical projects in Mannheim.

The genre of the idyll had been given a
firm footing in eighteenth-century writing by the
Swiss author Salomon Geßner. Müller wished to
steer clear of artifice and convention, and although his treatments of biblical and classical
themes may contain much traditional material,
they have unique qualities of fantasy and imagina-
tiveness. Customarily Müller's idylls are thought
to fall into three categories: those with a classical
setting, which largely adhere to the traditional conventions of the idyll; those that deal with biblical
material in the rhetorical manner of Ossian; and
those with contemporary or historical German settings.

The short prose idyll "Der Faun" (1775) is elegiac in mood. The faun Molon mourns the
death of his wife, telling of her qualities as a faithful spouse and mother and arranging for the funeral pyre to be lit in the evening; the bereaved
children weep. The two other idylls with a classical setting are very different in mood from "Der
Faun." *Der Satyr Mopsus* (1775) is a humorous narrative in three sections about the courtship of the
satyr Mopsus and the water nymph Persina. In
his preface to *Bacchidon und Milon* (1775) Müller
claims that this idyll is ancient Greek in spirit,

Müller as a faun; drawing by Genelli (Gustav Könnecke,
Bilderatlas zur Geschichte der deutschen National-
litteratur [Graz: Akademische Druck- und Verlags-
gesellschaft 1981])

but he introduces the costume of Rhineland peasants. The ever-thirsty satyr Bacchidon is invited
into the cave of the young Milon; there Milon
tries to read Bacchidon a poem he has composed, but Bacchidon pays scant attention.

Adams erstes Erwachen und erste seelige Nächte
(Adam's First Awakening and First Blissful
Nights, 1778) is an extended narrative based on
the Bible. Adam, Eve, their son Abel, and their
(nonbiblical) daughters Melboe and Tirza are
gathered beneath a tree in the evening. Adam relates his memories of the creation of the world–
how he heard the voice of God after the first rising of the sun, how the animals paid homage to
him, how God first revealed Eve to him in a
dream, and how the fruits of the earth were
made available to them. The style is elevated and
rhapsodic. The death of Abel at Cain's hands,
and thereby the introduction of mankind to mor-
tality, was described in an earlier sketch, "Der
erschlagene Abel" (The Slain Abel, 1775).

In *Die Schaaf-Schur* (The Sheep-Shearing,
1775) and "Das Nuß-Kernen" (The Nut-shelling,
1811) Müller makes his most original and characteristic contributions to the idyll. Both works are
in dialogue form with elements of dramatic ten-

sion, and both alternate prose and verse. Each
idyll brings together a group of people for
shared work connected with the farm; this work
is an annual event which allows for an occasion
of social celebration. The opening scene of *Die
Schaaf-Schur* shows Walter, a sheep farmer, and
young Veitel shearing the sheep while Walter's
daughters Guntel and Lotte gather the wool.
Veitel, who was adopted by Walter when his father died, is to depart the next day, but Walter,
not yet realizing that Veitel and Lotte are in love,
fails to understand why Lotte is dispirited and unable to sing one of her father's favorite songs. Walter prefers the traditional folk songs, while the
local schoolmaster, who is a friend of the family,
has an intellectual approach to music that often appears as pedantry. When Walter realizes the seriousness of the young people's feelings, he agrees
to their wish to marry and makes them various
gifts.

In "Das Nuß-Kernen," a sequel to *Die Schaaf-
Schur*, the group meets at the farm of Schulz, a
neighbor and friend of Walter's; the latter joins
the group accompanied by his now-pregnant
daughter Lotte, while her sister is being courted
by Fröhlich, an articulate and confident young
man who turns out to be a long-absent son of the
village. The schoolmaster tells sad stories of frus-
trated lovers, but the older generation gives its
blessing to the marriage of Guntel and Fröhlich,
and Walter's aged mother donates her savings to
enable the couple to get off to a good start. "Das
Nuß-Kernen" has inset narratives which are dis-
proportionately long and irrelevant, but it is in
general a vigorous and imaginative work. "Der
Christabend," first published in Otto Heuer's
1914 edition of *Idyllen*, has formal relationships
to *Die Schaaf-Schur* and "Das Nuß-Kernen"; a
group of people come together to celebrate an annual event. Christmas is the occasion which
brings together a family and friends. The action
involves the condemnation and arrest of a corrupt official by the ruling count. In subplots a na-
tivity play prepared by the schoolmaster is presented to the company, and a young man accepts
his duty to marry a young woman who is pregnant with their child. Müller introduces several
themes of Sturm und Drang writing–social criticism, the triumph of true love, the virtue of stay-
ing close to nature, the praise of folk poetry, the
desirability of transcending class barriers–all
based on his personal experiences.

"Ulrich von Coßheim" (1811), subtitled
"Deutsche Idylle" (German idyll), centers on a

Title page for Müller's idyll about a sheep-shearing

young knight who plans to join the service of the emperor Henry IV in the latter half of the eleventh century. His life is greatly changed through a chance meeting near Bingen with Weidmann, an older shepherd, who tells a story of a French knight who betrayed the love of the young woman who enabled him to escape from his imprisonment. While this inset narrative is somber, the framework action concludes with the happy betrothal of Ulrich and Weidmann's daughter Agnes, whose three brothers are to be introduced by Ulrich to the service of the emperor. The manner and setting of this idyll caused Müller to be spoken of as the Romantic among the writers of the Sturm und Drang.

In 1778 Müller raised from patrons sufficient money to pay the cost of travel to Rome, where he planned to devote himself to painting and the study of art history. Soon after settling in Rome Müller converted to Catholicism. Paintings and sketches which he sent to Goethe some

months after his arrival in Rome made a disappointing impression: Goethe's classicist tastes reacted unsympathetically to the freer, more independent style Müller had adopted. This setback coincided with a serious illness. Goethe's hostile reaction to the paintings was sufficiently influential to reduce Müller's chances of success and cause him to lose confidence in his creative ability. He lived precariously for years; at times he acted as a travel guide to German visitors and as a dealer in antiques. During the French occupation of Rome in 1798-1799 Müller's rooms were pillaged, and many of his papers were lost. The pension he received in Rome was small and irregular, and it was not until 1823 that it was somewhat improved.

Ludwig Tieck was mainly responsible for initiating the publication of three volumes of Müller's writings in 1811, but it was Georg Anton Batt who did most of the work and who kept in touch with the author. Tieck had withdrawn from personal contact with Müller because his sister, when in Rome, had asked Müller to arrange for her a loan of a considerable sum; she then refused to repay the debt, and it took Müller many years to get the money back.

Müller wrote one full-length, five-act historical drama, *Golo und Genovefa*, which was finished in 1791 and first published in complete form in 1811. Duke Siegfried of the Palatinate is setting out as leader of an expedition to help defend French territory against the invading Moors. There is surprise at his decision to appoint Golo, who is young and considered immature, to be in charge during his absence. In an early monologue Golo declares his obsessive love for Genovefa, the wife Siegfried is leaving behind. The melancholy and indecisive Golo is manipulated into unscrupulous acts by the widowed Mathilde, who later reveals to Golo that she is his mother. Golo incarcerates Genovefa through false accusations when she resists his advances. While imprisoned she gives birth to her and Siegfried's son, Schmerzenreich. Golo defends himself in single combat with the knight Karl; a court servant and a gardener have already been killed to further his misrule. In act five, four years have passed; Genovefa has been freed from prison through the actions of a loyal servant. Golo is living restlessly, away from Siegfried's castle, while Genovefa is bringing up her child in hiding in the forest. Mathilde, who has married the Duke of Swabia, dies from the accidental consumption of poison. Finally Genovefa

Pen-and-ink drawing by Müller of a farm girl and sheep (Goethemuseum, Frankfurt am Main)

is reunited with her husband, and Golo meets his death by Siegfried's sword. *Golo und Genovefa* is an ambitiously designed play with plentiful opportunities for pageantry; there is a great variety of settings for the often complex action. A professional production of the play took place in Mannheim in 1924.

Less substantial than *Golo und Genovefa*, *Niobe* (1778), a verse play in three acts, is operatic in style and shows the author experimenting with the serious treatment of classical myth. Diana and Apollo are indignant at the declaration of independence of Niobe, who, along with her fourteen children, defies the traditional divine powers; her rebellion has disastrous consequences.

Müller published two sections from a prose play on the Faust theme. *Fausts Leben, dramatisirt* (Faust's Life Dramatized, 1778) opens with a midnight meeting of devils at which Mephistopheles reports that he has his eye on a likely candidate for hell. In Ingolstadt Faust reveals in his initial monologue his discontent that man in his imagination but not in reality is a powerful being and a master of all arts. Debts, incurred primarily through generosity to others, are the immediate cause of Faust's difficulties; the lawyer Knellius and grasping moneylenders are putting pressure

on him. As soldiers surround the building where he has been gambling away what money he has left in the vain hope of recovering his losses, Faust seeks to turn through necromancy to a new life in which he shall have pleasure and wealth. As midnight approaches, Faust's discontent asserts itself above weariness or piety: ". . . warum hat meine Seele den unersättlichen Hunger, den nie zu erstillenden Durst nach Können und Vollbringen, Wissen und Würken, Hoheit und Ehre–das mächtige Gefühl, das mich aus diesem Gedränge von Niedrigkeit immer und immer hinaufruft. . . ?" (. . . why is my soul possessed by insatiable hunger and the unquenchable thirst for power and accomplishment, knowledge and action, glory and honor–the mighty emotion that continually calls me upwards, away from these pressures of baseness. . . ?). *Fausts Leben, dramatisirt* closes with a monologue from Mephistopheles as Faust lies sleeping. The much shorter excerpt *Situation aus Fausts Leben* (Situation from Faust's Life, 1776 consists of two scenes which belong to a later part of the story. In one scene Mephistopheles joins three infernal companions and relates that twelve years of his pact with Faust have passed. The other scene is at the royal palace of Madrid, where Faust, desirous of inti-

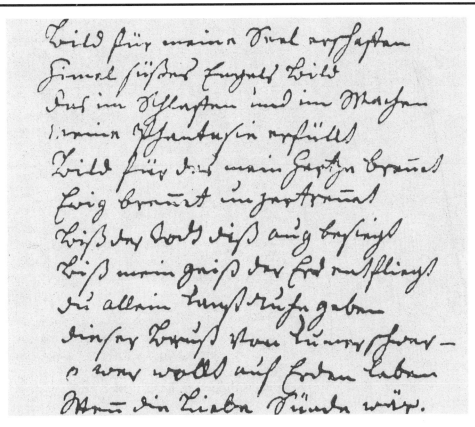

Part of a manuscript for a poem by Müller, written circa 1774 (Gustav Könnecke, Bilderatlas zur Geschichte der deutschen Nationallitteratur [Graz: Akademische Druck- und Verlagsanstalt, 1981])

macy with the king's sister, is reminded by Mephistopheles of the limited duration of his pact with him. Müller later returned to the Faust theme and wrote a complete eight-act metrical version of the work which has not been published.

In 1820 Müller composed an epitaph for himself which appears to be a wry comment by the author on his life and work:

> Wenig gekannt und wenig geschätzt, hab' ich beim
>   Wirken
>   Nach dem Wahren gestrebt, und mein höchster
>   Genuß
> War die Erkenntnis des Schönen und Großen—*ich
>   habe gelebt!*—
>   Daß Fortuna nie mich geliebt, verzeih' ich ihr
>   gern.

> (Little known and slightly esteemed, I have in my
>   activities
>   Striven for truth, and my highest pleasure
> Was the recognition of the beautiful and the
>   great—*I have lived!*—
>   I gladly forgive Fortune for never loving me.)

In 1821 and 1822 Müller underwent several eye operations. After a first stroke in 1824, a second and fatal stroke occurred in Rome in 1825.

Müller certainly had more than his share of disappointments and frustrations in the course of his life, but he is well remembered today. A Müller club has been established in Kreuznach, and in 1988 an exhibition of his literary and artistic work was held at the library of the University of Saarbrücken, where a collected edition of his works is in preparation. Gerhard Sauder, Rolf Paulus, and Christoph Weiß are editing Müller's correspondence for publication.

Bibliographies:

Friedrich Meyer, *Maler-Müller-Bibliographie* (Leipzig: 1912; reprinted, Hildesheim & New York: Olms, 1974);

Rolf Paulus, "Kleine Maler-Müller-Bibliographie: Werke und Forschungsliteratur in Auswahl," in *Maler-Müller-Almanach 1980*, edited by Paulus, Emil Walter Rabold, and Wolfgang Schlegels (Landau: Pfälzer Kunst, 1980), pp. 95-106.

Müller in 1816; pencil sketch by Ludwig Emil Grimm (Goethe-Museum, Düsseldorf)

References:

A. Beck, "Goethes *Iphigenie* und Maler Müllers *Niobe*," *Dichtung und Volkstum*, 40 (1939): 157-174;

Renate Böschenstein, "Maler Müller," in *Deutsche Dichter des 18. Jahrhunderts*, edited by Benno von Wiese (Berlin: Schmidt, 1977), pp. 641-657;

Felix Cambon, "Maler Müller–ein Pfälzer Vorkämpfer der Romantik? Mit einem Nach-

wort von Wolfgang Schlegel," *Blätter der Carl Zuckmayer-Gesellschaft*, 8 (1982): 71-122;

Ferdinand Denk, *Friedrich Müller der Malerdichter und Dichtermaler* (Speyer: Pfälzische Gesellschaft zur Förderung der Wissenschaften, 1930);

Willy Mathern, *Maler Müller 1749-1825: Leben und Werk des Maler-Dichters* (Bad Kreuznach: Raab, 1974);

K. Möllenbrock, "Die Idyllen des Maler Müller," *Dichtung und Volkstum*, 40 (1939): 145-157;

Willy Oeser, *Maler Müller: Neuwertung seines Schaffens* (Mannheim: Gremm, 1928);

Rolf Paulus, Emil Walter Rabold, and Wolfgang Schlegel, eds., *Maler-Müller-Almanach 1980* (Landau: Pfälzer Kunst, 1980);

Paulus, Rabold, and Schlegel, eds., *Maler-Müller-Almanach 1983* (Landau: Pfälzische Verlagsanstalt, 1983);

Paulus, Rabold, Gerhard Sauder, and Schlegel, eds., *Maler-Müller-Almanach 1987* (Bad Kreuznach: Fiedler, 1987);

Paulus, Rabold, Sauder, and Schlegel, eds., *Maler-Müller-Almanach 1988* (Bad Kreuznach: Fiedler, 1988);

Bernhard Seuffert, *Maler Müller: Im Anhang Mittheilungen aus Müllers Nachlaß* (Berlin: Weidmann, 1877);

James Trainer, "Anatomy of a Debt: Friedrich 'Maler' Müller and the Tiecks. With Unpublished Correspondence," *Oxford German Studies*, 11 (1980): 146-177;

Christoph Weiß, ed., *Maler Müller 1749-1825: Schriftsteller und Maler* (Saarbrücken: Universität des Saarlandes, 1988).

Papers:

There are Müller archives at the Freie Deutsche Hochstift, Frankfurt am Main, and at the Staatsbibliothek Preußischer Kulturbesitz, West Berlin.

Johann Heinrich Pestalozzi

(12 January 1746 - 17 February 1827)

Dieter Jedan
Murray State University

BOOKS: *Zuverlässige Nachricht von der Erziehungs-Anstalt des Herrn Pestalozze* (N.p., 1778);

Lienhard und Gertrud: Ein Buch für das Volk, 4 volumes, anonymous (volume 1, Berlin & Leipzig: Decker, 1781; volumes 2-4, Frankfurt am Main & Leipzig, 1783-1787); revised as *Lienhard und Gertrud: Ein Versuch, die Grundsätze der Volksbildung zu vereinfachen*, 3 volumes, as Pestalozzi (Zurich & Leipzig: Ziegler, 1790-1792); excerpts translated anonymously as *Leonard and Gertrude: A Popular Story, Written Originally in German; Translated into French, and Now Attempted in English; with the Hope of Its Being Useful to All Classes of Society* (Philadelphia: Printed for and sold by Joseph Groff, 1801; 2 volumes, London: Mawmann, 1825); translated and abridged by Eva Channing as *Pestalozzi's Leonard and Gertrude* (Boston: Ginn, Heath, 1885; reprinted, New York: Gordon Press, 1977);

Christoph und Else: Mein zweytes Volks Buch, 2 volumes, anonymous (Zurich & Dessau: Füßli, 1782);

Ueber Gesetzgebung und Kindermord: Wahrheiten und Träume, Nachforschungen und Bilder, anonymous (Frankfurt am Main & Leipzig: Published by the author, 1783);

Figuren zu meinem ABC Buch oder Zu den Anfangsgründen meines Denkens (Basel: Flick, 1797); republished as *Fabeln* (Basel: Flick, 1803);

Meine Nachforschungen über den Gang der Natur in der Entwicklung des Menschengeschlechts: Von dem Verfasser Lienhard und Gertrud, anonymous (Zurich: Geßner, 1797);

An mein Vaterland! (N.p., 1798);

Wach auf, Volk!: Ein Revolutionsgespräch zwischen den Bürgern Hans und Jacob (N.p., 1798);

Ein Wort an die Gesetzgebenden Räthe Helvetiens (Aarau, 1798);

Ueber den Zehnden (Aarau: Bek, 1798);

Anweisung zum Buchstabieren- und Lesenlernen (Bern: National-Buchdruckerey, 1801);

*Wie Gertrud ihre Kinder lehrt: Ein Versuch, den Müttern Anleitung zu geben, ihre Kinder selbst zu un-

Etching by Johann Heinrich Lips of a drawing by Diogg

terrichten, in Briefen* (Bern & Zurich: Geßner, 1801); translated by Lucy E. Holland and Francis C. Turner and edited by Ebenezer Cooke as *How Gertrude Teaches Her Children: An Attempt to Help Mothers to Teach Their Own Children and an Account of The Method. A Report to the Society of the Friends of Education, Burgdorf* (London: Sonnenschein / Syracuse, N.Y.: Bardeen, 1894; reprinted, London: Remax House, 1966; New York: Gordon Press, 1973);

Pestalozzi's farm, Neuhof, where he started his first school and to which he retired; engraving by J. Aschmann of a drawing by J. H. Schulthess, 1780

Ansichten über die Gegenstände, auf welche die Gesetzgebung Helvetiens ihr Augenmerk zu richten hat (Bern: Geßner, 1802);

ABC der Anschauung oder Anschauungslehre der Massverhältnisse (Zurich & Bern: Geßner, 1803);

Anschauungslehre der Zahlenverhältnisse (Zurich: Geßner / Tübingen: Cotta, 1803);

Buch der Mütter oder Anleitung für Mütter, ihre Kinder bemerken und reden zu lehren (Zurich & Bern: Geßner / Tübingen: Cotta, 1803);

Wochenschrift für Menschenbildung, 4 volumes (Aarau: Sauerlander, 1805-1811);

Ansichten, Erfahrungen und Mittel zur Beförderung einer der Menschennatur angemessenen Erziehungsweise: 1. Bandes 1. Heft (Leipzig: Gräff, 1807);

Das Pestalozzische Institut an das Publikum: Eine Schutzrede gegen verläumderische Angriffe (Yverdon, 1811);

Erklärung gegen Herrn Chorherr Bremi's Drey Dutzend Bürkli'sche Zeitungsfragen (Yverdon, 1812);

Pestalozzi an Herrn Geheimrath Delbrük, Erzieher Sr. Kögl. Hoheit des Kronprinzen von Preußen (Yverdon, 1813);

An die Unschuld, den Ernst und den Edelmuth meines Zeitalters und meines Vaterlandes: Ein Wort der Zeit (Yverdon: Published by the author, 1815);

The Address of Pestalozzi to the British Public Soliciting Them to Aid by Subscriptions His Plan of Preparing School Masters and Mistresses for the People, that Mankind May in Time Receive the First Principles of Intellectual Instruction from Their Mothers (Yverdon: Fiva, 1818);

Rede von Pestalozzi an sein Haus, an seinem zwei und siebzigsten Geburtstage, den 12. Jänner 1818 (Zurich: Orell & Füßli, 1818);

Bilder aus dem Leben Ulrichs Zwingli (Zurich, 1819);

Pestalozzi's sämtliche Schriften, 15 volumes (Stuttgart & Tübingen: Cotta, 1819-1826);

Ein Wort über den gegenwärtigen Zustand meiner pädagogischen Bestrebungen und über die neue Organi-

sation meiner Anstalt (Zurich: Orell & Füßli, 1820);

Meine Lebensschicksale als Vorsteher meiner Erziehungsinstitute in Burgdorf und Iferten (Leipzig: Fleischer, 1826);

Die Abendstunde eines Einsiedlers, edited by J. P. Scheuenstuhl (Erlangen: Published by the editor, 1845); excerpts translated by Robert Ulich as "Evening Hour of a Hermit," in his *Three Thousand Years of Educational Wisdom* (Cambridge: Harvard University Press, 1954), pp. 480-485;

Pestalozzi's sämtliche Werke: Gesichtet, vervollständigt und mit erläuternden Einleitungen versehen, edited by L. W. Seyffarth (16 volumes, Berlin: Eisenschmidt, 1881; revised, 12 volumes, Liegnitz: Seyffarth, 1899-1902);

Sämtliche Werke, 29 volumes, edited by Artur Buchenau, Eduard Spranger, and Hans Stettbacher (Berlin: De Gruyter / Zurich: Orell & Füßli, 1927-1978);

Werke: Gedenkausgabe zu seinem zweihundertsten Geburtstage, 8 volumes, edited by Paul Baumgartner (Zurich: Rotapfel, 1944-1949);

Werke in vier Bänden: Aufgrund wissenschaftlich-kritischer Ausgabe, 4 volumes, edited by Adolf A. Steiner (Zurich: Stauffacher, 1972).

Editions in English: *Letters on Early Education: Addressed to J. P. Greaves, Esq.: Translated from the German Manuscript*, translated anonymously (London: Sherwood, Gilbert & Piper, 1827; reprinted, Ann Arbor, Mich.: University Microfilms, 1971);

Letters of Pestalozzi on the Education of Infancy: Addressed to Mothers, translated anonymously (Boston: Carter & Hendee, 1830);

Pestalozzi's Educational Writings, edited by John Alfred Green and Frances A. Collie (New York: Longmans, Green / London: Arnold, 1912);

The Education of Man: Aphorisms, translated by Heinz and Ruth Norden (New York: Philosophical Library, 1951).

OTHER: *Journal für die Erziehung: Ersten Bandes erstes Heft*, edited by Pestalozzi (Leipzig: Gräff, 1807).

Johann Heinrich Pestalozzi, the most important educational thinker of the Enlightenment, was born in Zurich on 12 January 1746 to Johann Baptist Pestalozzi, a surgeon, and Susanne Pestalozzi, née Hotz. He was descended from an Italian family that had settled in Zurich in the six-

Pestalozzi and the Orphans in Stans; *oil painting by A. Anker, 1870, in the Kunsthaus, Zurich (courtesy of the Pestalozzi Foundation, New York)*

teenth century. After his father died in 1751, Pestalozzi experienced a sheltered childhood; he remembered that he was guarded like a sheep that was not allowed to leave the barn; he never met boys of his own age on the street; he knew none of their games or their secrets; he felt awkward among them.

After graduation from the Collegium Humanitas, a Zurich secondary school, Pestalozzi studied theology and then law at the University of Zurich. Influenced by the ideas of Montesquieu and Jean-Jacques Rousseau, he became a member of the Helvetic Society, a reformist Swiss political organization. After learning how to run a farm from a relative in Richterswyl and a landowner in Kirchberg, in 1767 he acquired a piece of moorland near Birr in Canton Aargau and established a farm he called "Neuhof." In 1769 he married Anna Schulthess. In 1775 he transformed the farm into a school for fifty poor children. At Neuhof, Pestalozzi tried to counter the purely verbal education that was typical of the time by allowing his pupils "Anschauung" (sense perception), that is, a direct acquaintance with

Pestalozzi in the classroom at Stans (Hermann Krüsi, Pestalozzi: His Life, Work, and Influence)

physical objects rather than only with books. The Neuhof enterprise failed in 1780 because of poor financial management, but Pestalozzi gained insights from the experience that are reflected in *Die Abendstunde eines Einsiedlers* (1845; excerpts translated as "Evening Hour of a Hermit," 1954), a collection of aphorisms Pestalozzi wrote after the closure of the school. The work, which advocates the combining of liberal and vocational education and emphasizes the importance of the mother in the education of the child, was first published in a periodical by Pestalozzi's friend, the editor Isaak Iselin.

In 1781 Pestalozzi wrote the first volume of what was to become his best-known work, *Lienhard und Gertrud* (1781-1787; excerpts translated as *Leonard and Gertrude,* 1801), completing the book in a matter of weeks. When he showed the manuscript to a publisher in Zurich he was told that the punctuation and spelling were all wrong and that the book's language and style were too coarse to be considered for publication. Pestalozzi turned to Iselin, who took the manu-

script to the publisher Decker in Berlin; Decker agreed to publish it. Written as a popular romance, *Lienhard und Gertrud* portrays the struggle between good and evil in the village of Bonnal. Evil is personified in Hummel, Bonnal's richest man and the town's only employer, innkeeper, judge, and policeman; Hummel is a person who has no interest other than personal gain. Gertrud represents the ideal mother-teacher in a family of working people. Through Gertrud, Pestalozzi shows how the education of young children should be placed in the hands of mothers. While Gertrud fights to save her family from destruction, her husband, Lienhard, is torn between Hummel's continuous temptations to drink away his earnings and his loyalty to Gertrud and his children. The book, which was an immediate bestseller, made Pestalozzi famous. As a result, he was invited to become a member of the "Illuminatenorden" (Order of Enlightenment), an exclusive society which enabled Pestalozzi to correspond with members of the various European courts. Three additional volumes appeared, in

1783, 1785, and 1787, respectively.

In December 1798, to show his opposition to the bloodshed of the French Revolution, Pestalozzi went to Stans, the site of a battle between the Swiss and the French. There he asked for and was put in charge of a school for war orphans in a converted convent. The Stans school was short-lived; it was closed in July 1799 to be converted into a military hospital. Shortly before the closing, Pestalozzi wrote that the education at Stans was successful in every respect.

Following Stans, Pestalozzi operated schools at Burgdorf in Canton Bern from 1799 to 1804, at Münchenbuchsee in Canton Bern from June to October 1804, and, most successfully, at Yverdon in Canton Vaud from 1805 to 1825. The attention of European and American educators was drawn to his methods, which emphasized individual differences, sense perception, the student's self-activity rather than rote learning, graduated learning based on the natural stages of the child's maturation, and the raising of the lower classes through an educational system which enabled the potential of all children to develop to the fullest.

In 1801 Pestalozzi published *Wie Gertrud ihre Kinder lehrt* (translated as *How Gertrude Teaches Her Children*, 1894), one of his most profound and important pedagogical writings. The title is a badly chosen one, since the name Gertrud appears not even once in the work. A collection of letters addressed to his assistants at Burgdorf, the book outlines Pestalozzi's teaching methods.

Pestalozzi's writing is generally obscure and confused, interspersed with brilliant insights; his thoughts are often poorly organized. Pestalozzi used his writings to spur public interest in education. He was by no means a natural writer with a gift for words; he became a writer, he said, to clarify his educational ideas to himself. Pestalozzi's writings did not earn him enough to support his wife and son; his income was largely derived from his schools.

Pestalozzi maintained that the primary concern of the school should not be to inculcate information but to stimulate and develop the latent powers within each child. In his schools teachers were not allowed to stifle a pupil's natural talents; instead, formal education was to be harmonized with each pupil's internal development.

Pestalozzi's principle of "Anschauung" held that the first lessons of children should be experiences of objects rather than books. Learners should discover the world around them, begin-

ning with the immediate environment before progressing to more distant places. For example, Pestalozzi argued that number instruction should always begin with concrete objects. Thus, he began his number teaching exercises by presenting his pupils with pebbles, peas, beans, or the like. Based on these experiences, Pestalozzi designed at Yverdon an "ABC der Zahlen" (ABC of Numbers) to facilitate the teaching of arithmetic. For the teaching of form Pestalozzi designed the "ABC der Formen" (ABC of Forms) to familiarize the pupils with the different geometrical forms, develop their sense of proportion, and exercise their ability to observe objects correctly with respect to size, shape, width, and height.

Pestalozzi believed that language evolved gradually in imitation of the sounds of nature, and that each human being repeated the evolution of man in the development of speech. Thus, in teaching a child language, we must follow the course of nature. Pestalozzi divided language teaching into three stages: the teaching of individual sounds and words; the teaching of grammar and sentence structure; and the teaching of language as meaning.

At Yverdon Pestalozzi reached the peak of his educational career. Pupils and teachers came from all over the Continent to learn and teach in a home-school environment. Pestalozzi's classes, which were often visited by observers, showed him to be a father figure and friend, constantly stressing the powers of love and understanding in the educational process. At Yverdon schooling served a double function: it provided the pupil with the necessary intellectual, moral, and physical stimuli to become a useful and responsible member of society, and it sheltered the child in a familylike atmosphere of cooperation, love, and affection.

In 1826 Pestalozzi, whose wife had died in 1815, returned to Neuhof to live with his grandson. There he dictated his last book, an autobiography, *Pestalozzi's Schwanengesang* (Pestalozzi's Swan Song, 1826), which appeared as volume 13 of his collected writings (1819-1826). Summarizing with warmth and lucidity the major themes and experiences of Pestalozzi's life and work as a writer, teacher, and educational thinker, the work is considered by many to be the equal of Goethe's autobiography, *Dichtung und Wahrheit* (Poetry and Truth, 1811-1833).

Pestalozzi died at Brugg on 17 February 1827.

Pestalozzi's school in Burgdorf, where he taught from 1799 to 1804

Letters:

Sämtliche Briefe, 13 volumes, edited by the Pestalozzianum and by the Zentralbibliothek in Zurich (Zurich: Füßli, 1946-1971).

Bibliographies:

August Israel, *Versuch einer Zusammenstellung der Schriften von und über Pestalozzi* (Zschopau: Gensel & Raschke, 1894);

Willibald Klinke, "Pestalozzi-Bibliographie," *Zeitschrift für Geschichte der Erziehung und des Unterrichts*, 11-13 (1921-1923);

Job-Guenter Klink and Lieselotte Klink, *Bibliographie Johann Heinrich Pestalozzi: Schrifttum 1923-1965* (Weinheim, Berlin & Basel: Beltz, 1968);

Gerhard Kuhlemann, "Pestalozzi-Bibliographie 1966-1977," *Pädagogische Rundschau*, 34 (1980): 189-202.

Biographies:

Charles Mayo, *A Lecture on the Life of Pestalozzi* (London: Hamilton, Adams, 1873);

Hermann Krüsi, *Pestalozzi: His Life, Work, and Influence* (Cincinnati & New York: Wilson, Hinkle, 1875);

John A. Green, *Life and Work of Pestalozzi* (Baltimore: Warwick & York, 1913);

Kate Silber, *Pestalozzi: The Man and His Work* (New York: Schocken, 1973).

References:

Theodor Ballauf, *Vernünftiger Wille und gläubige Liebe: Interpretation zu Kants und Pestalozzis Werk* (Meisenheim an Glan: Hain, 1957);

Henry Barnard, "Pestalozzi, Fellenberg, Wehrli," *Barnard's American Journal of Education*, 21 (1869): 565-576;

Edward Biber, *Henry Pestalozzi and His Plan of Education* (London: Souter, 1831);

Life mask of Pestalozzi, taken in 1809 by I. M. Christen (Pestalozzianum, Zurich)

Helen Bosshard, *Pestalozzis Staats- und Rechtsverständnis und seine Stellung in der Aufklärung* (Frankfurt am Main: Lang, 1983);

Arthur Brühlmeier, *Wandlungen im Denken Pestalozzis: Von der "Abendstunde" bis zu den Nachforschungen"* (Zurich: Juris, 1976);

F. Busse, "Object Teaching—Principles and Methods," *American Journal of Education*, 30 (1880): 417-450;

Norman Allison Calkins, "History of Object Teaching," *American Journal of Education*, 12 (1863): 633-645;

Jules G. Compayre, *Pestalozzi and Elementary Education*, translated from the French by R. P. Jago (New York: Crowell, 1907);

Jacqueline Cornaz-Besson, *Qui êtes-vous Monsieur Pestalozzi?* (Yverdon: Editions de la Thièle, 1977);

Roger De Guimps, *Pestalozzi: His Aim and Work*, translated from the French by Margaret Cuthbertson Crombie (Syracuse: Bardeen, 1889);

Emanuel M. Dejung, *Pestalozzi–Kritische Ausgabe: Jahresbericht des Redaktors* (Winterthur: Dejung, 1971);

Dejung, *Übersicht der wichtigeren Ausgaben von Werken und Briefen Pestalozzis: In chronologischer Ordnung* (Zurich: Verlag des Pestalozzianums, 1972);

Dejung, *Verlorene Schriften Pestalozzis* (Basel: Beltz, 1971);

Robert Downs, *Heinrich Pestalozzi: Father of Modern Pedagogy* (Boston: Twayne, 1975);

C. D. Gardette, "Pestalozzi in America," *Galaxy*, 4 (August 1867): 432-439;

Hermann Levin Goldschmidt, *Pestalozzis unvollendete Revolution* (Schaffhausen: Novalis, 1977);

John A. Green, *The Educational Ideas of Pestalozzi* (London: Clive / University Tutorial Press, 1905);

Green and Frances Collie, *Pestalozzi's Educational Writings* (New York: Longmans, Green, 1916);

Gerald L. Gutek, *Pestalozzi and Education* (New York: Random House, 1968);

Fritz-Peter Hager, *Pestalozzi und Rousseau: Pestalozzi als Vollender und als Gegner Rousseaus* (Bern, 1975);

William T. Harris, "Herbart and Pestalozzi Compared," *Educational Review*, 5 (May 1893): 417-423;

Frank H. Hayward, *The Educational Ideas of Pestalozzi and Froebel* (London: Holland, 1905);

Michael R. Heafford, *Pestalozzi: His Thought and Relevance Today* (London: Methuen, 1967);

Dieter Jedan, *Johann Heinrich Pestalozzi and the Pestalozzian Method of Language Teaching* (Bern: Lang, 1981);

Jedan, "Joseph Neef: Innovator or Imitator?," *Indiana Magazine of History*, 78 (December 1982): 323-340;

Johann Heinrich Pestalozzi: Vermächtnis und Verpflichtung. Gedenkfeiern im Aargau zum 150. Todesjahr (Zurich: Schweizerischer Lehrerverein, 1977);

Dietfrid Krause-Vilmar, *Liberales Plädoyer und radikale Demokratie: H. Pestalozzi und die Stäfner Volksbewegung* (Meisenheim: Hain, 1978);

Max Liedtke, *Johann Heinrich Pestalozzi: In Selbstzeugnissen und Bilddokumenten* (Reinbek: Rowohlt, 1974);

William S. Monroe, *History of the Pestalozzian Movement in the United States* (Syracuse: Bardeen, 1907);

Monroe, "Pestalozzi Literature in America," *Kindergarten Magazine*, 6 (May 1894): 673-676;

William F. Phelps, *Pestalozzi* (New York: Phillips & Hunt, 1897);

Georges Piaton, *Henri Pestalozzi: La présence de l'amour* (Toulouse: Privat, 1982);

Auguste Pinloche, *Pestalozzi and the Foundation of the Modern Elementary Schools* (New York: Scribners, 1901);

Johannes Schurr, *Pestalozzis "Abendstunde": Versuch einer einführenden Meditation* (Passau: Passavia, 1984);

Michel Soëtard, *Pestalozzi; ou, La naissance de l'éducateur: Etude sur l'évolution de la pensée et de l'action du pédagogue suisse (1746-1827)* (Bern: Lang, 1981);

Heinz Stübig, *Pädagogik und Politik in der preußischen Reformzeit: Studien zur Nationalerziehung und Pestalozzi-Rezeption* (Weinheim: Beltz, 1982);

Mary R. Walch, *Pestalozzi and the Pestalozzian Theory of Education* (Washington, D.C.: Catholic University Press, 1952).

Papers:

The bulk of Johann Heinrich Pestalozzi's papers is at the university library of the University of Zurich. Other materials are at the Pestalozzianum, Zurich. The Workingmen's Institute in New Harmony, Indiana, has letters and manuscripts that relate to the Americanization of Pestalozzianism. A few letters are in the Gratz Collection of the Historical Society of Pennsylvania, Philadelphia.

Johann Paul Friedrich Richter
(Jean Paul)

(21 March 1763 - 14 November 1825)

Wulf Koepke
Texas A & M University

BOOKS: *Grönländische Prozesse oder Satirische Skizzen*, anonymous, 2 volumes (Berlin: Voß, 1783; revised edition, Berlin: Vossische Buchhandlung, 1822);

Auswahl aus des Teufels Papieren, nebst einem nöthigen Aviso vom Juden Mendel, as J. P. F. Hasus (Gera: Beckmann, 1789);

Die unsichtbare Loge: Eine Biographie, 2 volumes (Berlin: Matzdorff, 1793; revised edition, Berlin: Reimer, 1822); translated by Charles T. Brooks as *The Invisible Lodge* (New York: Holt, 1883);

Hesperus, oder 45 Hundsposttage: Eine Biographie (3 volumes, Berlin: Matzdorff, 1795; revised and enlarged, 4 volumes, 1798); translated by Brooks as *Hesperus; or, Forty-five Dog-postdays: A Biography*, 2 volumes (New York: Lovell, 1864; London: Trübner, 1865);

Leben des Quintus Fixlein, aus fünfzehn Zettelkästen gezogen: Nebst einem Mustheil und einigen Jus de tablette (Bayreuth: Lübeck, 1796; revised and enlarged, 1801); translated by Thomas Carlyle as "Life of Quintus Fixlein, Extracted from Fifteen Letter-Boxes," in his *German Romance: Specimens of Its Chief Authors, with Biographical and Critical Notices*, volume 3 (Edinburgh & London: Tait, 1827); volume 2 (Boston: Munroe, 1841);

Blumen- Frucht- und Dornenstücke oder Ehestand, Tod und Hochzeit des Armenadvokaten F. St. Siebenkäs im Reichsmarktflecken Kuhschnappel (3 volumes, Berlin: Matzdorff, 1796-1797; revised and enlarged edition, 4 volumes, Berlin: Realschulbuchhandlung, 1818); translated by Edward Henry Noel as *Flower, Fruit, and Thorn Pieces; or, The Married Life, Death, and Wedding of the Advocate of the Poor, Firmian Stanislaus Siebenkäs*, 2 volumes (London: Smith, 1845; Boston: Munroe, 1845);

Jean Paul's biographische Belustigungen unter der Gehirnschale einer Riesin: Erstes Bändchen (Berlin: Matzdorff, 1796);

Engraving by Adrian Schluch of a painting by Friedrich Meier, 1811

Geschichte meiner Vorrede zur zweiten Auflage des Quintus Fixlein (Bayreuth: Lübeck, 1797);

Der Jubelsenior: Ein Appendix (Leipzig: Beygang, 1797);

Das Kampaner Thal oder Über die Unsterblichkeit der Seele: Nebst einer Erklärung der Holzschnitte unter den 10 Geboten des Katechismus (Erfurt: Hennings, 1797); translated by Juliette

Bauer as *The Campaner Thal; or, Discourses on the Immortality of the Soul* (London: Gilpin, 1848);

Palingenesien, 2 volumes (Leipzig & Gera: Heinsius, 1798);

Jean Pauls Briefe und bevorstehender Lebenslauf (Gera & Leipzig: Heinsius, 1799);

Titan, 4 volumes (Berlin: Matzdorff, 1800-1803); translated by Brooks as *Titan: A Romance*, 2 volumes (Boston: Ticknor & Fields, 1862; London: Trübner, 1863);

Komischer Anhang zum Titan, 2 volumes (Berlin: Matzdorff, 1800-1801);

Clavis Fichtiana seu Leibgeberiana: Anhang zum I. komischen Anhang des Titans (Erfurt: Hennings, 1800);

Das heimliche Klaglied der jezigen Männer: Eine Stadtgeschichte; und Die wunderbare Gesellschaft in der Neujahrsnacht (Bremen: Wilmans, 1801);

Vorschule der Aesthetik, nebst einigen Vorlesungen in Leipzig über die Parteien der Zeit, 3 volumes (Hamburg: Perthes, 1804; revised and enlarged edition, Stuttgart & Tübingen: Cotta, 1813); translated by Margaret R. Hale as *Horn of Oberon: Jean Paul Richter's School for Aesthetics* (Detroit: Wayne State University Press, 1973);

Flegeljahre: Eine Biographie, 4 volumes (Tübingen: Cotta, 1804-1805); translated by Eliza Buckminster Lee as *Walt and Vult; or, The Twins*, 2 volumes (Boston: Munroe / New York: Wiley & Putnam, 1846);

Jean Paul's Freiheits-Büchlein oder Dessen verbotene Zueignung an den regierenden Herzog August von Sachsen-Gotha; dessen Briefwechsel mit ihm;— und die Abhandlung über die Preßfreiheit (Tübingen: Cotta, 1805);

Levana oder Erziehungslehre (2 volumes, Brunswick: Vieweg, 1807; revised and enlarged edition, 3 volumes, Stuttgart & Tübingen: Cotta, 1814); translated by "A. H." as *Levana; or, The Doctrine of Education* (London: Longman, Brown, Green & Longmans, 1848; Boston: Ticknor & Fields, 1861);

Ergänzungs-Blatt zur Levana (Brunswick: Vieweg, 1807);

Friedens-Predigt an Deutschland gehalten von Jean Paul (Heidelberg: Mohr & Zimmer, 1808);

Des Feldpredigers Schmelzle Reise nach Flätz mit fortgehenden Noten: Nebst der Beichte des Teufels bey einem Staatsmanne (Tübingen: Cotta, 1809); translated by Carlyle as "Army Chaplain Schmelzle's Journey to Flaetz," in his *German Romance*, volume 3 (volume 2 of American edition);

Dr. Katzenbergers Badereise: Nebst einer Auswahl verbesserter Werkchen, 2 volumes (Heidelberg: Mohr & Zimmer, 1809; revised and enlarged edition, Breslau: Max, 1823);

Dämmerungen für Deutschland (Tübingen: Cotta, 1809);

Herbst-Blumine oder Gesammelte Werkchen aus Zeitschriften, 3 volumes (Stuttgart & Tübingen: Cotta, 1810-1820);

Leben Fibels, des Verfassers der Bienrodischen Fibel (Nuremberg: Schrag, 1812);

Museum (Stuttgart & Tübingen: Cotta, 1814);

Mars und Phöbus: Thronwechsel im J. 1814. Eine scherzhafte Flugschrift (Tübingen: Cotta, 1814);

Politische Fastenpredigten während Deutschlands Marterwoche (Stuttgart & Tübingen: Cotta, 1817);

Ueber die deutschen Doppelwörter: Eine grammatische Untersuchung in zwölf alten Briefen und zwölf neuen Postskripten (Stuttgart & Tübingen: Cotta, 1820);

Der Komet oder Nikolaus Marggraf: Eine komische Geschichte, 3 volumes (Berlin: Reimer, 1820-1822);

Kleine Bücherschau: Gesammelte Vorreden und Rezensionen, nebst einer kleinen Nachschule zur ästhetischen Vorschule, 2 volumes (Breslau: Max, 1825);

Wahrheit aus Jean Paul's Leben, edited by Christian Otto and Ernst Förster, 8 volumes (Breslau: Max, 1826-1833)—includes, as volume 1, *Selberlebensbeschreibung*;

Jean Paul's sämmtliche Werke, 65 volumes (Berlin: Reimer, 1826-1838);

Selina oder Über die Unsterblichkeit (Stuttgart & Tübingen: Cotta, 1827);

Politische Nachklänge: Wiedergedrucktes und Neues, edited by Ernst Förster (Heidelberg: Winter, 1832);

Der Papierdrache: Jean Paul's letztes Werk. Aus des Dichters Nachlaß, edited by Förster, 2 volumes (Frankfurt am Main: Literarische Anstalt, 1845);

Jean Paul's Werke, 60 volumes (Berlin: Hempel, 1867-1879);

Jean Paul's sämtliche Werke: Historisch-kritische Ausgabe, herausgegeben von der Preußischen Akademie der Wissenschaften in Verbindung mit der Akademie zur wissenschaftlichen Erforschung und zur Pflege des Deutschtums (Deutsche Akademie) und der Jean-Paul-Gesellschaft, edited by

Eduard Berend, 33 volumes (Weimar: Böhlau, 1927-1964);

Werke, edited by Norbert Miller, 10 volumes (Munich: Hanser, 1959-1980).

Editions in English: *The Death of an Angel and Other Pieces*, translated by A. Kenney (London, 1829);

Reminiscences of the Best Hours of Life for the Hour of Death, translated anonymously (Boston: Dowe, 1841);

Extracts from the Works of Jean Paul F. Richter, selected and translated by Georgiana Lady Chatterton (London: Parker, 1859);

The Campaner Thal, and Other Writings, translated by Juliette Bauer, Thomas Carlyle, and Thomas De Quincey (Boston: Ticknor & Fields, 1864);

"Life of the Cheerful Schoolmaster Maria Wutz," translated by John D. Grayson, in *Nineteenth-Century German Tales*, edited by Angel Flores (New York: Doubleday, 1959), pp. 1-37.

OTHER: *Taschenbuch für 1801*, edited by Richter, F. Genz, and Johann Heinrich Voß (Brunswick: Vieweg, 1800);

Sinngrün: Eine Folge romantischer Erzählungen, edited, with contributions by Richter and others (Uthe-Spazier & Berlin: Enslin, 1819).

PERIODICAL PUBLICATIONS: "Saturnalien, den die Erde 1818 regierenden Hauptplaneten Saturn betreffend; in sieben Morgenblättern mitgetheilt von Dr. Jean Paul Fr. Richter," 9 installments, *Morgenblatt für gebildete Stände*, 1-3, 5-10 January 1818;

"Traum eines bösen Geistes vor seinem Abfalle," *Taschenbuch für Damen auf das Jahr 1819* (1818): 251-257;

"Unternacht-Gedanken über den magnetischen Weltkörper im Erdkörper; nebst heun magnetischen Gesichten," 10 installments, *Morgenblatt für gebildete Stände*: January 1819;

"Briefblättchen an die Leserinnen des Damen-Taschenbuchs bey gegenwärtiger Uebergabe meiner abgerissenen Gedanken vor dem Frühstück und dem Nachtstück in Löbischau," *Taschenbuch für Damen auf das Jahr 1821* (1820): 285-318;

"Gesichte einer griechischen Mutter: Ein Traum; in den letzten Tage des Juli-Monats," *Morgenblatt für gebildete Stände*, 14 August 1821, pp. 773-774;

"Politisches und poetisches Allerlei," *Taschenbuch für Damen auf das Jahr 1822* (1821): 150-175;

"Die Anbeter des Luzifers und des Hesperus. Ein Beytrag zur ältesten Kirchengeschichte," *Morgenblatt für gebildete Stände*, 1-7 January 1822;

"Jean Paul's Wetterprophezeiungen zum Beßten der Reisenden, Spaziergengehenden und Gartenbauenden. Höchst wahrscheinliche Mutmaßungen über das Wetter der nächsten 6 Monate, an meinem Geburtstage, den 21. März, mildthätig, an Wetter-Laien ausgetheilt," *Abend-Zeitung*, 19 June 1823, p. 583;

"Ausschweife für künftige Fortsetzungen von vier Werken," 9 installments, *Morgenblatt für gebildete Stände*, 20, 22-24, 26-27, 29, 31 December 1823, 1 January 1824.

Johann Paul Friedrich Richter created for his first published novel, *Die unsichtbare Loge* (1793; translated as *The Invisible Lodge*, 1883), a narrator called "Jean Paul," and that name has been transferred to Richter himself. German patriots who considered Richter's work very "German" never liked this name and at least pronounced *Paul* in the German and not in the French way. "Jean Paul" is a clear allusion to Richter's great model, Jean-Jacques Rousseau. It is not really a pseudonym, since Richter never wanted to hide his authorship. But the creation of a narrator both identical and nonidentical with his author made possible a series of role-playing games in which fiction and reality merged. The narrator "Jean Paul" could meet the characters of his novels; on the other hand, Richter's audience, the women in particular, identified him as "Jean Paul" and carried the novels over into real life. Thus, while his book sales do not bear out the legend that Richter was the most popular writer of his time—far from it—he and his novel *Hesperus, oder 45 Hundsposttage* (1795; translated as *Hesperus; or, Forty-five Dog-post Days*, 1864) had real fans who cut off locks of his or his dog's hair, proposed marriage to "Jean Paul," and named their daughters after his heroine.

Although he lived at the time of German Classicism and Romanticism, Richter did not belong to any group or "school." His novels and shorter narratives can be seen in the context of the European humoristic novel from François Rabelais's *Gargantua and Pantagruel* (1532-1564) and Miguel de Cervantes's *Don Quixote* (1605-1615) to Jonathan Swift's *Gulliver's Travels* (1726) and Laurence Sterne's *Tristram Shandy* (1760-1767). Noteworthy among Richter's German predecessors is Theodor Gottlieb von

The house in Wunsiedel where Richter was born (George Wilhelm Meister, Jean Paul *[Öttingen: Frankish-Schwäbischer Heimatverlag, 1968])*

Hippel with his *Lebensläufe nach auftsteigender Linie* (Biographies in an Ascending Line, 1778-1781). Richter's popularity in his own time rested mainly on his novel *Hesperus*. Other works, notably *Titan* (1800-1803; translated, 1862) and *Flegeljahre* (Adolescence, 1804-1805; translated as *Walt and Vult; or, The Twins*, 1846), had a considerable impact on the younger Romantics. Richter's fame faded away in the late nineteenth century; but he was rediscovered around 1900, and the modernity of his narrative style and structures has been recognized ever since. While he continues to impress writers and individual readers and is acknowledged by scholars as one of the truly important writers of his age, his work remains unknown to a general audience; and its complexity has prevented most of it from being included in school reading lists. Thus his novels with their interesting narrative style, their many-layered depictions of German life in the late eighteenth century, and their portrayal of the aspirations of the best people of the time are left to the specialists and the few fans. Richter's life can be divided into three periods: his early career of starvation and frustration, until around 1790; his writing of his best-known works from *Die unsichtbare Loge* to *Flegeljahre*; his family life and writing in Bayreuth from 1804 to his death in 1825.

Richter was born on 21 March 1763 in Wunsiedel, the oldest son of Johann Christian Christoph Richter, who taught at the local school, and Sophia Rosina Kuhn Richter, the daughter of a well-to-do textile manufacturer from Hof. Wunsiedel is a small town east of the Fichtel mountains in the northeast corner of Bavaria. Richter's father, the son of a village schoolmaster, was a gifted musician and an impressive conversationalist. In 1765 he was able to find patronage to be appointed minister of the Lutheran church in the village of Joditz, and by 1776 he had risen to the position of head pastor in the town of Schwarzenbach. But his earlier life of poverty and his inability to pursue a career in music resulted in increasingly severe spells of depression. He became aloof and dogmatic, and he inflicted the worst possible private education on the two oldest of his five sons: memorizing meaningless grammatical items in Latin. In spite of clear indications of musical talent, "Fritz," the eldest, never received any instruction in music. Endowed with a vivid imagination, the boy began to create his own inner world, nourished by books. *Robinson Crusoe* (1719) was one of his earliest and most lasting impressions.

In Schwarzenbach a colleague of Richter's father, Johann Samuel Völkel, taught him some geography, gave him Johann Christoph Gottsched's *Erste Gründe der gesamten Weltweisheit* (First Elements of Philosophy, 1734), and introduced him to enlightened Lutheran theology.

Erhard Friedrich Vogel, a vicar in a neighboring village, opened his personal library to the boy. Around 1778, Richter began to write down excerpts from Vogel's journals and books—which he could never afford to own himself—and collected them in bound volumes (not in Zettelkästen [filing cabinets], as legend has it). He later established elaborate indexes and thus had a ready-to-use reservoir of quotations for all possible topics. He also began to compose his own aphorisms and ideas, indexing them in the same way. The majority of his aphorisms, one of the largest collections of any German writer, remain unpublished.

Early in 1779 Richter was sent to the gymnasium in Hof to prepare for university studies. While he became the butt of the jokes of his classmates because of his naive trust in people, he was an outstanding student who even embarrassed the teachers with his intelligence and knowledge. In April 1779 his father died, leaving behind a mountain of debts. Richter went to the University of Leipzig in spring 1781 with a *testimonium paupertatis* in hand. Realizing after one semester of theology that he would never follow in the footsteps of his father, he decided to become a writer. Had he not lived such an isolated life, he would have seen the misery of the many writers who were trying to make a living in the city of book fairs.

In 1780 Richter wrote a series of brief essays on issues in philosophy, theology, and popular science which he called "Übungen im Denken" (Exercises in Thinking). He then imitated Johann Martin Miller's sentimental novel *Siegwart* (1776) in an immature epistolary novel, "Abelard und Heloise" (published in 1928 in Eduard Berend's edition of Richter's collected works). In the spring of 1781 he wrote a long essay, "Über den Menschen" (On Man), with many echoes from the second epistle of Alexander Pope's *Essay on Man* (1733-1734); it seems to have been the first piece he submitted for publication—without success. He reworked and condensed his "Übungen im Denken" as "Rhapsodien" (Rhapsodies), including some ideas which came to him through the only professor at Leipzig who made an impression on him: Ernst Platner, a then-popular philosopher. But life in poverty and the constant struggle with what he considered mediocre, bigoted people had changed his initial confidence and trust. He began to diagnose the dominant ill of society as "Dummheit" (stupidity) and to fight for the legitimate place of extraordinary people, even if they

appear to be "Narren" (fools). Taking his cue from Erasmus, he wrote a satirical work titled "Lob der Dummheit" (Praise of Stupidity) but found it unsatisfactory. Then he produced a collection of satirical essays which he called *Grönländische Prozesse* (Greenland Trials) since in Greenland, he had read somewhere, disputes were settled by the opponents satirizing each other. Broad attacks on the nobility, courtiers, women, hack writers, and the clergy, the satires are harsh and radical, with details intended to shock the readers; the language abounds in imagery, metaphors, and similes, a style that makes it hard to follow the author's arguments. It is obvious to the reader that the author has read many books, from Juvenal to Swift, but does not know much about the real world.

Unlikely though it was that such a book could attract a large audience, the respected publisher Christian Friedrich Voß of Berlin accepted the manuscript and paid Richter a generous honorarium. The first volume appeared in spring 1783, the second in the fall. After the second volume, Voß refused to continue. The few reviews were hostile, noting the negativism and the sometimes shocking and overcharged language; sales must have been minimal. Richter continued to write in the same vein but had extreme difficulty placing his manuscripts. His mounting debts finally led him to flee from Leipzig under an assumed name on 12 November 1784 and return to his family, then living in Hof.

The fortunes of his family had gone from bad to worse. Richter's grandfather had died, but his estate had been squandered through litigation brought by spiteful relatives. The family lived in cramped quarters and abject poverty. The next-oldest brothers showed few signs of working toward stable careers. The family's situation was so bad that it drove Heinrich, the second youngest, to suicide in April 1789. Nobody in Hof understood why Richter kept on writing under such conditions. His unusual clothes—including open shirts "à la Hamlet"—and refusal to wear a wig in the fashion of the day kept the "society" of Hof away from him. In 1787 he became the tutor of the younger brother of a deceased friend in nearby Töpen, and from 1790 to 1794 he taught a group of seven children of friends in Schwarzenbach.

In the meantime, he continued to write. A new collection went through several versions and after many delays was published in 1789 as *Auswahl aus des Teufels Papieren* (Selection from

Illustration by Daniel Chodowiecki for Richter's novel Die unsichtbare Loge: *Gustav is brought out of the cave where he has been educated for the first eight years of his life*

the Devil's Papers) by an obscure publishing house. This collection contained satires with more narrative elements and more direct social criticism than *Grönländische Prozesse* and also included some serious essays. The book was published under the pen name "J. P. F. Hasus." As grim as Richter's life was, there were moments of joy in it, especially with friends such as Vogel and Christian Otto. Richter had an uncanny ability to maintain his hope and good spirits, although he had not really regained the belief in the existence of God and the progress of humankind that he had lost in Leipzig. To stimulate himself to write he began to drink strong coffee; he later switched to alcohol, especially beer, which be-

came indispensable for his writing for the rest of his life.

During the fall and winter of 1790 and 1791 Richter weathered a psychological crisis; on 15 November–which he afterward called the most important evening of his life–he had a vision of his death. Among the pieces he wrote for a planned collection to be titled "Bairische Kreuzerkomödie" (Bavarian Penny Theater) was a horrifying speech in which the dead Shakespeare tells dead listeners in a church that there is no God. The collection was never completed, but the speech would later become the famous "Rede des toten Christus vom Weltgebäude herab, daß kein Gott sei" (Speech of the Dead Christ from the Top of the Universe that There Is No God, 1797). This somber mood is discernible in Richter's first novel, which he wrote from spring 1791 to spring 1792. He finished the manuscript in a state of exhaustion, feeling only partially satisfied with the novel's incomplete plot. He sent the manuscript, which he titled "Mumien" (Mummies), to one of his favorite writers, Karl Philipp Moritz, in Berlin, and asked him to help in finding a publisher. Moritz responded enthusiastically and gave the manuscript to his brother-in-law, the publisher Matzdorff. It appeared in two little volumes in 1793 under the title *Die unsichtbare Loge*, with the innovative story "Das Leben des vergnügten Schulmeisterlein Wuz in Auenthal" (translated as "Life of the Cheerful Schoolmaster Maria Wutz," 1959), written in early 1791, as one of its appendices.

The plot of *Die unsichtbare Loge* would have required another volume to be completed. But considering its similarities with *Tristram Shandy*, completion may have been doubtful from the beginning. The book shows the influences of Rousseau's *Émile* (1762), Christoph Martin Wieland's Bildungsroman *Geschichte des Agathon* (Story of Agathon, 1766-1767), Swift's satire, Goethe's novel *Die Leiden des jungen Werthers* (The Sorrows of Young Werther, 1774), and Sterne's humor. In spite of these and other discernible influences, *Die unsichtbare Loge* is an original work that sets a new tone in German literature. For the first eight years of his life Gustav, the protagonist, is educated in a cave by a genius from Herrnhut, the center of the Moravians; during this time Gustav has no contact with anyone other than his teacher. Later he receives instruction from a second tutor, the narrator Jean Paul. As a young man he is brought to the court of Scheerau, a fictitious German state, where he is subjected to many intrigues, first as an officer, then as a diplomat. He falls in love with a girl named Beata but is seduced by a lady at the court; and it is only at the end, in a new spring– the seasons are of great significance in Richter's stories–that he is reunited with Beata, with Jean Paul, and with his friend Ottomar, half brother of the prince. The novel ends with Gustav being caught in a cave with a conspiratorial group and taken prisoner. If one can judge from the plots of Richter's later novels *Hesperus* and *Titan*, Gustav might have turned out to be the prince's son and the successor to the throne had the work been completed.

The book receives its distinctive character through its narrative tone. The narrator Jean Paul is a humorist capable both of satire and of sublime vision, but he is always good-hearted. Jean Paul adds quite a few materials that are not directly related to the plot: mostly satires but also serious essays such as "Vom hohen Menschen" (Of High People), which maintains that extraordinary human beings such as Plato and Shakespeare are not characterized by great-ness in the traditional sense but by their elevation above ordinary life and their expectation of a "zweites Leben" (second life). These sections for-eign to the plot are called "Extrablätter" (extra pages). They are more numerous in the first vol-ume, less conspicuous and much better structur-ally integrated in the second. Richter continued to adorn his stories with such materials, but after *Hesperus* he put them into appendixes rather than interrupting the plot. The digressive man-ner of the narrator with his flowery imagery may confuse the reader more than the "Extrablätter."

Equally important are the extraordinary scenes Richter brings about: the "resurrection" of Gustav from his life in the cave and his first experi-ence of a sunrise; the death of Gustav's friend Amandus during an eclipse of the moon; Ottomar's awakening in a grave after having been believed dead; declarations of friendship and love, usually in a park. Such sublime mo-ments prefiguring a second life were the favor-ites of his readers. All his novels combine sublim-ity, satire, a politically revolutionary spirit, a humorous view of the insignificance of this life, and tolerance for human weakness.

Matzdorff's honorarium ended the years of starvation for Richter's family, but he continued to teach. When his oldest pupils in Schwar-zenbach were ready for the gymnasium in 1794, he returned to Hof. There he finished his sec-

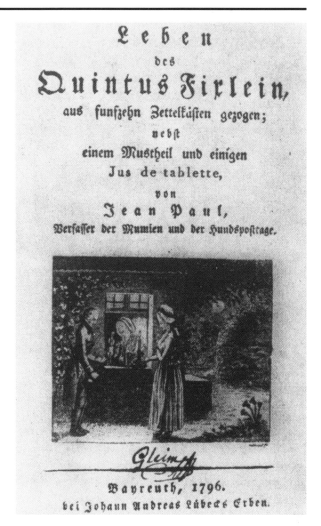

Title page, with engraving by Nahsbügel, for Richter's novel about a good-hearted hypochondriac

ond novel, *Hesperus, oder 45 Hundsposttage*, which appeared in 1795. *Die unsichtbare Loge* had not done well commercially, so Matzdorff offered him a less favorable contract. Richter did not stipu-late the number of copies to be printed for the first edition, so although *Hesperus* became a popu-lar success, it is uncertain how many books were ac-tually sold. A second edition appeared in 1798, a third in 1819.

In *Hesperus* the narrator Jean Paul lives on a small artificial island in a lake. He receives the ma-terials for his "Biographie" –Richter tended to call his fictional works "biographies" rather than novels–from an unknown correspondent who sends them via a dog ("Hundspost"). In the princi-pality of Flachsenfingen, an English aristocrat, Lord Horion, is in charge of the education of the prince's five sons and wants to ensure a transi-tion to a better rule. The story of separated and reunited brothers, interwoven with an account of the dawn of a new social system, is reminiscent of the complex plot of an anonymous novel, *Dya-Na-Sore* (1787-1789), part of which Richter had read in 1787. The protagonist is the young doctor Viktor, presumably the son of the lord, to whom the lord entrusts his affairs at court. Viktor becomes embroiled in a complex court intrigue; falls in love with Klotilde, who thinks she is a courtier's daughter; develops a friendship with Flamin, who is supposedly the son of a Lutheran minister; and becomes the target of Flamin's jealousy when Flamin also falls in love with Klotilde. Viktor early on learns that Klotilde is Flamin's half-sister, but Flamin and Klotilde do not know this. Flamin is drawn into a political conspiracy by triplets from England. In the end, those triplets, Flamin, and the narrator Jean Paul all turn out to be the sons of the prince, and Flamin the heir to the throne. Viktor finds out that he is really the Lutheran minister's son; thus there is a huge social difference between him and Klotilde, who is really the illegitimate daughter of the prince. Social standing, however, will not matter in the new world of Flachsenfingen, and Viktor and Klotilde will be married.

Hesperus, while continuing in the vein of *Die unsichtbare Loge*, was more accessible, more sentimental, even more realistic; the audience could more easily identify with its characters, and Flachsenfingen was perceived as a typical German court. Many readers, especially women, enjoyed the escape the novel afforded them from the miseries of life. For them, Richter *was* Jean Paul, and they treated him as such. He responded in kind, playing the role of the witty and sentimental narrator he had created.

Richter distinguished three types of stories in his oeuvre. The first type, exemplified by *Die unsichtbare Loge*, *Hesperus*, and later *Titan*, revolves around a small court in Germany, a "hidden prince" who is the successor to the throne, and a change of the social system for the better. It also involves love and friendship on a high level and visions of a "second life." In contrast, the second type is a village story, describing the life of humble and poor people, especially schoolmasters and vicars. The third type takes place in a small town and shows an idealistic young man struggling with bourgeois prejudice and pettiness and with poverty. The second type is best exemplified by the story of the Schulmeisterlein Wuz, who survives incredible poverty by his imagination and his talent for finding the sunny side of

every moment. He is a "Kauz" (odd character): he likes to read, but since he is too poor to buy books he obtains the catalog of the book fair, finds titles that interest him, then writes books to go with the titles: thus there are Wuz's versions of Friedrich Gottlieb Klopstock's *Der Messias* (The Messiah), Immanuel Kant's *Kritik der reinen Vernunft* (Critique of Pure Reason), and the like.

Wuz's first successor in Richter's work was Quintus Fixlein, described in *Leben des Quintus Fixlein* (1796; translated as "Life of Quintus Fixlein," 1827). Fixlein, a poor teacher, receives a vicarage through a clerical error. His idyllic life is disturbed by a prediction that he will die in his thirty-second year, as his ancestors did. He survives to that age and marries, but then documents are found which prove that his birthdate is really later than had been thought, and the critical time is impending. Initially almost insane with fear, Fixlein is calmed by the narrator, who is able to persuade him that he is a child playing with toys. Richter provides some counterpoints to this heartwarming story with two satires written earlier, and collected with it: the story of Freudel, whose life is made unbearable by his extreme absentmindedness; and the story of an excursion to the Fichtel mountains by the school principal Fälbel and his students. Fälbel is as inhumane a pedagogue as possible, the very model of the "Schultyrann" (school tyrant) well known in modern German literature. Richter also added a significant essay, "Über die natürliche Magie der Einbildungskraft" (On the Natural Magic of Imagination), which gives clues to his ideas on poetic imagination and its close relationship to dream language. Although Richter was for some time chiefly known for these "idyllic" village stories, he actually did not write many of them. The year after *Leben des Quintus Fixlein* appeared he published *Der Jubelsenior* (The Senior's Anniversary Celebration, 1797), an idyllic story about a village Lutheran minister's silver anniversary; in a comedy-of-errors subplot the minister tries to discover whether or not his son has been approved to be appointed as his vicar. Also involved is a visit from the narrator, Jean Paul, in his role as a prince from Flachsenfingen.

Richter's next major work after *Leben des Quintus Fixlein* was a novel of the third type, describing life in a small town. He gave it a long and baroque title, *Blumen- Frucht- und Dornenstükke oder Ehestand, Tod und Hochzeit des Armenadvokaten F. St. Siebenkäs im Reichsmarktflecken Kuhschnappel* (1796-1797; translated

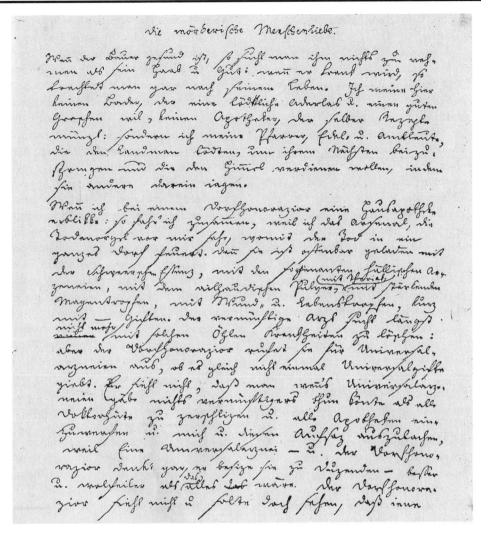

First page of a manuscript by Richter (Friedrich Vogt and Max Roch, Geschichte der deutschen Literatur von den ältesten Zeiten bis zur Gegenwart, volume 3 [Leipzig: Bibliographisches Institut, 1920])

as *Flower, Fruit, and Thorn Pieces; or, The Married Life, Death, and Wedding of the Advocate of the Poor, Firmian Stanislaus Siebenkäs*, 1845). Kuhschnappel is a republican "free city"; but it is too small really to be called a city and is ruled not by its citizenry but by a clique of wealthy businessmen. Siebenkäs returns to his hometown with his law degree and marries Lenette, a simple woman from Augsburg. Their prospects for happiness are shattered when Siebenkäs's guardian, the privy counselor von Blaise, one of the most prominent citizens, denies him his inheritance of 1,200 gulden plus interest, on the grounds that Siebenkäs has exchanged names with his friend and look-alike Leibgeber. Siebenkäs's suit against Blaise becomes his only activity as a lawyer. Living from occasional book reviews and from pawning possessions, Siebenkäs writes a collection of satires titled *Auswahl aus des Teufels Papieren*. Siebenkäs is rescued in the spring, the season of hope and new beginnings, by Leibgeber, who invites him to Bayreuth; there he meets and falls in love with Blaise's niece, Natalie. The designated fiance of Natalie, Everard Rosa von Meyern, a lothario, tries to seduce Lenette while Siebenkäs is competing for the title of Schützenkönig (best marksman). Rosa von Meyern's actions contribute to the estrangement of the couple, but other factors—their poverty and Lenette's love for the school superintendent Stiefel—are more important in driving them apart. Leibgeber and Siebenkäs tell Natalie about Rosa von Meyern's true character, and she cancels her engagement to him. Leibgeber conceives a plan whereby Siebenkäs fakes his own death and then takes Leibgeber's place as a counselor to the count of Vaduz; Leibgeber goes off to wander around the world. A year later Siebenkäs is passing through Kuhschnappel and learns that after a second, happier marriage to Stiefel, Lenette has died in childbirth. At her graveside (and supposedly his own) he meets Natalie, who believed him dead. United at last, Siebenkäs and Natalie look forward to a happy life together.

Critics found the mock death with its grotesque details objectionable. They even charged Richter with condoning insurance fraud: Siebenkäs had taken out a life insurance policy in Natalie's favor, and she, of course, had collected on it. On the other hand, they were favorably impressed–though sometimes shocked–by the depiction of the two friends. Leibgeber is a radical humorist, a free spirit who shuns all conventions, who criticizes all social institutions, who does not believe in God but would like to, and who laughs about humankind and himself, sometimes with a laughter of despair. Siebenkäs, on the other hand, while he considers the world as ridiculous and insignificant as Leibgeber does, empathizes with the ordinary people and smiles at their weaknesses and prejudices. He is an amiable humorist, while Leibgeber scorns ordinary life and people in a Swiftian manner. Richter appended to the novel "Rede des toten Christus vom Weltgebäude herab, daß kein Gott sei." The narrator carefully declares that this nightmare vision is indeed a dream and says that it shocked him into believing in God again. But this declaration can hardly offset the impact of the speech, in which Jesus Christ comes to tell humankind that there is no God, no father for them all. "Rede des toten Christus" has remained one of Richter's most anthologized pieces. Through a translation of parts of it into French in Madame de Staël's seminal book *De l'Allemagne* (On Germany, 1813), it found a large international audience and had an impact especially on French Romantics.

In June 1796 Richter sent off the last part of the manuscript of *Siebenkäs* to his publisher. The next day he departed on foot for a visit to Weimar at the invitation of Charlotte von Kalb, Friedrich Schiller's former friend. For Richter, Weimar was the holy city of the great geniuses of his age. Next to Goethe, he wanted to meet Johann Gottfried Herder, whose works had deeply impressed him since his student days in Leipzig. Richter must have envisioned Weimar as a community of "hohe Menschen," but what he found was

a small town rife with gossip and literary and political disputes. Goethe and Herder were not on speaking terms. Richter was well received by Goethe and Schiller but quickly sided with Herder, whose friendship he treasured. The acquaintance with important men and women gave a new quality to his writing. Herder introduced him to great literary works, such as the Greek classics, and to a new understanding of history, and he began to moderate his digressive style in favor of more unified structures. Weimar was also the beginning of the end of Richter's idealistic view of people and his hope for a future utopian society.

In 1796 appeared the novel fragment *Jean Paul's biographische Belustigungen unter der Gehirnschale einer Riesin* (Jean Paul's Biographical Enjoyments under the Skull of a Female Giant), a tale of a Scottish nobleman disappointed in the outcome of the French Revolution, his return to Scotland, and his marital problems. It was followed in 1797 by *Das Kampaner Thal oder Über die Unsterblichkeit der Seele* (translated as *The Campaner Thal; or, Discourses on the Immortality of the Soul*, 1848). The narrator Jean Paul goes to the valley of Campan in the Pyrenees, where a group of friends are engaging in platonic dialogues on immortality; Jean Paul is especially intent on refuting the Kantian position that there is no proof for the immortality of the soul, that the idea is only helpful in a moral sense. The work ends with a rise in a balloon at sunset, a lofty image of sublimity.

After his mother's death in July 1797 Richter left Hof to look for a place to settle. Leipzig, where he stayed from 1797 to 1798, disappointed him. During this time his youngest brother, Samuel, whose university studies Richter was financing, became a gambler and fled with all of Richter's money. Richter lived in Weimar from 1798 to 1800, enjoying Herder's friendship and instruction. In *Palingenesien* (Palingeneses, 1798), a work that grew out of the offer for a second edition of *Auswahl aus des Teufels Papieren*, Richter combined a small selection of reworked satires with the story of a trip to Nuremberg, where the narrator Jean Paul and his wife meet Siebenkäs and Natalie–Siebenkäs, according to the novel *Siebenkäs*, being the author of the original *Auswahl aus des Teufels Papiere*. The same narrator couples a collection of essays in the form of letters with an enthusiastic description of his future life with Hermine in an idyllic countryside in *Jean Pauls Briefe und bevorstehender Lebenslauf* (Jean Paul's Letters and Future Biography,

Richter in 1797; engraving by Johann Heinrich Pfenninger (Eduard Berend, Jean-Paul-Bibliographie)

1799). For a time, this inviting picture of married life was a favorite among Richter's women readers.

In 1799 Richter wrote a political essay, "Der 17. Juli oder Charlotte Corday" (The 17th of July; or, Charlotte Corday), in which he defended Charlotte Corday's assassination of Jean Paul Marat and the position of the Girondists against the Jacobins. Over the years this essay attracted much attention, some of it unwanted: the university student Karl Ludwig Sand declared that he was inspired by the essay to kill the playwright August von Kotzebue in 1819. During this time Richter attracted many women, several of whom proposed marriage to him; he was engaged several times. Finally, in Berlin, where he lived from 1800 to 1801, he met Karoline Mayer, who was fourteen years younger than he. They were married in 1801. The couple moved to Meiningen in 1801 and to Coburg in 1803.

Since 1792 Richter had been planning and writing what he called his "Kardinalroman" (principal novel), *Titan.* In his impatience to see it fi-

nally in print he published it in four individual volumes from 1800 to 1803. This mode of publication was one of the reasons for the work's lack of commercial success. Originally, Richter wanted to write a novel about a genius who was both good and evil, like the protagonist of Friedrich Heinrich Jacobi's epistolary novel *Eduard Allwill's Briefsammlung* (Eduard Allwill's Correspondence, 1792) about the young Goethe. Subsequently, Richter separated the good and evil aspects into two characters, Albano and Roquairol, and integrated into the novel his experiences in Weimar. His reading of Goethe's *Wilhelm Meisters Lehrjahre* (Wilhelm Meister's Apprenticeship, 1795-1796) also had its impact. For Richter, the age was characterized by self-centered titanic tendencies overreaching the limits of human existence: classicistic aestheticism, which implies moral indifference; excessive emotionalism; a creation of the world in one's own image through Kantian and Fichtean idealism. Such one-sided attacks on organic order and harmony were "einkräftig" (single-powered) and were to be countered by a

Richter in 1798; painting by Pfenninger
(Gleimhaus, Halberstadt)

new breed of active people whom Richter called "allkräftig" (all-powered).

Albano, the protagonist of *Titan*, is once more the hidden prince, the successor to the throne brought up with an assumed identity. His supposed father, Gaspard von Zesara, a count with Spanish connections and a Goethelike figure, wants to rule Hohenfließ through Albano and his presumed ward Linda, who is actually his own daughter. Even more complicated intrigues surround this plan, giving occasion for many elements of the gothic novel to be used. Albano's real education comes mainly through Dian, a Greek architect and Herderlike figure who introduces him to Shakespeare and Rousseau and Herderian ideas; and through the humorist Schoppe, who is actually Leibgeber from *Siebenkäs*. Before meeting Linda, his destined bride, however, Albano falls in love with the oversensitive Liane and becomes close friends with her brother Roquairol. Diabolical court intrigues intervene, and Liane dies after being told that Albano is not to be hers. Albano's rage and sor-

row are soothed by a trip to Italy, where he decides to go to France to fight for the revolution. But then he meets Linda and falls in love with her. In Pestiz, the capital of Hohenfließ, he encounters the enmity of Roquairol, who loved Linda but was rebuffed. Meanwhile Schoppe, suspecting Albano's true identity, disturbs Gaspard's plans; and Gaspard's brother, a frightful baldheaded ventriloquist, pursues him and finally drives him insane. Roquairol seduces Linda one night by imitating Albano's voice; then he performs his own life onstage and commits suicide at the end of the play. The novel ends with Albano's succession to the throne and a palingenesis of his former companions: he will marry Idoine, Liane's look-alike, and will be counseled by Siebenkäs, who arrives when Schoppe dies. Gaspard and Linda leave Hohenfließ for an unknown destination.

An expression of Schoppe's insanity, and one of its causes, is his adherence to the idealistic philosophies of Johann Gottlieb Fichte and Friedrich Wilhelm Joseph Schelling. Richter attacked these philosophies in his satirical *Clavis Fichtiana seu Leibgeberiana* (The Leibgeberian Key to Fichtiana), which he published separately in 1800 but considered part of *Titan*. *Titan* has several comic appendices, the most notable being "Des Luftschiffers Giannozo Seebuch" (The Logbook of the Balloonist Giannozzo), the diary of a friend of Schoppe's. Giannozzo, another wild humorist, roams Europe in a balloon until he meets his death in a thunderstorm over the waterfalls of the Rhine at Schaffhausen. The diary is "edited" by the narrator Jean Paul, who has found it. The perspective from the air, between sublimity and satire, gives rise to some of Richter's most unusual scenic descriptions.

In political terms, the utopian society of Hohenfließ at the end of *Titan* may have been obsolete in 1803, when Napoleon was bringing an end to the small German principalities and when people's aspirations were oriented toward a constitutional government rather than a philosopher-king. The work's message, directed against self-centered titanic arrogance, never stirred any debate. In literary terms, the last volume of *Titan* may be Richter's most outstanding achievement in style, character development, and presentation of tragic conflicts. Readers were most impressed by the tragic figures of Schoppe, Linda, and Roquairol.

During his work on *Titan* Richter thought of appending a contrasting story of idyllic charac-

Karoline Mayer Richter, whom Richter married in 1801; drawing by Ernst Förster, 1826 (Joseph Kürschner, ed., Deutsche National-Litteratur, volume 130 [Berlin, n.d.])

ter in the manner of *Leben des Quintus Fixlein.* This story grew into one of his major novels, *Flegeljahre*. It is a hilarious and melancholy tale of the twins Walt and Vult Harnisch, who cannot live without each other but cannot live together either; they are too close to be friends. A rich man, van der Kabel (whose real name is Richter), leaves his fortune to poor young Walt instead of to his seven distant relatives, stipulating that Walt has to accomplish a series of tasks before the fortune will be his. There are penalties for mistakes, and it is foreseeable that the young poet Walt, in his naive trust of people, will incur so many penalties that little or nothing will be left in the end. After four volumes, however, most of the tests still lie ahead. Vult, who has tried in vain to make his brother more realistic, grows bitter and jealous when they both fall in love with Wina and she prefers Walt. All that is left of their friendship is the novel they wrote together, which was rejected by a publisher because it reminded him too much of the novels of Jean Paul.

After a climactic masked ball and a grandiose dream which Walt relates to Vult, the disappointed if not desperate Vult leaves Walt and the novel breaks off. Vult, the humorist, will never find a home; Walt, the poet, will never under-

stand reality. The novel is serene, but it is also a farewell to the hopes and illusions of youth. There is a constant irony from this double perspective on life, and there are also scenes of elementary comic power. One of the best known is the opening scene, in which van der Kabel declares in his will that he will leave his house to whichever of his disinherited relatives is the first to shed tears over his death. Walt, the idealistic dreamer, often seems to be a Don Quixote who cannot distinguish fantasy from reality. Nevertheless, he is a real poet, and the reader likes him even while laughing at him. The narrator recreates Walt's enthusiasm and poetic power while keeping an ironic distance from his protagonist. *Flegeljahre* is possibly Richter's best book; it is certainly one of his most complex (for example, during the story he tells how it was written). It is also one of Richter's most accessible books. It was, however, anything but a success, which may have discouraged its author from completing it.

In 1804 Richter moved to Bayreuth, where he was to live for the rest of his life. He was at the height of his powers. He had thought about literature for more than twenty years, and he brought his thoughts together in *Vorschule der Aesthetik* (School for Aesthetics, 1804). Richter first defines the ascending scale of creative powers from imitation to creative genius; one category is that of the "passive Genie" (passive genius), that of the writer like Herder who is creative through receptivity rather than original production. Richter contrasts antique and modern poetry and art and defends modern Romantic poetry: Romanticism, he says, has created "das romantisch Komische" (the romantic comic), which is humor. Richter offers a penetrating analysis of humor, excluding satire from "poetic" literature although he includes in his definition of humor much of what is commonly called satire—Swift, for instance. Equally important are Richter's reflections on imagery, especially metaphor. Metaphors are anything but embellishments of style; metaphorical comparisons and combinations are "heuristic," a means of finding truth through the creation of images. *Vorschule der Aesthetik* itself states many of its results in images rather than in "scientific" terms.

After the theoretical first two parts of *Vorschule der Aesthetik*, Richter offers a third, narrative part in which Jean Paul tries to give lectures on contemporary literature during a book fair in Leipzig. With his first lecture, on poetic "materialists"—prosaic realists such as Friedrich

Richter's house in Bayreuth, where he moved in 1804; lithograph by Stelzner (Josef Nadler, Literaturgeschichte des deutschen Volkes, *volume 2 [Berlin: Propyläen, 1938])*

Nicolai–he drives away most of the crowd. His second lecture deals with poetic "nihilists" whose concern for poetic form annihilates all real-life substance and makes their works, like those of some younger Romantics, poetry about poetry. For the third lecture, on real poetic poetry that uses the elements of real life to make the "second life" reflected in ordinary life, only one listener shows up: Albano from *Titan*. He is the lone recipient not only of Jean Paul's thoughts on literature in general but also of his moving eulogy of Herder, who had died at the end of 1803.

Vorschule der Aesthetik is a valiant attempt to give an account of the achievements of German literature; it offers assessments of Gotthold Ephraim Lessing, Klopstock, Wieland, Herder, Schiller, and especially Goethe. It is less fair to Schiller than to the others, for he considered Schiller's style pedestrian and too apolitical, and he did not personally like Schiller. While critical of trends of the Romantic school, it recognizes quality in individual writers, such as Novalis and Heinrich von Kleist.

Levana oder Erziehungslehre (1807; translated as *Levana; or, The Doctrine of Education*, 1848), Richter's response to Rousseau's *Émile*, is based on his experiences as a student, teacher, and father. The book deals primarily not with institutional instruction but with teaching by parents and tutors. It contains much concrete and practical advice, especially for the education of younger children, and mothers at the time found it useful. It also offers an ideal view of what a human being should be, and thus is part of the new definition of "Bildung" (education) by German neohumanism. In contrast to Rousseau's "natural man," Richter defines the goal of education as an "Idealmensch" (ideal person) who lives in and for society but has developed his own ideas and the will power to resist the temptations of fashion and corruption. Firmness of character rather than the development of the powers of emotion and imagination is the main purpose of the educational process. While Richter advocates education for girls, he, like almost everybody else in his time, sees their role as essentially tied to the household. For this reason he thought their education should be practical, not abstract. Although he is keenly aware of the momentous reforms going on in the gymnasium and the university, Richter stresses, as Rousseau does, the personal relationship of teacher and pupil and the responsibilities of parents and tutors. An outstanding feature of his work, which he shared with the Swiss educator Johann Heinrich Pestalozzi, is respect for the child's mentality and world.

Richter had three children: Emma, born in 1802, who became the wife of the painter and art historian Ernst Förster; Maximilian, born in 1803; and Odilie, born in 1804. He decided to have only three children and apparently stopped having sexual intercourse at that point. His marriage, happy at first, went through several crises, and he and his wife were more than once on the verge of separation or divorce. Until he was close to forty years old Richter had been slim and youthful looking; but rather suddenly he became fat and looked much older than his years, certainly not least because of his heavy consumption of beer. The excellence of local beer had been a major factor in the choice of Bayreuth as his final residence.

Bayreuth was then Prussian territory and was affected by the war between France and Prussia in 1806 and 1807. The following years brought French occupation, much soul-searching and attempts at reorientation in German intellectual circles, and a severe economic crisis that directly affected a free-lance writer with family obligations. Richter took an active interest in the events of the time, but he never became a superpatriot, never hated the French, and never liked war. In his *Freiheits-Büchlein* (Little Book on Liberty, 1805) Richter had written a forceful indictment of censorship. The occasion was a witty dedication of *Vorschule der Aesthetik* to the duke of Gotha which the censors, professors in Jena, may not have understood but in any case refused to pass. Richter published the relevant correspondence together with his own commentary. After 1807, with a general feeling of crisis in the air, he spoke out in *Friedens-Predigt an Deutschland* (Sermon for Peace to Germany, 1808) and then in the more extensive *Dämmerungen für Deutschland* (Twilights for Germany, 1809). Other essays and narrative texts, some of them first published in Cotta's *Morgenblatt*, were collected and updated in *Politische Fastenpredigten während Deutschlands Marterwoche* (Political Lenten Sermons during Germany's Passion Week, 1817).

Richter spoke to many but pleased few. He opposed the German patriots who supported rearmament; but Goethe, who admired Napoleon, made fun of Richter's apparent indecisiveness in a satirical poem. Richter tried to be impartial in a partisan atmosphere. He also insisted on a moral renewal at a time when people were thinking politically. He tried to maintain a Herderian liberal attitude and give a balanced view of the good and the bad the French occupation had brought to Germany. He was not blind to the progress in civil liberties and legal protection which the "Rheinbund" (Rhenish Alliance) under Napoleon's protectorate introduced into western Germany. One of the most forceful sections of *Dämmerungen für Deutschland* is "Kriegserklärung gegen den Krieg" (Declaration of War against War), which holds that liberation of Germany should come through moral, cultural, economic, and political rather than military means. Richter warned against a new barbaric fanaticism and maintained that freedom comes with political maturity and can neither be imposed nor taken away.

In practical terms, the Rheinbund was good for Richter. Its leader, Karl Theodor von Dalberg, granted him an annual pension from 1808 to 1813. The pension was reinstated after 1815 by the king of Bavaria. Richter contributed some of his significant later essays to the *Museum* in Frankfurt, for instance his long essay on dream language and the subconscious. Compared to the political censorship after 1815, even in liberal Bavaria (Napoleon had made Bayreuth part of Bavaria), there was much freedom of opinion in the Napoleonic era. Richter maintained his liberal and cosmopolitan views, although he also felt touched by the new patriotism, especially in that beginning in October 1813 when Germany was evacuated by the French. But while the younger generation respected him as a great German and patriot, he was clearly out of place in the new era of nationalism.

There is much social criticism and a good measure of self-criticism in the narrative works after *Flegeljahre*; a tone of satire and disillusionment is unmistakable. Still, they are humorous and even contain lofty moments. *Des Feldpredigers Schmelzle Reise nach Flätz mit fortgehenden Noten* (1808; translated as "Army Chaplain Schmelzle's Journey to Flaetz," 1827) is a character study of a coward whose too-vivid imagination makes him afraid of improbable dangers such as meteors raining down upon him. "Ehrlosigkeit" (lack of

Richter on his way to the Rollwenzelei, an inn outside Bay-reuth where he liked to work; woodcut by T. von Oer (Georg Wilhelm Meister, Jean Paul [Öttingen: Frankisch-Schwäbischer Heimatverlag, 1968])

honor) was for Richter one of the major reasons for the German defeats and moral crisis. He included in this indictment a good part of the intelligentsia. Such intellectuals are depicted in *Dr. Katzenbergers Badereise* (Dr. Katzenberger's Trip to a Spa, 1809). While Dr. Katzenberger is a cold and cynical scientist who enjoys terrifying or nauseating others, the playwright Nieß is a vain and self-centered fraud. We should not look to such intellectuals for moral guidance but to simple, truthful, and courageous people like the mathematician and artillery captain Theudobach and Katzenberger's honest and loving daughter Theoda.

Even the idyllic village of Wuz and Fixlein is colored with satire in *Leben Fibels, des Verfassers der Bienrodischen Fibel* (Life of Fibel, the Author of the Bienroda Primer, 1812), in which Richter invents a biography for the author of a ridiculous primer. Fibel (whose name means primer in German) becomes wealthy from the sales of this primer; his vanity increases to absurd propor-

tions and is reinforced by flattering biographers. Suddenly, however, he comes to his senses. The narrator Jean Paul, who reconstructs the biography from documents which are being used as grocery bags, finds Fibel himself: he is a very old man, reborn and far removed from earthly vanity.

A project of a large comic novel that was to be the crowning achievement of his career and a counterpart to *Don Quixote* went through many stages but never materialized as such. It produced, however, the three volumes of *Der Komet* (The Comet, 1820-1822) and a fragment of autobiography, *Selberlebensbeschreibung* (Description of My Own Life), written in 1818 and 1819 and published posthumously in 1826.

Der Komet, Richter's last novel, is unfinished, like *Die unsichtbare Loge* and *Flegeljahre.* It tells the story of Nikolaus Marggraf, a pharmacist who is made to believe that he is the illegitimate son of a prince. Suddenly becoming rich by producing artificial diamonds, he collects an entourage and sets out to look for his purported father, as well as for a princess whom he had seen in his childhood and whose wax bust he carries with him. His entourage of friends and spongers includes one Kandidat Richter from Hof, who can predict the weather (one of the author's lifelong hobbies). Kandidat Richter is one of the few people who see Marggraf as a real prince. The progress of Marggraf 's party and his ridiculous princely demeanor give occasion for a series of comic scenes, mostly bordering on the grotesque. The grotesque becomes a central element, both in its funny and its frightful aspects, when Marggraf encounters the "Ledermensch" (leather man), who speaks at times with the voice of the devil. Though the work is subtitled *Eine komische Geschichte* (A Comic Story), it ends on a frightening note.

Richter liked to escape to a country inn outside of Bayreuth, the "Rollwenzelei," where he could work upstairs and Mrs. Rollwenzel would care for him. He felt isolated and out of place in Bayreuth but never moved; instead, he took summer trips to more lively cities. The most enjoyable of these trips was one in 1817 to Heidelberg, where he was given an honorary doctorate at the instigation of the philosopher G. W. F. Hegel. He had to write for money and produced many journal articles of uneven quality. He spent much time on revisions for new editions; *Siebenkäs,* in particular, was changed considerably. He also spent time defending dubious linguistic theories, like eliminating the *s* in the middle of compound nouns. Larger projects remained unfinished as he experienced increasing difficulties in writing. Among them was a plan to write against "Über-Christentum" (Super Christianity), a new wave of emotional, fanatical, sometimes fundamentalist Christian faith which made the rounds of the younger generation after 1815. Richter's own son Max was affected by this movement when he went to Heidelberg to study philosophy. In the fall of 1821 Max fell ill, probably with typhoid fever, and came home to Bayreuth in a state of exhaustion but also with symptoms of a nervous breakdown. On 25 September 1821 Max died; he was not quite eighteen years old. After this blow Richter vowed to devote his time to writing about immortality.

Ever since the publication of *Das Kampaner Thal* he had thought of writing a revision or continuation of the work. Now he transplanted the same group of characters into the present and added to them a new generation of figures in *Selina oder Über die Unsterblichkeit* (Selina; or, On Immortality, 1827). From 1823 until his death on 14 November 1825 Richter devoted his main energy to this work, and he finished about two thirds of it; it was published posthumously in 1827. While it seems to represent a stubborn adherence to problems of the eighteenth century which the nineteenth century had laid aside, the work is interesting not only for its new arguments and perspectives but also for its introduction of social and historical reality, including events of the Greek war of liberation. The narrator Jean Paul, once more moving among his characters, wrote for himself a fitting testament with this combination of narration, philosophy, religion, and visions of a "second world."

Richter, who was sick and almost blind at the end, negotiated the publication of his collected works (1826-1838) with Reimer, Matzdorff's successor. Reimer had also published *Der Komet*, which had sold well, and had offered Richter a supplemental payment that Richter declined because he thought Reimer had been fair with him. The money from the collected works was substantial and was important for Richter's widow, who survived him by thirty-five years. The princely funeral in Bayreuth gave more honor to him than he had ever received in his lifetime. The most memorable eulogy was pronounced two weeks later in Frankfurt by Ludwig Börne, who saw Jean Paul as the prophet of the twentieth century, an age of liberty and justice.

German writers of the first half of the nineteenth century were clearly under the spell of Richter's work and style. Later, realists such as Gottfried Keller tried to distance themselves from him, and later in the century his major novels were seldom read; only "Das Leben des vergnügten Schulmeisterlein Wuz in Auenthal" seemed to survive. Literary historians had difficulties fitting his work into Classicism or Romanticism. At the turn of the century the neoclassicist Stefan George rediscovered the "sublime" Jean Paul, and around this time serious work began on editions of his work. Eduard Berend's critical edition (1927-1964), however, was interrupted by the Nazi takeover and then by the division of Germany after 1945 and may remain unfinished forever.

It is not difficult to discover modern features in Richter's work, and writers and scholars since 1945 have increasingly done so. It makes little sense, however, to overemphasize the political content of *Hesperus* and *Titan*, as Wolfgang Harich of the German Democratic Republic did in 1974; calling the novels a direct response to the French Revolution raises false expectations. Richter was, as many since Börne have noted, politically progressive, and he was sympathetic to the ideals of the French Revolution. But he dealt with the problems of his age on a human level and wanted to change people, not institutions.

There is no shortcut for the reader of Richter's works. Since they deal with the social reality of their time, the last decades of the Holy Roman Empire, the reader needs an encyclopedia to understand the facts and allusions. But the reader also needs to follow the game of the narrator, who demonstrates how he fashions the text and still remains in it. Heinrich Heine noted in *Die romantische Schule* (The Romantic School, 1836) that Richter offers a work in progress rather than a finished product, and that he includes the description of the process of narration. Thus the reader is invited to engage in a complex dialogue with the narrator which requires repeated readings and an agile mind. Such a writer cannot expect to be popular but will have a real impact on those readers who enter into such a dialogue. Richter's narrator Jean Paul has an unmistakable tone and voice within the tradition of the European humorous novel from Cervantes and Rabelais to Fielding, Sterne, Charles Dickens, Fyodor Dostoyevski, Thomas Mann, Günter Grass, and Arno Schmidt.

The upstairs room at the Rollwenzelei where Richter did his writing; lithograph by Stelzner (Josef Nadler, Literaturgeschichte des deutschen Volkes, *volume 2 [Berlin: Propyläen, 1938])*

Letters:

Jean Paul's Briefe an Friedrich Heinrich Jacobi (Berlin: Reimer, 1828);

Jean Pauls Briefwechsel mit seinem Freunde Christian Otto, 4 volumes, edited by Ernst Förster (Berlin: Reimer, 1829-1833; reprinted, 1 volume, Berlin & New York: De Gruyter, 1978);

Briefe an eine Jugendfreundin, edited by J. F. Täglichsbeck (Brandenberg: Müller, 1858);

Jean Paul's Blätter der Verehrung: Briefwechsel mit großen Männern, edited by Förster (Munich: Fleischmann, 1865);

Jean Paul's Briefwechsel mit seinen Freunden: Emanuel Osmund, Friedrich von Oertel und Paul Theriot (Munich: Fleischmann, 1865);

Jean Pauls Briefwechsel mit seiner Frau und Christian Otto, edited by Paul Nerrlich (Berlin: Weidmann, 1902);

Die Briefe Jean Pauls, 4 volumes, edited by Eduard Berend (Munich: Müller, 1922-1926);

Jean Paul und Frau von Krüdener im Spiegel ihres Briefwechsels, edited by Dorothea Berger (Wiesbaden: Limes, 1957);

Jean Paul und Herder: Der Briefwechsel Jean Pauls und Karoline Richters mit Herder und der Herderschen Familie in den Jahren 1785 bis 1805, edited by Paul Stapf (Bern: Francke, 1959).

Bibliographies:

Eduard Berend, *Jean-Paul-Bibliographie,* revised by Johannes Krogoll (Stuttgart: Klett, 1963);

Eike Fuhrmann, "Jean-Paul-Bibliographie 1963-1965," *Jahrbuch der Jean-Paul-Gesellschaft,* 1 (1966): 163-179;

Renate Merwald: "Jean-Paul-Bibliographie 1966-1969," *Jahrbuch der Jean-Paul-Gesellschaft,* 5 (1970): 185-219;

Sabine Müller, "Jean Paul-Bibliographie 1970-1983," *Jahrbuch der Jean-Paul-Gesellschaft,* 19 (1984): 137-205.

Biographies:

Paul Nerrlich, *Jean Paul: Sein Leben und seine*

Unfinished watercolor of Richter by an unknown artist (center, standing) at a picnic given in his honor in Stuttgart in June 1819 by Count von Beroldingen (Schiller-Nationalmuseum, Marbach)

Werke (Berlin: Weidemann, 1889);

Walter Harich, *Jean Paul* (Leipzig: Haessel, 1925; reprinted, New York: AMS Press, 1971);

Günter de Bruyn, *Das Leben des Jean Paul Friedrich Richter* (Halle: Mitteldeutscher Verlag, 1975).

References:

Beate Allert, *Die Metapher und ihre Krise: Zur Dynamik der Bilderschrift Jean Pauls* (New York, Bern, Frankfurt am Main & Paris: Lang, 1987);

Heinz Ludwig Arnold, ed., *Jean Paul: Sonderband text & kritik* (Munich: Edition text & kritik, 1970; revised, 1983);

Hans Bach, *Jean Pauls Hesperus* (Berlin: Mayer & Müller, 1929);

Heidemarie Bade, *Jean Pauls politische Schriften* (Tübingen: Niemeyer, 1974);

Eduard Berend, *Jean Pauls Ästhetik* (Berlin: Dunkker, 1909);

Berend, ed., *Jean Pauls Persönlichkeit in Berichten der Zeitgenossen* (Berlin & Weimar: Akademie & Böhlau, 1956);

Dorothea Berger, *Jean Paul Friedrich Richter* (New York: Twayne, 1970);

Hendrik Birus, *Vergleichung: Goethes Einführung in die Schreibweise Jean Pauls* (Stuttgart: Metzler, 1986);

Ludwig Börne, *Denkrede auf Jean Paul* (Frankfurt am Main [actually Erfurt], 1826);

Bernhard Böschenstein, "Jean Pauls Romankonzeption," "Leibgeber und die Metapher der Hülle," in his *Studien zur Dichtung des Absoluten* (Zurich & Freiburg: Atlantis, 1968) pp. 25-50;

Heinrich Bosse, *Theorie und Praxis bei Jean Paul: Sektion 74 der "Vorschule der Ästhetik" und Jean Pauls erzählerische Technik, besonders im "Titan"* (Bonn: Bouvier, 1970);

Edward V. Brewer, "The New England Interest in Jean Paul Friedrich Richter," *University of California Publications in Modern Philology* 27, no. 1 (1943): 1-26;

Hans Esselborn, *Das Universum der Bilder: Die Naturwissenschaft in den Schriften Jean Pauls* (Tübingen: Niemeyer, 1989);

Ernst Förster, ed., *Denkwürdigkeiten aus dem Leben von Jean Paul Friedrich Richter: Zur Feier seines hundertjährigen Geburtstages herausgegeben*, 4 volumes (Munich: Fleischmann, 1863);

Marie-Luise Gansberg, "Welt-Verlachung und das 'rechte Land,' " *Deutsche Vierteljahrsschrift für Literaturwissenschaft und Geistesgeschichte*, 42 (1968): 373-398;

Hansjörg Garte, "Kunstform Schauerroman: Eine morphologische Begriffsbestimmung des Sensationsromans im 18. Jahrhundert von Walpoles 'Castle of Otranto' bis zu Jean Pauls 'Titan,' " Ph.D. dissertation, University of Leipzig, 1935;

Ursula Gauhe, *Jean Pauls Trawndichtungen* (Bonn: Scheur, 1936);

Käthe Hamburger, "Das Todesproblem bei Jean Paul," *Deutsche Vierteljahrsschrift für Literaturwissenschaft und Geistesgeschichte*, 7 (1929): 446-474;

Wolfgang Harich, *Jean Pauls Kritik des philosophischen Egoismus* (Frankfurt am Main: Suhrkamp, 1968);

Harich, *Jean Pauls Revolutionsdichtung: Versuch einer neuen Deutung seiner heroischen Romane* (Berlin: Akademie-Verlag, 1974);

Hesperus: Blätter der Jean-Paul-Gesellschaft, edited by Theodor Langemaier, nos. 1-30 (1951-1966);

Margaret R. Higonnet, "Jean Paul Richter: Kunstrichter," *Journal of English and German Philology*, 76 (1977): 471-490;

Jahrbuch der Jean-Paul-Gesellschaft, edited by Kurt Wölfel (1966-);

Jean-Paul-Blätter, edited by August Caselmann, Georg Regler, and Johannes Wirth, 1-19 (1926-1944);

Jean-Paul-Jahrbuch, edited by Eduard Berend, 1 (1925);

Wulf Koepke, *Erfolglosigkeit: Zum Frühwerk Jean Pauls* (Munich: Fink, 1977);

Koepke, ". . . von den Weibern geliebt: Jean Paul und seine Leserinnen," in *Die Frau von der Reformation zur Romantik: Die Situation der Frau vor dem Hintergrund der Literatur- und Sozialgeschichte*, edited by Barbara Becker-Cantarino (Bonn: Bouvier, 1980), pp. 217-242;

Max Kommerell, *Jean Paul* (Frankfurt am Main: Klostermann, 1933; fifth edition, 1977);

Burckhardt Lindner, *Jean Paul: Scheiternde Aufklärung und Autorrolle* (Darmstadt: Agora, 1976);

Peter Michelsen, *Laurence Sterne und der deutsche Roman des achtzehnten Jahrhunderts*, revised edition (Göttingen: Vandenhoeck & Ruprecht, 1972);

Götz Müller, *Jean Pauls Ästhetik und Naturphilosophie* (Tübingen: Niemeyer, 1983);

Ursula Naumann, *Predigende Poesie: Zur Bedeutung von Predigt, geistlicher Rede und Predigertum für das Werk Jean Pauls* (Nuremberg: Carl, 1976);

Eckart Oehlenschläger, *Närrische Phantasie: Zum metaphorischen Prozeß bei Jean Paul* (Tübingen: Niemeyer, 1980);

Hanns-Josef Ortheil, *Jean Paul in Selbstzeugnissen und Bilddokumenten* (Reinbek: Rowohlt, 1984);

Claude Pichois, *L'image de Jean-Paul dans les lettres françaises* (Paris: Cort, 1963);

Ulrich Profitlich, *Der seelige Leser: Untersuchungen zur Dichtungstheorie Jean Pauls* (Bonn: Bouvier, 1968);

Wolfgang Proß, *Jean Pauls geschichtliche Stellung* (Tübingen: Niemeyer, 1975);

Wolfdietrich Rasch, *Die Erzählweise Jean Pauls: Metaphernspiele und dissonante Strukturen* (Munich: Hanser, 1961);

Walther Rehm, *Jean Paul–Dostojewski: Eine Studie zur dichterischen Gestaltung des Unglaubens* (Göttingen: Vandenhoeck & Ruprecht, 1962);

Rehm, "Roquairol: Eine Studie zur Geschichte des Bösen," in his *Begegnungen und Probleme* (Bern: Francke, 1957); pp. 155-242;

Richard Rohde, *Jean Pauls Titan: Untersuchungen über Entstehung, Ideengehalt und Form des Romans* (Berlin: Mayer & Müller, 1920);

Heinz Schlaffer, "Epos und Roman: Tat und Bewußtsein. Jean Pauls Titan," in his *Der Bürger als Held: Sozialgeschichtliche Auflösungen literarischer Widersprüche*, third edition (Frankfurt am Main: Suhrkamp, 1981), pp. 15-50;

Wilhelm Schmidt-Biggemann, *Maschine und Teufel: Jean Pauls Jugendsatiren nach ihrer Modellgeschichte* (Freiburg & Munich: Alber, 1975);

Monika Schmitz-Emans, *Schnupftuchsknoten oder Sternbild: Jean Pauls Ansätze zu einer Theorie der Sprache* (Bonn: Bouvier, 1986);

Ferdinand Josef Schneider, *Jean Pauls Jugend und erstes Auftreten in der Literatur* (Berlin: Behr, 1905);

Rüdiger Scholz, *Welt und Form des Romans bei Jean Paul* (Bern: Francke, 1973);

Uwe Schweikert, *Jean Paul* (Stuttgart: Metzler, 1970);

Schweikert, *Jean Pauls Komet: Selbstparodie der Kunst* (Stuttgart: Metzler, 1971);

Schweikert, ed., *Jean Paul* (Darmstadt: Wissenschaftliche Buchgesellschaft, 1974);

Schweikert, Gabriele Schweikert, and Wilhelm Schmidt-Biggemann, eds., *Jean Paul Chronik: Daten zu Leben und Werk* (Munich: Hanser, 1975);

J. W. Smeed, "Jean Paul," in *German Men of Letters*, volume 5, edited by Alex Natan (London: Wolff, 1969), pp. 31-47;

Smeed, *Jean Paul's Dreams* (London, New York & Toronto: Oxford University Press, 1966);

Hans Michael Speier, *Die Ästhetik Jean Pauls in der Dichtung des deutschen Symbolismus* (Frankfurt am Main: Fischer, 1979);

Peter Sprengel, *Innerlichkeit: Jean Paul oder Das Leiden an der Gesellschaft* (Munich: Hanser, 1977);

Sprengel, ed., *Jean Paul im Urteil seiner Kritiker: Dokumente zur Wirkungsgeschichte Jean Pauls in Deutschland* (Munich: Beck, 1980);

Emil Staiger, "Jean Pauls 'Titan': Vorstudien zu einer Auslegung, " in his *Meisterwerke deutscher Sprache aus dem neunzehnten Jahrhundert* (Zurich: Atlantis, 1943), pp. 39-81;

Engelhard Weigl, *Aufklärung und Skeptizismus: Untersuchungen zu Jean Pauls Frühwerk* (Hildesheim: Gerstenberg, 1980);

Waltraud Wiethölter, *Witzige Illumination: Studien zur Ästhetik Jean Pauls* (Tübingen: Niemeyer, 1979);

Gisela Wilkending, *Jean Pauls Sprachauffassung in ihrem Verhältnis zu seiner Ästhetik* (Marburg: Elwert, 1966);

Kurt Wölfel, *Jean-Paul-Studien*, edited by Bernhard Buschendorf (Frankfurt am Main: Suhrkamp, 1989);

Wölfel, ed., "Sammlung zeitgenössischer Rezensionen von Jean Pauls Werken," 4 installments, *Jahrbuch der Jean-Paul-Gesellschaft*, 13 (1978), 16 (1981), 18 (1983), 23 (1988);

Ralph-Rainer Wuthenow, *Jean-Paul-Aufsätze* (Frankfurt am Main: Insel, 1975).

Papers:

Johann Paul Friedrich Richter's papers are in the Staatsbibliothek Berlin, East Berlin, and in the Eduard Berend Collection of the Deutsches Literaturarchiv, Marbach, Federal Republic of Germany.

Friedrich Schiller
(10 November 1759 - 9 May 1805)

John D. Simons
Florida State University

BOOKS: *Versuch über den Zusammenhang der thierischen Natur des Menschen mit seiner geistigen: Eine Abhandlung welche in höchster Gegenwart Sr. Herzoglichen Durchlaucht, während den öffentlichen akademischen Prüfungen vertheidigen wird Johann Christoph Friedrich Schiller, Kandidat der Medizin in der Herzoglichen Militair-Akademie* (Stuttgart: Cotta, 1780); translated by Kenneth Dewhurst and Nigel Reeves as "An Essay on the Connection between the Animal and Spiritual Nature of Man," in their *Friedrich Schiller: Medicine, Psychology, and Literature* (Berkeley: University of California Press, 1978), pp. 253-285;

Die Räuber: Ein Schauspiel, anonymous (Frankfurt am Main & Leipzig: Privately printed, 1781); revised as *Die Räuber: Ein Trauerspiel. Neue für die Mannheimer Bühne verbesserte Auflage*, as Schiller (Mannheim: Schwan, 1782); revised as *Die Räuber: Ein Schauspiel in fünf Akten* (Frankfurt am Main & Leipzig: Löffler, 1782); translated by Alexander F. Tytler as *The Robbers* (London: Robinson, 1792; New York: Printed for S. Campbell, 1793);

Elegie auf den frühzeitigen Tod Johann Christian Weckerlins: Von seinen Freunden, anonymous (Stuttgart: Mäntler, 1781);

Der Venuswagen, anonymous (Stuttgart: Metzler, 1781);

Anthologie auf das Jahr 1782, anonymous (Tobolsko: Gedruckt in der Buchdruckerei, 1782);

Todenfeyer am Grabe des hochwohlgebornen Herrn, HERRN Philipp Friderich von Rieger, Generalmajors und Chefs eines Infanterie-Bataillons, Kommandanten der Vestung Hohenasperg, und des herzoglich militairischen St. Karls Ordens Ritters, welcher im sechzigsten Jahr seines Alters am 15ten May 1782 zu Hohenasperg an einem Schlagflusse seelig verschied, und den 18ten des Monats feierlich zur Erde bestattet wurde, Ihm zum Ehrendenkmal geweyht von sämmtlicher Herzoglich-Wirtembergischen Generalität, anonymous (Stuttgart: Erhard, 1782);

Friedrich Schiller; painting by Anton Graff, circa 1786-1791 (Deutsche Fotothek, Dresden)

Die Verschwörung des Fiesko zu Genua: Ein republikanisches Trauerspiel (Mannheim: Schwan, 1783); translated by George Henry Noehden and Sir John Stoddart as *Fiesco; or, The Genoese Conspiracy* (London: Johnson, 1796);

Kabale und Liebe: Ein bürgerliches Trauerspiel in fünf Aufzügen (Mannheim: Schwan, 1784); translated by Matthew Gregory Lewis as *The Minister: A Tragedy in Five Acts* (London: Bell, 1797); translation revised as *The Harper's Daughter; or, Love and Ambition* (Philadelphia: Carey, 1813);

An die Freude: Ein Rundgesang für freye Männer. Mit Musik (N.p., 1786);

Dom Karlos, Infant von Spanien (Leipzig: Göschen, 1787); translated by Noehden and Stoddart as *Don Carlos, Infant of Spain* (London: Miller, 1798);

Der Geisterseher: Eine interessante Geschichte aus den Papieren des Grafen von O*** herausgegeben aus Herrn Schillers Thalia (Berlin & Leipzig, 1788); republished as *Der Geisterseher: Eine Geschichte aus den Memoires des Grafen von O*** (Leipzig: Göschen, 1789); translated by Daniel Boileau as *The Ghost-seer; or, The Apparitionist* (London: Vernor, 1795; New York: Printed for T. & J. Swords, 1796);

Geschichte des Abfalls der vereinigten Niederlande von der Spanischen Regierung: Erster Theil enthaltend die Geschichte der Rebellionen bis zur Utrechtischen Verbindung (Leipzig: Crusius, 1788); translated by Edward Backhouse Eastwick as *History of the Defection of the United Netherlands from the Spanish Empire* (Frankfurt am Main: Krebs, 1844);

Was heißt und zu welchem Ende studiert man Universalgeschichte?: Eine akademische Antrittsrede bey Eröffnung seiner Vorlesungen gehalten von Friedrich Schiller, Professor der Geschichte in Jena (Jena: Akademische Buchhandlung, 1789);

Historischer Calender für Damen für das Jahr 1791 (-1793): Geschichte des Dreißigjährigen Kriegs, 3 volumes (Leipzig: Göschen, 1791-1793); translated by William Blaquiere as *History of the Thirty Years' War*, 2 volumes (London: Miller, 1799);

Kleinere prosaische Schriften von Schiller: Aus mehrern Zeitschriften vom Verfasser selbst gesammelt und verbessert, 4 volumes (Leipzig: Crusius, 1792-1802);

Über Anmuth und Würde: An Carl von Dalberg in Erfurth, anonymous (Leipzig: Göschen, 1793);

Gedichte, 2 volumes (Leipzig: Crusius, 1800-1803);

Wallenstein: Ein dramatisches Gedicht, 2 volumes (Tübingen: Cotta, 1800)—comprises in volume 1, *Wallensteins Lager*, translated by F. L. Gower as *The Camp of Wallenstein* (London: Murray, 1830); *Die Piccolomini*, translated by Samuel Taylor Coleridge as *The Piccolomini; or, The First Part of Wallenstein, a Drama in Five Acts* (London: Longman & Rees, 1800); as volume 2, *Wallensteins Tod*, translated by Coleridge as *The Death of Wallenstein* (London: Longman & Rees, 1800);

Maria Stuart: Ein Trauerspiel (Tübingen: Cotta, 1801); translated by Joseph C. Mellish as

Mary Stuart: A Tragedy (London: Printed by G. Auld, 1801);

Turandot, Prinzessin von China: Ein tragicomisches Mährchen nach Gozzi (Tübingen: Cotta, 1802);

Kalendar auf das Jahr 1802: Die Jungfrau von Orleans. Eine romantische Tragödie (Berlin: Unger, 1802); translated by Henry Salvin as *The Maid of Orleans* in his *Mary Stuart and The Maid of Orleans* (London: Longman, 1824);

Die Braut von Messina oder Die feindlichen Brüder: Ein Trauerspiel mit Chören (Tübingen: Cotta, 1803); translated by G. Irvine as *The Bride of Messina* (London: Macrone, 1837);

Wilhelm Tell: Ein Schauspiel. Zum Neujahrsgeschenk auf 1805 (Tübingen: Cotta, 1804); translated anonymously as *William Tell* (London: Bull, 1829);

Die Huldigung der Künste: Ein lyrisches Spiel (Tübingen: Cotta, 1805); translated by A. I. du Pont Coleman as "Homage to the Arts," in *The German Classics of the Nineteenth and Twentieth Centuries*, volume 3, edited by Kuno Francke and William G. Howard (New York: German Publication Society, 1913), pp. 366-377;

Theater, 5 volumes (Tübingen: Cotta, 1805-1807);

Friedrich v. Schillers sämmtliche Werke, 12 volumes, edited by Christian Gottfried Körner (Stuttgart & Tübingen: Cotta, 1812-1815; revised, 1835);

Schiller's erste bis jetzt unbekannte Jugendschrift: Die Tugend in ihren Folgen betrachtet. Rede zur Feier des Geburtsfestes der Frau Reichsgräfin von Hohenheim auf gnädigsten Befehl Seiner Herzoglichen Durchlaucht verfertigt vom Eleve Schiller (Amberg: Klöber, 1839);

Nachlese zu Schillers Werken nebst Variantensammlung: Aus seinem Nachlaß, 4 volumes, edited by Karl Hoffmeister (Stuttgart & Tübingen: Cotta, 1840-1841);

Aventuren des neuen Telemachs oder Leben und Exsertionen Koerners des decenten, consequenten, piquanten u.s.f. von Hogarth in schönen illuminierten Kupfern abgefaßt und mit befriedigenden Erklärungen versehen von Winkelmann: Rom, 1786, drawings by Schiller, texts by Ludwig Ferdinand Huber, edited by Carl Künzel (Leipzig: Payne, 1862);

Ich habe mich rasieren lassen: Ein dramatischer Scherz, edited by Künzel (Leipzig: Payne, 1862);

Schillers dramatische Entwürfe zum erstenmal veröffentlicht durch Schillers Tochter, edited by Emilie

Freifrau von Gleichen-Rußwurm (Stuttgart: Cotta, 1867);

Schillers sämmtliche Schriften: Historisch-kritische Ausgabe, 16 volumes, edited by Karl Goedeke and others (Stuttgart: Cotta, 1867-1876);

Schiller's Werke: Nach den vorzüglichen Quellen revidirte Ausgabe, 16 volumes (Berlin: Hempel, 1868-1874);

Aus dem Schiller-Archiv: Ungedrucktes und unbekanntes zu Schillers Leben und Schriften, edited by J. Minor (Weimar: Böhlau, 1890);

Deutsche Größe: Ein unvollendetes Gedicht Schillers. 1801. Nachbildung der Handschrift im Auftrage des Vorstandes der Goethe-Gesellschaft, edited by Bernhard Suphan (Weimar, 1902);

Sämtliche Werke: Säkular-Ausgabe in sechzehn Bänden, 16 volumes, edited by E. von der Hellen (Stuttgart: Cotta, 1904-1905);

Werke: Nationalausgabe. Im Auftrag des Goethe- und Schiller-Archivs, des Schiller-Nationalmuseums und der Deutschen Akademie, 35 volumes to date, edited by Julius Petersen and Gerhard Fricke (Weimar: Böhlau, 1943-   );

Sämtliche Werke, 5 volumes, edited by Fricke, Herbert G. Göpfert, and Herbert Stubenrauch (Munich: Hanser, 1958-1960).

Editions in English: *Historical Works*, 2 volumes, translated by George Moir (Edinburgh: Constable / London: Hurst, 1828);

Philosophical and Aesthetic Letters, translated by Joseph Weiss (London: Chapman, 1844);

Essays: The Aesthetic Letters, Essays, and the Philosophical Letters, translated by Weiss (Boston: Little, Brown, 1845);

Works, Historical and Dramatic, 4 volumes (London: Bohn, 1846-1849; New York: Harper, 1855);

Poems of Schiller, Complete, Including All His Early Suppressed Poems, translated by Edgar Alfred Bowring (London: Parker, 1851; revised edition, London: Bell, 1874, New York: Lovell, 1884);

Complete Works, 2 volumes, edited by Carl J. Hempel (Philadelphia: Kohler, 1861; revised, 1870);

Essays Aesthetical and Philosophical: Translated by Various Hands (London: Bell, 1875);

The Revolt of the United Netherlands, translated by Alexander James W. Morrison (London: Bell, 1889);

Works, 7 volumes (London: Bell, 1897-1903);

"The Sport of Destiny," translated by Marian Klopfer, in *Great German Short Novels and Sto-*

ries, edited by Victor Lange (New York: Random House, 1952), pp. 100-109;

William Tell, translated by Sidney E. Kaplan (Woodbury, N.Y.: Barron's Educational Series, 1954);

Wallenstein: A Historical Drama in Three Parts, translated by Charles E. Passage (London: Owen, 1958; New York: Ungar, 1958; revised edition, New York: Ungar, 1960);

Mary Stuart: A Tragedy, translated by Sophie Wilkins (Woodbury, N.Y.: Barron's Educational Series, 1959);

The Maiden of Orleans: A Romantic Tragedy, translated by John T. Krumpelmann (Chapel Hill: University of North Carolina Press, 1959; revised, 1962);

Don Carlos, Infante of Spain, translated by Passage (New York: Ungar, 1959);

Friedrich Schiller: An Anthology for Our Time, in New English Translations and the Original German. With an Account of His Life and Work by Frederick Ungar, translations by Passage, Jane Bannard Greene, and Alexander Gode-von Aesch (New York: Ungar, 1959);

Mary Stuart; The Maid of Orleans: Two Historical Plays, translated by Passage (New York: Ungar, 1961);

The Bride of Messina; or, The Enemy Brothers: A Tragedy with Choruses; William Tell; Demetrius; or, The Blood Wedding in Moscow: A Fragment, translated by Passage (New York: Ungar, 1962);

Love and Intrigue; or, Louisa Miller, translated by Frederick Rolf (Great Neck, N.Y.: Barron's Educational Series, 1962);

Wilhelm Tell: A Verse Translation, translated by Gilbert J. Jordan (Indianapolis: Bobbs-Merrill, 1964);

On the Aesthetic Education of Man, in a Series of Letters, translated by Reginald Snell (New York: Ungar, 1965);

Naive and Sentimental Poetry, and On the Sublime: Two Essays, translated by Julius A. Elias (New York: Ungar, 1967);

On the Aesthetic Education of Man, in a Series of Letters, edited and translated by Elizabeth M. Wilkinson and Leonard A. Willoughby (Oxford: Clarendon Press, 1968);

Wilhelm Tell, translated by John Prudhoe (Manchester, U.K.: Manchester University Press / New York: Barnes & Noble, 1970);

Intrigue and Love: A Bourgeois Tragedy, translated by Passage (New York: Ungar, 1971);

William Tell, translated by William F. Mainland (Chicago & London: University of Chicago Press, 1972);

"The Philosophy of Physiology," translated by Kenneth Dewhurst and Nigel Reeves in their *Friedrich Schiller: Medicine, Psychology, and Literature* (Berkeley: University of California Press, 1978), pp. 149-167;

Love and Intrigue, translated and edited by Johanna Setzer and Elaine Gottesmann (Flushing, N.Y.: Setzer-Gottesmann, 1978);

The Robbers; Wallenstein, translated by F. J. Lamport (Harmondsworth, U.K. & New York: Penguin, 1979);

On the Naive and Sentimental in Literature, translated by Helen Wantanabe-O'Kelly (Manchester, U.K.: Carcanet New Press, 1981);

Plays, edited by Walter Hinderer (New York: Continuum, 1983).

OTHER: *Wirtembergisches Repertorium der Litteratur: Eine Vierteljahr-Schrift*, 2 volumes, edited by Schiller (N.p., 1782);

Rheinische Thalia: Erstes Heft, edited by Schiller (Mannheim: Auf dasigem kaiserl. freien R. Postamt & Schwan, 1785);

Thalia, 12 volumes, edited by Schiller (Leipzig: Göschen, 1786-1791);

Geschichte der merkwürdigsten Rebellionen und Verschwörungen aus den mittleren und neuern Zeiten: Bearbeitet von verschiedenen Verfassern. Erster Band, edited by Schiller (Leipzig: Crusius, 1788);

Euripides, *Iphigenie in Aulis: Ein Trauerspiel in fünf Aufzügen. Aus dem Griechischen*, translated by Schiller (Cologne: Langen, 1790);

Allgemeine Sammlung historischer Memoires vom zwölften Jahrhundert bis auf die neuesten Zeiten durch mehrere Verfasser übersetzt, mit den nöthigen Anmerkungen versehen, und jedesmal mit einer universalhistorischen Uebersicht begleitet, edited by Schiller, 7 volumes (Jena: Mauke, 1790-1792);

Geschichte des Maltheserordens nach Vertot von M. N. bearbeitet, 2 volumes, foreword by Schiller (Jena: Cuno, 1792-1793);

Merkwürdige Rechtsfälle als ein Beitrag zur Geschichte der Menschheit: Nach dem französischen Werk des Pitaval durch mehrere Verfasser ausgearbeitet und mit einer Vorrede begleitet, 4 volumes, edited by Schiller (Jena: Cuno, 1792-1795);

Neue Thalia, 4 volumes, edited by Schiller (Leipzig: Göschen, 1792-1793);

Die Horen: Eine Monatsschrift, 12 volumes, edited by Schiller (Tübingen: Cotta, 1795-1797);

Musen-Almanach für das Jahr 1796, edited by Schiller (Neustrelitz: Michaelis, 1796);

Musen-Almanach für das Jahr 1797, edited by Schiller (Tübingen: Cotta, 1797);

Musen-Almanach für das Jahr 1798, edited by Schiller (Tübingen: Cotta, 1798);

Musen-Almanach für das Jahr 1799, edited by Schiller (Tübingen: Cotta, 1799);

Musen-Almanach für das Jahr 1800, edited by Schiller (Tübingen: Cotta, 1800);

William Shakespeare, *Macbeth: Ein Trauerspiel*, translated and adapted by Schiller (Tübingen: Cotta, 1801);

Jean Racine, *Phädra: Trauerspiel*, translated by Schiller (Tübingen: Cotta, 1805);

Louis-Benoit Picard, *Der Parasit oder Die Kunst sein Glück zu machen: Ein Lustspiel nach dem Französischen*, adapted by Schiller (Tübingen: Cotta, 1806);

Picard, *Der Neffe als Onkel: Lustspiel in drey Aufzügen. Aus dem Französischen*, translated by Schiller (Tübingen: Cotta, 1807);

Johann Wolfgang von Goethe, *Goethe's Egmont für die Bühne bearbeitet*, adapted by Schiller (Stuttgart & Augsburg: Cotta, 1857).

A universal genius generally regarded as the greatest German dramatist, Friedrich Schiller dominates a period of German literary history as no one else before or since. Schiller revealed more vividly than any of his predecessors the power of drama and poetry to convey a philosophy; his works contain the strongest assertions of human freedom and dignity and the worth of the individual in all German literature. After his death he rapidly became part of the cultural environment: streets and schools were named after him, statues and monuments were raised to his memory, his birthday was declared a national holiday, and his major works became part of the educational curriculum.

To modern English-speaking people the mystique surrounding Schiller may seem hard to fathom. Yet to study how Germans perceive Schiller is to study how they perceive themselves. He appeared at a time when German literature was dominated by the monumental achievements of England, France, and Italy; there was even serious debate about whether the German language was a fit vehicle for literary expression. Schiller furnished proof of Germany's high cultural achievement. His stature was recognized even in

Schiller's parents, Johann Caspar Schiller and Elisabetha Dorothea Kodweis Schiller; oil paintings by Ludovike Simanowitz, 1793 (Schiller-Nationalmuseum, Marbach)

his lifetime: on 17 September 1801 he attended a performance of his *Die Jungfrau von Orleans* (1802; translated as *The Maid of Orleans*, 1824) at Leipzig. After the first act the audience exploded in shouts of "Es lebe Schiller!" (Long live Schiller), accompanied by cheers and applause. After the curtain fell on the last act, he was treated to a standing ovation. When he appeared at the exit, the throng fell silent. Baring their heads, they parted so as to form a corridor for him to pass. Here and there a parent lifted up a child and pointed out the honored man. Schiller had become, and remains, an icon.

Johann Christoph Friedrich Schiller was born in obscurity on 10 November 1759 in Marbach. His father, Johann Kaspar Schiller, was a captain in the army of Karl Eugen, duke of Württemberg. In 1749 he had married Elisabeth Dorothea Kodweiß, the daughter of a Marbach innkeeper. Though a captain's salary was not large, it provided the family with a modest standard of living and a happy home environment for the future poet. In later years Schiller looked back on his childhood as an idyllic time of simplicity and serenity. In 1762 the family moved to Ludwigsburg. In 1763 Johann Kaspar was sent to Schwäbisch-Gmünd as recruiting officer; the family followed in 1764. To save money they decided to live in the nearby hamlet of Lorch on the Rems. In 1766 the captain was posted back to Ludwigsburg. From 1767 to 1773 Schiller attended the local Latin school, where he received instruction in religion, Latin, Greek, Hebrew, and German.

Schiller's ambition in these early years was to become a clergyman. It was planned that he should attend the monastery school at Blaubeuren and then complete his studies at the Tübinger Stift (Tübinger Seminary). These plans were abruptly terminated in 1773 when the duke, who was absolute dictator in all but name, forced the thirteen-year-old to enroll in his newly established military academy at Solitude, two miles west of Stuttgart. Founded in 1770 as the Militärwaisenhaus (Military Orphanage), the school had been renamed the Militär Pflanzschule (Military Cadet School) in 1771. As the duke's pedagogical designs became more grandiose, he moved the school to Stuttgart in 1775 and changed its name to the Herzogliche Militärakademie (Ducal Military Academy). The institution was generally known as the "Karlsschule" (Karl's School).

Thus began for Schiller eight grueling years of rigid discipline and petty rules. Cadets were forbidden to leave the school, receive visitors, or write letters; their activities were organized and monitored around the clock. This experience left its mark on Schiller's personality and on his literary productions. His hostility toward and contempt for arbitrary political power and despotic rulers runs like a leitmotif throughout his works.

The Karlsschule offered several subjects in which students could specialize. Schiller first chose law, then transferred to medicine when that subject was added in 1775. Determined to make his school the envy of Germany, Karl Eugen hired the best teachers he could find; consequently, Schiller received an excellent education. In addition to courses in medicine and military science, he received instruction in Greek, Latin, French, English, classical mythology, theology, philosophy, history, literature, physics, chemistry, botany, and mathematics. Since the Karlsschule aimed at producing officers and gentlemen, students received instruction in dance, horsemanship, fencing, and court etiquette. When Schiller graduated he would have the intellectual training and social graces necessary for entry into polite society.

In 1779 Schiller completed his course work and submitted a dissertation, "Die Philosophie der Physiologie" (translated as "The Philosophy of Physiology," 1978). The committee rejected it, primarily because he had had the temerity to dispute the teachings of some traditional authorities. Schiller was particularly incensed when told that he would have to spend another year at the school. In 1780 his second dissertation, *Versuch über den Zusammenhang der Rierischen Natur des Menschen mit seiner geistigen* (1780; translated as "An Essay on the Connection between the Animal and Spiritual Nature of Man," 1978), was accepted, and he was allowed to graduate and take up his duties as a regimental surgeon in Stuttgart. Since the Karlsschule was not a university Schiller could not be granted the title M.D. with the license to practice medicine; instead, he was something like a paramedic, a position of little pay and less prestige. Schiller realized that all he could look forward to was the distasteful life of servitude laid out for him by the duke.

Schiller was delivered from his misery by his first drama, *Die Räuber* (1781; translated as *The Robbers*, 1792). Little is known about the genesis of the play other than that he had begun work on it when still a teenager. Once he was free of the academy he concentrated his energy and finished it in 1781. Unable to find a publisher, he borrowed the money and paid for the printing himself. Because of its many inflammatory passages, he decided to publish it anonymously outside the duchy. A vital, energetic, and troubling work, it soon caught the eye of Wolfgang Heribert von Dalberg, director of the Mannheim National Theater in the neighboring duchy of Hesse, who decided to bring it to the stage. Schiller left his post in Stuttgart without leave to attend the premiere on 13 January 1782. The play was a sensation. Much of its appeal resides in Schiller's choice of the archetypal theme of hostile brothers. The jealous and greedy Franz von Moor tricks his father, the ruling count, into disinheriting his elder brother, Karl, who is away at the university. He then imprisons his father and seizes the land and title for himself and tries to terrorize Karl's beloved, Amalia, into concubinage. Learning of his disinheritance, Karl drops out of school and becomes the leader of a band of robbers. No ordinary hoodlum, he is consumed by a demonic craving for justice; he has the noble but misguided notion that he can right the wrongs of the world by taking the law into his own hands. But the frightening violence that attends each raid begins to plague his conscience. His final catastrophic effort to bring his brother to justice ends in Franz's suicide and the deaths of the count, Amalia, and Karl's closest friend. In the end Karl realizes that he has done more harm than good. His last act, turning himself in to the police, amounts to a cry from the heart for lost ideals.

The drama introduces two themes that were to occupy Schiller for the rest of his life. The first is that of the criminal hero, the man inspired by lofty goals who employs immoral methods to achieve them. The second is that of the idealistic reformer betrayed by institutionalized hypocrisy and greed; in his hero's fall Schiller consistently underscores the futility inherent in the pursuit of ideals. The play also reveals Schiller's innate grasp of what constitutes drama. As a piece of stagecraft *Die Räuber* has it all: sibling rivalry, armed robberies, an evil tyrant, a captive maiden, raging battles, tender love, and the conflict between good and evil. The language and the characterization are shamelessly overblown, but they matched the epic proportions of the ac-

The Herzogliche Militärakademie ("Karlsschule") after its move to Stuttgart in 1775. Schiller studied at the school from 1773 to 1780. Engraving of a drawing by Conz.

tion and struck a responsive chord in the viewers. The play was one of the most astonishing hits in the annals of the German stage, and the critics were no less enthralled than the public. In short order *Die Räuber* was playing all over the country. Since the production broke all house records at the Mannheim National Theater, Dalberg promised to produce any other play Schiller might write.

During the following months Schiller made several clandestine trips to Mannheim. The duke eventually learned of his secret life, jailed him for two weeks, and ordered him to cease all literary activity. Unwilling to sacrifice his talent to the duke's whim, on 22 September 1782 Schiller deserted the army–a capital offense–and fled to Mannheim. He was somewhat naive in expecting Dalberg's protection and assistance; frightened of the duke's wrath, the director refused to have anything to do with the young playwright until the matter was settled. The prospect of being kidnapped and returned to face the duke's capricious brand of justice forced Schiller into hiding under the alias Dr. Ritter at the Bauerbach estate

of Frau Henriette von Wolzogen in distant Thuringia from December 1782 until July 1783. There he finished his second drama, *Die Verschwörung des Fiesko zu Genua* (1783; translated as *Fiesco: or, The Genoese Conspiracy*, 1796). Based on Count Fiesco's revolt against Andrea Doria in 1547, the play dramatizes the metamorphosis of an idealistic political reformer into an egotist hungry for power. Suspecting his ulterior motives, one of his coconspirators, the arch-republican Verrina, pushes Fiesko from a gangway, and he drowns. *Die Verschwörung des Fiesko zu Genua* is not a particularly deep or revealing examination of history, but it is a riveting drama. Nevertheless, when it premiered in Bonn on 20 July 1783 it received a mixed reception. The problem is that the hero is actually a villain involved in the ruthless pursuit of self-interest, and as Aristotle pointed out in his *Poetics*, if the hero is a villain it is not possible for the audience to experience the primary ingredients of tragedy, pity, and fear. Though *Die Verschwörung des Fiesko zu Genua* is much better constructed than *Die Räuber* is, it lacks both the idealistic fervor and the engaging characterizations of Schiller's first play.

By July 1783 it had become clear that Karl Eugen intended to ignore Schiller's desertion, and Dalberg decided that it was safe to hire Schiller as resident playwright to deliver three plays a year. Schiller assumed his new duties on 1 September, and *Die Verschwörung des Fiesko zu Genua* was produced at the National Theater on 11 January 1784. The first play Schiller wrote for Dalberg was *Kabale und Liebe* (Intrigue and Love, 1784; translated as *The Minister*, 1797). The play deals with one of the most controversial issues of the day: class discrimination. Ferdinand von Walter is the son of President von Walter, the unscrupulous chief administrator of a duchy. Ferdinand loves Luise Miller, the daughter of a lowborn musician. To break up the affair, which he regards as a threat to his political ambitions, the president employs the services of a slick opportunist, Wurm. Together they launch a cabal to convince Ferdinand that Luise is promiscuous. Believing the lies, Ferdinand poisons Luise and himself; he realizes the truth just before he dies. Justice–of a kind–is when the president and Wurm turn upon and destroy each other.

The most prominent theme of the play is the conflict between the decadent moral system of the aristocracy and the new morality emerging from the Enlightenment. Representative of the former is the president and his group, who treat the lower classes with contempt. They feel no obligation to respect laws, tradition, or even common decency in their pursuit of power and privilege. Luise, by contrast, represents traditional morality. She stands for custom, traditional values, honesty, and respect for the rights of others. Although the play ends with her death, the morality she represents triumphs.

The drama also displays another of Schiller's favorite themes, that of the hero who wears a mask of idealism to conceal motives of personal gain. Full of revolutionary enthusiasm, Ferdinand professes noble principles in defying his father, but the real reason is his passion for Luise. Furthermore, his idealism is selectively applied: he knows that his father gained power through mendacity and murder, but he feels no impulse to denounce him; nor does he object when his father's influence gets him the rank of major.

Schiller's year as official playwright was anything but serene: he quarreled with the actors and became involved in several intrigues. Dalberg was highly displeased with the failure of *Die Verschwörung des Fiesko zu Genua* and the poor at-

Title page for Schiller's first play. The vignette depicts Karl Moor swearing revenge on his brother Franz for cheating him out of his inheritance.

tendance at *Kabale und Liebe*. When Schiller failed to deliver the third play he had promised, Dalberg refused to renew the contract, which expired in August 1784. Schiller found himself in serious financial trouble. He had borrowed heavily, and his creditors were pressing for payment. To support himself he decided to launch a literary journal, *Die rheinische Thalia*, later renamed *Thalia*. He hoped that it would bring him a thousand talers a year. The journal did not sell well, however, and he fell even further into debt. To complicate matters he had fallen deeply in love with Charlotte von Kalb, the wife of major Heinrich von Kalb. This affair, Benno von Wiese thinks, prompted Schiller more than anything else to leave Mannheim.

Help arrived from an unexpected source. Christian Gottfried Körner, a wealthy official in the Kingdom of Saxony, and some of his friends wrote Schiller expressing their admiration, offering support, and extending an invitation to live

Schiller at age twenty-six; painting attributed to Reinhard (Gustav Könnecke, Bilderatlas zur Geschichte der deutschen Nationallitteratur *[Graz; Akademische Druck- und Verlagsanstalt, 1981])*

with them at Leipzig. Schiller accepted. He wrote that his requirements were modest: a room to receive visitors, a place to work and sleep, and above all, companionship. Although he needed solitude for composition, he was gregarious by nature. He often said that he would rather not eat at all if he had to dine alone. His lifelong work habits began to emerge about this time. To avoid interruptions and still fulfill his duties as houseguest he decided to write at night, sustaining himself with large quantities of coffee. He worked usually until four o'clock in the morning and slept until eleven.

Schiller lived with the Körners from April 1785 until July 1787. His gratitude for their generosity and warm hospitality is reflected in *An die Freude* (To Joy, 1786). His best-known poem of this period, it is a paean to friendship, universal brotherhood, peace on earth, and good will to men; its appeal resides in its youthful vigor and in its image of an ideal world based on love. Ludwig van Beethoven immortalized the poem when he set it to music in the final movement of his Ninth Symphony. Besides other poetry of some merit, the chief product of this period was the drama *Dom Karlos, Infant von Spanien* (1787; translated as *Don Carlos, Infant of Spain*, 1798; in later German editions the spelling of the title character's name was changed to *Don Carlos*). The action is based loosely on the short life and mysterious death in 1568 of Don Carlos, son of Philip II and heir to the Spanish throne. Virtually everything is invented, including the central character, the Marquis Posa, an idealistic young man of uncommon abilities who tries to overthrow Philip II and place his intimate friend, Don Carlos, on the throne. Posa and Carlos plan to inaugurate a new order based on idealistic principles of freedom and dignity. These are noble goals, but Posa's devious means lead him ever deeper into a web of deception, secrecy, and betrayal involving not only Don Carlos but the queen–Carlos's stepmother, to whom Carlos was once engaged and whom he still loves–as well. Eventually, through a series of miscalculations, Posa loses control of events, and the king has him shot as a traitor. In the final scenes Philip turns his son over to the Inquisition.

This drama, with its ideal of freedom, its vision of a better future, and its merciless attack on political absolutism, earned a special place with the public, particularly the younger generation. For over a century Posa was hailed as the paragon of noble virtues, the perfect example of "the lionhearted German youth," as one early critic put it. This one-sided view has been considerably modified as critics have realized that Schiller's hero has serious flaws. Posa, like Fiesko and Ferdinand before him, uses idealism to conceal motives of self-aggrandizement. Although his dedication to the idea of freedom is genuine, he is also driven by the desire to go down in history as a great man. He pursues both aims in cold blood: he lies to and manipulates Carlos shamelessly, he maneuvers the queen into putting her life in danger, and he betrays the king in the most heartless way. In the final analysis, he tramples underfoot the very ideals he professes to uphold. Thus, the drama does not end on a note of moral triumph, for Schiller wanted to show how fanatical idealism is defeated by its own extreme. The drama premiered on 29 August 1787 in Hamburg; it was a success, and soon it was playing throughout the country. King Friedrich Wilhelm II attended a performance in Berlin and was deeply moved, especially by the scenes in which Philip's trust in Posa is betrayed. Despite the popular acclaim, the drama is seriously flawed technically. Directors had to edit it extensively, for it is constructed more like a thrilling novel than high tragedy.

Schiller was well aware that he needed both to perfect his craft and to think through certain fundamental philosophical principles; also, although the Körners were providing for his material needs, he wanted to regain his independence. On 20 July 1787 he moved to Weimar, which had the largest concentration of intellectual talent in Germany, and took up the study of history; he wrote no more plays and little poetry for the next ten years. It was widely held that there is a suprapersonal force at work within the phenomenal world directing the course of civilization; many, including Schiller, thought that this force could be grasped through the study of history. His study of the revolt of the Netherlands from Spain (1788; translated, 1844) attracted favorable attention and in January 1789 resulted in his appointment as an unsalaried professor of history at the university in nearby Jena. Schiller married Charlotte von Lengefeld on 22 February 1790. They had four children: Emilie, Ernst, Karl, and Karoline. Since the professorship carried no stipend, Schiller was forced to earn his living by writing popular histories, translating, and editing. One of his better-known literary products of this period is the unfinished novel *Der Geisterseher* (1788; translated as *The Ghost-seer; or, The Apparitionist*, 1795). It is his only effort in the colportage genre. With it he sought to capitalize on the contemporary fascination with the supernatural and the mysterious which was being promoted by such famous charlatans as Alessandro Cagliostro and Franz Mesmer. A German prince in Venice falls victim to the deceptions of a secret society which drives him to Catholicism and in the end is supposed to incite him to a crime disrupting the order of succession to the Austrian throne. Schiller himself had a low opinion of the project and before completing it decided his energy could be better employed elsewhere. The twentieth century judges the work more favorably than Schiller did: the language seems almost contemporary, and the novel is a masterpiece of suspense, adventure, and description.

Schiller's academic career came to an abrupt end in January 1791 when overwork and earlier privations brought on a pulmonary disorder, probably pneumonia, which was later complicated by pleurisy. He lay near death for weeks,

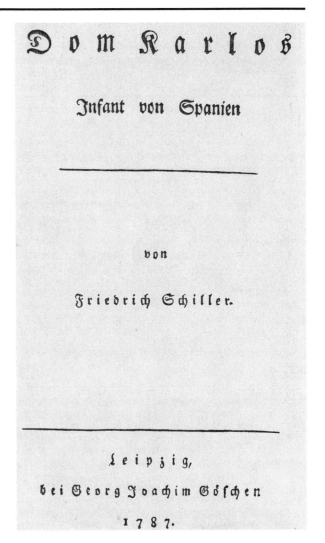

Dom Karlos

Infant von Spanien

von

Friedrich Schiller.

Leipzig,

bei Georg Joachim Göschen

1 7 8 7.

Title page for Schiller's play about an attempt to overthrow the king of Spain

and in the summer he traveled to the spas of Carsbad and Erfurt. He never fully recovered his health, and for the rest of his life he suffered a succession of illnesses, including whooping cough. Schiller was taller than six feet, with reddish-brown hair and blue eyes; before 1791 he had been robust and vigorous, but after the illness he became thin and bony with hollow cheeks and watery, bloodshot eyes. He suffered almost constantly from abdominal cramps, dyspnea, and insomnia. For months at a time he would not leave his house. Aside from trips to Württemberg from June 1793 to May 1794, to Leipzig in 1801, and to Berlin in May 1804, he never again left the vicinity of Weimar.

Although Schiller's body was wasted by disease, his mind and personality remained unaffected. In addition to his intellectual brilliance, the one trait virtually every visitor remarked upon was his enormous personal magnetism. He seems to have cast a spell over people, and the most independent-minded soon found themselves drawn into his orbit. The diplomat and linguist Wilhelm von Humboldt, who later founded the Humboldt University at Berlin, moved to Jena for the sole purpose of being near Schiller. Schiller, however, never seemed to be fully aware of his effect on people.

The severity of Schiller's illness had caused false reports of his death to circulate, and the loss of so great a talent was acutely felt by his admirers at the Danish court. When he learned that the rumor was false, Prince Christian Friedrich von Augustenburg of Denmark conferred upon Schiller a stipend of a thousand talers a year for three years, beginning in December 1791, so that he could convalesce properly. Freed from financial worries, Schiller took up the study of aesthetics and Kantian philosophy. This period marked the great intellectual and literary turning point of his life. He produced a series of analytical essays on tragedy, the sublime, spiritual rebirth, and grace and dignity, with his career culminating in two key essays on the role and nature of the fine arts: "Über die ästhetische Erziehung des Menschen in einer Reihe von Briefen" (On the Aesthetic Education of Man in a Series of Letters, 1795) and "Über naive und sentimentalische Dichtung" (On Naive and Sentimental Poetry, 1795-1796). Both essays were published in three parts in *Die Horen,* a monthly journal Schiller founded in 1795.

"Über die ästhetische Erziehung des Menschen in einer Reihe von Briefen" is a program for the improvement of man, society, and the state. Civilizations progress through three distinct stages, Schiller says: the natural state, the aesthetic state and the moral state. In the natural state individuals are ruled by their emotions and compelled by their physical needs. Since such people cannot be trusted to obey the law of their own free will, the state maintains order by brute force or the threat of it. Contemporary European society is near the end of the natural state but finds itself unable to take the next crucial step. An unsuccessful attempt to do so was underway in France: the French Revolution had begun with great promise but had turned into a bloodbath. The events in France proved that the average citizen was unable to cope with the freedom and the sophisticated moral principles promulgated by the reformers. Since political and so-

Charlotte von Lengefeld, whom Schiller married on 22 February 1790; oil painting by Simanowitz (Gustav Könnecke, Bilderatlas zur Geschichte der deutschen National-litteratur [Graz: Akademische Druck- und Verlagsanstalt, 1981])

cial institutions emanate from the character of the citizenry, it follows that if society is to be changed for the better the citizen must be changed first.

To change the character of the modern individual it is necessary to harmonize the forces operating within the human psyche. In our daily activities we are compelled on the one hand by the impulses emanating from our animal side, which Schiller calls the *Stofftrieb* (sense-drive). The Stofftrieb includes sense perception, the emotions, and the appetites. The other force, which arises from the rational faculty, he calls the *Formtrieb* (form-drive). It is the source of such abstractions as duty, law, justice, and moral principles. At present these two drives are in conflict, pulling the individual in opposite directions, with the sense-drive usually dominant. This inner disharmony is the primary cause of individual and social misery and misfortune. For further progress to occur, the two drives must work in concert. Both must be developed equally so that neither infringes on the territory of the other. This harmonization can be achieved by cultivating the *Spieltrieb* (drive to play). Play involves both drives and satisfies the demands of each simultaneously. Schiller defines play as whatever is done for its own sake; it is an end in itself, devoid of any ulterior motive. We sing, dance, play games, or listen to music purely for the pleasure involved, and that pleasure is the sensation of harmony. The delight in play derives precisely from its non-utilitarian character: if something could be gained by it, our pleasure in it would cease, and play would become work. Work is goal-oriented, play is process-oriented. Play and work are equivalent to freedom and servitude, respectively.

Schiller draws a close parallel between play and beauty: both are compounded of the sense-drive and the form-drive, both are disinterested, and both exert the same synthesizing effect on the psyche. The aesthetic state is the condition of harmony between reason and feeling: we are transported into this state of mind both through play and through the enjoyment and creation of beauty. He coins the term, "ästhetische Freiheit" (aesthetic freedom) to signify our liberation from the one-sided compulsion of either drive. Schiller's innovation is in tying art and beauty to our mimetic faculty. Since human beings learn through imitation, imitate what they see, and so become what they imitate, he proposes the aesthetic education of man as the way to equalize the discordant elements of the psyche. When sense and reason compel us equally, the moral state is possible. Schiller defines this state as any political body whose organization derives from laws and principles. In such a state we obey the law of our own free will. Projecting this scheme into the future, he says that once we approximate ideal harmony, we ourselves become the state; political organizations as we know them will no longer exist. Public pressure will be the only force needed to insure conformity to the ideal.

In "Über naive und sentimentalische Dichtung" Schiller examines the problems raised in the essay on aesthetic education from a different angle. His purpose is to elucidate two fundamentally different modes of perceiving the world and the two types of poetry which spring from these modes. Children exemplify the naive mode of perception: they are characterized above all by their straightforwardness and lack of guile. There is no difference between what they are and what they seem to be. Furthermore, they make no distinction between the world as it is and as it appears to be. They exist in a state of oneness with nature and with themselves. This child-like unity also characterizes the ancient Greeks: both in their moral behavior and in their poetry there is a certain unreflective spontaneity, almost as if nature herself were whispering directions. The naive orientation to life and poetry recurs from time to time in the modern age, notably in Shakespeare and Goethe. Modern civilization is largely to blame for our separation from nature and the accompanying destruction of our inner unity. When, as children, we are forced to obey rules and social conventions which are contrary to nature, we find that the promptings of the heart are at odds with the dictates of duty. As a consequence we become "sentimentalisch" (sentimental), a word which Schiller uses in its older connotation of intellectual, rational activity: with nature no longer available to guide us, we must reflect on our actions. The sentimental poet's alienation is reflected in his poetry; every word is the result of calculation and choice. The metaphors and symbols are carefully woven into the poem according to a preconceived plan to achieve a calculated effect. Until the sentimental poet overcomes his alienation, he will be able to write in only two modes: the satirical and the elegiac. The poet writes in the first mode if he is either angered or amused by the discrepancy between the ideal and its translation into reality; his language is flavored with sarcasm, ridicule, or irony. The elegiac mode, by contrast, expresses sadness at something lost or unattainable; the language here is colored with nostalgia and lament. Once human beings have harmonized the discordant elements of the psyche and the ideal has become reality, the poet's language will be filled with praise and exclamations of satisfaction. These are the characteristics of the sentimental idyll, the art form of the Golden Age. Believing in the perfectibility of man, Schiller is convinced that we can attain the ideal—not by returning to a state of nature as advocated by some contemporaries but by going forward. He assigns to the poets of the world the task of showing the way.

Schiller's essay can be read as an analysis of himself and Goethe. Though the two poets had been introduced in 1788, they remained cool to each other for several years because of the great difference in their temperaments. Schiller's mind was bent toward the abstract, the theoretical, and the ideal, whereas Goethe was this-worldly, practical, and realistic—naive in Schiller's sense of the word. Writing, for Schiller, was hard work, involving careful planning and self-discipline; he bitterly resented Goethe's presumably spontaneous and effortless composition. For his part, Goethe was well aware that he had been born with an enormous natural talent and was himself somewhat mystified by its independent nature. In his twenties he had discovered that he was unable to compose by conscious effort; verse came to him automatically at irregular intervals. Goethe was at first cool to Schiller because the ten-year-younger Schiller reminded him of his own Sturm und Drang youth and outlook on life. In his essay Schiller identifies the difficulty he had in relating to the naive poets as his habit of separating the author from his work; one of his greatest insights was the realization that in naive poetry it is not possible to make this separation. The two are a unity. Once Schiller grasped the fundamental difference between himself and Goethe, the way to friendship was cleared. From July 1794 until Schiller's death each served as an inspiration to the other. The completion of Goethe's *Faust*, Part I (1808), for instance, was due largely to Schiller's prodding. The chief product of their relationship is a correspondence of about one thousand letters which deal primarily with literary matters. In 1796 they collaborated on "Xenien" (Xenia), a series of satirical distichs in which they put to scorching ridicule a host of literary philistines and pretentious, self-appointed critics. "Xenien" was published in Schiller's journal, the *Musen-Almanach für das Jahr 1797*.

By 1795 Schiller had developed the firm theoretical foundation he had sought, and he felt ready to take up poetry again. The contrast between the new verse and his earlier efforts is most striking. His development as a poet is usually divided into three periods. The productions of his early youth display all the faults of someone not yet in control of an immense talent. Typical is "Der Eroberer" (The Conqueror), first published in the *Schwäbisches Magazin* in 1777. Grandiloquent, emotionally excessive, and often bizarre, it is a moral condemnation of excessive ambition. Other pieces addressed to the fictitious "Laura" are written in the same superheated fashion and take the same delight in rhetorical embellishment. Above all, they are testimony to the youth's awakening libido. The second period covers the years 1785 to 1789. Although Schiller still indulges his gift for rhetoric, the language of the poems of this period is more refined and elevated, and the content inclines toward philosophical ideas. "Resignation," published in Schiller's journal *Thalia* in February 1786, focuses on true and false virtue. A man dies and appears before

the judgment seat. He tells the judge that he had renounced all earthly pleasure in favor of compensation in the Hereafter; now he wants to collect his reward. Much to his distress he discovers that he has been laboring under a misapprehension. The judge tells him that humans can choose between hope and enjoyment; whoever picks the one must not covet the other. His reward for abstinence consisted in the pleasure he derived from self-denial. The poem ends with the remark that whatever we pass up in this life is not going to be waiting for us in eternity. A good deed performed with an eye toward a reward is not virtue. Like play, virtue is something we do purely for the pleasure involved. Another poem representative of the middle period is "Die Götter Griechenlandes" (The Gods of Greece), published in *Der Teutsche Merkur* in March 1788. It celebrates the ancient Greek view of religion and life to the detriment of the Christian. Schiller argues in the poem that if we look upon ourselves as helpless, sinful worms in a chain of being spiraling up to the Almighty, that simply makes Him the first and noblest worm. "Die Künstler" (The Artists), published in *Der Teutsche Merkur* in March 1789, is the last poem of the second period and probably the most significant. Schiller had by this time abandoned the study of history because it did not reveal the force responsible for social evolution. In this poem he says that art is this force, and he traces the role of art in civilization from earliest epochs to the eighteenth century. He went on to develop this idea in his essay on aesthetic education.

When Schiller resumed writing poetry in 1795 he was at the summit of his powers. His verse from this period has the ring of the self-confident master. Most of the poems are Gedankenlyrik (philosophical poetry); each is structured around a philosophical principle. Schiller believed that the poet's task is not to entertain but to inform, instruct, and improve the reader. The grand style is his mode of expression; his subjects are the rise and fall of civilizations, the destiny of mankind, the human condition. A particularly prominent motif is that of transcending through art and beauty the workaday world that inhibits the full development of our potential; only in the realm of ideals, truth, and beauty can we escape the enslaving forces of reality. He expresses this idea in such poems as "Der Tanz" (The Dance), published in the *Musen-Almanach für das Jahr 1796*, and particularly in his most profound philosophical poem, "Das Ideal und das

Leben" (The Ideal and Life), published in *Die Horen* in September 1795, in which he advises that one "fliehet aus dem engen, dumpfen Leben / In des Idealen Reich" (leave life's stupefying narrowness / For the realm of ideals).

Among Schiller's favorite subjects is the ascent of mankind from nomadism through the development of agriculture to the rise of cities. "Der Spaziergang" (The Walk), published in *Die Horen* in November 1795, focuses on the relation between nature and the development of civilization. In the beginning nature is our companion and protector. As we become more civilized, nature is made our servant. This is a positive development; trouble arises only when we try to dispense with nature altogether or when we act contrary to its laws. Without nature as its guiding principle, civilization loses its orientation and its roots. This kind of freedom is dangerous and can lead to social chaos. We must learn to live in harmony with nature.

In the *Musen-Almanach für das Jahr 1798* (1798) Schiller published a collection of ballads which included "Der Ring des Polykrates" (The Ring of Polykrates), "Die Kraniche des Ibykus" (The Cranes of Ibycus), "Der Taucher" (The Diver), and "Der Handschuh" (The Glove). The plot of "Der Ring des Polykrates" comes from a story found in the third book of Herodotus. As tyrant of Samos in the sixth century B.C. Polykrates, through dishonest means, dominated the eastern Aegean and amassed great wealth. In the poem the visiting Egyptian king warns him that the gods shower good fortune on those they have marked for destruction. To win their favor he should sacrifice his most esteemed possession. Polykrates agrees and casts his fabulous ring into the sea. The next day, while dressing a fresh fish, the cook finds the ring and returns it. Convinced that Polykrates' days are numbered, the Egyptian king hastily leaves Samos. By ending the ballad here, instead of going on to relate how Polykrates was soon lured to the mainland and crucified by the governor of Sardis, Schiller creates a mood of foreboding and doom.

"Die Kraniche des Ibykus" also dramatizes an incident from antiquity. The Greek poet Ibykus sets out to participate in the poetry competitions at Corinth. His journey happens to coincide with the migration of the cranes, whom he addresses as his friends. On the highway two robbers attack and murder him. With his dying breath he calls on the cranes to avenge him. The murderers continue to Corinth, where they enjoy the festival. One day, while they are attending a tragedy, a large flock of cranes suddenly flies over the ampitheater, provoking one of the murderers to exclaim without thinking: "Sieh da, sieh da, Timotheus, / Die Kraniche des Ibykus" (Look, look Timotheus, / The cranes of Ibykus). The robbers are arrested and brought to justice.

"Der Taucher" and "Der Handschuh" illustrate Schiller's concept of play. In the letters on aesthetic education, play is defined as any activity done merely for the pleasure involved without any thought of gain. If reward becomes the motivating factor the purity of the act is destroyed. In "Der Taucher" the king and his court are assembled on the cliffs of Messina overlooking the whirlpool known as Charybdis. Being in a playful mood, the king throws a golden goblet into the maelstrom and announces that whoever is intrepid enough to retrieve it can keep it as a symbol of his prowess. When none of the knights volunteers, a young squire steps forward, disrobes, and dives. A few minutes later he emerges with the goblet. Thrilled by the exploit and curious to hear more about the abyss and the gliding shadows the youth has described, the king announces that if he will dive a second time a fabulous ring and the king's beautiful daughter will be the reward. Even though the youth knows the danger, he dives. He never returns. Schiller's message is that when we act solely in accordance with reward, we corrupt not only the act but also ourselves.

In a letter to Goethe Schiller referred to "Der Handschuh" as a sequel to "Der Taucher." In this ballad the king and his court are seated around an arena containing a lion, tiger, and two leopards. Lady Kunigunde tosses her glove among the beasts, turns to the knight Delorges, and tells him that he can prove his love for her by retrieving the glove. Delorges casually descends among the animals, picks up the glove, and returns amid shouts of praise and wonder. Lady Kunigunde greets him with an expression promising sweet reward. At that moment he throws the glove in her face with the words "Den Dank, Dame, begehr ich nicht" (Thanks, lady, I don't desire) and leaves her forever. As with the first dive in "Der Taucher," Delorges performs his feat as an end in itself; when he realizes that Kunigunde thinks he risked his life for her reward, his reaction is the natural and spontaneous expression of utter contempt for someone who has entirely misjudged him.

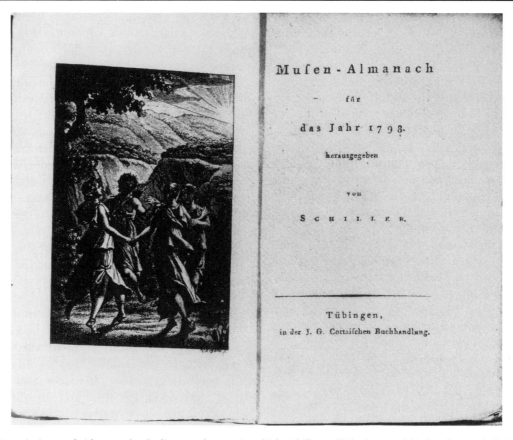

Frontispiece and title page for the literary almanac in which Schiller published some of his best-known ballads

These ballads in the *Musen-Almanach für das Jahr 1798*, and others which soon followed, are more responsible than any other factor for Schiller's popularity among the general public. Drawing his material from the widest range of literature, myth, philosophy, and history, he deals with ultimate questions about truth, beauty, and justice. After reading one of his ballads, one has the sensation of having undergone an elevating experience. The ballads are uneven in quality. Many are set in the Middle Ages, and he was not entirely successful in capturing the spirit of that time. He is at his best when he takes his material from classical antiquity, a subject which had fascinated him for years. "Die Kraniche des Ibykus," generally regarded as his finest ballad, has the force of an Aeschylean chorus.

In 1797 Schiller began work on the trilogy *Wallenstein* (1800; translated, 1800, 1830), which is often cited as the greatest German tragedy. Of all Schiller's historical plays, this one follows the actual events most closely. The play, which reflects his study of the Thirty Years War (published in 1791-1793), has a fearful, paranoid, doom-laden feeling. Schiller portrays a cold, cruel, and murderous world where power is the medium of exchange and lies, betrayal, and intrigue are the norm. Against this somber background looms the protagonist, Albrecht von Wallenstein, commander in chief of the Catholic army. An ambiguous figure, he is an austere, ambitious man driven to become central Europe's most powerful warlord and to found a new dynasty, even if these goals require him to rebel against Ferdinand, the Hapsburg emperor, and to plunge the entire continent into civil war. When the action begins he has already won the allegiance of the army and most of the officer corps away from Ferdinand. Yet he hesitates to come out in open revolt because he is not sure that the time is ripe. His irresolution does not spring from any inner struggle between right and wrong, for he is amoral. In this respect he stands in sharp contrast to Schiller's earlier creations, Karl Moor and the Marquis of Posa. Though they, too, rebel against established authority, they do so in the name of humanity. Wallenstein believes in nothing. He is motivated neither by guiding principle nor moral law. Believing that necessity rules the universe, he denies the possibility of free choice and claims that all human actions are predictable.

It is precisely Wallenstein's amoral and deterministic philosophy that leads him to make the mistakes which end in his downfall. His failure to give Ferdinand his full moral support arouses the emperor's suspicion; his belief in the predictability of human behavior causes him to misjudge the loyalty of his most trusted general, Octavio Piccolomini, as well as that of the army. By the time he realizes the magnitude of his errors it is too late. Deserted by the army and abandoned by his friends, he knows that there is not much point in fighting on; yet he perseveres with increasing energy and determination, thus evoking the audience's admiration, even though it knows that General Buttler and his assassins are on the move and that the duke is doomed. Ultimately, it is Wallenstein's self-assertion in the face of fortune which makes his death tragic. The play made a massive impression throughout Germany. Until then German literature could not boast of a drama of such magnitude, depth, sweep, and excellence. For the most part, the critics were overawed and contented themselves with trying to outdo one another in praising the work.

Following *Wallenstein* Schiller chose another historical subject, the three days preceding the execution of Mary Stuart, Queen of Scots, in 1587. The action of *Maria Stuart* (1801; translated as *Mary Stuart*, 1801) begins when Maria learns that the royal commission appointed by Elisabeth I has found her guilty of conspiring with others to assassinate the English queen. While Elisabeth procrastinates in signing the order of execution, Maria frantically tries to avert her fate. After Maria's failure in act 3 to persuade Elisabeth to release her, Mortimer, her jailer's nephew, heads a conspiracy to free her by force; he is driven by his passion for Maria. Leicester informs on him, and Mortimer kills himself as he is arrested. After an attempt by one of Mortimer's allies to assassinate her, Elisabeth signs the order of execution. It is carried out the next day.

The historical events provide the background for a story about rage, crime, remorse, and spiritual rebirth. In the first four acts Maria is not a heroine with whom audiences are expected to sympathize. She is a petty, vain, and insulting woman consumed by hatred for Elisabeth. Because of the many crimes of her youth, especially her complicity in the murder of her hus-

Watercolor by L. Wolf of act 5, scene 6 of Schiller's Maria Stuart: *Melvil kneels before Maria as she goes to her execution; Lord Leicester (right) looks on (Schiller National-Museum, Marbach)*

band, Lord Darnley, Maria's rage contains a quotient of self-condemnation; it is this remorse that eventually leads to her spiritual regeneration. One of Schiller's primary principles concerning the human condition, propounded in his theoretical writings on the sublime act, holds that a person who regrets a crime can regain peace of mind through voluntary self-punishment. The suffering brings about a change in character which amounts to a spiritual rebirth. For technical reasons, which he discusses in his theoretical writings, Schiller chose not to stage the moment of Maria's transformation but rather its effect on her character and bearing. To this end he uses the technique of contrast. First, he shows the unreconstructed Maria at her worst when she confronts Elisabeth in the third act. In this scene Maria loses her self-control and vents her pent-up hatred in a stream of verbal abuse culminating in the unparalleled and unforgivable insult: "Der Thron von England ist durch einen Bastard / Entweiht" (The throne of England is by a bas-

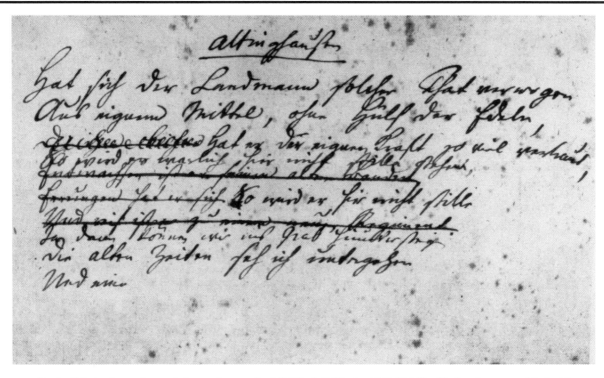

Draft of Attinghausen's speech in act 4, scene 2 of Schiller's Wilhelm Tell *(Schiller-Nationalmuseum, Marbach)*

tard / Profaned). Her transformation begins that night, when she realizes that the general uproar in the castle is not caused by her rescuers but by the workmen who are preparing her place of execution. Following an inner struggle, which happens offstage, she overcomes the negative qualities which led her not only into her earlier crimes but also into her present predicament. She even perceives a way to turn her execution for treason, of which she is innocent, into the means of her redemption: she chooses to regard her death as an atonement for her husband's murder. The effect of her inner transformation is seen through her serene speech and dignified bearing, which stand out in sharp contrast to the snarling shrew who called the queen of England a bastard. In the final scenes she projects an image of inner harmony and quiet tranquillity.

The first performance on 14 June 1800 at Weimar was a resounding success. After the play was issued in book form the following year, the literary critics spoke up. While praising the work's dramatic and linguistic qualities, they took its author to task for deviating from historical fact. They pointed out that the two queens had never met, that Elizabeth was not like Schiller's portrayal of her, that Mortimer never existed, and so on. Schiller shrugged off the criticism, for he had long since come to the conviction that art is not in the service of history. It is the dramatist's business to tell how things could or should have been, not how they were.

For the subject of his next play Schiller turned to the Joan of Arc legend. Beneath the surface action of *Die Jungfrau von Orleans*, which follows the historical events fairly closely until the final act, there is a conflict between duty and inclination, spirit and flesh. In the prologue Schiller emphasizes the conditions of Johanna's mission, which she will later violate: she is to lead the French army against the English, liberate Rheims, and crown the dauphin King Charles VII, and she will be given divine power to accomplish the task; under no circumstances, however, is she to entertain erotic thoughts but is to live by spirit alone. Johanna pursues her object relentlessly until, at the peak of fortune, she is suddenly paralyzed by a blind infatuation for a handsome young English officer, Lionel. Her divine powers vanish, and she is plunged into misery. Overcome with shame, guilt, and remorse she submits to her father's misguided accusations and to her unjust banishment from court for witchcraft as the means to atone for breaking her vow to God. After putting herself through more suffering and hardship, she emerges purified. With her charisma and powers restored she breaks out of the English prison and leads the French to victory. Schiller digresses considerably from history when he has her die of wounds received in battle.

The play premiered on 11 September 1801 at Leipzig and swept the audience off its feet; the reaction was repeated in succeeding performances around the country. The critics, of course, were upset at his deviation from the facts, but hardly anyone paid any attention to them. *Die Jungfrau von Orleans* was Schiller's most popular play and remained in the permanent repertoires of almost all German theaters throughout the nineteenth century. The drama was largely responsible for overturning the prevailing notion–propounded in Voltaire's scurrilous *La Pucelle* (1755)–that Joan of Arc was a charismatic charlatan who whored her way through regiments to achieve dubious ends: such was the influence of this play that historians and the clergy reopened the case and got at the facts. That Joan of Arc was finally canonized in 1920 can be traced directly back to Schiller's drama.

Schiller's long fascination with classical antiquity inspired him to write a tragedy in the style of the Athenian tragic poets. *Die Braut von Messina oder Die feindlichen Brüder* (The Bride of Messina; or, The Enemy Brothers, 1803; translated as *The Bride of Messina*, 1837) incorporates such features as the chorus, pity and fear, recognition-reversal, tragic error, and catharsis. And, as in the ancient tragedies, within the classical structure unfolds a most unsavory tale of outrages against nature. An old king, enraged at his son's eloping with the woman he desired for himself, rapes her and then lays a curse on her progeny. Prophecies and dreams of doom foretell the birth of a daughter who will cause the dynasty's destruction. Transgressing against nature, the new king orders the infant, Beatrice, flung into the sea. Queen Isabella, however, spirits the child away to a convent, where she matures into a ravishing beauty. Ignorant of her true identity, her brothers Cesar and Manuel, who are divided by an unnatural and morbid hatred, meet and fall in love with her. In a jealous fury Cesar kills Manuel. The catastrophe is brought on not only by the abnormal deeds of the individual characters but also by the unnatural presence of the family in Messina. Several times the chorus complains that the ancestors of the ruling family came from across the seas to conquer and then to divide into warring camps a people who had lived in peace-

Schiller in 1804; drawing by J. Gottfried Schadow Nationalgalerie, Berlin)

ful harmony with themselves and with nature. The play is one of Schiller's strongest depictions of what can happen when human beings violate the natural order. Structurally, *Die Braut von Messina* is the most carefully composed of Schiller's dramas; it is noted for its economy of form and its symmetry. Yet he was unable to breathe life into it, and the play remains a passive experience. He avoided the very things in which he excelled: portraying vividly drawn characters in vigorous action and speaking virtuoso dialogue. Most critics agree that it is an interesting experiment which failed. It premiered on 19 March 1803 in Weimar and closed after a few performances.

After the cold, gray aloofness of *Die Braut von Messina*, Schiller wrote a hit noted for its color and warmth. *Wilhelm Tell* (1804; translated as *William Tell*, 1829) is his most widely known drama outside Germany. Few people have not heard the legend of how Geßler, the cruel Austrian governor of the Cantons Schwyz and Uri, places his hat atop a pole and commands the people to bow to it. Tell does not bow and as punish-

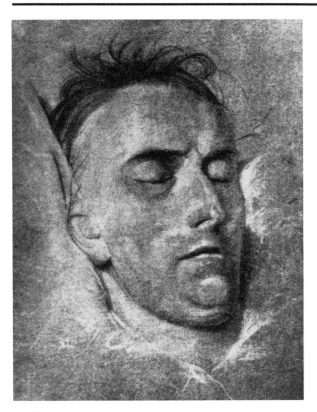

Schiller on his deathbed; pastel drawing by F. Jagemann (Gustav Könnecke, Bilderatlas zur Geschichte der deutschen Nationallitteratur *[Graz: Akademische Druck- und Verlagsanstalt, 1981])*

ment must pierce with an arrow an apple on his son's head. Geßler arrests Tell by trickery, but Tell escapes from the prison ship and slays the tyrant. Parallel to Tell's adventure run two other independent plots. The first is known as the Rütli Confederacy. During the night of 7-8 November 1307 representatives from three cantons meet at a clearing in the forest called the Rütli to plan an armed revolt. They decide to strike after Christmas. The second plot involves the young Swiss nobleman Rudenz von Attinghausen, who has turned his back on his countrymen because he loves the beautiful Berta von Bruneck. When he learns that he can win her only through Swiss independence, he has a change of heart. The three independent plots come together in act 5: when the Rütli Confederacy learns of Geßler's death the leaders decide to launch the revolt immediately, and Rudenz joins them. Most of act 5 is devoted to the storming of the castles and the expulsion of the last Austrian governor. At this point Schiller added a scene which is extraneous to the action: Duke Johannes of Swabia, called Parricida in the play, has assassinated the Austrian emperor Ferdinand for withholding his inheritance.

Pursued by soldiers, he seeks out Tell to beg for help because, as he explains, their deeds are similar. Tell stoutly denies any resemblance between them but gives assistance when he sees that Parricida is remorseful and wants to expiate his crime. This scene has often been criticized as gratuitous and out of harmony with the rest of the play, and it is almost always omitted when the play is performed. Yet Schiller felt compelled to justify Tell even more by contrasting his deed with Parricida's purely selfish, revengeful act.

The play dramatizes Schiller's thoughts on revolution (when it is justified, and that force should be applied without bloodshed) and his theory of social evolution. In his essay on aesthetic education he links civilization's upward course to the development of the rational faculty. In the figure of Wilhelm Tell he demonstrates how an individual, and by extension humanity, might progress from a naive state of oneness with nature through the moral state to the aesthetic state. In the first half of the play Tell displays the qualities of a person living in a state of nature: he is a unity within himself and lives at one with his environment. The basis of his morality is feeling, not reason. His actions are spontaneous and unpremeditated, as when he rescues Baumgarten from the pursuing soldiers in act 1. His naive simplicity is also apparent in his speech: a man of few words, he usually confines himself to proverbs. Tell's oneness is destroyed when Geßler orders him to risk his son's life, thereby forcing him to act contrary to his nature and to nature itself. At this point Tell is driven from the natural state into the moral state. In his essay "Über das Erhabene" (On the Sublime), written in 1793 and published in volume 3 of his *Kleinere prosaische Schriften* (Shorter Prose Writings, 1792-1802) in 1801, Schiller says that such an event always happens suddenly and without warning. From this point forward Tell is a different person. The change is at once apparent in his manner of speech: it is no longer a series of set phrases, as can be seen, for instance, in his vivid account of how he escaped from Geßler's ship and in his conversation with Johannes Parricida in act 5. As he awaits Geßler at the Hohle Gasse, Tell delivers a monologue in which he recalls his former inner unity and oneness with nature, then reflects upon how he has changed. He reasons that he must kill Geßler to protect not only his own family but also the Swiss people. He does not shoot Geßler in a blind fury as Cesar stabs his brother; rather, it is a premeditated act performed in full awareness of its necessity. In Schiller's terminology, Tell is forced to act sublimely; that is, he must overcome his natural feeling of revulsion at taking a human life and act solely according to what reason tells him is required. Tell's reason has been brought fully into play and can now operate in concert with his feelings. In the final scenes Tell has achieved that higher synthesis of the sense-drive and the form-drive that constitutes the aesthetic state.

For his next play Schiller turned to the life of Demetrius, the false czar. From the many fragments and notes he left behind it is possible to say that the work promised to be his crowning achievement; but he was unable to complete it. Early in 1805 his health began a rapid deterioration. On 1 May he contracted double pneumonia. Until his death on 9 May he drifted in and out of delirium. Among his last words, spoken in hallucination, were: "Ist das eure Himmel, ist das eure Hölle?" (Is that your heaven, is that your hell?). Schiller was first buried in the St. Jakobskirche cemetery in Weimar. From there his remains were removed to the Weimar Princes' Mausoleum. His coffin lies next to Goethe's.

Schiller's influence has been profound and far-reaching. The psychologist Carl Gustav Jung, for example, devotes two chapters of his *Psychologische Typen* (Psychological Types, 1921) to a discussion of "Über Naive und sentimentalische Dichtung" and stresses the importance of Schiller's typology of human nature to the development of his own theory. Friedrich Nietzsche's distinction between the Apollonian and the Dionysian can be traced directly to Schiller's essay. In aesthetics, Georg Wilhelm Friedrich Hegel's *Phenomenologie des Geistes* (Phenomenology of Spirit, 1807) was deeply indebted to Schiller on the crucial point of the dialectical reconciliation of opposites and the dynamic concept of harmony, which Hegel formulates in his triad of thesis-antithesis-synthesis. Schiller's concept of art as aesthetic play has given rise to many play theories of art and education. In political theory Schiller's most notable influence is found in the early writings of Karl Marx. Schiller's remarks about the negative effect of the division of labor on the human psyche led Marx to work out his whole-man theory, according to which the task of the state is to create conditions which will promote the harmonious coordination of all of each person's forces and faculties; the ultimate result, as in Schiller's program, will be the gradual disappearance of the state as a political organization.

Schiller's life and works continue to be studied and analyzed with an intensity accorded those of few other writers. Essays and monographs number in the thousands. The average German citizen regards the author as something like a national monument. Schiller's legacy shows few signs of fading away.

Letters:
Briefwechsel zwischen Schiller und Goethe in den Jahren 1794 bis 1805, 4 volumes (Stuttgart & Tübingen: Cotta, 1828-1829);
Correspondence of Schiller with Körner, Comprising Sketches and Anecdotes of Goethe, the Schlegels, Wieland, and Other Contemporaries, 3 volumes, translated by Leonard Simpson (London: Bentley, 1849);
Briefwechsel zwischen Schiller und Cotta, edited by Wilhelm Vollmer (Stuttgart: Cotta, 1876);
Briefe: Kritische Gesamtausgabe, 7 volumes, edited by Fritz Jonas (Stuttgart: Deutsche Verlags-Anstalt, 1892-1896);
Ausgewählte Briefe, edited by Henry B. Garland (Manchester, U.K.: Manchester University Press, 1959);
Der Briefwechsel zwischen Schiller und Goethe, edited by Paul Stapf (Berlin: Tempel, 1960);
Der Briefwechsel zwischen Friedrich Schiller und Wilhelm von Humboldt, 2 volumes, edited by Siegfried Seidel (Berlin: Aufbau, 1962);
Der Briefwechsel zwischen Schiller und Goethe, edited by Emil Staiger (Frankfurt am Main: Insel, 1966);
Briefe: In zwei Bänden, 2 volumes, edited by Karl-Heinz Hahn (Berlin & Weimar: Aufbau, 1968);
Briefe des jungen Schiller (1776-1789), edited by Karl Pörnbacher (Munich: Kösel, 1969);
Schillers Briefe, edited by Erwin Streitfeld (Königstein: Athenäum, 1983).

Bibliographies:
Wolfgang Vulpius, *Schiller Bibliographie 1893-1958* (Weimar: Arion, 1959);
Richard Pick, "Schiller in England 1787-1960: A Bibliography," *Publications of the English Goethe Society*, 30 (1961): 832-862;
Vulpius, *Schiller Bibliographie 1959-1963* (Berlin & Weimar: Aufbau, 1967);
Herbert Marcuse, ed., *Schiller-Bibliographie* (Hildesheim: Gerstenberg, 1971);
Peter Wersig, *Schiller Bibliographie 1964-1974* (Berlin & Weimar: Aufbau, 1977);

*Schiller's final resting place: the Princes' Mausoleum, Weimar; engraving by Nemetschek of an 1828 drawing by Stark
(Gustav Könnecke, Bilderatlas zur Geschichte der deutschen Nationallitteratur
[Graz: Akademische Druck- und Verlagsanstalt, 1981])*

Ingrid Hannich-Bode, "Schiller Bibliographie 1974-1978 und Nachträge," *Jahrbuch der Deutschen Schillergesellschaft* (1979): 549-612.

Biographies:

Thomas Carlyle, *The Life of Friedrich Schiller* (London: Chapman & Hall, 1825);

Heinrich Düntzer, *Schillers Leben* (Leipzig: Fues, 1881); translated by Percey Pinkerton as *The Life of Schiller* (London: Macmillan, 1883);

Calvin Thomas, *The Life and Works of Friedrich Schiller* (New York: Holt, 1901);

Reinhard Buchwald, *Schiller: Leben und Werk*, 2 volumes (Leipzig: Insel, 1937);

Benno von Wiese, *Schiller: Einführung in Leben und Welt* (Stuttgart: Reclam, 1959);

Friedrich Burschell, *Schiller* (Hamburg: Rowohlt, 1968);

Peter Lahnstein, *Schillers Leben* (Munich: List, 1981);

Eike Middell, *Friedrich Schiller: Leben und Werk*, second edition (Leipzig: Reclam, 1982).

References:

Rainer Blesch, *Drama und wirkungsästhetische Praxis: Zum Problem der ästhetischen Vermittlung bei Schiller* (Frankfurt am Main: Fischer, 1981);

Paul Böckmann, *Strukturprobleme in Schillers "Don Karlos"* (Heidelberg: Winter, 1982);

Albert James Camigliano, *Friedrich Schiller and Christian Gottfried Körner: A Critical Relationship* (Stuttgart: Heinz, 1976);

Ronald L. Crawford, *Images of Transience in the Poems and Ballads of Friedrich Schiller* (Bern: Lang, 1977);

Hans-Dietrich Dahnke, *Goethe und Schiller: Werk und Wirkung* (Weimar: Nationale Forschungs- und Gedenkstätten der klassischen deutschen Literatur, 1981);

Peter M. Daly, *Text- und Variantenkonkordanz zu Schillers "Kabale und Liebe"* (Berlin: De Gruyter, 1976);

Kenneth Dewhurst, and Nigel Reeves, *Friedrich Schiller: Medicine, Psychology, and Literature* (Berkeley: University of California Press, 1978);

Christina Didier, *Das Schillerhaus in Weimar* (Weimar: Nationale Forschungs- und Gedenkstätten der klassischen deutschen Literatur, 1979);

Hermann Fähnrich, *Schillers Musikalität und Musikanschauung* (Hildesheim: Gerstenberg, 1977);

John R. Frey, ed., *Schiller 1759-1959: Commemorative American Studies* (Urbana: University of Illinois Press, 1959);

Friedrich Schiller: Kunst, Humanität und Politik in der späten Aufklärung: Ein Symposium (Tübingen: Niemeyer, 1982);

Henry B. Garland, *Schiller* (London: Harrap, 1949);

Dietrich Germann, *Ich habe dir also von Schiller zu erzählen: Dokumente und Zeugnisse aus Schillers Jenaer Jahren* (Jena: Stadtmuseum, 1982);

Alfons Glück, *Schillers Wallenstein* (Munich: Fink, 1976);

Ilse Graham, *Schiller's Drama: Talent and Integrity* (New York: Barnes & Noble, 1974);

André von Gronicka, "Friedrich Schiller's Marquis Posa: A Character Study," *Germanic Review*, 26 (1951): 196-214;

Hans Henning, ed., *Schillers "Kabale und Liebe" in der zeitgenössischen Rezeption* (Leipzig: Zentralantiquariat, 1976);

Walter Hinderer, *Der Mensch in der Geschichte: Ein Versuch über Schillers Wallenstein* (Königstein: Athenäum, 1980);

Hinderer, ed., *Schillers Dramen: Neue Interpretationen* (Stuttgart: Reclam, 1979);

Rolf Hochhuth, *Räuber-Rede: Drei deutsche Vorwürfe. Schiller, Lessing, Geschwister Scholl* (Reinbek: Rowohlt, 1982);

Renate Homann, *Erhabenes und Satirisches: Zur Grundlegung einer Theorie ästhetischer Literatur bei Kant und Schiller* (Munich: Fink, 1977);

Falk Horst, *Der Leitgedanke von der Vollkommenheit der Natur in Schillers klassischem Werk* (Cirencester: Lang, 1980);

Karl-Heinz Hucke, *Jene "Scheu vor allem Mercantilischen": Schillers "Arbeits- und Finanzplan"* (Tübingen: Niemeyer, 1984);

Rudolf Ibel, *Friedrich Schiller: Die Räuber* (Frankfurt am Main: Diesterweg, 1982);

Rolf-Peter Janz, *Autonomie und soziale Funktion der Kunst: Studien zur Ästhetik von Schiller und Novalis* (Stuttgart, 1973);

Gerhard Kaiser, *Von Arkadien nach Elysium: Schiller-Studien* (Göttingen: Vandenhoeck & Ruprecht, 1978);

Helmut Koopman, *Friedrich Schiller*, 2 volumes (Stuttgart: Metzler, 1966; revised, 1977);

Koopman, *Schiller-Forschung: 1970-1980. Ein Bericht* (Marbach am Neckar: Deutsche Schillergesellschaft, 1982);

Irmgard Kowatzki, *Der Begriff des Spiels als ästhetisches Phänomen: Von Schiller bis Benn* (Bern: Lang, 1973);

Herbert Kraft, *Um Schiller betrogen* (Pfullingen: Neske, 1978);

Fritz Kühnlenz, *Schiller in Thüringen: Stätten seines Lebens und Wirkens*, second edition (Rudolstadt: Greifenverlag, 1976);

Marietta Kuntz, *Schillers Theaterpraxis* (Zurich: Juris, 1979);

Eduard Lachmann, *Die Natur des Demetrius* (Hildesheim: Gerstenberg, 1975);

Rolf N. Linn, *Schillers junge Idealisten* (Berkeley & London: University of California Press, 1973);

William P. Mainland, *Schiller and the Changing Past* (London: Heinemann, 1957);

Heinrich Mettler, *Entfremdung und Revolution: Brennpunkt des Klassischen. Studien zu Schillers Briefen "Über die ästhetische Erziehung des Menschen" im Hinblick auf die Begegnung mit Goethe* (Bern: Francke, 1977);

Peter Michelsen, *Der Bruch mit der Vater-Welt: Studien zu Schillers "Räubern"* (Heidelberg: Winter, 1979);

Wolfgang Militz, *Friedrich Schiller: Ein Weg zum Geist* (Stuttgart, 1974);

R. D. Miller, *The Drama of Schiller* (Harrogate, U.K.: Duchy Press, 1963);

Horst Nitschack, *Kritik der ästhetischen Wirklichkeitskonstitution: Eine Untersuchung zu den ästhetischen Schriften Kants und Schillers* (Frankfurt am Main: Roter Stern, 1976);

Birgit Osterwald, *Das Demetrius-Thema in der russischen und deutschen Literatur: Dargestellt an A. P. Sumarokovs "Dimitrij Samozvanec," A. S. Puskins "Boris Godunov" und F. Schillers "Demetrius"* (Münster: Aschendorff, 1982);

Charles E. Passage, *Friedrich Schiller* (New York: Ungar, 1975);

Helmut Pillau, *Die fortgedachte Dissonanz: Hegels Tragödientheorie und Schillers Tragödie. Deutsche Antworten auf die Französische Revolution* (Munich: Fink, 1981);

Hans-Georg Pott, *Die schöne Freiheit: Eine Interpretation zu Schillers Schrift Über die ästhetische Erziehung des Menschen in einer Reihe von Briefen* (Munich: Fink, 1980);

Deric Regin, *Freedom and Dignity: The Historical and Philosophical Thought of Schiller* (The Hague: Nijhoff, 1965);

Vicky Rippere, *Schiller and "Alienation"* (Bern: Lang, 1981);

Henning Rischbieter, *Friedrich Schiller*, 2 volumes, second edition (Munich: Deutscher Taschenbuch Verlag, 1969-1975);

Willy Rosalewski, *Schillers Ästhetik im Verhältnis zur Kantischen* (Nendeln, Liechtenstein: Kraus, 1978);

Georg Ruppelt, *Schiller im nationalsozialistischen Deutschland: Der Versuch einer Gleichschaltung* (Stuttgart: Metzler, 1979);

Friedegard Schaefer, *Friedrich Schiller* (Berlin: Stadtbibliothek, 1980);

Joachim Schmidt-Neubauer, *Tyrannei und der Mythos zum Glück: Drei Essays zu Lessing, Schiller und Goethe* (Frankfurt am Main: Fischer, 1981);

Hans H. Schulte, *"Werke der Begeisterung": Friedrich Schiller–Idee und Eigenart seines Schaffens* (Bonn: Bouvier, 1980);

Lesley Sharpe, *Schiller and the Historical Character: Presentation and Interpretation in the Historiographical Works and in the Historical Dramas* (Oxford: Oxford University Press, 1982);

Sigrid Siedhoff, *Der Dramaturg Schiller, "Egmont": Goethes Text, Schillers Bearbeitung* (Bonn: Bouvier, 1983);

Andreas Siekmann, *Drama und sentimentalisches Bewußtsein: Zur klassischen Dramatik Schillers* (Frankfurt am Main: Haag-Herchen, 1980);

John D. Simons, *Friedrich Schiller* (Boston: Twayne, 1981);

E. L. Stahl, *Friedrich Schiller's Drama: Theory and Practice* (Oxford: Clarendon Press, 1954);

Emil Staiger, *Friedrich Schiller* (Zurich: Atlantis, 1967);

Staiger, *Friedrich Schlegels Sieg über Schiller* (Heidelberg: Winter, 1981);

Paul Steck, *Schiller und Shakespeare: Idee und Wirklichkeit* (Frankfurt am Main: Lang, 1977);

Gerhard Storz, *Der Dichter Friedrich Schiller* (Stuttgart: Klett, 1963);

Heinrich Teutschmann, *Schillers verborgene Schöpfung* (Dornach, Switzerland: Philosophisch-Anthroposophischer Verlag, 1977);

Peter Utz, *Die ausgehöhlte Gasse: Stationen der Wirkungsgeschichte von Schillers "Wilhelm Tell"* (Königstein: Forum Academicum, 1984);

Julia Wernly, *Prolegomena zu einem Lexikon der ästhetisch-ethischen Terminologie Friedrich Schillers* (Hildesheim: Gerstenberg, 1975);

Leonard P. Wessell, *The Philosophical Background to Friedrich Schiller's Aesthetics of Living Form* (Frankfurt am Main: Lang, 1982);

Benno von Wiese, *Friedrich Schiller*, fourth edition (Stuttgart: Metzler, 1978);

Kenneth Parmelee Wilcox, *Anmut und Würde: Die Dialektik der menschlichen Vollendung bei Schiller* (Bern: Lang, 1981);

Gero von Wilpert, *Schiller-Chronik: Sein Leben und Schaffen* (Stuttgart: Kröner, 1958);

Andreas Wirth, *Das schwierige Schöne: Zu Schillers Ästhetik. Auch eine Interpretation der Abhandlung "Über Matthissons Gedichte," 1794* (Bonn: Bouvier, 1975);

William Witte, *Schiller* (Oxford: Blackwell, 1949);

Wolfgang Wittkowski, ed., *Friedrich Schiller: Ein Symposium* (Tübingen: Niemeyer, 1982);

Helga Zepp-LaRouche, *Das geheime Wissen des Friedrich Schiller* (Wiesbaden: Campaigner, 1979);

Theodore Ziolkowski, *The Classical German Elegy* (Princeton: Princeton University Press, 1980), pp. 3-134.

Papers:

More than half of Friedrich Schiller's papers are in the Schiller National-Museum at Marbach am Neckar. The remainder are deposited in the Goethe-und-Schiller Archiv, Weimar. A selection from his personal library and memorabilia is on display at his house in Weimar, Schillerstaße 12, which is now a museum.

August Wilhelm Schlegel

(5 September 1767 - 12 May 1845)

Thomas G. Sauer
University of Virginia

BOOKS: *De geographia Homerica commentatio, quae in concertatione civium academiae Georgiae Augustae IV Junii proxime ad praemium accessisse pronuntiata est* (Hannover: Schmidt, 1788);

Gedichte (Tübingen: Cotta, 1800);

Ehrenpforte und Triumphbogen für den Theater-Präsidenten von Kotzebue bey seiner gehofften Rückkehr ins Vaterland, anonymous (Leipzig, 1801);

Charakteristiken und Kritiken, 2 volumes, by Schlegel and Friedrich Schlegel (Königsberg: Nicolovius, 1801)–includes "Über Shakespeares Romeo und Julie," translated by Julius Charles Hare as "A. W. Schlegel on Shakespeare's *Romeo and Juliet,* with Remarks upon the Character of German Criticism," *Olliers Literary Miscellany,* 1 (1820): 1-29;

An das Publikum: Rüge einer in der Jenaischen Allgemeinen Literatur-Zeitung begangnen Ehrenschändung (Tübingen: Cotta, 1802);

Ion: Ein Schauspiel (Hamburg: Perthes, 1803);

Rom: Elegie (Berlin: Unger, 1805);

Comparaison entre la Phèdre de Racine et celle d'Euripide (Paris: Tourneisen, 1807); translated into German by H. J. von Collin as *Vergleichung der Phädra des Racine mit der des Euripides* (Vienna: Printed by A. Pichler, 1808);

Über dramatische Kunst und Litteratur: Vorlesungen, 2 volumes in 3 (Heidelberg: Mohr & Zimmer, 1809-1811); translated by John Black as *A Course of Lectures on Dramatic Art and Literature* (2 volumes, London: Printed for Baldwin, Cradock & Joy, 1815; 1 volume, Philadelphia: Hogan & Thompson, 1833); translation revised by A. J. W. Morrison (London: Bohn, 1846; reprinted, New York: AMS Press, 1973);

Poetische Werke, 2 volumes (Heidelberg: Mohr & Zimmer, 1811);

Werke, 3 volumes (Upsala: Bruzelius, 1812-1817);

Betrachtungen über die Politik der dänischen Regierung (Berlin: Reimer, 1813);

Proclamation Sr. Königl. Hoheit des Kronprinzen von Schweden und im Hauptquartier der vereinigten

Oil painting by H. C. Kolbe, circa 1820 (Josef Körner, ed., Briefe von und an August Wilhelm Schlegel, *1930)*

Armee von Nord-Deutschland bekannt gemachte Berichte vom Anfang der Kriegs-Operationen bis zum 10. Nov. 1813 (Göttingen: Dieterich, 1813);

Remarques sur un article de la Gazette de Leipsic du 5. octobre 1813: Relatif au prince royal de Suède (Leipzig & Altenburg: Brockhaus, 1813); German version published as *Bemerkungen über einen Artikel der Leipziger Zeitung vom 5ten Oktober 1813* (Göttingen, 1813); revised as *Ueber Napoleon Buonaparte und den*

Kronprinzen von Schweden, eine Parallele in Beziehung auf einen Artikel der Leipziger Zeitung vom 5ten Oktober 1813 (N.p., 1814);

Sur le système continental et sur ses rapports avec la suède (Hamburg, 1813); German version published as *Ueber das Continentalsystem und den Einfluß desselben auf Schweden* (Berlin: Reimer, 1813); translated anonymously as *The Continental System and Its Relations with Sweden* (London: Stockdale, 1813);

Réflexions sur l'état actuel de la Norvège (London, 1814);

Tableau de l'état politique et moral de l'empire français en 1813 (Hannover & London, 1814);

Lettre aux éditeurs de la bibliothèque italienne, sur les chevaux de bronze de Venise (Florence: Marenigh, 1816);

Rezension von Niebuhrs Römischer Geschichte (Hannover, 1816);

Le couronnement de la Sainte Vierge, et les miracles de Saint-Dominique: Tableau de Jean de Fiesole, publié en quinze planches par Guillaume Ternite. Avec une notice sur la vie du peintre et une explication du tableau par A.-G. de Sch. (Paris, 1817); German version published as *Mariä Krönung und die Wunder des heiligen Dominicus nach Johann von Fiesole, in fünfzehn Blättern; gezeichnet von Wilhelm Ternite: Nebst einer Nachricht vom Leben des Malers und Erklärung des Gemäldes* (Paris, 1817);

Observations sur la langue et la littérature provençales (Paris: Librairie grecque-latine-allemande, 1818);

Vorlesungen über Theorie und Geschichte der bildenden Künste: Gehalten in Berlin, im Sommer 1827 (Berlin: Schlesinger, 1827);

Berichtigung einiger Mißdeutungen (Berlin: Reimer, 1828);

Kritische Schriften, 2 volumes (Berlin: Reimer, 1828);

Réflexions sur l'étude des langues asiatiques adressées à Sir James Mackintosh, suivies d'une lettre à M. Horace Hayman Wilson (Bonn: Weber, 1832);

Essais littéraires et historiques (Bonn: Weber, 1842);

Oeuvres de M. Auguste-Guillaume de Schlegel écrites en français, 3 volumes, edited by Eduard Böcking (Leipzig: Weidmann, 1846);

Sämmtliche Werke, 12 volumes, edited by Böcking (Leipzig: Weidmann, 1846-1847; reprinted, Hildesheim & New York: Olms, 1971);

Opuscula quae Augustus Guilelmus Schlegelius latine scripta reliquit, edited by Böcking (Leipzig: Weidmann, 1848);

Vorlesungen über schöne Litteratur und Kunst, 3 volumes, edited by Jakob Minor (Heilbronn: Henninger, 1884; reprinted, Nendeln: Kraus, 1968);

Vorlesungen über philosophische Kunstlehre, edited by August Wünsche (Leipzig: Dieterich, 1911);

Geschichte der deutschen Sprache und Poesie: Vorlesungen, gehalten an der Universität Bonn seit dem Wintersemester 1818/19, edited by Josef Körner (Berlin: Behr, 1913; reprinted, Nendeln, Liechtenstein: Kraus, 1968);

Vorlesungen über dramatische Kunst und Litteratur, 2 volumes, edited by Giovanni V. Amoretti (Bonn: Schroeder, 1923);

Kritische Schriften und Briefe, 7 volumes, edited by Edgar Lohner (Stuttgart: Kohlhammer, 1962-1974);

Kritische Schriften, edited by Emil Staiger (Zurich: Artemis, 1963);

Vorlesungen über das akademische Studium, edited by Frank Jolles (Heidelberg: Stiehm, 1971).

Edition in English: *Ariadne*, translated by Elfa L. Harvey (Frankfurt am Main, 1847).

OTHER: Joachim Rendorp, *Geheime Nachrichten zur Aufklärung der Vorfälle während des letzten Krieges zwischen England und Holland*, translated by Schlegel (Leipzig: Brockhaus, 1793);

William Shakespeare, *Dramatische Werke*, 9 volumes, translated by Schlegel (Berlin: Unger, 1797-1810);

Athenaeum: Eine Zeitschrift, 3 volumes, edited, with contributions, by Schlegel and Friedrich Schlegel (volume 1, Berlin: Vieweg, 1798; volumes 2-3, Berlin: Fröhlich, 1799-1800);

Shakespeare, *Hamlet*, translated, with preface, by Schlegel (Berlin: Unger, 1800);

Horace Walpole, *Historische, literarische und unterhaltende Schriften*, translated by Schlegel (Leipzig: Hartknoch, 1800);

Johann Gottlieb Fichte, *Friedrich Nicolai's Leben und sonderbare Meinungen: Ein Beitrag zur Litteraturgeschichte des vergangenen und zur Pädagogik des angehenden Jahrhunderts*, edited by Schlegel (Tübingen: Cotta, 1801);

Musen-Almanach für das Jahr 1802, edited by Schlegel and Ludwig Tieck (Tübingen: Cotta, 1802);

Spanisches Theater, 2 volumes, translated and edited by Schlegel (volume 1, Berlin: Unger, 1803; volume 2, Hitzig, 1809);

Wilhelm von Schütz, *Lacrimas: Ein Schauspiel*, edited by Schlegel (Berlin: Realschulbuchhandlung, 1804);

Blumensträuße italiänischer, spanischer und portugiesischer Poesie, translated and edited and with contributions, by Schlegel (Berlin: Realschulbuchhandlung, 1804);

Pellegrin (Friedrich de la Motte-Fouqué), *Dramatische Spiele*, edited by Schlegel (Berlin: Unger, 1804);

Dépêches et lettres interceptées par des partis détachés de l'armée combinée du nord de l'Allemagne, edited by Schlegel (Paris: Les marchands de nouveautés, 1814); translated anonymously into German as *Interessante Staatsschriften und Briefe aufgefangen von Streif-Partheien der vereinigten Armee von Nord-Deutschland* (Hannover: Hahn, 1814); translated anonymously as *Copies of the Original Letters and Despatches of the Generals, Ministers, Grand Officers of State, &c. at Paris, to the Emperor Napoleon, at Dresden: Intercepted by the Advanced Troops of the Allies in the North of Germany* (London: Printed for John Murray by W. Clowes, 1814);

Anne Louise Germaine de Staël, *Considérations sur les événements principaux de la révolution française, ouvrage posthume, publié par M. le Duc de Broglie et M. le Baron de Staël*, 3 volumes, edited by Schlegel (Paris: Delaunay, Bossange & Masson, 1818);

Albertine Necker de Saussure, *Über den Charakter und die Schriften der Frau von Staël*, translated by Schlegel (Paris, London & Strasbourg: Treuttel, 1820);

Sophie Bernhardi, *Flore und Blanchefleur: Romantisches Gedicht in zwölf Gesängen*, edited by Schlegel (Berlin: Reimer, 1822);

Bhagavad-Gita, id est Thespesion melos sive almi Krishnae et Arjunae colloquium de rebus divinis, Bharateae episodium, edited and translated by Schlegel (Bonn: Weber, 1823);

Indische Bibliothek: Eine Zeitschrift, 3 volumes, edited, with contributions, by Schlegel (Bonn: Weber, 1823-1830);

Hitopadesas, id est, Institutio salutarius, 2 volumes, edited and translated by Schlegel and Christian Lassen (Bonn: Weber, 1829-1831);

Ramayana, id est, carmen epicum de Ramae rebus gestis poetae antiqissimi Valmicis opus, 4 volumes, edited and translated by Schlegel (Bonn: Weber, 1829-1846);

J. C. Prichard, *Darstellung der Aegyptischen Mythologie*, translated by L. Haymann, preface by Schlegel (Bonn: Weber, 1837);

Verzeichniß einer von Eduard Alton hinterlassenen Gemäldesammlung: Nebst einer Vorerinnerung und

ausführlicher Beurtheilung dreier darin befindlicher Bilder, edited by Schlegel (Bonn, 1840);

Shakespeare, *A. W. Schlegels erste Übersetzung des Sommernachtstraums*, edited by Frank Jolles (Göttingen: Vandenhoeck & Ruprecht, 1967).

The lectures, essays, and translations of August Wilhelm Schlegel count among the most significant productions of German Early Romanticism. One of the great intermediaries in the history of literature, he awakened Germany through his translations and critical essays to previously unknown or unappreciated works and traditions. Moreover, through his *Über dramatische Kunst und Litteratur: Vorlesungen* (1809-1811; translated as *A Course of Lectures on Dramatic Art and Literature*, 1815), which was quickly translated into French, English, and Italian, he established German literary theory and criticism as an international model whose influence pervaded the first half of the nineteenth century. If there is one figure who can be called central to Romanticism as an international phenomenon, it is Schlegel. His primary achievement as a critic was to synthesize, systematize, and clarify the program of Early Romanticism, but he brought to that program a distinct emphasis which was his own: a view of the unity of the work of art as the product of the consummate technical skill and "tiefe Absichtlichkeit" (deep intentionality) of the artist.

Schlegel was born on 5 September 1767 in Hannover, the fourth son of Johann Adolph Schlegel and Christiane Erdmuthe Hübsch Schlegel. His father was a Lutheran pastor with a minor literary career and the brother of the dramatist Johann Elias Schlegel. After completing his schooling in Hannover in the spring of 1786 he went to the University of Göttingen, where he began studying theology but soon switched to ancient and modern literature. He studied Greek and Roman literature under Christian Gottlob Heyne and published a treatise in Latin on Homer's geography (1788); he wrote poetry and translated Shakespeare and Petrarch under his other mentor, the poet Gottfried August Bürger. His poems appeared in Dietrich's *Musenalmanach* between 1788 and 1792 and in Bürger's *Akademie der schönen Redekunste* in 1790. He also wrote a series of reviews for the *Göttingische Anzeigen von gelehrten Sachen* between 1789 and 1791 and in 1791 published in Bürger's *Akademie der schönen Redekünste* his first important critical studies, a discussion of Friedrich Schiller's "Die Künstler" (The Artists,

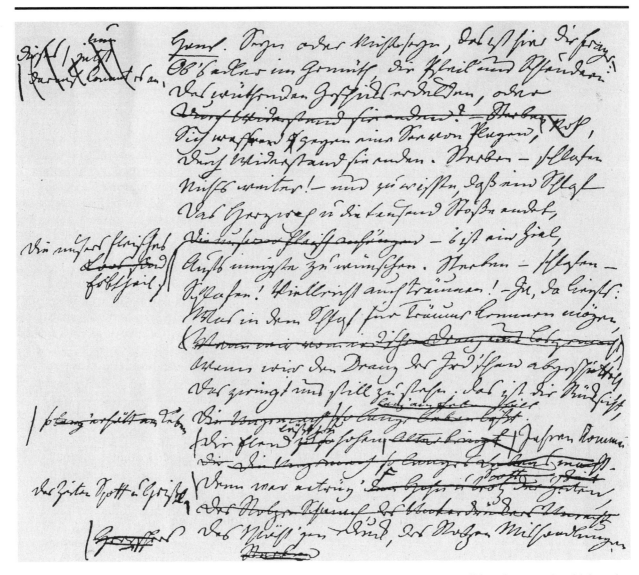

Manuscript for Schlegel's translation of the soliloquy from Hamlet *(Gustav Könnecke,* Bilderatlas zur Geschichte der deutschen Nationallitteratur *[Graz: Akademische Druck- und Verlagsanstalt, 1981])*

1789) and an essay on Dante's *Divine Comedy*.

At the completion of his studies in 1791 his hopes for a diplomatic career went unfulfilled. He accepted a position as tutor in the household of a wealthy businessman in Amsterdam, where he remained for four years. During this time he began the intellectual interchange with his younger brother Friedrich that was to have a profound influence on his work. He translated sections of the *Divine Comedy* and of Shakespeare's *Romeo and Juliet* and, at Friedrich's suggestion, began working on *Hamlet*. Schiller invited him to publish his translations in his journal *Die Horen* and soon considered Schlegel one of his most important contributors. Schlegel returned to Ger-

many in the summer of 1795 and lived in Brunswick until the following spring. In May 1796, at Schiller's suggestion, he moved to Jena. In Brunswick, on 1 July, he married Caroline Michaelis Böhmer, whom he had known in Göttingen and had helped to rescue from political imprisonment in Mainz in 1793. The Schlegel house in Jena became the center of Early Romanticism.

In 1796 and 1797 Schlegel published in *Die Horen* two essays—one on *Hamlet* and Goethe's *Wilhelm Meisters Lehrjahre* (Wilhelm Meister's Apprenticeship, 1795-1796) and one on *Romeo and Juliet*—that served as a call for a translation of Shakespeare's works into German verse. He argued that a work of art is an organic whole whose unity derives from the skill of the artist; Germans could not, therefore, properly appreciate Shakespeare, since they knew the plays only in prose versions. Between 1797 and 1801 he published his translations of sixteen of Shakespeare's plays into blank verse. These translations, along with a seventeenth published in 1810 and thirteen by Ludwig Tieck's daughter Dorothea and her husband Wolf Heinrich Graf von Baudissin, are known collectively as the "Schlegel-Tieck" translation and have themselves become major works within German culture.

During his years in Jena Schlegel wrote, with Caroline's assistance, some 350 reviews for the *Jenaer Allgemeine Literaturzeitung*. While most of them, like the works they treat, no longer warrant reading, his discussion of Goethe's *Hermann und Dorothea* (1798) stands out as a strong piece of criticism. He corresponded and met with Goethe frequently, advising him on the meter of the "Römische Elegien" (Roman Elegies, 1795) while Goethe read and commented on Schlegel's translations of Shakespeare. Schlegel also continued to write poetry, much of which Schiller included in his *Musenalmanach* for several years, even though Schiller broke off friendly relations with Schlegel after Friedrich Schlegel attacked *Die Horen* in a review. In 1798 Schlegel was named a visiting professor at the University of Jena, where he gave lectures on aesthetics. That same year Friedrich and he founded the *Athenaeum*, the organ of the Romantic movement. Besides functioning as coeditor Schlegel contributed poems, translations, a few aphorisms, and essays on art.

By the summer of 1800 Schlegel had become restless in provincial Jena and longed for the cultural and social attractions of Berlin. His marriage to Caroline, which had always been shaky, was over, although a divorce was not granted until 17 May 1803. (She then married the philosopher F. W. J. Schelling.) During 1800 Schlegel published his collected poetry under the title *Gedichte* (Poems) and a translation of a volume of Horace Walpole's works. These efforts were followed in 1801 by a two-volume collection of his and Friedrich's essays, *Charakteristiken und Kritiken* (Characterizations and Critiques).

Schlegel arrived in Berlin in February 1801. His talent for sharp, humorous satire was displayed in two works in 1801: *Ehrenpforte und Triumphbogen für den Theater-Präsidenten von Kotzebue* (Gate of Honor and Triumphal Arch for the President of the Theater von Kotzebue), aimed at the popular dramatist August von Kotzebue,

and the preface to Johann Gottlieb Fichte's book on Friedrich Nicolai, the self-proclaimed defender of rationalism. With Tieck he edited and contributed to the *Musen-Almanach für das Jahr 1802*. His only play, *Ion*, based upon Euripides' work of the same name, was produced in Weimar and Berlin in 1802 and appeared in print the following year. Goethe's support notwithstanding, the play was a failure. In 1803 the first volume of *Spanisches Theater*, his influential translations of Calderón's plays, was published and his essay on the Spanish drama appeared in Friedrich's journal *Europa*. In 1804 a collection of his translations of poetry from Italian, Spanish, and Portuguese was published. But the main endeavor of his years in Berlin were three subscription series of lectures known collectively as "Vorlesungen über schöne Litteratur und Kunst" (Lectures on Literature and Art).

During the winter of 1801-1802 Schlegel lectured on aesthetics, in 1802-1803 on classical literature, and in 1803-1804 on romantic literature. The lectures were not published until 1884, although excerpts from them appeared in *Europa* in 1803, in *Prometheus* in 1808, and in Friedrich's *Deutsches Museum* in 1812. In the summer of 1803 he gave a series of lectures titled "Enzyklopädie der Wissenschaften" (Encyclopedia of the Sciences); only three fragments of these lectures have been published (in a 1929 article by Josef Körner and a 1961 dissertation by Franz Finke), and according to Rudolf Haym and Josef Körner they are rather superficial and derivative. His lectures on literature and art, however, are generally considered the single best compendium of the literary theory and criticism of Early Romanticism.

In the spring of 1804 Madame de Staël arrived in Berlin with a letter of introduction to Schlegel from Goethe. She offered Schlegel a salary of twelve thousand francs per year to join her household as her adviser on German literature and culture and as her children's tutor. He accepted and left Germany in June, not to return permanently for fourteen years. Much of the time until 1812 was spent at Coppet, Madame de Staël's estate near Lausanne in Switzerland, with frequent trips to Italy, Austria, France, and Geneva. In 1805 Schlegel published his elegy *Rom* (Rome), which is generally considered his best poetic work. He kept up his contact with the German literary scene through his correspondence and occasional essays in journals. He also decided to try his hand at writing in French and in 1807 attacked French neoclassicism in *Comparaison entre la Phèdre de Racine et celle d'Euripide* (Comparison between the *Phèdre* of Racine and That of Euripides), an exaggerated rejection of Racine that identified what Schlegel considered the proper form of tragedy among modern European writers: that of Shakespeare and especially of Calderón.

In January 1808 Schlegel accompanied Madame de Staël to Vienna, and in the spring he delivered there a subscription series of fifteen lectures on drama. The "Vorlesungen über Dramaturgie" (Lectures on Dramaturgy) were well received, and negotiations to publish them were under way even before Schlegel left Vienna in late May. When they did appear in 1809 and late 1810 (dated 1811), Schlegel had greatly expanded the lectures on French tragedy, on Shakespeare, and on other English dramatists to include specific comments on an enormous number of plays. The "lecture" on Shakespeare, for example, runs to more than 240 pages. The large amount of practical critical commentary notwithstanding, *Über dramatische Kunst und Litteratur* is primarily a summary presentation of Schlegel's historical, theoretical, and critical views on literature as they apply to drama. *Über dramatische Kunst und Litteratur* was Schlegel's most popular and influential book; a second edition was required in 1817, by which time it had been translated into French, English, and Italian. In France it led to the characterization of critics as either followers of Boileau (Nicolas Boileau-Despréaux) or followers of Schlegel; in Russia Aleksandr Pushkin and in England Samuel Taylor Coleridge, to give just two examples, were strongly influenced by it; and its appearance in Bohn's Standard Library in 1846 turned it into a handbook on drama for English-speaking countries for the rest of the century.

After returning from Vienna Schlegel translated two more plays of Calderón and Shakespeare's *Richard III*. In April 1810 the de Staël household took up residence in the castle of Chaumont-sur-Loire, near Tours. Shortly after Schlegel finished the manuscript for *Über dramatische Kunst und Litteratur*, Madame de Staël was ordered out of France by the government of Napoleon, and all copies of her *De l'Allemagne* (On Germany) at the printer were ordered confiscated. One copy was saved, however, and Schlegel secretly took it to Vienna to deposit it with Friedrich in the summer of 1811.

Schlegel in 1793; painting by Friedrich August Tischbein (collection of Ernst Behler)

The previous December Schlegel had moved to Bern, where he worked on notes he had been assembling on the *Nibelungenlied* (Song of the Nibelungen) since his time in Berlin and published a series of essays on it, including an announcement of an edition he intended to bring out, in the *Deutsches Museum* in 1812. Madame de Staël was forced to flee Coppet on 23 May 1812, and Schlegel accompanied her to Vienna, Moscow, Petersburg, and Stockholm. When she went on to the safety of London, where she published *De l'Allemagne* from the copy Schlegel had saved, he remained in Stockholm and became secretary to Crown Prince Bernadotte of Sweden. He devoted his energies during 1813 to writing pamphlets in support of the allied war effort against Napoleon. That year he began signing his name "von Schlegel," which he claimed was justified by a patent of nobility granted his family by Emperor Ferdinand III in the seventeenth century. As soon as hostilities ended in April 1814 he joined Madame de Staël in London, then traveled with her to Paris.

From 1814 until Madame de Staël's death on 14 July 1817, Schlegel was in Italy, at Coppet, or in Paris. He wrote several short studies on various works of art and worked with Provençal manuscripts in Paris; the latter investigations led to his 1818 book on the Provençal language and literature. In the winter of 1816-1817 he resumed the study of Sanskrit, which he had begun two years earlier in Paris. After Madame de Staël's death he edited her *Considérations sur les événements principaux de la révolution française* (Considerations Concerning the Principal Events of the French Revolution, 1818). In December 1817, while engaged in this task, he received an offer of a professorship at the University of Berlin. In May 1818 he returned to Germany, and after visiting Friedrich in Frankfurt he went to Heidelberg. On 30 August Schlegel married Sophie Paulus, the twenty-eight-year-old daughter of Heinrich Paulus, a professor of theology whom Schlegel had known since he was in Jena. Sophie and her parents wanted Schlegel to stay in Heidelberg, and as a compromise Schlegel obtained permission from the Prussian authorities to assume a professorship at the newly founded University of Bonn instead of Berlin. But Sophie refused to leave her parents' household, and when Schlegel departed Heidelberg for Bonn she did not accompany him. There was never a divorce; Schlegel remained married, though alone, for the rest of his life.

Schlegel joined the faculty at Bonn in November 1818 as professor of literature and art history. During the final twenty-seven years of his life his main interest was ancient Indian language and literature. He founded, edited, and contributed to the journal *Indische Bibliothek* (Indian Library, 1823-1830) and prepared critical editions with Latin translations of the *Bhagavad-Gita* (1823) and the *Ramayana* (1829-1846). He is generally credited with being the founder of Sanskrit studies in Germany. He continued through the 1820s and 1830s to lecture on the history of German language and literature and the history of art. The former lectures were published posthumously (1913), as was a course of lectures on academic study (1971). Lectures on the fine arts delivered in Berlin in 1827 and poorly received as outdated were printed at the time and translated into French and Spanish. In 1829 and 1831 he wrote a long two-part article on the history of India for the *Berliner Kalender*, but much of his

writing from these years consists of occasional prefaces and of editions of his earlier works. *Berichtigung einiger Mißdeutungen* (Correction of Several Misinterpretations) and additions to his collected *Kritische Schriften* (Critical Writings), both published in 1828, are attempts—not always totally honest ones—to distance himself from an earlier interest in Catholicism (he had flirted with the idea of conversion from time to time between 1808 and 1816) and also from his brother, with whom he had broken over Friedrich's religious and political views and over a loan Friedrich had failed to repay. (Friedrich died the following year.) Through the 1830s he remained a famous personage, receiving many foreign visitors. In 1842 he published his collected French writings as *Essais littéraires et historiques* (Literary and Historical Essays). But his role in the literary and intellectual life of Germany was a thing of the past. By the time he died on 12 May 1845 he was, for the most part, either forgotten or ridiculed.

Schlegel's posthumous reputation in Germany is to a large extent embodied in Heinrich Heine's devastating portrait in *Die romantische Schule* (The Romantic School, 1835). There is, to be sure, much in Heine's treatment that is correct: Schlegel's overweening vanity intruded everywhere in his life and work, and a good deal of his thought does indeed derive from that of his brother Friedrich. Until the 1950s Heine's dismissal was countered only by the recognition of Schlegel as more systematic in his writings and less mystical in his thought than Friedrich or the other Early Romantics. Even Josef Körner, who is responsible for much of what is known about Schlegel, saw him primarily as a popularizer. It was René Wellek in 1955 who offered a major reassessment of Schlegel's place in the history of German criticism and theory. There remains, however, much to be done. There still exists no critical edition of his works, nor even a complete edition; no scholarly biography; no comprehensive monograph; and no unified collection of his vast correspondence. Scholars must be content with reprints of nineteenth-century editions and must scour a small library of diverse collections of letters, some of them in journals. Despite these hindrances, it is finally being recognized that Schlegel should be judged for what he contributed to Romantic criticism and theory, not for what he did not.

As a translator Schlegel was a major force in acquainting German readers and authors with new realms of literature, from Dante to Calderón

Portrait of Schlegel by P. Busch (Bildarchiv der Österreichischen Nationalbibliothek, Vienna)

erature embodies the total form of its culture it is admirable. The distinctions, then, between classical and romantic literature are those between the culture of ancient Greece and that of Christian Europe. Neoclassicism is unacceptable because it seeks to use a form borrowed from an alien culture. The mythology, religion, and fine arts of Europe are romantic, and European literature must have a form consistent with its culture. Romantic literature is not better than classical literature, only different. Since Germans are Europeans, they must look to other European, romantic traditions for models for the further development of their literature. Shakespeare and Calderón serve as examples of how the consummately skilled artist creates a work whose form is organic within itself and also within its culture. Romantic literature is for Schlegel not a speculative concept, as it was for the other early Romantics, but a historically, theoretically, and critically specifiable one.

Schlegel's statements, whether a "Fragment" in the *Athenaeum*, a German rendering of a well-known line in Shakespeare, or a sentence in a lecture, are well-turned, rhetorically finished phrases. While some have attacked his work for being poetic but shallow, his style is consistent with his view of literature as the product of one who has mastered the possibilities of expression in language.

to the verse of Shakespeare. Within German literature he argued for greater attention to medieval poetry, especially the *Nibelungenlied*. In his essays and lectures, moreover, he sought to underline the formal aesthetic qualities of these works. Schlegel wished to compile a body of exemplary texts and theory that would demonstrate the direction in which German literature should develop. Such a program was common to all the Early Romantics, but Schlegel stressed the craftsman's skill of the artist in the production of his work, though not in the sense of neoclassical imitation of foreign forms. To counteract such a misunderstanding he underscored the role of the imagination in the production of art and referred to "organisch" (organic) form to express the way the artist's intentionality infuses the entirety of work.

This notion of total form is also central to his division between classical and romantic literature, for just as an individual work is a unified totality, so, too, is a culture. "Classical" and "romantic" do not refer to narrowly delimited literary periods but to types of literature. Each type is a product of a specific culture, and insofar as any lit-

Letters:

Aus Schleiermachers Leben: In Briefen, 4 volumes, edited by Wilhelm Dilthey and Ludwig Jonas (Berlin: Reimer, 1858-1863); volumes 1 and 2 translated by Frederica Rowan as *The Life of Schleiermacher as Unfolded in His Autobiography and Letters*, 2 volumes (London: Smith, Elder, 1860);

Aus Schellings Leben: In Briefen, 3 volumes, edited by Gustav Plitt (Leipzig: Hirzel, 1869-1870);

Friedrich Schlegels Briefe an seinen Bruder August Wilhelm, edited by Oskar F. Walzel (Berlin: Speyer & Peters, 1890);

Briefwechsel zwischen Wilhelm von Humboldt und August Wilhelm Schlegel, edited by Albert Leitzmann (Halle: Niemeyer, 1908);

Briefwechsel A. W. von Schlegel, Christian Lassen, edited by W. Kirfel (Bonn: Cohen, 1914);

August Wilhelm Schlegels Briefwechsel mit seinen Heidelberger Verlegern, edited by Erich Jenisch (Heidelberg: Winter, 1922);

August Wilhelm und Friedrich Schlegel im Briefwechsel mit Schiller und Goethe, edited by Josef Körner and Ernst Wieneke (Leipzig: Insel, 1926);

Briefe von und an Friedrich und Dorothea Schlegel, edited by Körner (Berlin: Askanischer Verlag, 1926);

Ludwig Tieck und die Brüder Schlegel: Briefe mit Einleitung und Anmerkungen, edited by Henry Lüdeke (Frankfurt am Main: Baer, 1930);

Briefe von und an August Wilhelm Schlegel, 2 volumes, edited by Körner (Zurich: Amalthea, 1930);

Krisenjahre der Frühromantik: Briefe aus dem Schlegelkreis, 3 volumes, edited by Körner (Brünn: Rohrer, 1936-1958);

Ausgewählte Briefe, volume 7 of *Kritische Schriften und Briefe*, edited by Edgar Lohner (Stuttgart: Kohlhammer, 1974).

Bibliography:

Eduard Böcking, "Verzeichnis der von Aug. Wilh. von Schlegel verfaßten gedruckten Schriften," in *Katalog der von Aug. Wilh. von Schlegel ... nachgelassenen Büchersammlung: Welche Montag den 1ten Dezember 1845 und an den folgenden Tagen Abends 5 Uhr präcise bei J. M. Heberle in Bonn öffentlich versteigert und den Letztbietenden gegen gleich Zahlung verabfolgt wird* (Bonn: Georgi, 1845), pp. i-xxviii.

Biographies:

Bernhard von Brentano, *August Wilhelm Schlegel: Geschichte eines romantischen Geistes* (Stuttgart: Cotta, 1943);

Ruth Schirmer, *August Wilhelm Schlegel und seine Zeit: Ein Bonner Leben* (Bonn: Bouvier, 1986).

References:

Ernst Behler, *Die Zeitschriften der Brüder Schlegel: Ein Beitrag zur Geschichte der deutschen Romantik* (Darmstadt: Wissenschaftliche Buchgesellschaft, 1983);

Michael Bernays, *Zur Entstehungsgeschichte des Schlegelschen Shakespeare* (Leipzig: Hirzel, 1872);

Alfred Besenbeck, *Kunstanschauung und Kunstlehre August Wilhelm Schlegels* (Berlin: Ebering, 1930);

Otto Brandt, *August Wilhelm Schlegel: Der Romantiker und die Politik* (Stuttgart: Deutsche Verlags-Anstalt, 1919);

Hans Dietrich Dahnke, "August Wilhelm Schlegels Berliner und Wiener Vorlesungen und ihre Stellung in der romantischen Literatur," in *Begegnung und Bündnis: Sowjetische und deutsche Literatur*, edited by Gerhard Ziegengeist (Berlin: Akademie, 1972), pp. 470-481;

Ralph Ewton, *The Literary Theories of August Wilhelm Schlegel* (The Hague: Mouton, 1972);

H. G. Fiedler, ed., *A. W. Schlegel's Lectures on German Literature from Gottsched to Goethe Given at the University of Bonn and Taken Down by George Toynbee* (Oxford: Blackwell, 1944);

Franz Finke, "Die Brüder Schlegel als Literarhistoriker," Ph.D. dissertation, University of Kiel, 1961;

Peter Gebhardt, *A. W. Schlegels Shakespeare-Übersetzungen: Untersuchungen zu seinem Übersetzungsverfahren am Beispiel des Hamlet* (Göttingen: Vandenhoeck & Ruprecht, 1970);

Karl S. Guthke, "Benares am Rhein–Rom am Ganges: Orient und Okzident im Denken August Wilhelm Schlegels," *Das Abenteuer der Literatur* (Bern: Francke, 1981), pp. 242-258;

Rudolf Haym, *Die romantische Schule* (Berlin: Wiedmann, 1928);

Heinrich Heine, *Historisch-kritische Gesamtausgabe der Werke*, volume 8, edited by Manfred Windfuhr (Hamburg: Hoffmann & Campe, 1979), pp. 121-249;

Walter Jesinghaus, *August Wilhelm Schlegels Meinungen über die Ursprache mit einem Abdruck aus Schlegels Manuscript zu den Berliner Vorlesungen über eine Encyclopädie der Wissenschaften* (Düsseldorf: Jesinghaus, 1913);

Josef Körner, "August Wilhelm Schlegel: Die griechische und lateinische Sprache, Charakteristiken," *Romantik-Forschungen: Deutsche Vierteljahrsschrift für Literaturwissenschaft und Geistesgeschichte*, 16 (1929): 51-62;

Körner, *Die Botschaft der deutschen Romantik an Europa* (Augsburg: Filser, 1929);

Körner, *Romantiker und Klassiker: Die Brüder Schlegel in ihren Beziehungen zu Goethe und Schiller* (Berlin: Askanischer Verlag, 1924);

Edgar Lohner, "August Wilhelm Schlegel," in *Deutsche Dichter der Romantik*, edited by Benno von Wiese (Berlin: Schmidt, 1971), pp. 135-162;

Gregory Thomas Mico, "August Wilhelm Schlegel: The Berlin Lectures and the Romantic Theory of Language and Literature," Ph.D. dissertation, Stanford University, 1980;

Chetana Nagavajara, *August Wilhelm Schlegel in Frankreich: Sein Anteil an der französischen Literaturkritik 1807-35* (Tübingen: Niemeyer, 1966);

Georg Reichard, *August Wilhelm Schlegels "Ion": Das Schauspiel und die Aufführungen unter der Leitung von Goethe und Iffland* (Bonn: Bouvier, 1987);

Thomas G. Sauer, *A. W. Schlegel's Shakespearean Criticism in England, 1811-1846* (Bonn: Bouvier, 1981);

Walter Schirmer, *Kleine Schriften* (Tübingen: Niemeyer, 1950);

Günther Schmidt, *Herder und A. W. Schlegel* (Berlin: Blanke, 1917);

Karl Wilhelm Ferdinand Solger, "Beurteilung der *Vorlesungen über Kunst und Literatur*," in his *Nachgelassene Schriften und Briefwechsel*, volume 2, edited by Ludwig Tieck and Friedrich von Raumer (Heidelberg: Schneider, 1973), pp. 492-628;

Emil Sulger-Gebing, *A. W. und F. Schlegel in ihrem Verhältnis zur bildenden Kunst: Mit ungedruckten Briefen und Aufsätzen A. W. Schlegels* (Munich: Haushalter, 1897);

René Wellek, "August Wilhelm Schlegel," in his *A History of Modern Criticism*, volume 2 (New Haven: Yale University Press, 1955), pp. 36-73, 354-366;

Hans Zehnder, *Die Anfänge von August Wilhelm Schlegels kritischer Tätigkeit* (Mulhouse: Alsatia, 1930).

Papers:

August Wilhelm Schlegel's papers are in the Sächsische Landesbibliothek, Dresden.

Johann Gottfried Seume
(29 January 1763 - 13 June 1810)

Erich P. Hofacker, Jr.
University of Michigan

BOOKS: *Sinnlichkeit Ist Nicht Liebe oder Der Mann ohne vesten Charakter: Schauspiel* (Frankfurt am Main & Leipzig, 1791);

Arma veterum cum nostris breviter comparata (Leipzig, 1792);

Ueber Prüfung und Bestimmung junger Leute zum Militär (Warsaw: Dufour, 1793);

Einige Nachrichten über die Vorfälle in Polen im Jahre 1794 (Leipzig: Martini, 1796);

Obolen, 2 volumes (Leipzig: Martini, 1796-1798);

Rückerinnerungen, by Seume and Karl Ludwig August, Freiherr Münchhausen (Frankfurt am Main: Varrentrapp & Venner, 1797);

Ueber das Leben und den Karakter der Kaiserin von Rußland Katharina II. Mit Freymüthigkeit und Unparteylichkeit (Altona [actually Leipzig: Göschen], 1797);

Zwey Briefe über die neuesten Veränderungen in Rußland seit der Thronbesteigung Pauls des Ersten (Zurich & Leipzig: Göschen, 1797);

Gedichte (Leipzig: Hartknoch, 1801; enlarged, N.p., 1804; enlarged again, N.p., 1810; enlarged again, edited by Christian August Heinrich Clodius, Leipzig: Hartknoch, 1815; enlarged again, Leipzig: Hartknoch, 1843);

Zwey romantische Erzählungen, by Seume and J. C. H. Gitterman (Frankfurt am Main: Wilmans, 1802)–includes "Adelaide," by Seume;

Spaziergang nach Syrakus im Jahre 1802 (Brunswick & Leipzig: Vieweg, 1803); enlarged, 3 volumes (Leipzig: Hartknoch, 1811)–volume 3 titled *Apokryphen*; translated by Alexander and Elizabeth Henderson as *A Stroll to Syracuse* (London: Wolff, 1964; New York: Ungar, 1965); German version republished (Nördlingen: Greno, 1985);

Ueber Bewaffnung (Leipzig: Hartknoch, 1804);

Mein Sommer 1805 (Leipzig: Steinacker, 1806); translated anonymously as *A Tour through Part of Germany, Poland, Russia, Sweden, Denmark, &c. during the Summer of 1805* (London: Printed for R. Phillips, 1807); German

Undated engraving by F. Müller

version republished (Berlin: Rütten & Loening, 1968);

Miltiades: Ein Trauerspiel in fünf Aufzügen (Leipzig: Hartknoch, 1808);

Abschied und Vermächtniß nebst biographischer Skizze und einigen erläuternden Notizen, edited by W. Lohmann (Goslar, 1810);

Ein Nachlaß moralisch-religiösen Inhalts: Kurzes Pflichten- und Sittenbuch für Landleute (Leipzig: Göschen, 1811);

Mein Leben, completed by Georg Joachim Göschen and Christian August Heinrich Claudius (Leipzig: Göschen, 1813); edited by J. Henry Senger (Boston: Ginn, 1899); ex-

267

cerpts translated by M. Woelfel as "Memoirs of a Hessian Conscript: J. G. Seume's Reluctant Voyage to America," in *William and Mary Quarterly: A Magazine of Early American History*, 5 (1948): 553-570; German version reprinted (Nördlingen: Greno, 1986);

J. G. Seumes gesammelte Schriften, 5 volumes, edited by J. P. Zimmerman (Wiesbaden: Schellenberg, 1823-1826);

J. G. Seumes sämmtliche Werke, 12 volumes (Leipzig: Hartknoch, 1826-1827);

Sämmtliche Werke: Einzig rechtmässige Gesamt-Ausgabe in einem Bande, edited by Adolph Wagner (Leipzig: Hartknoch, 1835);

Sämmtliche Werke, 8 volumes (Leipzig: Hartknoch, 1839);

Prosaische und Poetische Werke, 10 volumes (Berlin: Hempel, 1867-1876).

Edition in English: "Extract from the Diary of the ... Poet and Adventurer, J. G. Seume, a Hessian Soldier and Participator on the Voyage," in *The Voyage of the First Hessian Army from Portsmouth to New York, 1776*, by Albert von Pfister, translated by Carl F. Heartman (New York: Printed for C. F. Heartman, 1915).

OTHER: *Honorie Warren: Roman aus dem Englischen*, 2 volumes, translated by Seume (Frankfurt am Main & Leipzig, 1788);

Johann Baptist von Alxinger, *Bliomberis*, edited by Seume (Leipzig: Göschen 1802);

Robert Percival, *Beschreibung des Vorgebirges der guten Hoffnung: Aus dem Englischen*, translated with foreword by Seume (Leipzig: Rhein, 1805);

Journal für deutsche Frauen, edited by Seume, 3 volumes (Leipzig: Göschen, 1805-1806).

In his determination to gain freedom and justice for the common people, Johann Gottfried Seume never ceased to oppose the reactionary political tendencies of his day. Shortly before his death, he acknowledged that his thinking was not in harmony with his age: "Meine Ideen sind nicht von heute und leider nicht für heute" (My ideas are not those of today and, unfortunately, are not for today). He was an outspoken late Enlightener living in the period of German Romanticism, a time that seemed intent on destroying the progress made by the earlier Rationalists and the French Revolution. An observant wayfarer in Europe and America, Seume added new dimensions to the travel literature which was then popular

with his vivid portrayals of depressing social conditions in Germany and abroad. He waged an unremitting crusade against the privileges and abuses of the nobility which, he believed, contributed greatly to the misery of the poor. A lively style and fascinating content assured the success of his works, but his relentless struggle for a more just and democratic society brought him into frequent difficulty with censors.

Seume was born on 29 January 1763 in the village of Poserna in Saxony, not far from Weißenfels. His father, Andreas Seume, was an itinerant cooper who had come from Thuringia and had married Regina Liebling, the daughter of a prosperous farmer. Andreas Seume's opposition to control by the landowning nobility and the church officials of the region had given him a reputation for steadfastness and independence, qualities which he passed on to his son. Johann Gottfried Seume's childhood years were happy ones, spent close to nature. Eventually, disagreements over taxation with local secular and ecclesiastical authorities threatened the elder Seume with arrest. In order to "dem Teufel und seiner Hölle [zu] entlaufen" (escape the devil and his hell), Andreas Seume sold the farm and moved the family to Knautkleeberg, near Leipzig, where he leased an inn and an adjoining farm. Johann Gottfried Seume was soon outperforming all the other pupils at his new school and was sometimes put in charge of the class while the teacher tended his garden. Bad weather in 1771 and 1772 caused crop losses on the Seume farm, but the landowner nevertheless demanded full payment of the rent. Its savings depleted, the family was reduced to farming a much smaller tract as tenant farmers. Illness soon incapacitated the father, but the landowner's overseer again demanded full payment and ridiculed the dying man for his inability to work. This bitter experience made a lasting impression on Seume. His autobiography, *Mein Leben* (My Life, 1813), identified this occurrence as the original spark in his later fight against injustice. In 1776 the elder Seume died at the age of thirty-seven, leaving 200 talers to his wife and five children. It sufficed for the purchase of a cottage, after which the family was dependent on the community for support.

Seume was about to leave school to become a blacksmith when his academic potential was recognized by the count of Hohenthal-Knauthain, one of the wealthiest landowners in the Leipzig area. The count sent him to the Borna "La-

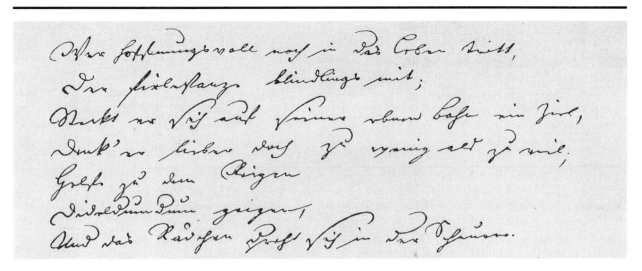

Manuscript for a poem by Seume (Gustav Könnecke, Bilderatlas zur Geschichte der deutschen Nationallitteratur [Graz: Akademische Druck- und Verlagsanstalt, 1981])

teinschule" (a school that taught the classical languages), where he lived with the principal. In his autobiography Seume relates that he threw himself into the study of Latin and Greek "wie ein Pferd, das doppeltes Futter braucht" (like a horse that needs twice the usual ration of fodder). He collected many Latin proverbs pertaining to character, courage, and love of country. Within two years he had moved to the head of the class. In 1779 the count sent him to the "Nikolai-Schule" in Leipzig. There he was less content, for the principal, Martini, was a melancholy man who was stingy with rations. Other teachers won his praise, however. At the "Nikolai-Schule" he was introduced to German literature; but he preferred the works of the ancients, who excelled, he felt, at the portrayal of the great human struggles. His meager scholarship of ten thalers monthly enabled him to visit the theater only occasionally, but since this was his great passion, he willingly missed meals to attend performances. After two years at the "Nikolai-Schule" he was admitted to the University of Leipzig, then attended by many well-to-do young men, to study theology. The cosmopolitan air of the town of twenty-seven thousand contrasted sharply with the narrow dogmatism of the theological faculty, and he preferred the lectures on history, philosophy, and the classical authors. He read the English Enlighteners Bolingbroke and Shaftesbury and the Frenchmen Pierre Bayle, Voltaire, Jean-Jacques Rousseau, and Louis Sébastien Mercier.

Seume had many difficulties with church doctrine, and although he did not express his doubts publicly, his poor record of church attendance and sometimes questionable social behavior lost him the favor of his aristocratic benefactor. Since he could not in good conscience continue in theology and had no hope of persuading the count to support his study in another field, he left Leipzig in June 1781. With nine talers in his pocket, he set out on foot in the direction of France. Soon, however, Seume was captured by Hessian "Werber" (recruiters), who intended to sell his services to the British to fight against the Americans in the Revolutionary War: the Landgrave of Cassel was to receive twenty-one million talers from England for twelve thousand conscripts. Seume writes that the conscripts, who had no quarrel "mit den armen Teufeln von Amerikanern" (with the poor American devils), unsuccessfully attempted to flee their captors. In June 1782 they were placed aboard British ships and began a twenty-two-week voyage under intolerable conditions. In *Mein Leben* he graphically describes the details of this experience; the worm-infested food and cramped quarters remind the reader of conditions on slave ships. Seume fared better than most of the other conscripts because he was able to ingratiate himself with the captain, who gave him better food and allowed him to read books from the captain's own library. Seume had also brought along his favorite classical works and read of the heroes of Sparta, Athens, and Rome; sitting in the crow's nest with the *Aeneid*, he compared Virgil's description of a storm at sea with his own experience. Sailing by way of Greenland, his ship landed in Halifax,

Nova Scotia, in December 1782. The German conscripts were not needed for combat, since the outcome of the war had been decided by the time of their arrival. Seume spent the next ten months in a military camp subsisting mainly on bread, butter, and smoked salmon, supplemented by an occasional dog or cat. The return trip to Germany took only twenty-three days.

When Seume landed in October 1782 he immediately deserted, but he was captured by the Prussians at Minden and pressed into military service once again. Escaping, he made his way to the duke of Oldenburg, with whom he had discussed his plans for the future. But as he left the ducal residence in a Prussian uniform he was recaptured and imprisoned for desertion. On his cell door he wrote in chalk "Tu ne cede malis, sed contra audentior ito" (Don't give in to misfortune but face it head on), one of the Latin quotes he had learned in school. His court-martial turned into a dispute over poetic meter, which allowed him to escape punishment. After the trial he was assigned to teach Latin and Greek to the children of the Prussian general Baron Guillaume René Courbière.

Even though he enjoyed the favor of his superiors, his years of service with the Prussian army were among the most bitter of his life. Following a failed attempt at desertion in January 1787 he was sentenced "zum zwölfmaligen Spießrutenlaufen" (to run the gauntlet twelve times). Only the pleas of General Courbière's children spared Seume this often-fatal ordeal, in which the condemned man was struck innumerable blows as he repeatedly ran past as many as three hundred stick-wielding soldiers. In May 1787 he finally secured his freedom by purchasing a "furlough" with eighty talers borrowed from a friendly merchant in Emden and returned to Knautkleeberg. The next year Seume paid back the loan with money he received for the translation of an English novel, *Honorie Warren* (1788). At this point he became "bewußt politisiert" (consciously politicized) and critically engaged in the events of society. He returned to the university and in 1792 received a degree in philosophy with a Habilitationsschrift (dissertation) which compared ancient and modern weapons. The same year he traveled to Russia as the confidential secretary to General Otto Heinrich Baron von Igelström, the brother of a Livonian count whose son he had formerly tutored. The German empress of Russia, Catherine II, convinced him of her enlightened outlook and her in-

tention to better the conditions of the peasants. Commissioned a lieutenant, Seume accompanied Igelström and the Russian army of occupation to Warsaw in January 1793. In charge of the general's German and French correspondence, he witnessed the diplomatic maneuvering which followed the second partition of Poland. There he composed his "Elegie auf einem Feste zu Warschau" (Elegy on the Occasion of a Celebration in Warsaw); the Poles had been forced to celebrate with the Russian occupation forces the loss of Polish territory–"weiss der Himmel mit welcher Mischung von Gefühlen" (heaven knows with what mixed feelings), as he wrote to Friedrich Schiller in his request for anonymous publication of the poem in the latter's journal, *Thalia*. Schiller prudently chose to avoid potential political consequences by printing instead Seume's earlier poem, "Der Wilde" (The Man of the Wilds), a 113-line Rousseauistic comparison of the generous American Indian and the decadent, greedy, and materialistic European. While in Warsaw, Seume narrowly escaped the uprising of the Polish nobility in which many of the occupation troops died; he was briefly imprisoned until the arrival of a Russian army of intervention, which defeated the Polish nobles. In 1796 he published *Einige Nachrichten über die Vorfälle in Polen im Jahre 1794* (Some Reports concerning the Events in Poland in 1794). He had praise for Gen. Tadeusz Kościuszko, the leader of the uprising and a man who had fought with the Americans in the Revolutionary War. Seume believed that the uprising had been provoked by Catherine II to justify the third partition of Poland in 1795, in which the country ceased to exist as a political entity. News of Catherine's death reached him while on furlough in Leipzig in 1796; declining to return to his garrison for official discharge, Seume forfeited his eligibility for a military pension. Living modestly as a private teacher of French and English, he courted the rich and beautiful Wilhelmine Röder; she, however, could not bring herself to marry a financially insecure scholar and writer.

Seume took to the pen because he felt driven to speak out concerning conditions and events of his day. In particular, he was provoked by the remnants of serfdom and other types of involuntary servitude he had seen and experienced. His *Ueber das Leben und den Karakter der Kaiserin von Rußland Katharina II.* (On the Life and Character of Empress Catherine II of Russia, 1797) expresses surprising praise for

Portrait of Seume, circa 1800, by Veit Hans Schnorr von Carolsfeld (Heimatmuseum, Lützen)

Catherine's "kühne Fortschritte auf allen menschlichen Gebieten" (bold progress in every field of humanity), despite her annexation of Polish territory. *Zwey Briefe über die neuesten Veränderungen in Rußland seit der Thronbesteigung Pauls des Ersten* (Two Letters concerning the Most Recent Changes in Russia since the Accession to the Throne of Paul I, 1797) deplores the increased power of the aristocracy under the new czar. Seume also condemned the resurgence of serfdom, and the increase in censorship under Paul I: "kosmische Wirkungen" (cosmic effects) should not be imputed to books or their authors since most of the good and bad in the world has been created without their influence.

The two-volume collection of essays *Obolen* (1796-1798) derived its title from the obolus, a small coin of ancient Greece. In "Rhapsodie über Atheismus" (Rhapsody for Atheism) Seume, a religious skeptic but not a confessed atheist, defends nonbelievers as good citizens. In a clear rejection of all belief in the world beyond he declares "die beste Religion ist diejenige, welche den Menschen hier am glücklichsten macht" (the best religion is the one which brings happiness here on earth). He also says that Immanuel Kant's

dream of eternal peace can be realized only when "die Begriffe von Bürgerfreiheit und allgemeiner Gerechtigkeit" (the concepts of universal freedom and justice) determine the policies of the state.

From 1797 until 1801 Seume was employed as a proofreader for Göschen, the respected publisher of the works of Goethe, Schiller, and Christoph Martin Wieland. Although this was a scholarly position, Seume found the work unrewarding and remained only until the completion of his most important assignment, an edition of the works of Friedrich Gottlieb Klopstock. He next gathered his poems, which had been appearing in various journals, into a collection which was reprinted in five successively enlarged editions between 1801 and 1843. The preface voices Seume's concern for the truth and his admiration of the noble, good, and beautiful. Not a sentimental lyricist, he primarily addresses the evils and abuses in society.

Despite his unhappy years in the Prussian army, Seume now hoped to become a commissioned officer in that army; but that aspiration could not be realized since he was not of the nobility. After visiting Goethe, Schiller, Wieland, and

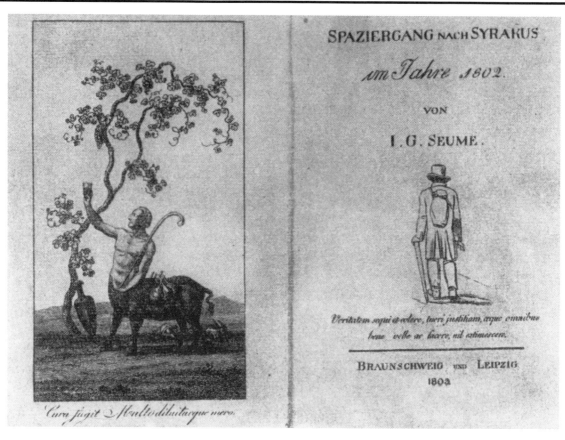

Frontispiece and title page for Seume's account of his "stroll to Syracuse"

August von Kotzebue in Weimar, he decided to make a tour of Italy, a popular goal of adventurous travelers of the day. His would be a "Fußtour" (walking tour), "um mich auszulaufen" (to stretch my legs). At the prospect of the danger presented by highwaymen and bandits, he bitterly remarked that his country would consider his death no loss, a reference to his ineligibility for an army commission. He chose to walk in order to see more of the world, since travel by vehicle would put him "um einige Grade von der ursprünglichen Humanität" (several degrees distant from the essence of humanity). He called his tour "ein [en] Spaziergang" (a stroll), not in understatement but to say something about the way he intended to travel: since a stroll lacks a specific destination, the stroller's attention will not be fixed on a goal and he will be more likely to make observations along the way. In undertaking the trip, Seume also wished "ein Mann zu werden" (to become a man) and to learn to overcome hardships. Said to have been the last stoic of the age of Romanticism, he practiced "Standhaftigkeit" (steadfastness), self-control, and self-sufficiency,

letting himself be guided by the Latin and Greek exhortations he had learned in school. Seume demonstrated remarkable bravery in his fearless trek through territory said to be infested with murderous highwaymen, and great physical prowess in covering, mostly on foot, 3,600 miles of often rugged terrain. On the return trip he crossed France to visit Paris, the center of the Enlightenment, then journeyed on to Leipzig via Nancy, Strasbourg, Mainz, and Frankfurt.

As Seume became politically oriented and more involved with the ideas of the Enlightenment, he became increasingly concerned with the question of man's purpose on earth. Of what use is an existence without direction, without concern for the future or a sense of duty toward one's fellows? To Seume, the course most beneficial to humanity seemed to be the struggle for universal justice and freedom, and the most effective means of personal social engagement seemed to be communication through the printed word. Accounts of his experiences and observations served him as an avenue for social action. On his return from Italy in 1802 he wrote a vivid and compelling narrative of his trip titled *Spaziergang nach Syrakus* (A Stroll to Syracuse, 1803), in which he registered his shock and dismay at the dire poverty and countless beggars he encountered. He saw the beggars among the ruins of the Colosseum with quite different eyes than his predecessor Goethe had: Goethe had focused on the aesthetics of the "romantic" scene, whereas Seume could see only the broken remains of ancient Rome and the tragedy of broken lives. In Sicily he visited the old port city of Syracuse, read Greek pastoral poetry, and peered into the crater of Etna. He compares the misery of the island with its former greatness in "Klage des Ceres" (Lament of Ceres [the patron goddess of Sicily]): "Meine Wiege, wie bist du verödet, du liebliches Eiland, / Ach, wie bist du verödet, du herrlicher Garten der Erde, / Wo die Götter mit Sterblichen einst den Olympus vergaßen!" (How desolate you are, you lovely island, my cradle, / Oh, how desolate you are, you glorious garden of the earth, / Where the gods together with mortals once forgot Mount Olympus!). *Spaziergang nach Syrakus* was widely read in its day, being distinguished from the many other travel accounts by the author's sensitivity to social conditions and courageous presentation of his observations. The book's harsh criticism of the Roman Catholic church, however, later led to censorship problems for Seume.

In Leipzig he continued to write short pieces and to tutor; fearful of losing his independence, he rejected offers to edit periodicals, such as Kotzebue's journal *Der Freimüthige* (although he did join Schiller and Friedrich Rochlitz in publishing the *Journal für deutsche Frauen* [1805-1806]). He fell in love with Johanna Loth, a girl some twenty years his junior to whom he had been giving Italian lessons for three years; but by the time he declared himself she had become engaged to another. To escape the resulting depression Seume set out in April 1805 on a six-month trip to the north, visiting Breslau, Warsaw, St. Petersburg, Moscow, Finland, Sweden, and Denmark; this time he rode most of the way. He declined a new commission in the Russian army and a professional post at the University of Tartu in the Republic of Estonia, for he could not bear the sight of the serfdom that would surround him: under Czar Paul I conditions in Russia had worsened in the past decade. On the return trip to Leipzig, Seume encountered the armies of Napoleon in Prussia and predicted the victory of the new France, which had been mor-

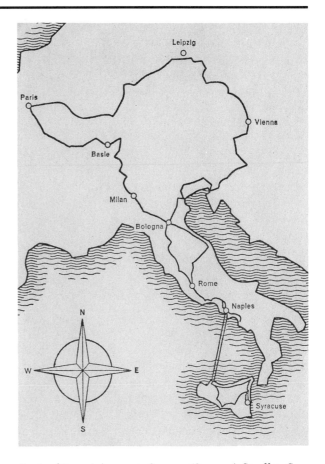

Route of Seume's journey to Syracuse (Seume, A Stroll to Syracuse, translated by Alexander and Elizabeth Henderson)

ally strengthened by the Revolution.

When *Mein Sommer 1805* (translated as *A Tour through Part of Germany, Poland, Russia, Sweden, Denmark, &c. in the Summer of 1805*, 1807) appeared in 1806, it was widely banned for its sharp political criticism. Following the battle of Jena and the French occupation of Leipzig in 1806, Seume was unable to publish his collection of political aphorisms, even in a Latin translation prefaced to a commentary on Plutarch: so fiery was his call for equality, justice, and freedom that the censor feared their publication even in scholarly form. Published posthumously in 1811 under the title *Apokryphen* (Apocrypha) as the third volume of an enlarged edition of *Spaziergang nach Syrakus*, the collection of aphorisms continued to be heavily edited until late in the century. (The commentary on Plutarch was published in 1820 as an appendix to the fourth edition of *Spaziergang nach Syrakus*.) In 1808 Seume was given permission to publish a less-provocative work, the five-act drama *Miltiades*, the story of the unshakeable love of country of the winner of the Greek marathon.

In *Apokryphen* Seume warned society of the dangers of aristocratic privilege ("Das erste Privilegium ist der erste Ansatz zum Krebs des Staatskörpers" [the first instance of privilege is the onset of cancer in the body of the state]) and of serfdom ("Wo die Möglichkeit des Lehnrechts stattfindet, ist der erste Schritt zur Sklaverei getan" [wherever the possibility of serfdom occurs the first step toward slavery has been taken]). He considered Germany to be at the mercy of princes who preferred to rule over slaves rather than free citizens who exercise self-determination. The scholar of the Enlightenment who hoped to create a better world through the education of rulers was also a peasant's son who knew that those in power would never grant self-determination to their subjects. In rejecting a request to write patriotic songs, Seume made it clear that he hoped Napoleon would defeat Prussia: "Es ist freilich auch philosophisch besser, Unrecht leiden als Unrecht tun, aber es gibt ein Drittes, das vernünftiger und edler ist als beides: mit Mut und Kraft verhindern, daß durchaus kein Unrecht geschehe" (From a philosophical standpoint, it is better to suffer injustice than to create injustice, but there is a third alternative that is more reasonable and noble than either of these: to impede injustice through courage and strength). Nevertheless, he knew that Napoleon had rejected the French Revolution: "Ich habe wider Bonaparte weiter nichts, als daß er auf alle Weise in der Vernunft rückwärts statt vorwärts geht" (I have nothing against Bonaparte except that in all aspects of rationality he is moving backward rather than forward).

In June 1808 Seume suffered an attack of the gout; it marked the onset of a two-year physical decline. During short periods of improvement he began his autobiography, *Mein Leben*. It remained a fragment but gave a vivid account of his early years until his return from America. (After his death the account was continued by his publisher, Georg Joachim Göschen, and his friend Christian August Heinrich Clodius, who gleaned autobiographical information from Seume's other writings.) Generally unable to work and without income, he was dependent on the assistance of friends. A former student took him in and a physician treated him free of charge. Through the intercession of Wieland and the Weimar court he was finally granted a pension as a former Russian officer, but this help

came too late. Seume died on 13 June 1810 at the mineral baths in Teplitz, in what is now Czechoslovakia. The censors, controlled by the privileged class Seume had sought to displace, continued until 1870 to prevent the publication of an unedited collection of his works, and the first uncensored collection was published by Hempel in 1879.

Letters:

"Ungedruckte Briefe Seumes," edited by Louise Devrient, *Unsere Zeit*, 7 (1880): 64-76;

Briefe an Cotta: Das Zeitalter Goethes und Napoleons, 1794-1815, edited by Maria Fehling, volume 1 (Stuttgart & Berlin: Cotta, 1925), pp. 127-134;

"Unbekannte Briefe Johann Gottfried Seumes an Karl Ludwig Frhr. von Münchhausen, 1792-1806," edited by Rolf Kraft, *Euphorion*, 63, no. 1/2 (1969): 167-206.

Biography:

Oskar Planer and Camillo Reissman, *Johann Gottfried Seume: Geschichte seines Lebens und seiner Schriften* (Leipzig: Göschen, 1898).

References:

Gertrude Elisabeth Grisham, "Johann Gottfried Seume: Eine Monographie," Ph.D. dissertation, Northwestern University, 1976;

Johann Höltl, "Johann Gottfried Seume: Die Entwicklung seines literarischen Schaffens zur zeitgemässen Publizistik," Ph.D. dissertation, University of Vienna, 1937;

Inge Jensen, "Der geistige Gehalt in J. G. Seumes Lyrik," Ph.D. dissertation, University of Halle, 1951;

Robert L. Kahn, "Seume and the English," *Studies in German*, 55 (1969): 47-68;

Kahn, "Seume's Knowledge of English Literature," *Symposium*, 8 (Winter 1954): 249-272;

Kahn, "Seume's Knowledge of the English Language," *Germanic Review*, 29 (1954): 131-145;

Kahn, "Seume's Reception in England and America," *Modern Language Review*, 52 (1957): 65-71;

Klaus Walter Klemm, "Johann Gottfried Seumes Schriften: Politisch-historisches Denken zur Revolution und Resignation," Ph.D. dissertation, University of Bonn, 1970;

Gert Kostenecki, *Johann Gottfried Seume: Absicht, Selbstdarstellung, Gedankenwelt. Versuch einer Revision* (Frankfurt am Main: Lang, 1979);

Gerard Kozietek, "Johann Gottfried Seumes Stellung zum polnischen Aufstand von 1794," *Impulse*, 2 (1979): 234-258;

Felix von Kozlowski, "Die Stellung Gleims und seines Freundeskreises zur französischen Revolution," *Euphorion*, 13 (1906): 71-79;

R. Kratzmann, *J. G. Seume als Patriot und patriotischer Dichter* (Leipzig: Naumann, 1897);

Lothar Pikulik, "Johann Gottfried Seume," in *Deutsche Dichter des 18. Jahrhunderts*, edited by Benno von Wiese (Berlin: Schmidt, 1977), pp. 972-994;

Hermann Schweppenhäuser, "Citoyen in Deutschland: Zu Seumes Apokryphen," in *Apokryphen*, by Seume (Frankfurt am Main: Insel, 1966), pp. 137-163;

Hildegard Siegmeth, "Johann Gottfried Seumes Leben und dichterisches Werk," Ph.D. dissertation, University of Vienna, 1943;

Ulrich Sonnemann, "Unangepaßtheit als kritische Prophetie: Zur deutschen Vergessenheit und Aktualität J. G. Seumes," in *Eingebildete Texte*, edited by Jochen Hörisch and Georg Christoph Tholen (Munich: Fink, 1985), pp. 91-102;

Inge Stephan, *Johann Gottfried Seume: Ein politischer Schriftsteller der deutschen Spätaufklärung* (Stuttgart: Metzler, 1973);

Hans Störel, "J. G. Seume und Rußland: Eine Darstellung seiner Rußlandbeziehungen und seines Rußlandbildes anhand seiner Werke und Briefe," Ph.D. dissertation, University of Leipzig, 1971;

Gertrud Wimmer, "J. G. Seumes 'Spaziergang nach Syrakus im Jahre 1802': Untersuchungen zu Erzähltechnik, Sprachkunst und literarischer Form," Ph.D. dissertation, University of Vienna, 1970.

Papers:
Manuscripts of Johann Gottfried Seume are in the Kleinhaus at Halberstadt and in the museum library at Weissenfels. Letters by Seume are in the Landesbibliothek in Dresden and in the Deutsche Bücherei in Leipzig.

Christian Graf zu Stolberg
(15 October 1748 - 18 January 1821)

Herbert Rowland
Purdue University

BOOKS: *Gedichte der Brüder Christian und Friedrich Leopold Grafen zu Stolberg*, edited by Heinrich Christian Boie (Leipzig: Weygand, 1779; enlarged, 3 volumes, Vienna: Bauer, 1817);

Schauspiele mit Choeren von den Brüdern Christian und Friedrich Leopold Grafen zu Stolberg: Erster Theil (Leipzig: Göschen, 1787);

Die weiße Frau: Ein Gedicht in sieben Balladen (Berlin: Hitzig, 1814);

Vaterländische Gedichte von Christian und Friedrich Leopold Grafen zu Stolberg (Hamburg: Perthes & Besser, 1815);

Gesammelte Werke der Brüder Christian und Friedrich Leopold Grafen zu Stolberg, 20 volumes (Hamburg: Perthes & Besser, 1820-1825; reprinted, Hildesheim & New York: Olms, 1974);

Kurzer Lebensabriß des Grafen Friedrich Leopold zu Stolberg (Leipzig, 1821).

Edition in English: "To My Brother," translated anonymously in *The Poets and Poetry of Europe*, edited by Henry Wadsworth Longfellow (Philadelphia: Porter / London: Chapman, 1845).

OTHER: *Gedichte aus dem Griechischen übersetzt*, translated by Stolberg (Hamburg: Bohn, 1782);

Sophocles, *Sofokles übersetzt*, 2 volumes, translated by Stolberg (Leipzig: Göschen, 1787);

Friedrich Leopold Grafen zu Stolberg kurze Abfertigung der langen Schmähschrift des Herrn Hofraths Voß wider ihn: Nach dem Tode des Verfassers vollendet, edited by Stolberg (Hamburg: Perthes & Besser, 1820).

Christian Graf zu Stolberg is remembered less for his own work than for his close relationship to many of the luminaries of a particularly lustrous firmament in German letters. The older brother of the more gifted and productive Friedrich Leopold zu Stolberg and the friend of Friedrich Gottlieb Klopstock, Johann Wolfgang von Goethe, and many others, Stolberg played a

Painting by Anton Graff, 1784-1785 (in possession of Erik Graf Holstein-Holsteinborg, Holsteinborg)

minor role in the revival of German literature that began around 1770.

Born in Hamburg on 15 October 1748 to Christian Günther and Friederike Christiane zu Stolberg, Stolberg grew up in small towns and rural areas in present-day Schleswig-Holstein and Denmark, enjoying the advantages of the physical and intellectual culture of the north German nobility. His outlook and work were shaped both by his pietistically inclined mother and his reform-minded father, who participated in the abolition of serfdom in the north. Together with his brother, he studied philosophy and law in Halle from 1770 to 1772 and in Göttingen from 1772 to 1773.

At the University of Göttingen, Christian and Friedrich Leopold met the young poets of the Göttinger Hainbund (Fraternity of the Göttingen Grove), and they became members of the group in December 1772. With these contemporaries they shared a boundless enthusiasm for Homer, Shakespeare, Ossian, and especially for Klopstock, as well as for the characteristic ideals of the 1770s–nature, genius, virtue, emotion, friendship, freedom, and the "Germanic." The brothers' interest turned increasingly from their professional training to literature, including the study of Greek, and both contributed poems to the organ of the Hainbund, the *Göttinger Musenalmanach*. In September 1773 they left Göttingen and moved to Hamburg.

In April 1775 the Stolbergs set out on an extended trip to Switzerland. In Frankfurt they met the young Goethe, who was then enjoying the unparalleled success of his novel *Die Leiden des jungen Werthers* (The Sorrows of Young Werther, 1774), and convinced him to join them. Clad in the "Werther-costume" of blue jacket and yellow pants and vest, the new friends made a youthfully exuberant journey, meeting many literary figures along the way.

Unlike Friedrich Leopold, Christian led a relatively uneventful life after the return from Switzerland. In 1776 he was named Danish chamberlain, and he served from 1777 to 1800 as magistrate in Tremsbüttel. He married Friederike Luise von Gramm in 1777 and enjoyed a happy but childless marriage. From 1800 until his death on 18 January 1821 he lived on his estate, Windbye, near Eckernförde; he was named a counselor to the Schleswig Provincial Court in 1806. Stolberg spent his adult life attending to his duties as a government official; maintaining close contact with friends and relatives, particularly some politically and religiously conservative groups in Emkendorff, Eutin, and Münster; and creating a modest literary oeuvre.

Stolberg's work was indelibly marked by Klopstock and ancient Greek literature. Typical is the poem "An Bürger" (To Bürger, 1773), dedicated to the poet Gottfried August Bürger. Written in Asclepiadean strophes and evincing "Germanic" motifs and a forceful tone, the piece laments the cultural subservience of Germany

Friederike Luise Gräfin zu Stolberg, née von Gramm, whom Stolberg married in 1777; painting by Graff, 1784-1785 (in possession of Erik Graf Holstein-Holsteinborg, Holsteinborg)

and the loss of old "German" virtues such as justice. The theme of freedom implicit here represents one of Stolberg's principal concerns and assumed a decidedly more pragmatic aspect around 1813, as Prussia and its allies sought to liberate themselves from Napoleon's rule. "Die geweihte Fahne" (The Consecrated Flag) spurs the freedom fighters on to battle for the *German* fatherland, evoking the ideal of unification, while "Leipzigs Schlacht" (The Battle of Leipzig) celebrates the decisive, avenging victory over the French. "An die deutsche Rathsversammlung in Wien" (To the German Congress in Vienna, 1814) expresses hope for a rejuvenation of the old "Holy German [!] Empire" and indicates that Stolberg's criticism of tyranny served the purposes of aristocratic restoration rather than bourgeois liberalism, as was long held.

Well over half of Stolberg's poems fall under the category of occasional poetry, and it was here that he did his best work. Form and content rarely go beyond the commonplace, but certain of the pieces–for example, "Nach einem

unerwarteten genußreichen Besuch" (After an Unexpected, Pleasurable Visit, 1787)–reveal a felici-
tous hand. Especially vis-à-vis the younger generation, the mature Stolberg at times displays an
unwonted human warmth and cavalier playful-
ness, as in "An die junge Gräfin Henriette von
Baudissin" (To the Young Countess Henriette
von Baudissin, 1788) and "Eingeschrieben in das
Stammbuch meiner Nichte, Nandine" (Written in
the Album of My Niece, Nandine, 1813). The religious poetry that became prominent in his work
after 1806 is unremarkable. Stolberg tried his
hand at forms as disparate as the sonnet and free
verse but achieved his greatest success in simpler
ballad stanzas. His imitations of ancient Greek
ode strophes are characterized by convoluted syn-
tax, owing in part to a heavy use of inverted
word order.

The influence of ancient Greece on
Stolberg's contributions to *Schauspiele mit Choeren*
(Plays with Choirs, 1787), written with his
brother, was perhaps even less fortunate. The numerous and often lengthy odes spoken by the
choirs in *Belsazer* and *Otanes* seem to exist more
for their own sake than for that of the plot and
tend to impede the action. Although based on
stories in the Bible and Herodotus, the plays are
quite topical in their criticism of despotism. Similarly infelicitous is the superimposition of ancient
Greek motifs and the Medea story on a medieval
Christian tale in the long narrative poem *Die
weiße Frau: Ein Gedicht in sieben Balladen* (The
Woman in White: A Poem in Seven Ballads,
1814).

Stolberg's interest in ancient Greek literature led to extensive translation during the
1780s. *Gedichte aus dem Griechischen übersetzt*
(Poems Translated from the Greek, 1782) includes works by Homer, Anacreon, and many others, while *Sofokles übersetzt* (Sophocles Translated,
1787) contains all seven extant tragedies.
Though generally accurate, Stolberg's renderings
are stiff and metrically awkward and could not
compete with the endeavors of translators such
as Johann Heinrich Voß.

Letters:
Stolberg in den letzten zwei Jahrzehnten seines Lebens,
edited by Johann Heinrich Hennes (Mainz:
Kirchheim, 1875);
*Briefwechsel zwischen Klopstock und den Grafen Chri-
stian und Friedrich Leopold zu Stolberg: Mit
einem Anhang: Briefwechsel zwischen Klopstock
und Herder*, edited by Jürgen Behrens (Neumünster: Wachholtz, 1964).

References:
Jürgen Behrens, "Wieland und die Brüder Christian und Friedrich Leopold Grafen zu Stolberg," *Jahrbuch des Wiener Goethe-Vereins*, 65
(1961): 45-67;
Johannes Janssen, *Friedrich Leopold Graf zu Stolberg: Größtentheils aus dem bisher noch ungedruckten Familiennachlaß* (Freiburg: Herder,
1877);
Theodor Menge, *Der Graf Friedrich Leopold Stolberg und seine Zeitgenossen* (Gotha: Perthes,
1862);
C. Schüddekopf, "Zu Christian und Friedrich Leopold von Stolbergs Jugendgedichten," *Zeitschrift für deutsche Philologie*, 18 (1886):
477-484;
Detlev W. Schumann, "Goethe and the Stolbergs:
A Friendship of the Storm and Stress," *Journal of English and Germanic Philology*, 48 (October 1949): 483-504;
Schumann, "Goethe and the Stolbergs After
1775: The History of a Problematic Relationship," *Journal of English and Germanic Philology*, 50 (1951): 22-59.

Papers:
Christian Graf zu Stolberg's papers are at the
Freies Deutsches Hochstift in the Frankfurter
Goethemuseum, Frankfurt am Main; and the
Schleswig-Holsteinische Landesbibliothek, Kiel.

Friedrich Leopold Graf zu Stolberg

(7 November 1750 - 5 December 1819)

Herbert Rowland
Purdue University

BOOKS: *Freiheits-Gesang aus dem Zwanzigsten Jahr-hundert: Manuscript für Freunde* (Zurich, 1775);

Gedichte der Brüder Christian und Friedrich Leopold Grafen zu Stolberg, edited by Heinrich Christian Boie (Leipzig: Weygand, 1779); enlarged edition, 3 volumes (Vienna: Bauer, 1817);

Jamben (Leipzig: Weidmann & Reich, 1784);

Timoleon: Ein Trauerspiel mit Chören. Manuscript für Freunde (Copenhagen: Thiele, 1784);

Schauspiele mit Choeren von den Brüdern Christian und Friedrich Leopold Grafen zu Stolberg: Erster Theil (Leipzig: Göschen, 1787)—includes Friedrich Leopold Graf zu Stolberg's *Timoleon, Theseus, Servius Tullius, Apollons Hain, Der Säugling*;

Die Insel (Leipzig: Göschen, 1788; reprinted, Heidelberg: Schneider, 1966);

Reise in Deutschland, der Schweiz, Italien und Sicilien in den Jahren 1791 und 1792, 4 volumes (Königsberg & Leipzig: Nicolovius, 1794); translated by Thomas Holcroft as *Travels through Germany, Switzerland, Italy, and Sicily*, 2 volumes (London: Printed for G. G. & J. Robinson, 1796-1797); German version reprinted, 2 volumes (Bern: Lang, 1971);

Schreiben eines Holsteinischen Kirchspielvogts an seinen Freund in Schweden über die neue Kirchen-Agende, anonymous (Hamburg: Perthes, 1798);

Geschichte der Religion Jesu Christi, 15 volumes (Hamburg: Perthes, 1806-1818);

Vaterländische Gedichte von Christian und Friedrich Leopold Grafen zu Stolberg (Hamburg: Perthes & Besser, 1815);

Ueber den Vorrang des Apostels Petrus vor den andern Aposteln und seiner Nachfolger vor den andern Bischöfen (Hamburg: Perthes, 1815);

Leben Alfred des Großen, Königes in England (Münster: Aschendorff, 1815);

Drey kleine Schriften (Münster: Theissing, 1818)—comprises "Die Sinne, ein Gespräch,"

Engraving by J. G. von Müller of a painting by J. C. Rincklake (Gustav Könnecke, Bilderatlas zur Geschichte der deutschen Nationallitteratur [Graz: Akademische Druck- und Verlagsanstalt, 1981])

"Ueber unsere Sprache, eine Abhandlung," "Gedanken ueber den Geist der Zeit"; *Leben des heiligen Vincentius von Paulus nebst desselben Ordensregeln, und ein aus dem Italienischen übersetztes Gespräch der heiligen Katharina von Siena* (Münster: Aschendorff, 1818);

Betrachtungen und Beherzigungen der heiligen Schrift, 2 volumes (Hamburg: Perthes & Besser, 1819-1821);

Ein Büchlein von der Liebe (Münster: Aschendorff, 1820); translated by Joseph Dalton as *A Little Book of the Love of God* (London: Burns, 1849);

Friedrich Leopold Grafen zu Stolberg kurze Abfertigung der langen Schmähschrift des Herrn Hofraths Voß wider ihn: Nach dem Tode des Verfassers vollendet von dem Bruder herausgegeben, edited by Christian Graf zu Stolberg (Hamburg: Perthes & Besser, 1820);

Gesammelte Werke der Brüder Christian und Friedrich Leopold Grafen zu Stolberg, 20 volumes (Hamburg: Perthes & Besser, 1820-1825; reprinted, Hildesheim & New York: Olms, 1974);

Unterricht über einige Unterscheidungslehren der katholischen Kirche, edited by G. Kellermann (Münster, 1842);

Die Zukunft: Ein bisher ungedrucktes Gedicht des Grafen Friedrich Leopold zu Stolberg aus den Jahren 1779-1782, Nach der einzigen bisher bekannt gewordenen Handschrift, edited by Otto Hartwig (Leipzig: Teubner, 1885);

Numa: Ein Roman, edited by Jürgen Behrens (Neumünster: Wachholtz, 1968);

Über die Fülle des Herzens: Frühe Prosa, edited by Behrens (Stuttgart: Reclam, 1970).

Editions in English: *Hymn to the Earth,* translated by Joseph Whitehouse (London: Cadell, 1801);

"Ode to a Mountain Torrent," translated by George Borrow, in his *Targum; or, Metrical Translations from Thirty Languages and Dialects* (St. Petersburg: Schulz & Beneze, 1835).

OTHER: Homer, *Homers Ilias verdeutscht,* 2 volumes, translated by Stolberg (Flensburg & Leipzig: Korten, 1778);

Ludwig Christoph Heinrich Hölty, *Gedichte,* edited by Stolberg and Johann Heinrich Voß (Hamburg: Bohn, 1783);

Plato, *Auserlesene Gespräche des Platon,* 3 volumes, translated by Stolberg (Königsberg: Nicolovius, 1796-1797);

Aeschylus, *Vier Tragödien des Aeschylos,* translated by Stolberg (Hamburg: Perthes, 1802);

St. Augustine, *Zwo Schriften des heiligen Augustinus von der wahren Religion und von den Sitten der katholischen Kirche: Mit Beilagen und Anmerkungen,* translated by Stolberg (Münster & Leipzig: Waldeck, 1803);

James Macpherson, *Die Gedichte von Ossian, dem Sohne Fingals,* 3 volumes, translated by Stolberg (Hamburg: Perthes, 1806);

Die heiligen sonn- und festtäglichen Episteln und Evangelien, nebst der Leidensgeschichte des Herrn nach den Evangelisten Matthäus und Johannes: Zum Gebrauche für Kirchen und Schulen übersetzt, translated by Stolberg (Münster: Theissing, 1823).

Friedrich Leopold Graf zu Stolberg is known in the history of German letters as the younger and more talented and prolific of the Stolberg brothers who arrived on the literary scene with the dynamic generation of the 1770s. While his work includes a novel and several plays, only a few of his poems and shorter essays survived the vicissitudes of nineteenth-century canonization. These works, however, disclose an almost paradigmatic figure of German Sentimentalism and suggest the need for an expanded and intensified resumption of the Stolberg scholarship that occurred in the 1960s.

Born on 7 November 1750 in Bramstedt, a small town in present-day Schleswig-Holstein, Stolberg was formatively influenced by both his introspective and humane father, Christian Günther zu Stolberg, who helped abolish serfdom in north Germany and Denmark, and his vivacious and imaginative mother, Friederike Christiane, who was inclined toward Pietism. He spent a happy childhood and youth on country estates and in small towns amid the culturally favored nobility of north Germany. Following an apparently uneventful two years at the University of Halle, Stolberg and his brother Christian continued their studies in Göttingen from 1772 to 1773.

Some two months after their arrival the brothers became members of the Göttinger Hainbund (Fraternity of the Göttingen Grove), a group of young sentimental poets and disciples of Friedrich Gottlieb Klopstock, and turned their attention increasingly from philosophy and law to literature. In addition to Klopstock, Friedrich Leopold Stolberg was particularly interested in Milton, Oliver Goldsmith, Shakespeare, Thomas Percy's collection of ballads, Ossian, the Bible, and the ancient Greeks, especially Homer and Plutarch. In January 1773 he began an intensive study of the ancient Greek language. At the same time he was writing lyrics on the themes of free-

Stolberg's parents, Christian Günther Graf zu Stolberg and Friederike Christiane Gräfin zu Stolberg; paintings by an unknown artist (in possession of Franz Graf zu Stolberg Stolberg, Hasselburg)

dom, nature, friendship, virtue, and the fatherland. In September 1773 the brothers moved to Hamburg to be near Klopstock and the poets Matthias Claudius and Heinrich Wilhelm von Gerstenberg.

In April 1775 the Stolbergs set off on a trip to Switzerland. Passing through Frankfurt they met the young Goethe, who was enjoying the extraordinary success of his novel *Die Leiden des jungen Werthers* (The Sorrows of Young Werther, 1774). Friedrich Leopold's rhapsodic enthusiasm moved Goethe to accompany them on what became known as the Geniereise (journey of geniuses). Wearing blue jackets and yellow pants and vests in imitation of Werther, the three indulged themselves in nude bathing and other behavior designed to scandalize the good burghers along the way–acts more of youthful high-spiritedness than of genius. On the other hand, they met Jakob Michael Reinhold Lenz, Friedrich Maximilian Klinger, and other members of the Sturm und Drang movement, as well as elder statesmen such as Voltaire and Christoph Martin Wieland; and they experienced the natural and political freedom of republican Switzerland.

On returning from the journey in 1776 Stolberg was named Danish chamberlain and, a year later, head cupbearer and envoy of the prince-bishop of Oldenburg-Lübeck in Copenhagen. During the ensuing few years he composed a series of short essays which reveal his basic views of art and life. The most important is "Über die Fülle des Herzens" (On the Fullness of the Heart, 1777), in which he says that the heart is the wellspring of all noble sentiments and of art, and that religion is the molder of the heart. In "Vom Dichten und Darstellen" (On Writing and Representation, 1780) he holds that a poem is a forceful release of the fullness of the heart. And in "Über die Begeistrung" (On Inspiration, 1782) he presents his subject as a prerational gift of divinity, independent of the individual's will, and the poet as a prophet who gives form to his momentary visions in freedom from all rules. Throughout these essays Stolberg employs an appropriately "dithyrambic" style. In 1778 his rendering of Homer's *Iliad* was published; it is more the product of enthusiastic dilettantism than of sustained effort and philological expertise.

Agnes Gräfin zu Stolberg, née von Witzleben, whom Stolberg married in 1782; painting by Anton Graff, 1784-1785 in Gräfl. Bylandt-Rheydtschem Besitz, Vienna)

Stolberg had published individual poems as early as 1774 in the *Göttinger Musenalmanach*, the influential organ of the Hainbund and the younger generation. His first collection, which also included works by his brother, appeared in 1779 under the title *Gedichte der Brüder Christian und Friedrich Leopold Grafen zu Stolberg* (Poems of the Brothers Counts Christian and Friedrich Leopold zu Stolberg). The early poetry is dominated by the ideas of the essays, as expressed, for example, in "Der Genius" and "Die Begeistrung: An Voß" (Inspiration: To [Johann Heinrich] Voß). Of particular interest is the notion of freedom, which manifests itself in various ways. It assumes the form of inward or artistic freedom in "Der Felsenstrom" (The Mountain Stream), which is reminiscent of Goethe's "Mahomets-Gesang" (Song of Mohammed, 1774) and is one of Stolberg's most noteworthy efforts in Klopstockian free rhythms. The concept is clearly political in "Freiheitsgesang aus dem Zwanzigsten Jahrhundert" (Song of Freedom from the Twentieth Century), which projects a victorious battle against tyranny into the future in the most

hymnic and freest of free rhythms. The theme of nature, as in "An die Natur" (To Nature), is also central to Stolberg's lyrics. Stolberg demonstrates that he has greater control over the ballad stanza than the Greek ode forms in such poems as "Elise von Mannsfeld: Eine Ballade aus dem 10. Jahrhundert" (Elise von Mannsfeld: A Ballad of the Tenth Century).

Between 1780 and 1782 Stolberg's spirit was tried by the deaths of several relatives and friends, as well as by the fall of his friend Count Andreas Peter von Bernstorff from the foreign ministry of Denmark. Consequently, he requested his discharge as envoy and was granted a long leave, which he spent in Copenhagen, Tremsbüttel, and Eutin. In the latter city he added the post of deputy chamberlain to his remaining duties.

A new life began for Stolberg in 1782 with his marriage to Agnes von Witzleben, with whom he shared, by all accounts, an unusually intimate and fulfilling relationship. Indeed, his family life and writing compensated for what he experienced as the "judicial yoke" about his neck following his move to Neuenburg as magistrate in 1785. Although his love poetry is generally Anacreontic in character, he composed several personal poems for his family–for example, "Lied für Agnes, ihren Kleinen in Schlaf zu singen" (Song for Agnes to Sing Her Little Boy to Sleep)– that call his friend Claudius to mind.

In the mid 1780s Stolberg began trying his hand at various genres, with varying success. *Jamben* (Iambs, 1784) is a boisterously satirical settling of accounts with abuses and abusers such as despotism, poetasters, and effusive sentimentalists; it includes an overt jibe at the controversial Hamburg pastor Johann Melchior Goeze. Stolberg is represented by five plays in *Schauspiele mit Choeren* (Plays with Choirs), which he published with his brother in 1787. *Timoleon, Theseus,* and *Servius Tullius* draw on the history or legends of antiquity to characterize the ideal ruler and to criticize tyranny. *Apollons Hain* (Apollo's Grove) is a satyr play in praise of the true poet and in criticism of the poetaster. Similar views are expressed in *Der Säugling* (The Infant), a dramatic fantasy on the childhood of Homer as the son of Apollo. The plays are neither dramatic nor the fruit of long labor, in accordance with Stolberg's view of the artwork as the result of the first, lucky coup. The dialogue is in blank verse, the choirs in Greek ode forms. In the words of a sympathetic writer, the functions of the choir of antiquity are

First page of manuscript for a poem by Stolberg (Gustav Könnecke, Bilderatlas zur Geschichte der deutschen Nationallitteratur *[Graz: Akademische Druck- und Verlagsanstalt, 1981])*

Stolberg's second wife, Sophie Charlotte Eleonore Gräfin zu Stolberg, née von Redern, whom he married in 1790; pastel by H. Schmidt, 1790 (in possession of Hedwig Gräfin zu Stolberg Stolberg, Bad Hall, Tirol)

fulfilled only "in theory." *Apollons Hain* is the most successful of the plays.

Among the most ambitious of Stolberg's early works is *Die Insel* (The Island, 1788), an eclectic idyll in the utopian tradition. Composed of dialogues, narrative hexameters, lyrics, and choral songs, the work draws on Plato, patriarchalism, and Jean-Jacques Rousseau without arriving at a coherent vision. Founded on sociopolitical and economic equality, the community depicted in the work evinces at the same time a minimum of codified laws and the strictest order. The work includes a few verses from *Die Zukunft* (The Future, 1885), a hexameter poem which was begun in 1779 and reached five cantos before being abandoned around 1782.

The death of his wife in 1788 marked a turning point in Stolberg's life. Incapacitated by grief, he again petitioned for release from his duties. In 1789 he became the Danish envoy in Berlin, where he met and married Countess Sophie Charlotte Eleonore von Redern the following

year. Finding Berlin uncongenial, he accepted a position in Eutin in 1791 as president of the Lübeck Chamber of Deputies. He immediately received a leave of absence, which he used for a trip to Italy. His account of this journey appeared in four volumes in 1794 under the title *Reise in Deutschland, der Schweiz, Italien und Sicilien in den Jahren 1791 und 1792* (translated as *Travels through Germany, Switzerland, Italy, and Sicily,* 1796-1797). Preferred by some contemporaries to Goethe's *Italienische Reise* (Italian Journey, 1816-1817), the work presents the South from the perspective of a sincere but amateurish enthusiast. During a sojourn in Münster, Stolberg met Princess Amalia Galizyn, the center of a mystically inclined group of Catholics, and formed a close and consequential friendship with her.

During the final decade of the century Stolberg's spirit and convictions were increasingly put to the test. The political and material misery of the French revolutionary war years in particular took its toll. Enthusiastic over the outbreak of the revolution and the prospect of freedom, he was horrified by the Terror and the rise of Napoleon. While his poetry decreased both in quantity and lyricism following his first wife's death, the political lyric occupied greater space and became more topical. "Die Westhunnen" (The Western Huns, 1793), for example, is a vitriolic attack on the godlessness and brutality of the revolution, while "Ode: Kassandra" (1796) warns of the danger threatening Germany from abroad. The novel *Numa* must be seen as an indirect response to the political situation in Europe. Written in the early 1790s but published only in 1968, it deals with yet another model ruler of antiquity. A source of respite during these trying times, Stolberg's love of the ancient Greeks resulted in the publication of *Auserlesene Gespräche des Platon* (Selected Dialogues of Plato) in 1796 and 1797 and *Vier Tragödien des Aeschylos* (Four Tragedies of Aeschylus) in 1802. Executed quickly, like so much of Stolberg's work, the translations of *Prometheus Bound, Seven against Thebes, Persae,* and *Eumenides* nonetheless enjoyed some success even with so astute a critic as Friedrich Schiller.

Even more unsettling than the developments in France were Kantian philosophy—indeed, the whole radicalized Enlightenment—and a Lutheranism which to Stolberg's mind led to deism and atheism. He was also deeply affected by the deaths of several of his children and of Bernstorff, as well as by his own serious illness in 1797. Coupled with his emotional spiritual-

*Front and side views of a marble bust of Stolberg by Luigi Acquisti, sculpted in 1794 (in possession of Franz
Graf zu Stolberg Stolberg, Wiesbaden)*

ity and the influence of his friends in Münster, these factors moved him to convert to Catholicism in 1800. In an age and place characterized by confessional chauvinism, Stolberg's conversion created enormous controversy. Exploited polemically by Catholics and Protestants alike, it resulted in many breaches of friendship, most bitterly with Voß. Feeling that he could no longer remain in the Protestant North, Stolberg resigned his post and moved to Münster later in 1800.

Following his conversion Stolberg's belletristic productivity diminished dramatically. Aside from his poetry he devoted his energies primarily to religious writing. His major work was *Geschichte der Religion Jesu Christi* (History of the Religion of Jesus Christ, 1806-1818), a fifteen-volume popular rather than scholarly attempt to trace the progress of Providence through secular history; it met with a warm reception. In 1806 he paid tribute to a hero of his youth with the translation *Die Gedichte von Ossian, dem Sohne Fingals* (The Poems of Ossian, the Son of Fingal).

In 1812 Stolberg moved to the estate

Tatenhausen near Bielefeld and in 1816 to the Osnabrück manor Sondermühlen, where he led a quiet, contented life with his family, friends, and work. Toward the end of the Napoleonic Wars he joined his brother in writing about the struggle against and victory over the French in poems such as "Napoleon" (1814) and "Blücher" (1814), the latter dedicated to Germany's Wellington. In "Deutschlands Beruf" (Germany's Calling, 1815) he envisions Germany as the heart of Europe and source of truth and virtue. In *Leben Alfred des Großen, Königes in England* (The Life of Alfred the Great, King of England, 1815) he delved into the past for the final time to find qualities of the ideal ruler for the present. In addition to the patriotic poems, Stolberg's late poetry largely comprises occasional pieces, for example, the fine "Andenken des Wandsbecker Boten" (Commemoration of the Wandsbeck Courier, 1816), written on the passing of Claudius, and "Schwanengesang" (Swan Song, 1819), in which the poet returns to the dithyrambic style of his youth in praise of the story of salvation.

Eventually daunted by the monumentality of the *Geschichte der Religion Jesu Christi*, Stolberg in 1819 turned with joy to the writing of *Betrachtungen und Beherzigungen der heiligen Schrift* (Reflections and Mementos of the Holy Scripture, 1819-1821), in which he was able to deal directly with the Bible and his own reaction to it. His final work was a self-defense, written in response to Voß's renewed attack, under the title *Friedrich Leopold Grafen zu Stolberg kurze Abfertigung der langen Schmähschrift des Herrn Hofraths Voß wider ihn* (Count Friedrich Leopold zu Stolberg's Brief Rebuff of Court Counselor Voß's Long Diatribe against Him), which was completed and published by Christian in 1820. More characteristic of the man, however, was *Ein Büchlein von der Liebe* (1820; translated as *A Little Book of the Love of God*, 1849), which in the manner of *Betrachtungen und Beherzigungen der heiligen Schrift* ascribes various manifestations of love to the infinite love of Christ. Just as he escaped the egotism of nobility, Stolberg avoided the zealotry of the convert and lived his ideal of tolerance. He died at Sondermühlen on 5 December 1819 at the age of sixty-nine.

Letters:

"Briefe F. L. Stolbergs an Gerstenberg," *Morgenblatt für gebildete Stände*, 29, nos. 156-157 (1835);

Friedrich Leopold Graf zu Stolberg und Herzog Peter Friedrich Ludwig von Oldenburg: Aus ihren Briefen und andern archivalischen Quellen, edited by Johann Heinrich Hennes (Mainz: Kirchheim, 1870);

Stolberg in den letzten zwei Jahrzehnten seines Lebens edited by Hennes (Mainz: Kirchheim, 1875);

Briefe Friedrich Leopolds Grafen zu Stolberg und der Seinigen an Voß, edited by Otto Hellinghaus (Münster: Aschendorff, 1891);

Briefwechsel zwischen Klopstock und den Grafen Christian und Friedrich Leopold zu Stolberg: Mit einem Anhang: Briefwechsel zwischen Klopstock und Herder, edited by Jürgen Behrens (Neumünster: Wachholtz, 1964);

"Johann Heinrich Voß und Friedrich Leopold Graf zu Stolberg: Neun bisher unveröffentlichte Briefe," edited by Behrens, *Jahrbuch des Freien Deutschen Hochstifts* (1965): 49-87;

Friedrich Leopold Graf zu Stolberg: Briefe, edited by Behrens (Neumünster: Wachholtz, 1966).

Bibliography:

Karl Goedeke, "Friedrich Leopold Graf zu Stol-

berg," in his *Grundriß zur Geschichte der deutschen Dichtung aus den Quellen*, third edition, volume 6, part 1 (Dresden: Ehlermann, 1916), pp. 1024-1038.

Biographies:

Christian Graf zu Stolberg, *Kurzer Lebensabriß des Grafen Friedrich Leopold zu Stolberg* (Leipzig, 1821);

Theodor Menge, *Der Graf Friedrich Leopold Stolberg und seine Zeitgenossen* (Gotha: Perthes, 1862);

Johann Heinrich Hennes, *Aus Friedrich Leopold v. Stolberg's Jugendjahren: Nach Briefen der Familie und andern handschriftlichen Nachrichten* (Frankfurt am Main: Sauerländer, 1876);

Johannes Janssen, *Friedrich Leopold Graf zu Stolberg: Größtentheils aus dem bisher ungedruckten Familiennachlaß* (Freiburg im Breisgau: 1877).

References:

Adolf Beck, *Die Äschylos-Übersetzung des Grafen F. L. zu Stolberg* (Berlin: Heine, 1937);

Beck, "Hölderlin und Friedrich Leopold Graf zu Stolberg: Die Anfänge des hymnischen Stils bei Hölderlin," in *Forschung und Deutung: Ausgewählte Aufsätze zur Literatur*, edited by Ulrich Fülleborn (Frankfurt am Main & Bonn, 1966), pp. 236-264;

Ingeborg and Jürgen Behrens, eds., *Friedrich Leopold Graf zu Stolberg: Verzeichnis sämtlicher Briefe* (Bad Homburg: Gehlen, 1968);

Behrens and Behrens, eds., "Nachtrag zum Verzeichnis sämtlicher Briefe des Grafen Friedrich Leopold zu Stolberg," *Jahrbuch des Freien Deutschen Hochstifts* (1971): 479-482;

Jürgen Behrens, "Friedrich Leopold Graf zu Stolberg: Bemerkungen zu einigen zeitgenössischen Schriftstellern," *Literaturwissenschaftliches Jahrbuch der Görresgesellschaft*, new series 9 (1968): 141-157;

Behrens, "Friedrich Leopold Graf zu Stolberg: Porträt eines Standesherrn," in *Staatsdienst und Menschlichkeit: Studien zur Adelskultur des späten 18. Jahrhunderts in Schleswig-Holstein und Dänemark*, edited by Christian Degn and Dieter Lohmeier (Neumünster: Wachholtz, 1980), pp. 151-165;

Behrens, "*Numa:* Ein unveröffentlichter Roman von Friedrich Leopold Graf zu Stolberg," *Jahrbuch des Wiener Goethe-Vereins*, 69 (1968): 103-120;

Behrens, "Wieland und die Brüder Christian und Friedrich Leopold Grafen zu Stolberg-Stolberg," *Jahrbuch des Wiener Goethe-Vereins,* new series 65 (1961): 45-67;

Pierre Brachin, *Le cercle de Münster (1779-1806) et la pensée religieuse de F. L. Stolberg* (Lyon & Paris: IAC, 1952);

Brachin, "Friedrich Leopold von Stolberg und die deutsche Romantik," *Literaturwissenschaftliches Jahrbuch der Görresgesellschaft,* new series 1 (1960): 117-131;

F. Heyer, "Kleuker und Graf Stolberg," *Nordelbingen,* 34 (1965): 148-160;

Michel Kauffmann, "Notes sur l'évolution politique de F. L. Stolberg et J. H. Voß," in *Méditations ou le métier de germaniste: Mélanges offerts à Pierre Bertaux* (Asnières: Institut d'Allemand d'Asnières, 1977), pp. 138-147;

Wolfgang Kehn, "Kultur als Verwirklichung der Natur: Über den Zusammenhang von Landschaftsgartenkunst, Menschenbild und aristokratischem Selbstverständnis in den Briefen des Grafen F. L. Stolberg," *Nordelbingen,* 52 (1983): 59-85;

Wilhelm Keiper, *Friedrich Leopold Stolbergs Jugendpoesie* (Berlin: Mayer & Müller, 1893);

Françoise Knopper, "L'île de F. L. Stolberg: Poesie et Renoncement," *Travaux et mémoires de l'Université de Limoges: Colloque Allemand,* 1 (1976): 47-65;

I. Markus-Grimm, "Stolbergs Beziehungen zu Klopstock nach seiner Konversion," in *Fürstenberg, Fürstin Gallitzin und ihr Kreis: Quellen und Forschungen,* edited by Erich Trunz (Münster: Aschendorff, 1955), pp. 92-99;

Hans-Werner Nieschmidt, "Stürzende Wasser: Zum Motiv des Wasserfalls in Gedichten Stolbergs, Goethes und Mörikes," *Journal of the Australasian Universities Language and Literature Association,* 38 (1972): 143-158;

L. Pfleger, "Friedrich Schlegel und Leopold Graf zu Stolberg: Ein Beitrag zu Schlegels Konversionsgeschichte," *Historisch-politische Blätter für das katholische Deutschland,* 149 (1911): 495-504;

Leo Scheffczyk, *Friedrich Leopold zu Stolbergs Geschichte der Religion Christi: Die Abwendung der katholischen Kirchengeschichtsschreibung von der Aufklärung und ihre Neuorientierung im Zeitalter der Romantik* (Munich: Zink, 1952);

Karl August Schleiden, "Über ein unbekanntes Gedicht des Grafen Friedrich Leopold zu Stolberg," *Jahrbuch der Deutschen Schillergesellschaft,* 6 (1963): 35-65;

George C. Schoolfield, "Schubert-Stolberg-Diktonius," in *Aufnahme, Weitergabe: Literarische Impulse um Lessing und Goethe: Festschrift für Heinz Moenkemeyer zum 68. Geburtstag,* edited by John A. McCarthy and Albert A. Kipa (Hamburg: Buske, 1982), pp. 263-280;

C. Schüddekopf, "Zu Christian und Friedrich Leopold von Stolbergs Jugendgedichten," *Zeitschrift für deutsche Philologie,* 18 (1886): 477-484;

Detlev W. Schumann, "Friedrich Leopold Graf zu Stolberg," in *Deutsche Dichter des 18. Jahrhunderts: Ihr Leben und Werk,* edited by Benno von Wiese (Berlin: Schmidt, 1977), pp. 726-746;

Schumann, "Friedrich Leopold Stolbergs Übertritt zur katholischen Kirche," *Euphorion,* 50 (1956): 271-306;

Schumann, "Goethe and the Stolbergs: A Friendship of the Storm and Stress," *Journal of English and Germanic Philology,* 48 (1949): 483-504;

Schumann, "Goethe and the Stolbergs after 1775: The History of a Problematic Relationship," *Journal of English and Germanic Philology,* 50 (1951): 22-59;

Otto Graf zu Stolberg-Wernigerode, "Friedrich Leopold Graf zu Stolberg-Stolberg (1750-1819) und seine Zeit," *Archiv für Kulturgeschichte,* 57 (1975): 195-210;

Siegfried Sudhof, "Goethe und Stolberg," in *Festschrift für Detlev Schumann zum 70. Geburtstag,* edited by Albert R. Schmitt (Munich: Delp, 1970), pp. 97-109;

Sudhof, "Herder und der 'Kreis von Münster': Ein Beitrag zur Beurteilung von F. L. Stolbergs Konversion," *Wissenschaftliches Jahrbuch der Görres-Gesellschaft,* new series 1 (1960): 133-147;

Harro Zimmermann, "Der Antiquar und die Revolution: Friedrich Leopold von Stolbergs *Reise in Deutschland, der Schweiz, Italien und Sizilien,*" in *Reise und soziale Realität am Ende des 18. Jahrhunderts,* edited by Wolfgang Griep and Hans-Wolf Jäger (Heidelberg, 1983), pp. 94-126.

Papers:

Friedrich Leopold Graf zu Stolberg's papers are at the Freies Deutsches Hochstift, Frankfurter Goethemuseum, Frankfurt am Main; and the Schleswig-Holsteinische Landesbibliothek, Kiel.

Friederike Helene Unger
(1741? - 21 September 1813)

Susanne Zantop
Dartmouth College

BOOKS: *Die Damen dürfen doch auch ein Wort mitreden? Eine Scene aus dem Visiten-Zimmer; beym Caffee übers neue Gesangbuch,* anonymous (Berlin: Matzdorf, 1781);

Vermischte Erzählungen und Einfälle zur angenehmen Unterhaltung, 4 volumes, anonymous (Berlin: Unger, 1783-1786);

Julchen Grünthal: Eine Pensionsgeschichte. Mit allergnädigsten Freiheiten, anonymous (Berlin: Unger, 1784; revised, 1787; revised and enlarged, 2 volumes, 1798);

Neuestes Berlinisches Kochbuch oder Anweisung, alle Speisen und Saucen zuzurichten, 2 volumes, anonymous (Berlin: Unger, 1785); revised and enlarged as *Neuestes Berlinisches Kochbuch oder Anweisung, Speisen, Saucen und Gebacknes schmackhaft zuzurichten; desgleichen auch allerlei Arten Früchte einzumachen; nebst verschiedenen Anmerkungen und Kunstgriffen der Kochkunst,* 3 volumes, anonymous (Berlin: Unger, 1790);

Naturkalender zur Unterhaltung der heranwachsenden Jugend, anonymous (Berlin: Unger, 1789);

Vaterländisches Lesebuch für Land- und Soldatenschulen (Berlin: Unger, 1799);

Gräfinn Pauline, anonymous, 2 volumes (Berlin: Unger, 1800);

Rosalie und Nettchen: Ein Roman, anonymous (Berlin: Unger, 1801);

Prinz Bimbam: Ein Mährchen für Jung und Alt, anonymous (Berlin: Unger, 1802);

Mährchen, anonymous, attributed to Unger and to Karoline von Günderrode (Berlin: Ungers Journalhandlung, 1802);

Bekenntnisse einer Giftmischerin: Von ihr selbst geschrieben, anonymous, attributed to Unger and to Friedrich Buchholz (Berlin: Unger, 1803);

Melanie, das Findelkind, anonymous (Berlin: Unger, 1804);

Albert und Albertine, anonymous (Berlin: Unger, 1804);

Bekenntnisse einer schönen Seele: Von ihr selbst geschrieben, anonymous, also attributed to Buchholz

Friederike Helene Unger; drawing by J. Gottfried Schadow, circa 1800 (Josef Nadler, Literaturgeschichte des deutschen Volkes *[Berlin: Propyläen, 1938])*

and to Charlotte von Ahlefeld (Berlin: Unger, 1806);

Die Franzosen in Berlin oder Serene an Clementinen in den Jahren 1806, 7, 8: Ein Sittengemälde, anonymous (Leipzig, Züllichau & Freystadt: Darnmann, 1809);

Der junge Franzose und das deutsche Mädchen: Wenn man will, ein Roman, anonymous (Hamburg: Hoffmann, 1810).

OTHER: Jean-Jacques Rousseau, *J. J. Rousseaus Bekenntnisse,* 2 volumes, translated by Unger (Berlin: Unger, 1782);

Rousseau, *J. J. Rousseaus Selbstgespräche auf einsamen Spaziergängen: Ein Anhang zu den Bekennt-*

nissen, translated by Unger (Berlin: Unger, 1782);

Simon Nicolas Henri Linguet, *Denkwürdigkeiten der Bastille und die Gefangenschaft des Verfassers in diesem Königlichen Schlosse vom 27. September 1780 bis zum 19. Mai 1782*, translated by Unger (Berlin: Unger, 1783);

Linguet, *Beschreibung und Geschichte der Bastille während der Regierungen Ludwig des Vierzehnten, Funfzehnten und Sechszehnten*, translated by Unger (Berlin: Unger, 1784);

Pierre-Augustin Caron de Beaumarchais, *Der lustige Tag oder: Figaro's Hochzeit*, translated by Unger (Berlin: Unger, 1785);

Anonymous, *Maria, eine Geschichte in zwei Bänden: Aus dem Englischen übersetzt*, 2 volumes, translated by Unger (Berlin: Unger, 1786);

Louis Sebastien Mercier, *Mercier's Nachtmütze: Dritter Band. Mit chursächsischem Privilegium*, translated by Unger (Berlin: Unger, 1786);

Mme. de Montolien (Elisabeth Jeanne Pauline Portier de Bottens), *Karoline von Lichtfeld: Eine Geschichte in 2 Theilen*, translated by Unger (Berlin: Unger, 1787);

Molière, *Der Betbruder: Ein Lustspiel in fünf Aufzügen. Nach Molier's [sic] Tartüffe frei übersetzt*, translated by Unger (Berlin: Unger, 1787);

Molière, *Der adelsüchtige Bürger: Eine Posse. Mit Tanz untermischt*, translated by Unger (Berlin: Unger, 1788);

Dumaniant (Antoine Jean Bourlin), *Die Abenteuer einer Nacht oder Die zwei lebenden Todten: Ein Lustspiel in drei Akten. Aus dem Französischen*, translated by Unger (Berlin: Unger, 1789);

Dumaniant, *Die magnetische Wunderkraft oder Aller Welt zum Trotz doch ein Arzt: Ein Lustspiel in drei Aufzügen vom Verfasser der offenen Fehde. Aus dem Französischen frey übersetzt*, translated by Unger (Berlin: Unger, 1790);

Anonymous, *Der Mondkaiser: Eine Posse in drey Aufzügen. Aus dem Französischen frei übersetzt*, translated by Unger (Berlin: Unger, 1790);

Pierre Carlet de Chamblain de Marivaux, *Marianen's Begebenheiten: Aus dem Französischen des Marivaux*, 3 volumes, translated by Unger (Berlin: Unger, 1791-1792);

Joseph Gorani, *Geheime und kritische Nachrichten von Italien nebst einem Gemälde der Höfe: Regierungen und Sitten der vornehmsten Staaten dieses Landes. Von Joseph Gorani, französischem Bürger*, 3 volumes, translated by Unger (Frankfurt am Main & Leipzig, 1794).

PERIODICAL PUBLICATIONS: "Uebersicht der Geschichte Ludwig des funfzehnten," *Berlinisches Magazin der Wissenschaften und Künste*, 1, no. 3 (1782): 90-163;

"Etwas über das weibliche Gesinde. (Von einer Hausfrau)," as F. U.... geb. R., *Berlinische Monatsschrift*, 11 (January-June 1788): 676-684;

"Über Berlin: Aus Briefen einer reisenden Dame an ihren Bruder in H," *Jahrbücher der Preußischen Monarchie unter der Regierung Friedrich Wilhelms des Dritten*, 2 (1798): 17-33, 133-143, 287-302; republished as *Briefe über Berlin aus Briefen einer reisenden Dame an ihren Bruder in H.: Von Helene Friederike Unger* (Berlin: Aldus, 1930);

"Louis und Louise," as Die Verfasserin der Gräfinn Pauline, *Irene: Eine Monatsschrift*, 1 (1802): 125-164;

"Auguste von Friedenheim," *Berlinischer Damen-Kalender auf das Schaltjahr 1804* (1803): 1-192.

Among German women writers of the eighteenth century, Friederike Helene Unger occupies both a privileged and an enigmatic position. Of aristocratic descent, unusually well educated, married to the Berlin printer and publisher Johann Friedrich Unger, and childless, she had the preparation, time, and access to the world of letters that many of her female contemporaries could only dream of. Yet being neither daughter, wife, lover, nor muse of any of the literary "giants," she never even carved out a space in their biographies. Her many works appeared anonymously and have often been attributed to other authors. Except for an occasional mention in nineteenth-century dictionaries and in histories of printing, no information is available about this writer who was a best-selling author in her lifetime, known for her sharp and witty pen and her satirical depictions of courtly and bourgeois mores.

Friederike Helene von Rothenburg was probably born in 1741–not in 1751, as most biographers claim–as the daughter of the Prussian general Friedrich Rudolf Graf von Rothenburg, one of Frederick II's favorites. Little is known of her mother, a Marquise de Vieuville, daughter of the French general Marquis de Parabère, whom Rothenburg, then an officer in French service, married in 1735. Unger refers to her mother only once, and indirectly, when she writes in a letter that French was her mother tongue. In 1741

Frederick II called Rothenburg back to Prussia, where he had a distinguished military career until he died in 1751 from the aftereffects of wounds suffered in the Silesian Wars. Throughout her life Unger preserved an almost mystic veneration for her father, for the Great Frederick, and for Prussian military glory, in spite of her growing abhorrence of the disastrous effects of war.

Presumably after her father's premature death, but possibly even before (according to one biography, Rothenburg died "childless"), Friederike was raised in the house of the court preacher Johann Peter Bamberger, where she received a thorough education in French literature, history, and English. While working as a governess she met the printer and wood engraver Johann Friedrich Unger, whom she married around 1785. Johann Friedrich Unger became one of Berlin's leading publishers (he published Goethe's *Wilhelm Meisters Lehrjahre* [Wilhelm Meister's Apprenticeship, 1795-1796], August Wilhelm Schlegel's Shakespeare translations [1797-1810], and many works by the Romantics), an ingenious printer (inventor of the "Unger Fraktur" typeface), a successful bookseller, and a professor of wood engraving at the Academy of Fine Arts in Berlin. Throughout her married years, Friederike Helene Unger remained her husband's closest collaborator. She translated autobiographies (including Jean-Jacques Rousseau's *Confessions* [1782] and *Rêveries d'un promeneur solitaire* [1782]), novels (including Marivaux's *Vie de Marianne* [1791-1792]), and plays for his press, wrote articles and reviews for his journals, and kept a literary salon. She also served as his adviser in literary matters—to the great dismay of Friedrich Schlegel, who in 1798 apparently invented a love affair with the fifty-seven-year-old "Ungeheuerin" (she-monster), as he calls her in his letters, in retaliation for Unger's derogatory remarks about Jewish *salonnières* and her rejection of the novel *Florentin* (1801), written by Schlegel's companion Dorothea Mendelssohn-Veit. Unger's complicated, competitive relationship with the Schlegels (her husband was involved in a lawsuit against August Wilhelm) and their friends translated into the satirical asides against anything "Romantic" that abound in Unger's works.

In 1804 her husband died at the age of fifty-one. Unger took on the management of the music and book printeries and the bookshop, despite the enterprise's precarious financial situation. She repeatedly attempted to secure royal support for the failing business, which finally collapsed during the Napoleonic Wars. In 1811 Unger was forced to declare bankruptcy and sell the publishing house to pay the debts. A two-hundred-taler pension which King Friedrich Wilhelm finally granted the destitute widow came too late: Unger died on 21 September 1813.

Although Unger wrote in a wide range of genres—she published a popular cookbook (1785), a calendar (1789), a reader (1783-1786), and many translations—she made her reputation as a novelist. Her eight novels explore the difficult socialization processes women face in a society that knows only one compound female role, that of wife, housewife, and mother, and only one female virtue, chastity. In their advocacy of a pragmatic, rational approach to male-female relationships and in their fierce opposition to self-indulgent Sentimentalism, Unger's works form a bridge between the Enlightenment philosophy of Sophie von La Roche and the republicanism of writers in the 1830s and 1840s.

In Unger's first and most acclaimed novel, *Julchen Grünthal* (1784), based on Marivaux's *La paysanne parvenue* (1735), Julchen's father, Magistrate Grünthal (Greenvale), tells the story of his daughter's "fall" due to miseducation. Sent to a French boarding school in Berlin by her ambitious mother, the innocent country girl is corrupted by the immoral headmistress and by her aristocratic fellow students. Corrupted by fashion, balls, and French novels of passion such as Rousseau's *La nouvelle Héloïse* (1791) into a life of dissipation, Julchen has an affair with a married man, later marries the adulterer, and, after he has gambled away their fortune, elopes with a Russian prince, never to be heard of again.

The novel, which appeared anonymously, was an immediate success. The *Göttingische Gelehrte Anzeiger*, normally not a forum for the discussion of novels, printed a glowing review recommending the book as an invective against French schools and as a warning to those parents who wanted to educate their daughters beyond their "natural" station. A revised edition appeared in 1787, and in 1788 Pastor Johann Jakob Stutz published a sequel, also anonymously, in which a repenting Julchen returns home to start her own German boarding school. All responses identified with the position of the narrator-father, ignoring the woman whose desire for education beyond the household had ended in disaster. In 1798 Unger published another revised version of *Julchen Grünthal*, with her own sequel in a second

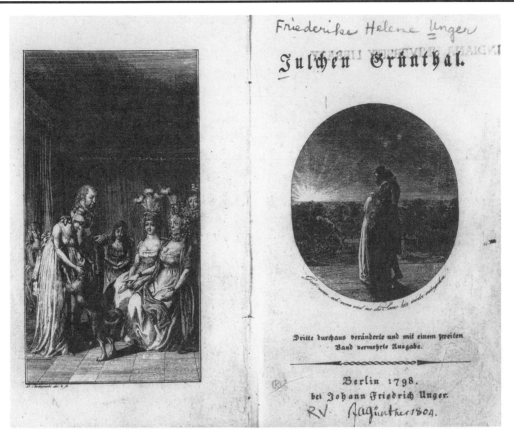

Frontispiece and title page for the enlarged third edition of Unger's novel about a girl who is corrupted as a result of a bad education

volume. Julchen, who has returned to her father, now tells her own story of conflict between desire and duty. She describes the battles she had to wage to fend off the advances of the Russian prince–particularly after she found out that he was married–and of a lesbian countess in whose house she had sought shelter. Julchen's narrative is corroborated by the "confessions" of her friend Minna, another victim of an overly strict, bigoted home and an overly permissive, sensuous city education, and by the success story of Julchen's cousin Karoline Falk. In all three cases, painful experiences are shown to be necessary steps toward a fuller, more consciously moral existence. As Grünthal says of his daughter: "Was sie zu werden versprach, ist nichts gegen das, was sie geworden ist" (What she promised to become is nothing compared to what she became), and of Karoline: "es scheint mir oft, als habe es so seyn müssen, wie alles gewesen ist, damit jede ihrer schönen Anlagen sich entwickeln konnte" (I often think that everything had to be the way it was so that each of her beautiful talents could de-

velop). "Tugend" (female virtue) is not something a woman can lose, but something she can gain–through suffering and struggle.

The idea that there is more than one female virtue and that "virtue" is the result of experiences that can in fact empower women is elaborated in Unger's subsequent novels, *Gräfinn Pauline* (Countess Pauline, 1800), *Rosalie und Nettchen* (1801), *Melanie, das Findelkind* (Melanie, the Foundling, 1804), and *Albert und Albertine* (1804). All of them attempt to create a female Bildungsroman, a novel of character formation–*Charakterbildung*, as Unger calls it–in opposition to the concept of an unchanging, and therefore unformable, female nature. *Gräfinn Pauline*, an Entsagungsroman (novel of renunciation) that Friedrich Schiller cherished, tells the story of an almost superhuman inner struggle between love and duty which ends in the protagonist's voluntary renunciation of her love and her subsequent death. While Countess Pauline's self-sacrifice transforms her into a true "heroine" in the tradition of Goethe's Iphigenie or Wilhelmine

Karoline von Wobeser's Elise, the story of her suffering actually undercuts the moment of transcendence and raises doubts as to Unger's seriousness when she composed another of these self-sacrificial plots. In *Rosalie und Nettchen*, a hybrid between court satire and bourgeois tragedy, Unger's tone is less melodramatic, and the ending is happy: the women's constancy is rewarded with marital bliss; their unswerving love eventually "conquers" and "civilizes" the lovers. In *Melanie, das Findelkind*, a female counterpart to *Wilhelm Meisters Lehrjahre*, Melanie's renunciation of her lover constitutes one of many tests she has to undergo before legitimately coming into her own. A foundling raised in a noble family, she is pushed out and earns her living as an actress, governess, and lady's companion until she is recognized by her legitimate father, the prince, and allowed to assume the elevated social station she had morally held all along. Albertine, the least self-effacing and most sensuous of Unger's heroines, is rewarded for her independence of judgment, her ironic distance from Romantic Empfindsamkeit (Sentimentality), and her stoic endurance of hardship with the love of Albert, her true soul mate. And what is more, in *Albert und Albertine* it is the man who has to endure and make sacrifices to become worthy of the woman he loves. In these novels Unger thus not only expands and revises conventional models of the eternal feminine–the passive "virtue in distress," the disembodied "beautiful soul," and the selfless "Entsagende" (renunciant)–to create rational, pragmatic, active heroines, but she also develops new visions of the eternal male.

The question of independence of judgment is central to Unger's last three novels, which she wrote after her husband's death and in the midst of warfare and economic hardship. *Bekenntnisse einer schönen Seele: Von ihr selbst geschrieben* (Confessions of a Beautiful Soul: Written by Herself, 1806) relates the story of an "independent" woman who, in a letter to a friend, tries to answer what she considers to be the main question of her life: how she managed to remain single despite her physical and intellectual charms, and why she prefers the single state over marriage and motherhood. In contrast to Goethe's Beautiful Soul, who clearly served as an ironic foil, Unger's heroine is not religious, nor does she appear particularly troubled or neurotic–which is possibly why Goethe, in his review of the novel, called it "die Kopfgeburt eines verständigen Mannes" (the brainchild of a sensible man), not

the product of a woman's imagination. In *Die Franzosen in Berlin* (The Frenchmen in Berlin, 1809) the protagonist Serena, a widow and head of a large Berlin household, describes in letters to her French friend Clementina the trials and tribulations under French occupation. In this book, as in her subsequent novel, *Der junge Franzose und das deutsche Mädchen* (The Young Frenchman and the German Girl, 1810), a French-German love story set during the Napoleonic Wars, Unger attacks nationalist prejudice and pleads for the toleration of difference–no small achievement in view of the rising nationalism and shrill francophobia of the time. In these late works Unger transcends the limits of women's writing of the period not only thematically but also formally, mixing the private with the public, the effusive letter with historical and political discourse. Her digressions into Prussian history and her observations on current events (for example, the impact of French occupation on the economy and morals of the Berlin population) open up new areas for women writers; they anticipate the work of later political analysts and activists such as Louise Otto and Louise Aston.

In spite of enthusiastic responses to Unger's works during her lifetime, she remained practically forgotten until 1919, when Christine Touaillon recognized her as one of the most important representatives of the "rationalist novel." The more recent interest in what Marion Beaujean and others have termed "Trivialliteratur" and the current attempts to unearth and reevaluate women's writing have caused critics such as Magdalene Heuser to take a fresh look at the "author of Julchen Grünthal" and to assess her contribution to the female novel of formation. As a consequence of this renewed interest the Georg Olms publishing house in Hildesheim has published new editions of *Julchen Grünthal*, *Bekenntnisse einer schönen Seele*, and *Albert und Albertine*. These editions will provide access to some of the more influential and interesting early modern women's novels and to a woman author who, though she shared some of the limitations of her generation, surpassed many other writers of that generation in her wit and satire.

Letters:

Johann Friedrich Unger im Verkehr mit Goethe und Schiller: Briefe und Nachrichten, edited by Flodoard von Biedermann (Berlin: Berthold, 1927), pp. 67-69, 172;

Krisenjahre der Frühromantik: Briefe aus dem Schlegelkreis, 2 volumes, second edition, edited by Josef Körner (Bern & Munich: Francke, 1969), I: 194-195, 241-243, 551-554, 651-652; II: 25-27, 208-209.

References:

J. W. von Archenholz, "Ungers Tod," *Minerva*, 1 (1805): 175-180;

Dietlinde S. Bailet, *Die Frau als Verführte und als Verführerin in der deutschen und französischen Literatur des 18. Jahrhunderts* (Bern, Frankfurt am Main & Las Vegas: Lang, 1981), pp. 1-50;

Marion Beaujean, *Der Trivialroman in der zweiten Hälfte des 18. Jahrhunderts* (Bonn: Bouvier, 1964), pp. 39-41;

Jeannine Blackwell, "Bildungsroman mit Dame: The Heroine in the German 'Bildungsroman' from 1770 to 1900," Ph.D. dissertation, Indiana University, 1982, pp. 129-158;

Ernst Crous, *Die Schriftgießereien in Berlin von Thurneysser bis Unger* (Berlin: Berthold, 1928), pp. 86ff;

Dagmar Grenz, *Mädchenliteratur* (Stuttgart: Metzler, 1981), pp. 145-158;

Natalie Halperin, "Die deutschen Schriftstellerinnen in der zweiten Hälfte des 18. Jahrhunderts," Ph.D. dissertation, University of Frankfurt am Main, 1935, pp. 45-47;

Ernst L. Hauswedell and Christian Voigt, eds., *Buchkunst und Literatur in Deutschland 1750 bis 1850*, volume 1 (Hamburg: Maximilian Gesellschaft, 1977), pp. 25-29;

Manfred W. Heiderich, *The German Novel of 1800: A Study of Popular Prose Fiction* (Bern & Frankfurt am Main: Lang, 1982), pp. 230-232;

Magdalene Heuser, " 'Spuren trauriger Selbstvergessenheit.' Möglichkeiten eines weiblichen Bildungsromans um 1800: Friederike Helene Unger," in *Frauensprache-Frauenliteratur?: Für und wider eine Psychoanalyse literarischer Werke. Kontroversen, alte und neue. Akten des VI. Internationalen Germanisten-Kongresses*, volume 6, edited by Inge Stephan and Carl Pietzcker (Tübingen: Niemeyer, 1986), pp. 30-42;

Eberhard Hölscher, "Johann Friedrich Unger," *Imprimatur*, 6 (1935): 121-137;

Helga Meise, *Die Unschuld und die Schrift: Deutsche Frauenromane im 18. Jahrhundert* (Berlin & Marburg: Guttandin & Hoppe, 1983), pp. 51-65;

Meise, "Papierne Mädchen: Ansichten von der Unschuld im Frauenroman des 18. Jahrhunderts," in *Frauensprache-Frauenliteratur?*, volume 6, edited by Stephan and Pietzcker, pp. 18-23;

August Potthast, *Geschichte der Buchdruckerkunst in Berlin im Umriß*, edited by Crous (Berlin: Verein der Berliner Buchdruckerei-Besitzer, 1926), pp. 43ff;

Lydia Schieth, *Die Entwicklung des deutschen Frauenromans im ausgehenden 18. Jahrhundert: Ein Beitrag zu einer Gattungsgeschichte* (Frankfurt am Main, Bern & New York: Lang, 1986);

Werner E. Stichnote, "Goethe und Unger," *Das Druckgewerbe*, 2, no. 17 (1949): 291-292;

Christine Touaillon, *Der deutsche Frauenroman des 18. Jahrhunderts* (Vienna & Leipzig: Braumüller, 1919), pp. 244-261;

Susanne Zantop, Afterword to Unger's *Albert und Albertine* (Hildesheim: Olms, forthcoming 1990);

Zantop, Afterword to Unger's *Bekenntnisse einer schönen Seele: Von ihr selbst geschrieben* (Hildesheim: Olms, forthcoming 1990);

Zantop, Afterword to Unger's *Julchen Grünthal* (Hildesheim: Olms, forthcoming 1990);

Zantop, "Aus der Not eine Tugend: Tugendgebot und Öffentlichkeit bei Friederike Helene Unger," in *Der deutsche Roman von Frauen im ausgehenden 18. Jahrhundert*, edited by Heuser and Helga Gallas (Tübingen: Niemeyer, forthcoming 1990);

Zantop, "The Beautiful Soul Writes Herself: Friederike Helene Unger and the 'Große Göthe,' " in *In the Shadow of Olympus*, edited by Katharine Goodman and Edith Waldstein (Albany: State University of New York Press, forthcoming 1990).

Papers:
Most of Friederike Helene Unger's correspondence and all of the papers belonging to the Unger Verlag were lost during World War II. The few remaining documents can be found in the Staatsbibliothek Preußischer Kulturbesitz, West Berlin; the Staats- und Universitätsbibliothek, Hamburg; the Stadt-Archiv, Hannover; the Deutsches Buch- und Schriftmuseum der Deutschen Bücherei, Leipzig; the Deutsches Literaturarchiv, Marbach; the Zentrales Staatsarchiv der DDR, Merseburg; the Pennsylvania Historical Society, Philadelphia; and the Biblioteka Jagiellónska, Kraków.

Heinrich Leopold Wagner

(19 February 1747 - 4 March 1779)

Christopher L. Dolmetsch
Marshall University

BOOKS: *Apolls des ersten Bänkelsängers Leben und Thaten auf dieser Welt nebst seiner letzten Willens-Ordnung allen seinen unächten Söhnen die nichts von ihm erhalten haben, zum Aergerniss, dem Herrn, Herrn David Friedrich Döllin Med. Lt. bey seiner Abreise von Strassburg, zur nöthigen Einsicht kund gemacht und übergeben von einigen seiner zärtlichsten Freunde*, anonymous (Strasbourg: Lorenz, 1772);

Phaeton, eine Romanze, dem durchlauchtigsten Fürsten von Nassau-Saarbrücken in tiefster Ehrfurcht erzählt von Heinrich Leopold Wagner (Saarbrükken: Hofer, 1774);

Chronologisches Spiel, zum Gebrauch der Jugend, entworfen von Heinrich Leopold Wagner (Frankfurt am Main: Eichenberg, 1774)—includes "Ein Brief an Herrn Hofrath Pfeffel in Colmar, die nöthigsten Erläuterungen und Regeln meines chronologischen Spiels enthaltend";

Confiskable-Erzählungen: Wien, bey der Bücher-Censur, anonymous (Gießen: Krieger, 1774);

Prometheus, Deukalion und seine Recensenten: Voran ein Prologus und zuletzt ein Epilogus, anonymous (Frankfurt am Main: Eichenberg, 1775);

Der wolthätige Unbekannte: Eine Familien-Scene (Frankfurt am Main: Eichenberg, 1775); translated by Wagner as *L'Inconnu bienfésant: Drame en un acte* (Frankfurt am Main: Eichenberg, 1775);

Die Reue nach der That: Ein Schauspiel, anonymous (Frankfurt am Main: Eichenburg, 1775);

Rheinischer Most: Erster Herbst, anonymous (N.p., 1775);

Q. D. BV. Dissertatio Inauguralis: Historico-Juridica De Aurea Bulla non solorum electorum sed omnium statuum consensu condita, quam Deo solo praeside ex honorifico illustris facultatis juridicae decreto in alma argentoratensium universitate pro licentia summos in utroque jure honores et privilegia doctoralia rite consequendi solemni eruditorum examini ad diem XXVIII. Aug. submittit auc-

Silhouette of Heinrich Leopold Wagner, circa 1770 (Freies Deutsches Hochstift, Frankfurter Goethe-Museum, Frankfurt am Main)

tor Henricus Leopold Wagner Argentinensis. MDCCLXXVI (Strasbourg: Lorenz, 1776);

Leben und Tod Sebastian Silligs: Ein Roman für allerley Leser zur Warnung, nicht zur Nachfolge, anonymous (Frankfurt am Main & Leipzig: Eichenberg, 1776);

Epilog bey Eröffnung des Herrschaftlichen Theaters in Mainz, gesprochen von Madame Seyler, den 17. Juni 1777 (Mainz: Kunze, 1776);

Die Kindermörderinn: Ein Trauerspiel, anonymous (Leipzig: Schwickert, 1776); revised by Karl Gotthelf Lessing as *Die Kindermörderinn: Ein Trauerspiel in fünf Aufzügen. Neue umgearbeitete Auflage* (Berlin: Himburg, 1777);

Briefe, die Seylerische Schauspielergesellschaft und ihre Vorstellungen zu Frankfurt am Mayn betreffend, anonymous (Frankfurt am Main: Eichenberg, 1776);

Apolls Abschied von den Musen: Ein allegorischer Prolog mit welchem sich Einem Hochedlen und Hochweisen Magistrat wie auch dem gesammten nach Standes Gebühr geehrten Publiko der kaiserlichen freyen Reichs-, Wahl- und Handelstadt Frankfurt am Mayn unterthänigst empfehlen wollte und sollte die Seylerische Schauspielergesellschaft, anonymous (Frankfurt am Main: Eichenberg, 1777);

Voltaire am Abend seiner Apotheose: Aus dem Französischen, anonymous (Frankfurt am Main & Leipzig: Gebhardt, 1778);

Theaterstücke (Frankfurt am Main: Garbe, 1779)—comprises "Dédicace à Heribert von Dalberg"; *Evchen Humbrecht oder Ihr Mütter merkts Euch!: Ein Schauspiel in fünf Aufzügen; Macbeth: Ein Trauerspiel in fünf Aufzügen nach Shackespear;*

Gesammelte Schauspiele fürs deutsche Theater, 4 volumes (Frankfurt am Main: Garbe, 1780);

Gesammelte Werke in fünf Bänden: Zum ersten Mal vollständig, edited by Leopold Hirschberg, only one volume published (Potsdam: Hadern, 1923).

OTHER: Charles-Louis de Secondat, Baron de La Brède et de Montesquieu, *Der Tempel zu Gnidus: Aus dem Französischen des Herrn von Montesquieu übersetzt von H. L. W.,* translated by Wagner (Strasbourg: Heitz, 1770);

Louis Sébastien Mercier, *Der Schubkarn des Essighändlers: Ein Lustspiel in drey Aufzügen, aus dem Französischen des Herrn Mercier,* translated by Wagner (Frankfurt am Main: Eichenberg: 1775);

Die Königs-Krönung: Aufgefuhrt auf dem Theater zu Renne in Gegenwart Ihro Durchlaucht der Prinzessin von Lamballe, translated by Wagner (The Hague [actually Frankfurt am Main: Deinet], 1775);

Maximilian Joseph Graf von Lamberg, *Tagebuch eines Weltmanns,* 2 volumes, translated by Wagner (Frankfurt am Main: Eichenberg, 1775);

Mercier, *Neuer Versuch über die Schauspielkunst: Aus dem Französischen. Mit einem Anhang aus Goethes Brieftasche,* translated by Wagner and Johann Wolfgang Goethe (Leipzig: Schwickert, 1776).

PERIODICAL PUBLICATIONS: "Moropolis, Lieder für die Söhne der Dummheit," *Frankfurter gelehrte Anzeigen* (1774): 424;

"Der Sudelkoch," *Frankfurter gelehrte Anzeigen* (1774): 762;

"Neujahrswunsch," *Saarbrücken Wochenblatt* (January 1774);

"Die verbotene Verwandlung: Eine Romanze gesungen am Neujahrstage," *Almanach der deutschen Musen,* Leipzig (1775): 7-11;

"Erklärung an alle Schönen," *Almanach der deutschen Musen,* Leipzig (1776): 103;

"Ernestinchens Empfindungen an dem Grabe der hochseel. Frau Landgräfinn von Darmstadt," "An den Mond," "Ein Abschiedsliedchen," *Almanach der deutschen Musen,* Leipzig (1776): 153-160;

"Der reiche Stax," *Almanach der deutschen Musen,* Leipzig (1776): 269;

"Die vergebliche Warnung: Ein Lied," *Bürgerfreund,* Strasbourg, 1 (1776): 260;

"Bitte an die Vorsicht," *Bürgerfreund,* Strasbourg, 1 (1776): 342-343;

"Lob der Freundschaft," *Bürgerfreund,* Strasbourg, 1 (1776): 390-392;

"Kinderpastorale aufzuführen am Geburtstage eines rechtschaffenen Vaters," *Bürgerfreund,* Strasbourg, 2 (1776): 154-160;

"Der Fürst und der Naturkündiger," *Almanach der deutschen Musen,* Leipzig (1777): 57;

"Der Edelmann und sein Knecht," *Almanach der deutschen Musen,* Leipzig (1777): 110;

"Der Wittwer bey seiner Frauen Grabe," *Almanach der deutschen Musen,* Leipzig (1777): 233;

"An Thaliens jüngste Schülerin, Lotte Grosmann, auf ihren zweyten Geburtstag, den 9. September 1777," *Berliner Litteratur- und Theaterzeitung,* 1 (1777): 322-323;

"Fragment eines Nachspiels, Jedem sein Lohn," *Theaterjournal,* 10 (1779): 14-42;

"Von Wagners Schatten," *Berliner Litteratur- und Theaterzeitung* (1780): 85-87.

Heinrich Leopold Wagner has been described as "the least noteworthy of the German Storm and Stress writers" and as having been "tactless," "indiscreet," "affected," and above all "unpleasant." His contemporary Philipp Karl Diehl noted in a letter of March 1775 that "seine Gesichtsbildung ist mehr faunisch, als natürlich oder menschlich, und zum aushönen ist er geboren; ich möchte nicht mit ihm umgehen, viel weniger Freund von ihm seyn" (his appearance is more lascivious than natural or human, and he was born to deride. I would not like to associate with him, much less be a friend of his). Even his faithful nineteenth-century biographer Erich Schmidt concluded an analysis of Wagner: "Ich möchte ihm nicht gern zu nahe treten, aber einen erfreulichen Eindruck macht er mir nicht" (I do not wish to be too harsh, but he does not make an agreeable impression on me). Wagner's literary reputation owes a great deal to his much-publicized break with Goethe over *Prometheus, Deukalion und seine Recensenten* (Prometheus, Deukalion and Its Reviewers, 1775), Wagner's droll, anonymous satire of the criticism of Goethe's novel *Die Leiden des jungen Werthers* (The Sorrows of Young Werther, 1774). This discord led not only to Wagner's immediate expulsion from most contemporary German literary circles but also contributed to his reputation among later Goethe worshipers as a charlatan.

The rejection of Wagner by both his contemporaries and later scholars is unfortunate, since he was, in many respects, the quintessential Sturm und Drang author, rivaled only by his longtime friend and fellow tutor J. M. R. Lenz. Both of Wagner's major dramas, *Die Reue nach der That* (The Remorse after the Deed, 1775) and *Die Kindermörderinn* (The Child-killer, 1776), along with his lesser satirical prose works, his poetry and translations, and the unfinished novel *Leben und Tod Sebastian Silligs* (Life and Death of Sebastian Sillig, 1776), should have earned him greater respect and renown. His use of local dialect and of actual city landmarks from his native Strasbourg in *Die Kindermörderinn*, for instance, certainly foreshadowed their application by nineteenth-century German naturalists and went far beyond the usual conventions of his day. His dramatic plots were ingenious and contained bourgeois themes later found in the works of Goethe and Friedrich Schiller. And his satirical writings were no less witty or masterful than those of more celebrated eighteenth-century authors. Nonetheless, Wagner's foreshortened life, his stormy relationship with the great Goethe, and his frank and forthright demeanor all contributed to his unjustly tarnished reputation as a writer.

Wagner was born in Strasbourg on 19 February 1747, the eldest of six children of Heinrich Leopold and Katharina Salome Steinbach Wagner. He attended primary and secondary schools in his native city, whose mingling of French and German languages, cultures, and customs had a pro-

found and lasting impact on him. Strasbourg's university was already an intellectual mecca of the fine arts and literature when Wagner matriculated as a student of law there in 1770. With this reputation, the university was beginning to attract such highly talented students as Johann Gottfried Herder, Johann Heinrich Jung-Stilling, Lenz, and, of course, Goethe. In such esteemed company Wagner quickly produced his first literary texts, a translation from the French of Montesquieu's *The Temple of Gnidus* in 1770 and his own satirical poem of erotic fantasy, *Apolls des ersten Bänkelsängers Leben und Thaten auf dieser Welt* (The Life and Deeds of Apollo, the First Ballad Singer, in This World) in 1772. Although he was praised by local critics for the translation, the Alsatian puritanism of the Strasbourg censors prevented his second piece from being distributed and a proposed collection of short poems from being published.

Compelled by his family's mounting financial difficulties to quit the university early in 1772, Wagner sought a position as tutor. After working briefly for the young Count Löwenstein-Wertheim in Strasbourg, Wagner was employed as a tutor in the home of Maximilian Freiherr von Günderrode in Saarbrücken on 17 February 1773. From his two years there come the majority of surviving documents and letters by and pertaining to Wagner. He became an ardent admirer of Christoph Martin Wieland, to whom he sent letters but from whom he never received any replies, and Friedrich Nicolai. He also composed occasional poems, principally for his patrons, the Günderrodes; several of these poems were reproduced in the local weekly newspaper. As to the quality of his early verse little is now known, since all of it vanished with the issues of the paper in which it appeared. Wagner's request to have a volume of these poems published was denied by Günderrode. Although the titles of several occasional poems are known—for example, "Der Fuchs als Gratulant" (The Fox as Congratulator), presented to Günderrode's children on 9 March 1773, and "Neujahrswunsch" (New Year's Wish) from January 1774—only one complete text has survived: "Kinderpastorale aufzuführen am Geburtstage eines rechtschaffenen Vaters" (Children's Pastorale Performed on the Birthday of a Righteous Father), written for his young charges in the late summer of 1773 and published in 1776 in the Strasbourg periodical *Bürgerfreund*. His next literary contribution was a locally printed poetic romance, *Phaeton* (1774), dedicated to the Prince of Nassau-Saarbrücken. Unbeknownst to Wagner, the prince and Günderrode were then quarreling, and so his seemingly innocent gift to the regent led to Wagner's dismissal from the Günderrode household at the end of May 1774.

His next destination was Gießen, where he had applied for the position of house tutor with Administrative Secretary Wiessner. He continued writing for a youthful audience with *Chronologisches Spiel, zum Gebrauch der Jugend* (Chronological Game, for the Youngster's Use, 1774), a work intended as a playful device for memorizing world history. More important, however, the summer of 1774 witnessed the first serious publication of Wagner's poetry in the Leipzig *Almanach der deutschen Musen*, an event which motivated the young writer to quickly draft eleven humorous poems which appeared in a slender volume titled *Confiskable-Erzählungen: Wien, bey der Bücher-Censur* (Confiscatable Tales: Vienna, at the Office of the Book Censor, 1774). In such poems as "Die unheilbare Krankheit" (The Incurable Sickness), "Der Schinken" (The Ham), and "Das ***Fest" (The *** Festival) Wagner's style is reminiscent, perhaps even imitative, of that of Hans Sachs. Although this style had been acceptable in sixteenth-century Germany, the critics of the eighteenth century were not amused. Perhaps anticipating a chilly reception Wagner omitted his name from the title page and dedicated this supposedly anonymous work to the "unbefleckten, aetherisch-reinen, fanatisch-ehrbaren und mehr als strengen" (immaculate, ethereally pure, fanatically honorable and more than strict) book censor in Vienna.

In the autumn of 1774 Wagner attended the fair in Frankfurt; there he met Johann Konrad Deinet, who urged Wagner to move permanently to Frankfurt to assist in the editing of Deinet's periodical, the *Frankfurter gelehrte Anzeigen*. Wagner's chief responsibilities were those of reviewer and contributing poet. In Frankfurt, Wagner renewed his acquaintance with his former fellow law student, Goethe. By this time Goethe was becoming the leading literary celebrity in Germany. The publication of *Die Leiden des jungen Werthers* late in the summer of 1774 had made him the focus of unprecedented public attention and adoration. Many of Goethe's fellow literati soon came to envy and ridicule this formidable recognition. Wagner was so outraged by their censure that he sprang to Goethe's defense: in February 1775 he cleverly satirized the critics

of Goethe's novel in the anonymously published *Prometheus, Deukalion und seine Recensenten*. Again using Sachs's rhyming couplets, Wagner combined classical fable motifs, using animals and gods to represent the critical authors and including many direct references to the current literary scene.

The text Wagner created was brazen, to say the least. Opening in English with what later was to be referred to as Wagner's motto–"Let 'em censure: What care I? / The herd of critiks I defy, / Let the wretches know; I write / Regardless of their graces, or spite"–the work moves on to a prologue which immediately sets forth its premise: "Kann's nit länger mehr ansehn, / Wie die Kerls mit dem guten W** umgehen" (I can no longer stand the way these knaves treat the good W[erther]). Thereafter each of the characters appears in the form of a woodcut with an accompanying verse. Since the book appeared anonymously, reviewers at first attributed it to Goethe. Their generally positive remarks were quickly supplanted by words of anger and dismay when it was revealed that Wagner, and not the great Goethe, was responsible for the work. Goethe even went so far as to publish a special notice in several periodicals, including Deinet's *Frankfurter gelehrte Anzeigen* (21 April 1775), which declared: "Nicht ich, sondern Heinrich Leopold Wagner hat den Prometheus gemacht und drucken lassen, ohne mein Zuthun, ohne mein Wissen. Mir war's, wie meinen Freunden, und dem Publiko, ein Räzel, wer meine Manier in der ich manchmal Scherz zu treiben pflege, so nachahmen, und von gewissen Anecdoten unterrichtet seyn könnte, ehe sich mir der Verfasser vor wenig Tagen entdeckte. Ich glaube diese Erklärung denen schuldig zu seyn, die mich lieben und mir aufs Wort trauen. Übrigens war mir's ganz recht, bei dieser Gelegenheit verschiedne Personen, aus ihrem Betragen gegen mich, in der Stille näher kennen zu lernen. Frankfurt, am 9. April 1775" (Not I, but rather Heinrich Leopold Wagner composed *Prometheus* and had it printed without my permission, without my knowledge. It was a puzzle to me, as well as to my friends and the public, as to who was imitating the style in which I sometimes attempt to produce humorous works, and who could have been so knowledgeable of particular anecdotes, before the author revealed himself to me a few days ago. I believe I owe this explanation to those who love me and who trust my word. In any case, I think it was useful on this occasion quietly to get to know various persons better as a result of their conduct toward me. Frankfurt, April 9, 1775). While even this direct disclaimer did not end all suspicion of Goethe's involvement, Schmidt and August Sauer, among others, have since proved Wagner's authorship beyond any doubt. Following Goethe's revelation, the backlash against Wagner was immediate and severe. Most of his fellow writers–save for Lenz, Friedrich Maximilian Klinger, and the kindhearted Deinet–turned their backs on him, and he was soon beset with serious financial difficulties.

Wagner is known today principally as a dramatist. His interest in the theater may have been sparked by a project he had inherited from Goethe before their break. The publication in 1773 of the French dramatist Louis Sébastien Mercier's treatise on the new bourgeois theater, *Du théâtre ou nouvel essai sur l'art dramatique* (On the Theater; or A New Essay on the Dramatic Arts), so excited Goethe that he immediately began translating the work into German, with the announced intention of completing the task within a year. By the spring of 1775 the job was far from complete, however, and in the wake of his success with *Die Leiden des jungen Werthers* Goethe had lost interest in seeing the project through. Wagner assumed the responsibility and later the credit for the published translation, *Neuer Versuch über die Schauspielkunst* (New Essay on the Art of Theater, 1776). Mercier's analysis of popular bourgeois characters and themes, elements already employed by many German playwrights, so fascinated Wagner that while translating the theoretical text he also found the time to draft and publish his own first drama, *Der wohlthätige Unbekannte* (The Benevolent Stranger, 1775). The story, thought to have been based on an anecdote from the life of Montesquieu, focuses on the Robert family. The mother, son, and daughter endure a life of extreme deprivation and toil to save enough money to buy the freedom of the enslaved father. By chance the son encounters at the harbor a benevolent stranger who, upon being told of the family's misfortune, informs the youth that he has already freed the father and brought him safely home. Neither the reunited family nor the audience ever learns the true identity of the benefactor.

The success of the drama on both sides of the Rhine, thanks in part to Mercier's Paris production of the author's own French translation, was sufficiently encouraging to prompt Wagner to write a second play, a six-act bourgeois tragedy which appeared at Easter 1775. *Die Reue nach der That* was based on a recent incident in Vienna. Assistant Judge Langen loves Friederike Walz, the daughter of a coachman; but his mother, the proud, class-conscious wife of a judicial councilor, forbids their marriage. Langen's proposal, without his mother's consent, is refused by Friederike. The mother contrives to part the two young lovers for good by arranging for Friederike's banishment to a convent. The heartbroken girl poisons herself; Langen succumbs to madness and must be incarcerated; and his mother goes mad with remorse.

Upon the publication of the drama the critics voiced almost universal praise of this new creative genius; they proclaimed him another "master" and ranked him alongside Goethe and Lenz. Yet, although the play was staged to great acclaim, first in Hamburg and then in a revised five-act version called *Der Familienstolz* (The Family's Pride) in Mannheim, interest in the work did not endure. Neither of the other two dramas Wagner published in 1775 seems to have garnered much attention: a translation of Mercier's *La brouette du vinaigrier* (The Wheelbarrow of the Vinegar Merchant) under the title *Der Schubkarn des Essighändlers* and another translation from the French, *Die Königs-Krönung* (The Coronation of the King). In 1775 Wagner also published, at the behest of Deinet, a translation of the prose narrative *Mémorial d'un Mondain* (Recollections of a World Traveler, 1774) by Maximilian Joseph Graf von Lamberg in two volumes as *Tagebuch eines Weltmanns* (Diary of a Cosmopolitan), with the full cooperation of the author, who was then a noted resident of Landshut. Booksellers anticipated a curious, erudite public who would gladly thumb through the travel reminiscences and musings of an educated, well-traveled Austrian count, a writer of noble birth connected to many royal courts, a long-term resident of France whose nearest relations had played prominent roles in Berlin and Vienna; but despite Lamberg's pronouncement that Wagner's translation was "masterful," the book experienced only fleeting success.

To save himself, in Schmidt's words, "aus dem kümmerlichen Litterathenthum" (from the wretched realm of literature), and to find "einen sicheren Hafen" (a safer haven), Wagner resumed his legal studies in Strasbourg in May 1776. On 28 August he successfully defended his doctoral dissertation, a discourse on the Golden Bull, and on 21 September he took the legal oath and was also granted citizenship in Frankfurt. On 7 October he married Theodora Magdalena Müller (born Frieß), a widow eighteen years his senior. Little is known about Wagner's married life save that his wife died on 10 May 1778, whereupon his sister Christine moved in and assumed management of the household.

In 1776 Wagner's close friend Klinger became theater poet of the renowned Seyler Theater Troop, leading to Wagner's association with the company as both legal adviser and house poet. The most notable products of this relationship were a series of dramatic introductions or prologues which Wagner composed for the troupe's openings in Frankfurt and Mannheim and eighteen letters in praise of its productions and performers, none of which are of historical or literary consequence. Of greater importance were two independent literary contributions, the tragedy *Die Kindermörderinn* and *Leben und Tod Sebastian Silligs*, an unfinished picaresque novel in the manner of Tobias Smollet, Henry Fielding, and Laurence Sterne. *Die Kindermörderinn* has been compared favorably with Gotthold Ephraim Lessing's *Emilia Galotti* (1772) and Friedrich Schiller's *Kabale und Liebe* (Intrigue and Love, 1784). It is by far Wagner's best-known and most-performed work, with thirty-nine productions between 1776 and 1976.

The theme of infanticide was surprisingly popular during this period. In addition to Wagner, both Gottfried August Bürger and Anton Matthias Sprickmann wrote tales recounting a child's murder. Goethe, however, is considered the master of this motif, and Goethe's Gretchen from the then incomplete and unpublished *Faust*, part 1 (1808) served as the principal inspiration and model for Wagner's drama. Years later Goethe recalled, with restrained indignation, having read the pertinent passages of his manuscript to an appreciative Wagner, only to find them pilfered not long thereafter. There can be no doubt that the similarities in plot as well as in characters—for example, Wagner's Frau Marthan and Goethe's Marthe Schwerdtlein—were more than just coincidence.

Die Kindermörderinn is set in Strasbourg, using actual city landmarks and regional dialect. The butcher Martin Humbrecht's wife and his daughter, Evchen, become the victims of Lieutenant von Gröningseck's position and charm. Evchen is raped and then promised marriage after the mother consumes a sleeping potion. Her father's gruff demeanor compels the pregnant daughter to take refuge with the washerwoman Frau Marthan to give birth. Despite the taunts of Hasenpoth, a fellow officer, von Gröningseck resolves to make good his pledge, but he and the contrite butcher arrive too late to prevent Evchen from killing her infant. The laws of the day, the subject of considerable controversy, mandate death for Evchen.

The strength of this play lies in the outstanding characterizations of the proud but provincial Humbrecht and of the locally garrisoned officer corps, the sort of undisciplined and unprincipled cadre that was also the focus of Lenz's drama of the same year, *Die Soldaten* (The Soldiers). So much alike are the portrayals of regimental hauteur in the two works that some contemporaries credited Wagner's anonymous text to Lenz. The completed six-act play received scant notice upon its appearance in print, but within the year it debuted in Pressburg. More important, it attracted the attention of the Berlin theater director Karl Lessing, who mentioned it favorably to his famous brother. Also thinking the work to be by Lenz, Karl Lessing revised it—eliminating the offending first act, with the rape of Evchen in a Strasbourg bordello, and substituting a lengthy prologue explaining the circumstances that led to the rest of the action. Additional changes included the renaming of some supporting characters, the purification of Wagner's salty dialogue, the elimination of regional dialect and of references to Strasbourg, and the omission of some short transitional scenes. This version appeared in print in Berlin at the end of February 1777. Its title page stated that the work "auf dem deutschen Theater zu Berlin im Januar 1777 aufgeführt worden ist" (has been performed at the German Theater in Berlin in January 1777); this assumption by the publisher was erroneous, however, since, much to Wagner's glee, the police in Berlin forbade the performance to take place.

Partly to show his anger at Lessing's unauthorized edition and partly to enable his work to be staged, Wagner made his own revisions. Retitled *Evchen Humbrecht oder Ihr Mütter merkts Euch!* (Evchen Humbrecht; or, You Mothers Watch Out!), omitting the killing of the child, and, like Lessing's version, deleting the first act, the play was published posthumously in a volume of Wagner's dramas in 1779. Of all of Wagner's works, *Die Kindermörderinn* has had the greatest and most enduring impact on the public. Although the play was virtually forgotten in the nineteenth century, the twentieth century has witnessed many revivals of this Sturm und Drang masterpiece, starting with a production at the Volkstheater in Munich in the spring of 1904. In 1957 the East German playwright and director Peter Hacks staged Wagner's drama in a production designed to emphasize the socioeconomic themes in the work.

Wagner's only novel, *Leben und Tod Sebastian Silligs*, was originally conceived as a multivolume work. Only the first part–a prologue–appeared in print at Easter 1776. In the midst of writing the second part Wagner was suddenly overwhelmed with the fear of being labeled a poor imitator of Sterne rather than a true successor, and he ceased work on it. During 1777 and 1778 he devoted most of his time to the theater while continuing to be a prolific contributor to Deinet's Frankfurt journal. In 1778 he completed one of the many eighteenth-century German translations of Shakespeare's *Macbeth*, a wholly undistinguished version when compared to Wieland's masterful rendition from the same period. This translation also appeared in the 1779 edition of Wagner's theatrical works.

After the death of his wife and with his own health failing, Wagner's literary productivity decreased markedly in 1778. Posthumously published fragments suggest that he had intended to concentrate on writing plays, yet his last completed work marked a return to the form of writing which had first brought him to the public's attention only four years before: the satire. The butt of his biting wit was Voltaire, who was then at the height of his success with his new drama *Irène*. All of Paris was praising this theatrical triumph. Wagner, with his usual insolence, paid his respects in a different way. *Voltaire am Abend seiner Apotheose: Aus dem Französischen* (Voltaire on the Evening of His Apotheosis: From the French, 1778) is, in Schmidt's words, "zwar eine Crudität, aber eine höchst ergetzliche" (to be sure a crudity but a most amusing one). What sets this dramatic farce apart from other satires of the period is Wagner's clever and creative vision of Voltaire's reputation as an author exactly one century later. A passing spirit gives Voltaire a book published in 1875 that chronicles the literature of France in the previous century. Distressed by the harsh judgment given his peers, Voltaire turns to his own entry and is shocked to learn that his beloved *Irène* has been totally forgotten. Such is the blow to his ego that Voltaire collapses.

Like the Voltaire of his final work, Wagner may well have worried about his own reputation.

Although he was well known during his lifetime, he faded into obscurity not long after his death on 4 March 1779. The illness which ended his life at age thirty-two was never definitely diagnosed, although Schmidt speculates that it was tuberculosis.

Heinrich Leopold Wagner cannot be considered among the great German writers of the eighteenth century. Still, the tendency of nineteenth-century scholars to dismiss him merely because of his coarseness and candor ignores the creative inspiration and artistic expression Wagner brought to works such as *Prometheus*, *Die Reue nach der That*, and *Die Kindermörderinn*.

Letters:

"Verteidigung vor der Frankfurter Zensurbehörde," *Euphorion: Zeitschrift für Literaturgeschichte*, Stuttgart, 30 (1929): 281-289.

Bibliographies:

Ernst Schulte-Strathaus, *Bibliographie der Originalausgaben deutscher Dichtung im Zeitalter Goethes*, volume 1, part 1 (Munich & Leipzig: Müller, 1913), pp. 165-182;

Karl Goedeke, *Grundriß zur Geschichte der deutschen Dichtung*, volume 4, part 1 (Berlin: Akademie-Verlag, 1955), pp. 766-773.

References:

Jörg-Ulrich Fechner, ed., *Die Kindermörderin* (Stuttgart: Reclam, 1983);

Johannes Froitzheim, *Goethe und Heinrich Leopold Wagner* (Strasbourg: Heitz, 1889);

Froitzheim, *Lenz, Goethe und Cleophe Fibich von Straßburg* (Strasbourg: Heitz, 1888);

Elisabeth Genton, "La mort de Heinrich Leopold Wagner: Une lettre inédite de Christine Wagner à Anton Matthias Sprickmann," *Études Germaniques*, 21 (1966): 63-68;

Genton, *La vie et les opinions de Heinrich Leopold Wagner (1747-1779)* (Frankfurt am Main, Bern & Cirencester: Lang, 1981);

Herbert Haffner, *Heinrich Leopold Wagner, Peter Hacks, "Die Kindermörderin": Original und Bearbeitung im Vergleich* (Paderborn: Schöningh, 1982);

Gerhard Sauder, "Kein Sturm und Drang in Saarbrücken: Heinrich Leopold Wagners Hofmeisterzeit," *Saarheimat* (Saarbrücken), 23 (1979): 57-62;

Erich Schmidt, "Heinrich Leopold Wagner, " in *Allgemeine deutsche Biographie*, volume 50

(Leipzig: Duncker & Humblot, 1896), pp. 502-506;

Schmidt, *Heinrich Leopold Wagner: Goethes Jugendgenosse. Nebst neuen Briefen und Gedichten von Wagner und Lenz* (Jena: Frommann, 1875; revised, 1879);

Schmidt, "Nachträge zu Heinrich Leopold Wagner," *Zeitschrift für deutsches Altertum*, new series 19 (1876): 372-385;

Schmidt, "Von und über Heinrich Leopold Wagner," *Archiv für Literaturgeschichte*, 6 (1877): 522-525;

Johannes Werner, *Gesellschaft in literarischer Form: H. L. Wagners "Kindermörderin" als Epochen- und Methodenparadigma* (Stuttgart: Klett, 1977);

John Whiton, "Faith and the Devil in H. L. Wagner's *Die Kindermörderin*," *Lessing Yearbook*, 16 (1984): 221-228;

Karl Wolff, "Heinrich Leopold Wagners Verteidigung vor der Frankfurter Zensurbehörde," *Euphorion*, 30 (1929): 281-289.

Papers:

A collection of manuscripts and documents pertaining to Heinrich Leopold Wagner was donated by Wilhelm Frels to the Literary Archive of the Preußische Staatsbibliothek (Prussian State Library), Berlin, in 1930. Among these papers, according to Erich Schmidt, were manuscripts for several unpublished pieces, including "An Herrn von Tückheim am Tage seiner Vermählung" (To Mr. von Tückheim on the Day of His Wedding), "Der Fuchs als Gratulant" (The Fox as Well-Wisher), "An Madame Abt" (To Madame Abt), "An Chloe" (To Chloe), "Der Schmetterling" (The Butterfly), and "Die Neuen Schauspieler in Mannheim: Vorspiel und Prolog, welches bei Eröffnung des Mannheimer deutschen Theaters hätte gegeben werden können" (The New Actors in Mannheim: Curtain-raiser and Prologue Which Could Have Been Given at the Opening of the Mannheim German Theater). All seem to have been lost or destroyed during World War II. With the exception of a few documents and letters reproduced by Schmidt, Elisabeth Genton, and others, Wagner's papers now appear forever lost.

Zacharias Werner

(18 November 1768 - 17 January 1823)

Colin Walker
Queen's University of Belfast

BOOKS: *Gedichte* (Königsberg: Hartung, 1789);

Die Söhne des Thales: Ein dramatisches Gedicht, 2 volumes, anonymous (Berlin: Sander, 1803-1804)—comprises volume 1, *Die Templer auf Cypern*; volume 2, *Die Kreuzesbrüder*; revised and enlarged (1807-1819); volume 1 translated by Elizabeth Alicia Maria Lewis as *The Templars in Cyprus: A Dramatic Poem* (London: Bell, 1886); volume 2 translated as *The Brethren of the Cross* (London & New York: Bell, 1892);

Das Kreuz an der Ostsee: Ein Trauerspiel vom Verfasser der Söhne des Thales. Erster Theil: Die Brautnacht, anonymous (Berlin: Sander, 1806);

Einige Worte an das Publikum über das Schauspiel die Weyhe der Kraft: Vom Verfasser desselben, anonymous (Berlin: Realschulbuchhandlung, 1806);

Martin Luther oder Die Weihe der Kraft: Eine Tragödie vom Verfasser der Söhne des Thales, anonymous (Berlin: Sander, 1807);

Historischer Vorbericht zum ersten Theile der Söhne des Thals genannt die Templer auf Cypern: Vom Verfasser, anonymous (Berlin: Sander, 1807);

Attila, König der Hunnen: Eine romantische Tragödie in fünf Akten (Berlin: Realschulbuchhandlung, 1808);

Lied der heiligen drei Könige aus der Nibelungen Land: Zum 30. Jänner 1809, anonymous (N.p., 1809);

Werners Klagen um seine Königin, Luisa von Preußen: Rom, den 4ten August 1810 (Rome [actually Berlin: Haude & Spener], 1810);

Wanda, Königin der Sarmaten: Eine romantische Tragödie mit Gesang in fünf Akten (Tübingen: Cotta, 1810);

Kriegslied für die zum heiligen Kriege verbündeten deutschen Heere (Frankfurt am Main: Wenner, 1813);

Theater: Wörtlich nach der Original-Ausgabe, 6 volumes (Vienna: Wallishausser, 1813-1815; revised and enlarged edition, Vienna: Grund, 1816-1818);

Zacharias Werner; etching by Johann Ender (Gustav Könnecke, Bilderatlas zur Geschichte der deutschen Nationallitteratur [Graz: Akademische Druck- und Verlagsanstalt, 1981])

Die Weihe der Unkraft: Ein Ergänzungsblatt zur deutschen Haustafel (Frankfurt am Main: Andreä, 1813 [dated 1814]);

Te Deum zur Feyer der Einnahme von Paris durch die zum heiligen Kriege verbündeten Heere: Nach dem lateinischen Hymnus der heiligen Kirchenlehrer Ambrosius und Augustinus, mit beygefügtem Urtexte (Frankfurt am Main: Andreä, 1814);

Cunegunde die Heilige, Römisch-Deutsche Kaiserin: Ein romantisches Schauspiel in fünf Akten (Leipzig & Altenburg: Brockhaus, 1815);

Der vierundzwanzigste Februar: Eine Tragödie in einem Akt (Leipzig & Altenburg: Brockhaus, 1815); translated by Edmund Riley as *The*

Twenty-fourth of February: A Tragedy in One Act (London: Hughes, 1844); German version reprinted, edited by Johannes Krogoll (Stuttgart: Reclam, 1967);

Predigt, vorgetragen bey dem jährlichen Dankfeste des Handlungs-Kranken-Instituts in der Kapelle des heiligen Schutzpatrons Joseph am Pfingstmontage dem 15. Mai 1815 (Vienna: Gerold, 1815);

Rede am Fest des heil. Augustinus: Vorgetragen den 3ten September 1813 in der Pfarrkirche der ehrwürdigen P. P. Augustiner zu Wien von Friedrich Ludwig Zacharias Werner, Weltpriester und Großherzoglich Hessisch-Darmstadtischem Hofrath (Vienna: Tendler, 1815);

Geistliche Uebungen für drey Tage (Vienna: Wallishausser, 1818);

Die Mutter der Makkabäer: Tragödie in fünf Akten (Vienna: Wallishausser, 1820);

Lied zum Gedächtnisse des Hochwürdigsten, Hochseligen Herrn Sigismund Anton, aus dem Hause der Grafen von Hohenwart in Gerlachstein, Fürst-Erzbischof zu Wien . . . : Im Namen seiner Getreuen gedichtet (Vienna: Wallishausser, 1820);

Kurze Biographie von Friedrich Ludwig Zacharias Werner: Aus dem Felder'schen, jetzt Waitzenegger'schen Gelehrten- und Schriftsteller-Lexikon für dessen Freunde und Verehrer eigens abgedruckt (Landshut: Thomann, 1822);

Letzte Lebenstage und Testament: Nebst einem hierher gehörigen, im Jahre 1812 zu Florenz begonnenen Aufsatze des Verblichenen (Vienna: Wallishausser, 1823);

Die Posaunen des Weltgerichts: Eine Predigt (Würzburg: Etlinger, 1825);

Geistes-Funken, aufgefangen im Umgange mit weiland F. L. Z. Werner, edited by "Isidorus Regiomontanus" (Würzburg: Etlinger, 1827);

Nachgelassene Predigten: Gehalten in den Jahren 1814 bis 1816 in Wien, so wie in und bei Aschaffenburg (Vienna: Wallishausser, 1836);

Ausgewählte Schriften: Aus seinem handschriftlichen Nachlasse herausgegeben von seinen Freunden. Einzige rechtmäßige Gesammtausgabe, 15 volumes (Grimma: Verlags-Comptoir, 1840-1841)—includes as volumes 14-15, *Zacharias Werner's Biographie und Characteristik, nebst Original-Mittheilungen aus dessen handschriftlichen Tagebüchern,* edited by Professor Dr. Schütz; volumes 1-13 republished as *Sämmtliche Werke: Aus seinem handschriftlichen Nachlasse herausgegeben von seinen Freunden,* 13 volumes (Grimma: Verlags-Comptoir,

1840-1844); original 15-volume collection reprinted in 5 volumes (Bern: Lang, 1970);

Dramen, edited by Paul Kluckhohn (Leipzig: Reclam, 1937; reprinted, Darmstadt: Wissenschaftliche Buchgesellschaft, 1971);

Die Tagebücher des Dichters Zacharias Werner: Kritisch durchgesehene und erläuterte Gesamtausgabe, 2 volumes, edited by Oswald Floeck (Leipzig: Hiersemann, 1939-1940).

OTHER: A. A. L. de Lehndorff-Bandels, *Traité des mésalliances: Traduit sur l'original Latin, avec des annotations pratiques,* translated by Werner (Berlin: Unger, 1792);

Thomas à Kempis, *Von der Nachfolge Christi,* translated by J. P. Silbert, foreword by Werner (Vienna: Wallishausser, 1822).

In most of his writings Zacharias Werner comes across as an eccentric propagandist; yet he was the most gifted dramatist of German Romanticism, and his stage successes in the first decade of the nineteenth century led many contemporaries to believe that he was the natural successor to Friedrich Schiller. He has been remembered in the twentieth century largely as the progenitor of the genre of fate tragedy, a reputation which many critics have come to dispute.

Born in Königsberg (now Kaliningrad, U.S.S.R.) on 18 November 1768, Friedrich Ludwig Zacharias Werner was the third and only surviving child of Jakob Friedrich Werner, professor of history and rhetoric at Königsberg University, and Luise Henriette Werner, née Pietsch. Since his father was also the theater censor in Königsberg, the boy gained an insight into staging techniques and the irregularities of theatrical life; he planned to become an actor. His mother had a markedly Pietist outlook and lapsed into periodic bouts of religious mania. Werner's remorse over his quarrels with her is a recurrent theme in his writings. Shortly before his sixteenth birthday he began to study law at Königsberg University; there he attended lectures by Immanuel Kant, who apparently introduced him to the works of Jean-Jacques Rousseau (later one of Werner's "saints," whose birthday he treated for a while as New Year's Day). He left the university after sixteen terms of desultory study and without a degree, determined on a literary career. He obtained a humble civil-service post in Prussian-occupied Poland and lived an unstable existence: between 1792 and 1806 he was married and divorced three times. In 1792 he married

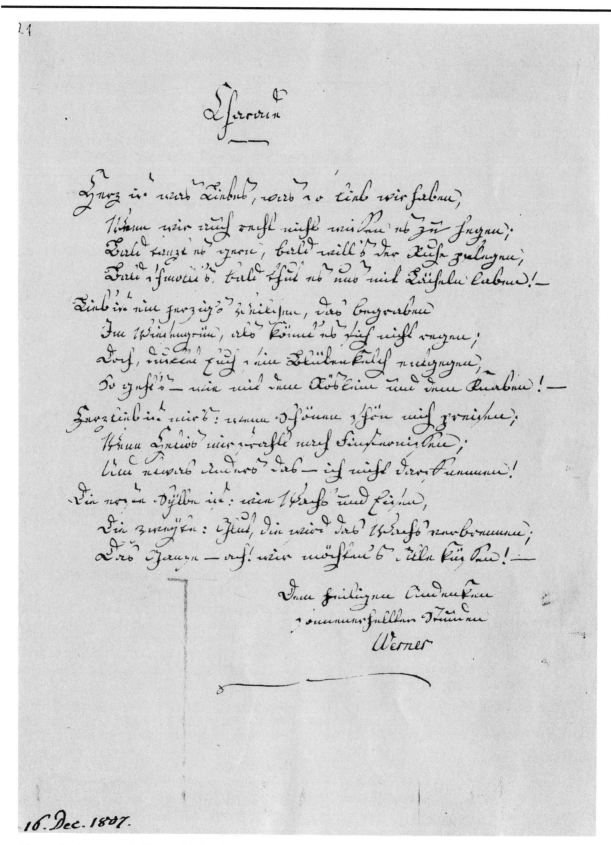

Manuscript for a poem by Werner (Nationale Forschungs- und Gedenkstätten der klassischen deutschen Literatur, Weimar)

Drawing of Werner by L. F. Schnorr von Carolsfeld (Bildredaktionsarchiv)

Friederike Schultz; they were divorced in 1794. His second marriage, to Karoline Friederike Luise Jorzig, lasted from 1799 to 1801. In the latter year he married Matgorzata Marchwiatowska; the marriage ended in 1806. None of the marriages produced any children.

Werner's early writings reveal formal facility and outspoken advocacy of what had become the conventions of the Enlightenment. In 1792 he joined a Königsberg Masonic lodge, and he gave radical support to the libertarian ideals of the French Revolution; his poem "An die Freiheit" (To Freedom), published in the *Preußisches Archiv* in 1790, accepts the execution of those who hinder freedom. Even more surprising from a Prussian civil servant are the poems in praise of the Polish people's resistance to foreign oppression, such as "Schlachtgesang der Polen unter Kosziusko" (Battle-song of the Poles under Kosciusko) and "An ein Volk" (To a People). By the end of the 1790s he was coming increasingly under the influence of Romantic writers and philosophers, especially Friedrich and August Wilhelm Schlegel, Novalis, Johann Heinrich Wackenroder, Friedrich Schleiermacher, and Johann Gottlieb Fichte.

In what many experienced as the millenarian intellectual climate at the turn of the century Werner felt called upon to bring to the German people a new gospel, a "System der Liebe" (system of love) which was an arcane combination of Masonic fraternalism, Pietist mysticism, Romantic aesthetics, and his own apparently irrepressible sensuality. Werner hoped to gather around him a band of disciples who would live and preach a religion of selflessness, renunciation, and suffering. His chief medium of evangelism was art, which was for him essentially synonymous with religion, and his chosen art was drama. He wished to reveal to his audiences how one could commune with the divine—indeed, even merge with the divine—through the ecstatic abandonment of one's individuality. This dissolution of the personality could be achieved through love in all its forms and, supremely, in death. The trinity of art, love, and death were the true "Mittler" (intermediaries) which enabled one to attain to God. He believed that in the theater such themes could be most evocatively decked out in the colorful forms of Catholic mythology.

Initially Werner thought that a rejuvenated Freemasonry could best proclaim his doctrine of selflessness; indeed, he held that its fundamental teaching of self-abnegation was the same as that of primitive Christianity and that Christ was the only supreme master of Masonry. The latter-day corruption of Masonry through rationalism and also its potential for revival are the underlying themes of his two-part drama in blank verse, *Die Söhne des Thales* (The Sons of the Vale, 1803-1804; part 1, *Die Templer auf Cypern*, translated as *The Templars in Cyprus*, 1886; part 2, *Die Kreuzesbrüder*, translated as *The Brethren of the Cross*, 1892), which depicts the destruction of the Templar Order under its Grand Master Jakob Molay (Jacques de Molay) in the years 1306 to 1314. Molay's sacrifice at the stake is supposed to exemplify the ideal of self-immolation (though his longing for the bliss of annihilation paradoxically gives the impression of self-indulgence). The Sons of the Vale in the play's title is a secret and all-powerful society that engineers the Templars' downfall and is confident that one day a purified Order will be born anew. The first part of the play, *Die Templer auf Cypern*, was staged in Berlin in 1807.

Das Kreuz an der Ostsee (The Cross on the Baltic Sea, 1806) was also to be a two-part drama, but only the first part, *Die Brautnacht* (The Wedding Night), was completed. It remained Wer-

Illustration for Werner's play Martin Luther oder Die Weihe der Kraft *(Josef Nadler,* Literaturgeschichte des deutschen Volkes, *volume 2 [Berlin: Propyläen, 1938])*

ner's favorite play, and many critics have found its portrayal of the clash of cultures in thirteenth-century Poland, with the heathen Prussians ranged against the Christian Poles (aided by the Teutonic Knights), to be his most imaginative poetic achievement. He draws on local folklore as well as Christian legend (though a couple of minor scenes express some of the most cruel anti-Semitism in German Romantic literature). In the planned second part, some of which was written but none of which is extant, the impetus for the reconciliation of the two nations under the cross was to be the Christian martyrdom of the young lovers, the Polish girl Malgona and the Prussian Warmio, who, having vowed chastity, were to achieve the ideal consummation of their love in an ecstatic Liebestod (love-death). Werner planned to combine the two parts into a compact stage version, to be titled "Der Ostermorgen" (Easter Morning); a fragment of this work has sur-

vived and was published by Birgit Heinemann in the *Jahrbuch des Freien Deutschen Hochstifts* in 1962.

The leading actor-director of the time, August Wilhelm Iffland, declined to stage *Die Brautnacht* at the National Theater in Berlin—much to the disappointment not only of Werner but also of E. T. A. Hoffmann, who had written the incidental music for it. Iffland agreed, however, to play the major role in Werner's next play, *Martin Luther oder Die Weihe der Kraft* (Martin Luther; or, The Consecration of Strength, 1807), hoping that it would be less marred by mysticism. Werner included two tiresome little guardian angels, but he did rely rather more on authentic historical detail. Not that he had abandoned his "system": the consecration of Luther's strength of which the subtitle speaks is the purification and new determination he attains when he recognizes the self-denying devotion of his future wife, the nun Katharina von Bora, when he feels desolate and betrayed. She assures him that she is ready to die for him, moving him to confess that for the cause of God he would be prepared not only to die but to undergo the supreme form of self-denial by sacrificing her life. Iffland's realistic acting as well as Werner's gift for succinct characterization and eye for striking scenic effect made the play a sensational success, though many Berlin Protestants were outraged at the depiction of the great reformer onstage and especially by the play's alleged "Catholicizing" tendencies. This succès de scandale is a background theme in Theodor Fontane's *Schach von Wuthenow* (1882).

Werner's next three full-length plays followed the pattern he had established. *Attila, König der Hunnen* (Attila, King of the Huns, 1808), first performed in Bamberg in 1808, portrays the predestined love of the Christian Princess Honoria and the "Scourge of God" as he lays siege to Rome. But the Princess Hildegunde of Burgundy takes murderous revenge on Attila, and angel choirs sing him sweetly to his rest. *Wanda, Königin der Sarmaten* (Wanda, Queen of the Sarmatians, 1810), like *Das Kreuz an der Ostsee*, has a legendary Polish setting, though this time there is no religious clash. Tragedy occurs because of conflicting oaths taken by the former lovers Rüdiger, prince of the Rugians, and Wanda, queen of the Sarmatians. He has sworn to his army that he will conquer her lands and make her his wife; she has sworn to her people that she will never marry. At the climax of their renewed passion Wanda lovingly thrusts her sword into Rüdiger's heart as he lies in her arms, and

Illustration by Study for Werner's play Attila, König der Hunnen *(Gero von Wilpert,* Deutsche Literatur in Bildern *[Stuttgart: Kröner, 1965])*

then, in the rays of the rising sun, she flings herself into the waters of the Vistula. Goethe, who had encouraged Werner to write the play, had it produced at the Weimar theater on 30 January 1808–two days before rejecting Heinrich von Kleist's *Penthesilea* (1808). *Cunegunde die Heilige, Römisch-Deutsche Kaiserin* (Conegonde the Saintly, Holy Roman Empress, 1815), written in 1808-1809 and first performed in Danzig (now Gdansk) in 1815, portrays the trials and temptations of the empress, who has vowed perpetual chastity but is falsely accused of adultery. At the end she and her husband look forward to eternal union in Heaven.

Literary historians have associated Werner primarily with his next play, the one-act tragedy *Der vierundzwanzigste Februar* (1815; translated as *The Twenty-fourth of February,* 1844), since it gave impetus to the vogue for fate tragedy in Germany and elsewhere. It was written at Weimar in

1809 with Goethe's encouragement and was first publicly performed there on 24 February 1810. It can be calculated that the events of the play take place around midnight on 24 February 1804, the day on which Werner's mother died. It is a gloomy and terrifying treatment of a tale familiar in folk mythology of the long-lost son who returns home to his impoverished parents and, unrecognized, is murdered by his father for his money. A heavy atmosphere of doom hangs over the action: the parents believe that it is because of a paternal curse that all the calamities that have befallen the family in the course of twenty-eight years have occurred on the "dies fatalis," 24 February. Werner depicts the mounting desperation of the couple with convincing psychological realism.

In recent years many critics have argued that the parents are driven into the crime only by their superstitious fears–by fatalism rather than fate–and that the dying son's words of forgiveness at the end of the play show that temptation and guilt can be overcome by reliance on God's grace. These critics have therefore held that the play is anything but a fate tragedy, and that the spate of trivial imitations by such authors as Adolf Müllner, Ernst von Houwald, and Ernst Raupach were based on a misunderstanding of the work. But it is difficult to explain away the fact that all of the family's catastrophes have occurred on the fatal day, at seven-year intervals; and the prologue Werner wrote in 1814 for the publication of the play seems to support the view that behind the events there is a supernatural and malevolent power–the power of Satan–which does not directly control the characters' lives but leads them into temptation, which they could resist through trust in God. It has also been argued that Werner's portrayal of physical and mental squalor, of the compulsive attraction of gold, and of the father's recourse to alcohol all point forward to the conventions of environmental determinism of Naturalist drama.

By 1810 Werner's personal life had become increasingly restless and unhappy. He had ranged through Germany, to Switzerland and northern Italy, to Paris, through Germany again, back to Switzerland, and had wound up in Italy. In salon and palace he had read from his works and expounded his system, doubting more and more whether he was leaving disciples behind him, or indeed whether he deserved to do so. He was still tormented by guilt over his treatment of his mother, and he found forgiveness and a new

Drawing of Werner (1812) by E. T. A. Hoffmann (Gero von Wilpert, Deutsche Literatur in Bildern *[Stuttgart: Kröner, 1965])*

sense of security when he was received into the Catholic church in Rome on 19 April 1810. His poetry and diaries of this period offer moving insight into his release from his anguish, although the faith he gained was never to be serene. In a poetic confession, *Die Weihe der Unkraft* (The Consecration of Weakness, 1813), he denounced most of his preconversion writings and what he thought was their widespread influence on the German public. He also summoned his fellow Germans to turn from the sins of egoism and religious indifference and factionalism. Thus cleansed, the German people could respond to God's inspiration and lead the nations of Europe in a holy crusade against the satanic Napoleon. This is the theme, too, of several of his battle songs for the Wars of Liberation, poems that reek of incense rather than gun smoke.

After training for the priesthood in Rome and Aschaffenburg he was ordained in 1813. He moved to Vienna in 1814 and soon joined the circle of the Redemptorist Clement Maria Hofbauer. He seemed to have exchanged the

stage for the pulpit, and the Vienna of the Congress period offered eager audiences. The beau monde crowded to hear his histrionic preaching, though his published sermons are not as graphically self-condemnatory as some contemporary accounts allege. Of particular interest are his patriotic sermons, some of which were probably heard by delegates to the Congress, and which rank with those of Schleiermacher.

He had not abandoned the theater entirely: he attempted to have *Cunegunde die Heilige, Römisch-Deutsche Kaiserin* staged in Vienna; and in 1816 he wrote *Die Mutter der Makkabäer* (The Mother of the Maccabeans, 1820) specifically for performance in Vienna, apparently to follow the local vogue for spectacular biblical plays. It is the least esoteric of his dramas but also by general consent the weakest. It follows 2 Macc. 7 in depicting the fervent stoicism of the Maccabean mother and her seven sons in defense of the Jewish law as they are tormented to death by the Syrian tyrant Antiochus Epiphanes; some scholars have found it reminiscent of baroque martyr tragedy, though it is doubtful whether that was Werner's intention. This grisly piece was not staged, and it is surprising that following some emendations by Werner it was passed for performance by the notoriously severe censorship of Vienna's police chief, Count Sedlnitzky, after being given reluctant approval by Vienna's archbishop. In 1821 Werner joined the Redemptorist order, but its rigors were too much for his enfeebled health, and he left before taking his monastic vows. He insisted on maintaining a vigorous regime of preaching until almost the end. He died in Vienna on 17 January 1823 and was buried beside his friend and mentor Hofbauer in what became known as the "Romantikerfriedhof" (Cemetery of the Romantics) at Maria Enzersdorf, near Vienna.

Letters:

Briefe des Dichters Friedrich Ludwig Zacharias Werner: Kritisch durchgesehene und erläuterte Gesamtausgabe, 2 volumes, edited by Oswald Floeck (Munich: Müller, 1914);

Fernand Baldensperger, "Lettres inédites de Zacharias Werner à Madame de Staël," *Revue de Littérature Comparée,* 3 (1923): 112-133;

Augustinus Bludau, "Zwei Briefe des Dichters Zacharias Werner," *Zeitschrift für die Geschichte und Altertumskunde Ermlands,* 23 (1927): 123-146;

Floeck, "Unbekannte Briefe von Zacharias Werner," *Hochland*, 27 (1929-1930): 329-353, 446-462, 550-557;

Gerard Kozielek, "Briefe Zacharias Werners an J. F. Cotta," *Germanica Wratislaviensia*, 5 (1960): 79-115;

Kozielek, "Ein Romantiker in preußischen Diensten: Unbekannte Briefe Zacharias Werners," *Germanica Wratislaviensia*, 7 (1962): 95-113;

Birgit Witte-Heinemann, "Zehn bisher nicht bekannte Briefe Zacharias Werners," *Jahrbuch des Freien Deutschen Hochstifts* (1963): 251-295;

Kozielek, "Briefe Zacharias Werners an Sophie von Schardt," *Germanica Wratislaviensia*, 15 (1971): 99-140.

References:

Herbert Breyer, *Das Prinzip von Form und Sinn im Drama Zacharias Werners* (Breslau: Priebatsch, 1933);

Gretel Carow, *Zacharias Werner und das Theater seiner Zeit*, Theater und Drama, no. 3 (Clausthal: Pieper, 1933);

Hildegard Dauer, "Das Todesproblem bei Zacharias Werner," Ph.D. dissertation, University of Frankfurt, 1946;

Jonas Fraenkel, *Zacharias Werners "Weihe der Kraft": Eine Studie zur Technik des Dramas*, Beiträge zur Ästhetik, no. 9 (Hamburg & Leipzig: Voss, 1904);

Giuseppe Gabetti, *Il dramma di Zacharias Werner* (Turin: Fratelli Bocca, 1916);

Louis Guinet, *De la Franc-Maçonnerie mystique au sacerdoce, ou La Vie romantique de Friedrich-Ludwig-Zacharias Werner (1768-1823)* (Caen: Association des Publications de la Faculté des Lettres et Sciences Humaines de l'Université de Caen, 1964);

Guinet, *Zacharias Werner et l'ésotérisme maçonnique*, Société et idéologies, Ie Série, Études V (Paris & The Hague: Mouton, 1962);

Paul Hankamer, *Zacharias Werner: Ein Beitrag zur Darstellung des Problems der Persönlichkeit in der Romantik* (Bonn: Cohen, 1920);

Birgit Heinemann, "Ein Fragment des Dramas 'Der Ostermorgen' von Zacharias Werner," *Jahrbuch des Freien Deutschen Hochstifts* (1962): 69-96;

Heinemann, "Geschichte und Mythos in Zacharias Werners Drama 'Das Kreuz an der Ostsee,'" Ph.D. dissertation, University of Göttingen, 1960;

Lee B. Jennings, "The Freezing Flame: Zacharias Werner and The Twenty-fourth of February," *Symposium*, 20 (1966): 24-42;

R. Kann, "Konversion und Predigt in der Restaurationszeit, 1814-1848: Zacharias Werner und Johann Emanuel Veith," *Vierteljahresschrift des A. Stifter-Instituts des Landes Oberösterreich*, 30, no. 1-2 (1981): 46-60;

Gerard Kozielek, *Das dramatische Werk Zacharias Werners*, Travaux de la Société des Sciences et des Lettres de Wroclaw, Seria A, Nr. 120 (Wroclaw: Société des Sciences et des Lettres de Wroclaw, 1967);

Kozielek, "Friedrich Ludwig Zacharias Werner," in *Deutsche Dichter der Romantik: Ihr Leben und Werk*, revised edition, edited by Benno von Wiese (Berlin: Schmidt, 1983), pp. 485-504;

Kozielek, *Friedrich Ludwig Zacharias Werner: Sein Weg zur Romantik*, Travaux de la Société des Sciences et des Lettres de Wroclaw, Seria A, Nr. 88 (Wroclaw: Société des Sciences et des Lettres de Wroclaw, 1963);

Kozielek, "Prediger und Poet: Zacharias Werners Wirken in Wien," *Aurora*, 41 (1981): 93-104;

Johannes Krogoll, Postscript, in Werner's *Der vierundzwanzigste Februar: Eine Tragödie in einem Akt* (Stuttgart: Reclam, 1967), pp. 77-96;

Konrad Maria Krug, "Zacharias Werner und die Bühne," Ph.D. dissertation, University of Münster, 1924;

Otto Mann, "Zacharias Werner," *Deutsche Vierteljahrsschrift für Literaturwissenschaft und Geistesgeschichte*, 7 (1929): 475-488;

Heinz Moenkemeyer, "Motivierung in Zacharias Werners Drama 'Der 24. Februar,'" *Monatshefte*, 50 (1958): 105-110;

Theo Pehl, "Zacharias Werner und der Pietismus: Studien zur religiösen Lebensform des frühen Zacharias Werner," Ph.D. dissertation, University of Frankfurt, 1933;

Margit Pflagner, "Zacharias Werner und das Wirken des Wiener Hofbauer-Kreises," *Lenau-Almanach* (1979): 221-260;

Kurt Sommer, "Die Entwicklung der Lyrik von Zacharias Werner," Ph.D. dissertation, Jena University, 1954;

Elisabeth Stopp, "A Romantic Reaction to 'Die Wahlverwandtschaften': Zacharias Werner and Goethe," *Literaturwissenschaftliches Jahrbuch*, 11 (1970): 67-85;

Stopp, "'Ein Sohn der Zeit': Goethe and the Romantic Plays of Zacharias Werner," *Publica-*

tions of the English Goethe Society, 40 (1970): 123-150;

Franz Stuckert, *Das Drama Zacharias Werners: Entwicklung und literaturgeschichtliche Stellung,* Deutsche Forschungen, no. 15 (Frankfurt am Main: Diesterweg, 1926);

Bruce Thompson, "The Limitations of Freedom: A Comparative Study of Schiller's 'Die Braut von Messina' and Werner's 'Der 24. Februar,'" *Modern Language Review,* 73 (April 1978): 328-336;

E. Vierling, *Zacharias Werner (1768-1823): La conversion d'un romantique* (Paris: Didier, 1908);

Colin Walker, "Temptation and salvation in Zacharias Werner's 'Der vierundzwanzigste Februar,'" *Literaturwissenschaftliches Jahrbuch,* 15 (1974): 17-37;

Walker, "Zacharias Werner and the Crusade against Napoleon," *Bulletin of the John Rylands University Library of Manchester,* 71 (Autumn 1989): 141-157;

Walker, "Zacharias Werner and the 'Martyrdom' of Abraham," *Modern Language Review,* 70 (April 1975): 333-346;

Walker, "Zacharias Werner's 'Die Mutter der Makkabäer' and Biblical Drama in Vienna," *Forum for Modern Language Studies,* 18 (January 1982): 23-38.

Papers:

Zacharias Werner bequeathed his papers to the Redemptorist Order in Vienna, but they probably did not survive the expulsion of the Redemptorists from the city in April 1848. Manuscripts of letters, poems, and fragments of his plays are held by many European libraries and archives, including the Märkisches Museum, Berlin; the Staats-Bibliothek, Berlin; the Goethe-Schiller-Archiv, Weimar; the Landes-Bibliothek Thüringen, Weimar; the Schiller National-Museum, Marbach; and the Stadtbibliothek, Vienna.

Johann Karl Wezel

(31 October 1747 - 28 January 1819)

Phillip S. McKnight
University of Kentucky

BOOKS: *Filibert und Theodosia: Ein dramatisches Gedicht* (Leipzig: Hilscher, 1772);

Lebensgeschichte Tobias Knauts des Weisen, sonst der Stammler genannt: Aus Familiennachrichten gesammelt, 4 volumes (Leipzig: Crusius, 1773-1776);

Der Graf von Wickham: Ein Trauerspiel in fünf Aufzügen (Leipzig: Crusius, 1774);

Epistel an die deutschen Dichter (Leipzig: Crusius, 1775)—includes "Die unvermuthete Nachbarschaft, oder Über die rechte Schätzung des Lebens," "Die wahre Welt oder Der rechte Gesichtspunkt, die Scenen dieser Welt zu beurtheilen";

Belphegor, oder die wahrscheinlichste Geschichte unter der Sonne, 2 volumes (Leipzig: Crusius, 1776);

Satirische Erzählungen, 2 volumes (Leipzig: Crusius, 1777-1778)—comprises in volume 1, "Silvans Bibliothek oder Die gelehrten Abenteuer," "Der Streit über das Gnaseg-chub: Eine Geschichte aus einem anderen Welttheile," "Die Erziehung der Moahi"; in volume 2, "Die unglückliche Schwäche," "Einige Gedanken und Grundsäzte meines Lehrers, des großen Euphrosinopatorius," "Johannes Düc, der Lustige, oder Geschichte eines Mannes von guter Laune";

Appellation der Vokalen an das Publikum: Geschrieben im Jahre 1776 (Frankfurt am Main & Leipzig, 1778);

Pädagogische Unterhandlungen, hrsg. von dem Dessauischen Erziehungsinstitut: Zweytes Jahr. Erstes Quartal (Dessau, 1778)—comprises "Präliminarien über deutsche Erziehung," "Über die Erziehungsschriften," "Welche Seite der Welt soll man jungen Leuten zeigen," "Noch eine Apologie des Ehrtriebes";

Lustspiele, 4 volumes (Leipzig: Dyk, 1778-1787)—comprises in volume 1, *Rache für Rache; Ertappt! ertappt!;* in volume 2 (1779), *Eigensinn und Ehrlichkeit; Die seltsame Probe;* in volume 3 (1784), *Der blinde Lärm oder Zwey Wittwen; Die komische Familie; Wildheit und Großmuth;*

Johann Karl Wezel; engraving by C. G. Geyser

Der erste Dank; Zelmor und Ermide: Ein musikalisches Schauspiel; Die Komödianten: Ein theatralisches Sittengemälde; in volume 4, *Der kluge Jakob: Eine komische Oper; Kutsch und Pferde; Herr Quodlibet;*

Die wilde Betty: Eine Ehestandsgeschichte (Leipzig: Dyk, 1779);

Peter Marks: Eine Ehestandsgeschichte. Vom Verfasser neu überarbeitet (Leipzig: Dyk, 1779);

Briefwechsel über einige Recensionen der neuesten Wezelischen Schriften (Leipzig, 1779);

Robinson Krusoe: Neu bearbeitet (Leipzig: Dyk, 1780); republished as *Robinson's Kolonie oder Die Welt im Kleinen* (Leipzig: Dyk, 1795);

Herrmann und Ulrike, 4 volumes (Leipzig: Dyk, 1780);

Ueber Sprache, Wissenschaften und Geschmack der Teutschen (Leipzig: Dyk, 1781);

Nachricht von J. K. Wezels Aufforderung an Herrn Doktor Plattner zu Leipzig (Halle, 1781);

Untersuchung über das Platnerische Verfahren gegen J. K. Wezel und gegen sein Urtheil von Leibnitzen (Leipzig: Schneider, 1781);

Mein letzter Wille: Mit gelehrten Anmerkungen begleitet von Ernst Maria Pumpelmus (Dessau: Buchhandlung der Gelehrten, 1781);

Zwei Gedichte (Leipzig, 1782);

Wilhelmine Arend, oder die Gefahren der Empfindsamkeit, 2 volumes (Dessau: Buchhandlung der Gelehrten, 1782);

Kakerlak, oder Geschichte eines Rosenkreuzers aus dem vorigen Jahrhundert (Leipzig: Dyk, 1784);

Versuch über die Kenntniß des Menschen, 2 volumes (Leipzig: Dyk, 1784-1785);

Prinz Edmund: Eine komische Erzählung (Leipzig: Dyk, 1785).

Modern Editions: *Herrmann und Ulrike*, edited by Carl Georg von Maaßen (Munich: Müller, 1919);

Herrmann und Ulrike, edited by Alfred Gerz (Potsdam: Rütten & Loening, 1943);

Belphegor, oder die wahrscheinlichste Geschichte unter der Sonne, edited by Walter Dietze (Berlin: Rütten & Loening, 1965);

Belphegor, oder die wahrscheinlichste Geschichte unter der Sonne, edited by Herbert Gersch (Frankfurt am Main: Insel, 1965);

Peter Marks; Die wilde Betty, edited by Hans Henning (Leipzig: Edition Leipzig, 1969);

Wilhelmine Arend, oder die Gefahren der Empfindsamkeit (Frankfurt am Main: Minerva, 1970);

Kritische Schriften, 3 volumes, edited by Albert R. Schmitt (Stuttgart: Metzler, 1971-1975);

Lebensgeschichte Tobias Knaut des Weisen, sonst der Stammler genannt, edited by Victor Lange (Stuttgart: Metzler, 1971);

Herrmann und Ulrike, edited by Eva Becker (Stuttgart: Metzler, 1971);

Versuch über die Kenntniß des Menschen (Frankfurt am Main: Athenäum, 1971);

Belphegor, oder die wahrscheinlichste Geschichte unter der Sonne, edited by Lenz Prütting (Frankfurt am Main: Verlag 2001, 1978);

Robinson Krusoe, edited by Anneliese Klingenberg (Berlin: Rütten & Loening, 1979);

Herrmann und Ulrike, edited by Gerhard Steiner (Leipzig: Insel, 1980);

Robinson Krusoe, edited by Rolf Strube (Berlin: Freitag, 1982);

Satirische Erzählungen, edited by Klingenberg (Berlin: Rütten & Loening, 1983);

Kakerlak, oder Geschichte eines Rosenkreuzers aus dem vorigen Jahrhundert, edited by Henning (Berlin: Rütten & Loening, 1984);

Belphegor, oder Die wahrscheinlichste Geschichte unter der Sonne (Nördlingen: Greno, 1986);

Lebensgeschichte Tobias Knaut des Weisen, sonst der Stammler genannt, edited by Klingenberg (Berlin: Rütten & Loening, 1990).

OTHER: *Komisches Theater der Franzosen für Deutschen*, edited by Johann Gottfried Dyk (Leipzig: Dyk, 1777-1786)–includes in volume 5 (1779), *Die galante Betrügerey*, adapted by Wezel from *Le Galant Escroc* by Charles Colle, pp. 1-46; *Die falsche Vergiftung*, adapted by Wezel from *Le faux Empoisennement*, by Carmontelle, pp. 199-240;

Daniel Defoe, *Robinson Krusoe*, volume 1, translated by Wezel (Leipzig: Dyk, 1779);

Oliver Goldsmith, *Der Weltbürger, oder Briefe eines chinesischen Philosophen aus London an seine Freunde im Orient*, 2 volumes, translated by Wezel (Leipzig: Schwickert, 1781);

Elizabeth Craven, *Anekdoten aus der alten Familie der Kinkvervänkotsdarspräkengotschderns: Ein Weihnachtsmärchen*, translated by Wezel (Leipzig: Schwickert, 1781).

Johann Karl Wezel's novel *Herrmann und Ulrike* (1780) was read by his contemporaries and praised for its wit, piquant humor, innovative insight into human motivation, and impeccable style. But his embittered withdrawal from public life, which coincided with the changing aesthetics of emerging German Classicism and Romanticism, caused Wezel to be almost forgotten until 1919. That year Carl Georg von Maaßen edited *Herrmann und Ulrike*, which he claimed unequivocally to be the best novel of the eighteenth century–echoing a comment made by Christoph Martin Wieland in the year of its original publication. One of the most individualistic personalities of eighteenth-century letters, Wezel gained considerable notoriety as a result of his vindictive satirical attacks on political corruption and abuse of power, on the self-compromising position of writers who were dependent on patronage, on the melancholy sentimentalism that swept over Germany in the late 1760s and 1770s, and because of his anthropomorphic view of religion.

The golden coach of Prince Heinrich I of Schwarzburg-Sondershausen, imported from Paris at a cost of ten thousand talers. Such displays of wealth, and the corruption that went with them, made a strong impression on the young Wezel (Sondershausen Museum).

The negative reception of Wezel is partly the fault of his early biographers, who destroyed his literary reputation with conjectures about his purported insanity during the last thirty years of his life. Probably inspired in part by Christian Heinrich Spieß's *Biographien der Wahnsinnigen* (Biographies of the Insane, 1795-1796), accounts of Wezel between 1796 and 1805 held that his ambitious nature and unorthodox views constituted a fundamental immorality that led to his "deserved" physical and mental demise. Although unsubstantiated and unverifiable speculation about Wezel's illness has frequently overshadowed the reception of his literary production, during the "Wezel Renaissance" of the 1970s and 1980s it was realized that no author provides a more realistic glimpse into everyday life of eighteenth-century German society and culture, from the peasantry to the nobility and from the village to the metropolis. The major satirist in eighteenth-century Germany, Wezel redirected satire from its harmless function as a corrective for socially unacceptable behavior to an aggressive and critical

agitation to be employed in the socialization and politicalization of the reading public. With *Herrmann und Ulrike* he created a major Entwicklungsroman (developmental novel) years before Goethe's *Wilhelm Meisters Lehrjahre* (Wilhelm Meister's Apprenticeship, 1795-1796). Wezel was the first author of such a novel to set his plot in contemporary Germany, and *Herrmann and Ulrike* is often regarded as the first German national novel. Viewing the system of patronage as tantamount to renouncing freedom of the press, Wezel was, as far as can be ascertained, one of the first German authors to support himself solely on the income of his own literary production for a prolonged period. The entire body of his work, which includes eight novels, fourteen plays, and several scholarly and philosophical books, was written in just fifteen years, from 1772 to 1787.

Wezel's antifeudalistic political views, his defense of Voltaire and other progressive French writers, his determined effort to expose the social conditions of the lower and middle classes,

First page of Wezel's first letter to the author Christoph Martin Wieland, dated 6 November 1773, asking Wieland to become his mentor (Nationale Forschungs- und Gedenkstätten der klassischen deutschen Literatur in Weimar) his incompatability with the prevalent idealistic optimism, and his rejection of the popular Sturm und Drang movement's linguistic excesses and exaltation of personal suffering make it difficult to place him in the traditional categories of literary history. As Albert R. Schmitt has pointed out, Wezel was in agreement with the social-reform ideas underlying many of the Sturm und Drang writings, particularly those of J. M. R. Lenz; but he remained essentially loyal to the principles of the late Enlightenment, which he felt provided a more pragmatic approach for a direct, if gradual, improvement of the social order.

Wezel was born in Sondershausen, at that time a town of about twenty-one thousand inhabitants and the residential seat for the principality Schwarzburg-Sondershausen, on 31 October 1747. Karl-Heinz Meyer and Gerhard Steiner have advanced the somewhat unlikely notion that he may have been the illegitimate son of the bachelor petty prince Heinrich I rather than of Johann Christoph Wezel, royal cook and confidante to the prince. Wezel's mother, Julianne Blättermann Wezel, was the daughter of the royal cutlery servant. (And it was with dinnerware servants–the Baer family–that Wezel would find lodging after his self-imposed retirement and exile to Sondershausen around 1789.) Heinrich, known as the "diamond prince" for his collection of precious gems, amassed a fortune of some half-million talers and flaunted his status with displays of grandeur before his subjects, including a golden carriage imported from Paris at a cost of ten thousand thalers (now on display in the Sondershausen Museum). Prince Heinrich and Johann Christoph Wezel died on the same day in 1758. Heinrich's nephew and successor, Prince Christian Günther II, uncovered a staggering amount of corruption at court and immediately had some 350 people arrested under suspicion of illegally trading and selling offices and titles. In fact, Heinrich himself had made his fortune from selling offices and titles as well as from commissions on local products and services and from the sale of soldiers and officers as mercenaries. An administrator of his, Hendrich, had made as much as seventy-five hundred talers a year on bribes and kickbacks as one of the prince's middlemen.

The milieu in which Wezel grew up provided him with an intimate view of the tension between the proud and decadent nobility, the impoverished peasantry, and the bourgoisie with its small-town mentality. His observation of citizens scrambling in a sea of envy and greed for titles and courtly favor provided a wealth of material for his prose. It is little wonder that Wezel came to reject the fools and social deviants of Saxon comedy as the source of the degeneration of society, the fall of empires, or the transformation of men into "zu habsüchtigen, treulosen, auflauernden Wölfen" (greedy, disloyal, opportunistic wolves); instead, the root of the problem was to be found in political abuses. Wezel would dare to attack the cause at its source, the upper echelons of society where the power lay, rather than concentrating on correcting middle- and lower-class behavior.

Wezel was raised by his maternal grandparents. His grandfather provided a private tutor for him until the fourth grade, when he was enrolled in the public school. There Gottfried Konrad Böttger and Nikolaus Dietrich Giseke gave the gifted child a solid background in languages and stimulated his interest in literature. Giseke recommended Wezel to his friend, the prominent novelist and man of letters Christian Fürchtegott Gellert, who agreed to provide him with an attic room in his house in Leipzig. On 8 May 1765 Wezel enrolled at the University of Leipzig as a student of theology, then changed to law and finally to philosophy. He did not earn a degree during his four and a half years at the university, but he made contact with the important intellectual circles there through his friendship with Gellert. Wezel felt that he had the choice of becoming a disciple of the Leibnizian philosopher Christian Wolff–the university was dominated by the thinking of Leibniz and Wolff–or of Christian August Crusius, who had taken issue with Wolff's formulations of the Leibnizian doctrines of preestablished harmony and the principle of sufficient reason. Although the philosophical dialogue in Leipzig provided Wezel with ample material for satire in his first novel, *Lebensgeschichte Tobias Knauts des Weisen, sonst der Stammler genannt* (History of Tobias Knaut the Wise, also Known as the Stutterer, 1773-1776), he remained unconvinced by either side. Instead, John Locke's *Essay Concerning Human Understanding* (1689) profoundly influenced his thinking and ultimately led him to extensive studies of French materialists such as Claude-Adrien Helvétius, Julien Offroy de La Mettrie, Étienne Bonnot de Condillac, Samuel August André David Tissot, and, from the French sector of Switzerland, Charles Bonnet.

Wezel's observation of Gellert's deterioration into acute depression, which occurred in spite of the adulation he constantly received from his public, undoubtedly left a profound impression on the young student. In *Lebensgeschichte Tobias Knauts* Wezel would incorporate many aspects of Gellert's personality into the character of Selmann, with his optimism and his compulsion to seek out suffering people, thoroughly convinced that he could solve their problems. Wezel's depiction of Selmann was to be the beginning of his commentary on the German national spirit, a spirit depressed from within and suppressed from without, capable of thinking far beyond its ability to act, ultimately driven to complacency, despair, melancholy, and nervous breakdown by its self-consuming emotional excess and by the discrepancy between its rational idealism and the reality of social conditions.

Shortly before his death in 1769 Gellert recommended Wezel as a tutor for two children of Johann Wilhelm Traugott von Schönberg in Bautzen. Von Schönberg's official duties brought Wezel into contact with the political and economic affairs of Saxony, an economy being rebuilt with a manufacturing base under the leadership of Thomas Fritsch, a middle-class organizer and pragmatic reformer who had risen to a position of unusual trust and authority; Gerhard Steiner has pointed out that Fritsch became the model for bourgeois emancipation envisioned by Wezel in *Herrmann und Ulrike*. Wezel also became aware of the tensions remaining from the peasant uprisings of 1765 and the continued plight of most of the peasants as bonded serfs. Von Schönberg seems to have viewed institutional religion with considerable skepticism and, like Immanuel Kant, as a tool to abuse power and to deprive the masses of their will to assume self-responsibility. Wezel's discussions with von Schönberg triggered a crisis in his thinking that would be manifested in his anticlerical *Prinz Edmund* (1785); in the grotesque portrayal of the power-crazed Pope Alexander VI in his second novel, *Belphegor, oder die wahrscheinlichste Geschichte unter der Sonne* (Belphegor; or, The Most Probable Story under the Sun, 1776), and in the persiflage directed at asceticism in his version of *Robinson Krusoe* (1780). He also began to formulate the ideas for his *Versuch über die Kenntniß des Menschen* (Essay on the Knowledge of Man, 1784-1785) on tracing the origin of religion to superstition and to a historical manifestation of evolving cultural needs.

Wezel was able to find time to think and write at the estate of von Schönberg's wife in Trattlau (today Kostrzyna, Poland). By 1771 he had written a translation of the first four books of Homer's *Iliad* in hexameters and sent a sample of his work to the publisher Friedrich Nicolai in Berlin. Nothing came of it, and none of the manuscripts have ever been found. The only copy ever found of his first publication, the operetta libretto *Filibert und Theodosia* (1772), turned up in the Johann Wilhelm Ludwig Gleim collection in Halberstadt around 1981. The first volume of *Lebensgeschichte Tobias Knauts* in 1773 sold out quickly, however, and went into a second edition the same year. Encouraged, Wezel wrote to Wieland in 1773, asking him to replace his deceased friends Giseke and Gellert as his mentor; he enclosed a few of his manuscripts. Wieland responded enthusiastically, praised *Lebensgeschichte Tobias Knauts* in the *Teutsche Merkur,* and resolved to make Wezel the "German Fielding." *Lebensgeschichte Tobias Knauts,* with its ironic narrator who interrupts the story, was clearly in the tradition of Laurence Sterne—or perhaps even more accurately, in the narrative tradition of Wieland's early prose.

In his arduous development from "Dummkopf" (dunce) to "Tor" (fool) Tobias, who starts out with no innate qualities, is subjected to the arbitrary will and whims of the author. Tobias's virtue consists in his lack of sensitivity, his refusal to let himself become emotionally wrought; and his behavior, which defies logical expectations, parodies the then-current expositions of the doctrine of sufficient reason. Often overlooked in the novel is Wezel's controlled character development, the deliberate socialization process of Tobias in the course of his exposure to his cultural and political environment. When Tobias realizes that his naive wit has only been exploited for the amusement of the idle rich, he rejects the traditional role of court jester, and his own vanity and ambition are awakened.

Wezel followed up on this idea in his *Epistel an die deutschen Dichter* (Epistle to German Poets, 1775), which he sent to Wieland in December 1775. The work is an exhortation to German poets to extricate themselves from the demeaning burden of patronage: "Nur sprich, wie man sie [die Prinzen] lobt und auch die Wahrheit sagt?" (How can you praise them [the princes] and tell the truth at the same time?) Wezel asks. Wieland, himself heavily dependent on his pension, returned the work as unsuitable for the *Merkur* with a laconic note pointing out that he, Wieland, was also a poet. The year before, after

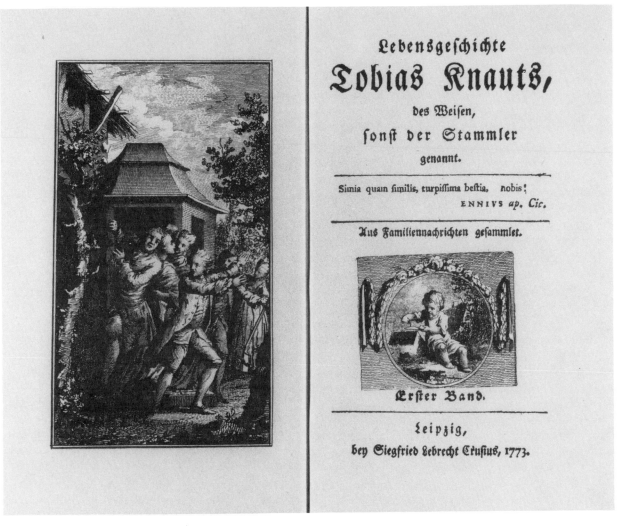

Frontispiece and title page for the first volume of Wezel's first novel

the appearance of the second volume of *Lebensgeschichte Tobias Knauts,* Wezel had left his position in Bautzen to strike out on his own.

In the summer or fall of 1775 Wezel visited Weimar and met Wieland, who published Wezel's short comic novel "Ehestandsgeschichte des Herrn Philipp Peter Marks" (Marriage History of Herr Philipp Peter Marks) in three parts in the *Merkur* from January to March 1776 (it was republished in book form, with a slightly different title, in 1779). By this time, however, Wieland may have realized that he was dealing with the "German Swift" rather than the "German Fielding." Volume three of *Lebensgeschichte Tobias Knauts* was not reviewed in the *Merkur,* possibly because of Wezel's switch in tone from light irony to satire. Wieland commissioned Joachim Heinrich Merck to write a review of volume four for the March

issue but cautioned him to take it easy on Wezel as the latter was still contributing popular stories to the *Merkur.* In volume four Wezel had switched from light satire and parody of anacreontic and sentimental themes to ridicule of "Genie" (genius) fever, the sudden popularity of "Bardendichtung" (bardpoetry) and ancient folk poetry, and opportunistic writers imitating the style of the Sturm und Drang. At the same time Wezel offered a hint of his own forthcoming excesses by defining in the last volume of *Lebensgeschichte Tobias* the satirical approach he would take in *Belphegor,* which appeared later in 1776: "Von nun an wollen wir nicht mehr Menschen, wie andre seyn: was andre schätzen, lieben, begehren, das wollen wir verachten; was sie glauben, verfechten: wir wollen das ewige Widerspiel des menschlichen Geschlechts seyn"

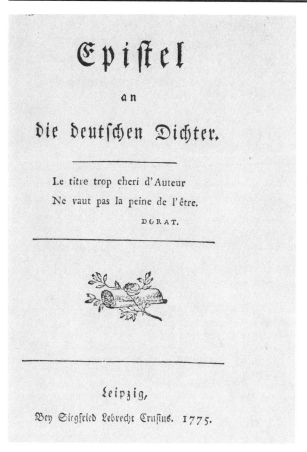

*Title page for Wezel's exhortation to German poets to reject
the bonds of patronage*

(From now on we will not be like other people;
that which others value, love, desire, we will de-
spise; what they believe we will denounce: we
will become the eternal counterpart to the
human race.)

Merck's review indicated that Wezel was over-
stepping the limits of acceptability to the Weimar
circle with his repeated exposés of corrupt and
self-indulgent nobility, and it warned that Wezel's
reputation could be severely damaged by a less restrained review. The appearance of *Belphegor*
shortly thereafter brought the irreconcilable differences between Wezel and Wieland to a head.
Merck's scathing review of *Belphegor* in the July
issue of the *Merkur* was directly solicited by Wieland, who instructed Merck not to restrain himself in condemning the book. Shocked and enraged, Wezel immediately requested Wieland to
return the rest of his pending manuscripts.

This largely unjustified review, along with
several of Wieland's letters to Wezel that were published in the nineteenth century, are among the
primary factors in the negative reception of

Wezel. In 1961 Arno Schmidt perpetuated the
image of Wezel as a misanthrope that emerged
from Merck's review with his *Belphegor, oder wie
ich euch hasse* (Belphegor; or, How I Hate You), a
radio play that revived interest in Wezel in the
1960s.

In fact, *Belphegor* is one of the most univer-
sally European works to come out of eighteenth-
century Germany and is one of the few novels of
the period that is still readable by the nonspecial-
ist. Walter Dietze has demonstrated that the crisis
in Enlightenment optimism apparent in Voltaire's
Candide (1759) provided a loose framework from
which Wezel constructed his own story. Those
two works, together with Samuel Johnson's *The
History of Rasselas, Prince of Abissinia* (1759), constitute a major antiutopian thrust directed at the
Leibniz-Wolffian school. In Wezel's view, an abun-
dance of idealistic literature impedes the concrete
action needed for the progress of civilization and
for the emancipation of the lower and middle
classes. This was a particularly sensitive point in
Germany, which had maintained its authoritarian
political structure during an age of revolution.
Operating against the grain of the "Mitleid-
Generation" (compassionate generation) in Germany, Wezel attacked the notorious resignation
of the German intelligentsia and stated in the foreword that envy and ambition were the dominant
motivating factors for both good and evil in
human behavior. Enough idyllic utopias had
been published, according to Wezel, and it was
time that the negative side of human nature be exposed to balance the picture of man emerging in
the eighteenth century. The idealistic Belphegor
is placed in the contrasting company of the unscrupulous, fatalistic, and Machiavellian Fromal; the
passive Wolffian Medardus, forever reliant on
providence; and the opportunistic but totally exploited female character Akante, who delivers a remarkable tirade on the historical suppression of
women. The friends end their misadventures by
tending their gardens in Virginia, as in *Candide*.
But Wezel concludes the novel with the irrepressible Belphegor going off to join the American Revolution. Many modern critics, assuming Fromal
to be Wezel's chief theoretician in the work, have
accepted Volker-Ulrich Müller's argument that
the enthusiastic Belphegor is just engaging in
one more futile adventure bound to end in
disaster. By pointing out the parallels to Thomas Hobbes in Wezel's text, however, Dietrich
Naumann argues that Belphegor is placed in a series of situations under natural law—*bellum om-*

nium contra omnes (Wezel's motto for the first volume)–in order to portray the consequences of a society without a social contract. The conclusion would have to be that such a contract is needed to avoid chaos and for mankind to become civilized. Like Merck, most critics of *Belphegor* tend to overlook the satirical aspects: Belphegor's final action upholds the satirical agitation employed by Wezel to expose a reality in need of change. The agitation is the hidden agenda of the book; or, as Regine Seibert puts it, the moral force of satire is intended to sensitize the reader in favor of social justice. For Belphegor to remain in Virginia tending his garden would have been an admission that Fromal's fatalistic and cynical minihistory of mankind was correct, would have left Belphegor to join the national "noble resignation," and would have effectively eliminated the element of satirical agitation.

Just prior to his break with Wieland, Wezel had gone to Berlin to take a position as tutor in the house of the Prussian minister of justice, Ernst Friedemann von Münchhausen, whose wife's family had come from the Sondershausen area. Münchhausen, a nephew of the famous Hannover minister Gerlach Adolf Münchhausen, was lord of various properties in Eckartsberga, held offices in Dresden, and was president of the Berlin district court. Münchhausen was embroiled in controversy with the king due to Friedrich's refusal to acknowledge liberties taken with the law by members of the privileged nobility, and Wezel gained firsthand knowledge of the absolute rule of the "enlightened, anti-Machiavellian" Prussian ruler. He was also exposed to merchant financiers, courtly parasites, metropolitan life, luxury and privilege, and the exaggerated gallicization of language and culture. Illness forced Wezel to resign after about six months, but he remained in Berlin until about the spring of 1777, becoming friends with the poet Karl Wilhelm Ramler and probably developing contacts with Moses Mendelssohn, Johann Jakob Engel, Johann Erich Biester, and Nicolai.

In 1777 he returned to Leipzig and began the most productive years of his life. He completed the two volumes of *Satirische Erzählungen* (Satirical Tales, 1777-1778), for his publisher, Siegfried Leberecht Crusius. The work consists of short stories with educational and philosophical themes and satires, including a travesty of small-town mentality based on an incident in Bautzen, a variation of Swift's *Battle of the Books* (1704),

Frontispiece for Wezel's second novel, Belphegor, oder die wahrscheinlichste Geschichte unter der Sonne: *Akante kicks Belphegor out of his idealistic fantasies into the real world*

and a tale of how a good-natured character is transformed into a biting satirist by the hypocrisy and discrimination he encounters in high society. A close friendship soon developed between Wezel and Johann Gottfried Dyk, who was a playwright as well as a publisher. Dyk invited Wezel to contribute to the various journals and anthologies he was editing, especially the *Taschenbuch für Dichter und Dichterfreunde,* the *Komisches Theater der Franzosen für Deutschen,* and the most important organ of the Leipzig Enlightenment, the *Neue Bibliothek der freyen Künste und schönen*

Wissenschaften, which was edited by Dyk and Christian Felix Weiße. Wezel's literary criticism in the *Neue Bibliothek* would later be remembered as having stirred as much interest and provocation as Gotthold Ephraim Lessing had done earlier with his journal *Literaturbriefe* (Letters on Literature, 1759-1765). In his important reviews of Johann Timotheus Hermes's *Sophiens Reise von Memel nach Sachsen* (Sophie's Journey from Memel to Saxony, 1769-1773), J. M. R. Lenz's *Zerbin oder Die neuere Philosophie* (Zerbin; or, The New Philosophy, 1776), Wieland's *Oberon* (1780), and the rival journal *Deutsches Museum,* Wezel stressed the need to incorporate political and social realism in fiction without the prevalent moralizing tone common to the literature of the Enlightenment. He rejected the imitators of Shakespeare and Goethe for overworking suicide and murder motifs and took issue with the aesthetics of the Sturm und Drang writers and the Göttinger Hain poets. His contemptuous review of *Oberon* drew the line between realistic and idealistic writers, categorizing Wieland, whose *Merkur* reviews had admonished Wezel for his lack of verisimilitude, as a writer who did not portray real events or people. Wezel's long and well-argued criticism of Wieland's creations of supernatural beings to help superhuman heroes revealed his disdain for what he must have regarded as Wieland's double standard.

In 1778 the first volume of Wezel's four-volume *Lustspiele* (Comedies) appeared. All the plays in the first three volumes were reprinted in the Viennese collection *Deutsche Schaubühne* (German Stage, 1765-1804); the first two volumes reappeared in the Schmieder pirate edition series; and two plays were translated into French and had popular runs at a theater in Paris. Wezel's plays were only moderately successful in Germany, however. His strengths were his critical observation of human nature, his true-to-life characters, his comic dialogue, and his situation comedy. Most of Wezel's comedies bear a great deal of resemblance to the Enlightenment comedies of the 1760s and 1770s, but without their overbearing moralization. Not all the plays were comedies. Fritz Martini has described Wezel's *Eigensinn und Ehrlichkeit* (Ego and Honesty, 1779) as a conscious alternative to Sturm und Drang plays. The plot, which is partially repeated in *Herrmann und Ulrike,* concerns a tutor torn between his fiancée and his love for the countess whose child is in his charge. When pressed to make a choice, he "follows his heart" and chooses the countess, an impos-

sible union for a bourgeois intellectual. Other theatrical endeavors include pedagogical themes (*Der erste Dank,* [The First Thanks, 1782]), literary satire (*Die Komödianten* [The Actors, 1784]), comic-operetta librettos (*Zelmor und Ermide* [1779], *Der kluge Jakob* [Clever Jacob, 1784]), and a series of love comedies and intrigues.

In 1778 Wezel was recommended by Weiße and the widely respected Leipzig reformed Protestant preacher Georg Joachim Zollikofer for a position at Johann Bernhard Basedow's famous Philanthropinum in Dessau, the center for progressive and experimental educational ideas. After a visit to Dessau he decided not to return to teaching, but he agreed to write several essays on educational theory for the institute's journal, *Pädagogische Unterhandlungen.* (These important essays were virtually lost until Anneliese Klingenberg located copies of the journal in the late 1970s.) In these essays, Wezel expresses his opposition to authoritarian, repressive forms of education and maintains that natural human drives, including sex, ambition, and Eigenliebe (self-love) should be treated as though they were, indeed, natural and should be given positive reinforcement. Young people should grow up with less religious training and more direct awareness of political reality. The essays also include a defense of self-interest and personal ambition. Finding positive ways to direct ambition and ego was an educational priority for Wezel that reflected his study of Adam Smith's theories of self-interest. (In 1780, with a notice in the *Deutsches Museum,* Wezel would announce his intention to establish his own academy for the education of twelve-to-eighteen-year-olds; but his secular approach and liberal principles did not appeal to parents in Germany at the time).

While in Dessau Wezel met Joachim Heinrich Campe, a popular philosopher. As a project for the Philanthropinum each began independently to translate Daniel Defoe's *Robinson Crusoe* (1719). Campe's book was oriented to younger readers and went on to appear in more than a hundred editions; Wezel's translation of the first part, aimed at the adult reader, was only printed once. Wezel, however, decided to write a sequel—titled, like his translation, *Robinson Krusoe* (1780)—about the generations of civilization on the island after Crusoe, and he created one of the most unusual antiutopian works of the eighteenth century. Every conceivable form of government—democratic, dictatorial, republican, socialist—comes into power, flourishes for a short

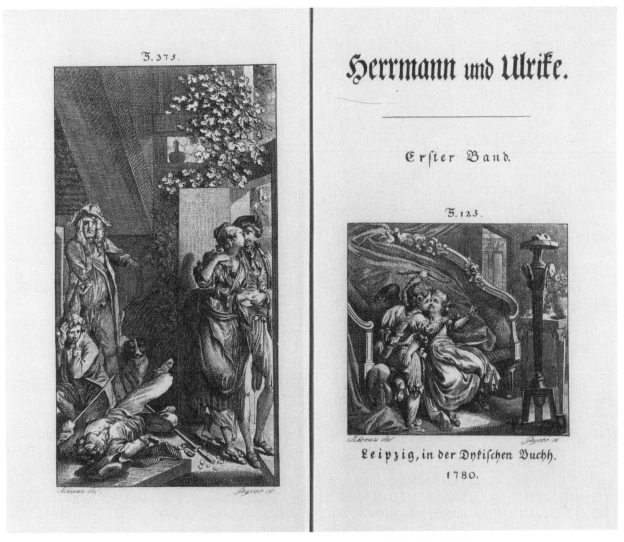

Frontispiece and title page for the first volume of Wezel's socially critical Bildungsroman

while, then self-destructs and begins a new cycle. The message seemed to be that it was futile to flee to the New World, because the same problems would eventually manifest themselves again. The strong dose of anticlericism in Wezel's sequel and his "sacrilegious" treatment of Jean-Jacques Rousseau in the foreword caused problems with the Leipzig censorship commission, directed by Johann Gottlob Böhme. The comments on Rousseau were banned, but Wezel had the foreword printed outside Leipzig to be inserted in the local copies of the book. This act earned author and publisher a subpoena to appear before the commission on 11 July 1780; but Dyk appeared alone while Wezel went to Gotha to stay with his friend Friedrich Wilhelm Gotter, a theater director and dramatist with whom Wezel had worked for

Dyk's *Komisches Theater der Franzosen.* Several of Wezel's plays had been staged in Gotha in 1778 and 1779, and Wezel hoped to work with Gotter to "rescue" the German language and theater from the "Originalgenies" (original geniuses) of the Sturm und Drang.

Robinson Krusoe was the last of Wezel's "pessimistic" works and concluded his literary portrayal of the crisis of reason in the eighteenth century. In *Herrmann und Ulrike,* the story of Herrmann's forcefully prohibited teenage love of the young noblewoman Ulrike, the harsh discrimination he experiences, his loss of innocence, his disillusionment with the Rousseauean "back to nature" solution, and his ultimate rise to a position of political power and marriage to Ulrike, Wezel struggled to find a rational answer to the class struggle and the dilemma of the individual in eighteenth-century society without misleading his readers about what was politically feasible. Although Herrmann makes adjustments in his character and attitude to achieve his goals, Wezel did not allow him the compromise indulged in by many of his contemporaries, including Goethe: when offered a title in recognition of his service, Herrmann keeps things in proper perspective and turns the offer down.

After eleven months of deliberation–during which Böhme died–the courts in Dresden accepted Dyk's apology for the *Robinson Krusoe* affair on 29 June 1781. Dyk was, however, required to pay the court costs.

In 1781 appeared Wezel's detailed aesthetic and cultural study *Ueber Sprache, Wissenschaften und Geschmack der Teutschen* (On Language, Science and Good Taste of the Germans), a response to Frederick the Great's famous repudiation of the German language, *De la littérature allemande* (1780). In the book Wezel called Leibniz's works unreadable; the statement set off an exchange of pasquinades between himself and the Leipzig professor Ernst Platner, whose students rallied with some twenty-five-odd anti-Wezel pamphlets, creating–on the heels of the *Robinson Krusoe* affair–an intolerable situation for Wezel in Leipzig.

After *Ueber Sprache, Wissenschaften und Geschmack der Teutschen*, Wezel did not publish anything with Dyk until 1784. Meanwhile he kept himself afloat with the private publication of *Wilhelmine Arend, oder die Gefahren der Empfindsamkeit* (Wilhelmine Arend; or, The Dangers of Sentimentality, 1782). The novel describes the nervous breakdown and death of a woman unable to cope with her adulterous husband and unable to perceive the genuine love of another man– who provides emotional support and wants to be her companion–as anything other than adultery on her part. The novel reworks the central issues of Gellert's *Leben der schwedischen Gräfin von G . . .* (Life of the Swedish Countess von G . . . , 1747-1748) in the context of the anthropological-psychological discussion current in France and Germany at the time concerning the physical damage caused by extreme psychic stress. The subtitle indicated Wezel's attitude that the prevalent hypersensitive form of Sentimentality evident in Johann Martin Miller's *Siegwart* (1776) and in Goethe's *Die Leiden des jungen Werthers* (The Sorrows of Young Werther, 1774) was a national epidemic linked with the widespread resignation

and melancholy experienced by middle-class intellectuals since 1770.

In the winter of 1781 Wezel moved to Vienna, where Joseph II had begun his reforms with the tolerance edict of October 1781. Although he received a gold medallion of appreciation from the emperor, he was unsuccessful in his efforts to break into the inner circle of the Viennese National Theater. The rejection of his comic-opera libretto *Der kluge Jakob* led Wezel to write the satirical play *Die Komödianten*, which took the theater establishment–particularly actor-writers such as the brothers Christian Gottlob and Gottlieb Stephanie–to task.

Wezel returned to Leipzig sometime in 1783 and wrote *Kakerlak, oder Geschichte eines Rosenkreuzers aus dem vorigen Jahrhundert* (Kakerlak; or, The Story of a Rosicrucian from the Previous Century, 1784), an ironical rendition of the Faust motif in a prose-and-verse "Feenmärchen" (fairy tale). The protagonist finally becomes bored with the incessant worldly struggle and returns to the sanctuary of his books and studies. The hidden agenda of the work seems to have been a parody of contemporary figures which has yet to be decoded.

In 1784 and 1785 the first two volumes of Wezel's major philosophical treatise, *Versuch Über die Kenntniß des Menschen*, appeared in Leipzig. These volumes were essentially finished in 1781, while he was writing *Wilhelmine Arend*. Wezel's anthropological discussion of the physical-psychic condition of man not only develops the thoughts of French materialism but, as Hans Henning has shown, deals with major philosophical issues in Germany at the time. The first two volumes explore the influence of geography, cultural trends, religion, and particularly the self-interest drive on human consciousness. Wezel's anthropomorphic explanation of religion as a sociopolitical phenomenon created by man to justify customs and to explain life and death plunged him into strife with the university censorship commission in Leipzig. Wezel had submitted the manuscript for volume three, which dealt with the formulation of ideas, but he was so incensed by the censorship that he withdrew the manuscript, returned the advance payment to Dyk, and swore never to publish anything in Saxony again. In 1787 he wrote to Nicolai in Berlin to ask him to publish the third volume. No reply has ever been found, and neither Nicolai nor anyone else published the manuscript as far as has been ascertained. The fourth volume was to have analyzed will and action as well as certain anomalous phenomena such as dreams, mental illness, and Schwärmerei (revelry), and the fifth volume was to have treated speculative and hypothetical problems.

In 1788 Wezel wrote a desperate letter to Dessau, asking for a job there in return for nothing more than room and board and thirty to fifty thalers per year. The letter was addressed "Werther Herr" (Valued Sir). According to Anneliese Klingenberg, it was probably intended for Christian Heinrich Wolcke; by 1788, however, Wolcke was no longer in Dessau. There is no known response. The following year he moved to his birthplace, Sondershausen, where he attempted to organize his financial affairs. He disregarded a public plea by Dyk to resubmit part three of *Versuch über die Kenntniß des Menschen*. His attempts to recover his physical and financial health proved futile, and he remained in Sondershausen disillusioned and withdrawn, unable or unwilling to write or publish anything else until his death thirty years later on 28 January 1819, a fate reminiscent of that of Friedrich Hölderlin. Whether or not Wezel was mentally ill during this time has occupied Wezel scholars and biographers since the early nineteenth century. In 1799 he was sent by unknown parties to Dr. Samuel Hahnemann in Hamburg for about six weeks; suspicion exists that the motivation was less to cure Wezel than to get at his manuscripts, some of which may have been altered and printed without his knowledge. Wezel's posthumous papers disappeared, however, and it is unlikely that any certainty will ever be established about the last thirty years of his life. Wezel's withdrawal, whether it had mental or physiological causes, played a large role in his negative reception. His unorthodox views about religion, his radical political ideas, and his rejection of pity in favor of self-interest all were "shown" by his biographers to be contributing factors to his misanthropy and ultimate demise. Wezel's writings were not accorded their rightful place in literary history for some two hundred years after his brief period of productivity and popularity had ended.

Bibliographies:

Phillip S. McKnight, "Versuch einer Gesamtbibliographie über Johann Karl Wezel," in Wezel's *Kritische Schriften*, volume 2, edited by Albert R. Schmitt (Stuttgart: Metzler, 1971), pp. 813-836;

Albert R. Schmitt, "Bibliographie: Nachträge und Korrekturen," in Wezel's *Kritische Schriften*, volume 3, edited by Schmitt (Stuttgart: Metzler, 1975), pp. 523-527;

Schmitt, review of *Das Groteske in der deutschen Literatur der Spätaufklärung: Ein Versuch über das Erzählwerk Johann Karl Wezels*, by Wolfgang Jansen, *German Quarterly*, 55, no. 1 (1982): 117;

Hans Henning, " 'Denn haben meine Schriften wahren Werth . . .' (Wezel): Zum Stand der Wezel-Forschung," *Das achtzehnte Jahrhundert: Mitteilungen der Deutschen Gesellschaft für die Erforschung des achtzehnten Jahrhunderts*, 11, no. 2 (1987): 79-85;

McKnight, "Wezelforschung in der DDR: Miszellaneen, Material und Mutmaßungen aus Sondershausen und Leipzig," *Lessing Yearbook*, 19 (1987): 223-266.

Biographies:

Jonas Ludwig von Hess, *Durchflüge durch Deutschland, die Niederlande und Frankreich*, volume 1 (Hamburg: Bachmann & Gundermann, 1793), pp. 190-194;

J. N. Becker, *Wezel seit seines Aufenthaltes in Sondershausen: Ein Nachtrag zu Herrn von Hessens Durchflügen durch Deutschland und eine Aufforderung an alle Freunde der schönen Literatur, die eines der trefflichsten deutschen Genies nicht länger in unwürdiger Abgeschiedenheit schmachten lassen wollen* (Erfurt: Neumann, 1799);

Fr. J., "Wezel in Sondershausen," *Der Reichs-Anzeiger*, edited by Rudolf Zacharias Becker, no. 105 (1799);

Dr. L. Vogel, "Betrachtungen über die sicherste und leichteste Methode, die Geisteszerrüttung des unglücklichen Wezels zu heben," *Der Reichs-Anzeiger*, edited by Becker, no. 118 (1799);

G., "Auch ein Wort über Wezel," *Der Reichs-Anzeiger*, edited by Becker, no. 154 (1799);

Vogel, "Noch ein Wort über Wezel's Rettung," *Der Reichs-Anzeiger*, edited by Becker, no. 197 (1799);

Günther von Ziegeler, "Wezel zu Sondershausen," *Zeitung für die elegante Welt*, 23 April 1805, cols. 385-388;

Friedrich Carl Ludloff, "Wezel als Schriftsteller," 6 installments, *Gemeinnützige Blätter für Schwarzburg*, nos. 26-31 (1808);

Ziegeler, "Etwas über den jetzigen Zustand Wezels," *Zeitung für die elegante Welt*, 18 February 1812, cols. 276-279;

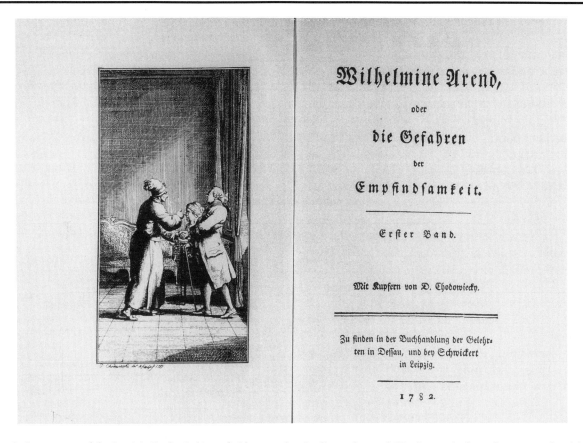

Frontispiece, engraved by Daniel Chodowiecki, and title page for the first volume of Wezel's novel about the nervous breakdown and death of a woman caught between an adulterous husband and a strict moral code that will not allow her to accept emotional support from another man

Ziegeler, "Nachtrag zu dem Aufsatz über Wezel in Nr. 35 dieser Blätter," *Zeitung für die elegante Welt*, 16 March 1812, cols. 425-429;

Ziegeler, "Nachtrag zu dem Aufsatz über Wezel: Beschluß," *Zeitung für die elegante Welt*, 17 March 1812, cols. 433, 435;

August von Blumröder, "Johann Karl Wezel, Fragmente über sein Leben und seinen Wahnsinn," *Zeitgenossen: Ein biographisches Magazin für die Geschichte unserer Zeit*, 4 (1833): 141-172;

Hermann Marggraff, "J. K. Wezel, der Sonderling aus Sondershausen," in his *Bücher und Menschen* (Bunzlau: Appuns, 1837), pp. 177-207;

Carl Schüddekopf, *Klassische Findlinge: Freundesgaben für C. A. H. Burkhard* (Weimar: Böhlau, 1900), pp. 89-119;

Günter Lutze, "Ein vergessener Dichter," in his *Aus Sondershausens Vergangenheit: Ein Beitrag zur Kultur und Sittengeschichte früherer Jahrhunderte*, volume 2 (Sondershausen: Eupel, 1909), pp. 189-213;

Carl Georg von Maassen, Introduction to Wezel's *Herrmann und Ulrike* (Munich: Müller, 1919), pp. vii-xliii;

Kurt Adel, *Johann Karl Wezel: Ein Beitrag zur Geistesgeschichte der Goethezeit* (Vienna: Notring, 1968);

Anneliese Klingenberg, Afterword to Wezel's *Robinson Krusoe* (Berlin: Rütten & Loening, 1979), pp. 263-292;

Gerhard Steiner, "Zerstörung einer Legende oder das wirkliche Leben Johann Karl Wezels," *Sinn und Form*, 31, no. 3 (1979): 699-710;

Steiner, Afterword to Wezel's *Herrmann und Ulrike* (Leipzig: Insel, 1980), pp. 823-882;

Albert R. Schmitt, "Paralipomena zu Gerhard Steiners Wezel-Aufsatz," *Sinn und Form*, 32, no. 2 (1980): 492-497;

Karl-Heinz Meyer, ed., *Neues aus der Wezel-Forschung*, 2 volumes (Sondershausen: Arbeitskreis des Kulturbandes der DDR, 1980-1984);

Steiner, "Johann Karl Wezels Behandlung durch Dr. Samuel Hahnemann," *Jahrbuch der Deutschen Schillergesellschaft*, 25 (1981): 229-237.

References:

Kurt Adel, "Eine vergessene Faust-Dichtung des 18. Jahrhunderts: J. K. Wezels *Kakerlak*," *Jahrbuch des Wiener-Goethe Vereins*, 66 (1962): 61-74;

Monika Ammermann, *Gemeines Leben: Gewandelter Naturbegriff und literarische Spätaufklärung. Lichtenberg, Wezel, Garve* (Bonn: Bouvier, 1978);

Pierre Chevalier, "Quelques emplois du mot 'Révolution' dans l'oeuvre de Johann Karl Wezel," *Etudes Germaniques*, 38 (1983): 229-233;

Walter Dietze, "Elend und Glanz eines 'Deutschen Candide.' Vorläufige Bemerkungen zu Johann Karl Wezels Roman 'Belphegor oder die wahrscheinlichste Geschichte unter der Sonne,' " *Wissenschaftliche Zeitschrift der Karl-Marx Universität Leipzig*, 14 (1965): 771-796;

Steffen Dietzsch, "Aufklärungsquerelen: Anmerkungen zur Wezel-Platner-Debatte 1781/82. Ein Streit um Leibniz' Theodizee," *Weimarer Beiträge*, 35, no. 5 (1989): 861-868;

Liselotte Grevel, *Johann Karl Wezel: Illuminismo in Controluce* (Pisa: Giardini Editori E Stampatori, 1979);

Hans Henning, "Johann Karl Wezels 'Versuch über die Kenntniß des Menschen' (1784/85)," *arcadia*, 15, no. 3 (1980): 258-277;

Henning, "Satire, Aufklärung und Philosophie–Johann Karl Wezel," *Goethe Jahrbuch*, 104 (1987): 332-349;

Elisabeth Holzhey-Pfenniger, *Der desorientierte Erzähler: Studien zu J. C. Wezels "Lebensgeschichte Tobias Knauts"* (Bern, Frankfurt am Main & Munich: Lang, 1976);

Wolfgang Jansen, *Das Groteske in der deutschen Literatur der Spätaufklärung: Ein Versuch über das Erzählwerk Johann Karl Wezels* (Bonn, Bouvier, 1980);

Anneliese Klingenberg, "Radicale Aufklärung und ihr Preis: Johann Karl Wezel (1747-1819), *Colloquia Germanica*, 22, no. 1 (1989): 12-20;

Klingenberg, "Wezels 'Lebensgeschichte Tobias Knauts des Weisen, sonst der Stammler genannt,' " *Weimarer Beiträge*, 35, no. 3 (1989): 430-449;

Klingenberg, ed., *Johann Karl Wezel und die Aufklärung: Protokollband der Wezel-Konferenz am 20.*

Sept. in Weimar (Weimar: Selbstverlag des Kulturbundes, 1989);

Alexander Kosenina, *Ernst Platners Anthropologie und Philosophie: Der "Philosophische Arzt" und seine Wirkung auf Johann Karl Wezel und Jean Paul* (Würzburg: Königshausen & Neumann, 1989);

Detlef Kremer, *Wezel: Über die Nachtseite der Aufklärung. Skeptische Lebensphilosophie zwischen Spätaufklärung und Frühromantik* (Munich: Fink, 1984);

Fritz Martini, "Johann Karl Wezels verspätete Lustspiele," in *Aspekte der Goethezeit: Festschrift für Viktor Lange*, edited by Stanley A. Corngold and others (Göttingen: Vandenhoeck & Ruprecht, 1977), pp. 38-67;

Phillip S. McKnight, "Folgenreiche Weichenstellung: Weimars Nicht-Rezeption der Dichtungs- und Gesellschaftskritik J. K. Wezels," in *Verlorene Klassik?*, edited by Wolfgang Wittkowski (Tübingen: Niemeyer, 1986), pp. 131-143;

McKnight, *The Novels of Johann Karl Wezel: Satire, Realism and Social Criticism in Late 18th Century Literature*, New York University Ottendorfer Series 14 (Bern, Frankfurt am Main & Las Vegas: Lang, 1981);

Volker-Ulrich Müller, "Aufklärung als traurige Wissenschaft: Johann Carl Wezels 'Belphegor oder die wahrscheinlichste Geschichte unter der Sonne,' " in *Reise und Utopie: Zur Literatur der Spätaufklärung*, edited by Hans Joachim Piechotta (Frankfurt am Main: Insel, 1976), pp. 170-221;

Dietrich Naumann, "Utopie und Kritik der Utopie," in his *Politik und Moral: Studien zur Utopie der deutschen Aufklärung* (Heidelberg: Winter, 1977), pp. 247-267;

Wolfgang Promies, *Die Bürger und der Narr oder das Risiko der Phantasie* (Munich: Hanser, 1966);

Arno Schmidt, *Belphegor: Nachrichten von Büchern und Menschen* (Karlsruhe: Stahlberg, 1961);

Albert R. Schmitt, "Englische Einflüße in den Schriften Johann Carl Wezels," *Wissenschaftliche Zeitschrift der Wilhelm-Pieck-Universität Rostock*, 31 (1982): 23-29; translated by Schmitt as "English Influences in the Writings of Johann Carl Wezel," *Modern Language Studies*, 15, no. 1 (1985): 69-79;

Schmitt, "Wezel und Wieland," in *Christoph Martin Wieland: Nordamerikanische Forschungsbeiträge zur 250. Wiederkehr seines Geburtstages*

1983, edited by Hansjörg Schelle (Tübingen: Niemeyer, 1984), pp. 251-275;

Jörg Schönert, "Fragen ohne Antwort: Zur Krise der literarischen Aufklärung im Roman des späten 18. Jahrhunderts. Wezels 'Belphegor,' Klingers 'Faust,' und die 'Nachtwachen des Bonaventura,' " *Jahrbuch der Deutschen Schiller-Gesellschaft*, 14 (1970): 183-229;

Schönert, *Roman und Satire im 18. Jahrhundert* (Stuttgart: Metzler, 1969);

Regine Seibert, *Satirische Empirie: Literarische Struktur und geschichtlicher Wandel der Satire in der Spätaufklärung* (Würzburg: Königshausen & Neumann, 1981);

Rolf-Günter Strube, *Die Physiognomie der Unvernunft: Studien zur Rolle der Einbildungskraft im erzählerischen Werk Johann Karl Wezels* (Heidelberg: Winter, 1980);

Hans Peter Thurn, *Der Roman der unaufgeklärten Gesellschaft: Untersuchungen zum Prosawerk Johann Karl Wezels* (Stuttgart: Kohlhammer, 1973);

Maria Tronskaja, *Die deutsche Prosasatire der Aufklärung*, translated from the Russian by Brigitta Schröder, volume 28 of *Neue Beiträge zur Literaturwissenschaft*, edited by Werner Krauss and Walter Dietze (Berlin: Rütten & Loening, 1970).

Papers:

The last person known to have seen Johann Karl Wezel's papers was August von Blumröder, who saw them shortly after Wezel's death in 1819. All efforts to locate these papers have thus far proven futile. Karl Ludloff, one of Wezel's early biographers, also had access to Wezel's papers; Ludloff's papers, which were discovered in 1979 in File Z of the Staatsarchiv Rudolstadt in the German Democratic Republic, included copies of some of Wezel's poems and letters, but none of Wezel's original papers. Letters to and from Wezel may be found in the Nationale Foschungs- und Gedenkstätten der Klassischen Deutschen Literatur in Weimar, the Deutsches Literaturarchiv in Marbach, the Staatsbibliothek Preußischer Kulturbesitz in Berlin, the Archiv des Germanischen National-Museums in Nuremberg, and the Zentralarchiv der Akademie der Wissenschaften der DDR in Berlin.

Heinrich Zschokke

(22 March 1771 - 27 June 1848)

Donald H. Crosby
University of Connecticut

BOOKS: *Graf Monaldeschi oder Männerbund und Weiberwuth: Trauerspiel in fünf Aufzügen*, anonymous (Küstrin: Oehmigke, 1790);

Die schwarzen Brüder: Eine abentheuerliche Geschichte, 3 volumes, as M. J. R. (volume 1, Berlin & Frankfurt an der Oder: Kunze, 1791; volume 2, N.p., 1793; volume 3, Leipzig & Frankfurt an der Oder: Apitz, 1795); republished as *Die Männer der Finsterniß: Roman und kein Roman. Ein modernes Clairobscüre für Seher und Zeichendeuter*, 1 volume, anonymous (Frankfurt an der Oder: Apitz, 1795);

Der Schriftstellerteufel, anonymous (Berlin, 1791);

Schwärmerey und Traum in Fragmenten, Romanen und Dialogen, 2 volumes, as Johann von Magdeburg (Stettin: Kaffke, 1791-1794); republished as *Kleine Schriften*, 2 volumes, as Zschokke (Stettin: Kaffke, 1800);

Die Bibliothek nach der Mode: Erstes Bändchen, anonymous (Frankfurt an der Oder: Kunze, 1793);

Dissertatio hypothesium diiudicationem sistens (Frankfurt an der Oder, 1793);

Ideen zur psychologischen Ästhetik (Berlin & Frankfurt an der Oder: Kunze, 1793);

Abällino der große Bandit, anonymous (Frankfurt an der Oder & Leipzig: Apitz, 1793); translated by Matthew Gregory Lewis as *The Bravo of Venice: A Romance* (London: Printed by D. N. Shury for Hughes, 1804; New York: Cassell, 1804; reprinted, with an introduction by Davendra P. Varma, New York: Arno Press, 1972);

Charlotte Corday oder Die Rebellion von Calvados: Ein republikanisches Trauerspiel in vier Akten vom Verfasser des "Abellino," anonymous (Stettin: Kaffke, 1794);

Die sieben Teufelsproben: Eine ehrwürdige Legende für Katholiken und Protestanten, anonymous, attributed to Zschokke (Stettin: Kaffke, 1794);

Abällino der große Bandit: Ein Trauerspiel in fünf Aufzügen, nach der Geschichte dieses Namens von demselben Verfasser, anonymous (Leipzig & Frankfurt an der Oder: Apitz, 1795; re-

Heinrich Zschokke (Schiller-Nationalmuseum / Deutsches Literaturarchiv, Marbach)

vised, 1796); translated by William Dunlap as *Abellino, the Great Bandit* (New York: Longworth, 1802); German version revised as *Abellino: Schauspiel in fünf Aufzügen* (Aarau: Sauerländer, 1828);

Der Freiheitsbaum: Lustspiel (Frankfurt an der Oder: Apitz, 1795);

Kuno von Kyburg nahm die Silberlocke des Enthaupteten und ward Zerstörer des heiligen Vehm-Gerichts: Eine Kunde der Väter, erzählt vom Verfasser der schwarzen Brüder, 2 volumes, anonymous (Berlin: Maurer, 1795-1799);

Arkadien, oder Gemälde nach der Natur, gesammelt auf einer Reise von Berlin nach Rom, anonymous (Bayreuth: Lübeck, 1796);

Coronata oder Der Seeräuberkönig auf Coronata: Vom Verfasser des Aböllino, anonymous (Bayreuth: Lübeck, 1796);

Julius von Sassen: Ein Trauerspiel in vier Aufzügen vom Verfasser des Aböllino, anonymous (Zurich: Orell, Geßner & Füßli, 1796);

Salomonische Nächte, anonymous (N.p., 1796);

Über die Schul- und Erziehungsanstalt zu Reichenau, bei Chur: In einem Sendschreiben an den Herrn Gymnasiarch Michael von Wagner, zu Bern (N.p., 1796);

Stephan Bathori, König von Polen: Ein historisch-romantisches Gemählde in zwei Büchern (Bayreuth: Lübeck, 1796);

Meine Wallfahrt nach Paris, 2 volumes, anonymous (Zurich: Orell & Füßli, 1796-1797);

Die drey ewigen Bünde im hohen Rhätien: Historische Skizze, 2 volumes (Zurich: Orell, Geßner & Füßli, 1798); revised as *Geschichte des Freystaats der drey Bünde im hohen Rhätien*, 1 volume (Zurich: Orell & Füßli, 1817);

Freie Bündner, verlaßt die braven Schweizer nicht!: Nothwendiger und letzter Zuruf an biedere, nachdenkende Vaterlandsfreunde (Chur: Otto, 1798);

Das Mißverständniß: Ein Schauspiel in vier Aufzügen von dem Verfasser des Aböllino, anonymous, attributed to Zschokke (Augsburg: Stage, 1798);

Schreiben . . . an die Patrioten Graubündens . . ., anonymous (N.p., 1798);

Das neue und nützliche Schulbüchlein, zum Gebrauch und Unterricht für die wißbegierige Jugend im Bündnerlande . . . : Verfasset und herausgegeben von einem Freunde der guten und fleißigen Kinder des Bündnerlandes. Auf Kosten wohlthätiger Bündner, anonymous (Malans: Berthold, 1798);

Soll Bünden sich an die vereinte Schweiz schließen? Soll Bünden ein eigner Staat bleiben?: Ein vaterländisches Wort an das freie Bündnervolk und dessen Regierung (Chur: Otto, 1798);

Verfassung der Litterarischen Societaet des Cantons Lucern, zur Beförderung der Aufklärung, des Gemeingeistes und der Industrie in Helvetien, anonymous (Lucerne: Meyer, 1798);

Die Zauberinn Sidonia: Schauspiel in vier Aufzügen (Berlin: Maurer, 1798);

Zuschrift des Herrn Dr. Heinrich Zschokke, an den Hochlöblichen Landtag der Republik Graubünden, in Chur versammelt (Chur: Otto, 1798);

Kurze, doch deutliche Anweisung für Schullehrer auf dem Lande, wie sie ihre Jugend wohl unterrichten, und die Anfangsschulen so einrichten können, daß dieselben zur Ehre Gottes, zum Nutzen des Vaterlandes und zur zeitlichen und ewigen Wohlfahrt der Kinder gereichen mögen (Lucerne: Meyer, 1799);

Rechenschaft und Verzeichniß der freywilligen Beyträge edler Schweizer und Schweizerinnen zur Unterstützung der leidenden Menschheit im Kanton Waldstätten (Lucerne: Meyer, 1799);

Geschichte vom Kampf und Untergang der schweizerischen Berg- und Waldkantone, besonders des alten eidgenössischen Kantons Schwyz (Bern & Zurich: Geßner, 1801); translated anonymously from a French translation by J. B. Briatte as *History of the Invasion of Switzerland by the French, and the Destruction of the Democratical Republics of Schwitz, Uri, and Unterwalden* (London: Longman & Rees, 1803);

Vignetten, gezeichnet vom Verfasser des Aböllino, anonymous (Basel: Flick, 1801);

Alamontade der Galeeren-Sklav: Vom Verfasser des Aböllino, 2 volumes, anonymous (Zurich: Orell & Füßli, 1803); republished as *Lebensgemälde vom Verfasser des Aböllino*, 2 volumes (Zurich: Orell & Füßli, 1803); translated by John Turner Sargent Sullivan as *The Galley Slave* (Philadelphia: Joy, 1849);

Hippolyt und Roswida: Schauspiel in vier Aufzügen (Zurich: Orell & Füßli, 1803);

Die Nonne: Vom Verfasser des Aböllino, anonymous, attributed to Zschokke (Frankfurt am Main, 1803);

Schattirungen (Basel: Flick, 1803);

Die Alpenwälder: Für Naturforscher und Forstmänner (Tübingen: Cotta, 1804);

Die einsame Larve: Trauerspiel in fünf Akten (Bayreuth: Lübeck, 1804);

Der Marschall von Sachsen: Schauspiel in vier Aufzügen (Bayreuth: Lübeck, 1804);

Die Prinzessin von Wolfenbüttel: Vom Verfasser des Alamontade, 2 volumes, anonymous (Zurich: Orell & Füßli, 1804); translated by M. A. Faber as "The Princess of Brunswick-Wolfenbüttel," in his *The Princess of Brunswick-Wolfenbüttel and Other Tales* (Leipzig: Tauchnitz / London: Low, Marston, 1867);

Schauspiele: Erster Band, 2 volumes (Bayreuth: Lübeck, 1804);

Giulio degli Obizzi oder Aböllino unter den Calabresen, 2 volumes, anonymous (Basel & Aarau: Flick, 1805-1806);

Der schweizerische Gebürgs-Förster oder Deutliche und genaue Anweisung für Forstbediente usw., 2 volumes (Basel & Aarau: Flick, 1806);

Wird die Menschheit bey den politischen Verwandlungen unseres Welttheils gewinnen oder verlieren? (Gera: Heinsius, 1807);

Die einsame Wohnung oder Das Archiv des Bundes: Vom Verfasser der schwarzen Brüder, anonymous, attributed to Zschokke (Berlin: Privately printed, 1807);

Stunden der Andacht zur Beförderung wahren Christenthums und häuslicher Gottesverehrung, 8 volumes (Aarau: Sauerländer, 1809-1816); translated anonymously as *Hours of Devotion* (New York: Bliss & Wadsworth / Philadelphia: James Kay / Pittsburgh: John I. Kay, 1834); translated by Edward John Burrow as *Hours of Devotion, for the Promotion of True Christianity and Family Worship* (London: Printed for J. G. & F. Rivington, 1838);

Der Krieg Österreichs gegen Frankreich und den rheinischen Bund im Jahre 1809: Ein historischer Überblick (Aarau: Sauerländer, 1810);

Der Feuergeist: Eine Geschichte aus dem 16. Jahrhundert, getreu nach einer alten Handschrift des Herrn G. L. W. in Landsberg (Aarau: Sauerländer, 1812);

Der Krieg Napoleons gegen den Aufstand der spanischen und portugiesischen Völker: Erster Theil (Aarau: Sauerländer, 1813);

Der Baierischen Geschichten, 4 volumes (Aarau: Sauerländer, 1813-1818; revised, 1821);

Von der Freiheit und den Rechten der Kantone Bern, Aargau und Waadt (Aarau: Sauerländer, 1814);

Über die Salzquellen im Sulzthal des Kantons Aargau: Eine Vorlesung. Statistischer Abriß des Cantons Aargau, ein Neujahrsgeschenk für Aargauer Jünglinge (N.p., 1816);

Das Goldmacher-Dorf: Eine anmuthige und wahrhafte Geschichte vom aufrichtigen und wohlerfahrnen Schweizerboten, anonymous (Aarau: Sauerländer, 1817); translated anonymously as *Goldenthal: A Tale* (London: Whittaker, 1833); translated anonymously as *The Goldmakers' Village* (London: Burns, 1845; New York: Appleton, 1845);

Kleine Erzählungen und Gedichte für Erholungsstunden: Aus den beliebten Erheiterungen besonders abgedruckt, 4 volumes (Aarau: Sauerländer, 1818);

Leitfaden für Vorträge über Staatswirtschaft im Lehrverein (Aarau: Sauerländer, 1819);

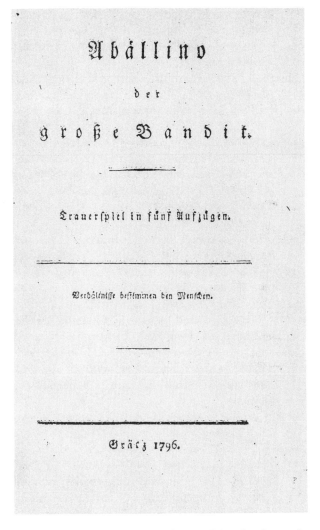

Title page for one of the many editions of the play that made Zschokke famous (courtesy of Staatsarchiv des Kantons Aargau)

Darstellung gegenwärtiger Ausbreitung des Christenthums auf dem Erdball (Aarau: Sauerländer, 1819);

Vom Geist des deutschen Volks im Anfang des neunzehnten Jahrhunderts (Aarau: Sauerländer, 1820);

Anleitung zur zweckmäßigen Anordnung und richtigen Beurtheilung der Blitzableiter (Aarau: Sauerländer, 1821);

Des Schweizerlands Geschichten für das Schweizervolk (Aarau: Sauerländer, 1822); translated by W. Howard Howe as *Popular History of Switzerland: From the German, with the Author's Subsequent Alterations of the Original Work* (Frankfurt am Main: Sauerländer, 1833); translation republished as *The History of Switzerland, from Its Earliest Origin to the Present Time: A Popular Description and Faithful Pic-*

ture of the Gradual Rise and Progress of the Swiss Nation (London: Wilson, 1834);

Die Wirren des Jahrhunderts und des Jahres (Aarau: Sauerländer, 1823);

Betrachtung einer großen Angelegenheit des eidgenössischen Vaterlandes (Aarau: Sauerländer, 1824);

Bilder aus der Schweiz, 5 volumes (Aarau: Sauerländer, 1824-1826);

Ausgewählte Schriften, 40 volumes (Aarau: Sauerländer, 1825-1828);

Die farbigen Schatten, ihr Entstehen und Gesetz: Vorlesung, gehalten in der naturforschenden Gesellschaft zu Aarau den 10. Januar 1826 (Aarau: Sauerländer, 1826);

Lieder der Gesellschaft für vaterländische Cultur im Canton Aargau (N.p., 1829);

Rede an die Helvetische Gesellschaft zu Schinznach (Aarau: Sauerländer, 1829);

Der Creole: Eine Erzählung (Aarau: Sauerländer, 1830); translated by Gustaf Clemens Hebbe as The Creole (New York: Colyer, 1846);

Ueber die grundlosen Drohungen, daß sich fremde Mächte in die Angelegenheiten unserer Kantone einmischen können (Aarau: Sauerländer, 1830);

Der Kanton Aargau neben den andern (Aarau: Sauerländer, 1830);

Allgemeiner Bericht über die, in Bezug auf Verfassungsbesserung und Gesetzgebung eingekommenen, Bittschriften, Anträge und Wünsche, dem Verfassungsrath des Kantons Aargau abgestattet, anonymous (Aarau: Sauerländer, 1831);

Ausgewählte Novellen und Dichtungen (8 volumes, Aarau: Sauerländer, 1836; enlarged, 16 volumes, 1838-1839; revised, 6 volumes, 1841; enlarged, 10 volumes, 1843); enlarged as Novellen und Dichtungen, 15 volumes (Aarau: Sauerländer, 1851-1853);

Volksbildung ist Volksbefreiung!: Eine Rede gehalten in der Versammlung des schweizerischen Volksbildungsvereins zu Laufen den 10. April 1836 (Sissach: Aktien-Buchdruck, 1836);

Die Brannteweinpest: Eine Trauergeschichte zur Warnung und Lehre für Reich und Arm, Alt und Jung (Aarau: Sauerländer, 1837); translated anonymously as The Rum-Plague: A Narrative for the Admonition and Instruction of Both Old and Young, and Rich and Poor (New York: Taylor, 1853);

Kurze Geschichte des Vaterlandes für schweizerische Anfangsschulen und Taubstummenanstalten (Aarau: Sauerländer, 1839);

Die Allmacht Gottes in den Werken der Natur: Ein Volksbuch zur wahren Erkenntniß Gottes und zur Beleh-

rung für alle Stände (Aarau: Sauerländer, 1840);

Die römische Curie und die kirchlichen Wirren in der Schweiz: Gegenstück zu den kirchlichen Wirren Europas, anonymous (Offenbach: Kohler & Teller, 1841);

Lichtstrahlen beleuchtend Religion, Christenthum und Welt, aus H. Zschokke's Werken: Gesammelt und mit dessen Zustimmung allen Freunden des Gerechten, Wahren und Guten dargeboten, edited by Georg Rittschlag (Weimar: Voigt, 1842);

Eine Selbstschau, 2 volumes (Aarau: Sauerländer, 1842); volume 1 translated anonymously as Autobiography of Heinrich Zschokke (London: Chapman & Hall, 1845); German version reprinted, edited by Rémy Charbon (Bern: Haupt, 1977);

Heinrich Zschokke's Aehrenlese, 4 volumes (Aarau: Sauerländer, 1844-1847)—comprises in volume 1, "Pandora: Civilisation, Demoralisation und Todesstrafen: In Briefen an einen jungen Fürsten," "Die Rose von Disentis"; in volume 2, "Die Rose von Disentis (Beschluß)"; in volumes 3 and 4, "Lyonel Harlington"; "Die Rose von Disentis" translated by James J. D. Trevor as The Rose of Disentis: A Novel (New York: Sheldon, 1873);

Meister Jordan oder Handwerk hat goldenen Boden: Ein Feierabendbüchlein für Lehrlinge, verständige Gesellen und Meister (Aarau: Sauerländer, 1845); translated by John Yeats as Labour Stands on Golden Feet; or, The Life of a Foreign Workman: A Holiday Story (London: Groombridge, 1852; New York: Dodd & Mead, 1870);

Gesammelte Volksschriften: Für Volksbibliotheken und Lesevereine zu Stadt und Land (Aarau: Sauerländer, 1846);

Familien-Andachtsbuch: Aus den "Stunden der Andacht" zum Besten minderbemittelter Personen und Haushaltungen umgearbeitet und zusammengeordnet von deren Verfasser (Aarau: Sauerländer, 1848);

Feldblumen: Eine andere Selbstschau in poetischen Gedenkblättern, edited by Emil Zschokke (Frankfurt am Main: Sauerländer, 1850);

Gesammelte Schriften (35 volumes, Aarau: Sauerländer, 1851-1854; enlarged, 36 volumes, 1856-1859);

Sämmtliche Novellen, 12 volumes (Berlin: Merten, 1863);

Addrich im Moos: Historischer Roman (Berlin: Buchverlag Der Morgen, 1966);

Die Walpurgisnacht und andere Erzählungen, edited by Günther Albrecht and Barbara Albrecht (Berlin: Verlag der Nation, 1975);

Hans Dampf in allen Gassen: Humoristische Erzählungen, Novellen und Fabeln, edited by Volker Michels (Frankfurt am Main: Insel, 1980).

Editions in English: *The Polish Chieftain: A Romance*, translated anonymously (London, 1806);

The Sleepwalker: A Tale from the German, translated anonymously (Boston: Munroe, 1842);

Incidents of Social Life amid the European Alps, translated by Louis Strack (New York & Philadelphia: Appleton, 1844); republished as *The Fool of the Nineteenth Century; and Other Tales* (New York & Philadelphia: Appleton, 1845)—comprises "Florian: The Fugitive of the Jura," "Marble and Conrad: Mend the Hole in Your Sleeve," "Olivier Flyeln: A Fool of the Nineteenth Century," "Hortensia: Asleep and Awake";

The Refugee in the Mountains of Jura, translated by Parke Godwin (New York: Winchester, 1844);

The Journal of a Poor Vicar, The Walpurgisnacht, and Other Stories, translated anonymously (Philadelphia: Carey & Hart, 1845);

The Prime Minister; or, The Singular Fortunes of a Peasant and a Peer, translated anonymously (London: Clarke, 1845);

Tales: From the German of Heinrich Zschokke, translated by Godwin (New York: Wiley & Putnam, 1845)—comprises "The Fool of the XIX Century," "Harmonius," "Jack Steam," "Floretta," "New Year's Eve," "Illumination," "The Broken Cup," "Jonathan Frock," "The Involuntary Journey," "Leaves from the Journal of a Poor Vicar in Wiltshire";

Wanderings of a Phil-Hellene, translated by Gustaf Clemens Hebbe (New York: Daggers, 1845);

Veronica; or, The Free Court of Aarau, translated by Samuel Spring (New York: Harper, 1845);

Journal of a Poor Vicar, translated anonymously (New York: Taylor, 1852);

Julius, and Other Tales from the German, translated by William Henry Furness (Philadelphia: Parry & McMillan, 1856);

The Eccentric, translated by George C. McWhorter (New York, 1869);

The Dead Guest: A Mysterious Story, translated by McWhorter (New York: Appleton, 1869);

The Dead Guest, translated anonymously (Chicago: Donnelley, Loyd, 1878);

A Sylvester Night's Adventure, translated by M. B. W. (Cincinnati: Clarke, 1884).

OTHER: *Frankfurter Ephemeriden für Weltbürger*, edited by Zschokke and others (Frankfurt an der Oder: Apitz, 1793);

Literarisches Pantheon, 2 volumes, edited by Zschokke (Frankfurt an der Oder: Apitz, 1794);

Der aufrichtige und wohlerfahrene Schweizerbote, edited by Zschokke (Aarau: Sauerländer, 1798-1800, 1804-1837);

Der helvetische Genius: Eine periodische Schrift, 2 volumes, edited, with contributions, by Zschokke (Lucerne & Zurich: Geßner, 1799);

Historische Denkwürdigkeiten der helvetischen Staatsumwälzung, 3 volumes, edited by Zschokke (Winterthur: Steiner, 1803-1805);

Isis: Eine Monatsschrift deutscher und schweizerischer Gelehrten, edited by Zschokke and others (Zurich, 1805-1806);

Molière, *Lustspiele und Possen: Für die deutsche Bühne*, translated and adapted by Zschokke (Zurich: Geßner, 1805-1806);

Miscellen für die neuste Weltkunde, 7 volumes, edited by Zschokke (Aarau: Sauerländer, 1807-1813);

Stéphanie Félicité Ducrest de Saint-Aubin, Comtesse de Genlis, *Belisar: Aus dem Französischen der Frau von Genlis. Begleitet von einer biographischen Skizze des Feldherrn*, translated, with additions, by Zschokke (Aarau: Sauerländer, 1808);

Erheiterungen: Eine Monatsschrift für gebildete Leser, 17 volumes, edited, with contributions, by Zschokke and others (Aarau: Sauerländer, 1811-1827);

Johann Rudolf Meyer, *Reise auf die Eisgebirge des Kantons Bern und Ersteigung ihrer höchsten Gipfel im Sommer 1812: Mit einer Karte der bereiseten Gletscher*, edited by Zschokke (Aarau: Sauerländer, 1813);

Ueberlieferungen zur Geschichte unserer Zeit, 7 volumes, edited by Zschokke (Aarau: Sauerländer, 1817-1823);

T. von Haupt, *Unsere Vorzeit*, 4 volumes, introduction by Zschokke (Frankfurt am Main: Sauerländer, 1828);

Prometheus: Für Licht und Recht, 3 volumes, edited by Zschokke and others (Aarau: Sauerländer, 1832-1833);

P. Usteri, *Kleine gesammelte Schriften*, edited by Zschokke (Aarau: Sauerländer, 1832);

Frontispiece and title page for one of Zschokke's works on the history of Switzerland (courtesy of Staatsarchiv des Kantons Aargau)

Carl Gustav Jochmann, *Reliquien: Aus seinen nachgelassenen Papieren*, 3 volumes, edited by Zschokke (Hechingen: Ribler, 1836-1838); volume 3 republished as *Zur Naturgeschichte des Adels* (Heidelberg: Winter, 1982);

Die klassischen Stellen der Schweiz und deren Hauptorte in Originalansichten dargestellt, gezeichnet von Gustav Adolph Müller, auf Stahl gestochen von Henry Winkles und den besten englischen Künstlern, texts by Zschokke (Karlsruhe & Leipzig: Kunstverlag & Creuzbauer, 1838);

Rodolphe Töpffer, *Genfer Novellen: Nach dem Französischen*, edited and translated by Zschokke (2 volumes, Aarau: Sauerländer, 1839; enlarged, 1 volume, 1845).

Although Heinrich Zschokke has become little more than a footnote to the history of German literature, he was one of the best-known and most prolific authors of his day and forged a career over his long lifetime that bears more

than a superficial resemblance to that of his great contemporary Johann Wolfgang von Goethe. Like Goethe, Zschokke showed precocious learning ability; found early fame as a bestselling author; had a love for and practical experience in the theater; served with distinction as a minister of state; and attained stature as a serious scientist whose publications earned him the respect of the scientific community. Unlike Goethe, however, Zschokke was not considered a "Dichter" (major poet) by his contemporaries; instead, he was regarded as a "Schriftsteller" (popular and prolific author). It is a judgment with which Zschokke, a modest and fair-minded man, would have concurred; had he designated a legacy to posterity, it would surely have sprung from his tireless efforts to bring constitutional democracy to his beloved adopted homeland, Switzerland.

Johann Heinrich Daniel Zschokke was born in Magdeburg, Prussia, on 22 March 1771 into a large and financially secure family. His mother died while Zschokke was still an infant; when he was eight, the death of his father brought an end to what had been a peaceful and stable childhood. Taken into the home of an older brother, Zschokke was shunted off to an uncongenial religious boarding school. There the future scholar and pedagogue was branded a slow learner; only the intervention of a sympathetic older sister spared the sensitive boy from being apprenticed to a trade. A change of schools proved beneficial, but even Zschokke's improved grades could not convince his practical-minded brother that study at a gymnasium would be anything but a waste of time.

Zschokke was in effect a prisoner in the home of his brother, but the resourceful boy soon found an avenue of escape: through the precocious use of the facile pen which was to serve him for a lifetime, he created a private, fictive world which knew nothing of bills, receipts, profits, or losses. These imaginative flights were furthered by whatever books he could lay hands on in his pedestrian surroundings. Neither threats nor punishments inhibited him from smuggling forbidden volumes into his bedroom, where he often read by the light of a lamp he had made from a hollowed-out turnip. This taste of the forbidden fruits of learning only whetted Zschokke's appetite for Bildung (higher learning, culture), and at the age of twelve, exasperated by the unyielding hostility of his foster parents, he took the bold step of going over their heads and carrying his plea for the right to a better education directly to the chief administrator of the Obervormundschaftsamt (Guardianship Office). Within a few days he found himself emancipated from his foster parents, transferred to the care of a kindly retired school principal, and enrolled in a gymnasium. Zschokke proved to be a brilliant student despite his late start and was soon at the head of his class. Upon completion of his studies he was eager to continue his quest for Bildung at a university. This time, however, he had less luck in obtaining the necessary permission and funds from his guardian, who felt that the seventeen-year-old was not up to the rigors of university life.

Zschokke was not one to ignore the possibilities inherent in this forced hiatus in his academic career. In his autobiography, *Eine Selbstschau* (A Look at Myself, 1842; translated in part as *Autobiography of Heinrich Zschokke*, 1845), he refers to his flight from his native city while waiting for

Zschokke circa 1810 (Bildarchiv Preußischer Kulturbesitz)

his guardian to have a change of heart; but in reality what Zschokke undertook was a time-honored Wanderjahr (year of journeying), that rite of passage then favored by young Germans both in fiction and in life. A summary of Zschokke's adventures over the next two years reads like a condensation of Goethe's *Wilhelm Meisters Lehrjahre* (Wilhelm Meister's Apprenticeship, 1795-1796): encounters with several helpful mentors, a period as an actor, and employment as a part-time playwright with an itinerant stage ensemble. Yet Zschokke never lost sight of his serious goals, and in his autobiography he recounts how he gradually turned away from "this rabble of lazy apprentices, runaway wives, prodigal sons, sentimental girls, worthless students, etc." and found solace again in his beloved books.

At the age of nineteen Zschokke at last obtained the permission of his guardian to matriculate at the University of Frankfurt an der Oder. He registered for lectures in theology (his major subject), philosophy, and law–passing over medicine, as he explained, because of an aversion to corpses and autopsies; but the sterility of the subject matter, combined with the stuffiness of the lecturers, left him bored and embittered. Yet Zschokke was anything but a poor student, and by the end of his third year he had so impressed his professors that he was encouraged to complete a doctorate in theology and to accept an appointment as a Privat-Dozent (unpaid lecturer). Hence at the age of twenty-two the erstwhile "slow learner" was lecturing at the university level on critical theology, aesthetics, and moral philosophy.

For all his academic accomplishments, Zschokke was also a man of action. Although he turned his back on the usual excesses of university students, especially drinking and dueling, he proved a congenial companion to classmates who shared his seriousness of purpose. He also continued the dramatic writing he had begun during his vagabond years with the itinerant theater troupe. Even before entering the university he had published his first play, *Graf Monaldeschi oder Männerbund und Weiberwuth* (Count Monaldeschi; or, The League of Men and Rage of Women, 1790); at the insistence of his close friends, he completed the draft of a play called *Aballino der große Bandit* (1795; translated as *Abellino, the Great Bandit*, 1802). Although Zschokke later deprecated the blood-and-thunder drama as being little more than a potboiler, the play immediately caught the public fancy; like Goethe's *Götz von Berlichingen* (1773), it made its author famous virtually overnight.

Characteristically, Zschokke did not allow the success of *Aballino* to turn his head. He had already made up his mind to pursue an academic career, and he never regarded creative writing as his prime vocation. Although several adventure novels followed *Aballino* in the next few years, Zschokke directed most of his energies into preparation for a professorship. He also served a trial appointment as a part-time pastor and found time to edit a journal, the *Literarisches Pantheon* (1794).

The year 1794 was a pivotal one for Zschokke. From semester to semester his reputation as a popular lecturer had been growing, and with a successful postdoctoral examination behind him he felt confident of attaining a tenured professorship. To his surprise he was told that he was too young to be considered for the position and was counseled to be patient for a few years. Whether Zschokke's youth really was the reason, or whether his outspoken support of the French Revolution had offended the conservative Prus-

sian minister of education, is open to speculation; in any case, Zschokke severed his ties to the university, sold his books and furniture, and left Frankfurt in the spring of 1795.

Rather to his chagrin, Zschokke discovered that his reputation as the author of *Aballino* had preceded him to Berlin, Leipzig, Bayreuth, and every other German city that could boast of a stage–as virtually every German city could. Although Zschokke enjoyed the new acquaintances he made everywhere, he found it impossible to settle down; it was as though some force were drawing him ineluctably southward. Years earlier, in one of his foster homes, he had gazed longingly at a map of Switzerland and wondered whether his travels would ever take him beyond the walls of Magdeburg to this distant alpine paradise. Upon reaching the shore of Lake Constance, Zschokke felt that his youthful dream was about to be realized. In his autobiography, written fifty years later, Zschokke vividly recalled the exhilaration he felt at his first glimpse of the "giant piles and summits of the Alps, with all their towers of icy peaks and fields of silver...." He recalled, too, his first steps on "the dear adopted soil," how he literally kissed the ground of this "rocky fortress of freedom."

Zschokke was at first enchanted by his travels through what he called "the promised land": the bright sky, the green hills, the blue streams, the cheerful villages with their neatly dressed inhabitants, the variety of national costumes, and above all the majestic Alps made his Prussian homeland seem drab by comparison. Yet the keen-eyed observer soon discovered that Switzerland was far from being a paradise, or even a "rocky fortress of freedom": the mountains and valleys which gave the land its beauty also impeded mobility and communication; inbred, insular attitudes resisted any form of innovation and modernization. Even in more cosmopolitan areas, such as Zurich, Zschokke found a distressing cleavage between "haves" and "have-nots" and was appalled to discover that the underprivileged suffered deprivations reminiscent of serfdom.

Sobered by this confrontation with reality, Zschokke made no attempt to establish roots during his first visit to Switzerland; instead, he set his course for Paris. A staunch defender of the French Revolution, Zschokke had hoped to find its ringing ideals translated into practice; what he found instead was anarchy, despotism, and an undemocratic redistribution of privilege. Convinced that the French had merely substituted one set of masters for another, the disillusioned idealist packed his bags once more. His goal this time was Rome, not because the Eternal City held out any promise of realizing his utopian hopes for democracy but because–like Goethe before him–he felt that a sojourn in Rome might develop his talents as a painter.

On his first trip to Switzerland, Zschokke had met the renowned educator Heinrich Pestalozzi, whose progressive theories of education paralleled Zschokke's own convictions. Although Zschokke's training had prepared him for a career as a university professor, his discussions with Pestalozzi had rekindled the memory of his turbulent years as a primary and secondary pupil in Magdeburg, where memorization, examinations, and routine canings constituted the accepted pedagogy. Passing through Switzerland on his way to Rome in 1796, he visited the Seminar Reichenau, a school roughly equivalent to a German gymnasium, in the Canton of the Grisons. A replacement was being sought for the retiring director, under whose stewardship the school had become demoralized and poorly attended. In spite of his lack of experience in school administration Zschokke was promptly installed as the new director of the Seminar. With a free hand to revise the curriculum and to pioneer new methods of instruction, he quickly raised morale at the school; within a year enrollment had increased fivefold. As Zschokke's reputation grew, so did his attachment to his new homeland, so that neither his postponed art studies in Rome nor the belated offer of a professorship from his former university could tempt him to leave the Grisons. In 1798 he was accorded Swiss citizenship, an honor rarely bestowed on foreigners.

That same year Napoleon, eager to bring northern Italy and the western part of Switzerland under French hegemony, sent his troops across the border to establish a Helvetic Republic. In exchange for close ties with France, Napoleon offered the fledgling republic freedom of the press and religion, as well as emancipation from the vestiges of feudal servitude. In reaction, the Hapsburgs of Austria, reluctant to see Switzerland fall under Napoleon's domination, exerted pressure on the Swiss cantons to remain within the Austrian sphere of influence. The Grisons, the largest land in the Swiss Confederation, was caught in the middle of this political tug-of-war. Zschokke's idealism and sympathy with the oppressed led him to support Napoleon's initiative, and soon his energies and his prolific pen were

Zschokke in 1825; engraving by M. Eßlinger of a drawing by J. Notz

marshaled in support of the Helvetic Republic. But in a plebiscite the majority of his fellow citizens rejected affiliation with the Helvetic Republic in favor of continued ties with Austria. The victorious pro-Hapsburg faction promptly mounted a vicious campaign of retribution. Vilified as a traitor and with a price on his head, Zschokke was forced to flee for his life.

He sought refuge in Aarau, the provisional capital of the Helvetic Republic, where he became the spokesman for his fellow refugees. To disseminate his populist manifesto he founded *Der aufrichtige und wohlerfahrene Schweizerbote* (The Honest and Experienced Swiss Messenger), a weekly newspaper written in a language designed to make it accessible to all classes. The political acumen displayed by the young editor did not go unnoticed, and Zschokke was entrusted with troubleshooting diplomatic assignments. Although he was in his twenties and had only recently immigrated to Switzerland, Zschokke so impressed the regional authorities that in 1799 he was appointed governor of the Canton Waldstätten.

Indeed, once initiated into the realpolitik of strife-torn Switzerland, Zschokke showed such political skill that he became a sort of minister-at-large to the Cantons of Tessin and Basel. With tact, tolerance, liberalism, patience, energy, and courage, Zschokke almost single-handedly healed old wounds, restored morale, and channeled financial assistance to war-devastated areas.

Zschokke's tireless efforts as a diplomat were crowned in 1801 by the Treaty of Lunéville, which seemed to guarantee Switzerland the right to shape its own destiny. But when, at Napoleon's instigation, the treaty was undermined by selfish oligarchs within Switzerland itself, Zschokke resigned his diplomatic offices and resumed his career as an author and publisher. The pent-up literary energies released produced many tales, novellas, and novels, as well as articles and monographs devoted to forestry and to recent Swiss history. In 1804 the Sauerländer Verlag, the publishing house which was to serve as a conduit for Zschokke's writings for the rest of his life, was established in Aarau.

Zschokke's extensive travels, combined with his prominence as an author, statesman, pedagogue, and scientist, brought him into contact with leading figures in the spheres of activity he pursued. It was through his friendship with Heinrich von Kleist that Zschokke has earned at least a passing reference in histories of German literature. In 1802, as Zschokke tells the story in his autobiography, he, Kleist, and Ludwig Wieland—the son of the well-known German author Christoph Martin Wieland—engaged in a friendly competition to give a literary interpretation of an engraving, "La Cruche Cassée" (The Broken Jug), which Zschokke had mounted on the wall of his apartment in Bern. Wieland promised a satire, Zschokke a prose narrative, and Kleist a comedy; thus was born Kleist's masterful comedy Der zerbrochne Krug (The Broken Jug, 1811), which has held the boards long after the contributions of Wieland and Zschokke have been forgotten.

With the defeat of Napoleon in 1813 a wave of political reaction began to spread through Switzerland; Swiss liberals, appalled by the threat to the fragile foundations of republican equality in the cantons, turned once again to Heinrich Zschokke. Happily married since 1805 and with a growing brood of children to care for, Zschokke was at first reluctant to return to public service; characteristically, however, he put the interests of his fellow citizens first and accepted an appointment to the Grand Council of Aarau. Thanks to his prestige, energy, and political vision, his adopted canton soon became a model of religious tolerance and democracy. In his ecumenical weekly Stunden der Andacht (1809-1816; translated as Hours of Devotion, 1834), one of the most influential religious tracts of its time, Zschokke argued vigorously against intolerance. Politically, he envisioned a united Switzerland modeled after the United States of America, in which the central government would allow the component states a reasonable degree of autonomy, but regional differences would be subordinated to the needs of the nation.

In 1829 Zschokke once again retired from public life. With undiminished energy he returned to the activities he loved: writing, editing, scientific research, and pedagogy. He established a foundation that encouraged impoverished youths to study at universities, which in Zschokke's day tended to serve the middle and upper classes. Moved by the plight of the many Swiss handicapped by speech and hearing impairment—they were often stigmatized as "cretins" and denied education and employment—he persuaded educational authorities in Aarau to open Switzerland's first school for the speech- and hearing-impaired. Zschokke and his wife personally took charge of this institution, which, as he had hoped, became a model for similar schools throughout Switzerland.

Despite the many claims on his time, Zschokke continued his long career as a writer of fiction. The year 1837 brought the publication of one of his most popular tales, Die Brannteweinpest (translated as The Rum-Plague, 1853), which, like his earlier tale Das Goldmacher-Dorf (The Goldmakers' Village, 1817; translated as Goldenthal, 1833), illustrated his facility for combining entertaining prose with an educational mission. In Das Goldmacher-Dorf Zschokke had pilloried the greed and materialism bred by what he called the "Kantönligeist" (insular mentality) of some of his fellow citizens; in the later story he used a fictional framework to inveigh against alcoholism, which was rapidly becoming a nationwide social problem. Although Zschokke had a gift for coating the pill of moral suasion with palatable prose, little of his fiction survived his lifetime; a narrow focus on a problem affecting a small group of people at a particular time is not the stuff of which durable literature is made. Besides, Zschokke was simply not a great author. One need only compare his diffuse tale "Der zerbrochene Krug"

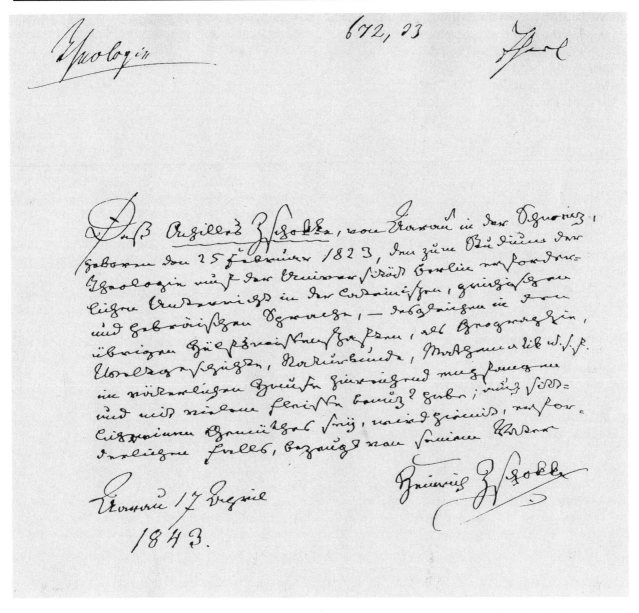

Letter of recommendation from Zschokke to the University of Berlin on behalf of his son, Achilles, dated 17 April 1843
(Staatsarchiv des Kantons Bern)

(1813; translated as "The Broken Cup," 1845) with Kleist's taut comedy on the same subject to perceive the difference between a merely good writer and a great one.

Yet Zschokke cannot be casually dismissed as a literary personality, even though changing tastes and times have consigned his fictional oeuvre to obscurity. His wit and gift for characterization bear comparison with those of Jean Paul Richter; his penchant for inserting himself into his stories, thereby creating what would later be called an "alienation effect," aligns him with Lud-

wig Tieck and other writers of the German Romantic movement; his tales of robbers and adventure anticipated those of his popular contemporary Christian Vulpius; his historical novels were among the first to strive for verisimilitude by reference to a historical "chronicle," a device employed by such writers as Kleist, Conrad Ferdinand Meyer, and Thomas Mann; he was among the pioneers in creating the genre of the Dorfgeschichte (village tale); he made innovative use of the language of Luther's Bible; and he ranks with Matthias Claudius and Johann Peter

Hebel as one of the most original and influential writers for the common people of his day.

Blessed with robust health well into his eighth decade and undaunted by the rigors of travel, Zschokke undertook extensive journeys to France, Holland, and various cities in Germany. At home in Aarau there was a constant stream of visitors coming to see the famous author, statesman, scientist, and pedagogue; and he continued to produce well-turned fiction, translations, and essays. Only in 1847, when Zschokke was seventy-six, did his enormous vitality begin to ebb; by the year's end he was bedridden with a terminal illness. He lived long enough to see one final, fervent wish realized: the birth of the modern Republic of Switzerland. On the day the Swiss Constitution was ratified–27 June 1848–Heinrich Zschokke died.

Biographies:

W. Neumann, *Heinrich Zschokke: Eine Biographie* (Cassel, 1853);

Emil Zschokke, *Heinrich Zschokke: Ein biographischer Umriß*, second edition (Berlin: Lüdersitz, 1869);

J. J. Bäbler, *Heinrich Zschokke: Ein Lebensbild* (Aarau: Sauerländer, 1884);

Carl Günther, *Heinrich Zschokkes Jugend und Bildungsjahre bis 1798: ein Beitrag zu seiner Lebensgeschichte* (Aarau: Sauerländer, 1918).

References:

Percy Willoughby Ames, "The Supposed Source of *The Vicar of Wakefield* and Its Treatment by Zschokke and Goldsmith," *Royal Society of Literature of the United Kingdom, London*, 19 (1898): 93-106;

Holger Böning, *Heinrich Zschokke und sein "Aufrichtiger und wohlerfahrener Schweizerbote: Die Aufklärung in der Schweiz* (Bern: Lang, 1983);

Emil Dietsch, *Heinrich Zschokkes Rechts- und Staatsdenken* (Aarau: Sauerländer, 1957);

J. Keller, *Beiträge zur politischen Tätigkeit Heinrich Zschokkes in den Revolutionsjahren 1789-1801* (Aarau: Sauerländer, 1888);

E. E. Kluge, "Heinrich Zschokke und die Freiheit der Presse," *Rote Revue* (Zurich), 18 (1938): 2-22;

Ernst Reichmann, *Die philosophischen Anschauungen des jungen Zschokke* (Leipzig: Borna, 1936);

Paul Schaffroth, *Heinrich Zschokke als Politiker und Publizist während der Restauration und Regeneration* (Aarau: Sauerländer, 1950);

M. Schneiderreit, *Heinrich Zschokke, seine Weltanschauung und Lebensweisheit* (Berlin, 1904);

Martin Schulz, *Heinrich Zschokke als Dramatiker* (Stuttgart: Metzler, 1914);

R. Wernly, *Vater Heinrich Zschokke: Ein Lebens- und Charakterbild* (Aarau: Sauerländer, 1894).

Papers:

Some of Heinrich Zschokke's manuscripts are in the Bundesarchiv in Bern and in the Aargauisches Staatsarchiv in Aargau, Switzerland.

Books for Further Reading

Blackall, Eric A. *The Emergence of German as a Literary Language, 1700-1775*, 2nd edition. Ithaca, N.Y.: Cornell University Press, 1978.

Borchmeyer, Dieter. *Die Weimarer Klassik: Eine Einführung*. Königstein / Ts: Athenäum, 1980.

Bruford, Walter H. *Culture and Society in Classical Weimar, 1775-1806*. London: Cambridge University Press, 1962.

Bruford, *The German Tradition of Self Cultivation. 'Bildung' from Humboldt to Thomas Mann*. London: Cambridge University Press, 1975.

Bruford, *Germany in the Eighteenth Century: The Social Background of the Literary Revival*. Cambridge: Cambridge University Press, 1935.

Bruford, *Theatre, Drama, and Audience in Goethe's Germany*. London: Routledge & Kegan Paul, 1950.

Burckhardt, Sigurd. *The Drama of Language: Essays on Goethe and Kleist*. Baltimore: Johns Hopkins University Press, 1970.

Cassirer, Ernst. *The Philosophy of the Enlightenment*. Princeton: Princeton University Press, 1951.

Conrady, Karl Otto, ed. *Deutsche Literatur zur Zeit der Klassik*. Stuttgart: Reclam, 1977.

Garland, Henry and Mary. *The Oxford Companion to German Literature*, 2nd edition. Oxford, New York: Oxford University Press, 1986.

Gay, Peter. *The Enlightenment: An Interpretation. The Rise of Modern Paganism*. New York: Knopf, 1966.

Graham, Ilse. *Goethe and Lessing: The Wellsprings of Creation*. New York: Barnes & Noble, 1973.

Guthke, Karl S. *Literarisches Leben im achtzehnten Jahrhundert in Deutschland und in der Schweiz*. Bern: Francke, 1975.

Hatfield, Henry C. *Aesthetic Paganism in German Literature. From Winckelmann to the Death of Goethe*. Cambridge: Harvard University Press, 1964.

Hettner, Hermann Julius. *Literaturgeschichte der Goethezeit*, edited by Johannes Anderegg. Munich: Beck, 1970.

Hinck, Walter, ed. *Europäische Aufklärung*. Frankfurt am Main: Athenaion, 1974.

Jacobs, Jürgen. *Wilhelm Meister und seine Brüder: Untersuchungen zum deutschen Bildungsroman*. Munich: Fink, 1972.

Kieffer, Bruce. *The Storm and Stress of Language: Linguistic Catastrophe in the Early Works of Goethe, Lenz, Klinger, and Schiller*. University Park: Pennsylvania State University Press, 1986.

Kluckhohn, Paul. *Die Auffassung der Liebe in der Literatur des 18 Jahrhunderts und in der deutschen Romantik*, 3rd edition. Tübingen: Niemeyer, 1966.

Lange, Victor. *The Classical Age of German Literature, 1740-1815*. New York: Holmes & Meier, 1982.

Newald, Richard. *Von Klopstock bis zu Goethes Tod*. Erster Teil: *Ende der Aufklärung und Vorbereitung der Klassik*. Munich: Beck, 1957.

Pascal, Roy. *The German Sturm und Drang*. Manchester: Manchester University Press, 1953.

Pasley, Malcolm. *Germany: A Companion to German Studies*, 2nd edition. London: Methuen, 1982.

Reed, T. J. *The Classical Centre. Goethe and Weimar 1775-1832*. London: Croom Helm, New York: Barnes & Noble, 1980.

Swales, Martin. *The German Bildungsroman from Wieland to Hesse*. Princeton: Princeton University Press, 1978.

Wiese, Benno von, ed. *Deutsche Dichter des 18. Jahrhunderts. Ihr Leben und Werk*. Berlin: Schmidt, 1977.

Ziolkowski, Theodore. *German Romanticism and its Institutions*. Princeton: Princeton University Press, 1990.

Contributors

Jeannine Blackwell ....*University of Kentucky*

Jane K. Brown...*University of Washington*

Bettina Kluth Cothran..*Georgia State University*

Donald H. Crosby...*University of Connecticut*

Christopher L. Dolmetsch..*Marshall University*

James Hardin ....*University of South Carolina*

Edward P. Harris ....*University of Cincinnati*

Erich P. Hofacker, Jr...*University of Michigan*

Dieter Jedan ....*Murray State University*

G. L. Jones ....*University College of Wales, Aberystwyth*

Gerda Jordan...*University of South Carolina*

Wulf Koepke ....*Texas A & M University*

Edward T. Larkin ....*University of New Hampshire*

Phillip S. McKnight...*University of Kentucky*

Max Reinhart ....*University of Georgia*

John F. Reynolds...*Longwood College*

Herbert Rowland ....*Purdue University*

Thomas P. Saine...*University of California, Irvine*

Thomas G. Sauer ....*University of Virginia*

Henry J. Schmidt ....*Ohio State University*

John D. Simons...*Florida State University*

Rita Terras...*Connecticut College*

H. M. Waidson...*University of Wales, Swansea*

Colin Walker...*Queen's University of Belfast*

Susanne Zantop ....*Dartmouth College*

Cumulative Index

Dictionary of Literary Biography, Volumes 1-94
Dictionary of Literary Biography Yearbook, 1980-1988
Dictionary of Literary Biography Documentary Series, Volumes 1-7

Cumulative Index

DLB before number: *Dictionary of Literary Biography,* Volumes 1-94
Y before number: *Dictionary of Literary Biography Yearbook,* 1980-1988
DS before number: *Dictionary of Literary Biography Documentary Series,* Volumes 1-7

A

Abbey Press..DLB-49

The Abbey Theatre and Irish
Drama, 1900-1945 ....DLB-10

Abbot, Willis J. 1863-1934 ....DLB-29

Abbott, Jacob 1803-1879 ....DLB-1

Abbott, Lyman 1835-1922 ....DLB-79

Abbott, Robert S. 1868-1940 ....DLB-29, 91

Abelard-Schuman DLB-46

Abell, Arunah S. 1806-1888 ....DLB-43

Abercrombie, Lascelles 1881-1938 ....DLB-19

Abrams, M. H. 1912- DLB-67

Abse, Dannie 1923- DLB-27

Academy Chicago Publishers DLB-46

Ace Books DLB-46

Acorn, Milton 1923-1986 ....DLB-53

Acosta, Oscar Zeta 1935?- DLB-82

Actors Theatre of Louisville DLB-7

Adair, James 1709?-1783? DLB-30

Adame, Leonard 1947- DLB-82

Adamic, Louis 1898-1951..........................DLB-9

Adams, Alice 1926- Y-86

Adams, Brooks 1848-1927 ....DLB-47

Adams, Charles Francis, Jr. 1835-1915 ....DLB-47

Adams, Douglas 1952- Y-83

Adams, Franklin P. 1881-1960 ....DLB-29

Adams, Henry 1838-1918...................DLB-12, 47

Adams, Herbert Baxter 1850-1901 ....DLB-47

Adams, J. S. and C. [publishing house].............DLB-49

Adams, James Truslow 1878-1949.................DLB-17

Adams, John 1735-1826.............................DLB-31

Adams, John Quincy 1767-1848....................DLB-37

Adams, Léonie 1899-1988 ....DLB-48

Adams, Samuel 1722-1803...........................DLB-31, 43

Adams, William Taylor 1822-1897 ....DLB-42

Adcock, Fleur 1934- DLB-40

Ade, George 1866-1944 ....DLB-11, 25

Adeler, Max (see Clark, Charles Heber)

Advance Publishing Company DLB-49

AE 1867-1935 ....DLB-19

Aesthetic Poetry (1873), by Walter Pater............DLB-35

Afro-American Literary Critics:
An Introduction DLB-33

Agassiz, Jean Louis Rodolphe 1807-1873 ....DLB-1

Agee, James 1909-1955................................DLB-2, 26

Aichinger, Ilse 1921- DLB-85

Aiken, Conrad 1889-1973.............................DLB-9, 45

Ainsworth, William Harrison 1805-1882 ....DLB-21

Aitken, Robert [publishing house].....................DLB-49

Akins, Zoë 1886-1958....................................DLB-26

Alain-Fournier 1886-1914 ....DLB-65

Alba, Nanina 1915-1968................................DLB-41

Albee, Edward 1928- DLB-7

Alcott, Amos Bronson 1799-1888........................DLB-1

Alcott, Louisa May 1832-1888.................DLB-1, 42, 79

Alcott, William Andrus 1798-1859.......................DLB-1

Alden, Henry Mills 1836-1919 ....DLB-79

Alden, Isabella 1841-1930..............................DLB-42

Alden, John B. [publishing house] DLB-49

Alden, Beardsley and Company DLB-49

Aldington, Richard 1892-1962 ....DLB-20, 36

Aldis, Dorothy 1896-1966 ....DLB-22

Aldiss, Brian W. 1925- DLB-14

Aldrich, Thomas Bailey 1836-1907
....DLB-42, 71, 74, 79

Alexander, Charles 1868-1923..........................DLB-91

Alexander, Charles Wesley

[publishing house] DLB-49

Alexander, James 1691-1756 ....DLB-24

Alexander, Lloyd 1924- DLB-52

Alger, Horatio, Jr. 1832-1899...............DLB-42

Algonquin Books of Chapel Hill DLB-46

Algren, Nelson 1909-1981 ....DLB-9; Y-81, 82

Allan, Andrew 1907-1974 ....DLB-88

Allan, Ted 1916- DLB-68

Allbeury, Ted 1917- DLB-87

Alldritt, Keith 1935- DLB-14

Allen, Ethan 1738-1789 ....DLB-31

Allen, George 1808-1876 ....DLB-59

Allen, Grant 1848-1899 ....DLB-70, 92

Allen, Henry W. 1912- Y-85

Allen, Hervey 1889-1949 ....DLB-9, 45

Allen, James 1739-1808.........................DLB-31

Allen, James Lane 1849-1925 ....DLB-71

Allen, Jay Presson 1922- DLB-26

Allen, John, and Company DLB-49

Allen, Samuel W. 1917- DLB-41

Allen, Woody 1935- DLB-44

Allingham, Margery 1904-1966 ....DLB-77

Allingham, William 1824-1889 ....DLB-35

Allison, W. L. [publishing house] DLB-49

Allott, Kenneth 1912-1973....................DLB-20

Allston, Washington 1779-1843 ....DLB-1

Alsop, George 1636-post 1673...............DLB-24

Alsop, Richard 1761-1815......................DLB-37

Altemus, Henry, and Company...............DLB-49

Altenberg, Peter 1885-1919 ....DLB-81

Alurista 1947- DLB-82

Alvarez, A. 1929- DLB-14, 40

Ambler, Eric 1909- DLB-77

*America: or, a Poem on the Settlement of the
    British Colonies* (1780?), by Timothy
    Dwight..DLB-37

American Conservatory Theatre DLB-7

American Fiction and the 1930s DLB-9

American Humor: A Historical Survey
    East and Northeast
    South and Southwest
    Midwest
    West..DLB-11

American News Company.....................DLB-49

The American Poets' Corner: The First
    Three Years (1983-1986)..................Y-86

American Publishing Company DLB-49

American Stationers' Company.............DLB-49

American Sunday-School Union DLB-49

American Temperance Union................DLB-49

American Tract Society DLB-49

The American Writers Congress
    (9-12 October 1981) Y-81

The American Writers Congress: A Report
    on Continuing Business....................Y-81

Ames, Fisher 1758-1808.......................DLB-37

Ames, Mary Clemmer 1831-1884 ....DLB-23

Amini, Johari M. 1935- DLB-41

Amis, Kingsley 1922- DLB-15, 27

Amis, Martin 1949- DLB-14

Ammons, A. R. 1926- DLB-5

Amory, Thomas 1691?-1788..................DLB-39

Anaya, Rudolfo A. 1937- DLB-82

Andersch, Alfred 1914-1980..................DLB-69

Anderson, Margaret 1886-1973.............DLB-4, 91

Anderson, Maxwell 1888-1959 ....DLB-7

Anderson, Patrick 1915-1979................DLB-68

Anderson, Paul Y. 1893-1938...............DLB-29

Anderson, Poul 1926- DLB-8

Anderson, Robert 1917- DLB-7

Anderson, Sherwood 1876-1941......DLB-4, 9, 86; DS-1

Andreas-Salomé, Lou 1861-1937...........DLB-66

Andres, Stefan 1906-1970......................DLB-69

Andrews, Charles M. 1863-1943............DLB-17

Andrews, Miles Peter ?-1814.................DLB-89

Andrieux, Louis (see Aragon, Louis)

Andrian, Leopold von 1875-1951 ....DLB-81

Andrus, Silas, and Son DLB-49

Angell, James Burrill 1829-1916 ....DLB-64

Angelou, Maya 1928- DLB-38

The "Angry Young Men"......................DLB-15

Anhalt, Edward 1914- DLB-26

Anners, Henry F. [publishing house].....DLB-49

Anthony, Piers 1934- DLB-8

Anthony Burgess's *99 Novels:* An Opinion Poll Y-84

Antin, Mary 1881-1949 ....Y-84

Antschel, Paul (see Celan, Paul)

Apodaca, Rudy S. 1939- DLB-82

Appleton, D., and Company DLB-49

Appleton-Century-Crofts DLB-46

Apple-wood Books DLB-46

Aquin, Hubert 1929-1977.............................DLB-53

Aragon, Louis 1897-1982.............................DLB-72

Arbor House Publishing Company DLB-46

Arcadia House DLB-46

Arce, Julio G. (see Ulica, Jorge)

Archer, William 1856-1924...........................DLB-10

Arden, John 1930- DLB-13

Arden of Faversham DLB-62

The Arena Publishing Company DLB-49

Arena Stage..DLB-7

Arensberg, Ann 1937- Y-82

Arias, Ron 1941- DLB-82

Arland, Marcel 1899-1986 ....DLB-72

Arlen, Michael 1895-1956............................DLB-36, 77

Armed Services Editions DLB-46

Arndt, Ernst Moritz 1769-1860 ....DLB-90

Arnim, Achim von 1781-1831 ....DLB-90

Arnim, Bettina von 1785-1859 ....DLB-90

Arno Press...DLB-46

Arnold, Edwin 1832-1904 ....DLB-35

Arnold, Matthew 1822-1888.........................DLB-32, 57

Arnold, Thomas 1795-1842...........................DLB-55

Arnow, Harriette Simpson 1908-1986.................DLB-6

Arp, Bill (see Smith, Charles Henry)

Arthur, Timothy Shay 1809-1885 ....DLB-3, 42, 79

Artmann, H. C. 1921- DLB-85

As I See It, by Carolyn Cassady.......................DLB-16

Asch, Nathan 1902-1964.............................DLB-4, 28

Ash, John 1948- DLB-40

Ashbery, John 1927- DLB-5; Y-81

Asher, Sandy 1942- Y-83

Ashton, Winifred (see Dane, Clemence)

Asimov, Isaac 1920- DLB-8

Asselin, Olivar 1874-1937 ....DLB-92

Atheneum Publishers DLB-46

Atherton, Gertrude 1857-1948.......................DLB-9, 78

Atkins, Josiah circa 1755-1781.......................DLB-31

Atkins, Russell 1926- DLB-41

The Atlantic Monthly Press DLB-46

Attaway, William 1911-1986 ....DLB-76

Atwood, Margaret 1939- DLB-53

Aubert, Alvin 1930- DLB-41

Aubin, Penelope 1685-circa 1731 ....DLB-39

Aubrey-Fletcher, Henry Lancelot (see Wade, Henry)

Auchincloss, Louis 1917- DLB-2; Y-80

Auden, W. H. 1907-1973.............................DLB-10, 20

Audio Art in America: A Personal
    Memoir..Y-85

Auernheimer, Raoul 1876-1948 ....DLB-81

Austin, Alfred 1835-1913.............................DLB-35

Austin, Mary 1868-1934..............................DLB-9, 78

Austin, William 1778-1841...........................DLB-74

The Author's Apology for His Book
    (1684), by John Bunyan DLB-39

An Author's Response, by Ronald Sukenick Y-82

Authors and Newspapers Association DLB-46

Authors' Publishing Company DLB-49

Avalon Books...DLB-46

Avendaño, Fausto 1941- DLB-82

Avison, Margaret 1918- DLB-53

Avon Books...DLB-46

Ayckbourn, Alan 1939- DLB-13

Aymé, Marcel 1902-1967 ....DLB-72

Aytoun, William Edmondstoune 1813-1865 ......DLB-32

B

Babbitt, Irving 1865-1933 ....DLB-63

Babbitt, Natalie 1932- DLB-52

Babcock, John [publishing house] DLB-49

Bache, Benjamin Franklin 1769-1798 ....DLB-43

Bachmann, Ingeborg 1926-1973 ....DLB-85

Bacon, Delia 1811-1859..............................DLB-1

Bacon, Thomas circa 1700-1768......................DLB-31

Badger, Richard G., and Company DLB-49

Bage, Robert 1728-1801 ....DLB-39

Bagehot, Walter 1826-1877 ....DLB-55

Bagley, Desmond 1923-1983...............................DLB-87

Bagnold, Enid 1889-1981 ....DLB-13

Bahr, Hermann 1863-1934 ....DLB-81

Bailey, Alfred Goldsworthy 1905- DLB-68

Bailey, Francis [publishing house] DLB-49

Bailey, H. C. 1878-1961 ....DLB-77

Bailey, Paul 1937- DLB-14

Bailey, Philip James 1816-1902.........................DLB-32

Baillargeon, Pierre 1916-1967 ....DLB-88

Baillie, Hugh 1890-1966 ....DLB-29

Baillie, Joanna 1762-1851 ....DLB-93

Bailyn, Bernard 1922- DLB-17

Bainbridge, Beryl 1933- DLB-14

Baird, Irene 1901-1981 ....DLB-68

The Baker and Taylor Company DLB-49

Baker, Houston A., Jr. 1943- DLB-67

Baker, Walter H., Company
   ("Baker's Plays")...DLB-49

Bald, Wambly 1902- DLB-4

Balderston, John 1889-1954 ....DLB-26

Baldwin, James 1924-1987 ....DLB-2, 7, 33; Y-87

Baldwin, Joseph Glover 1815-1864 ....DLB-3, 11

Ballantine Books..DLB-46

Ballard, J. G. 1930- DLB-14

Ballou, Maturin Murray 1820-1895...................DLB-79

Ballou, Robert O. [publishing house]................DLB-46

Bambara, Toni Cade 1939- DLB-38

Bancroft, A. L., and Company DLB-49

Bancroft, George 1800-1891 ....DLB-1, 30, 59

Bancroft, Hubert Howe 1832-1918...................DLB-47

Bangs, John Kendrick 1862-1922.................DLB-11, 79

Banks, John circa 1653-1706 ....DLB-80

Bantam Books..DLB-46

Banville, John 1945- DLB-14

Baraka, Amiri 1934- DLB-5, 7, 16, 38

Barbeau, Marius 1883-1969..............................DLB-92

Barber, John Warner 1798-1885 ....DLB-30

Barbour, Ralph Henry 1870-1944.....................DLB-22

Barbusse, Henri 1873-1935...............................DLB-65

Barclay, E. E., and Company DLB-49

Bardeen, C. W. [publishing house]....................DLB-49

Baring, Maurice 1874-1945...............................DLB-34

Barker, A. L. 1918- DLB-14

Barker, George 1913- DLB-20

Barker, Harley Granville 1877-1946 ....DLB-10

Barker, Howard 1946- DLB-13

Barker, James Nelson 1784-1858.......................DLB-37

Barker, Jane 1652-1727? DLB-39

Barks, Coleman 1937- DLB-5

Barlach, Ernst 1870-1938..................................DLB-56

Barlow, Joel 1754-1812 ....DLB-37

Barnard, John 1681-1770 ....DLB-24

Barnes, A. S., and Company...............................DLB-49

Barnes, Djuna 1892-1982 ....DLB-4, 9, 45

Barnes, Margaret Ayer 1886-1967 ....DLB-9

Barnes, Peter 1931- DLB-13

Barnes, William 1801-1886...............................DLB-32

Barnes and Noble Books....................................DLB-46

Barney, Natalie 1876-1972................................DLB-4

Baron, Richard W., Publishing Company DLB-46

Barr, Robert 1850-1912 ....DLB-70, 92

Barrax, Gerald William 1933- DLB-41

Barrie, James M. 1860-1937..............................DLB-10

Barrio, Raymond 1921- DLB-82

Barry, Philip 1896-1949 ....DLB-7

Barry, Robertine (see Françoise)

Barse and Hopkins...DLB-46

Barstow, Stan 1928- DLB-14

Barth, John 1930- DLB-2

Barthelme, Donald 1931-1989...................DLB-2; Y-80

Barthelme, Frederick 1943- Y-85

Bartlett, John 1820-1905...................................DLB-1

Bartol, Cyrus Augustus 1813-1900.....................DLB-1

Bartram, John 1699-1777 ....DLB-31

Bartram, William 1739-1823.............................DLB-37

Basic Books DLB-46

Bass, T. J. 1932- Y-81

Bassett, John Spencer 1867-1928 ....DLB-17

Bassler, Thomas Joseph (see Bass, T. J.)

Bate, Walter Jackson 1918- DLB-67

Bates, Katharine Lee 1859-1929........................DLB-71

Baum, L. Frank 1856-1919..............................DLB-22

Baum, Vicki 1888-1960...................................DLB-85

Baumbach, Jonathan 1933- Y-80

Bawden, Nina 1925- DLB-14

Bax, Clifford 1886-1962 ....DLB-10

Bayer, Eleanor (see Perry, Eleanor)

Bayer, Konrad 1932-1964 ....DLB-85

Bazin, Hervé 1911- DLB-83

Beach, Sylvia 1887-1962 ....DLB-4

Beacon Press DLB-49

Beadle and Adams...DLB-49

Beagle, Peter S. 1939- Y-80

Beal, M. F. 1937- Y-81

Beale, Howard K. 1899-1959............................DLB-17

Beard, Charles A. 1874-1948............................DLB-17

A Beat Chronology: The First Twenty-five
        Years, 1944-1969 ....DLB-16

Beattie, Ann 1947- Y-82

Beauchemin, Nérée 1850-1931..........................DLB-92

Beauchemin, Yves 1941- DLB-60

Beaulieu, Victor-Lévy 1945- DLB-53

Beaumont, Francis circa 1584-1616
        and Fletcher, John 1579-1625 ....DLB-58

Beauvoir, Simone de 1908-1986..............Y-86, DLB-72

Becher, Ulrich 1910- DLB-69

Becker, Carl 1873-1945...................................DLB-17

Becker, Jurek 1937- DLB-75

Becker, Jürgen 1932- DLB-75

Beckett, Samuel 1906-1989.........................DLB-13, 15

Beckford, William 1760-1844 ....DLB-39

Beckham, Barry 1944- DLB-33

Beecher, Catharine Esther 1800-1878.................DLB-1

Beecher, Henry Ward 1813-1887..................DLB-3, 43

Beer, George L. 1872-1920..............................DLB-47

Beer, Patricia 1919- DLB-40

Beerbohm, Max 1872-1956..............................DLB-34

Beer-Hofmann, Richard 1866-1945 ....DLB-81

Beers, Henry A. 1847-1926 ....DLB-71

Behan, Brendan 1923-1964..............................DLB-13

Behn, Aphra 1640?-1689...........................DLB-39, 80

Behn, Harry 1898-1973 ....DLB-61

Behrman, S. N. 1893-1973 ....DLB-7, 44

Belaney, Archibald Stansfeld (see Grey Owl)

Belasco, David 1853-1931 ....DLB-7

Belford, Clarke and Company..........................DLB-49

Belitt, Ben 1911- DLB-5

Belknap, Jeremy 1744-1798........................DLB-30, 37

Bell, James Madison 1826-1902........................DLB-50

Bell, Marvin 1937- DLB-5

Bell, Robert [publishing house] DLB-49

Bellamy, Edward 1850-1898.............................DLB-12

Bellamy, Joseph 1719-1790..............................DLB-31

Belloc, Hilaire 1870-1953 ....DLB-19

Bellow, Saul 1915- DLB-2, 28; Y-82; DS-3

Belmont Productions......................................DLB-46

Bemelmans, Ludwig 1898-1962........................DLB-22

Bemis, Samuel Flagg 1891-1973........................DLB-17

Benchley, Robert 1889-1945.............................DLB-11

Benedictus, David 1938- DLB-14

Benedikt, Michael 1935- DLB-5

Benét, Stephen Vincent 1898-1943...............DLB-4, 48

Benét, William Rose 1886-1950.........................DLB-45

Benford, Gregory 1941- Y-82

Benjamin, Park 1809-1864 ....DLB-3, 59, 73

Benn, Gottfried 1886-1956..............................DLB-56

Bennett, Arnold 1867-1931 ....DLB-10, 34

Bennett, Charles 1899- DLB-44

Bennett, Gwendolyn 1902- DLB-51

Bennett, Hal 1930- DLB-33

Bennett, James Gordon 1795-1872 ....DLB-43

Bennett, James Gordon, Jr. 1841-1918 ....DLB-23

Bennett, John 1865-1956 ....DLB-42

Benoit, Jacques 1941- DLB-60

Benson, Stella 1892-1933 ....DLB-36

Bentley, E. C. 1875-1956..................................DLB-70

Benton, Robert 1932- and Newman,
        David 1937- DLB-44

Benziger Brothers...DLB-49

Beresford, Anne 1929- DLB-40

Beresford-Howe, Constance 1922- DLB-88

Berford, R. G., Company DLB-49

Berg, Stephen 1934- DLB-5

Bergengruen, Werner 1892-1964 ....DLB-56

Berger, John 1926- DLB-14

Berger, Meyer 1898-1959 ....DLB-29

Berger, Thomas 1924- DLB-2; Y-80

Berkeley, Anthony 1893-1971 ....DLB-77

Berkeley, George 1685-1753 ....DLB-31

The Berkley Publishing Corporation DLB-46

Bernal, Vicente J. 1888-1915 ....DLB-82

Bernanos, Georges 1888-1948 ....DLB-72

Bernard, Harry 1898-1979 ....DLB-92

Bernard, John 1756-1828 ....DLB-37

Bernhard, Thomas 1931-1989 ....DLB-85

Berrigan, Daniel 1921- DLB-5

Berrigan, Ted 1934-1983 ....DLB-5

Berry, Wendell 1934- DLB-5, 6

Berryman, John 1914-1972 ....DLB-48

Bersianik, Louky 1930- DLB-60

Berton, Pierre 1920- DLB-68

Bessette, Gerard 1920- DLB-53

Bessie, Alvah 1904-1985 ....DLB-26

Bester, Alfred 1913- DLB-8

The Bestseller Lists: An Assessment Y-84

Betjeman, John 1906-1984 ....DLB-20; Y-84

Betts, Doris 1932- Y-82

Beveridge, Albert J. 1862-1927 ....DLB-17

Beverley, Robert circa 1673-1722 ....DLB-24, 30

Bibaud, Adèle 1854-1941 ....DLB-92

Bichsel, Peter 1935- DLB-75

Bickerstaff, Isaac John 1733-circa 1808 ....DLB-89

Biddle, Drexel [publishing house] DLB-49

Bidwell, Walter Hilliard 1798-1881 ....DLB-79

Bienek, Horst 1930- DLB-75

Bierbaum, Otto Julius 1865-1910 ....DLB-66

Bierce, Ambrose 1842-1914? DLB-11, 12, 23, 71, 74

Bigelow, William F. 1879-1966 ....DLB-91

Biggle, Lloyd, Jr. 1923- DLB-8

Biglow, Hosea (see Lowell, James Russell)

Billings, Josh (see Shaw, Henry Wheeler)

Binding, Rudolf G. 1867-1938 ....DLB-66

Bingham, Caleb 1757-1817 ....DLB-42

Binyon, Laurence 1869-1943 ....DLB-19

Biographical Documents I Y-84

Biographical Documents II Y-85

Bioren, John [publishing house] DLB-49

Bird, William 1888-1963 ....DLB-4

Birney, Earle 1904- DLB-88

Bishop, Elizabeth 1911-1979 ....DLB-5

Bishop, John Peale 1892-1944 ....DLB-4, 9, 45

Bissett, Bill 1939- DLB-53

Black, David (D. M.) 1941- DLB-40

Black, Walter J. [publishing house] DLB-46

Black, Winifred 1863-1936 ....DLB-25

The Black Arts Movement, by Larry Neal DLB-38

Black Theaters and Theater Organizations in
    America, 1961-1982: A Research List DLB-38

Black Theatre: A Forum [excerpts] DLB-38

Blackamore, Arthur 1679-? DLB-24, 39

Blackburn, Alexander L. 1929- Y-85

Blackburn, Paul 1926-1971 ....DLB-16; Y-81

Blackburn, Thomas 1916-1977 ....DLB-27

Blackmore, R. D. 1825-1900 ....DLB-18

Blackmur, R. P. 1904-1965 ....DLB-63

Blackwood, Caroline 1931- DLB-14

Blair, Eric Arthur (see Orwell, George)

Blair, Francis Preston 1791-1876 ....DLB-43

Blair, James circa 1655-1743 ....DLB-24

Blair, John Durburrow 1759-1823 ....DLB-37

Blais, Marie-Claire 1939- DLB-53

Blaise, Clark 1940- DLB-53

Blake, Nicholas 1904-1972 ....DLB-77
    (see also Day Lewis, C.)

Blake, William 1757-1827 ....DLB-93

The Blakiston Company DLB-49

Blanchot, Maurice 1907- DLB-72

Blanckenburg, Christian Friedrich von
    1744-1796 ....DLB-94

Bledsoe, Albert Taylor 1809-1877 ....DLB-3, 79

Blelock and Company DLB-49

Blish, James 1921-1975 ....DLB-8

Bliss, E., and E. White [publishing house] DLB-49

Bloch, Robert 1917- DLB-44

Block, Rudolph (see Lessing, Bruno)

Blondal, Patricia 1926-1959 ....DLB-88

Bloom, Harold 1930- DLB-67

Bloomer, Amelia 1818-1894 ....DLB-79

Bloomfield, Robert 1766-1823 ....DLB-93

Blume, Judy 1938- DLB-52

Blunck, Hans Friedrich 1888-1961 ....DLB-66

Blunden, Edmund 1896-1974 ....DLB-20

Blunt, Wilfrid Scawen 1840-1922 ....DLB-19

Bly, Nellie (see Cochrane, Elizabeth)

Bly, Robert 1926- DLB-5

Boaden, James 1762-1839 ....DLB-89

The Bobbs-Merrill Company DLB-46

Bobrowski, Johannes 1917-1965 ....DLB-75

Bodenheim, Maxwell 1892-1954 ......DLB-9, 45

Bodkin, M. McDonnell 1850-1933 ....DLB-70

Bodmershof, Imma von 1895-1982 ....DLB-85

Bodsworth, Fred 1918- DLB-68

Boehm, Sydney 1908- DLB-44

Boer, Charles 1939- DLB-5

Bogan, Louise 1897-1970 ....DLB-45

Bogarde, Dirk 1921- DLB-14

Boie, Heinrich Christian 1744-1806 ......DLB-94

Bok, Edward W. 1863-1930 ....DLB-91

Boland, Eavan 1944- DLB-40

Böll, Heinrich 1917-1985 ....Y-85, DLB-69

Bolling, Robert 1738-1775 ....DLB-31

Bolt, Carol 1941- DLB-60

Bolt, Robert 1924- DLB-13

Bolton, Herbert E. 1870-1953 ....DLB-17

Bonaventura..DLB-89

Bond, Edward 1934- DLB-13

Boni, Albert and Charles [publishing house].....DLB-46

Boni and Liveright DLB-46

Robert Bonner's Sons DLB-49

Bontemps, Arna 1902-1973 ....DLB-48, 51

The Book League of America DLB-46

Book Reviewing in America: I Y-87

Book Reviewing in America: II Y-88

Book Supply Company DLB-49

The Booker Prize
    Address by Anthony Thwaite, Chairman
      of the Booker Prize Judges
    Comments from Former Booker Prize
      Winners Y-86

Boorstin, Daniel J. 1914- DLB-17

Booth, Mary L. 1831-1889.....................DLB-79

Booth, Philip 1925- Y-82

Booth, Wayne C. 1921- DLB-67

Borchardt, Rudolf 1877-1945 ....DLB-66

Borchert, Wolfgang 1921-1947 ....DLB-69

Borges, Jorge Luis 1899-1986 ....Y-86

Börne, Ludwig 1786-1837......................DLB-90

Borrow, George 1803-1881................DLB-21, 55

Bosco, Henri 1888-1976.........................DLB-72

Bosco, Monique 1927- DLB-53

Botta, Anne C. Lynch 1815-1891 ....DLB-3

Bottomley, Gordon 1874-1948...............DLB-10

Bottoms, David 1949- Y-83

Bottrall, Ronald 1906- DLB-20

Boucher, Anthony 1911-1968.................DLB-8

Boucher, Jonathan 1738-1804 ....DLB-31

Boudreau, Daniel (see Coste, Donat)

Bourjaily, Vance Nye 1922- DLB-2

Bourne, Edward Gaylord 1860-1908......DLB-47

Bourne, Randolph 1886-1918.................DLB-63

Bousquet, Joë 1897-1950 ....DLB-72

Bova, Ben 1932- Y-81

Bove, Emmanuel 1898-1945 ....DLB-72

Bovard, Oliver K. 1872-1945.................DLB-25

Bowen, Elizabeth 1899-1973..................DLB-15

Bowen, Francis 1811-1890......................DLB-1, 59

Bowen, John 1924- DLB-13

Bowen-Merrill Company.........................DLB-49

Bowering, George 1935- DLB-53

Bowers, Claude G. 1878-1958.................DLB-17

Bowers, Edgar 1924- DLB-5

Bowles, Paul 1910- DLB-5, 6

Bowles, Samuel III 1826-1878................DLB-43

Bowles, William Lisles 1762-1850...........DLB-93

Bowman, Louise Morey 1882-1944 ....DLB-68

Boyd, James 1888-1944...........................DLB-9

Boyd, John 1919- DLB-8

Boyd, Thomas 1898-1935 ....DLB-9

Boyesen, Hjalmar Hjorth 1848-1895 ....DLB-12, 71

Boyle, Kay 1902- DLB-4, 9, 48, 86

Boyle, Roger, Earl of Orrery 1621-1679 ....DLB-80

Boyle, T. Coraghessan 1948- Y-86

Brackenbury, Alison 1953- DLB-40

Brackenridge, Hugh Henry 1748-1816........DLB-11, 37

Brackett, Charles 1892-1969 ....DLB-26

Brackett, Leigh 1915-1978 ....DLB-8, 26

Bradburn, John [publishing house] DLB-49

Bradbury, Malcolm 1932- DLB-14

Bradbury, Ray 1920- DLB-2, 8

Braddon, Mary Elizabeth 1835-1915..........DLB-18, 70

Bradford, Andrew 1686-1742....................DLB-43, 73

Bradford, Gamaliel 1863-1932....................DLB-17

Bradford, John 1749-1830 ....DLB-43

Bradford, Roark 1896-1948 ....DLB-86

Bradford, William 1590-1657 ....DLB-24, 30

Bradford, William III 1719-1791 ....DLB-43, 73

Bradlaugh, Charles 1833-1891....................DLB-57

Bradley, David 1950- DLB-33

Bradley, Ira, and Company....................DLB-49

Bradley, J. W., and Company DLB-49

Bradley, Marion Zimmer 1930- DLB-8

Bradley, William Aspenwall 1878-1939................DLB-4

Bradstreet, Anne 1612 or 1613-1672 ....DLB-24

Brady, Frederic A. [publishing house] DLB-49

Bragg, Melvyn 1939- DLB-14

Brainard, Charles H. [publishing house]...........DLB-49

Braine, John 1922-1986 ....DLB-15; Y-86

Braithwaite, William Stanley 1878-1962 ....DLB-50, 54

Bräker, Ulrich 1735-1798....................DLB-94

Bramah, Ernest 1868-1942....................DLB-70

Branagan, Thomas 1774-1843....................DLB-37

Branch, William Blackwell 1927- DLB-76

Branden Press....................DLB-46

Brault, Jacques 1933- DLB-53

Braun, Volker 1939- DLB-75

Brautigan, Richard 1935-1984 ....DLB-2, 5; Y-80, 84

Braxton, Joanne M. 1950- DLB-41

Bray, Thomas 1656-1730 ....DLB-24

Braziller, George [publishing house] DLB-46

The Bread Loaf Writers' Conference 1983...........Y-84

The Break-Up of the Novel (1922), by John Middleton Murry....................DLB-36

Breasted, James Henry 1865-1935....................DLB-47

Brecht, Bertolt 1898-1956 ....DLB-56

Bredel, Willi 1901-1964....................DLB-56

Bremser, Bonnie 1939- DLB-16

Bremser, Ray 1934- DLB-16

Brentano, Bernard von 1901-1964....................DLB-56

Brentano, Clemens 1778-1842....................DLB-90

Brentano's DLB-49

Brenton, Howard 1942- DLB-13

Breton, André 1896-1966 ....DLB-65

Brewer, Warren and Putnam DLB-46

Brewster, Elizabeth 1922- DLB-60

Bridgers, Sue Ellen 1942- DLB-52

Bridges, Robert 1844-1930....................DLB-19

Bridie, James 1888-1951....................DLB-10

Briggs, Charles Frederick 1804-1877 ....DLB-3

Brighouse, Harold 1882-1958....................DLB-10

Brimmer, B. J., Company DLB-46

Brinnin, John Malcolm 1916- DLB-48

Brisbane, Albert 1809-1890....................DLB-3

Brisbane, Arthur 1864-1936 ....DLB-25

Broadway Publishing Company DLB-46

Broch, Hermann 1886-1951 ....DLB-85

Brochu, André 1942- DLB-53

Brock, Edwin 1927- DLB-40

Brod, Max 1884-1968....................DLB-81

Brodhead, John R. 1814-1873 ....DLB-30

Brome, Richard circa 1590-1652 ....DLB-58

Bromfield, Louis 1896-1956 ....DLB-4, 9, 86

Broner, E. M. 1930- DLB-28

Brontë, Anne 1820-1849....................DLB-21

Brontë, Charlotte 1816-1855....................DLB-21

Brontë, Emily 1818-1848 ....DLB-21, 32

Brooke, Frances 1724-1789....................DLB-39

Brooke, Henry 1703?-1783 ....DLB-39

Brooke, Rupert 1887-1915.....................DLB-19

Brooker, Bertram 1888-1955 ....DLB-88

Brooke-Rose, Christine 1926- DLB-14

Brookner, Anita 1928- Y-87

Brooks, Charles Timothy 1813-1883 ....DLB-1

Brooks, Cleanth 1906- DLB-63

Brooks, Gwendolyn 1917- DLB-5, 76

Brooks, Jeremy 1926- DLB-14

Brooks, Mel 1926- DLB-26

Brooks, Noah 1830-1903....................DLB-42

Brooks, Richard 1912- DLB-44

Brooks, Van Wyck 1886-1963 ....DLB-45, 63

Brophy, Brigid 1929- DLB-14

Brossard, Chandler 1922- DLB-16

Brossard, Nicole 1943- DLB-53

Brother Antoninus (see Everson, William)

Brougham, John 1810-1880...................DLB-11

Broughton, James 1913- DLB-5

Broughton, Rhoda 1840-1920...................DLB-18

Broun, Heywood 1888-1939 ....DLB-29

Brown, Alice 1856-1948 ....DLB-78

Brown, Bob 1886-1959...................DLB-4, 45

Brown, Cecil 1943- DLB-33

Brown, Charles Brockden 1771-1810.....DLB-37, 59, 73

Brown, Christy 1932-1981..................DLB-14

Brown, Dee 1908- Y-80

Browne, Francis Fisher 1843-1913 ....DLB-79

Brown, Frank London 1927-1962 ....DLB-76

Brown, Fredric 1906-1972 ....DLB-8

Brown, George Mackay 1921- DLB-14, 27

Brown, Harry 1917-1986 ....DLB-26

Brown, Marcia 1918- DLB-61

Brown, Margaret Wise 1910-1952 ....DLB-22

Brown, Morna Doris (see Ferrars, Elizabeth)

Brown, Oliver Madox 1855-1874.........DLB-21

Brown, Sterling 1901-1989 ....DLB-48, 51, 63

Brown, T. E. 1830-1897....................DLB-35

Brown, William Hill 1765-1793 ....DLB-37

Brown, William Wells 1814-1884..........DLB-3, 50

Browne, Charles Farrar 1834-1867.........DLB-11

Browne, Michael Dennis 1940- DLB-40

Browne, Wynyard 1911-1964...................DLB-13

Brownell, W. C. 1851-1928 ....DLB-71

Browning, Elizabeth Barrett 1806-1861 ....DLB-32

Browning, Robert 1812-1889...................DLB-32

Brownjohn, Allan 1931- DLB-40

Brownson, Orestes Augustus 1803-1876.........DLB-1, 59, 73

Bruce, Charles 1906-1971 ....DLB-68

Bruce, Leo 1903-1979 ....DLB-77

Bruce, Philip Alexander 1856-1933...........DLB-47

Bruce Humphries [publishing house] DLB-46

Bruce-Novoa, Juan 1944- DLB-82

Bruckman, Clyde 1894-1955.................DLB-26

Brundage, John Herbert (see Herbert, John)

Bryant, William Cullen 1794-1878..........DLB-3, 43, 59

Buchan, John 1875-1940.................DLB-34, 70

Buchanan, Robert 1841-1901 ....DLB-18, 35

Buchman, Sidney 1902-1975 ....DLB-26

Buck, Pearl S. 1892-1973 ....DLB-9

Buckingham, Joseph Tinker 1779-1861 and Buckingham, Edwin 1810-1833...................DLB-73

Buckler, Ernest 1908-1984.................DLB-68

Buckley, William F., Jr. 1925- Y-80

Buckminster, Joseph Stevens 1784-1812............DLB-37

Buckner, Robert 1906- DLB-26

Budd, Thomas ?-1698......................DLB-24

Budrys, A. J. 1931- DLB-8

Buechner, Frederick 1926- Y-80

Buell, John 1927- DLB-53

Buffum, Job [publishing house]........DLB-49

Bugnet, Georges 1879-1981...............DLB-92

Bukowski, Charles 1920- DLB-5

Bullins, Ed 1935- DLB-7, 38

Bulwer-Lytton, Edward (also Edward Bulwer) 1803-1873 ....DLB-21

Bumpus, Jerry 1937- Y-81

Bunce and Brother DLB-49

Bunner, H. C. 1855-1896 ....DLB-78, 79

Bunting, Basil 1900-1985 ....DLB-20

Bunyan, John 1628-1688....................DLB-39

Burch, Robert 1925- DLB-52

Burciaga, José Antonio 1940- DLB-82

Bürger, Gottfried August 1747-1794 ....DLB-94

Burgess, Anthony 1917- DLB-14

Burgess, Gelett 1866-1951 ....DLB-11

Burgess, John W. 1844-1931................DLB-47

Burgess, Thornton W. 1874-1965 ....DLB-22

Burgess, Stringer and Company.....................DLB-49

Burk, John Daly circa 1772-1808....................DLB-37

Burke, Kenneth 1897- DLB-45, 63

Burlingame, Edward Livermore 1848-1922.......DLB-79

Burnett, Frances Hodgson 1849-1924...............DLB-42

Burnett, W. R. 1899-1982 ....DLB-9

Burney, Fanny 1752-1840 ....DLB-39

Burns, Alan 1929- DLB-14

Burns, John Horne 1916-1953....................Y-85

Burnshaw, Stanley 1906- DLB-48

Burr, C. Chauncey 1815?-1883...........DLB-79

Burroughs, Edgar Rice 1875-1950 ....DLB-8

Burroughs, John 1837-1921...............DLB-64

Burroughs, Margaret T. G. 1917- DLB-41

Burroughs, William S., Jr. 1947-1981 ....DLB-16

Burroughs, William Seward 1914-
...................................DLB-2, 8, 16; Y-81

Burroway, Janet 1936- DLB-6

Burt, A. L., and Company DLB-49

Burt, Maxwell S. 1882-1954..............DLB-86

Burton, Miles (see Rhode, John)

Burton, Richard F. 1821-1890 ....DLB-55

Burton, Virginia Lee 1909-1968.........DLB-22

Burton, William Evans 1804-1860.....................DLB-73

Busch, Frederick 1941- DLB-6

Busch, Niven 1903- DLB-44

Bussières, Arthur de 1877-1913 ....DLB-92

Butler, E. H., and Company.......................DLB-49

Butler, Juan 1942-1981 ....DLB-53

Butler, Octavia E. 1947- DLB-33

Butler, Samuel 1835-1902..............DLB-18, 57

Butor, Michel 1926- DLB-83

Butterworth, Hezekiah 1839-1905.....................DLB-42

B. V. (see Thomson, James)

Byars, Betsy 1928- DLB-52

Byatt, A. S. 1936- DLB-14

Byles, Mather 1707-1788................DLB-24

Bynner, Witter 1881-1968................DLB-54

Byrd, William II 1674-1744 ....DLB-24

Byrne, John Keyes (see Leonard, Hugh)

C

Cabell, James Branch 1879-1958 ....DLB-9, 78

Cable, George Washington 1844-1925 ....DLB-12, 74

Cahan, Abraham 1860-1951.....................DLB-9, 25, 28

Cain, George 1943- DLB-33

Caldwell, Ben 1937- DLB-38

Caldwell, Erskine 1903-1987 ....DLB-9, 86

Caldwell, H. M., Company................DLB-49

Calhoun, John C. 1782-1850 ....DLB-3

Calisher, Hortense 1911- DLB-2

Callaghan, Morley 1903- DLB-68

Callaloo..................................Y-87

A Call to Letters and an Invitation
    to the Electric Chair,
    by Siegfried Mandel DLB-75

Calmer, Edgar 1907- DLB-4

Calverley, C. S. 1831-1884 ....DLB-35

Calvert, George Henry 1803-1889 ....DLB-1, 64

Cambridge Press................................DLB-49

Cameron, Eleanor 1912- DLB-52

Camm, John 1718-1778 ....DLB-31

Campbell, Gabrielle Margaret Vere
    (see Shearing, Joseph)

Campbell, James Edwin 1867-1896 ....DLB-50

Campbell, John 1653-1728 ....DLB-43

Campbell, John W., Jr. 1910-1971 ....DLB-8

Campbell, Thomas 1777-1844 ....DLB-93

Campbell, William Wilfred
    1858-1918 ....DLB-92

Campbell, Roy 1901-1957 ....DLB-20

Campion, Thomas 1567-1620............DLB-58

Camus, Albert 1913-1960 ....DLB-72

Canby, Henry Seidel 1878-1961 ....DLB-91

Candelaria, Cordelia 1943- DLB-82

Candelaria, Nash 1928- DLB-82

Candour in English Fiction (1890),
    by Thomas Hardy DLB-18

Canetti, Elias 1905- DLB-85

Cannan, Gilbert 1884-1955 ....DLB-10

Cannell, Kathleen 1891-1974 ....DLB-4

Cannell, Skipwith 1887-1957 ....DLB-45

Cantwell, Robert 1908-1978 ....DLB-9

Cape, Jonathan, and Harrison Smith
    [publishing house] DLB-46

Capen, Joseph 1658-1725 ....DLB-24

Capote, Truman 1924-1984 ....DLB-2; Y-80, 84

Cardinal, Marie 1929- DLB-83

Carey, Henry circa 1687-1689-1743 ....DLB-84

Carey, M., and Company DLB-49

Carey, Mathew 1760-1839 ....DLB-37, 73

Carey and Hart DLB-49

Carlell, Lodowick 1602-1675 ....DLB-58

Carleton, G. W. [publishing house] DLB-49

Carman, Bliss 1861-1929 ....DLB-92

Carossa, Hans 1878-1956 ....DLB-66

Carr, Emily 1871-1945 ....DLB-68

Carrier, Roch 1937- DLB-53

Carlyle, Jane Welsh 1801-1866 ....DLB-55

Carlyle, Thomas 1795-1881 ....DLB-55

Carpenter, Stephen Cullen ?-1820?...................DLB-73

Carroll, Gladys Hasty 1904- DLB-9

Carroll, John 1735-1815...................................DLB-37

Carroll, Lewis 1832-1898 ....DLB-18

Carroll, Paul 1927- DLB-16

Carroll, Paul Vincent 1900-1968 ....DLB-10

Carroll and Graf Publishers DLB-46

Carruth, Hayden 1921- DLB-5

Carryl, Charles E. 1841-1920..............................DLB-42

Carswell, Catherine 1879-1946 ....DLB-36

Carter, Angela 1940- DLB-14

Carter, Henry (see Leslie, Frank)

Carter, Landon 1710-1778 ....DLB-31

Carter, Lin 1930- Y-81

Carter, Robert, and Brothers............................DLB-49

Carter and Hendee..DLB-49

Caruthers, William Alexander 1802-1846...........DLB-3

Carver, Jonathan 1710-1780 ....DLB-31

Carver, Raymond 1938-1988 ....Y-84, 88

Cary, Joyce 1888-1957....................................DLB-15

Casey, Juanita 1925- DLB-14

Casey, Michael 1947- DLB-5

Cassady, Carolyn 1923- DLB-16

Cassady, Neal 1926-1968..................................DLB-16

Cassell Publishing Company DLB-49

Cassill, R. V. 1919- DLB-6

Castlemon, Harry (see Fosdick, Charles Austin)

Caswall, Edward 1814-1878 ....DLB-32

Cather, Willa 1873-1947..............DLB-9, 54, 78; DS-1

Catherwood, Mary Hartwell 1847-1902 ....DLB-78

Catton, Bruce 1899-1978..................................DLB-17

Causley, Charles 1917- DLB-27

Caute, David 1936- DLB-14

Cawein, Madison 1865-1914 ....DLB-54

The Caxton Printers, Limited............................DLB-46

Cayrol, Jean 1911- DLB-83

Celan, Paul 1920-1970....................................DLB-69

Céline, Louis-Ferdinand 1894-1961 ....DLB-72

Center for the Book Research Y-84

Centlivre, Susanna 1669?-1723..........................DLB-84

The Century Company DLB-49

Cervantes, Lorna Dee 1954- DLB-82

Chacón, Eusebio 1869-1948 ....DLB-82

Chacón, Felipe Maximiliano
    1873-?..DLB-82

Challans, Eileen Mary (see Renault, Mary)

Chalmers, George 1742-1825.............................DLB-30

Chamberlain, Samuel S. 1851-1916...................DLB-25

Chamberland, Paul 1939- DLB-60

Chamberlin, William Henry 1897-1969 ....DLB-29

Chambers, Charles Haddon 1860-1921 ....DLB-10

Chamisso, Albert von 1781-1838........................DLB-90

Chandler, Harry 1864-1944...............................DLB-29

Chandler, Raymond 1888-1959 ....DS-6

Channing, Edward 1856-1931 ....DLB-17

Channing, Edward Tyrrell 1790-1856 ....DLB-1, 59

Channing, William Ellery 1780-1842 ....DLB-1, 59

Channing, William Ellery II 1817-1901 ....DLB-1

Channing, William Henry 1810-1884 ....DLB-1, 59

Chaplin, Charlie 1889-1977 ....DLB-44

Chapman, George 1559 or 1560-1634 ....DLB-62

Chappell, Fred 1936- DLB-6

Charbonneau, Jean 1875-1960 ....DLB-92

Charbonneau, Robert 1911-1967 ....DLB-68

Charles, Gerda 1914- DLB-14

Charles, William [publishing house]..................DLB-49

The Charles Wood Affair:
    A Playwright Revived Y-83

Charlotte Forten: Pages from her Diary.............DLB-50

Charteris, Leslie 1907- DLB-77

Charyn, Jerome 1937- Y-83

Chase, Borden 1900-1971 ....DLB-26

Chase, Edna Woolman 1877-1957 ....DLB-91

Chase-Riboud, Barbara 1936- DLB-33

Chauncy, Charles 1705-1787 ....DLB-24

Chávez, Fray Angélico 1910- DLB-82

Chayefsky, Paddy 1923-1981 ....DLB-7, 44; Y-81

Cheever, Ezekiel 1615-1708 ....DLB-24

Cheever, George Barrell 1807-1890 ....DLB-59

Cheever, John 1912-1982 ....DLB-2; Y-80, 82

Cheever, Susan 1943- Y-82

Chelsea House DLB-46

Cheney, Ednah Dow (Littlehale) 1824-1904 ....DLB-1

Cherry, Kelly 1940 ....Y-83

Cherryh, C. J. 1942- Y-80

Chesnutt, Charles Waddell 1858-1932...DLB-12, 50, 78

Chester, George Randolph 1869-1924 ....DLB-78

Chesterton, G. K. 1874-1936...........DLB-10, 19, 34, 70

Cheyney, Edward P. 1861-1947.........................DLB-47

Chicano History...DLB-82

Chicano Language...DLB-82

Child, Francis James 1825-1896 ....DLB-1, 64

Child, Lydia Maria 1802-1880.....................DLB-1, 74

Child, Philip 1898-1978 ....DLB-68

Childers, Erskine 1870-1922 ....DLB-70

Children's Book Awards and Prizes DLB-61

Childress, Alice 1920- DLB-7, 38

Childs, George W. 1829-1894 ....DLB-23

Chilton Book Company....................................DLB-46

Chittenden, Hiram Martin 1858-1917..............DLB-47

Chivers, Thomas Holley 1809-1858 ....DLB-3

Chopin, Kate 1850-1904 ....DLB-12, 78

Chopin, Rene 1885-1953....................................DLB-92

Choquette, Adrienne 1915-1973........................DLB-68

Choquette, Robert 1905- DLB-68

The Christian Publishing Company DLB-49

Christie, Agatha 1890-1976 ....DLB-13, 77

Church, Benjamin 1734-1778............................DLB-31

Church, Francis Pharcellus 1839-1906..............DLB-79

Church, William Conant 1836-1917..................DLB-79

Churchill, Caryl 1938- DLB-13

Ciardi, John 1916-1986..............................DLB-5; Y-86

Cibber, Colley 1671-1757..................................DLB-84

City Lights Books DLB-46

Cixous, Hélène 1937- DLB-83

Clapper, Raymond 1892-1944 ....DLB-29

Clare, John 1793-1864 ....DLB-55

Clark, Alfred Alexander Gordon (see Hare, Cyril)

Clark, Ann Nolan 1896- DLB-52

Clark, C. M., Publishing Company....................DLB-46

Clark, Catherine Anthony 1892-1977 ....DLB-68

Clark, Charles Heber 1841-1915 ....DLB-11

Clark, Davis Wasgatt 1812-1871 ....DLB-79

Clark, Eleanor 1913- DLB-6

Clark, Lewis Gaylord 1808-1873 ....DLB-3, 64, 73

Clark, Walter Van Tilburg 1909-1971.................DLB-9

Clarke, Austin 1896-1974 ....DLB-10, 20

Clarke, Austin C. 1934- DLB-53

Clarke, Gillian 1937- DLB-40

Clarke, James Freeman 1810-1888...............DLB-1, 59

Clarke, Rebecca Sophia 1833-1906....................DLB-42

Clarke, Robert, and Company DLB-49

Clausen, Andy 1943- DLB-16

Claxton, Remsen and Haffelfinger....................DLB-49

Clay, Cassius Marcellus 1810-1903 ....DLB-43

Cleary, Beverly 1916- DLB-52

Cleaver, Vera 1919- and
    Cleaver, Bill 1920-1981..............................DLB-52

Cleland, John 1710-1789...................................DLB-39

Clemens, Samuel Langhorne
1835-1910...........................DLB-11, 12, 23, 64, 74

Clement, Hal 1922- DLB-8

Clemo, Jack 1916- DLB-27

Clifton, Lucille 1936- DLB-5, 41

Clode, Edward J. [publishing house].................DLB-46

Clough, Arthur Hugh 1819-1861......................DLB-32

Cloutier, Cécile 1930- DLB-60

Coates, Robert M. 1897-1973 ....DLB-4, 9

Coatsworth, Elizabeth 1893- DLB-22

Cobb, Jr., Charles E. 1943- DLB-41

Cobb, Frank I. 1869-1923 ....DLB-25

Cobb, Irvin S. 1876-1944.......................DLB-11, 25, 86

Cobbett, William 1762-1835 ....DLB-43

Cochran, Thomas C. 1902- DLB-17

Cochrane, Elizabeth 1867-1922 ....DLB-25

Cockerill, John A. 1845-1896...........................DLB-23

Cocteau, Jean 1889-1963.................................DLB-65

Coderre, Emile (see Jean Narrache)

Coffee, Lenore J. 1900?-1984 ....DLB-44

Coffin, Robert P. Tristram 1892-1955 ....DLB-45

Cogswell, Fred 1917- DLB-60

Cogswell, Mason Fitch 1761-1830 ....DLB-37

Cohen, Arthur A. 1928-1986............................DLB-28

Cohen, Leonard 1934- DLB-53

Cohen, Matt 1942- DLB-53

Colden, Cadwallader 1688-1776..................DLB-24, 30

Cole, Barry 1936- DLB-14

Colegate, Isabel 1931- DLB-14

Coleman, Emily Holmes 1899-1974 ....DLB-4

Coleridge, Mary 1861-1907..............................DLB-19

Coleridge, Samuel Taylor 1772-1834 ....DLB-93

Colette 1873-1954...DLB-65

Colette, Sidonie Gabrielle (see Colette)

Collier, John 1901-1980 ....DLB-77

Collier, P. F. [publishing house] DLB-49

Collier, Robert J. 1876-1918.............................DLB-91

Collin and Small...DLB-49

Collins, Isaac [publishing house] DLB-49

Collins, Mortimer 1827-1876.......................DLB-21, 35

Collins, Wilkie 1824-1889..............................DLB-18, 70

Collyer, Mary 1716?-1763? DLB-39

Colman, Benjamin 1673-1747............................DLB-24

Colman, George, the Elder
1732-1794 ....DLB-89

Colman, George, the Younger
1762-1836 ....DLB-89

Colman, S. [publishing house] DLB-49

Colombo, John Robert 1936- DLB-53

Colter, Cyrus 1910- DLB-33

Colum, Padraic 1881-1972..............................DLB-19

Colwin, Laurie 1944- Y-80

Comden, Betty 1919- and Green,
Adolph 1918- DLB-44

The Comic Tradition Continued
[in the British Novel]..................................DLB-15

Commager, Henry Steele 1902- DLB-17

The Commercialization of the Image of
Revolt, by Kenneth Rexroth DLB-16

Community and Commentators: Black
Theatre and Its Critics..................................DLB-38

Compton-Burnett, Ivy 1884?-1969 ....DLB-36

Conference on Modern Biography...........................Y-85

Congreve, William 1670-1729 ....DLB-39, 84

Conkey, W. B., Company....................................DLB-49

Connell, Evan S., Jr. 1924- DLB-2; Y-81

Connelly, Marc 1890-1980..........................DLB-7; Y-80

Connolly, James B. 1868-1957...........................DLB-78

Connor, Ralph 1860-1937................................DLB-92

Connor, Tony 1930- DLB-40

Conquest, Robert 1917- DLB-27

Conrad, John, and Company...............................DLB-49

Conrad, Joseph 1857-1924 ....DLB-10, 34

Conroy, Jack 1899- Y-81

Conroy, Pat 1945- DLB-6

The Consolidation of Opinion: Critical
Responses to the Modernists DLB-36

Constantin-Weyer, Maurice
1881-1964 ....DLB-92

Constantine, David 1944- DLB-40

Contempo Caravan: Kites in a Windstorm Y-85

A Contemporary Flourescence of Chicano
Literature Y-84

The Continental Publishing Company DLB-49

A Conversation with Chaim Potok...........................Y-84

Conversations with Publishers I: An Interview
    with Patrick O'Connor......................................Y-84

The Conversion of an Unpolitical Man,
    by W. H. Bruford...DLB-66

Conway, Moncure Daniel 1832-1907..................DLB-1

Cook, David C., Publishing Company...............DLB-49

Cook, Ebenezer circa 1667-circa 1732...............DLB-24

Cook, Michael 1933- DLB-53

Cooke, George Willis 1848-1923 ....DLB-71

Cooke, Increase, and Company...........................DLB-49

Cooke, John Esten 1830-1886.............................DLB-3

Cooke, Philip Pendleton 1816-1850 ....DLB-3, 59

Cooke, Rose Terry 1827-1892 ....DLB-12, 74

Coolbrith, Ina 1841-1928..................................DLB-54

Coolidge, George [publishing house] DLB-49

Coolidge, Susan (see Woolsey, Sarah Chauncy)

Cooper, Giles 1918-1966...................................DLB-13

Cooper, James Fenimore 1789-1851.....................DLB-3

Cooper, Kent 1880-1965...................................DLB-29

Coover, Robert 1932- DLB-2; Y-81

Copeland and Day...DLB-49

Coppel, Alfred 1921- Y-83

Coppola, Francis Ford 1939- DLB-44

Corcoran, Barbara 1911- DLB-52

Corelli, Marie 1855-1924 ....DLB-34

Corle, Edwin 1906-1956...................................Y-85

Corman, Cid 1924- DLB-5

Cormier, Robert 1925- DLB-52

Corn, Alfred 1943- Y-80

Cornish, Sam 1935- DLB-41

Cornwell, David John Moore
    (see le Carré, John)

Corpi, Lucha 1945- DLB-82

Corrington, John William 1932- DLB-6

Corrothers, James D. 1869-1917 ....DLB-50

Corso, Gregory 1930- DLB-5, 16

Cortez, Jayne 1936- DLB-41

Corvo, Baron (see Rolfe, Frederick William)

Cory, William Johnson 1823-1892......................DLB-35

Cosmopolitan Book Corporation......................DLB-46

Costain, Thomas B. 1885-1965...........................DLB-9

Coste, Donat 1912-1957 ....DLB-88

Cotter, Joseph Seamon, Sr.
    1861-1949 ....DLB-50

Cotter, Joseph Seamon, Jr.
    1895-1919 ....DLB-50

Cotton, John 1584-1652 ....DLB-24

Coulter, John 1888-1980...................................DLB-68

Cournos, John 1881-1966 ....DLB-54

Coventry, Francis 1725-1754 ....DLB-39

Coverly, N. [publishing house] DLB-49

Covici-Friede...DLB-46

Coward, Noel 1899-1973 ....DLB-10

Coward, McCann and Geoghegan......................DLB-46

Cowles, Gardner 1861-1946...............................DLB-29

Cowley, Hannah 1743-1809...............................DLB-89

Cowley, Malcolm 1898-1989.................DLB-4, 48; Y-81

Cox, A. B. (see Berkeley, Anthony)

Cox, Palmer 1840-1924 ....DLB-42

Coxe, Louis 1918- DLB-5

Coxe, Tench 1755-1824.....................................DLB-37

Cozzens, James Gould 1903-1978 ....DLB-9; Y-84; DS-2

Crabbe, George 1754-1832 ....DLB-93

Craddock, Charles Egbert (see Murfree, Mary N.)

Cradock, Thomas 1718-1770............................DLB-31

Craig, Daniel H. 1811-1895 ....DLB-43

Craik, Dinah Maria 1826-1887 ....DLB-35

Cranch, Christopher Pearse 1813-1892..........DLB-1, 42

Crane, Hart 1899-1932 ....DLB-4, 48

Crane, R. S. 1886-1967 ....DLB-63

Crane, Stephen 1871-1900 ....DLB-12, 54, 78

Crapsey, Adelaide 1878-1914 ....DLB-54

Craven, Avery 1885-1980...................................DLB-17

Crawford, Charles 1752-circa 1815 ....DLB-31

Crawford, F. Marion 1854-1909.........................DLB-71

Crawford, Isabel Valancy
    1850-1887 ....DLB-92

Crawley, Alan 1887-1975 ....DLB-68

Crayon, Geoffrey (see Irving, Washington)

Creasey, John 1908-1973 ....DLB-77

Creative Age Press...DLB-46

Creel, George 1876-1953 ....DLB-25

Creeley, Robert 1926- DLB-5, 16

Creelman, James 1859-1915 ....DLB-23

Cregan, David 1931- DLB-13

Creighton, Donald Grant 1902-1979.................DLB-88

Crèvecoeur, Michel Guillaume Jean de
    1735-1813 ....DLB-37

Crews, Harry 1935- DLB-6

Crichton, Michael 1942- Y-81

A Crisis of Culture: The Changing Role
    of Religion in the New Republic DLB-37

Crispin, Edmund 1921-1978.............................DLB-87

Cristofer, Michael 1946- DLB-7

"The Critic as Artist" (1891), by Oscar Wilde....DLB-57

Criticism In Relation To Novels (1863),
    by G. H. Lewes DLB-21

Crockett, David (Davy) 1786-1836.................DLB-3, 11

Croft-Cooke, Rupert (see Bruce, Leo)

Crofts, Freeman Wills 1879-1957 ....DLB-77

Croly, Herbert 1869-1930 ....DLB-91

Croly, Jane Cunningham 1829-1901 ....DLB-23

Crosby, Caresse 1892-1970 ....DLB-48

Crosby, Caresse 1892-1970 and Crosby,
    Harry 1898-1929 ....DLB-4

Crosby, Harry 1898-1929................................DLB-48

Crossley-Holland, Kevin 1941- DLB-40

Crothers, Rachel 1878-1958.............................DLB-7

Crowell, Thomas Y., Company.........................DLB-49

Crowley, John 1942- Y-82

Crowley, Mart 1935- DLB-7

Crown Publishers...DLB-46

Crowne, John 1641-1712 ....DLB-80

Crowninshield, Frank 1872-1947......................DLB-91

Croy, Homer 1883-1965 ....DLB-4

Crumley, James 1939- Y-84

Cruz, Victor Hernández 1949- DLB-41

Csokor, Franz Theodor 1885-1969 ....DLB-81

Cullen, Countee 1903-1946.....................DLB-4, 48, 51

Culler, Jonathan D. 1944- DLB-67

The Cult of Biography
    Excerpts from the Second Folio Debate:
      "Biographies are generally a disease of

English Literature"–Germaine Greer,
    Victoria Glendinning, Auberon Waugh,
    and Richard Holmes Y-86

Cumberland, Richard 1732-1811 ....DLB-89

Cummings, E. E. 1894-1962 ....DLB-4, 48

Cummings, Ray 1887-1957 ....DLB-8

Cummings and Hilliard DLB-49

Cummins, Maria Susanna 1827-1866.................DLB-42

Cuney, Waring 1906-1976...............................DLB-51

Cuney-Hare, Maude 1874-1936.......................DLB-52

Cunningham, J. V. 1911- DLB-5

Cunningham, Peter F. [publishing house]..........DLB-49

Cuomo, George 1929- Y-80

Cupples and Leon DLB-46

Cupples, Upham and Company.........................DLB-49

Cuppy, Will 1884-1949 ....DLB-11

Currie, Mary Montgomerie Lamb Singleton,
    Lady Currie (see Fane, Violet)

Curti, Merle E. 1897- DLB-17

Curtis, Cyrus H. K. 1850-1933 ....DLB-91

Curtis, George William 1824-1892.................DLB-1, 43

D

D. M. Thomas: The Plagiarism Controversy Y-82

Dabit, Eugène 1898-1936.................................DLB-65

Daborne, Robert circa 1580-1628......................DLB-58

Daggett, Rollin M. 1831-1901...........................DLB-79

Dahlberg, Edward 1900-1977 ....DLB-48

Dale, Peter 1938- DLB-40

Dall, Caroline Wells (Healey) 1822-1912.............DLB-1

Dallas, E. S. 1828-1879...................................DLB-55

The Dallas Theater Center DLB-7

D'Alton, Louis 1900-1951 ....DLB-10

Daly, T. A. 1871-1948.....................................DLB-11

Damon, S. Foster 1893-1971 ....DLB-45

Damrell, William S. [publishing house].............DLB-49

Dana, Charles A. 1819-1897 ....DLB-3, 23

Dana, Richard Henry, Jr. 1815-1882 ....DLB-1

Dandridge, Ray Garfield DLB-51

Dane, Clemence 1887-1965...............................DLB-10

Danforth, John 1660-1730 ....DLB-24

Danforth, Samuel I 1626-1674 ....DLB-24

Danforth, Samuel II 1666-1727.......................DLB-24

Dangerous Years: London Theater,
   1939-1945 ....DLB-10

Daniel, John M. 1825-1865 ....DLB-43

Daniel, Samuel 1562 or 1563-1619....................DLB-62

Daniells, Roy 1902-1979....................................DLB-68

Daniels, Josephus 1862-1948 ....DLB-29

Danner, Margaret Esse 1915- DLB-41

Dantin, Louis 1865-1945....................................DLB-92

Darwin, Charles 1809-1882................................DLB-57

Darwin, Erasmus 1731-1802.............................DLB-93

Daryush, Elizabeth 1887-1977 ....DLB-20

Dashwood, Edmée Elizabeth Monica
   de la Pasture (see Delafield, E. M.)

d'Aulaire, Edgar Parin 1898- and
   d'Aulaire, Ingri 1904- DLB-22

Davenant, Sir William 1606-1668 ....DLB-58

Davenport, Robert ?-? DLB-58

Daves, Delmer 1904-1977 ....DLB-26

Davey, Frank 1940- DLB-53

Davidson, Avram 1923- DLB-8

Davidson, Donald 1893-1968............................DLB-45

Davidson, John 1857-1909 ....DLB-19

Davidson, Lionel 1922- DLB-14

Davie, Donald 1922- DLB-27

Davies, Robertson 1913- DLB-68

Davies, Samuel 1723-1761................................DLB-31

Davies, W. H. 1871-1940...................................DLB-19

Daviot, Gordon 1896?-1952 ....DLB-10
   (see also Tey, Josephine)

Davis, Charles A. 1795-1867 ....DLB-11

Davis, Clyde Brion 1894-1962...........................DLB-9

Davis, Dick 1945- DLB-40

Davis, Frank Marshall 1905-? DLB-51

Davis, H. L. 1894-1960.....................................DLB-9

Davis, John 1774-1854 ....DLB-37

Davis, Margaret Thomson 1926- DLB-14

Davis, Ossie 1917- DLB-7, 38

Davis, Rebecca Harding 1831-1910.................DLB-74

Davis, Richard Harding 1864-1916.................DLB-12,
   23, 78, 79

Davis, Samuel Cole 1764-1809...........................DLB-37

Davison, Peter 1928- DLB-5

Davys, Mary 1674-1732.....................................DLB-39

DAW Books DLB-46

Dawson, William 1704-1752..............................DLB-31

Day, Benjamin Henry 1810-1889 ....DLB-43

Day, Clarence 1874-1935 ....DLB-11

Day, Dorothy 1897-1980 ....DLB-29

Day, Frank Parker 1881-1950 ....DLB-92

Day, John circa 1574-circa 1640 ....DLB-62

Day, The John, Company DLB-46

Day Lewis, C. 1904-1972............................DLB-15, 20
   (see also Blake, Nicholas)

Day, Mahlon [publishing house] DLB-49

Day, Thomas 1748-1789 ....DLB-39

Deacon, William Arthur 1890-1977 ....DLB-68

Deal, Borden 1922-1985 ....DLB-6

de Angeli, Marguerite 1889-1987......................DLB-22

De Bow, James Dunwoody Brownson
   1820-1867 ....DLB-3, 79

de Bruyn, Günter 1926- DLB-75

de Camp, L. Sprague 1907- DLB-8

The Decay of Lying (1889),
   by Oscar Wilde [excerpt]............................DLB-18

Dedication, *Ferdinand Count Fathom* (1753),
   by Tobias Smollett DLB-39

Dedication, *Lasselia* (1723), by Eliza
   Haywood [excerpt] DLB-39

Dedication, *The History of Pompey the
   Little* (1751), by Francis Coventry DLB-39

Dedication, *The Wanderer* (1814),
   by Fanny Burney DLB-39

Defense of *Amelia* (1752), by Henry Fielding.....DLB-39

Defoe, Daniel 1660-1731...................................DLB-39

de Fontaine, Felix Gregory 1834-1896 ....DLB-43

De Forest, John William 1826-1906...................DLB-12

de Graff, Robert 1895-1981 ....Y-81

Deighton, Len 1929- DLB-87

DeJong, Meindert 1906- DLB-52

Dekker, Thomas circa 1572-1632.....................DLB-62

Delacorte, Jr., George T. 1894- DLB-91

Delafield, E. M. 1890-1943 ....DLB-34

Delahaye, Guy 1888-1969 ....DLB-92

de la Mare, Walter 1873-1956..........................DLB-19

Deland, Margaret 1857-1945 ....DLB-78

Delaney, Shelagh 1939- DLB-13

Delany, Martin Robinson 1812-1885 ....DLB-50

Delany, Samuel R. 1942- DLB-8, 33

de la Roche, Mazo 1879-1961 ....DLB-68

Delbanco, Nicholas 1942- DLB-6

De León, Nephtalí 1945- DLB-82

Delgado, Abelardo Barrientos 1931- DLB-82

DeLillo, Don 1936- DLB-6

Dell, Floyd 1887-1969 ....DLB-9

Dell Publishing Company..............................DLB-46

delle Grazie, Marie Eugene 1864-1931 ....DLB-81

del Rey, Lester 1915- DLB-8

de Man, Paul 1919-1983 ....DLB-67

Demby, William 1922- DLB-33

Deming, Philander 1829-1915 ....DLB-74

Demorest, William Jennings 1822-1895 ....DLB-79

Denham, Sir John 1615-1669 ....DLB-58

Denison, Merrill 1893-1975 ....DLB-92

Denison, T. S., and Company..........................DLB-49

Dennie, Joseph 1768-1812...............DLB-37, 43, 59, 73

Dennis, Nigel 1912-1989...........................DLB-13, 15

Dent, Tom 1932- DLB-38

Denton, Daniel circa 1626-1703.......................DLB-24

DePaola, Tomie 1934- DLB-61

Derby, George Horatio 1823-1861 ....DLB-11

Derby, J. C., and Company.............................DLB-49

Derby and Miller DLB-49

Derleth, August 1909-1971.............................DLB-9

The Derrydale Press....................................DLB-46

Desaulniers, Gonsalve 1863-1934 ....DLB-92

Desbiens, Jean-Paul 1927- DLB-53

des Forêts, Louis-René 1918- DLB-83

DesRochers, Alfred 1901-1978 ....DLB-68

Desrosiers, Léo-Paul 1896-1967.......................DLB-68

Destouches, Louis-Ferdinand (see Céline,
    Louis-Ferdinand)

De Tabley, Lord 1835-1895 ....DLB-35

Deutsch, Babette 1895-1982 ....DLB-45

Deveaux, Alexis 1948- DLB-38

The Development of Lighting in the Staging
    of Drama, 1900-1945 [in Great Britain]......DLB-10

de Vere, Aubrey 1814-1902 ....DLB-35

The Devin-Adair Company.............................DLB-46

De Voto, Bernard 1897-1955 ....DLB-9

De Vries, Peter 1910- DLB-6; Y-82

Dewdney, Christopher 1951- DLB-60

Dewdney, Selwyn 1909-1979 ....DLB-68

DeWitt, Robert M., Publisher DLB-49

DeWolfe, Fiske and Company..........................DLB-49

Dexter, Colin 1930- DLB-87

de Young, M. H. 1849-1925...........................DLB-25

The Dial Press..DLB-46

Diamond, I. A. L. 1920-1988 ....DLB-26

Di Cicco, Pier Giorgio 1949- DLB-60

Dick, Philip K. 1928- DLB-8

Dick and Fitzgerald DLB-49

Dickens, Charles 1812-1870.................DLB-21, 55, 70

Dickey, James 1923- DLB-5; Y-82; DS-7

Dickey, William 1928- DLB-5

Dickinson, Emily 1830-1886 ....DLB-1

Dickinson, John 1732-1808.............................DLB-31

Dickinson, Jonathan 1688-1747 ....DLB-24

Dickinson, Patric 1914- DLB-27

Dickinson, Peter 1927- DLB-87

Dickson, Gordon R. 1923- DLB-8

Didion, Joan 1934- DLB-2; Y-81, 86

Di Donato, Pietro 1911- DLB-9

Dillard, Annie 1945- Y-80

Dillard, R. H. W. 1937- DLB-5

Dillingham, Charles T., Company....................DLB-49

The G. W. Dillingham Company......................DLB-49

Dintenfass, Mark 1941- Y-84

Diogenes, Jr. (see Brougham, John)

DiPrima, Diane 1934- DLB-5, 16

Disch, Thomas M. 1940- DLB-8

Disney, Walt 1901-1966.................................DLB-22

Disraeli, Benjamin 1804-1881.....................DLB-21, 55

Ditzen, Rudolf (see Fallada, Hans)

Dix, Dorothea Lynde 1802-1887 ....DLB-1

Cumulative Index

Dix, Dorothy (see Gilmer, Elizabeth Meriwether)

Dix, Edwards and Company DLB-49

Dixon, Paige (see Corcoran, Barbara)

Dixon, Richard Watson 1833-1900 ....DLB-19

Dobell, Sydney 1824-1874...................................DLB-32

Döblin, Alfred 1878-1957 ....DLB-66

Dobson, Austin 1840-1921 ....DLB-35

Doctorow, E. L. 1931- DLB-2, 28; Y-80

Dodd, William E. 1869-1940 ....DLB-17

Dodd, Mead and Company..................................DLB-49

Doderer, Heimito von 1896-1968......................DLB-85

Dodge, B. W., and Company..............................DLB-46

Dodge, Mary Mapes 1831?-1905 ....DLB-42, 79

Dodge Publishing Company DLB-49

Dodgson, Charles Lutwidge (see Carroll, Lewis)

Dodson, Owen 1914-1983 ....DLB-76

Doesticks, Q. K. Philander, P. B. (see Thomson,
    Mortimer)

Donahoe, Patrick [publishing house].................DLB-49

Donald, David H. 1920- DLB-17

Donleavy, J. P. 1926- DLB-6

Donnadieu, Marguerite (see Duras, Marguerite)

Donnelley, R. R., and Sons Company DLB-49

Donnelly, Ignatius 1831-1901...........................DLB-12

Donohue and Henneberry..................................DLB-49

Doolady, M. [publishing house].........................DLB-49

Dooley, Ebon (see Ebon)

Doolittle, Hilda 1886-1961............................DLB-4, 45

Dor, Milo 1923- DLB-85

Doran, George H., Company.............................DLB-46

Dorgelès, Roland 1886-1973 ....DLB-65

Dorn, Edward 1929- DLB-5

Dorr, Rheta Childe 1866-1948 ....DLB-25

Dorst, Tankred 1925- DLB-75

Dos Passos, John 1896-1970 ....DLB-4, 9; DS-1

Doubleday and Company...................................DLB-49

Dougall, Lily 1858-1923....................................DLB-92

Doughty, Charles M. 1843-1926..................DLB-19, 57

Douglas, Keith 1920-1944 ....DLB-27

Douglas, Norman 1868-1952 ....DLB-34

Douglass, Frederick 1817?-1895.........DLB-1, 43, 50, 79

Douglass, William circa 1691-1752....................DLB-24

Dover Publications..DLB-46

Dowden, Edward 1843-1913.............................DLB-35

Downes, Gwladys 1915- DLB-88

Downing, J., Major (see Davis, Charles A.)

Downing, Major Jack (see Smith, Seba)

Dowson, Ernest 1867-1900................................DLB-19

Doxey, William [publishing house]....................DLB-49

Doyle, Sir Arthur Conan 1859-1930 ....DLB-18, 70

Doyle, Kirby 1932- DLB-16

Drabble, Margaret 1939- DLB-14

Drach, Albert 1902- DLB-85

The Dramatic Publishing Company DLB-49

Dramatists Play Service.....................................DLB-46

Draper, John W. 1811-1882..............................DLB-30

Draper, Lyman C. 1815-1891 ....DLB-30

Dreiser, Theodore 1871-1945 ....DLB-9, 12; DS-1

Drewitz, Ingeborg 1923-1986 ....DLB-75

Drieu La Rochelle, Pierre 1893-1945.................DLB-72

Drinkwater, John 1882-1937 ....DLB-10, 19

The Drue Heinz Literature Prize
    Excerpt from "Excerpts from a Report
    of the Commission," in David
    Bosworth's *The Death of Descartes*
    An Interview with David Bosworth Y-82

Drummond, William Henry
    1854-1907 ....DLB-92

Dryden, John 1631-1700...................................DLB-80

Duane, William 1760-1835................................DLB-43

Dubé, Marcel 1930- DLB-53

Dubé, Rodolphe (see Hertel, François)

Du Bois, W. E. B. 1868-1963................DLB-47, 50, 91

Du Bois, William Pène 1916- DLB-61

Ducharme, Réjean 1941- DLB-60

Dudek, Louis 1918- DLB-88

Duell, Sloan and Pearce DLB-46

Duffield and Green DLB-46

Duffy, Maureen 1933- DLB-14

Dugan, Alan 1923- DLB-5

Dugas, Marcel 1883-1947..................................DLB-92

Duhamel, Georges 1884-1966...........................DLB-65

Dukes, Ashley 1885-1959 ....DLB-10

Dumas, Henry 1934-1968 ....DLB-41

Dunbar, Paul Laurence 1872-1906 ....DLB-50, 54, 78

Duncan, Norman 1871-1916.................................DLB-92

Duncan, Robert 1919-1988 ....DLB-5, 16

Duncan, Ronald 1914-1982..................................DLB-13

Duncan, Sara Jeannette
      1861-1922 ....DLB-92

Dunigan, Edward, and Brother DLB-49

Dunlap, John 1747-1812 ....DLB-43

Dunlap, William 1766-1839...................DLB-30, 37, 59

Dunn, Douglas 1942- DLB-40

Dunne, Finley Peter 1867-1936 ....DLB-11, 23

Dunne, John Gregory 1932- Y-80

Dunne, Philip 1908- DLB-26

Dunning, Ralph Cheever 1878-1930 ....DLB-4

Dunning, William A. 1857-1922 ....DLB-17

Plunkett, Edward John Moreton Drax,
      Lord Dunsany 1878-1957 ....DLB-10, 77

Durand, Lucile (see Bersianik, Louky)

Duranty, Walter 1884-1957...............................DLB-29

Duras, Marguerite 1914- DLB-83

Durfey, Thomas 1653-1723 ....DLB-80

Durrell, Lawrence 1912- DLB-15, 27

Durrell, William [publishing house] DLB-49

Dürrenmatt, Friedrich 1921- DLB-69

Dutton, E. P., and Company..............................DLB-49

Duvoisin, Roger 1904-1980................................DLB-61

Duyckinck, Evert Augustus 1816-1878 ....DLB-3, 64

Duyckinck, George L. 1823-1863 ....DLB-3

Duyckinck and Company DLB-49

Dwight, John Sullivan 1813-1893 ....DLB-1

Dwight, Timothy 1752-1817 ....DLB-37

Dyer, Charles 1928- DLB-13

Dyer, George 1755-1841 ....DLB-93

Dylan, Bob 1941- DLB-16

E

Eager, Edward 1911-1964...................................DLB-22

Earle, James H., and Company DLB-49

Early American Book Illustration,

      by Sinclair Hamilton DLB-49

Eastlake, William 1917- DLB-6

Eastman, Carol ?- DLB-44

Eastman, Max 1883-1969..................................DLB-91

Eberhart, Richard 1904- DLB-48

Ebner, Jeannie 1918- DLB-85

Ebner-Eschenbach, Marie von
      1830-1916 ....DLB-81

Ebon 1942- DLB-41

Ecco Press..DLB-46

Edes, Benjamin 1732-1803..................................DLB-43

Edgar, David 1948- DLB-13

The Editor Publishing Company DLB-49

Edmonds, Randolph 1900- DLB-51

Edmonds, Walter D. 1903- DLB-9

Edschmid, Kasimir 1890-1966 ....DLB-56

Edwards, Jonathan 1703-1758............................DLB-24

Edwards, Jonathan, Jr. 1745-1801.......................DLB-37

Edwards, Junius 1929- DLB-33

Edwards, Richard 1524-1566...............................DLB-62

Effinger, George Alec 1947- DLB-8

Eggleston, Edward 1837-1902 ....DLB-12

Eggleston, Wilfred 1901-1986 ....DLB-92

Ehrenstein, Albert 1886-1950............................DLB-81

Eich, Günter 1907-1972 ....DLB-69

Eichendorff, Joseph Freiherr von
      1788-1857 ....DLB-90

1873 Publishers' Catalogues...............................DLB-49

Eighteenth-Century Aesthetic Theories DLB-31

Eighteenth-Century Philosophical
      Background DLB-31

Eigner, Larry 1927- DLB-5

Eisenreich, Herbert 1925-1986...........................DLB-85

Eisner, Kurt 1867-1919......................................DLB-66

Eklund, Gordon 1945- Y-83

Elder, Lonne III 1931- DLB-7, 38, 44

Elder, Paul, and Company.................................DLB-49

Elements of Rhetoric (1828; revised, 1846),
      by Richard Whately [excerpt] DLB-57

Elie, Robert 1915-1973.....................................DLB-88

Eliot, George 1819-1880 ....DLB-21, 35, 55

Eliot, John 1604-1690..DLB-24

Eliot, T. S. 1888-1965 ....DLB-7, 10, 45, 63

Elizondo, Sergio 1930- DLB-82

Elkin, Stanley 1930- DLB-2, 28; Y-80

Elles, Dora Amy (see Wentworth, Patricia)

Ellet, Elizabeth F. 1818?-1877...........................DLB-30

Elliott, George 1923- DLB-68

Elliott, Janice 1931- DLB-14

Elliott, William 1788-1863 ....DLB-3

Elliott, Thomes and Talbot DLB-49

Ellis, Edward S. 1840-1916 ....DLB-42

The George H. Ellis Company DLB-49

Ellison, Harlan 1934- DLB-8

Ellison, Ralph 1914- DLB-2, 76

Ellmann, Richard 1918-1987 ....Y-87

The Elmer Holmes Bobst Awards
    in Arts and Letters Y-87

Emanuel, James Andrew 1921- DLB-41

Emerson, Ralph Waldo 1803-1882..........DLB-1, 59, 73

Emerson, William 1769-1811...............................DLB-37

Empson, William 1906-1984 ....DLB-20

The End of English Stage Censorship,
    1945-1968 ....DLB-13

Ende, Michael 1929- DLB-75

Engel, Marian 1933-1985 ....DLB-53

Engle, Paul 1908- DLB-48

English Composition and Rhetoric (1866),
    by Alexander Bain [excerpt].......................DLB-57

The English Renaissance of Art (1908),
    by Oscar Wilde DLB-35

Enright, D. J. 1920- DLB-27

Enright, Elizabeth 1909-1968 ....DLB-22

L'Envoi (1882), by Oscar Wilde DLB-35

Epps, Bernard 1936- DLB-53

Epstein, Julius 1909- and
    Epstein, Philip 1909-1952 ....DLB-26

Equiano, Olaudah circa 1745-1797 ....DLB-37, 50

Erichsen-Brown, Gwethalyn Graham
    (see Graham, Gwethalyn)

Ernst, Paul 1866-1933 ....DLB-66

Erskine, John 1879-1951 ....DLB-9

Ervine, St. John Greer 1883-1971 ....DLB-10

Eshleman, Clayton 1935- DLB-5

Ess Ess Publishing Company...............................DLB-49

Essay on Chatterton (1842),
    by Robert Browning DLB-32

Estes, Eleanor 1906-1988 ....DLB-22

Estes and Lauriat...DLB-49

Etherege, George 1636-circa 1692.....................DLB-80

Ets, Marie Hall 1893- DLB-22

Eudora Welty: Eye of the Storyteller.....................Y-87

Eugene O'Neill Memorial Theater Center..........DLB-7

Eugene O'Neill's Letters: A Review.....................Y-88

Evans, Donald 1884-1921....................................DLB-54

Evans, George Henry 1805-1856.......................DLB-43

Evans, Hubert 1892-1986 ....DLB-92

Evans, M., and Company DLB-46

Evans, Mari 1923- DLB-41

Evans, Mary Ann (see Eliot, George)

Evans, Nathaniel 1742-1767...............................DLB-31

Evans, Sebastian 1830-1909 ....DLB-35

Everett, Alexander Hill 1790-1847....................DLB-59

Everett, Edward 1794-1865 ....DLB-1, 59

Everson, R. G. 1903- DLB-88

Everson, William 1912- DLB-5, 16

Every Man His Own Poet; or, The
    Inspired Singer's Recipe Book (1877),
    by W. H. Mallock DLB-35

Ewart, Gavin 1916- DLB-40

Ewing, Juliana Horatia 1841-1885.....................DLB-21

Exley, Frederick 1929- Y-81

Experiment in the Novel (1929),
    by John D. Beresford DLB-36

F

"F. Scott Fitzgerald: St. Paul's Native Son
    and Distinguished American Writer":
    University of Minnesota Conference,
    29-31 October 1982.......................................Y-82

Faber, Frederick William 1814-1863 ....DLB-32

Fair, Ronald L. 1932- DLB-33

Fairfax, Beatrice (see Manning, Marie)

Fairlie, Gerard 1899-1983 ....DLB-77

Fallada, Hans 1893-1947 ....DLB-56

Fancher, Betsy 1928- Y-83

Fane, Violet 1843-1905.....................................DLB-35

Fantasy Press Publishers DLB-46

Fante, John 1909-1983......................................Y-83

Farber, Norma 1909-1984................................DLB-61

Farigoule, Louis (see Romains, Jules)

Farley, Walter 1920- DLB-22

Farmer, Philip José 1918- DLB-8

Farquhar, George circa 1677-1707 ....DLB-84

Farquharson, Martha (see Finley, Martha)

Farrar and Rinehart..DLB-46

Farrar, Straus and Giroux DLB-46

Farrell, James T. 1904-1979.............DLB-4, 9, 86; DS-2

Farrell, J. G. 1935-1979...................................DLB-14

Fast, Howard 1914- DLB-9

Faulkner, William 1897-1962
...................................DLB-9, 11, 44; DS-2; Y-86

Fauset, Jessie Redmon 1882-1961 ....DLB-51

Faust, Irvin 1924- DLB-2, 28; Y-80

Fawcett Books DLB-46

Fearing, Kenneth 1902-1961 ....DLB-9

Federal Writers' Project..................................DLB-46

Federman, Raymond 1928- Y-80

Feiffer, Jules 1929- DLB-7, 44

Feinberg, Charles E. 1899-1988 ....Y-88

Feinstein, Elaine 1930- DLB-14, 40

Fell, Frederick, Publishers DLB-46

Fels, Ludwig 1946- DLB-75

Felton, Cornelius Conway 1807-1862 ....DLB-1

Fennario, David 1947- DLB-60

Fenno, John 1751-1798 ....DLB-43

Fenno, R. F., and Company DLB-49

Fenton, James 1949- DLB-40

Ferber, Edna 1885-1968 ....DLB-9, 28, 86

Ferdinand, Vallery III (see Salaam, Kalamu ya)

Ferguson, Sir Samuel 1810-1886 ....DLB-32

Ferguson, William Scott 1875-1954 ....DLB-47

Ferland, Albert 1872-1943 ....DLB-92

Ferlinghetti, Lawrence 1919- DLB-5, 16

Fern, Fanny (see Parton, Sara
    Payson Willis)

Ferrars, Elizabeth 1907- DLB-87

Ferret, E., and Company DLB-49

Ferrini, Vincent 1913- DLB-48

Ferron, Jacques 1921-1985 ....DLB-60

Ferron, Madeleine 1922- DLB-53

Fetridge and Company DLB-49

Feuchtwanger, Lion 1884-1958......................DLB-66

Fichte, Johann Gottlieb 1762-1814 ....DLB-90

Ficke, Arthur Davison 1883-1945....................DLB-54

Fiction Best-Sellers, 1910-1945 ....DLB-9

Fiction into Film, 1928-1975: A List of Movies
    Based on the Works of Authors in
    British Novelists, 1930-1959 ....DLB-15

Fiedler, Leslie A. 1917- DLB-28, 67

Field, Eugene 1850-1895 ....DLB-23, 42

Field, Nathan 1587-1619 or 1620.....................DLB-58

Field, Rachel 1894-1942...........................DLB-9, 22

A Field Guide to Recent Schools of
    American Poetry...Y-86

Fielding, Henry 1707-1754 ....DLB-39, 84

Fielding, Sarah 1710-1768 ....DLB-39

Fields, James Thomas 1817-1881 ....DLB-1

Fields, Julia 1938- DLB-41

Fields, W. C. 1880-1946 ....DLB-44

Fields, Osgood and Company...........................DLB-49

Fifty Penguin Years...Y-85

Figes, Eva 1932- DLB-14

Filson, John circa 1753-1788............................DLB-37

Finch, Robert 1900- DLB-88

Findley, Timothy 1930- DLB-53

Finlay, Ian Hamilton 1925- DLB-40

Finley, Martha 1828-1909 ....DLB-42

Finney, Jack 1911- DLB-8

Finney, Walter Braden (see Finney, Jack)

Firbank, Ronald 1886-1926.............................DLB-36

Firmin, Giles 1615-1697...................................DLB-24

First Strauss "Livings" Awarded to Cynthia
    Ozick and Raymond Carver
    An Interview with Cynthia Ozick
    An Interview with Raymond Carver Y-83

Fischer, Karoline Auguste Fernandine
    1764-1842 ....DLB-94

Fish, Stanley 1938- DLB-67

Fisher, Clay (see Allen, Henry W.)

Fisher, Dorothy Canfield 1879-1958 .... DLB-9

Fisher, Leonard Everett 1924- DLB-61

Fisher, Roy 1930- DLB-40

Fisher, Rudolph 1897-1934 .... DLB-51

Fisher, Sydney George 1856-1927 .... DLB-47

Fisher, Vardis 1895-1968 .... DLB-9

Fiske, John 1608-1677 .... DLB-24

Fiske, John 1842-1901 .... DLB-47, 64

Fitch, Thomas circa 1700-1774 .... DLB-31

Fitch, William Clyde 1865-1909 .... DLB-7

FitzGerald, Edward 1809-1883 .... DLB-32

Fitzgerald, F. Scott 1896-1940
.... DLB-4, 9, 86; Y-81; DS-1

Fitzgerald, Penelope 1916- DLB-14

Fitzgerald, Robert 1910-1985 .... Y-80

Fitzgerald, Thomas 1819-1891 .... DLB-23

Fitzgerald, Zelda Sayre 1900-1948 .... Y-84

Fitzhugh, Louise 1928-1974 .... DLB-52

Fitzhugh, William circa 1651-1701 .... DLB-24

Flanagan, Thomas 1923- Y-80

Flanner, Hildegarde 1899-1987 .... DLB-48

Flanner, Janet 1892-1978 .... DLB-4

Flavin, Martin 1883-1967 .... DLB-9

Flecker, James Elroy 1884-1915 .... DLB-10, 19

Fleeson, Doris 1901-1970 .... DLB-29

Fleidser, Marieluise 1901-1974 .... DLB-56

Fleming, Ian 1908-1964 .... DLB-87

The Fleshly School of Poetry and Other
     Phenomena of the Day (1872), by Robert
     Buchanan DLB-35

The Fleshly School of Poetry: Mr. D. G.
     Rossetti (1871), by Thomas Maitland
     (Robert Buchanan) DLB-35

Fletcher, J. S. 1863-1935 .... DLB-70

Fletcher, John (see Beaumont, Francis)

Fletcher, John Gould 1886-1950 .... DLB-4, 45

Flieg, Helmut (see Heym, Stefan)

Flint, F. S. 1885-1960 .... DLB-19

Flint, Timothy 1780-1840 .... DLB-73

Follen, Eliza Lee (Cabot) 1787-1860 .... DLB-1

Follett, Ken 1949- Y-81, DLB-87

Follett Publishing Company DLB-46

Folsom, John West [publishing house] DLB-49

Foote, Horton 1916- DLB-26

Foote, Samuel 1721-1777 .... DLB-89

Foote, Shelby 1916- DLB-2, 17

Forbes, Calvin 1945- DLB-41

Forbes, Ester 1891-1967 .... DLB-22

Forbes and Company DLB-49

Force, Peter 1790-1868 .... DLB-30

Forché, Carolyn 1950- DLB-5

Ford, Charles Henri 1913- DLB-4, 48

Ford, Corey 1902-1969 .... DLB-11

Ford, Ford Madox 1873-1939 .... DLB-34

Ford, J. B., and Company DLB-49

Ford, Jesse Hill 1928- DLB-6

Ford, John 1586-? DLB-58

Ford, R. A. D. 1915- DLB-88

Ford, Worthington C. 1858-1941 .... DLB-47

Fords, Howard, and Hulbert DLB-49

Foreman, Carl 1914-1984 .... DLB-26

Forester, Frank (see Herbert, Henry William)

Fornés, Maria Irene 1930- DLB-7

Forrest, Leon 1937- DLB-33

Forster, E. M. 1879-1970 .... DLB-34

Forster, Georg 1754-1794 .... DLB-94

Forsyth, Frederick 1938- DLB-87

Forten, Charlotte L. 1837-1914 .... DLB-50

Fortune, T. Thomas 1856-1928 .... DLB-23

Fosdick, Charles Austin 1842-1915 .... DLB-42

Foster, Genevieve 1893-1979 .... DLB-61

Foster, Hannah Webster 1758-1840 .... DLB-37

Foster, John 1648-1681 .... DLB-24

Foster, Michael 1904-1956 .... DLB-9

Fouqué, Caroline de la Motte
     1774-1831 .... DLB-90

Fouqué, Friedrich de la Motte
     1777-1843 .... DLB-90

Four Essays on the Beat Generation,
     by John Clellon Holmes DLB-16

Four Seas Company DLB-46

Four Winds Press DLB-46

Fournier, Henri Alban (see Alain-Fournier)

Fowler and Wells Company DLB-49

Fowles, John 1926- DLB-14

Fox, John, Jr. 1862 or 1863-1919 ....DLB-9

Fox, Paula 1923- DLB-52

Fox, Richard K. [publishing house] DLB-49

Fox, Richard Kyle 1846-1922 ....DLB-79

Fox, William Price 1926- DLB-2; Y-81

Fraenkel, Michael 1896-1957 ....DLB-4

France, Richard 1938- DLB-7

Francis, C. S. [publishing house] DLB-49

Francis, Convers 1795-1863 ....DLB-1

Francis, Dick 1920- DLB-87

François 1863-1910 ....DLB-92

Francke, Kuno 1855-1930 ....DLB-71

Frank, Leonhard 1882-1961 ....DLB-56

Frank, Melvin (see Panama, Norman)

Frank, Waldo 1889-1967 ....DLB-9, 63

Franken, Rose 1895?-1988 ....Y-84

Franklin, Benjamin 1706-1790 ....DLB-24, 43, 73

Franklin, James 1697-1735 ....DLB-43

Franklin Library DLB-46

Frantz, Ralph Jules 1902-1979 ....DLB-4

Fraser, G. S. 1915-1980 ....DLB-27

Frayn, Michael 1933- DLB-13, 14

Frederic, Harold 1856-1898 ....DLB-12, 23

Freeling, Nicolas 1927- DLB-87

Freeman, Douglas Southall 1886-1953 ....DLB-17

Freeman, Legh Richmond 1842-1915 ....DLB-23

Freeman, Mary E. Wilkins 1852-1930 ....DLB-12, 78

Freeman, R. Austin 1862-1943 ....DLB-70

French, Alice 1850-1934 ....DLB-74

French, David 1939- DLB-53

French, James [publishing house] DLB-49

French, Samuel [publishing house] DLB-49

Freneau, Philip 1752-1832 ....DLB-37, 43

Fried, Erich 1921-1988 ....DLB-85

Friedman, Bruce Jay 1930- DLB-2, 28

Friel, Brian 1929- DLB-13

Friend, Krebs 1895?-1967? DLB-4

Fries, Fritz Rudolf 1935- DLB-75

Fringe and Alternative Theater
  in Great Britain DLB-13

Frisch, Max 1911- DLB-69

Frischmuth, Barbara 1941- DLB-85

Fritz, Jean 1915- DLB-52

Frost, Robert 1874-1963 ....DLB-54; DS-7

Frothingham, Octavius Brooks 1822-1895 ....DLB-1

Froude, James Anthony 1818-1894 ....DLB-18, 57

Fry, Christopher 1907- DLB-13

Frye, Northrop 1912- DLB-67, 68

Fuchs, Daniel 1909- DLB-9, 26, 28

The Fugitives and the Agrarians:
  The First Exhibition Y-85

Fuller, Charles H., Jr. 1939- DLB-38

Fuller, Henry Blake 1857-1929 ....DLB-12

Fuller, John 1937- DLB-40

Fuller, Roy 1912- DLB-15, 20

Fuller, Samuel 1912- DLB-26

Fuller, Sarah Margaret, Marchesa
  D'Ossoli 1810-1850 ....DLB-1, 59, 73

Fulton, Len 1934- Y-86

Fulton, Robin 1937- DLB-40

Furman, Laura 1945- Y-86

Furness, Horace Howard 1833-1912 ....DLB-64

Furness, William Henry 1802-1896 ....DLB-1

Furthman, Jules 1888-1966 ....DLB-26

The Future of the Novel (1899),
  by Henry James DLB-18

G

Gaddis, William 1922- DLB-2

Gág, Wanda 1893-1946 ....DLB-22

Gagnon, Madeleine 1938- DLB-60

Gaine, Hugh 1726-1807 ....DLB-43

Gaine, Hugh [publishing house] DLB-49

Gaines, Ernest J. 1933- DLB-2, 33; Y-80

Gaiser, Gerd 1908-1976 ....DLB-69

Galaxy Science Fiction Novels DLB-46

Gale, Zona 1874-1938 ....DLB-9, 78

Gallagher, William Davis 1808-1894 ....DLB-73

Gallant, Mavis 1922- DLB-53

Gallico, Paul 1897-1976.................................DLB-9

Galsworthy, John 1867-1933......................DLB-10, 34

Galvin, Brendan 1938- DLB-5

Gambit..DLB-46

Gammer Gurton's Needle...............................DLB-62

Gannett, Frank E. 1876-1957...........................DLB-29

García, Lionel G. 1935- DLB-82

Gardam, Jane 1928- DLB-14

Garden, Alexander circa 1685-1756...................DLB-31

Gardner, John 1933-1982.......................DLB-2; Y-82

Garis, Howard R. 1873-1962...........................DLB-22

Garland, Hamlin 1860-1940..................DLB-12, 71, 78

Garneau, Hector de Saint-Denys 1912-1943......DLB-88

Garneau, Michel 1939- DLB-53

Garner, Hugh 1913-1979...............................DLB-68

Garnett, David 1892-1981.............................DLB-34

Garraty, John A. 1920- DLB-17

Garrett, George 1929- DLB-2, 5; Y-83

Garrick, David 1717-1779.............................DLB-84

Garrison, William Lloyd 1805-1879..............DLB-1, 43

Garve, Andrew 1908- DLB-87

Gary, Romain 1914-1980...............................DLB-83

Gascoyne, David 1916- DLB-20

Gaskell, Elizabeth Cleghorn 1810-1865.............DLB-21

Gass, William Howard 1924- DLB-2

Gates, Doris 1901- DLB-22

Gates, Henry Louis, Jr. 1950- DLB-67

Gates, Lewis E. 1860-1924...........................DLB-71

Gauvreau, Claude 1925-1971...........................DLB-88

Gay, Ebenezer 1696-1787.............................DLB-24

Gay, John 1685-1732.................................DLB-84

The Gay Science (1866),
        by E. S. Dallas [excerpt]...................DLB-21

Gayarré, Charles E. A. 1805-1895...................DLB-30

Gaylord, Charles [publishing house]................DLB-49

Geddes, Gary 1940- DLB-60

Geddes, Virgil 1897- DLB-4

Geis, Bernard, Associates............................DLB-46

Geisel, Theodor Seuss 1904- DLB-61

Gelber, Jack 1932- DLB-7

Gélinas, Gratien 1909- DLB-88

Gellhorn, Martha 1908- Y-82

Gems, Pam 1925- DLB-13

A General Idea of the College of Mirania (1753),
        by William Smith [excerpts].................DLB-31

Genet, Jean 1910-1986..........................Y-86, DLB-72

Genevoix, Maurice 1890-1980.........................DLB-65

Genovese, Eugene D. 1930- DLB-17

Gent, Peter 1942- Y-82

George, Henry 1839-1897.............................DLB-23

George, Jean Craighead 1919- DLB-52

Gerhardie, William 1895-1977........................DLB-36

Germanophilism, by Hans Kohn......................DLB-66

Gernsback, Hugo 1884-1967............................DLB-8

Gerould, Katharine Fullerton 1879-1944..........DLB-78

Gerrish, Samuel [publishing house]..................DLB-49

Gerrold, David 1944- DLB-8

Geston, Mark S. 1946- DLB-8

Gibbon, John Murray 1875-1952.......................DLB-92

Gibbon, Lewis Grassic (see Mitchell, James Leslie)

Gibbons, Floyd 1887-1939............................DLB-25

Gibbons, William ?-?................................DLB-73

Gibson, Graeme 1934- DLB-53

Gibson, Wilfrid 1878-1962...........................DLB-19

Gibson, William 1914- DLB-7

Gide, André 1869-1951...............................DLB-65

Giguère, Diane 1937- DLB-53

Giguère, Roland 1929- DLB-60

Gilbert, Anthony 1899-1973..........................DLB-77

Gilbert, Michael 1912- DLB-87

Gilder, Jeannette L. 1849-1916......................DLB-79

Gilder, Richard Watson 1844-1909..............DLB-64, 79

Gildersleeve, Basil 1831-1924.......................DLB-71

Giles, Henry 1809-1882..............................DLB-64

Gill, William F., Company...........................DLB-49

Gillespie, A. Lincoln, Jr. 1895-1950................DLB-4

Gilliam, Florence ?-?................................DLB-4

Gilliatt, Penelope 1932- DLB-14

Gillott, Jacky 1939-1980............................DLB-14

Gilman, Caroline H. 1794-1888..................DLB-3, 73

Gilman, W. and J. [publishing house]...............DLB-49

Gilmer, Elizabeth Meriwether 1861-1951.........DLB-29

Gilmer, Francis Walker 1790-1826 ....DLB-37

Gilroy, Frank D. 1925- DLB-7

Ginsberg, Allen 1926- DLB-5, 16

Ginzkey, Franz Karl 1871-1963 ....DLB-81

Giono, Jean 1895-1970 ....DLB-72

Giovanni, Nikki 1943- DLB-5, 41

Gipson, Lawrence Henry 1880-1971 ....DLB-17

Girard, Rodolphe 1879-1956 ....DLB-92

Giraudoux, Jean 1882-1944 ....DLB-65

Gissing, George 1857-1903 ....DLB-18

Gladstone, William Ewart 1809-1898 ....DLB-57

Glaeser, Ernst 1902-1963 ....DLB-69

Glanville, Brian 1931- DLB-15

Glapthorne, Henry 1610-1643? DLB-58

Glasgow, Ellen 1873-1945 ....DLB-9, 12

Glaspell, Susan 1876-1948 ....DLB-7, 9, 78

Glass, Montague 1877-1934 ....DLB-11

Glassco, John 1909-1981 ....DLB-68

Glauser, Friedrich 1896-1938 ....DLB-56

F. Gleason's Publishing Hall DLB-49

Glück, Louise 1943- DLB-5

Godbout, Jacques 1933- DLB-53

Goddard, Morrill 1865-1937 ....DLB-25

Goddard, William 1740-1817 ....DLB-43

Godey, Louis A. 1804-1878 ....DLB-73

Godey and McMichael..DLB-49

Godfrey, Dave 1938- DLB-60

Godfrey, Thomas 1736-1763 ....DLB-31

Godine, David R., Publisher DLB-46

Godkin, E. L. 1831-1902......................................DLB-79

Godwin, Gail 1937- DLB-6

Godwin, Parke 1816-1904.................................DLB-3, 64

Godwin, William 1756-1836 ....DLB-39

Goes, Albrecht 1908- DLB-69

Goethe, Johann Wolfgang von
        1749-1832 ....DLB-94

Goffe, Thomas circa 1592-1629..........................DLB-58

Goffstein, M. B. 1940- DLB-61

Gogarty, Oliver St. John 1878-1957 ....DLB-15, 19

Goines, Donald 1937-1974 ....DLB-33

Gold, Herbert 1924- DLB-2; Y-81

Gold, Michael 1893-1967 ....DLB-9, 28

Goldberg, Dick 1947- DLB-7

Golding, William 1911- DLB-15

Goldman, William 1931- DLB-44

Goldsmith, Oliver 1730?-1774 ....DLB-39, 89

Goldsmith Publishing Company DLB-46

Gomme, Laurence James
        [publishing house] DLB-46

González-T., César A. 1931- DLB-82

The Goodman Theatre DLB-7

Goodrich, Frances 1891-1984 and
        Hackett, Albert 1900- DLB-26

Goodrich, S. G. [publishing house] DLB-49

Goodrich, Samuel Griswold 1793-1860 ...DLB-1, 42, 73

Goodspeed, C. E., and Company DLB-49

Goodwin, Stephen 1943- Y-82

Gookin, Daniel 1612-1687 ....DLB-24

Gordon, Caroline 1895-1981 ....DLB-4, 9; Y-81

Gordon, Giles 1940- DLB-14

Gordon, Mary 1949- DLB-6; Y-81

Gordone, Charles 1925- DLB-7

Gorey, Edward 1925- DLB-61

Görres, Joseph 1776-1848 ....DLB-90

Gosse, Edmund 1849-1928 ....DLB-57

Gotlieb, Phyllis 1926- DLB-88

Gould, Wallace 1882-1940 ....DLB-54

Goyen, William 1915-1983..........................DLB-2; Y-83

Gracq, Julien 1910- DLB-83

Grady, Henry W. 1850-1889 ....DLB-23

Graf, Oskar Maria 1894-1967............................DLB-56

Graham, George Rex 1813-1894 ....DLB-73

Graham, Gwethalyn 1913-1965 ....DLB-88

Graham, Lorenz 1902-1989 ....DLB-76

Graham, Shirley 1896-1977 ....DLB-76

Graham, W. S. 1918- DLB-20

Graham, William H. [publishing house] DLB-49

Graham, Winston 1910- DLB-77

Grahame, Kenneth 1859-1932............................DLB-34

Grainger, Martin Allerdale
        1874-1941 ....DLB-92

Gramatky, Hardie 1907-1979 ....DLB-22

Grandbois, Alain 1900-1975 ....DLB-92

Granich, Irwin (see Gold, Michael)

Grant, George 1918-1988....................................DLB-88

Grant, Harry J. 1881-1963 ....DLB-29

Grant, James Edward 1905-1966 ....DLB-26

Grass, Günter 1927- DLB-75

Grasty, Charles H. 1863-1924 ....DLB-25

Grau, Shirley Ann 1929- DLB-2

Graves, John 1920- Y-83

Graves, Richard 1715-1804 ....DLB-39

Graves, Robert 1895-1985 ....DLB-20; Y-85

Gray, Asa 1810-1888 ....DLB-1

Gray, David 1838-1861 ....DLB-32

Gray, Simon 1936- DLB-13

Grayson, William J. 1788-1863 ....DLB-3, 64

The Great War and the Theater, 1914-1918
 [Great Britain] DLB-10

Greeley, Horace 1811-1872 ....DLB-3, 43

Green, Adolph (see Comden, Betty)

Green, Duff 1791-1875 ....DLB-43

Green, Gerald 1922- DLB-28

Green, Henry 1905-1973 ....DLB-15

Green, Jonas 1712-1767 ....DLB-31

Green, Joseph 1706-1780 ....DLB-31

Green, Julien 1900- DLB-4, 72

Green, Paul 1894-1981 ....DLB-7, 9; Y-81

Green, T. and S. [publishing house] DLB-49

Green, Timothy [publishing house] DLB-49

Greenberg: Publisher DLB-46

Green Tiger Press DLB-46

Greene, Asa 1789-1838 ....DLB-11

Greene, Benjamin H. [publishing house] DLB-49

Greene, Graham 1904- DLB-13, 15, 77; Y-85

Greene, Robert 1558-1592 ....DLB-62

Greenhow, Robert 1800-1854 ....DLB-30

Greenough, Horatio 1805-1852 ....DLB-1

Greenwell, Dora 1821-1882 ....DLB-35

Greenwillow Books DLB-46

Greenwood, Grace (see Lippincott, Sara Jane Clarke)

Greenwood, Walter 1903-1974 ....DLB-10

Greer, Ben 1948- DLB-6

Greg, W. R. 1809-1881 ....DLB-55

Gregg Press DLB-46

Persse, Isabella Augusta,

Lady Gregory 1852-1932 ....DLB-10

Gregory, Horace 1898-1982 ....DLB-48

Grenfell, Wilfred Thomason
 1865-1940 ....DLB-92

Greve, Felix Paul (see Grove, Frederick Philip)

Greville, Fulke, First Lord Brooke
 1554-1628 ....DLB-62

Grey, Zane 1872-1939 ....DLB-9

Grey Owl 1888-1938 ....DLB-92

Grier, Eldon 1917- DLB-88

Grieve, C. M. (see MacDiarmid, Hugh)

Griffith, Elizabeth 1727?-1793 ....DLB-39, 89

Griffiths, Trevor 1935- DLB-13

Griggs, S. C., and Company DLB-49

Griggs, Sutton Elbert 1872-1930 ....DLB-50

Grignon, Claude-Henri 1894-1976 ....DLB-68

Grigson, Geoffrey 1905- DLB-27

Grimké, Angelina Weld 1880-1958 ....DLB-50, 54

Grimm, Hans 1875-1959 ....DLB-66

Grimm, Jacob 1785-1863 ....DLB-90

Grimm, Wilhelm 1786-1859 ....DLB-90

Griswold, Rufus Wilmot 1815-1857 ......DLB-3, 59

Gross, Milt 1895-1953 ....DLB-11

Grosset and Dunlap DLB-49

Grossman Publishers DLB-46

Grosvenor, Gilbert H. 1875-1966 ....DLB-91

Groulx, Lionel 1878-1967 ....DLB-68

Grove, Frederick Philip
 1879-1949 ....DLB-92

Grove Press DLB-46

Grubb, Davis 1919-1980 ....DLB-6

Gruelle, Johnny 1880-1938 ....DLB-22

Guare, John 1938- DLB-7

Guest, Barbara 1920- DLB-5

Guèvremont, Germaine 1893-1968 ....DLB-68

Guilloux, Louis 1899-1980 ....DLB-72

Guiney, Louise Imogen 1861-1920 ....DLB-54

Guiterman, Arthur 1871-1943 ....DLB-11

Günderrode, Caroline von
 1780-1806 ....DLB-90

Gunn, Bill 1934-1989 ....DLB-38

Gunn, James E. 1923- DLB-8

Gunn, Neil M. 1891-1973 ....DLB-15

Gunn, Thom 1929- DLB-27

Gunnars, Kristjana 1948- DLB-60

Gurik, Robert 1932- DLB-60

Gustafson, Ralph 1909- DLB-88

Gütersloh, Albert Paris 1887-1973 ....DLB-81

Guthrie, A. B., Jr. 1901- DLB-6

Guthrie, Ramon 1896-1973.................................DLB-4

The Guthrie Theater..DLB-7

Guy, Ray 1939- DLB-60

Guy, Rosa 1925- DLB-33

Gwynne, Erskine 1898-1948 ....DLB-4

Gysin, Brion 1916- DLB-16

H

H. D. (see Doolittle, Hilda)

Hackett, Albert (see Goodrich, Frances)

Hadden, Briton 1898-1929 ....DLB-91

Hagelstange, Rudolf 1912-1984..........................DLB-69

Haggard, H. Rider 1856-1925 ....DLB-70

Haig-Brown, Roderick 1908-1976 ....DLB-88

Hailey, Arthur 1920- DLB-88; Y-82

Haines, John 1924- DLB-5

Hake, Thomas Gordon 1809-1895 ....DLB-32

Haldeman, Joe 1943- DLB-8

Haldeman-Julius Company....................................DLB-46

Hale, E. J., and Son...DLB-49

Hale, Edward Everett 1822-1909 ....DLB-1, 42, 74

Hale, Leo Thomas (see Ebon)

Hale, Lucretia Peabody 1820-1900.....................DLB-42

Hale, Nancy 1908-1988 ....DLB-86; Y-80, 88

Hale, Sarah Josepha (Buell) 1788-1879 ...DLB-1, 42, 73

Haley, Alex 1921- DLB-38

Haliburton, Thomas Chandler 1796-1865.........DLB-11

Hall, Donald 1928- DLB-5

Hall, James 1793-1868 ....DLB-73, 74

Hall, Samuel [publishing house].........................DLB-49

Hallam, Arthur Henry 1811-1833......................DLB-32

Halleck, Fitz-Greene 1790-1867 ....DLB-3

Hallmark Editions DLB-46

Halper, Albert 1904-1984....................................DLB-9

Halstead, Murat 1829-1908.................................DLB-23

Hamburger, Michael 1924- DLB-27

Hamilton, Alexander 1712-1756 ....DLB-31

Hamilton, Alexander 1755?-1804........................DLB-37

Hamilton, Cicely 1872-1952................................DLB-10

Hamilton, Edmond 1904-1977 ....DLB-8

Hamilton, Gail (see Corcoran, Barbara)

Hamilton, Ian 1938- DLB-40

Hamilton, Patrick 1904-1962..............................DLB-10

Hamilton, Virginia 1936- DLB-33, 52

Hammett, Dashiell 1894-1961 ....DS-6

Hammon, Jupiter 1711-died between
    1790 and 1806....................................DLB-31, 50

Hammond, John ?-1663 ....DLB-24

Hamner, Earl 1923- DLB-6

Hampton, Christopher 1946- DLB-13

Handel-Mazzetti, Enrica von
    1871-1955....................................DLB-81

Handke, Peter 1942- DLB-85

Handlin, Oscar 1915- DLB-17

Hankin, St. John 1869-1909 ....DLB-10

Hanley, Clifford 1922- DLB-14

Hannah, Barry 1942- DLB-6

Hannay, James 1827-1873................................DLB-21

Hansberry, Lorraine 1930-1965 ....DLB-7, 38

Hapgood, Norman 1868-1937..........................DLB-91

Harcourt Brace Jovanovich DLB-46

Hardenberg, Friedrich von (see Novalis)

Hardwick, Elizabeth 1916- DLB-6

Hardy, Thomas 1840-1928..........................DLB-18, 19

Hare, Cyril 1900-1958.......................................DLB-77

Hare, David 1947- DLB-13

Hargrove, Marion 1919- DLB-11

Harlow, Robert 1923- DLB-60

Harness, Charles L. 1915- DLB-8

Harper, Fletcher 1806-1877 ....DLB-79

Harper, Frances Ellen Watkins
    1825-1911 ....DLB-50

Harper, Michael S. 1938- DLB-41

Harper and Brothers...DLB-49

Harris, Benjamin ?-circa 1720 ....DLB-42, 43

Harris, Christie 1907- DLB-88

Harris, George Washington 1814-1869 ....DLB-3, 11

Harris, Joel Chandler 1848-1908 ....
    DLB-11, 23, 42, 78, 91

Harris, Mark 1922- DLB-2; Y-80

Harrison, Charles Yale 1898-1954 ....DLB-68

Harrison, Frederic 1831-1923 ....DLB-57

Harrison, Harry 1925- DLB-8

Harrison, James P., Company DLB-49

Harrison, Jim 1937- Y-82

Harrison, Paul Carter 1936- DLB-38

Harrison, Tony 1937- DLB-40

Harrisse, Henry 1829-1910 ....DLB-47

Harsent, David 1942- DLB-40

Hart, Albert Bushnell 1854-1943 ....DLB-17

Hart, Moss 1904-1961 ....DLB-7

Hart, Oliver 1723-1795 ....DLB-31

Harte, Bret 1836-1902 ....DLB-12, 64, 74, 79

Hartlaub, Felix 1913-1945 ....DLB-56

Hartley, L. P. 1895-1972 ....DLB-15

Hartley, Marsden 1877-1943 ....DLB-54

Härtling, Peter 1933- DLB-75

Hartman, Geoffrey H. 1929- DLB-67

Hartmann, Sadakichi 1867-1944 ....DLB-54

Harvey, Jean-Charles 1891-1967 ....DLB-88

Harwood, Lee 1939- DLB-40

Harwood, Ronald 1934- DLB-13

Haskins, Charles Homer 1870-1937 ....DLB-47

The Hatch-Billops Collection DLB-76

Hauff, Wilhelm 1802-1827 ....DLB-90

A Haughty and Proud Generation (1922),
    by Ford Madox Hueffer DLB-36

Hauptmann, Carl 1858-1921 ....DLB-66

Hauptmann, Gerhart 1862-1946 ....DLB-66

Hauser, Marianne 1910- Y-83

Hawker, Robert Stephen 1803-1875 ....DLB-32

Hawkes, John 1925- DLB-2, 7; Y-80

Hawkins, Walter Everette 1883-? DLB-50

Hawthorne, Nathaniel 1804-1864 ....DLB-1, 74

Hay, John 1838-1905 ....DLB-12, 47

Hayden, Robert 1913-1980 ....DLB-5, 76

Hayes, John Michael 1919- DLB-26

Hayley, William 1745-1820 ....DLB-93

Hayne, Paul Hamilton 1830-1886 ....DLB-3, 64, 79

Haywood, Eliza 1693?-1756 ....DLB-39

Hazard, Willis P. [publishing house] DLB-49

Hazzard, Shirley 1931- Y-82

Headley, Joel T. 1813-1897 ....DLB-30

Heaney, Seamus 1939- DLB-40

Heard, Nathan C. 1936- DLB-33

Hearn, Lafcadio 1850-1904 ....DLB-12, 78

Hearst, William Randolph 1863-1951 ....DLB-25

Heath, Catherine 1924- DLB-14

Heath-Stubbs, John 1918- DLB-27

Hebel, Johann Peter 1760-1826 ....DLB-90

Hébert, Anne 1916- DLB-68

Hébert, Jacques 1923- DLB-53

Hecht, Anthony 1923- DLB-5

Hecht, Ben 1894-1964 ....DLB-7, 9, 25, 26, 28, 86

Hecker, Isaac Thomas 1819-1888 ....DLB-1

Hedge, Frederic Henry 1805-1890 ....DLB-1, 59

Hegel, Georg Wilhelm Friedrich
    1770-1831 ....DLB-90

Heidish, Marcy 1947- Y-82

Heine, Heinrich 1797-1856 ....DLB-90

Heinlein, Robert A. 1907- DLB-8

Heidsenbüttel 1921- DLB-75

Heinrich, Willi 1920- DLB-75

Heinse, Wilhelm 1746-1803 ....DLB-94

Heller, Joseph 1923- DLB-2, 28; Y-80

Hellman, Lillian 1906-1984 ....DLB-7; Y-84

Helprin, Mark 1947- Y-85

Helwig, David 1938- DLB-60

Hemingway, Ernest 1899-1961
    ....DLB-4, 9; Y-81, 87; DS-1

Hemingway: Twenty-Five Years Later Y-85

Hémon, Louis 1880-1913 ....DLB-92

Hemphill, Paul 1936- Y-87

Hénault, Gilles 1920- DLB-88

Henchman, Daniel 1689-1761 ....DLB-24

Henderson, Alice Corbin 1881-1949 ....DLB-54

Henderson, David 1942- DLB-41

Henderson, George Wylie 1904- DLB-51

Henderson, Zenna 1917- DLB-8

Henisch, Peter 1943- DLB-85

Henley, Beth 1952- Y-86

Henley, William Ernest 1849-1903.....................DLB-19

Henry, Buck 1930- DLB-26

Henry, Marguerite 1902- DLB-22

Henry, Robert Selph 1889-1970.....................DLB-17

Henry, Will (see Allen, Henry W.)

Henschke, Alfred (see Klabund)

Henty, G. A. 1832-1902 ....DLB-18

Hentz, Caroline Lee 1800-1856.....................DLB-3

Herbert, Alan Patrick 1890-1971 ....DLB-10

Herbert, Frank 1920-1986 ....DLB-8

Herbert, Henry William 1807-1858 ....DLB-3, 73

Herbert, John 1926- DLB-53

Herbst, Josephine 1892-1969............................DLB-9

Herburger, Günter 1932- DLB-75

Hercules, Frank E. M. 1917- DLB-33

Herder, B., Book Company...........................DLB-49

Hergesheimer, Joseph 1880-1954.....................DLB-9

Heritage Press..DLB-46

Hermlin, Stephan 1915- DLB-69

Hernton, Calvin C. 1932- DLB-38

"The Hero as Man of Letters: Johnson,
    Rousseau, Burns" (1841), by Thomas
    Carlyle [excerpt].................................DLB-57

The Hero as Poet. Dante; Shakspeare (1841),
    by Thomas Carlyle DLB-32

Herrick, E. R., and Company DLB-49

Herrick, Robert 1868-1938......................DLB-9, 12, 78

Herrick, William 1915- Y-83

Herrmann, John 1900-1959..............................DLB-4

Hersey, John 1914- DLB-6

Hertel, François 1905-1985..............................DLB-68

Hervé-Bazin, Jean Pierre Marie (see Bazin, Hervé)

Herzog, Emile Salomon Wilhelm (see Maurois, André)

Hesse, Hermann 1877-1962.............................DLB-66

Hewat, Alexander circa 1743-circa 1824...........DLB-30

Hewitt, John 1907- DLB-27

Hewlett, Maurice 1861-1923............................DLB-34

Heyen, William 1940- DLB-5

Heyer, Georgette 1902-1974............................DLB-77

Heym, Stefan 1913- DLB-69

Heyward, Dorothy 1890-1961 and
    Heyward, DuBose 1885-1940 ....DLB-7

Heyward, DuBose 1885-1940...................DLB-7, 9, 45

Heywood, Thomas 1573 or 1574-1641 ....DLB-62

Hickman, William Albert
    1877-1957 ....DLB-92

Hiebert, Paul 1892-1987 ....DLB-68

Higgins, Aidan 1927- DLB-14

Higgins, Colin 1941-1988 ....DLB-26

Higgins, George V. 1939- DLB-2; Y-81

Higginson, Thomas Wentworth
    1823-1911 ....DLB-1, 64

Highwater, Jamake 1942?- DLB-52; Y-85

Hildesheimer, Wolfgang 1916- DLB-69

Hildreth, Richard 1807-1865 ....DLB-1, 30, 59

Hill, Aaron 1685-1750 ....DLB-84

Hill, Geoffrey 1932- DLB-40

Hill, George M., Company...............................DLB-49

Hill, "Sir" John 1714?-1775 ....DLB-39

Hill, Lawrence, and Company, Publishers.........DLB-46

Hill, Leslie 1880-1960 ....DLB-51

Hill, Susan 1942- DLB-14

Hill, Walter 1942- DLB-44

Hill and Wang DLB-46

Hilliard, Gray and Company DLB-49

Hillyer, Robert 1895-1961 ....DLB-54

Hilton, James 1900-1954..........................DLB-34, 77

Hilton and Company......................................DLB-49

Himes, Chester 1909-1984.........................DLB-2, 76

Hine, Daryl 1936- DLB-60

Hinojosa-Smith, Rolando 1929- DLB-82

The History of the Adventures of Joseph Andrews
    (1742), by Henry Fielding [excerpt]............DLB-39

Hirsch, E. D., Jr. 1928- DLB-67

Hoagland, Edward 1932- DLB-6

Hoagland, Everett H. III 1942- DLB-41

Hoban, Russell 1925- DLB-52

Hobsbaum, Philip 1932- DLB-40

Hobson, Laura Z. 1900- DLB-28

Hochman, Sandra 1936- DLB-5

Hodgins, Jack 1938- DLB-60

Hodgman, Helen 1945- DLB-14

Hodgson, Ralph 1871-1962 ....DLB-19

Hodgson, William Hope 1877-1918..................DLB-70

Hoffenstein, Samuel 1890-1947......................DLB-11

Hoffman, Charles Fenno 1806-1884 ....DLB-3

Hoffman, Daniel 1923- DLB-5

Hoffmann, E. T. A. 1776-1822 ....DLB-90

Hofmann, Michael 1957- DLB-40

Hofmannsthal, Hugo von 1874-1929................DLB-81

Hofstadter, Richard 1916-1970 ....DLB-17

Hogan, Desmond 1950- DLB-14

Hogan and Thompson.....................................DLB-49

Hogg, James 1770-1835 ....DLB-93

Hohl, Ludwig 1904-1980 ....DLB-56

Holbrook, David 1923- DLB-14, 40

Holcroft, Thomas 1745-1809......................DLB-39, 89

Holden, Molly 1927-1981 ....DLB-40

Hölderlin, Friedrich 1770-1843 ....DLB-90

Holiday House DLB-46

Holland, Norman N. 1927- DLB-67

Hollander, John 1929- DLB-5

Holley, Marietta 1836-1926 ....DLB-11

Hollingsworth, Margaret 1940- DLB-60

Hollo, Anselm 1934- DLB-40

Holloway, John 1920- DLB-27

Holloway House Publishing Company DLB-46

Holme, Constance 1880-1955 ....DLB-34

Holmes, Oliver Wendell 1809-1894...................DLB-1

Holmes, John Clellon 1926-1988 ....DLB-16

Holst, Hermann E. von 1841-1904....................DLB-47

Holt, Henry, and Company DLB-49

Holt, John 1721-1784....................................DLB-43

Holt, Rinehart and Winston.............................DLB-46

Hölty, Ludwig Christoph Heinrich
        1748-1776 ....DLB-94

Holthusen, Hans Egon 1913- DLB-69

Home, Henry, Lord Kames 1696-1782..............DLB-31

Home, John 1722-1808..................................DLB-84

Home Publishing Company DLB-49

Home, William Douglas 1912- DLB-13

Homes, Geoffrey (see Mainwaring, Daniel)

Honig, Edwin 1919- DLB-5

Hood, Hugh 1928- DLB-53

Hooker, Jeremy 1941- DLB-40

Hooker, Thomas 1586-1647 ....DLB-24

Hooper, Johnson Jones 1815-1862 ....DLB-3, 11

Hopkins, Gerard Manley 1844-1889.........DLB-35, 57

Hopkins, John H., and Son DLB-46

Hopkins, Lemuel 1750-1801..........................DLB-37

Hopkins, Pauline Elizabeth 1859-1930..............DLB-50

Hopkins, Samuel 1721-1803 ....DLB-31

Hopkinson, Francis 1737-1791 ....DLB-31

Horgan, Paul 1903- Y-85

Horizon Press...DLB-46

Horne, Frank 1899-1974................................DLB-51

Horne, Richard Henry (Hengist) 1802
        or 1803-1884..DLB-32

Hornung, E. W. 1866-1921.............................DLB-70

Horovitz, Israel 1939- DLB-7

Horton, George Moses 1797?-1883?.................DLB-50

Horváth, Ödön von 1901-1938.........................DLB-85

Horwood, Harold 1923- DLB-60

Hosford, E. and E. [publishing house]..............DLB-49

Hotchkiss and Company DLB-49

Hough, Emerson 1857-1923..............................DLB-9

Houghton Mifflin Company DLB-49

Houghton, Stanley 1881-1913 ....DLB-10

Household, Geoffrey 1900-1988........................DLB-87

Housman, A. E. 1859-1936..............................DLB-19

Housman, Laurence 1865-1959.........................DLB-10

Houwald, Ernst von 1778-1845 ....DLB-90

Hovey, Richard 1864-1900................................DLB-54

Howard, Maureen 1930- Y-83

Howard, Richard 1929- DLB-5

Howard, Roy W. 1883-1964..............................DLB-29

Howard, Sidney 1891-1939.........................DLB-7, 26

Howe, E. W. 1853-1937 ....DLB-12, 25

Howe, Henry 1816-1893 ....DLB-30

Howe, Irving 1920- DLB-67

Howe, Julia Ward 1819-1910...............................DLB-1

Howell, Clark, Sr. 1863-1936..........................DLB-25

Howell, Evan P. 1839-1905.............................DLB-23

Howell, Soskin and Company.........................DLB-46

Howells, William Dean 1837-1920...DLB-12, 64, 74, 79

Hoyem, Andrew 1935- DLB-5

de Hoyos, Angela 1940- DLB-82

Hoyt, Henry [publishing house] DLB-49

Hubbard, Elbert 1856-1915 ....DLB-91

Hubbard, Kin 1868-1930 ....DLB-11

Hubbard, William circa 1621-1704....................DLB-24

Huber, Therese 1764-1829..............................DLB-90

Huch, Friedrich 1873-1913.............................DLB-66

Huch, Ricarda 1864-1947 ....DLB-66

Huck at 100: How Old Is
     Huckleberry Finn?....................................Y-85

Hudson, Henry Norman 1814-1886 ....DLB-64

Hudson and Goodwin..DLB-49

Huebsch, B. W. [publishing house] DLB-46

Hughes, David 1930- DLB-14

Hughes, John 1677-1720 ....DLB-84

Hughes, Langston 1902-1967 ....DLB-4, 7, 48, 51, 86

Hughes, Richard 1900-1976 ....DLB-15

Hughes, Ted 1930- DLB-40

Hughes, Thomas 1822-1896.............................DLB-18

Hugo, Richard 1923-1982................................DLB-5

Hugo Awards and Nebula Awards.....................DLB-8

Hull, Richard 1896-1973.................................DLB-77

Hulme, T. E. 1883-1917 ....DLB-19

Humboldt, Alexander von 1769-1859...............DLB-90

Humboldt, Wilhelm von 1767-1835 ....DLB-90

Hume, Fergus 1859-1932.................................DLB-70

Humorous Book Illustration.............................DLB-11

Humphrey, William 1924- DLB-6

Humphreys, David 1752-1818..........................DLB-37

Humphreys, Emyr 1919- DLB-15

Huncke, Herbert 1915- DLB-16

Huneker, James Gibbons 1857-1921 ....DLB-71

Hunt, Irene 1907- DLB-52

Hunt, William Gibbes 1791-1833 ....DLB-73

Hunter, Evan 1926- Y-82

Hunter, Jim 1939- DLB-14

Hunter, Kristin 1931- DLB-33

Hunter, N. C. 1908-1971 ....DLB-10

Hurd and Houghton..DLB-49

Hurst and Company..DLB-49

Hurst, Fannie 1889-1968................................DLB-86

Hurston, Zora Neale 1901?-1960 ....DLB-51, 86

Huston, John 1906- DLB-26

Hutcheson, Francis 1694-1746.........................DLB-31

Hutchinson, Thomas 1711-1780 ....DLB-30, 31

Hutton, Richard Holt 1826-1897......................DLB-57

Huxley, Aldous 1894-1963...............................DLB-36

Huxley, Elspeth Josceline 1907- DLB-77

Huxley, T. H. 1825-1895................................DLB-57

Hyman, Trina Schart 1939- DLB-61

I

The Iconography of Science-Fiction Art..............DLB-8

Iffland, August Wilhelm 1759-1814...................DLB-94

Ignatow, David 1914- DLB-5

Iles, Francis (see Berkeley, Anthony)

Imbs, Bravig 1904-1946 ....DLB-4

Inchbald, Elizabeth 1753-1821 ....DLB-39, 89

Inge, William 1913-1973..................................DLB-7

Ingelow, Jean 1820-1897..................................DLB-35

The Ingersoll Prizes Y-84

Ingraham, Joseph Holt 1809-1860 ....DLB-3

Inman, John 1805-1850 ....DLB-73

Innerhofer, Franz 1944- DLB-85

Innis, Harold Adams 1894-1952 ....DLB-88

Innis, Mary Quayle 1899-1972 ....DLB-88

International Publishers Company DLB-46

An Interview with Peter S. Prescott.........................Y-86

An Interview with Tom Jenks.................................Y-86

Introduction to Paul Laurence Dunbar,
     Lyrics of Lowly Life (1896),
     by William Dean Howells...........................DLB-50

Introductory Essay: *Letters of Percy Bysshe*
     Shelley (1852), by Robert Browning DLB-32

Introductory Letters from the Second Edition
     of *Pamela* (1741), by Samuel Richardson.....DLB-39

Irving, John 1942- DLB-6; Y-82

Irving, Washington
    1783-1859 ....DLB-3, 11, 30, 59, 73, 74

Irwin, Grace 1907- DLB-68

Irwin, Will 1873-1948 ....DLB-25

Isherwood, Christopher 1904-1986..........DLB-15; Y-86

The Island Trees Case: A Symposium on School
        Library Censorship
    An Interview with Judith Krug
    An Interview with Phyllis Schlafly
    An Interview with Edward B. Jenkinson
    An Interview with Lamarr Mooneyham
    An Interview with Harriet Bernstein Y-82

Ivers, M. J., and Company.................................DLB-49

J

Jackmon, Marvin E. (see Marvin X)

Jackson, Angela 1951- DLB-41

Jackson, Helen Hunt 1830-1885 ....DLB-42, 47

Jackson, Laura Riding 1901- DLB-48

Jackson, Shirley 1919-1965 ....DLB-6

Jacob, Piers Anthony Dillingham (see Anthony,
    Piers)

Jacobi, Friedrich Heinrich 1743-1819 ....DLB-94

Jacobs, George W., and Company DLB-49

Jacobson, Dan 1929- DLB-14

Jahnn, Hans Henny 1894-1959 ....DLB-56

Jakes, John 1932- Y-83

James, Henry 1843-1916 ....DLB-12, 71, 74

James, John circa 1633-1729.............................DLB-24

James Joyce Centenary: Dublin, 1982 ....Y-82

James Joyce Conference Y-85

James, P. D. 1920- DLB-87

James, U. P. [publishing house]..........................DLB-49

Jameson, Fredric 1934- DLB-67

Jameson, J. Franklin 1859-1937 ....DLB-17

Jameson, Storm 1891-1986 ....DLB-36

Jarrell, Randall 1914-1965............................DLB-48, 52

Jasmin, Claude 1930- DLB-60

Jay, John 1745-1829 ....DLB-31

Jeffers, Lance 1919-1985 ....DLB-41

Jeffers, Robinson 1887-1962...............................DLB-45

Jefferson, Thomas 1743-1826............................DLB-31

Jelinek, Elfriede 1946- DLB-85

Jellicoe, Ann 1927- DLB-13

Jenkins, Robin 1912- DLB-14

Jenkins, William Fitzgerald (see Leinster, Murray)

Jennings, Elizabeth 1926- DLB-27

Jens, Walter 1923- DLB-69

Jensen, Merrill 1905-1980...................................DLB-17

Jephson, Robert 1736-1803................................DLB-89

Jerome, Jerome K. 1859-1927 ....DLB-10, 34

Jesse, F. Tennyson 1888-1958............................DLB-77

Jewett, John P., and Company...........................DLB-49

Jewett, Sarah Orne 1849-1909......................DLB-12, 74

The Jewish Publication Society DLB-49

Jewsbury, Geraldine 1812-1880 ....DLB-21

Joans, Ted 1928- DLB-16, 41

John Edward Bruce: Three Documents.............DLB-50

John O'Hara's Pottsville Journalism........................Y-88

John Steinbeck Research Center.............................Y-85

John Webster: The Melbourne Manuscript............Y-86

Johnson, B. S. 1933-1973.............................DLB-14, 40

Johnson, Benjamin [publishing house]..............DLB-49

Johnson, Benjamin, Jacob, and
    Robert [publishing house]...........................DLB-49

Johnson, Charles 1679-1748 ....DLB-84

Johnson, Charles R. 1948- DLB-33

Johnson, Charles S. 1893-1956.....................DLB-51, 91

Johnson, Diane 1934- Y-80

Johnson, Edward 1598-1672.............................DLB-24

Johnson, Fenton 1888-1958 ....DLB-45, 50

Johnson, Georgia Douglas 1886-1966 ....DLB-51

Johnson, Gerald W. 1890-1980..........................DLB-29

Johnson, Helene 1907- DLB-51

Johnson, Jacob, and Company............................DLB-49

Johnson, James Weldon 1871-1938 ....DLB-51

Johnson, Lionel 1867-1902 ....DLB-19

Johnson, Nunnally 1897-1977 ....DLB-26

Johnson, Owen 1878-1952 ....Y-87

Johnson, Pamela Hansford 1912- DLB-15

Johnson, Pauline 1861-1913 ....DLB-92

Johnson, Samuel 1696-1772..............................DLB-24

Johnson, Samuel 1709-1784..............................DLB-39

Johnson, Samuel 1822-1882...............................DLB-1

Johnson, Uwe 1934-1984 ....DLB-75

Johnston, Annie Fellows 1863-1931..................DLB-42

Johnston, Basil H. 1929- DLB-60

Johnston, Denis 1901-1984 ....DLB-10

Johnston, George 1913- DLB-88

Johnston, Jennifer 1930- DLB-14

Johnston, Mary 1870-1936..............................DLB-9

Johnston, Richard Malcolm 1822-1898 ....DLB-74

Johnstone, Charles 1719?-1800?......................DLB-39

Jolas, Eugene 1894-1952...............................DLB-4, 45

Jones, Alice C. 1853-1933 ....DLB-92

Jones, Charles C., Jr. 1831-1893......................DLB-30

Jones, D. G. 1929- DLB-53

Jones, David 1895-1974...................................DLB-20

Jones, Ebenezer 1820-1860 ....DLB-32

Jones, Ernest 1819-1868.................................DLB-32

Jones, Gayl 1949- DLB-33

Jones, Glyn 1905- DLB-15

Jones, Gwyn 1907- DLB-15

Jones, Henry Arthur 1851-1929.......................DLB-10

Jones, Hugh circa 1692-1760...........................DLB-24

Jones, James 1921-1977..................................DLB-2

Jones, LeRoi (see Baraka, Amiri)

Jones, Lewis 1897-1939 ....DLB-15

Jones, Major Joseph (see Thompson, William
    Tappan)

Jones, Preston 1936-1979................................DLB-7

Jones, William Alfred 1817-1900 ....DLB-59

Jones's Publishing House DLB-49

Jong, Erica 1942- DLB-2, 5, 28

Jonke, Gert F. 1946- DLB-85

Jonson, Ben 1572?-1637..................................DLB-62

Jordan, June 1936- DLB-38

Joseph, Jenny 1932- DLB-40

Josephson, Matthew 1899-1978 ....DLB-4

Josiah Allen's Wife (see Holley, Marietta)

Josipovici, Gabriel 1940- DLB-14

Josselyn, John ?-1675.....................................DLB-24

Joudry, Patricia 1921- DLB-88

Joyaux, Philippe (see Sollers, Philippe)

Joyce, Adrien (see Eastman, Carol)

Joyce, James 1882-1941 ....DLB-10, 19, 36

Judd, Orange, Publishing Company...................DLB-49

Judd, Sylvester 1813-1853................................DLB-1

June, Jennie (see Croly, Jane Cunningham)

Jünger, Ernst 1895- DLB-56

Jung-Stilling, Johann Heinrich
    1740-1817 ....DLB-94

Justice, Donald 1925- Y-83

K

Kacew, Romain (see Gary, Romain)

Kafka, Franz 1883-1924...................................DLB-81

Kalechofsky, Roberta 1931- DLB-28

Kaler, James Otis 1848-1912............................DLB-12

Kandel, Lenore 1932- DLB-16

Kanin, Garson 1912- DLB-7

Kant, Hermann 1926- DLB-75

Kant, Immanuel 1724-1804 ....DLB-94

Kantor, Mackinlay 1904-1977...........................DLB-9

Kaplan, Johanna 1942- DLB-28

Kasack, Hermann 1896-1966............................DLB-69

Kaschnitz, Marie Luise 1901-1974.....................DLB-69

Kästner, Erich 1899-1974................................DLB-56

Kattan, Naim 1928- DLB-53

Katz, Steve 1935- Y-83

Kauffman, Janet 1945- Y-86

Kaufman, Bob 1925- DLB-16, 41

Kaufman, George S. 1889-1961.........................DLB-7

Kavanagh, Patrick 1904-1967......................DLB-15, 20

Kavanagh, P. J. 1931- DLB-40

Kaye-Smith, Sheila 1887-1956 ....DLB-36

Kazin, Alfred 1915- DLB-67

Keane, John B. 1928- DLB-13

Keating, H. R. F. 1926- DLB-87

Keats, Ezra Jack 1916-1983.............................DLB-61

Keble, John 1792-1866...............................DLB-32, 55

Keeble, John 1944- Y-83

Keeffe, Barrie 1945- DLB-13

Keeley, James 1867-1934 ....DLB-25

W. B. Keen, Cooke and Company.....................DLB-49

Keillor, Garrison 1942- Y-87

Keith, Marian 1874?-1961 ....DLB-92

Keller, Gary D. 1943- DLB-82

Kelley, Edith Summers 1884-1956 ....DLB-9

Kelley, William Melvin 1937- DLB-33

Kellogg, Ansel Nash 1832-1886.......................DLB-23

Kellogg, Steven 1941- DLB-61

Kelly, George 1887-1974..............................DLB-7

Kelly, Hugh 1739-1777 ....DLB-89

Kelly, Piet and Company DLB-49

Kelly, Robert 1935- DLB-5

Kemble, Fanny 1809-1893 ....DLB-32

Kemelman, Harry 1908- DLB-28

Kempowski, Walter 1929- DLB-75

Kendall, Claude [publishing company] DLB-46

Kendell, George 1809-1867 ....DLB-43

Kenedy, P. J., and Sons...............................DLB-49

Kennedy, Adrienne 1931- DLB-38

Kennedy, John Pendleton 1795-1870..................DLB-3

Kennedy, Leo 1907- DLB-88

Kennedy, Margaret 1896-1967 ....DLB-36

Kennedy, William 1928- Y-85

Kennedy, X. J. 1929- DLB-5

Kennelly, Brendan 1936- DLB-40

Kenner, Hugh 1923- DLB-67

Kennerley, Mitchell [publishing house]..............DLB-46

Kent, Frank R. 1877-1958............................DLB-29

Keppler and Schwartzmann...........................DLB-49

Kerner, Justinus 1776-1862 ....DLB-90

Kerouac, Jack 1922-1969.....................DLB-2, 16; DS-3

Kerouac, Jan 1952- DLB-16

Kerr, Charles H., and Company.......................DLB-49

Kerr, Orpheus C. (see Newell, Robert Henry)

Kesey, Ken 1935- DLB-2, 16

Kessel, Joseph 1898-1979.............................DLB-72

Kessel, Martin 1901- DLB-56

Kesten, Hermann 1900- DLB-56

Keun, Irmgard 1905-1982 ....DLB-69

Key and Biddle...DLB-49

Keyserling, Eduard von 1855-1918 ....DLB-66

Kiely, Benedict 1919- DLB-15

Kiggins and Kellogg....................................DLB-49

Kiley, Jed 1889-1962 ....DLB-4

Killens, John Oliver 1916- DLB-33

Killigrew, Thomas 1612-1683.........................DLB-58

Kilmer, Joyce 1886-1918 ....DLB-45

King, Clarence 1842-1901 ....DLB-12

King, Florence 1936 ....Y-85

King, Francis 1923- DLB-15

King, Grace 1852-1932 ....DLB-12, 78

King, Solomon [publishing house]....................DLB-49

King, Stephen 1947- Y-80

King, Woodie, Jr. 1937- DLB-38

Kinglake, Alexander William 1809-1891...........DLB-55

Kingsley, Charles 1819-1875.....................DLB-21, 32

Kingsley, Henry 1830-1876...........................DLB-21

Kingsley, Sidney 1906- DLB-7

Kingston, Maxine Hong 1940- Y-80

Kinnell, Galway 1927- DLB-5; Y-87

Kinsella, Thomas 1928- DLB-27

Kipling, Rudyard 1865-1936 ....DLB-19, 34

Kirk, John Foster 1824-1904..........................DLB-79

Kirkconnell, Watson 1895-1977.......................DLB-68

Kirkland, Caroline M. 1801-1864 ....DLB-3, 73, 74

Kirkland, Joseph 1830-1893 ....DLB-12

Kirkup, James 1918- DLB-27

Kirouac, Conrad (see Marie-Victorin, Frère)

Kirsch, Sarah 1935- DLB-75

Kirst, Hans Hellmut 1914-1989......................DLB-69

Kitchin, C. H. B. 1895-1967 ....DLB-77

Kizer, Carolyn 1925- DLB-5

Klabund 1890-1928 ....DLB-66

Klappert, Peter 1942- DLB-5

Klass, Philip (see Tenn, William)

Klein, A. M. 1909-1972...............................DLB-68

Kleist, Heinrich von 1777-1811 ....DLB-90

Klinger, Friedrich Maximilian
    1752-1831 ....DLB-94

Kluge, Alexander 1932- DLB-75

Knapp, Joseph Palmer 1864-1951 ....DLB-91

Knapp, Samuel Lorenzo 1783-1838 ....DLB-59

Knickerbocker, Diedrich (see Irving, Washington)

Knigge, Adolph Franz Friedrich Ludwig,
    Freiherr von 1752-1796 ....DLB-94

Knight, Damon 1922- DLB-8

Knight, Etheridge 1931- DLB-41

Knight, John S. 1894-1981.....................DLB-29

Knight, Sarah Kemble 1666-1727.................DLB-24

Knister, Raymond 1899-1932 ....DLB-68

Knoblock, Edward 1874-1945 ....DLB-10

Knopf, Alfred A. 1892-1984 ....Y-84

Knopf, Alfred A. [publishing house]................DLB-46

Knowles, John 1926- DLB-6

Knox, Frank 1874-1944 ....DLB-29

Knox, John Armoy 1850-1906.....................DLB-23

Knox, Ronald Arbuthnott 1888-1957................DLB-77

Kober, Arthur 1900-1975 ....DLB-11

Koch, Howard 1902- DLB-26

Koch, Kenneth 1925- DLB-5

Koenigsberg, Moses 1879-1945 ....DLB-25

Koeppen, Wolfgang 1906- DLB-69

Koestler, Arthur 1905-1983 ....Y-83

Kolb, Annette 1870-1967 ....DLB-66

Kolbenheyer, Erwin Guido 1878-1962...............DLB-66

Kolleritsch, Alfred 1931- DLB-85

Kolodny, Annette 1941- DLB-67

Komroff, Manuel 1890-1974 ....DLB-4

Konigsburg, E. L. 1930- DLB-52

Kopit, Arthur 1937- DLB-7

Kops, Bernard 1926?- DLB-13

Kornbluth, C. M. 1923-1958.....................DLB-8

Körner, Theodor 1791-1813 ....DLB-90

Kosinski, Jerzy 1933- DLB-2; Y-82

Kotzebue, August von 1761-1819.................DLB-94

Kraf, Elaine 1946- Y-81

Krasna, Norman 1909-1984 ....DLB-26

Krauss, Ruth 1911- DLB-52

Kreisel, Henry 1922- DLB-88

Kreuder, Ernst 1903-1972 ....DLB-69

Kreymborg, Alfred 1883-1966 ....DLB-4, 54

Krieger, Murray 1923- DLB-67

Krim, Seymour 1922- DLB-16

Krock, Arthur 1886-1974 ....DLB-29

Kroetsch, Robert 1927- DLB-53

Krutch, Joseph Wood 1893-1970.................DLB-63

Kubin, Alfred 1877-1959 ....DLB-81

Kubrick, Stanley 1928- DLB-26

Kumin, Maxine 1925- DLB-5

Kunnert, Günter 1929- DLB-75

Kunitz, Stanley 1905- DLB-48

Kunjufu, Johari M. (see Amini, Johari M.)

Kunze, Reiner 1933- DLB-75

Kupferberg, Tuli 1923- DLB-16

Kurz, Isolde 1853-1944 ....DLB-66

Kusenberg, Kurt 1904-1983 ....DLB-69

Kuttner, Henry 1915-1958.....................DLB-8

Kyd, Thomas 1558-1594 ....DLB-62

Kyger, Joanne 1934- DLB-16

Kyne, Peter B. 1880-1957 ....DLB-78

L

Laberge, Albert 1871-1960 ....DLB-68

Laberge, Marie 1950- DLB-60

Lacretelle, Jacques de 1888-1985..................DLB-65

Ladd, Joseph Brown 1764-1786.....................DLB-37

La Farge, Oliver 1901-1963.....................DLB-9

Lafferty, R. A. 1914- DLB-8

Lahaise, Guillaume (see Delahaye, Guy)

Laird, Carobeth 1895- Y-82

Laird and Lee DLB-49

Lalonde, Michèle 1937- DLB-60

Lamantia, Philip 1927- DLB-16

Lamb, Charles 1775-1834 ....DLB-93

Lambert, Betty 1933-1983 ....DLB-60

L'Amour, Louis 1908?- Y-80

Lampman, Archibald 1861-1899 ....DLB-92

Lamson, Wolffe and Company DLB-49

Lancer Books DLB-46

Landesman, Jay 1919- and
    Landesman, Fran 1927- DLB-16

Landor, William Savage 1775-1864....................DLB-93

Landry, Napoléon-P. 1884-1956.......................DLB-92

Lane, Charles 1800-1870.................................DLB-1

The John Lane Company DLB-49

Lane, Laurence W. 1890-1967.........................DLB-91

Lane, M. Travis 1934- DLB-60

Lane, Patrick 1939- DLB-53

Lane, Pinkie Gordon 1923- DLB-41

Laney, Al 1896- DLB-4

Langevin, André 1927- DLB-60

Langgässer, Elisabeth 1899-1950......................DLB-69

Lanham, Edwin 1904-1979 ....DLB-4

Lanier, Sidney 1842-1881 ....DLB-64

Lapointe, Gatien 1931-1983...........................DLB-88

Lapointe, Paul-Marie 1929- DLB-88

Lardner, Ring 1885-1933 ....DLB-11, 25, 86

Lardner, Ring, Jr. 1915- DLB-26

Lardner 100: Ring Lardner
Centennial Symposium...................................Y-85

Larkin, Philip 1922-1985 ....DLB-27

La Roche, Sophie von 1730-1807 ....DLB-94

La Rocque, Gilbert 1943-1984........................DLB-60

Laroque de Roquebrune, Robert
(see Roquebrune, Robert de)

Larrick, Nancy 1910- DLB-61

Larsen, Nella 1893-1964 ....DLB-51

Lasker-Schüler, Else 1869-1945 ....DLB-66

Lasnier, Rina 1915- DLB-88

Lathrop, Dorothy P. 1891-1980 ....DLB-22

Lathrop, George Parsons 1851-1898................DLB-71

Lathrop, John, Jr. 1772-1820 ....DLB-37

Latimore, Jewel Christine McLawler (see Amini,
Johari M.)

Laughlin, James 1914- DLB-48

Laumer, Keith 1925- DLB-8

Laurence, Margaret 1926-1987........................DLB-53

Laurents, Arthur 1918- DLB-26

Laurie, Annie (see Black, Winifred)

Laut, Agnes Christiana 1871-1936 ....DLB-92

Lavin, Mary 1912- DLB-15

Lawless, Anthony (see MacDonald, Philip)

Lawrence, David 1888-1973............................DLB-29

Lawrence, D. H. 1885-1930...................DLB-10, 19, 36

Lawson, John ?-1711 ....DLB-24

Lawson, Robert 1892-1957.............................DLB-22

Lawson, Victor F. 1850-1925 ....DLB-25

Layton, Irving 1912- DLB-88

Lea, Henry Charles 1825-1909.........................DLB-47

Lea, Tom 1907- DLB-6

Leacock, John 1729-1802...............................DLB-31

Leacock, Stephen 1869-1944 ....DLB-92

Lear, Edward 1812-1888................................DLB-32

Leary, Timothy 1920- DLB-16

Leary, W. A., and Company DLB-49

Léautaud, Paul 1872-1956 ....DLB-65

Leavitt and Allen...DLB-49

le Carré, John 1931- DLB-87

Lécavelé, Roland (see Dorgelès, Roland)

Lechlitner, Ruth 1901- DLB-48

Leclerc, Félix 1914- DLB-60

Le Clézio, J. M. G. 1940- DLB-83

Lectures on Rhetoric and Belles Lettres (1783),
by Hugh Blair [excerpts]..............................DLB-31

Leder, Rudolf (see Hermlin, Stephan)

Lederer, Charles 1910-1976............................DLB-26

Ledwidge, Francis 1887-1917 ....DLB-20

Lee, Dennis 1939- DLB-53

Lee, Don L. (see Madhubuti, Haki R.)

Lee, George W. 1894-1976 ....DLB-51

Lee, Harper 1926- DLB-6

Lee, Harriet (1757-1851) and
Lee, Sophia (1750-1824) DLB-39

Lee, Laurie 1914- DLB-27

Lee, Nathaniel circa 1645 - 1692 ....DLB-80

Lee, Vernon 1856-1935..................................DLB-57

Lee and Shepard DLB-49

Le Fanu, Joseph Sheridan 1814-1873 ....DLB-21, 70

Leffland, Ella 1931- Y-84

le Fort, Gertrud von 1876-1971 ....DLB-66

Le Gallienne, Richard 1866-1947 ....DLB-4

Legaré, Hugh Swinton 1797-1843 ....DLB-3, 59, 73

Legaré, James M. 1823-1859 ....DLB-3

Léger, Antoine-J. 1880-1950............................DLB-88

Le Guin, Ursula K. 1929- DLB-8, 52

Lehman, Ernest 1920- DLB-44

Lehmann, John 1907- DLB-27

Lehmann, Rosamond 1901- DLB-15

Lehmann, Wilhelm 1882-1968 ....DLB-56

Leiber, Fritz 1910- DLB-8

Leinster, Murray 1896-1975 ....DLB-8

Leisewitz, Johann Anton 1752-1806.................DLB-94

Leitch, Maurice 1933- DLB-14

Leland, Charles G. 1824-1903 ....DLB-11

Lemelin, Roger 1919- DLB-88

Le Moyne, Jean 1913- DLB-88

L'Engle, Madeleine 1918- DLB-52

Lennart, Isobel 1915-1971 ....DLB-44

Lennox, Charlotte 1729 or 1730-1804 ....DLB-39

Lenski, Lois 1893-1974 ....DLB-22

Lenz, Hermann 1913- DLB-69

Lenz, J. M. R. 1751-1792 ....DLB-94

Lenz, Siegfried 1926- DLB-75

Leonard, Hugh 1926- DLB-13

Leonard, William Ellery 1876-1944 ....DLB-54

LePan, Douglas 1914- DLB-88

Le Queux, William 1864-1927...........................DLB-70

Lerner, Max 1902- DLB-29

Lernet-Holenia, Alexander 1897-1976..............DLB-85

Le Rossignol, James 1866-1969 ....DLB-92

LeSieg, Theo. (see Geisel, Theodor Seuss)

Leslie, Frank 1821-1880................................DLB-43, 79

The Frank Leslie Publishing House DLB-49

Lessing, Bruno 1870-1940................................DLB-28

Lessing, Doris 1919- DLB-15; Y-85

LeSeur, William Dawson 1840-1917.................DLB092

Lettau, Reinhard 1929- DLB-75

Letter to [Samuel] Richardson on *Clarissa*
  (1748), by Henry Fielding...........................DLB-39

Lever, Charles 1806-1872 ....DLB-21

Levertov, Denise 1923- DLB-5

Levi, Peter 1931- DLB-40

Levien, Sonya 1888-1960 ....DLB-44

Levin, Meyer 1905-1981 ....DLB-9, 28; Y-81

Levine, Norman 1923- DLB-88

Levine, Philip 1928- DLB-5

Levy, Benn Wolfe 1900-1973....................DLB-13; Y-81

Lewes, George Henry 1817-1878 ....DLB-55

Lewis, Alfred H. 1857-1914................................DLB-25

Lewis, Alun 1915-1944....................................DLB-20

Lewis, C. Day (see Day Lewis, C.)

Lewis, Charles B. 1842-1924................................DLB-11

Lewis, C. S. 1898-1963 ....DLB-15

Lewis, Henry Clay 1825-1850 ....DLB-3

Lewis, Janet 1899- Y-87

Lewis, Matthew Gregory 1775-1818..................DLB-39

Lewis, Richard circa 1700-1734 ....DLB-24

Lewis, Sinclair 1885-1951 ....DLB-9; DS-1

Lewis, Wyndham 1882-1957....................................DLB-15

Lewisohn, Ludwig 1882-1955....................DLB-4, 9, 28

The Library of America................................DLB-46

The Licensing Act of 1737................................DLB-84

Lichtenberg, Georg Christoph 1742-1799 ....DLB-94

Liebling, A. J. 1904-1963 ....DLB-4

Lieutenant Murray (see Ballou, Maturin Murray)

Lighthall, William Douw 1857-1954..................DLB-92

Lilar, Françoise (see Mallet-Joris, Françoise)

Lillo, George 1691-1739.................................DLB-84

Lilly, Wait and Company DLB-49

Limited Editions Club DLB-46

Lincoln and Edmands DLB-49

Lindsay, Jack 1900- Y-84

Lindsay, Vachel 1879-1931................................DLB-54

Linebarger, Paul Myron Anthony (see
  Smith, Cordwainer)

Link, Arthur S. 1920- DLB-17

Linn, John Blair 1777-1804 ....DLB-37

Linton, Eliza Lynn 1822-1898...........................DLB-18

Linton, William James 1812-1897 ....DLB-32

Lion Books...DLB-46

Lionni, Leo 1910- DLB-61

Lippincott, J. B., Company DLB-49

Lippincott, Sara Jane Clarke 1823-1904............DLB-43

Lippmann, Walter 1889-1974 ....DLB-29

Lipton, Lawrence 1898-1975 ....DLB-16

Literary Documents: William Faulkner
and the People-to-People Program Y-86

Literary Documents II: *Library Journal–*
Statements and Questionnaires from
First Novelists Y-87

Literary Effects of World War II
[British novel] DLB-15

Literary Prizes [British] DLB-15

Literary Research Archives: The Humanities
Research Center, University of Texas...............Y-82

Literary Research Archives II: Berg
Collection of English and American Literature
of the New York Public Library.......................Y-83

Literary Research Archives III:
The Lilly Library Y-84

Literary Research Archives IV:
The John Carter Brown Library.......................Y-85

Literary Research Archives V:
Kent State Special Collections..........................Y-86

Literary Research Archives VI: The Modern
Literary Manuscripts Collection in the
Special Collections of the Washington
University Libraries Y-87

"Literary Style" (1857), by William
Forsyth [excerpt]..DLB-57

Literatura Chicanesca:
The View From Without.................................DLB-82

Literature at Nurse, or Circulating Morals (1885),
by George Moore DLB-18

Littell, Eliakim 1797-1870 ....DLB-79

Littell, Robert S. 1831-1896................................DLB-79

Little, Brown and Company..................................DLB-49

Littlewood, Joan 1914- DLB-13

Lively, Penelope 1933- DLB-14

Livesay, Dorothy 1909- DLB-68

Livesay, Florence Randal
1874-1953 ....DLB-92

Livings, Henry 1929- DLB-13

Livingston, Anne Howe 1763-1841 ....DLB-37

Livingston, Myra Cohn 1926- DLB-61

Livingston, William 1723-1790 ....DLB-31

Lizárraga, Sylvia S. 1925- DLB-82

Llewellyn, Richard 1906-1983 ....DLB-15

Lobel, Arnold 1933- DLB-61

Lochridge, Betsy Hopkins (see Fancher, Betsy)

Locke, David Ross 1833-1888 ....DLB-11, 23

Locke, John 1632-1704...DLB-31

Locke, Richard Adams 1800-1871......................DLB-43

Locker-Lampson, Frederick 1821-1895..............DLB-35

Lockridge, Ross, Jr. 1914-1948............................Y-80

Locrine and *Selimus*...DLB-62

Lodge, David 1935- DLB-14

Lodge, George Cabot 1873-1909........................DLB-54

Lodge, Henry Cabot 1850-1924 ....DLB-47

Loeb, Harold 1891-1974 ....DLB-4

Logan, James 1674-1751 ....DLB-24

Logan, John 1923- DLB-5

Logue, Christopher 1926- DLB-27

London, Jack 1876-1916...........................DLB-8, 12, 78

Long, H., and Brother DLB-49

Long, Haniel 1888-1956 ....DLB-45

Longfellow, Henry Wadsworth 1807-1882 ....DLB-1, 59

Longfellow, Samuel 1819-1892...........................DLB-1

Longley, Michael 1939- DLB-40

Longmans, Green and Company DLB-49

Longstreet, Augustus Baldwin
1790-1870 ....DLB-3, 11, 74

Longworth, D. [publishing house] DLB-49

Lonsdale, Frederick 1881-1954...........................DLB-10

A Look at the Contemporary Black Theatre
Movement DLB-38

Loos, Anita 1893-1981 ....DLB-11, 26; Y-81

Lopate, Phillip 1943- Y-80

López, Diana (see Isabella, Ríos)

Loranger, Jean-Aubert
1896-1942 ....DLB-92

The Lord Chamberlain's Office and Stage
Censorship in England DLB-10

Lorde, Audre 1934- DLB-41

Lorimer, George Horace 1867-1939 ....DLB-91

Loring, A. K. [publishing house] DLB-49

Loring and Mussey...DLB-46

Lossing, Benson J. 1813-1891..............................DLB-30

Lothar, Ernst 1890-1974 ....DLB-81

Lothrop, D., and Company...................................DLB-49

Lothrop, Harriet M. 1844-1924...........................DLB-42

The Lounger, no. 20 (1785), by Henry

Mackenzie DLB-39

Lounsbury, Thomas R. 1838-1915 ....DLB-71

Lovell, John W., Company..................................DLB-49

Lovell, Coryell and Company DLB-49

Lovesey, Peter 1936- DLB-87

Lovingood, Sut (see Harris, George Washington)

Low, Samuel 1765-? DLB-37

Lowell, Amy 1874-1925......................................DLB-54

Lowell, James Russell 1819-1891 ....DLB-1, 11, 64, 79

Lowell, Robert 1917-1977 ....DLB-5

Lowenfels, Walter 1897-1976.............................DLB-4

Lowndes, Marie Belloc 1868-1947.....................DLB-70

Lowry, Lois 1937- DLB-52

Lowry, Malcolm 1909-1957................................DLB-15

Lowther, Pat 1935-1975 ....DLB-53

Loy, Mina 1882-1966 ....DLB-4, 54

Lozeau, Albert 1878-1924..................................DLB-92

Lucas, Fielding, Jr. [publishing house]..............DLB-49

Luce, Henry R. 1898-1967.................................DLB-91

Luce, John W., and Company DLB-46

Lucie-Smith, Edward 1933- DLB-40

Ludlum, Robert 1927- Y-82

Ludwig, Jack 1922- DLB-60

Luke, Peter 1919- DLB-13

The F. M. Lupton Publishing Company DLB-49

Lurie, Alison 1926- DLB-2

Lyall, Gavin 1932- DLB-87

Lyly, John circa 1554-1606 ....DLB-62

Lyon, Matthew 1749-1822..................................DLB-43

Lytle, Andrew 1902- DLB-6

Lytton, Edward (see Bulwer-Lytton, Edward)

Lytton, Edward Robert Bulwer 1831-1891 ....DLB-32

M

Maass, Joachim 1901-1972 ....DLB-69

Mabie, Hamilton Wright 1845-1916..................DLB-71

Mac A'Ghobhainn, Iain (see Smith, Iain Crichton)

MacArthur, Charles 1895-1956...............DLB-7, 25, 44

Macaulay, David 1945- DLB-61

Macaulay, Rose 1881-1958 ....DLB-36

Macaulay, Thomas Babington 1800-1859 ....DLB-32, 55

Macaulay Company DLB-46

MacBeth, George 1932- DLB-40

Macbeth, Madge 1880-1965..............................DLB-92

MacCaig, Norman 1910- DLB-27

MacDiarmid, Hugh 1892-1978 ....DLB-20

MacDonald, George 1824-1905 ....DLB-18

MacDonald, John D. 1916-1986 ....DLB-8; Y-86

MacDonald, Philip 1899?-1980 ....DLB-77

Macdonald, Ross (see Millar, Kenneth)

MacDonald, Wilson 1880-1967 ....DLB-92

MacEwen, Gwendolyn 1941- DLB-53

Macfadden, Bernarr 1868-1955 ....DLB-25, 91

MacGregor, Mary Esther (see Keith, Marian)

Machar, Agnes Maule 1837-1927 ....DLB-92

Machen, Arthur Llewelyn Jones 1863-1947.......DLB-36

MacInnes, Colin 1914-1976 ....DLB-14

MacInnes, Helen 1907-1985 ....DLB-87

MacKaye, Percy 1875-1956 ....DLB-54

Macken, Walter 1915-1967 ....DLB-13

Mackenzie, Compton 1883-1972........................DLB-34

Mackenzie, Henry 1745-1831 ....DLB-39

Mackey, William Wellington 1937- DLB-38

Mackintosh, Elizabeth (see Tey, Josephine)

Macklin, Charles 1699-1797..............................DLB-89

MacLean, Katherine Anne 1925- DLB-8

MacLeish, Archibald 1892-1982.......DLB-4, 7, 45; Y-82

MacLennan, Hugh 1907- DLB-68

MacLeod, Alistair 1936- DLB-60

Macleod, Norman 1906- DLB-4

The Macmillan Company....................................DLB-49

MacNamara, Brinsley 1890-1963 ....DLB-10

MacNeice, Louis 1907-1963 ....DLB-10, 20

MacPhail, Andrew 1864-1938.............................DLB-92

Macpherson, Jay 1931- DLB-53

Macpherson, Jeanie 1884-1946..........................DLB-44

Macrae Smith Company DLB-46

Macy-Masius..DLB-46

Madden, David 1933- DLB-6

Maddow, Ben 1909- DLB-44

Madgett, Naomi Long 1923- DLB-76

Madhubuti, Haki R. 1942- DLB-5, 41

Madison, James 1751-1836 ....DLB-37

Mahan, Alfred Thayer 1840-1914 ....DLB-47

Maheux-Forcier, Louise 1929- DLB-60

Mahin, John Lee 1902-1984 ....DLB-44

Mahon, Derek 1941- DLB-40

Mailer, Norman 1923-
.................................DLB-2, 16, 28; Y-80, 83; DS-3

Maillet, Adrienne 1885-1963 ....DLB-68

Maillet, Antonine 1929- DLB-60

Main Selections of the Book-of-the-Month Club,
1926-1945 ....DLB-9

Main Trends in Twentieth-Century
Book Clubs DLB-46

Mainwaring, Daniel 1902-1977 ....DLB-44

Major, André 1942- DLB-60

Major, Clarence 1936- DLB-33

Major, Kevin 1949- DLB-60

Major Books..DLB-46

Makemie, Francis circa 1658-1708....................DLB-24

The Making of a People,
by J. M. Ritchie....................................DLB-66

Malamud, Bernard 1914-1986 ....DLB-2, 28; Y-80, 86

Malleson, Lucy Beatrice (see Gilbert, Anthony)

Mallet-Joris, Françoise 1930- DLB-83

Mallock, W. H. 1849-1923 ....DLB-18, 57

Malone, Dumas 1892-1986............................DLB-17

Malraux, André 1901-1976............................DLB-72

Malzberg, Barry N. 1939- DLB-8

Mamet, David 1947- DLB-7

Mandel, Eli 1922- DLB-53

Mandiargues, André Pieyre de 1909- DLB-83

Manfred, Frederick 1912- DLB-6

Mangan, Sherry 1904-1961............................DLB-4

Mankiewicz, Herman 1897-1953 ....DLB-26

Mankiewicz, Joseph L. 1909- DLB-44

Mankowitz, Wolf 1924- DLB-15

Manley, Delarivière 1672?-1724 ....DLB-39, 80

Mann, Abby 1927- DLB-44

Mann, Heinrich 1871-1950............................DLB-66

Mann, Horace 1796-1859............................DLB-1

Mann, Klaus 1906-1949............................DLB-56

Mann, Thomas 1875-1955 ....DLB-66

Manning, Marie 1873?-1945 ....DLB-29

Manning and Loring DLB-49

Mano, D. Keith 1942- DLB-6

Manor Books DLB-46

March, William 1893-1954............................DLB-9, 86

Marchessault, Jovette 1938- DLB-60

Marcus, Frank 1928- DLB-13

Marek, Richard, Books....................................DLB-46

Marie-Victorin, Frère
1885-1944 ....DLB-92

Marion, Frances 1886-1973............................DLB-44

Marius, Richard C. 1933- Y-85

The Mark Taper Forum....................................DLB-7

Markfield, Wallace 1926- DLB-2, 28

Markham, Edwin 1852-1940............................DLB-54

Markle, Fletcher 1921- DLB-68

Marlatt, Daphne 1942- DLB-60

Marlowe, Christopher 1564-1593 ....DLB-62

Marlyn, John 1912- DLB-88

Marmion, Shakerley 1603-1639 ....DLB-58

Marquand, John P. 1893-1960............................DLB-9

Marquis, Don 1878-1937............................DLB-11, 25

Marriott, Anne 1913- DLB-68

Marryat, Frederick 1792-1848 ....DLB-21

Marsh, George Perkins 1801-1882 ....DLB-1, 64

Marsh, James 1794-1842............................DLB-1, 59

Marsh, Capen, Lyon and Webb DLB-49

Marsh, Ngaio 1899-1982............................DLB-77

Marshall, Edward 1932- DLB-16

Marshall, James 1942- DLB-61

Marshall, Joyce 1913- DLB-88

Marshall, Paule 1929- DLB-33

Marshall, Tom 1938- DLB-60

Marston, John 1576-1634............................DLB-58

Marston, Philip Bourke 1850-1887....................DLB-35

Martens, Kurt 1870-1945............................DLB-66

Martien, William S. [publishing house].............DLB-49

Martin, Abe (see Hubbard, Kin)

Martin, Claire 1914- DLB-60

Martin du Gard, Roger 1881-1958....................DLB-65

Martineau, Harriet 1802-1876......................DLB-21, 55

Martínez, Max 1943- DLB-82

Martyn, Edward 1859-1923 ....DLB-10

Marvin X 1944- DLB-38

Marzials, Theo 1850-1920.................................DLB-35

Masefield, John 1878-1967 ....DLB-10, 19

Mason, A. E. W. 1865-1948 ....DLB-70

Mason, Bobbie Ann 1940- Y-87

Mason Brothers...DLB-49

Massey, Gerald 1828-1907 ....DLB-32

Massinger, Philip 1583-1640.........................DLB-58

Masters, Edgar Lee 1868-1950 ....DLB-54

Mather, Cotton 1663-1728........................DLB-24, 30

Mather, Increase 1639-1723 ....DLB-24

Mather, Richard 1596-1669 ....DLB-24

Matheson, Richard 1926- DLB-8, 44

Matheus, John F. 1887- DLB-51

Mathews, Cornelius 1817?-1889 ....DLB-3, 64

Mathias, Roland 1915- DLB-27

Mathis, June 1892-1927 ....DLB-44

Mathis, Sharon Bell 1937- DLB-33

Matthews, Brander 1852-1929...................DLB-71, 78

Matthews, Jack 1925- DLB-6

Matthews, William 1942- DLB-5

Matthiessen, F. O. 1902-1950 ....DLB-63

Matthiessen, Peter 1927- DLB-6

Maugham, W. Somerset 1874-1965 ....DLB-10, 36, 77

Mauriac, Claude 1914- DLB-83

Mauriac, François 1885-1970...........................DLB-65

Maurice, Frederick Denison 1805-1872 ....DLB-55

Maurois, André 1885-1967 ....DLB-65

Maury, James 1718-1769.................................DLB-31

Mavor, Elizabeth 1927- DLB-14

Mavor, Osborne Henry (see Bridie, James)

Maxwell, H. [publishing house]...........................DLB-49

Maxwell, William 1908- Y-80

May, Elaine 1932- DLB-44

May, Thomas 1595 or 1596-1650......................DLB-58

Mayer, Mercer 1943- DLB-61

Mayer, O. B. 1818-1891 ....DLB-3

Mayes, Wendell 1919- DLB-26

Mayfield, Julian 1928-1984........................DLB-33; Y-84

Mayhew, Henry 1812-1887...........................DLB-18, 55

Mayhew, Jonathan 1720-1766...........................DLB-31

Mayne, Seymour 1944- DLB-60

Mayor, Flora Macdonald 1872-1932..................DLB-36

Mayröcker, Friederike 1924- DLB-85

Mazursky, Paul 1930- DLB-44

McAlmon, Robert 1896-1956 ....DLB-4, 45

McArthur, Peter 1866-1924 ....DLB-92

McBride, Robert M., and Company DLB-46

McCaffrey, Anne 1926- DLB-8

McCarthy, Cormac 1933- DLB-6

McCarthy, Mary 1912-1989 ....DLB-2; Y-81

McCay, Winsor 1871-1934 ....DLB-22

McClatchy, C. K. 1858-1936 ....DLB-25

McClellan, George Marion 1860-1934 ....DLB-50

McCloskey, Robert 1914- DLB-22

McClung, Nellie Letitia
    1873-1951 ....DLB-92

McClure, Joanna 1930- DLB-16

McClure, Michael 1932- DLB-16

McClure, Phillips and Company........................DLB-46

McClure, S. S. 1857-1949.................................DLB-91

McClurg, A. C., and Company DLB-49

McCluskey, John A., Jr. 1944- DLB-33

McCollum, Michael A. 1946........................Y-87

McConnell, William C. 1917- DLB-88

McCord, David 1897- DLB-61

McCorkle, Jill 1958- Y-87

McCorkle, Samuel Eusebius 1746-1811 ....DLB-37

McCormick, Anne O'Hare 1880-1954................DLB-29

McCormick, Robert R. 1880-1955 ....DLB-29

McCourt, Edward 1907-1972...........................DLB-88

McCoy, Horace 1897-1955...........................DLB-9

McCrae, John 1872-1918 ....DLB-92

McCullagh, Joseph B. 1842-1896 ....DLB-23

McCullers, Carson 1917-1967........................DLB-2, 7

McDonald, Forrest 1927- DLB-17

McDougall, Colin 1917-1984 ....DLB-68

McDowell, Obolensky DLB-46

McEwan, Ian 1948- DLB-14

Morgan, Edmund S. 1916- DLB-17

Morgan, Edwin 1920- DLB-27

Morgner, Irmtraud 1933- DLB-75

Morin, Paul 1889-1963.....................DLB-92

Morison, Samuel Eliot 1887-1976.....................DLB-17

Moritz, Karl Philipp 1756-1793 ....DLB-94

Morley, Christopher 1890-1957..................DLB-9

Morley, John 1838-1923....................DLB-57

Morris, George Pope 1802-1864.....................DLB-73

Morris, Lewis 1833-1907.....................DLB-35

Morris, Richard B. 1904-1989 ....DLB-17

Morris, William 1834-1896...................DLB-18, 35, 57

Morris, Willie 1934- Y-80

Morris, Wright 1910- DLB-2; Y-81

Morrison, Arthur 1863-1945 ....DLB-70

Morrison, Charles Clayton 1874-1966...............DLB-91

Morrison, Toni 1931- DLB-6, 33; Y-81

Morrow, William, and Company DLB-46

Morse, James Herbert 1841-1923....................DLB-71

Morse, Jedidiah 1761-1826 ....DLB-37

Morse, John T., Jr. 1840-1937....................DLB-47

Mortimer, John 1923- DLB-13

Morton, John P., and Company DLB-49

Morton, Nathaniel 1613-1685....................DLB-24

Morton, Sarah Wentworth 1759-1846................DLB-37

Morton, Thomas circa 1579-circa 1647.............DLB-24

Mosley, Nicholas 1923- DLB-14

Moss, Arthur 1889-1969 ....DLB-4

Moss, Howard 1922- DLB-5

The Most Powerful Book Review in America
    [*New York Times Book Review*] Y-82

Motion, Andrew 1952- DLB-40

Motley, John Lothrop 1814-1877.............DLB-1, 30, 59

Motley, Willard 1909-1965....................DLB-76

Motteux, Peter Anthony 1663-1718 ....DLB-80

Mottram, R. H. 1883-1971....................DLB-36

Mouré, Erin 1955- DLB-60

Movies from Books, 1920-1974 ....DLB-9

Mowat, Farley 1921- DLB-68

Mowrer, Edgar Ansel 1892-1977....................DLB-29

Mowrer, Paul Scott 1887-1971...................DLB-29

Mucedorus..................................DLB-62

Muhajir, El (see Marvin X)

Muhajir, Nazzam Al Fitnah (see Marvin X)

Muir, Edwin 1887-1959....................DLB-20

Muir, Helen 1937- DLB-14

Mukherjee, Bharati 1940- DLB-60

Muldoon, Paul 1951- DLB-40

Müller, Friedrich (see Müller, Maler)

Müller, Maler 1749-1825 ....DLB-94

Müller, Wilhelm 1794-1827 ....DLB-90

Mumford, Lewis 1895- DLB-63

Munby, Arthur Joseph 1828-1910....................DLB-35

Munday, Anthony 1560-1633 ....DLB-62

Munford, Robert circa 1737-1783 ....DLB-31

Munro, Alice 1931- DLB-53

Munro, George [publishing house]....................DLB-49

Munro, H. H. 1870-1916 ....DLB-34

Munro, Norman L. [publishing house] DLB-49

Munroe, James, and Company DLB-49

Munroe, Kirk 1850-1930 ....DLB-42

Munroe and Francis.........................DLB-49

Munsell, Joel [publishing house]....................DLB-49

Munsey, Frank A. 1854-1925 ....DLB-25, 91

Munsey, Frank A., and Company....................DLB-49

Murdoch, Iris 1919- DLB-14

Murfree, Mary N. 1850-1922 ....DLB-12, 74

Muro, Amado 1915-1971....................DLB-82

Murphy, Arthur 1727-1805 ....DLB-89

Murphy, Beatrice M. 1908- DLB-76

Murphy, John, and Company DLB-49

Murphy, Richard 1927- DLB-40

Murray, Albert L. 1916- DLB-38

Murray, Gilbert 1866-1957 ....DLB-10

Murray, Judith Sargent 1751-1820....................DLB-37

Murray, Pauli 1910-1985...................DLB-41

Muschg, Adolf 1934- DLB-75

Musil, Robert 1880-1942....................DLB-81

Mussey, Benjamin B., and Company.................DLB-49

Myers, Gustavus 1872-1942 ....DLB-47

Myers, L. H. 1881-1944 ....DLB-15

Myers, Walter Dean 1937- DLB-33

N

Nabbes, Thomas circa 1605-1641 ....DLB-58

Nabl, Franz 1883-1974 ....DLB-81

Nabokov, Vladimir 1899-1977 ....DLB-2; Y-80; DS-3

Nabokov Festival at Cornell....................................Y-83

Nafis and Cornish...DLB-49

Naipaul, Shiva 1945-1985.......................................Y-85

Naipaul, V. S. 1932- Y-85

Nancrede, Joseph [publishing house]................DLB-49

Narrache, Jean 1893-1970 ....DLB-92

Nasby, Petroleum Vesuvius (see Locke, David Ross)

Nash, Ogden 1902-1971....................................DLB-11

Nast, Condé 1873-1942.....................................DLB-91

Nathan, Robert 1894-1985...................................DLB-9

The National Jewish Book Awards.........................Y-85

The National Theatre and the Royal Shakespeare
    Company: The National Companies...........DLB-13

Naughton, Bill 1910- DLB-13

Neagoe, Peter 1881-1960 ....DLB-4

Neal, John 1793-1876 ....DLB-1, 59

Neal, Joseph C. 1807-1847.................................DLB-11

Neal, Larry 1937-1981 ....DLB-38

The Neale Publishing Company.........................DLB-49

Neely, F. Tennyson [publishing house] DLB-49

"The Negro as a Writer," by
    G. M. McClellan DLB-50

"Negro Poets and Their Poetry," by
    Wallace Thurman DLB-50

Neihardt, John G. 1881-1973 ....DLB-9, 54

Nelligan, Emile 1879-1941................................DLB-92

Nelson, Alice Moore Dunbar
    1875-1935 ....DLB-50

Nelson, Thomas, and Sons..................................DLB-49

Nelson, William Rockhill 1841-1915 ....DLB-23

Nemerov, Howard 1920- DLB-5, 6; Y-83

Ness, Evaline 1911-1986....................................DLB-61

Neugeboren, Jay 1938- DLB-28

Neumann, Alfred 1895-1952...............................DLB-56

Nevins, Allan 1890-1971 ....DLB-17

The New American Library..................................DLB-46

New Directions Publishing Corporation............DLB-46

A New Edition of *Huck Finn* Y-85

New Forces at Work in the American Theatre:
    1915-1925 ....DLB-7

New Literary Periodicals: A Report
    for 1987...Y-87

New Literary Periodicals: A Report
    for 1988...Y-88

The New *Ulysses* Y-84

The New Variorum Shakespeare Y-85

A New Voice: The Center for the Book's First
    Five Years Y-83

The New Wave [Science Fiction] DLB-8

Newbolt, Henry 1862-1938 ....DLB-19

Newbound, Bernard Slade (see Slade, Bernard)

Newby, P. H. 1918- DLB-15

Newcomb, Charles King 1820-1894 ....DLB-1

Newell, Peter 1862-1924 ....DLB-42

Newell, Robert Henry 1836-1901 ....DLB-11

Newman, David (see Benton, Robert)

Newman, Frances 1883-1928 ....Y-80

Newman, John Henry 1801-1890 ....DLB-18, 32, 55

Newman, Mark [publishing house].....................DLB-49

Newsome, Effie Lee 1885-1979 ....DLB-76

Newspaper Syndication of American Humor....DLB-11

Nichol, B. P. 1944- DLB-53

Nichols, Dudley 1895-1960 ....DLB-26

Nichols, John 1940- Y-82

Nichols, Mary Sargeant (Neal) Gove
    1810-1884 ....DLB-1

Nichols, Peter 1927- DLB-13

Nichols, Roy F. 1896-1973 ....DLB-17

Nichols, Ruth 1948- DLB-60

Nicholson, Norman 1914- DLB-27

Ní Chuilleanáin, Eiléan 1942- DLB-40

Nicol, Eric 1919- DLB-68

Nicolay, John G. 1832-1901 and
    Hay, John 1838-1905 ....DLB-47

Niebuhr, Reinhold 1892-1971 ....DLB-17

Niedecker, Lorine 1903-1970 ....DLB-48

Nieman, Lucius W. 1857-1935...........................DLB-25

Niggli, Josefina 1910- Y-80

Niles, Hezekiah 1777-1839 ....DLB-43

Nims, John Frederick 1913- DLB-5

Nin, Anaïs 1903-1977....................................DLB-2, 4

1985: The Year of the Mystery:
A Symposium......................................Y-85

Nissenson, Hugh 1933- DLB-28

Niven, Frederick John 1878-1944 ....DLB-92

Niven, Larry 1938- DLB-8

Nizan, Paul 1905-1940 ....DLB-72

Nobel Peace Prize
The 1986 Nobel Peace Prize
Nobel Lecture 1986: Hope, Despair
and Memory
Tributes from Abraham Bernstein,
Norman Lamm, and John R. Silber Y-86

The Nobel Prize and Literary
Politics..Y-88

Nobel Prize in Literature
The 1982 Nobel Prize in Literature
Announcement by the Swedish Academy
of the Nobel Prize
Nobel Lecture 1982: The Solitude of Latin
America
Excerpt from *One Hundred Years
of Solitude*
The Magical World of Macondo
A Tribute to Gabriel García Márquez Y-82
The 1983 Nobel Prize in Literature
Announcement by the Swedish
Academy
Nobel Lecture 1983
The Stature of William Golding................Y-83
The 1984 Nobel Prize in Literature
Announcement by the Swedish
Academy
Jaroslav Seifert Through the Eyes of the
English-Speaking Reader
Three Poems by Jaroslav Seifert............Y-84
The 1985 Nobel Prize in Literature
Announcement by the Swedish
Academy
Nobel Lecture 1985...................................Y-85
The 1986 Nobel Prize in Literature
Nobel Lecture 1986: This Past Must
Address Its Present...............................Y-86
The 1987 Nobel Prize in Literature
Nobel Lecture 1987...................................Y-87
The 1988 Nobel Prize in Literature
Nobel Lecture 1988...................................Y-88

Noel, Roden 1834-1894 ....DLB-35

Nolan, William F. 1928- DLB-8

Noland, C. F. M. 1810?-1858.......................DLB-11

Noonday Press DLB-46

Noone, John 1936- DLB-14

Nordhoff, Charles 1887-1947 ....DLB-9

Norman, Marsha 1947- Y-84

Norris, Charles G. 1881-1945 ....DLB-9

Norris, Frank 1870-1902..............................DLB-12

Norris, Leslie 1921- DLB-27

Norse, Harold 1916- DLB-16

North Point Press.......................................DLB-46

Norton, Alice Mary (see Norton, Andre)

Norton, Andre 1912- DLB-8, 52

Norton, Andrews 1786-1853.........................DLB-1

Norton, Caroline 1808-1877 ....DLB-21

Norton, Charles Eliot 1827-1908...............DLB-1, 64

Norton, John 1606-1663 ....DLB-24

Norton, Thomas (see Sackville, Thomas)

Norton, W. W., and Company.......................DLB-46

Norwood, Robert 1874-1932 ....DLB-92

Nossack, Hans Erich 1901-1977 ....DLB-69

A Note on Technique (1926), by Elizabeth
A. Drew [excerpts].................................DLB-36

Nourse, Alan E. 1928- DLB-8

Novalis 1772-1801 ....DLB-90

The Novel in [Robert Browning's] "The Ring
and the Book" (1912), by Henry James DLB-32

The Novel of Impressionism,
by Jethro Bithell....................................DLB-66

Novel-Reading: *The Works of Charles Dickens,
The Works of W. Makepeace Thackeray* (1879),
by Anthony Trollope.............................DLB-21

The Novels of Dorothy Richardson (1918), by
May Sinclair DLB-36

Novels with a Purpose (1864),
by Justin M'Carthy DLB-21

Nowlan, Alden 1933-1983.............................DLB-53

Noyes, Alfred 1880-1958 ....DLB-20

Noyes, Crosby S. 1825-1908..........................DLB-23

Noyes, Nicholas 1647-1717 ....DLB-24

Noyes, Theodore W. 1858-1946.....................DLB-29

Nugent, Frank 1908-1965 ....DLB-44

Nye, Edgar Wilson (Bill) 1850-1896 ....DLB-11, 23

Nye, Robert 1939- DLB-14

O

Oakes, Urian circa 1631-1681 ....DLB-24

Oates, Joyce Carol 1938- DLB-2, 5; Y-81

Oberholtzer, Ellis Paxson 1868-1936 ....DLB-47

O'Brien, Edna 1932- DLB-14

O'Brien, Fitz-James 1828-1862............................DLB-74

O'Brien, Kate 1897-1974 ....DLB-15

O'Brien, Tim 1946- Y-80

O'Casey, Sean 1880-1964 ....DLB-10

Ochs, Adolph S. 1858-1935 ....DLB-25

O'Connor, Flannery 1925-1964.................DLB-2; Y-80

O'Dell, Scott 1903- DLB-52

Odell, Jonathan 1737-1818 ....DLB-31

Odets, Clifford 1906-1963 ....DLB-7, 26

O'Donnell, Peter 1920- DLB-87

O'Faolain, Julia 1932- DLB-14

O'Faolain, Sean 1900- DLB-15

Off Broadway and Off-Off-Broadway DLB-7

Off-Loop Theatres DLB-7

Offord, Carl Ruthven 1910- DLB-76

O'Flaherty, Liam 1896-1984 ....DLB-36; Y-84

Ogilvie, J. S., and Company................................DLB-49

O'Grady, Desmond 1935- DLB-40

O'Hagan, Howard 1902-1982............................DLB-68

O'Hara, Frank 1926-1966...............................DLB-5, 16

O'Hara, John 1905-1970 ....DLB-9, 86; DS-2

O. Henry (see Porter, William Sydney)

O'Keeffe, John 1747-1833 ....DLB-89

Old Franklin Publishing House DLB-49

Older, Fremont 1856-1935 ....DLB-25

Oliphant, Laurence 1829?-1888..........................DLB-18

Oliphant, Margaret 1828-1897 ....DLB-18

Oliver, Chad 1928- DLB-8

Oliver, Mary 1935- DLB-5

Ollier, Claude 1922- DLB-83

Olsen, Tillie 1913?- DLB-28; Y-80

Olson, Charles 1910-1970.............................DLB-5, 16

Olson, Elder 1909- DLB-48, 63

On Art in Fiction (1838), by
    Edward Bulwer...DLB-21

On Learning to Write...Y-88

On Some of the Characteristics of Modern
    Poetry and On the Lyrical Poems of Alfred
    Tennyson (1831), by Arthur Henry
    Hallam...DLB-32

"On Style in English Prose" (1898), by Frederic
    Harrison...DLB-57

"On Style in Literature: Its Technical Elements"
    (1885), by Robert Louis Stevenson..............DLB-57

"On the Writing of Essays" (1862),
    by Alexander Smith......................................DLB-57

Ondaatje, Michael 1943- DLB-60

O'Neill, Eugene 1888-1953 ....DLB-7

Oppen, George 1908-1984...................................DLB-5

Oppenheim, E. Phillips 1866-1946....................DLB-70

Oppenheim, James 1882-1932...........................DLB-28

Oppenheimer, Joel 1930- DLB-5

Optic, Oliver (see Adams, William Taylor)

Orczy, Emma, Baroness 1865-1947 ....DLB-70

Orlovitz, Gil 1918-1973 ....DLB-2, 5

Orlovsky, Peter 1933- DLB-16

Ormond, John 1923- DLB-27

Ornitz, Samuel 1890-1957 ....DLB-28, 44

Orton, Joe 1933-1967.......................................DLB-13

Orwell, George 1903-1950 ....DLB-15

The Orwell Year Y-84

Osbon, B. S. 1827-1912....................................DLB-43

Osborne, John 1929- DLB-13

Osgood, Herbert L. 1855-1918..........................DLB-47

Osgood, James R., and Company DLB-49

O'Shaughnessy, Arthur 1844-1881....................DLB-35

O'Shea, Patrick [publishing house]....................DLB-49

Oswald, Eleazer 1755-1795 ....DLB-43

Ostenso, Martha 1900-1963 ....DLB-92

Otero, Miguel Antonio 1859-1944 ....DLB-82

Otis, James (see Kaler, James Otis)

Otis, James, Jr. 1725-1783 ....DLB-31

Otis, Broaders and Company............................DLB-49

Ottendorfer, Oswald 1826-1900 ....DLB-23

Otway, Thomas 1652-1685 ....DLB-80

Ouellette, Fernand 1930- DLB-60

Ouida 1839-1908 ....DLB-18

Outing Publishing Company............................DLB-46

Outlaw Days, by Joyce Johnson.........................DLB-16

The Overlook Press..DLB-46

Overview of U.S. Book Publishing, 1910-1945....DLB-9

Owen, Guy 1925- DLB-5

Owen, John [publishing house]........................DLB-49

Owen, Wilfred 1893-1918...............................DLB-20

Owsley, Frank L. 1890-1956 ....DLB-17

Ozick, Cynthia 1928- DLB-28; Y-82

P

Pacey, Desmond 1917-1975 ....DLB-88

Pack, Robert 1929- DLB-5

Packaging Papa: *The Garden of Eden* Y-86

Padell Publishing Company DLB-46

Padgett, Ron 1942- DLB-5

Page, L. C., and Company DLB-49

Page, P. K. 1916- DLB-68

Page, Thomas Nelson 1853-1922 ....DLB-12, 78

Page, Walter Hines 1855-1918.....................DLB-71, 91

Paget, Violet (see Lee, Vernon)

Pain, Philip ?-circa 1666................................DLB-24

Paine, Robert Treat, Jr. 1773-1811 ....DLB-37

Paine, Thomas 1737-1809 ....DLB-31, 43, 73

Paley, Grace 1922- DLB-28

Palfrey, John Gorham 1796-1881..................DLB-1, 30

Palgrave, Francis Turner 1824-1897 ....DLB-35

Paltock, Robert 1697-1767 ....DLB-39

Panama, Norman 1914-   and
    Frank, Melvin 1913-1988   ....DLB-26

Pangborn, Edgar 1909-1976 ....DLB-8

"Panic Among the Philistines": A Postscript,
    An Interview with Bryan Griffin Y-81

Panneton, Philippe (see Ringuet)

Panshin, Alexei 1940- DLB-8

Pansy (see Alden, Isabella)

Pantheon Books..DLB-46

Paperback Library DLB-46

Paperback Science Fiction DLB-8

Paquet, Alfons 1881-1944 ....DLB-66

Paradis, Suzanne 1936- DLB-53

Parents' Magazine Press DLB-46

Parisian Theater, Fall 1984: Toward
    A New Baroque Y-85

Parizeau, Alice 1930- DLB-60

Parke, John 1754-1789.....................................DLB-31

Parker, Dorothy 1893-1967 ....DLB-11, 45, 86

Parker, James 1714-1770..................................DLB-43

Parker, Theodore 1810-1860............................DLB-1

Parkman, Francis, Jr. 1823-1893....................DLB-1, 30

Parks, Gordon 1912- DLB-33

Parks, William 1698-1750 ....DLB-43

Parks, William [publishing house] DLB-49

Parley, Peter (see Goodrich, Samuel Griswold)

Parrington, Vernon L. 1871-1929 ....DLB-17, 63

Parton, James 1822-1891 ....DLB-30

Parton, Sara Payson Willis 1811-1872.........DLB-43, 74

Pastan, Linda 1932- DLB-5

Pastorius, Francis Daniel 1651-circa 1720.........DLB-24

Patchen, Kenneth 1911-1972.......................DLB-16, 48

Pater, Walter 1839-1894..................................DLB-57

Paterson, Katherine 1932- DLB-52

Patmore, Coventry 1823-1896 ....DLB-35

Paton, Joseph Noel 1821-1901..........................DLB-35

Patrick, John 1906- DLB-7

Pattee, Fred Lewis 1863-1950...........................DLB-71

Pattern and Paradigm: History as
    Design, by Judith Ryan DLB-75

Patterson, Eleanor Medill 1881-1948 ....DLB-29

Patterson, Joseph Medill 1879-1946..................DLB-29

Pattillo, Henry 1726-1801 ....DLB-37

Paul, Elliot 1891-1958 ....DLB-4

Paul, Jean (see Richter,
    Johann Paul Friedrich)

Paul, Peter, Book Company DLB-49

Paulding, James Kirke 1778-1860 ....DLB-3, 59, 74

Paulin, Tom 1949- DLB-40

Pauper, Peter, Press.......................................DLB-46

Paxton, John 1911-1985..................................DLB-44

Payn, James 1830-1898 ....DLB-18

Payne, John 1842-1916 ....DLB-35

Payne, John Howard 1791-1852 ....DLB-37

Payson and Clarke DLB-46

Peabody, Elizabeth Palmer 1804-1894.................DLB-1

Peabody, Elizabeth Palmer [publishing
    house]...DLB-49

Peabody, Oliver William Bourn 1799-1848 ....DLB-59

Peachtree Publishers, Limited DLB-46

Pead, Deuel ?-1727 ....DLB-24

Peake, Mervyn 1911-1968 ....DLB-15

Pearson, H. B. [publishing house] DLB-49

Peck, George W. 1840-1916.........................DLB-23, 42

Peck, H. C., and Theo. Bliss [publishing
    house]...DLB-49

Peck, Harry Thurston 1856-1914................DLB-71, 91

Peele, George 1556-1596...................................DLB-62

Pellegrini and Cudahy.......................................DLB-46

Pelletier, Aimé (see Vac, Bertrand)

Pemberton, Sir Max 1863-1950 ....DLB-70

Penguin Books..DLB-46

Penn Publishing Company DLB-49

Penn, William 1644-1718 ....DLB-24

Penner, Jonathan 1940- Y-83

Pennington, Lee 1939- Y-82

Percy, Walker 1916- DLB-2; Y-80

Perec, Georges 1936-1982 ....DLB-83

Perelman, S. J. 1904-1979......................DLB-11, 44

Periodicals of the Beat Generation DLB-16

Perkins, Eugene 1932- DLB-41

Perkoff, Stuart Z. 1930-1974............................DLB-16

Permabooks...DLB-46

Perry, Bliss 1860-1954 ....DLB-71

Perry, Eleanor 1915-1981 ....DLB-44

"Personal Style" (1890), by John Addington
    Symonds...DLB-57

Perutz, Leo 1882-1957......................................DLB-81

Pestalozzi, Johann Heinrich 1746-1827 ....DLB-94

Peter, Laurence J. 1919-1990............................DLB-53

Peterkin, Julia 1880-1961 ....DLB-9

Petersham, Maud 1889-1971 and
    Petersham, Miska 1888-1960 ....DLB-22

Peterson, Charles Jacobs 1819-1887 ....DLB-79

Peterson, Len 1917- DLB-88

Peterson, Louis 1922- DLB-76

Peterson, T. B., and Brothers DLB-49

Petry, Ann 1908- DLB-76

Pharr, Robert Deane 1916-1989........................DLB-33

Phelps, Elizabeth Stuart 1844-1911 ....DLB-74

Philippe, Charles-Louis 1874-1909.....................DLB-65

Phillips, David Graham 1867-1911.................DLB-9, 12

Phillips, Jayne Anne 1952- Y-80

Phillips, Stephen 1864-1915...............................DLB-10

Phillips, Ulrich B. 1877-1934.............................DLB-17

Phillips, Willard 1784-1873................................DLB-59

Phillips, Sampson and Company DLB-49

Phillpotts, Eden 1862-1960...........................DLB-10, 70

Philosophical Library..DLB-46

"The Philosophy of Style" (1852), by
    Herbert Spencer.......................................DLB-57

Phinney, Elihu [publishing house].......................DLB-49

Phoenix, John (see Derby, George Horatio)

PHYLON (Fourth Quarter, 1950),
    The Negro in Literature:
    The Current Scene.....................................DLB-76

Pickard, Tom 1946- DLB-40

Pickthall, Marjorie 1883-1922............................DLB-92

Pictorial Printing Company...............................DLB-49

Pike, Albert 1809-1891......................................DLB-74

Pilon, Jean-Guy 1930- DLB-60

Pinckney, Josephine 1895-1957 ....DLB-6

Pinero, Arthur Wing 1855-1934........................DLB-10

Pinget, Robert 1919- DLB-83

Pinnacle Books..DLB-46

Pinsky, Robert 1940- Y-82

Pinter, Harold 1930- DLB-13

Piontek, Heinz 1925- DLB-75

Piper, H. Beam 1904-1964 ....DLB-8

Piper, Watty DLB-22

Pisar, Samuel 1929- Y-83

Pitkin, Timothy 1766-1847 ....DLB-30

The Pitt Poetry Series: Poetry
    Publishing Today Y-85

Pitter, Ruth 1897- DLB-20

Pix, Mary 1666-1709 ....DLB-80

The Place of Realism in Fiction (1895), by
George Gissing..DLB-18

Plante, David 1940- Y-83

Platen, August von 1796-1835 ....DLB-90

Plath, Sylvia 1932-1963 ....DLB-5, 6

Platt and Munk Company DLB-46

Playboy Press..DLB-46

Plays, Playwrights, and Playgoers.......................DLB-84

Playwrights and Professors, by Tom
Stoppard DLB-13

Playwrights on the Theater..............................DLB-80

Plenzdorf, Ulrich 1934- DLB-75

Plessen, Elizabeth 1944- DLB-75

Plievier, Theodor 1892-1955 ....DLB-69

Plomer, William 1903-1973................................DLB-20

Plumly, Stanley 1939- DLB-5

Plumpp, Sterling D. 1940- DLB-41

Plunkett, James 1920- DLB-14

Plymell, Charles 1935- DLB-16

Pocket Books..DLB-46

Poe, Edgar Allan 1809-1849..............DLB-3, 59, 73, 74

Poe, James 1921-1980...DLB-44

The Poet Laureate of the United States
Statements from Former Consultants
in Poetry...Y-86

Pohl, Frederik 1919- DLB-8

Poirier, Louis (see Gracq, Julien)

Poliakoff, Stephen 1952- DLB-13

Polite, Carlene Hatcher 1932- DLB-33

Pollard, Edward A. 1832-1872.........................DLB-30

Pollard, Percival 1869-1911..............................DLB-71

Pollard and Moss DLB-49

Pollock, Sharon 1936- DLB-60

Polonsky, Abraham 1910- DLB-26

Poole, Ernest 1880-1950....................................DLB-9

Poore, Benjamin Perley 1820-1887....................DLB-23

Popular Library..DLB-46

Porlock, Martin (see MacDonald, Philip)

Porter, Eleanor H. 1868-1920...........................DLB-9

Porter, Henry ?-? DLB-62

Porter, Katherine Anne 1890-1980........DLB-4, 9; Y-80

Porter, Peter 1929- DLB-40

Porter, William Sydney 1862-1910.........DLB-12, 78, 79

Porter, William T. 1809-1858........................DLB-3, 43

Porter and Coates DLB-49

Portis, Charles 1933- DLB-6

Poston, Ted 1906-1974.......................................DLB-51

Postscript to [the Third Edition of] *Clarissa*
(1751), by Samuel Richardson DLB-39

Potok, Chaim 1929- DLB-28; Y-84

Potter, David M. 1910-1971 ....DLB-17

Potter, John E., and Company...........................DLB-49

Pottle, Frederick A. 1897-1987 ....Y-87

Poulin, Jacques 1937- DLB-60

Pound, Ezra 1885-1972..........................DLB-4, 45, 63

Powell, Anthony 1905- DLB-15

Pownall, David 1938- DLB-14

Powys, John Cowper 1872-1963 ....DLB-15

Powys, T. F. 1875-1953 ....DLB-36

The Practice of Biography: An Interview with
Stanley Weintraub...Y-82

The Practice of Biography II: An Interview with
B. L. Reid...Y-83

The Practice of Biography III: An Interview with
Humphrey Carpenter Y-84

The Practice of Biography IV: An Interview with
William Manchester...Y-85

The Practice of Biography V: An Interview with
Justin Kaplan Y-86

The Practice of Biography VI: An Interview with
David Herbert Donald Y-87

Praeger Publishers...DLB-46

Pratt, E. J. 1882-1964...DLB-92

Pratt, Samuel Jackson 1749-1814 ....DLB-39

Preface to *Alwyn* (1780), by Thomas
Holcroft...DLB-39

Preface to *Colonel Jack* (1722), by Daniel
Defoe..DLB-39

Preface to *Evelina* (1778), by Fanny Burney.......DLB-39

Preface to *Ferdinand Count Fathom* (1753), by
Tobias Smollett DLB-39

Preface to *Incognita* (1692), by William
Congreve..DLB-39

Preface to *Joseph Andrews* (1742), by

Henry Fielding DLB-39

Preface to *Moll Flanders* (1722), by Daniel
Defoe...DLB-39

Preface to *Poems* (1853), by Matthew
Arnold...DLB-32

Preface to *Robinson Crusoe* (1719), by Daniel
Defoe...DLB-39

Preface to *Roderick Random* (1748), by Tobias
Smollett...DLB-39

Preface to *Roxana* (1724), by Daniel Defoe DLB-39

Preface to *St. Leon* (1799),
by William Godwin.........................DLB-39

Preface to Sarah Fielding's *Familiar Letters*
(1747), by Henry Fielding [excerpt]............DLB-39

Preface to Sarah Fielding's *The Adventures of
David Simple* (1744), by Henry Fielding.......DLB-39

Preface to *The Cry* (1754), by Sarah Fielding DLB-39

Preface to *The Delicate Distress* (1769), by
Elizabeth Griffin DLB-39

Preface to *The Disguis'd Prince* (1733), by Eliza
Haywood [excerpt] DLB-39

Preface to *The Farther Adventures of Robinson
Crusoe* (1719), by Daniel Defoe DLB-39

Preface to the First Edition of *Pamela* (1740), by
Samuel Richardson.....................................DLB-39

Preface to the First Edition of *The Castle of
Otranto* (1764), by Horace Walpole..............DLB-39

Preface to *The History of Romances* (1715), by
Pierre Daniel Huet [excerpts] DLB-39

Preface to *The Life of Charlotta du Pont* (1723),
by Penelope Aubin DLB-39

Preface to *The Old English Baron* (1778), by
Clara Reeve..DLB-39

Preface to the Second Edition of *The Castle of
Otranto* (1765), by Horace Walpole..............DLB-39

Preface to *The Secret History, of Queen Zarah, and
the Zarazians* (1705), by Delarivière
Manley...DLB-39

Preface to the Third Edition of *Clarissa* (1751),
by Samuel Richardson [excerpt]..................DLB-39

Preface to *The Works of Mrs. Davys* (1725), by
Mary Davys DLB-39

Preface to Volume 1 of *Clarissa* (1747), by
Samuel Richardson....................................DLB-39

Preface to Volume 3 of *Clarissa* (1748), by
Samuel Richardson....................................DLB-39

Préfontaine, Yves 1937- DLB-53

Prelutsky, Jack 1940- DLB-61

Premisses, by Michael Hamburger DLB-66

Prentice, George D. 1802-1870.....................DLB-43

Prentice-Hall.....................................DLB-46

Prescott, William Hickling 1796-1859......DLB-1, 30, 59

The Present State of the English Novel (1892),
by George Saintsbury DLB-18

Preston, Thomas 1537-1598 ....DLB-62

Price, Reynolds 1933- DLB-2

Price, Richard 1949- Y-81

Priest, Christopher 1943- DLB-14

Priestley, J. B. 1894-1984 ....DLB-10, 34, 77; Y-84

Prime, Benjamin Young 1733-1791 ....DLB-31

Prince, F. T. 1912- DLB-20

Prince, Thomas 1687-1758 ....DLB-24

The Principles of Success in Literature (1865), by
George Henry Lewes [excerpt]...................DLB-57

Pritchett, V. S. 1900- DLB-15

Procter, Adelaide Anne 1825-1864 ....DLB-32

The Progress of Romance (1785), by Clara Reeve
[excerpt]...DLB-39

Prokosch, Frederic 1906-1989 ....DLB-48

The Proletarian Novel...........................DLB-9

Propper, Dan 1937- DLB-16

The Prospect of Peace (1778), by Joel Barlow DLB-37

Proud, Robert 1728-1813.....................DLB-30

Proust, Marcel 1871-1922 ....DLB-65

Prynne, J. H. 1936- DLB-40

Przybyszewski, Stanislaw 1868-1927 ....DLB-66

The Public Lending Right in America
Statement by Sen. Charles McC. Mathias, Jr.
PLR and the Meaning of Literary Property
Statements on PLR by American Writers.........Y-83

The Public Lending Right in the United Kingdom
Public Lending Right: The First Year in the
United Kingdom Y-83

The Publication of English Renaissance
Plays DLB-62

Publications and Social Movements
[Transcendentalism] DLB-1

Publishers and Agents: The Columbia
Connection..Y-87

Publishing Fiction at LSU Press Y-87

Pugin, A. Welby 1812-1852..................................DLB-55

Pulitzer, Joseph 1847-1911 ....DLB-23

Pulitzer, Joseph, Jr. 1885-1955 ....DLB-29

Pulitzer Prizes for the Novel, 1917-1945 ....DLB-9

Purdy, Al 1918- DLB-88

Purdy, James 1923- DLB-2

Pusey, Edward Bouverie 1800-1882..................DLB-55

Putnam, George Palmer 1814-1872 ....DLB-3, 79

Putnam, Samuel 1892-1950 ....DLB-4

G. P. Putnam's Sons DLB-49

Puzo, Mario 1920- DLB-6

Pyle, Ernie 1900-1945 ....DLB-29

Pyle, Howard 1853-1911 ....DLB-42

Pym, Barbara 1913-1980 ....DLB-14; Y-87

Pynchon, Thomas 1937- DLB-2

Pyramid Books...DLB-46

Pyrnelle, Louise-Clarke 1850-1907 ....DLB-42

Q

Quad, M. (see Lewis, Charles B.)

The Queen City Publishing House....................DLB-49

Queneau, Raymond 1903-1976 ....DLB-72

The Question of American Copyright
    in the Nineteenth Century
      Headnote
      Preface, by George Haven Putnam
      The Evolution of Copyright, by Brander
        Matthews
      Summary of Copyright Legislation in the
        United States, by R. R. Bowker
      Analysis of the Provisions of the Copyright
        Law of 1891, by George Haven Putnam
      The Contest for International Copyright,
        by George Haven Putnam
      Cheap Books and Good Books,
        by Brander Matthews...................DLB-49

Quin, Ann 1936-1973..DLB-14

Quincy, Samuel of Georgia ?-? DLB-31

Quincy, Samuel of Massachusetts 1734-1789.....DLB-31

Quintana, Leroy V. 1944- DLB-82

Quist, Harlin, Books..DLB-46

Quoirez, Françoise (see Sagan, Françoise)

R

Rabe, David 1940- DLB-7

Radcliffe, Ann 1764-1823 ....DLB-39

Raddall, Thomas 1903- DLB-68

Radiguet, Raymond 1903-1923.........................DLB-65

Radványi, Netty Reiling (see Seghers, Anna)

Raimund, Ferdinand Jakob 1790-1836..............DLB-90

Raine, Craig 1944- DLB-40

Raine, Kathleen 1908- DLB-20

Ralph, Julian 1853-1903....................................DLB-23

Ralph Waldo Emerson in 1982 ....Y-82

Rambler, no. 4 (1750), by Samuel Johnson
    [excerpt]..DLB-39

Ramée, Marie Louise de la (see Ouida)

Ramsay, David 1749-1815 ....DLB-30

Rand, Avery and Company..................................DLB-49

Rand McNally and Company..............................DLB-49

Randall, Dudley 1914- DLB-41

Randall, Henry S. 1811-1876.............................DLB-30

Randall, James G. 1881-1953............................DLB-17

The Randall Jarrell Symposium: A Small
    Collection of Randall Jarrells
      Excerpts From Papers Delivered at
        the Randall Jarrell Symposium Y-86

Randolph, A. Philip 1889-1979 ....DLB-91

Randolph, Anson D. F. [publishing house]........DLB-49

Randolph, Thomas 1605-1635...........................DLB-58

Random House..DLB-46

Ranlet, Henry [publishing house].......................DLB-49

Ransom, John Crowe 1888-1974 ....DLB-45, 63

Raphael, Frederic 1931- DLB-14

Raphaelson, Samson 1896-1983........................DLB-44

Raskin, Ellen 1928-1984....................................DLB-52

Rattigan, Terence 1911-1977 ....DLB-13

Rawlings, Marjorie Kinnan 1896-1953...........DLB-9, 22

Raworth, Tom 1938- DLB-40

Ray, David 1932- DLB-5

Ray, Henrietta Cordelia 1849-1916...................DLB-50

Raymond, Henry J. 1820-1869....................DLB-43, 79

Raymond Chandler Centenary Tributes
    from Michael Avallone, James Elroy, Joe Gores,

and William F. Nolan Y-88

Reach, Angus 1821-1856.............................DLB-70

Read, Herbert 1893-1968 ....DLB-20

Read, Opie 1852-1939....................................DLB-23

Read, Piers Paul 1941- DLB-14

Reade, Charles 1814-1884..............................DLB-21

Reader's Digest Condensed Books DLB-46

Reading, Peter 1946- DLB-40

Reaney, James 1926- DLB-68

Rechy, John 1934- Y-82

Redding, J. Saunders 1906-1988.................DLB-63, 76

Redfield, J. S. [publishing house] DLB-49

Redgrove, Peter 1932- DLB-40

Redmon, Anne 1943- Y-86

Redmond, Eugene B. 1937- DLB-41

Redpath, James [publishing house] DLB-49

Reed, Henry 1808-1854 ....DLB-59

Reed, Henry 1914- DLB-27

Reed, Ishmael 1938- DLB-2, 5, 33

Reed, Sampson 1800-1880...............................DLB-1

Reedy, William Marion 1862-1920 ....DLB-91

Reese, Lizette Woodworth 1856-1935 ....DLB-54

Reese, Thomas 1742-1796 ....DLB-37

Reeve, Clara 1729-1807...................................DLB-39

Reeves, John 1926- DLB-88

Regnery, Henry, Company DLB-46

Reid, Alastair 1926- DLB-27

Reid, Christopher 1949- DLB-40

Reid, Helen Rogers 1882-1970 ....DLB-29

Reid, James ?-?..DLB-31

Reid, Mayne 1818-1883 ....DLB-21

Reid, Thomas 1710-1796 ....DLB-31

Reid, Whitelaw 1837-1912 ....DLB-23

Reilly and Lee Publishing Company DLB-46

Reimann, Brigitte 1933-1973 ....DLB-75

Reisch, Walter 1903-1983................................DLB-44

Remarque, Erich Maria 1898-1970...................DLB-56

"Re-meeting of Old Friends": The Jack Kerouac
    Conference..Y-82

Remington, Frederic 1861-1909 ....DLB-12

Renaud, Jacques 1943- DLB-60

Renault, Mary 1905-1983 ....Y-83

Rendell, Ruth 1930- DLB-87

Representative Men and Women: A Historical
    Perspective on the British Novel,
    1930-1960 ....DLB-15

(Re-)Publishing Orwell Y-86

Reuter, Gabriele 1859-1941 ....DLB-66

Revell, Fleming H., Company...........DLB-49

Reventlow, Franziska Gräfin zu
    1871-1918 ....DLB-66

Review of [Samuel Richardson's] *Clarissa* (1748),
    by Henry Fielding DLB-39

The Revolt (1937), by Mary
    Colum [excerpts] DLB-36

Rexroth, Kenneth 1905-1982 ....DLB-16, 48; Y-82

Rey, H. A. 1898-1977...........................DLB-22

Reynal and Hitchcock DLB-46

Reynolds, G. W. M. 1814-1879.........DLB-21

Reynolds, Mack 1917- DLB-8

Reznikoff, Charles 1894-1976.............DLB-28, 45

"Rhetoric" (1828; revised, 1859), by
    Thomas de Quincey [excerpt] DLB-57

Rhett, Robert Barnwell 1800-1876.........DLB-43

Rhode, John 1884-1964 ....DLB-77

Rhodes, James Ford 1848-1927 ....DLB-47

Rhys, Jean 1890-1979...........................DLB-36

Ricardou, Jean 1932- DLB-83

Rice, Elmer 1892-1967..........................DLB-4, 7

Rice, Grantland 1880-1954 ....DLB-29

Rich, Adrienne 1929- DLB-5, 67

Richards, David Adams 1950- DLB-53

Richards, George circa 1760-1814.........DLB-37

Richards, I. A. 1893-1979 ....DLB-27

Richards, Laura E. 1850-1943 ....DLB-42

Richards, William Carey 1818-1892 ......DLB-73

Richardson, Charles F. 1851-1913.........DLB-71

Richardson, Dorothy M. 1873-1957 .....DLB-36

Richardson, Jack 1935- DLB-7

Richardson, Samuel 1689-1761.............DLB-39

Richardson, Willis 1889-1977 ....DLB-51

Richler, Mordecai 1931- DLB-53

Richter, Conrad 1890-1968..................DLB-9

Richter, Hans Werner 1908- DLB-69

Richter, Johann Paul Friedrich
1763-1825 ....DLB-94

Rickword, Edgell 1898-1982 ....DLB-20

Riddell, John (see Ford, Corey)

Ridge, Lola 1873-1941 ....DLB-54

Ridler, Anne 1912- DLB-27

Riffaterre, Michael 1924- DLB-67

Riis, Jacob 1849-1914 ....DLB-23

Riker, John C. [publishing house] DLB-49

Riley, John 1938-1978 ....DLB-40

Rilke, Rainer Maria 1875-1926 ....DLB-81

Rinehart and Company DLB-46

Ringuet 1895-1960 ....DLB-68

Ringwood, Gwen Pharis 1910-1984 ....DLB-88

Rinser, Luise 1911- DLB-69

Ríos, Isabella 1948- DLB-82

Ripley, Arthur 1895-1961 ....DLB-44

Ripley, George 1802-1880 ....DLB-1, 64, 73

The Rising Glory of America: Three Poems DLB-37

The Rising Glory of America: Written in 1771
(1786), by Hugh Henry Brackenridge and
Philip Freneau DLB-37

Riskin, Robert 1897-1955 ....DLB-26

Risse, Heinz 1898- DLB-69

Ritchie, Anna Mowatt 1819-1870 ....DLB-3

Ritchie, Anne Thackeray 1837-1919 ....DLB-18

Ritchie, Thomas 1778-1854 ....DLB-43

Rites of Passage [on William Saroyan]........Y-83

The Ritz Paris Hemingway Award................Y-85

Rivard, Adjutor 1868-1945 ....DLB-92

Rivera, Tomás 1935-1984..............................DLB-82

Rivers, Conrad Kent 1933-1968 ....DLB-41

Riverside Press DLB-49

Rivington, James circa 1724-1802 ....DLB-43

Rivkin, Allen 1903- DLB-26

Robbe-Grillet, Alain 1922- DLB-83

Robbins, Tom 1936- Y-80

Roberts, Charles G. D. 1860-1943 ....DLB-92

Roberts, Dorothy 1906- DLB-88

Roberts, Elizabeth Madox 1881-1941............DLB-9, 54

Roberts, Kenneth 1885-1957 ....DLB-9

Roberts Brothers..DLB-49

Robertson, A. M., and Company......................DLB-49

Robinson, Casey 1903-1979 ....DLB-44

Robinson, Edwin Arlington 1869-1935 ....DLB-54

Robinson, James Harvey 1863-1936..............DLB-47

Robinson, Lennox 1886-1958 ....DLB-10

Robinson, Mabel Louise 1874-1962..............DLB-22

Robinson, Therese 1797-1870 ....DLB-59

Roblès, Emmanuel 1914- DLB-83

Rodgers, Carolyn M. 1945- DLB-41

Rodgers, W. R. 1909-1969 ....DLB-20

Rodriguez, Richard 1944- DLB-82

Roethke, Theodore 1908-1963 ....DLB-5

Rogers, Samuel 1763-1855 ....DLB-93

Rogers, Will 1879-1935 ....DLB-11

Rohmer, Sax 1883-1959................................DLB-70

Roiphe, Anne 1935- Y-80

Rojas, Arnold R. 1896-1988..........................DLB-82

Rolfe, Frederick William 1860-1913..............DLB-34

Rolland, Romain 1866-1944 ....DLB-65

Rolvaag, O. E. 1876-1931..............................DLB-9

Romains, Jules 1885-1972 ....DLB-65

Roman, A., and Company..............................DLB-49

Romero, Orlando 1945- DLB-82

Roosevelt, Theodore 1858-1919 ....DLB-47

Root, Waverley 1903-1982 ....DLB-4

Roquebrune, Robert de 1889-1978 ....DLB-68

Rose, Reginald 1920- DLB-26

Rosei, Peter 1946- DLB-85

Rosen, Norma 1925- DLB-28

Rosenberg, Isaac 1890-1918 ....DLB-20

Rosenfeld, Isaac 1918-1956..........................DLB-28

Rosenthal, M. L. 1917- DLB-5

Ross, Leonard Q. (see Rosten, Leo)

Ross, Sinclair 1908- DLB-88

Ross, W. W. E. 1894-1966..............................DLB-88

Rossen, Robert 1908-1966 ....DLB-26

Rossetti, Christina 1830-1894......................DLB-35

Rossetti, Dante Gabriel 1828-1882..............DLB-35

Rossner, Judith 1935- DLB-6

Rosten, Leo 1908- DLB-11

Roth, Gerhard 1942- DLB-85

Roth, Henry 1906?- DLB-28

Roth, Joseph 1894-1939 ....DLB-85

Roth, Philip 1933- DLB-2, 28; Y-82

Rothenberg, Jerome 1931- DLB-5

Routier, Simone 1901-1987.....................DLB-88

Rowe, Elizabeth 1674-1737 ....DLB-39

Rowe, Nicholas 1674-1718 ....DLB-84

Rowlandson, Mary circa 1635-circa 1678..........DLB-24

Rowley, William circa 1585-1626......................DLB-58

Rowson, Susanna Haswell circa 1762-1824........DLB-37

Roy, Camille 1870-1943 ....DLB-92

Roy, Gabrielle 1909-1983.........................DLB-68

Roy, Jules 1907- DLB-83

The Royal Court Theatre and the English
　　Stage Company...............................DLB-13

The Royal Court Theatre and the New
　　Drama DLB-10

The Royal Shakespeare Company
　　at the Swan.....................................Y-88

Royall, Anne 1769-1854.........................DLB-43

The Roycroft Printing Shop DLB-49

Rubens, Bernice 1928- DLB-14

Rudd and Carleton...............................DLB-49

Rudkin, David 1936- DLB-13

Ruffin, Josephine St. Pierre 1842-1924.............DLB-79

Ruggles, Henry Joseph 1813-1906 ....DLB-64

Rukeyser, Muriel 1913-1980 ....DLB-48

Rule, Jane 1931- DLB-60

Rumaker, Michael 1932- DLB-16

Rumens, Carol 1944- DLB-40

Runyon, Damon 1880-1946..................DLB-11, 86

Rush, Benjamin 1746-1813......................DLB-37

Ruskin, John 1819-1900..........................DLB-55

Russ, Joanna 1937- DLB-8

Russell, B. B., and Company DLB-49

Russell, Benjamin 1761-1845.....................DLB-43

Russell, Charles Edward 1860-1941 ....DLB-25

Russell, George William (see AE)

Russell, R. H., and Son DLB-49

Rutherford, Mark 1831-1913.............................DLB-18

Ryan, Michael 1946- Y-82

Ryan, Oscar 1904- DLB-68

Ryga, George 1932- DLB-60

Ryskind, Morrie 1895-1985 ....DLB-26

S

The Saalfield Publishing Company DLB-46

Saberhagen, Fred 1930- DLB-8

Sackler, Howard 1929-1982.........................DLB-7

Sackville, Thomas 1536-1608
　　and Norton, Thomas 1532-1584 ....DLB-62

Sackville-West, V. 1892-1962 ....DLB-34

Sadlier, D. and J., and Company........................DLB-49

Saffin, John circa 1626-1710.........................DLB-24

Sagan, Françoise 1935- DLB-83

Sage, Robert 1899-1962 ....DLB-4

Sagel, Jim 1947- DLB-82

Sahkomaapii, Piitai (see Highwater, Jamake)

Sahl, Hans 1902- DLB-69

Said, Edward W. 1935- DLB-67

Saiko, George 1892-1962 ....DLB-85

St. Johns, Adela Rogers 1894-1988 ....DLB-29

St. Martin's Press DLB-46

Saint-Exupéry, Antoine de 1900-1944 ....DLB-72

Saint Pierre, Michel de 1916-1987.......................DLB-83

Saintsbury, George 1845-1933...........................DLB-57

Saki (see Munro, H. H.)

Salaam, Kalamu ya 1947- DLB-38

Salas, Floyd 1931- DLB-82

Salemson, Harold J. 1910-1988 ....DLB-4

Salinas, Luis Omar 1937- DLB-82

Salinger, J. D. 1919- DLB-2

Salt, Waldo 1914- DLB-44

Salverson, Laura Goodman 1890-1970 ....DLB-92

Sampson, Richard Henry (see Hull, Richard)

Sanborn, Franklin Benjamin 1831-1917 ....DLB-1

Sánchez, Ricardo 1941- DLB-82

Sanchez, Sonia 1934- DLB-41

Sandburg, Carl 1878-1967.........................DLB-17, 54

Sanders, Ed 1939- DLB-16

Sandoz, Mari 1896-1966......................DLB-9

Sandwell, B. K. 1876-1954.......................DLB-92

Sandys, George 1578-1644.......................DLB-24

Santayana, George 1863-1952 ....DLB-54, 71

Santmyer, Helen Hooven 1895-1986......................Y-84

Sapir, Edward 1884-1939......................DLB-92

Sapper (see McNeile, Herman Cyril)

Sargent, Pamela 1948- DLB-8

Saroyan, William 1908-1981............DLB-7, 9, 86; Y-81

Sarraute, Nathalie 1900- DLB-83

Sarrazin, Albertine 1937-1967 ....DLB-83

Sarton, May 1912- DLB-48; Y-81

Sartre, Jean-Paul 1905-1980 ....DLB-72

Sassoon, Siegfried 1886-1967 ....DLB-20

Saturday Review Press.......................DLB-46

Saunders, James 1925- DLB-13

Saunders, John Monk 1897-1940 ....DLB-26

Saunders, Margaret Marshall
   1861-1947 ....DLB-92

Savage, James 1784-1873 ....DLB-30

Savage, Marmion W. 1803?-1872 ....DLB-21

Savard, Félix-Antoine 1896-1982.......................DLB-68

Sawyer, Ruth 1880-1970 ....DLB-22

Sayers, Dorothy L. 1893-1957 ....DLB-10, 36, 77

Sayles, John Thomas 1950- DLB-44

Scannell, Vernon 1922- DLB-27

Scarry, Richard 1919- DLB-61

Schaeffer, Albrecht 1885-1950 ....DLB-66

Schaeffer, Susan Fromberg 1941- DLB-28

Schaper, Edzard 1908-1984 ....DLB-69

Scharf, J. Thomas 1843-1898 ....DLB-47

Schelling, Friedrich Wilhelm Joseph von
   1775-1854 ....DLB-90

Schickele, René 1883-1940 ....DLB-66

Schiller, Friedrich 1759-1805.......................DLB-94

Schlegel, August Wilhelm 1767-1845.......................DLB-94

Schlegel, Dorothea 1763-1839 ....DLB-90

Schlegel, Friedrich 1772-1829.......................DLB-90

Schleiermacher, Friedrich 1768-1834.......................DLB-90

Schlesinger, Arthur M., Jr. 1917- DLB-17

Schlumberger, Jean 1877-1968.......................DLB-65

Schmid, Eduard Hermann Wilhelm
   (see Edschmid, Kasimir)

Schmidt, Arno 1914-1979 ....DLB-69

Schmidt, Michael 1947- DLB-40

Schmitz, James H. 1911- DLB-8

Schnitzler, Arthur 1862-1931 ....DLB-81

Schnurre, Wolfdietrich 1920- DLB-69

Schocken Books.......................DLB-46

The Schomburg Center for Research
   in Black Culture DLB-76

Schopenhauer, Arthur 1788-1860.......................DLB-90

Schopenhauer, Johanna 1766-1838.......................DLB-90

Schouler, James 1839-1920.......................DLB-47

Schrader, Paul 1946- DLB-44

Schreiner, Olive 1855-1920.......................DLB-18

Schroeder, Andreas 1946- DLB-53

Schubert, Gotthilf Heinrich 1780-1860.......................DLB-90

Schulberg, Budd 1914- DLB-6, 26, 28; Y-81

Schulte, F. J., and Company DLB-49

Schurz, Carl 1829-1906.......................DLB-23

Schuyler, George S. 1895-1977...............DLB-29, 51

Schuyler, James 1923- DLB-5

Schwartz, Delmore 1913-1966 ....DLB-28, 48

Schwartz, Jonathan 1938- Y-82

Science Fantasy.......................DLB-8

Science-Fiction Fandom and Conventions...........DLB-8

Science-Fiction Fanzines: The Time Binders.......DLB-8

Science-Fiction Films DLB-8

Science Fiction Writers of America and the
   Nebula Awards DLB-8

Scott, Duncan Campbell 1862-1947 ....DLB-92

Scott, Evelyn 1893-1963.......................DLB-9, 48

Scott, F. R. 1899-1985 ....DLB-88

Scott, Frederick George
   1861-1944 ....DLB-92

Scott, Harvey W. 1838-1910 ....DLB-23

Scott, Paul 1920-1978.......................DLB-14

Scott, Sarah 1723-1795.......................DLB-39

Scott, Tom 1918- DLB-27

Scott, Sir Walter 1771-1832.......................DLB-93

Scott, William Bell 1811-1890.......................DLB-32

Scott, William R. [publishing house] DLB-46

Scott-Heron, Gil 1949- DLB-41

Charles Scribner's Sons DLB-49

Scripps, E. W. 1854-1926..................................DLB-25

Scudder, Horace Elisha 1838-1902 ....DLB-42, 71

Scudder, Vida Dutton 1861-1954.....................DLB-71

Scupham, Peter 1933- DLB-40

Seabrook, William 1886-1945 ....DLB-4

Seabury, Samuel 1729-1796..............................DLB-31

Sears, Edward I. 1819?-1876 ....DLB-79

Sears Publishing Company.................................DLB-46

Seaton, George 1911-1979 ....DLB-44

Seaton, William Winston 1785-1866..................DLB-43

Sedgwick, Arthur George 1844-1915 ....DLB-64

Sedgwick, Catharine Maria 1789-1867..........DLB-1, 74

Sedgwick, Ellery 1872-1930 ....DLB-91

Seeger, Alan 1888-1916 ....DLB-45

Seers, Eugene (see Dantin, Louis)

Segal, Erich 1937- Y-86

Seghers, Anna 1900-1983 ....DLB-69

Seid, Ruth (see Sinclair, Jo)

Seidel, Frederick Lewis 1936- Y-84

Seidel, Ina 1885-1974..DLB-56

Séjour, Victor 1817-1874 ....DLB-50

Séjour Marcou et Ferrand,
    Juan Victor (see Séjour, Victor)

Selby, Hubert, Jr. 1928- DLB-2

Selden, George 1929- DLB-52

Selected English-Language Little Magazines and
    Newspapers [France, 1920-1939] DLB-4

Selected Humorous Magazines (1820-1950) DLB-11

Selected Science-Fiction Magazines and
    Anthologies...DLB-8

Seligman, Edwin R. A. 1861-1939 ....DLB-47

Seltzer, Chester E. (see Muro, Amado)

Seltzer, Thomas [publishing house]....................DLB-46

Sendak, Maurice 1928- DLB-61

Senécal, Eva 1905- DLB-92

Sensation Novels (1863), by H. L. Manse..........DLB-21

Seredy, Kate 1899-1975 ....DLB-22

Serling, Rod 1924-1975.....................................DLB-26

Service, Robert 1874-1958 ....DLB-92

Seton, Ernest Thompson
    1860-1942 ....DLB-92

Settle, Mary Lee 1918- DLB-6

Seume, Johann Gottfried 1763-1810.................DLB-94

Seuss, Dr. (see Geisel, Theodor Seuss)

Sewall, Joseph 1688-1769.................................DLB-24

Sewell, Samuel 1652-1730.................................DLB-24

Sex, Class, Politics, and Religion [in the British
    Novel, 1930-1959] DLB-15

Sexton, Anne 1928-1974....................................DLB-5

Shaara, Michael 1929-1988 ....Y-83

Shadwell, Thomas 1641?-1692 ....DLB-80

Shaffer, Anthony 1926- DLB-13

Shaffer, Peter 1926- DLB-13

Shairp, Mordaunt 1887-1939............................DLB-10

Shakespeare, William 1564-1616 ....DLB-62

Shange, Ntozake 1948- DLB-38

Shapiro, Karl 1913- DLB-48

Sharon Publications DLB-46

Sharpe, Tom 1928- DLB-14

Shaw, Albert 1857-1947 ....DLB-91

Shaw, Bernard 1856-1950............................DLB-10, 57

Shaw, Henry Wheeler 1818-1885 ....DLB-11

Shaw, Irwin 1913-1984 ....DLB-6; Y-84

Shaw, Robert 1927-1978 ....DLB-13, 14

Shay, Frank [publishing house]..........................DLB-46

Shea, John Gilmary 1824-1892 ....DLB-30

Shearing, Joseph 1886-1952..............................DLB-70

Shebbeare, John 1709-1788 ....DLB-39

Sheckley, Robert 1928- DLB-8

Shedd, William G. T. 1820-1894 ....DLB-64

Sheed, Wilfred 1930- DLB-6

Sheed and Ward DLB-46

Sheldon, Alice B. (see Tiptree, James, Jr.)

Sheldon, Edward 1886-1946...............................DLB-7

Sheldon and Company DLB-49

Shepard, Sam 1943- DLB-7

Shepard, Thomas I 1604 or 1605-1649 ....DLB-24

Shepard, Thomas II 1635-1677.........................DLB-24

Shepard, Clark and Brown DLB-49

Sheridan, Frances 1724-1766......................DLB-39, 84

Sheridan, Richard Brinsley 1751-1816...............DLB-89

Sherman, Francis 1871-1926.........................DLB-92

Sherriff, R. C. 1896-1975..................................DLB-10

Sherwood, Robert 1896-1955.......................DLB-7, 26

Shiels, George 1886-1949..................................DLB-10

Shillaber, B.[enjamin] P.[enhallow]
        1814-1890..DLB-1, 11

Shine, Ted 1931- DLB-38

Ship, Reuben 1915-1975.................................DLB-88

Shirer, William L. 1904- DLB-4

Shirley, James 1596-1666.................................DLB-58

Shockley, Ann Allen 1927- DLB-33

Shorthouse, Joseph Henry 1834-1903...............DLB-18

Showalter, Elaine 1941- DLB-67

Shulevitz, Uri 1935- DLB-61

Shulman, Max 1919-1988 ....DLB-11

Shute, Henry A. 1856-1943 ....DLB-9

Shuttle, Penelope 1947- DLB-14, 40

Sidney, Margaret (see Lothrop, Harriet M.)

Sidney's Press DLB-49

Siegfried Loraine Sassoon: A Centenary Essay
        Tributes from Vivien F. Clarke and
            Michael Thorpe Y-86

Sierra Club Books..DLB-49

Sigourney, Lydia Howard (Huntley)
        1791-1865.............................DLB-1, 42, 73

Silkin, Jon 1930- DLB-27

Silliphant, Stirling 1918- DLB-26

Sillitoe, Alan 1928- DLB-14

Silman, Roberta 1934- DLB-28

Silverberg, Robert 1935- DLB-8

Simak, Clifford D. 1904-1988 ....DLB-8

Simcox, George Augustus 1841-1905...............DLB-35

Sime, Jessie Georgina
        1868-1958 ....DLB-92

Simenon, Georges 1903-1989 ....DLB-72

Simmel, Johannes Mario 1924- DLB-69

Simmons, Herbert Alfred 1930- DLB-33

Simmons, James 1933- DLB-40

Simms, William Gilmore 1806-1870
        ....DLB-3, 30, 59, 73

Simon, Claude 1913- DLB-83

Simon, Neil 1927- DLB-7

Simon and Schuster..DLB-46

Simons, Katherine Drayton Mayrant 1890-1969.....Y-83

Simpson, Helen 1897-1940 ....DLB-77

Simpson, Louis 1923- DLB-5

Simpson, N. F. 1919- DLB-13

Sims, George 1923- DLB-87

Sims, George R. 1847-1922.........................DLB-35, 70

Sinclair, Andrew 1935- DLB-14

Sinclair, Bertrand William
        1881-1972 ....DLB-92

Sinclair, Jo 1913- DLB-28

Sinclair Lewis Centennial Conference Y-85

Sinclair, Lister 1921- DLB-88

Sinclair, May 1863-1946...................................DLB-36

Sinclair, Upton 1878-1968...................................DLB-9

Sinclair, Upton [publishing house] DLB-46

Singer, Isaac Bashevis 1904- DLB-6, 28, 52

Singmaster, Elsie 1879-1958 ....DLB-9

Siodmak, Curt 1902- DLB-44

Sissman, L. E. 1928-1976...................................DLB-5

Sisson, C. H. 1914- DLB-27

Sitwell, Edith 1887-1964 ....DLB-20

Skelton, Robin 1925- DLB-27, 53

Skinner, Constance Lindsay
        1877-1939 ....DLB-92

Skinner, John Stuart 1788-1851 ....DLB-73

Skipsey, Joseph 1832-1903...............................DLB-35

Slade, Bernard 1930- DLB-53

Slater, Patrick 1880-1951 ....DLB-68

Slavitt, David 1935- DLB-5, 6

A Slender Thread of Hope: The Kennedy
        Center Black Theatre Project DLB-38

Slick, Sam (see Haliburton, Thomas Chandler)

Sloane, William, Associates DLB-46

Small, Maynard and Company DLB-49

Small Presses in Great Britain and Ireland,
        1960-1985 ....DLB-40

Small Presses I: Jargon Society Y-84

Small Presses II: The Spirit That
        Moves Us Press Y-85

Small Presses III: Pushcart Press............................Y-87

Smart, Elizabeth 1913-1986 ....DLB-88

Smiles, Samuel 1812-1904..................................DLB-55

Smith, A. J. M. 1902-1980 ....DLB-88

Smith, Alexander 1829-1867 ....DLB-32, 55

Smith, Betty 1896-1972 ....Y-82

Smith, Carol Sturm 1938- Y-81

Smith, Charles Henry 1826-1903 ....DLB-11

Smith, Charlotte 1749-1806 ....DLB-39

Smith, Cordwainer 1913-1966 ....DLB-8

Smith, Dave 1942- DLB-5

Smith, Dodie 1896- DLB-10

Smith, Doris Buchanan 1934- DLB-52

Smith, E. E. 1890-1965.....................................DLB-8

Smith, Elihu Hubbard 1771-1798.....................DLB-37

Smith, Elizabeth Oakes (Prince) 1806-1893 ....DLB-1

Smith, George O. 1911-1981 ....DLB-8

Smith, H. Allen 1907-1976..........................DLB-11, 29

Smith, Harrison, and Robert Haas
    [publishing house] DLB-46

Smith, Iain Crichten 1928- DLB-40

Smith, J. Allen 1860-1924.................................DLB-47

Smith, J. Stilman, and Company DLB-49

Smith, John 1580-1631 ....DLB-24, 30

Smith, Josiah 1704-1781..................................DLB-24

Smith, Ken 1938- DLB-40

Smith, Lee 1944- Y-83

Smith, Mark 1935- Y-82

Smith, Michael 1698-circa 1771 ....DLB-31

Smith, Red 1905-1982......................................DLB-29

Smith, Roswell 1829-1892 ....DLB-79

Smith, Samuel Harrison 1772-1845...................DLB-43

Smith, Samuel Stanhope 1751-1819..................DLB-37

Smith, Seba 1792-1868.................................DLB-1, 11

Smith, Stevie 1902-1971.................................DLB-20

Smith, Sydney Goodsir 1915-1975 ....DLB-27

Smith, W. B., and Company DLB-49

Smith, William 1727-1803..............................DLB-31

Smith, William 1728-1793..............................DLB-30

Smith, William Gardner 1927-1974...................DLB-76

Smith, William Jay 1918- DLB-5

Smollett, Tobias 1721-1771 ....DLB-39

Snellings, Rolland (see Touré, Askia Muhammad)

Snodgrass, W. D. 1926- DLB-5

Snow, C. P. 1905-1980 ....DLB-15, 77

Snyder, Gary 1930- DLB-5, 16

Sobiloff, Hy 1912-1970 ....DLB-48

The Society for Textual Scholarship
    and *TEXT*...Y-87

Solano, Solita 1888-1975 ....DLB-4

Sollers, Philippe 1936- DLB-83

Solomon, Carl 1928- DLB-16

Solway, David 1941- DLB-53

Solzhenitsyn and America Y-85

Sontag, Susan 1933- DLB-2, 67

Sorrentino, Gilbert 1929- DLB-5; Y-80

Sotheby, William 1757-1833 ....DLB-93

Soto, Gary 1952- DLB-82

Sources for the Study of Tudor
    and Stuart Drama....................................DLB-62

Souster, Raymond 1921- DLB-88

Southerland, Ellease 1943- DLB-33

Southern, Terry 1924- DLB-2

Southern Writers Between the Wars DLB-9

Southerne, Thomas 1659-1746..........................DLB-80

Southey, Robert 1774-1843...............................DLB-93

Spark, Muriel 1918- DLB-15

Sparks, Jared 1789-1866 ....DLB-1, 30

Sparshott, Francis 1926- DLB-60

Späth, Gerold 1939- DLB-75

Spellman, A. B. 1935- DLB-41

Spencer, Anne 1882-1975.............................DLB-51, 54

Spencer, Elizabeth 1921- DLB-6

Spencer, Herbert 1820-1903.............................DLB-57

Spencer, Scott 1945- Y-86

Spender, Stephen 1909-..................................DLB-20

Spicer, Jack 1925-1965.................................DLB-5, 16

Spielberg, Peter 1929- Y-81

Spier, Peter 1927- DLB-61

Spinrad, Norman 1940- DLB-8

Spofford, Harriet Prescott 1835-1921 ....DLB-74

Squibob (see Derby, George Horatio)

Stafford, Jean 1915-1979 ....DLB-2

Stafford, William 1914- DLB-5

Stage Censorship: "The Rejected Statement"
    (1911), by Bernard Shaw [excerpts] DLB-10

Stallings, Laurence 1894-1968 ....DLB-7, 44

Stallworthy, Jon 1935- DLB-40

Stampp, Kenneth M. 1912- DLB-17

Stanford, Ann 1916- DLB-5

Stanton, Elizabeth Cady 1815-1902 ....DLB-79

Stanton, Frank L. 1857-1927 ....DLB-25

Stapledon, Olaf 1886-1950 ....DLB-15

Star Spangled Banner Office DLB-49

Starkweather, David 1935- DLB-7

Statements on the Art of Poetry DLB-54

Stead, Robert J. C. 1880-1959 ....DLB-92

Steadman, Mark 1930- DLB-6

The Stealthy School of Criticism (1871), by
    Dante Gabriel Rossetti DLB-35

Stearns, Harold E. 1891-1943 ....DLB-4

Stedman, Edmund Clarence 1833-1908 ....DLB-64

Steele, Max 1922- Y-80

Steele, Richard 1672-1729 ....DLB-84

Steele, Wilbur Daniel 1886-1970 ....DLB-86

Steere, Richard circa 1643-1721 ....DLB-24

Stegner, Wallace 1909- DLB-9

Stehr, Hermann 1864-1940 ....DLB-66

Steig, William 1907- DLB-61

Stein, Gertrude 1874-1946 ....DLB-4, 54, 86

Stein, Leo 1872-1947 ....DLB-4

Stein and Day Publishers DLB-46

Steinbeck, John 1902-1968 ....DLB-7, 9; DS-2

Steiner, George 1929- DLB-67

Stephen, Leslie 1832-1904 ....DLB-57

Stephens, Alexander H. 1812-1883 ....DLB-47

Stephens, Ann 1810-1886 ....DLB-3, 73

Stephens, Charles Asbury 1844?-1931 ....DLB-42

Stephens, James 1882?-1950 ....DLB-19

Sterling, George 1869-1926 ....DLB-54

Sterling, James 1701-1763 ....DLB-24

Stern, Richard 1928- Y-87

Stern, Stewart 1922- DLB-26

Sterne, Laurence 1713-1768 ....DLB-39

Sternheim, Carl 1878-1942 ....DLB-56

Stevens, Wallace 1879-1955 ....DLB-54

Stevenson, Anne 1933- DLB-40

Stevenson, Robert Louis 1850-1894 ....DLB-18, 57

Stewart, Donald Ogden 1894-1980 ....DLB-4, 11, 26

Stewart, Dugald 1753-1828 ....DLB-31

Stewart, George R. 1895-1980 ....DLB-8

Stewart and Kidd Company DLB-46

Stickney, Trumbull 1874-1904 ....DLB-54

Stiles, Ezra 1727-1795 ....DLB-31

Still, James 1906- DLB-9

Stith, William 1707-1755 ....DLB-31

Stockton, Frank R. 1834-1902 ....DLB-42, 74

Stoddard, Ashbel [publishing house] DLB-49

Stoddard, Richard Henry 1825-1903 ....DLB-3, 64

Stoddard, Solomon 1643-1729 ....DLB-24

Stoker, Bram 1847-1912 ....DLB-36, 70

Stokes, Frederick A., Company DLB-49

Stokes, Thomas L. 1898-1958 ....DLB-29

Stolberg, Christian Graf zu
    1748-1821 ....DLB-94

Stolberg, Friedrich Leopold Graf zu
    1750-1819 ....DLB-94

Stone, Herbert S., and Company DLB-49

Stone, Lucy 1818-1893 ....DLB-79

Stone, Melville 1848-1929 ....DLB-25

Stone, Samuel 1602-1663 ....DLB-24

Stone and Kimball DLB-49

Stoppard, Tom 1937- DLB-13; Y-85

Storey, Anthony 1928- DLB-14

Storey, David 1933- DLB-13, 14

Story, Thomas circa 1670-1742 ....DLB-31

Story, William Wetmore 1819-1895 ....DLB-1

Storytelling: A Contemporary Renaissance............Y-84

Stoughton, William 1631-1701 ....DLB-24

Stowe, Harriet Beecher 1811-1896 ....DLB-1, 12, 42, 74

Stowe, Leland 1899- DLB-29

Strand, Mark 1934- DLB-5

Stratemeyer, Edward 1862-1930 ....DLB-42

Stratton and Barnard DLB-49

Straub, Peter 1943- Y-84

Street, Cecil John Charles (see Rhode, John)

Street and Smith.................................DLB-49

Streeter, Edward 1891-1976 ....DLB-11

Stribling, T. S. 1881-1965 ....DLB-9

Stringer and Townsend DLB-49

Stringer, Arthur 1874-1950 ....DLB-92

Strittmatter, Erwin 1912- DLB-69

Strother, David Hunter 1816-1888.....................DLB-3

Stuart, Jesse 1906-1984.........................DLB-9, 48; Y-84

Stuart, Lyle [publishing house]...........................DLB-46

Stubbs, Harry Clement (see Clement, Hal)

The Study of Poetry (1880), by Matthew
    Arnold...DLB-35

Sturgeon, Theodore 1918-1985 ....DLB-8; Y-85

Sturges, Preston 1898-1959.............................DLB-26

"Style" (1840; revised, 1859), by Thomas
    de Quincey [excerpt]...................................DLB-57

"Style" (1888), by Walter Pater DLB-57

Style (1897), by Walter Raleigh [excerpt]...........DLB-57

"Style" (1877), by T. H. Wright [excerpt].........DLB-57

"Le Style c'est l'homme" (1892),
    by W. H. Mallock DLB-57

Styron, William 1925- DLB-2; Y-80

Suárez, Mario 1925- DLB-82

Such, Peter 1939- DLB-60

Suckling, Sir John 1609-1642 ....DLB-58

Suckow, Ruth 1892-1960.................................DLB-9

Suggs, Simon (see Hooper, Johnson Jones)

Sukenick, Ronald 1932- Y-81

Suknaski, Andrew 1942- DLB-53

Sullivan, Alan 1868-1947 ....DLB-92

Sullivan, C. Gardner 1886-1965 ....DLB-26

Sullivan, Frank 1892-1976 ....DLB-11

Summers, Hollis 1916- DLB-6

Sumner, Henry A. [publishing house] DLB-49

Surtees, Robert Smith 1803-1864 ....DLB-21

A Survey of Poetry
    Anthologies, 1879-1960 ....DLB-54

Surveys of the Year's Biography
    A Transit of Poets and Others: American
        Biography in 1982 ....Y-82

The Year in Literary Biography Y-83
The Year in Literary Biography Y-84
The Year in Literary Biography Y-85
The Year in Literary Biography Y-86
The Year in Literary Biography Y-87
The Year in Literary Biography Y-88

Surveys of the Year's Book Publishing
    The Year in Book Publishing................Y-86

Surveys of the Year's Drama
    The Year in Drama.....................................Y-82
    The Year in Drama.....................................Y-83
    The Year in Drama.....................................Y-84
    The Year in Drama.....................................Y-85
    The Year in Drama.....................................Y-87
    The Year in Drama.....................................Y-88

Surveys of the Year's Fiction
    The Year's Work in Fiction: A Survey..............Y-82
    The Year in Fiction: A Biased View.................Y-83
    The Year in Fiction.....................................Y-84
    The Year in Fiction.....................................Y-85
    The Year in Fiction.....................................Y-86
    The Year in the Novel.................................Y-87
    The Year in Short Stories...........................Y-87
    The Year in the Novel.................................Y-88
    The Year in Short Stories...........................Y-88

Surveys of the Year's Poetry
    The Year's Work in American Poetry.............Y-82
    The Year in Poetry Y-83
    The Year in Poetry Y-84
    The Year in Poetry Y-85
    The Year in Poetry Y-86
    The Year in Poetry Y-87
    The Year in Poetry Y-88

Sutherland, John 1919-1956 ....DLB-68

Sutro, Alfred 1863-1933 ....DLB-10

Swados, Harvey 1920-1972 ....DLB-2

Swain, Charles 1801-1874 ....DLB-32

Swallow Press...DLB-46

Swenson, May 1919-1989 ....DLB-5

Swerling, Jo 1897- DLB-44

Swift, Jonathan 1667-1745 ....DLB-39

Swinburne, A. C. 1837-1909.........................DLB-35, 57

Swinnerton, Frank 1884-1982.........................DLB-34

Swisshelm, Jane Grey 1815-1884 ....DLB-43

Swope, Herbert Bayard 1882-1958 ....DLB-25

Swords, T. and J., and Company DLB-49

Swords, Thomas 1763-1843 and
    Swords, James ?-1844.................................DLB-73

Symonds, John Addington 1840-1893...............DLB-57

Symons, Arthur 1865-1945.........................DLB-19, 57

Symons, Julian 1912- DLB-87

Symons, Scott 1933- DLB-53

Synge, John Millington 1871-1909...............DLB-10, 19

T

Tafolla, Carmen 1951- DLB-82

Taggard, Genevieve 1894-1948.........................DLB-45

Tait, J. Selwin, and Sons....................................DLB-49

Talvj or Talvi (see Robinson, Therese)

Taradash, Daniel 1913- DLB-44

Tarbell, Ida M. 1857-1944................................DLB-47

Tarkington, Booth 1869-1946............................DLB-9

Tashlin, Frank 1913-1972..................................DLB-44

Tate, Allen 1899-1979.............................DLB-4, 45, 63

Tate, James 1943- DLB-5

Tate, Nahum circa 1652-1715.............................DLB-80

Taylor, Bayard 1825-1878..................................DLB-3

Taylor, Bert Leston 1866-1921 ....DLB-25

Taylor, Charles H. 1846-1921 ....DLB-25

Taylor, Edward circa 1642-1729 ....DLB-24

Taylor, Henry 1942- DLB-5

Taylor, Sir Henry 1800-1886 ....DLB-32

Taylor, Mildred D. ?- DLB-52

Taylor, Peter 1917- Y-81

Taylor, William, and Company.........................DLB-49

Taylor-Made Shakespeare? Or Is
    "Shall I Die?" the Long-Lost Text
    of Bottom's Dream?........................Y-85

Teasdale, Sara 1884-1933.................................DLB-45

The Tea-Table (1725), by Eliza Haywood
    [excerpt]......................................DLB-39

Tenn, William 1919- DLB-8

Tennant, Emma 1937- DLB-14

Tenney, Tabitha Gilman 1762-1837 ....DLB-37

Tennyson, Alfred 1809-1892 ....DLB-32

Tennyson, Frederick 1807-1898 ....DLB-32

Terhune, Albert Payson 1872-1942.................DLB-9

Terry, Megan 1932- DLB-7

Terson, Peter 1932- DLB-13

Tesich, Steve 1943- Y-83

Tey, Josephine 1896?-1952 ....DLB-77

Thacher, James 1754-1844 ....DLB-37

Thackeray, William Makepeace
    1811-1863 ....DLB-21, 55

Thanet, Octave (see French, Alice)

The Theater in Shakespeare's Time DLB-62

The Theatre Guild DLB-7

Thelwall, John 1764-1834 ....DLB-93

Theriault, Yves 1915-1983 ....DLB-88

Thério, Adrien 1925- DLB-53

Theroux, Paul 1941- DLB-2

Thibaudeau, Colleen 1925- DLB-88

Thoma, Ludwig 1867-1921....................DLB-66

Thoma, Richard 1902- DLB-4

Thomas, Audrey 1935- DLB-60

Thomas, D. M. 1935- DLB-40

Thomas, Dylan 1914-1953 ....DLB-13, 20

Thomas, Edward 1878-1917 ....DLB-19

Thomas, Gwyn 1913-1981 ....DLB-15

Thomas, Isaiah 1750-1831.........................DLB-43, 73

Thomas, Isaiah [publishing house].................DLB-49

Thomas, John 1900-1932....................................DLB-4

Thomas, Joyce Carol 1938- DLB-33

Thomas, Lorenzo 1944- DLB-41

Thomas, R. S. 1915- DLB-27

Thompson, Dorothy 1893-1961.........................DLB-29

Thompson, Francis 1859-1907 ....DLB-19

Thompson, George Selden (see Selden, George)

Thompson, John 1938-1976 ....DLB-60

Thompson, John R. 1823-1873 ....DLB-3, 73

Thompson, Maurice 1844-1901...................DLB-71, 74

Thompson, Ruth Plumly 1891-1976 ....DLB-22

Thompson, William Tappan 1812-1882 ....DLB-3, 11

Thomson, Edward William
    1849-1924 ....DLB-92

Thomson, James 1834-1882.................................DLB-35

Thomson, Mortimer 1831-1875........................DLB-11

Thoreau, Henry David 1817-1862 ....DLB-1

Thorpe, Thomas Bangs 1815-1878...............DLB-3, 11

Thoughts on Poetry and Its Varieties (1833),
    by John Stuart Mill..DLB-32

Thurber, James 1894-1961 ....DLB-4, 11, 22

Thurman, Wallace 1902-1934..........................DLB-51

Thwaite, Anthony 1930- DLB-40

Thwaites, Reuben Gold 1853-1913 ....DLB-47

Ticknor, George 1791-1871.........................DLB-1, 59

Ticknor and Fields DLB-49

Tieck, Ludwig 1773-1853.................................DLB-90

Ticknor and Fields (revived)..............................DLB-46

Tietjens, Eunice 1884-1944.............................DLB-54

Tilton, J. E., and Company...............................DLB-49

Time and Western Man (1927), by Wyndham
    Lewis [excerpts] DLB-36

Time-Life Books DLB-46

Times Books DLB-46

Timothy, Peter circa 1725-1782 ....DLB-43

Timrod, Henry 1828-1867................................DLB-3

Tiptree, James, Jr. 1915- DLB-8

Titus, Edward William 1870-1952......................DLB-4

Toklas, Alice B. 1877-1967 ....DLB-4

Tolkien, J. R. R. 1892-1973 ....DLB-15

Tolson, Melvin B. 1898-1966 ....DLB-48, 76

Tom Jones (1749), by Henry
    Fielding [excerpt] DLB-39

Tomlinson, Charles 1927- DLB-40

Tomlinson, Henry Major 1873-1958 ....DLB-36

Tompkins, Abel [publishing house]....................DLB-49

Tompson, Benjamin 1642-1714 ....DLB-24

Tonks, Rosemary 1932- DLB-14

Toole, John Kennedy 1937-1969 ....Y-81

Toomer, Jean 1894-1967................................DLB-45, 51

Tor Books DLB-46

Torberg, Friedrich 1908-1979 ....DLB-85

Torrence, Ridgely 1874-1950...........................DLB-54

Toth, Susan Allen 1940- Y-86

Tough-Guy Literature DLB-9

Touré, Askia Muhammad 1938- DLB-41

Tourgée, Albion W. 1838-1905.........................DLB-79

Tourneur, Cyril circa 1580-1626 ....DLB-58

Tournier, Michel 1924- DLB-83

Tousey, Frank [publishing house].......................DLB-49

Tower Publications..DLB-46

Towne, Benjamin circa 1740-1793.....................DLB-43

Towne, Robert 1936- DLB-44

Tracy, Honor 1913- DLB-15

Train, Arthur 1875-1945..................................DLB-86

The Transatlantic Publishing Company DLB-49

Transcendentalists, American DS-5

Traven, B. 1882? or 1890?-1969? DLB-9, 56

Travers, Ben 1886-1980 ....DLB-10

Tremain, Rose 1943- DLB-14

Tremblay, Michel 1942- DLB-60

Trends in Twentieth-Century
    Mass Market Publishing DLB-46

Trent, William P. 1862-1939............................DLB-47

Trescot, William Henry 1822-1898....................DLB-30

Trevor, William 1928- DLB-14

Trilling, Lionel 1905-1975 ....DLB-28, 63

Triolet, Elsa 1896-1970...................................DLB-72

Tripp, John 1927- DLB-40

Trocchi, Alexander 1925- DLB-15

Trollope, Anthony 1815-1882 ....DLB-21, 57

Trollope, Frances 1779-1863 ....DLB-21

Troop, Elizabeth 1931- DLB-14

Trotter, Catharine 1679-1749 ....DLB-84

Trotti, Lamar 1898-1952.........................DLB-44

Trottier, Pierre 1925- DLB-60

Troupe, Quincy Thomas, Jr. 1943- DLB-41

Trow, John F., and Company DLB-49

Trumbo, Dalton 1905-1976..............................DLB-26

Trumbull, Benjamin 1735-1820........................DLB-30

Trumbull, John 1750-1831...............................DLB-31

T. S. Eliot Centennial Y-88

Tucholsky, Kurt 1890-1935..............................DLB-56

Tucker, George 1775-1861 ....DLB-3, 30

Tucker, Nathaniel Beverley 1784-1851 ....DLB-3

Tucker, St. George 1752-1827 ....DLB-37

Tuckerman, Henry Theodore 1813-1871 ....DLB-64

Tunis, John R. 1889-1975 ....DLB-22

Tuohy, Frank 1925- DLB-14

Tupper, Martin F. 1810-1889 ....DLB-32

Turbyfill, Mark 1896- DLB-45

Turco, Lewis 1934- Y-84

Turnbull, Gael 1928- DLB-40

Turner, Charles (Tennyson) 1808-1879 ....DLB-32

Turner, Frederick 1943- DLB-40

Turner, Frederick Jackson 1861-1932...............DLB-17

Turner, Joseph Addison 1826-1868 ....DLB-79

Turpin, Waters Edward 1910-1968 ....DLB-51

Twain, Mark (see Clemens, Samuel Langhorne)

The 'Twenties and Berlin,
    by Alex Natan...................................DLB-66

Tyler, Anne 1941- DLB-6; Y-82

Tyler, Moses Coit 1835-1900 ....DLB-47, 64

Tyler, Royall 1757-1826 ....DLB-37

Tylor, Edward Burnett 1832-1917.....................DLB-57

U

Udall, Nicholas 1504-1556 ....DLB-62

Uhland, Ludwig 1787-1862 ....DLB-90

Uhse, Bodo 1904-1963......................................DLB-69

Ulibarrí, Sabine R. 1919- DLB-82

Ulica, Jorge 1870-1926......................................DLB-82

Under the Microscope (1872), by A. C.
    Swinburne...DLB-35

Unger, Friederike Helene 1741-1813................DLB-94

United States Book Company DLB-49

Universal Publishing and Distributing
    Corporation DLB-46

The University of Iowa Writers'
    Workshop Golden Jubilee Y-86

"The Unknown Public" (1858), by
    Wilkie Collins [excerpt].................DLB-57

Unruh, Fritz von 1885-1970 ....DLB-56

Upchurch, Boyd B. (see Boyd, John)

Updike, John 1932- DLB-2, 5; Y-80, 82; DS-3

Upton, Charles 1948- DLB-16

Upward, Allen 1863-1926 ....DLB-36

Urista, Alberto Baltazar (see Alurista)

Urzidil, Johannes 1896-1976...........................DLB-85

Ustinov, Peter 1921- DLB-13

V

Vac, Bertrand 1914- DLB-88

Vail, Laurence 1891-1968 ....DLB-4

Vailland, Roger 1907-1965...............................DLB-83

Vajda, Ernest 1887-1954 ....DLB-44

Valgardson, W. D. 1939- DLB-60

Van Allsburg, Chris 1949- DLB-61

Van Anda, Carr 1864-1945...............................DLB-25

Vanbrugh, Sir John 1664-1726 ....DLB-80

Vance, Jack 1916?- DLB-8

Van Doren, Mark 1894-1972 ....DLB-45

van Druten, John 1901-1957 ....DLB-10

Van Duyn, Mona 1921- DLB-5

Van Dyke, Henry 1852-1933 ....DLB-71

Van Dyke, Henry 1928- DLB-33

Vane, Sutton 1888-1963 ....DLB-10

Vanguard Press...DLB-46

van Itallie, Jean-Claude 1936- DLB-7

Vann, Robert L. 1879-1940...............................DLB-29

Van Rensselaer, Mariana Griswold
    1851-1934 ....DLB-47

Van Rensselaer, Mrs. Schuyler (see Van
    Rensselaer, Mariana Griswold)

Van Vechten, Carl 1880-1964 ....DLB-4, 9

van Vogt, A. E. 1912- DLB-8

Varley, John 1947- Y-81

Varnhagen von Ense, Karl August
    1785-1858 ....DLB-90

Varnhagen von Ense, Rahel
    1771-1833 ....DLB-90

Vassa, Gustavus (see Equiano, Olaudah)

Vega, Janine Pommy 1942- DLB-16

Veiller, Anthony 1903-1965...............................DLB-44

Venegas, Daniel ?-?...DLB-82

Verplanck, Gulian C. 1786-1870........................DLB-59

Very, Jones 1813-1880...DLB-1

Vian, Boris 1920-1959......................................DLB-72

Vickers, Roy 1888?-1965 ....DLB-77

Victoria 1819-1901 ....DLB-55

Vidal, Gore 1925- DLB-6

Viebig, Clara 1860-1952.....................................DLB-66

Viereck, George Sylvester 1884-1962 ....DLB-54

Viereck, Peter 1916- DLB-5

Viewpoint: Politics and Performance, by David
Edgar DLB-13

Vigneault, Gilles 1928- DLB-60

The Viking Press DLB-46

Villanueva, Tino 1941- DLB-82

Villard, Henry 1835-1900 ....DLB-23

Villard, Oswald Garrison 1872-1949 ....DLB-25, 91

Villarreal, José Antonio 1924- DLB-82

Villemaire, Yolande 1949- DLB-60

Villiers, George, Second Duke
of Buckingham 1628-1687 ....DLB-80

Viorst, Judith ?- DLB-52

Voaden, Herman 1903- DLB-88

Volkoff, Vladimir 1932- DLB-83

Volland, P. F., Company DLB-46

von der Grün, Max 1926- DLB-75

Vonnegut, Kurt 1922- DLB-2, 8; Y-80; DS-3

Voß, Johann Heinrich 1751-1826 ....DLB-90

Vroman, Mary Elizabeth circa 1924-1967 ....DLB-33

W

Wackenroder, Wilhelm Heinrich
1773-1798 ....DLB-90

Waddington, Miriam 1917- DLB-68

Wade, Henry 1887-1969 ....DLB-77

Wagner, Heinrich Leopold 1747-1779 ....DLB-94

Wagoner, David 1926- DLB-5

Wah, Fred 1939- DLB-60

Waiblinger, Wilhelm 1804-1830 ....DLB-90

Wain, John 1925- DLB-15, 27

Wainwright, Jeffrey 1944- DLB-40

Waite, Peirce and Company DLB-49

Wakoski, Diane 1937- DLB-5

Walck, Henry Z. DLB-46

Walcott, Derek 1930- Y-81

Waldman, Anne 1945- DLB-16

Walker, Alice 1944- DLB-6, 33

Walker, George F. 1947- DLB-60

Walker, Joseph A. 1935- DLB-38

Walker, Margaret 1915- DLB-76

Walker, Ted 1934- DLB-40

Walker and Company DLB-49

Walker, Evans and Cogswell Company DLB-49

Walker, John Brisben 1847-1931 ....DLB-79

Wallace, Edgar 1875-1932 ....DLB-70

Wallant, Edward Lewis 1926-1962 ....DLB-2, 28

Walpole, Horace 1717-1797 ....DLB-39

Walpole, Hugh 1884-1941 ....DLB-34

Walrond, Eric 1898-1966 ....DLB-51

Walser, Martin 1927- DLB-75

Walser, Robert 1878-1956 ....DLB-66

Walsh, Ernest 1895-1926 ....DLB-4, 45

Walsh, Robert 1784-1859 ....DLB-59

Wambaugh, Joseph 1937- DLB-6; Y-83

Ward, Artemus (see Browne, Charles Farrar)

Ward, Arthur Henry Sarsfield
(see Rohmer, Sax)

Ward, Douglas Turner 1930- DLB-7, 38

Ward, Lynd 1905-1985 ....DLB-22

Ward, Mrs. Humphry 1851-1920 ....DLB-18

Ward, Nathaniel circa 1578-1652 ....DLB-24

Ward, Theodore 1902-1983 ....DLB-76

Ware, William 1797-1852 ....DLB-1

Warne, Frederick, and Company DLB-49

Warner, Charles Dudley 1829-1900 ....DLB-64

Warner, Rex 1905- DLB-15

Warner, Susan Bogert 1819-1885 ....DLB-3, 42

Warner, Sylvia Townsend 1893-1978 ....DLB-34

Warner Books DLB-46

Warr, Bertram 1917-1943 ....DLB-88

Warren, John Byrne Leicester (see De Tabley, Lord)

Warren, Lella 1899-1982 ....Y-83

Warren, Mercy Otis 1728-1814 ....DLB-31

Warren, Robert Penn 1905-1989 ....DLB-2, 48; Y-80

Washington, George 1732-1799 ....DLB-31

Wassermann, Jakob 1873-1934 ....DLB-66

Wasson, David Atwood 1823-1887 ....DLB-1

Waterhouse, Keith 1929- DLB-13, 15

Waterman, Andrew 1940- DLB-40

Waters, Frank 1902- Y-86

Watkins, Tobias 1780-1855 ....DLB-73

Watkins, Vernon 1906-1967 ....DLB-20

Watmough, David 1926- DLB-53

Watson, James Wreford (see Wreford, James)

Watson, Sheila 1909- DLB-60

Watson, Wilfred 1911- DLB-60

Watt, W. J., and Company DLB-46

Watterson, Henry 1840-1921 ....DLB-25

Watts, Alan 1915-1973 ....DLB-16

Watts, Franklin [publishing house]....................DLB-46

Waugh, Auberon 1939- DLB-14

Waugh, Evelyn 1903-1966............................DLB-15

Way and Williams DLB-49

Wayman, Tom 1945- DLB-53

Weatherly, Tom 1942- DLB-41

Weaver, Robert 1921- DLB-88

Webb, Frank J. ?-? DLB-50

Webb, James Watson 1802-1884 ....DLB-43

Webb, Mary 1881-1927.............................DLB-34

Webb, Phyllis 1927- DLB-53

Webb, Walter Prescott 1888-1963 ....DLB-17

Webster, Augusta 1837-1894 ....DLB-35

Webster, Charles L., and Company DLB-49

Webster, John 1579 or 1580-1634?...................DLB-58

Webster, Noah 1758-1843 ....DLB-1, 37, 42, 43, 73

Weems, Mason Locke 1759-1825...........DLB-30, 37, 42

Weidman, Jerome 1913- DLB-28

Weinbaum, Stanley Grauman 1902-1935 ....DLB-8

Weisenborn, Günther 1902-1969......................DLB-69

Weiß, Ernst 1882-1940 ....DLB-81

Weiss, John 1818-1879 ....DLB-1

Weiss, Peter 1916-1982 ....DLB-69

Weiss, Theodore 1916- DLB-5

Welch, Lew 1926-1971? DLB-16

Weldon, Fay 1931- DLB-14

Wellek, René 1903- DLB-63

Wells, Carolyn 1862-1942.............................DLB-11

Wells, Charles Jeremiah circa 1800-1879 ....DLB-32

Wells, H. G. 1866-1946 ....DLB-34, 70

Wells, Robert 1947- DLB-40

Wells-Barnett, Ida B. 1862-1931........................DLB-23

Welty, Eudora 1909- DLB-2; Y-87

Wendell, Barrett 1855-1921 ....DLB-71

Wentworth, Patricia 1878-1961 ....DLB-77

Werfel, Franz 1890-1945 ....DLB-81

The Werner Company......................................DLB-49

Werner, Zacharias 1768-1823...........................DLB-94

Wersba, Barbara 1932- DLB-52

Wescott, Glenway 1901- DLB-4, 9

Wesker, Arnold 1932- DLB-13

Wesley, Richard 1945- DLB-38

Wessels, A., and Company DLB-46

West, Anthony 1914-1988 ....DLB-15

West, Dorothy 1907- DLB-76

West, Jessamyn 1902-1984 ....DLB-6; Y-84

West, Mae 1892-1980.....................................DLB-44

West, Nathanael 1903-1940 ....DLB-4, 9, 28

West, Paul 1930- DLB-14

West, Rebecca 1892-1983 ....DLB-36; Y-83

West and Johnson DLB-49

Western Publishing Company DLB-46

Wetherell, Elizabeth (see Warner, Susan Bogert)

Wetzel, Friedrich Gottlob 1779-1819 ....DLB-90

Wezel, Johann Karl 1747-1819 ....DLB-94

Whalen, Philip 1923- DLB-16

Whalley, George 1915-1983.............................DLB-88

Wharton, Edith 1862-1937 ....DLB-4, 9, 12, 78

Wharton, William 1920s?- Y-80

What's Really Wrong With Bestseller Lists Y-84

Wheatley, Dennis Yates 1897-1977 ....DLB-77

Wheatley, Phillis circa 1754-1784................DLB-31, 50

Wheeler, Charles Stearns 1816-1843...................DLB-1

Wheeler, Monroe 1900-1988 ....DLB-4

Wheelock, John Hall 1886-1978.......................DLB-45

Wheelwright, John circa 1592-1679 ....DLB-24

Wheelwright, J. B. 1897-1940...........................DLB-45

Whetstone, Colonel Pete (see Noland, C. F. M.)

Whipple, Edwin Percy 1819-1886 ....DLB-1, 64

Whitaker, Alexander 1585-1617......................DLB-24

Whitaker, Daniel K. 1801-1881 ....DLB-73

Whitcher, Frances Miriam 1814-1852 ....DLB-11

White, Andrew 1579-1656 ....DLB-24

White, Andrew Dickson 1832-1918 ....DLB-47

White, E. B. 1899-1985 ....DLB-11, 22

White, Edgar B. 1947- DLB-38

White, Ethel Lina 1887-1944 ....DLB-77

White, Horace 1834-1916 ....DLB-23

White, Phyllis Dorothy James
    (see James, P. D.)

White, Richard Grant 1821-1885 ....DLB-64

White, Walter 1893-1955 ....DLB-51

White, William, and Company DLB-49

White, William Allen 1868-1944 ....DLB-9, 25

White, William Anthony Parker
    (see Boucher, Anthony)

White, William Hale (see Rutherford, Mark)

Whitechurch, Victor L. 1868-1933 ....DLB-70

Whitehead, James 1936- Y-81

Whitehead, William 1715-1785...........................DLB-84

Whitfield, James Monroe 1822-1871 ....DLB-50

Whiting, John 1917-1963 ....DLB-13

Whiting, Samuel 1597-1679 ....DLB-24

Whitlock, Brand 1869-1934 ....DLB-12

Whitman, Albert, and Company DLB-46

Whitman, Albery Allson 1851-1901 ....DLB-50

Whitman, Sarah Helen (Power) 1803-1878.........DLB-1

Whitman, Walt 1819-1892 ....DLB-3, 64

Whitman Publishing Company DLB-46

Whittemore, Reed 1919- DLB-5

Whittier, John Greenleaf 1807-1892 ....DLB-1

Whittlesey House...DLB-46

Wideman, John Edgar 1941- DLB-33

Wiebe, Rudy 1934- DLB-60

Wiechert, Ernst 1887-1950...............................DLB-56

Wied, Martina 1882-1957................................DLB-85

Wieners, John 1934- DLB-16

Wier, Ester 1910- DLB-52

Wiesel, Elie 1928- DLB-83; Y-87

Wiggin, Kate Douglas 1856-1923 ....DLB-42

Wigglesworth, Michael 1631-1705 ....DLB-24

Wilbur, Richard 1921- DLB-5

Wild, Peter 1940- DLB-5

Wilde, Oscar 1854-1900 ....DLB-10, 19, 34, 57

Wilde, Richard Henry 1789-1847 ....DLB-3, 59

Wilde, W. A., Company DLB-49

Wilder, Billy 1906- DLB-26

Wilder, Laura Ingalls 1867-1957.......................DLB-22

Wilder, Thornton 1897-1975 ....DLB-4, 7, 9

Wiley, Bell Irvin 1906-1980..............................DLB-17

Wiley, John, and Sons DLB-49

Wilhelm, Kate 1928- DLB-8

Wilkes, George 1817-1885 ....DLB-79

Wilkinson, Anne 1910-1961..............................DLB-88

Wilkinson, Sylvia 1940- Y-86

Wilkinson, William Cleaver 1833-1920 ....DLB-71

Willard, L. [publishing house] DLB-49

Willard, Nancy 1936- DLB-5, 52

Willard, Samuel 1640-1707..............................DLB-24

Williams, A., and Company DLB-49

Williams, C. K. 1936- DLB-5

Williams, Chancellor 1905- DLB-76

Williams, Emlyn 1905- DLB-10, 77

Williams, Garth 1912- DLB-22

Williams, George Washington 1849-1891 ....DLB-47

Williams, Heathcote 1941- DLB-13

Williams, Hugo 1942- DLB-40

Williams, Isaac 1802-1865................................DLB-32

Williams, Joan 1928- DLB-6

Williams, John A. 1925- DLB-2, 33

Williams, John E. 1922- DLB-6

Williams, Jonathan 1929- DLB-5

Williams, Raymond 1921- DLB-14

Williams, Roger circa 1603-1683 ....DLB-24

Williams, Samm-Art 1946- DLB-38

Williams, Sherley Anne 1944- DLB-41

Williams, T. Harry 1909-1979.........................DLB-17

Williams, Tennessee 1911-1983........DLB-7; Y-83; DS-4

Williams, Valentine 1883-1946..........................DLB-77

Williams, William Appleman 1921- DLB-17

Williams, William Carlos 1883-1963
    ....DLB-4, 16, 54, 86

Williams, Wirt 1921- DLB-6

Williams Brothers DLB-49

Williamson, Jack 1908- DLB-8

Willingham, Calder Baynard, Jr. 1922- DLB-2, 44

Willis, Nathaniel Parker 1806-1867 ...DLB-3, 59, 73, 74

Wilmer, Clive 1945- DLB-40

Wilson, A. N. 1950- DLB-14

Wilson, Angus 1913- DLB-15

Wilson, Arthur 1595-1652 ....DLB-58

Wilson, Augusta Jane Evans 1835-1909 ....DLB-42

Wilson, Colin 1931- DLB-14

Wilson, Edmund 1895-1972 ....DLB-63

Wilson, Ethel 1888-1980 ....DLB-68

Wilson, Harriet E. Adams 1828?-1863? DLB-50

Wilson, Harry Leon 1867-1939 ....DLB-9

Wilson, John 1588-1667 ....DLB-24

Wilson, Lanford 1937- DLB-7

Wilson, Margaret 1882-1973..................DLB-9

Wilson, Michael 1914-1978 ....DLB-44

Wilson, Woodrow 1856-1924 ....DLB-47

Wimsatt, William K., Jr. 1907-1975.........DLB-63

Winchell, Walter 1897-1972.................DLB-29

Winchester, J. [publishing house] DLB-49

Windham, Donald 1920- DLB-6

Winsor, Justin 1831-1897...................DLB-47

John C. Winston Company DLB-49

Winters, Yvor 1900-1968 ....DLB-48

Winthrop, John 1588-1649 ....DLB-24, 30

Winthrop, John, Jr. 1606-1676..............DLB-24

Wirt, William 1772-1834....................DLB-37

Wise, John 1652-1725 ....DLB-24

Wiseman, Adele 1928- DLB-88

Wisner, George 1812-1849...................DLB-43

Wister, Owen 1860-1938.....................DLB-9, 78

Witherspoon, John 1723-1794................DLB-31

Wittig, Monique 1935- DLB-83

Wodehouse, P. G. 1881-1975.................DLB-34

Wohmann, Gabriele 1932- DLB-75

Woiwode, Larry 1941- DLB-6

Wolcott, Roger 1679-1767...................DLB-24

Wolf, Christa 1929- DLB-75

Wolfe, Gene 1931- DLB-8

Wolfe, Thomas 1900-1938...............DLB-9; DS-2; Y-85

Wollstonecraft, Mary 1759-1797 ....DLB-39

Wondratschek, Wolf 1943- DLB-75

Wood, Benjamin 1820-1900..................DLB-23

Wood, Charles 1932- DLB-13

Wood, Mrs. Henry 1814-1887 ....DLB-18

Wood, Joanna E. 1867-1927.................DLB-92

Wood, Samuel [publishing house] DLB-49

Wood, William ?-?.........................DLB-24

Woodberry, George Edward 1855-1930........DLB-71

Woodbridge, Benjamin 1622-1684 ....DLB-24

Woodcock, George 1912- DLB-88

Woodhull, Victoria C. 1838-1927 ....DLB-79

Woodmason, Charles circa 1720-? DLB-31

Woodson, Carter G. 1875-1950 ....DLB-17

Woodward, C. Vann 1908- DLB-17

Woolf, David (see Maddow, Ben)

Woolf, Virginia 1882-1941 ....DLB-36

Woollcott, Alexander 1887-1943............DLB-29

Woolman, John 1720-1772...................DLB-31

Woolner, Thomas 1825-1892.................DLB-35

Woolsey, Sarah Chauncy 1835-1905..........DLB-42

Woolson, Constance Fenimore 1840-1894....DLB-12, 74

Worcester, Joseph Emerson 1784-1865 ....DLB-1

Wordsworth, William 1770-1850 ....DLB-93

The Works of the Rev. John Witherspoon
   (1800-1801) [excerpts].................DLB-31

A World Chronology of Important Science
   Fiction Works (1818-1979) DLB-8

World Publishing Company DLB-46

Worthington, R., and Company..............DLB-49

Wouk, Herman 1915- Y-82

Wreford, James 1915- DLB-88

Wright, Charles 1935- Y-82

Wright, Charles Stevenson 1932- DLB-33

Wright, Frances 1795-1852 ....DLB-73

Wright, Harold Bell 1872-1944 ....DLB-9

Wright, James 1927-1980...................DLB-5

Wright, Jay 1935- DLB-41

Wright, Louis B. 1899-1984................DLB-17

Wright, Richard 1908-1960 ....DS-2, DLB-76

Wright, Richard B. 1937- DLB-53

Wright, Sarah Elizabeth 1928- DLB-33

Writers and Politics: 1871-1918,
    by Ronald Gray...DLB-66

Writers' Forum..Y-85

Writing for the Theatre, by Harold Pinter........DLB-13

Wycherley, William 1641-1715 ....DLB-80

Wylie, Elinor 1885-1928................................DLB-9, 45

Wylie, Philip 1902-1971 ....DLB-9

Y

Yates, Dornford 1885-1960 ....DLB-77

Yates, J. Michael 1938- DLB-60

Yates, Richard 1926- DLB-2; Y-81

Yeats, William Butler 1865-1939 ....DLB-10, 19

Yep, Laurence 1948- DLB-52

Yerby, Frank 1916- DLB-76

Yezierska, Anzia 1885-1970...............................DLB-28

Yolen, Jane 1939- DLB-52

Yonge, Charlotte Mary 1823-1901 ....DLB-18

A Yorkshire Tragedy DLB-58

Yoseloff, Thomas [publishing house] DLB-46

Young, Al 1939- DLB-33

Young, Stark 1881-1963 ....DLB-9

Young, Waldeman 1880-1938 ....DLB-26

Young, William [publishing house]...................DLB-49

Yourcenar, Marguerite 1903-1987............DLB-72; Y-88

"You've Never Had It So Good," Gusted by
    "Winds of Change": British Fiction in the
    1950s, 1960s, and After DLB-14

Z

Zamora, Bernice 1938- DLB-82

Zand, Herbert 1923-1970 ....DLB-85

Zangwill, Israel 1864-1926 ....DLB-10

Zebra Books DLB-46

Zebrowski, George 1945- DLB-8

Zech, Paul 1881-1946 ....DLB-56

Zelazny, Roger 1937- DLB-8

Zenger, John Peter 1697-1746 ....DLB-24, 43

Zieber, G. B., and Company DLB-49

Zieroth, Dale 1946- DLB-60

Zimmer, Paul 1934- DLB-5

Zindel, Paul 1936- DLB-7, 52

Zolotow, Charlotte 1915- DLB-52

Zschokke, Heinrich 1771-1848 ....DLB-94

Zubly, John Joachim 1724-1781.........................DLB-31

Zu-Bolton II, Ahmos 1936- DLB-41

Zuckmayer, Carl 1896-1977 ....DLB-56

Zukofsky, Louis 1904-1978 ....DLB-5

zur Mühlen, Hermynia 1883-1951 ....DLB-56

Zweig, Arnold 1887-1968...................................DLB-66

Zweig, Stefan 1881-1942 ....DLB-81

(front endsheets)

ry Critics and Scholars, 1880-1900, edited by John W. Rathbun and Mon- *988)*

1930-1960, edited by Catharine Savage Brosman (1988)

Magazine Journalists, 1741-1850, edited by Sam G. Riley (1988)

can Short-Story Writers Before 1880, edited by Bobby Ellen Kimbel, with the assist-*ance* of William E. Grant (1988)

75: *Contemporary German Fiction Writers,* Second Series, edited by Wolfgang D. Elfe and James Hardin (1988)

76: *Afro-American Writers, 1940-1955,* edited by Trudier Harris (1988)

77: *British Mystery Writers, 1920-1939,* edited by Bernard Benstock and Thomas F. Staley (1988)

78: *American Short-Story Writers, 1880-1910,* edited by Bobby Ellen Kimbel, with the assist-ance of William E. Grant (1988)

79: *American Magazine Journalists, 1850-1900,* edited by Sam G. Riley (1988)

80: *Restoration and Eighteenth-Century Dramatists,* First Series, edited by Paula R. Backscheider (1989)

81: *Austrian Fiction Writers, 1875-1913,* edited by James Hardin and Donald G. Daviau (1989)

82: *Chicano Writers,* First Series, edited by Francisco A. Lomelí and Carl R. Shirley (1989)

83: *French Novelists Since 1960,* edited by Catharine Savage Brosman (1989)

84: *Restoration and Eighteenth-Century Dramatists,* Second Series, edited by Paula R. Backscheider (1989)

85: *Austrian Fiction Writers After 1914,* edited by James Hardin and Donald G. Daviau (1989)

86: *American Short-Story Writers, 1910-1945,* First Series, edited by Bobby Ellen Kimbel (1989)

87: *British Mystery and Thriller Writers Since 1940,* First Series, edited by Bernard Benstock and Thomas F. Staley (1989)

88: *Canadian Writers, 1920-1959,* Second Series, edited by W. H. New (1989)

89: *Restoration and Eighteenth-Century Dramatists,* Third Series, edited by Paula R. Backscheider (1989)

90: *German Writers in the Age of Goethe, 1789-1832,* edited by James Hardin and Christoph E. Schweitzer (1989)

91: *American Magazine Journalists, 1900-1960,* First Series, edited by Sam G. Riley (1990)

92: *Canadian Writers, 1890-1920,* edited by W. H. New (1990)

93: *British Romantic Poets, 1789-1832,* First Series, edited by John R. Greenfield (1990)

94: *German Writers in the Age of Goethe: Sturm und Drang to Classicism,* edited by James Hardin and Christoph E. Schweitzer (1990)

Documentary Series

1: *Sherwood Anderson, Willa Cather, John Dos Passos, Theodore Dreiser, F. Scott Fitzgerald, Ernest Hemingway, Sinclair Lewis,* edited by Margaret A. Van Antwerp (1982)

2: *James Gould Cozzens, James T. Farrell, William Faulkner, John O'Hara, John Steinbeck, Thomas Wolfe, Richard Wright,* edited by Margaret A. Van Antwerp (1982)

ul Bellow, Jack Kerouac, Norman Mailer, Vladimir Nabokov, John Updike, Kurt Vonnegut, ted by Mary Bruccoli (1983)

Tennessee Williams, edited by Margaret A. Van Antwerp and Sally Johns (1984)